Mixed Reality and Gamification for Cultural Heritage

Marinos Ioannides • Nadia Magnenat-Thalmann •
George Papagiannakis
Editors

Mixed Reality and Gamification for Cultural Heritage

Editors
Marinos Ioannides
Digital Heritage Research Lab
Cyprus University of Technology
Limassol, Cyprus

Nadia Magnenat-Thalmann
University of Geneva
Geneva, Switzerland

George Papagiannakis
Institute of Computer Science
Foundation for Research and Technology—Hellas
Heraklion, Greece

Department of Computer Science
University of Crete
Voutes Campus
Heraklion, Greece

ISBN 978-3-319-84198-4 ISBN 978-3-319-49607-8 (eBook)
DOI 10.1007/978-3-319-49607-8

Softcover reprint of the hardcover 1st edition 2017

Cover illustration: Florence, visualization of the point cloud of the Dome of the Sagrestia Nuova by Michelangelo, coloured by intensity values (© 2003 DIAPReM centre, reprinted with permission)

Printed on acid-free paper

This Springer imprint is published by Springer Nature
The registered company is Springer International Publishing AG
The registered company address is: Gewerbestrasse 11, 6330 Cham, Switzerland

Preface

There is tremendous interest among researchers and creative industries professionals for the development of virtual and augmented reality and gamification technologies for cultural heritage. To date, the major applications of these technologies include photogrammetric modeling, artifact-whole heritage site digitization, museum guides, and a wide range of virtual museum applications. Recently there has been a renewed rapid proliferation in virtual reality (VR) and augmented reality (AR)—together termed mixed reality (MR)—due to the renaissance in MR hardware (such as Oculus Rift, Google Cardboard, etc.) and respective intensive commitment from the ICT industrial sector (Google, Microsoft, Sony, Facebook, etc.) that propels this field dramatically by instilling "Presence" (feeling of being and doing there in the virtual or augmented world). To aid in this direction, recent advances in gamification (employment of game design elements in nongame contexts and activities) have become the central focus of the creative industries, resulting in a new breed of smart education and heritage applications. Many recent studies have identified the benefits of employing mixed reality in these applications by further fusing it with gamification principles.

This research volume on virtual and augmented reality and gamification for cultural heritage offers an insightful introduction to the theories, development, and applications of the latest advances in the enabling technologies of VR/AR and gamified interaction in cultural heritage and, in general, the creative industries. It is divided into two sections following a pedagogical model realized by the focus group of the first EU Marie S. Curie Fellowship Initial Training Network on Digital Cultural Heritage (ITN-DCH) project fellows, which has been undergoing such training:

- *Section I: Describes all recent advances in the enabling technologies of MR and gamification* that include chapters in the following *four parts*:

  (a) Part II: Digitization and Visualization (acquisition, capturing, modeling, Web3D–WebGL)

  (b) Part III: Content Use and Reuse (semantics, ontologies, and digital libraries)

(c) Part IV: Geospatial (3D cultural web GIS and historic BIM for VR/AR)
(d) Part V: Presence (mobile VR/AR, multisensory rendering, and multimodal serious games)

- *Section II: Describes all recent advances in interaction with 3D tangible and intangible cultural heritage* in the following *thematic areas:*

  (a) Part VI: Intangible Heritage (interactive virtual characters and ancient gamified sports simulation)
  (b) Part VII: Ambient Intelligence and Storytelling (robotic curators, gamified smart environments, and digital-epigraphy narratives)
  (c) Part VIII: Museum Applications (3D printing, e-learning, and 4D modeling)

This book is directed toward heritage professionals, scientists, researchers, professors, scholars, and students who wish to explore the enabling technologies and applications of virtual and augmented reality and gamification in cultural heritage and creative industries further.

Mixed reality (including virtual and augmented reality: VR/AR) and its creative concept of cyber-real space invoke interactive 3D digital narratives that promote new patterns of understanding in communicating *tangible* (such as monuments and artifacts) as well as *intangible* (such as oral practices-traditions/storytelling, performances) *cultural heritage*. The word "narrative" refers to a set of events happening during a certain period of time—and under different circumstances—providing aesthetic, dramaturgical, and emotional element recreation, as well as 3D static objects associated with their metadata and semantics, as *new information* storytelling *attitudes*.

Combining such aesthetic heritage reconstructions with virtual augmentations and adding dramatic tension has developed over the recent years these narrative patterns into an exciting *new* VR/AR *edutainment* and gamification medium for both computer science and digital humanities. The digital information fusion of virtual restitutions of static 3D cultural artifacts with interactive, augmented historical character-based event representations is an important component of this redefinition. Although several successful publications in cultural computing cover various case studies, the field still lacks a textbook that aims to train heritage researchers in employing digital documentation's engineering principles in their fields.

For digital narratives realized with mixed reality, the conditioned notion of a 3D artifact gives way to a far more liberated concept, as suspended in virtual and augmented reality space, the modern scholar or layman leaves the strict notions of petrified cultural heritage and emerges in a contextualized world of informative intangible and tangible sensation. In such a digital heritage world, "the dream of perfect FORMS becomes the dream of information and knowledge (the story)." The aim of this book is to *highlight* the extensive value *chain* in knowledge engineering for the documentation of the past by illustrating the *3D digital pipeline* from museums and artifacts to digital, mixed reality technologies via multiple disciplines examining their role in the redefinition of the cultural "memory institution" itself as "communication engine and storytelling machine."

Such "interactive contextualized narratives" and "hermeneutic experiences" are in fact stirring the fleeting notion of history and time travel, based on the new emerging cultural fabric of the twenty-first century (novel dynamic storytelling). These result in intriguing possibilities and advances as described in this book for new digital narratives based on computer vision, computer graphics, systems engineering, human-computer interaction, photogrammetry robotics, as well as knowledge engineering and archaeology, history, arts, and cultural studies. These computational digital humanities that will pervade the information age are now challenging and raising new issues on cultural heritage representation, space, time, interpretation, interaction, identity, and the real. With this book, a new, unique light is being shed in that particular area, where *3D real and virtual cultural heritage elements* are studied together as part of a *new creative gamified medium* for digital humanities and science students as well as cultural heritage and creative professionals.

The *aim* of this book is twofold: (a) it offers a *novel platform for researchers* in and across the cultural-related disciplines to share with peers and to critique and to reflect on each other's studies and (b) it serves as an introductory textbook to *train early-stage as well as experienced researchers* in the emerging field of interactive digital cultural heritage based on *VR/AR and gamification* enabling technologies (the *scope of this book*).

This book contains selected contributions from some of the most experienced researchers and professionals in the field of VR/AR, gamification, digital heritage, and documentation of the past, based in large part on their experience in the last decade. The aim of this book is to provide an insight into ongoing research worldwide and future directions in this novel, promising, and multidisciplinary evolving field, which lies at the intersection of VR/AR, serious games and gamification, digital heritage, digital humanity, archaeology, computer science, civil/electrical engineering, mathematics, material science, architecture, surveying engineering, and geoinformatics. The objective of this book is to illustrate the new avenues in the digital documentation of cultural heritage: A complete 3D digital pipeline from museums and artifacts to digital, mixed reality simulations in multiple disciplines is described in detail, highlighting a new, different model for creating, authoring, gamifying, and distributing knowledge (the story) in cultural heritage. Having as a starting point the *first international European-funded Initial Training Network in Digital Cultural Heritage (ITN-DCH: www.itn-dch.eu)*, this book aims to significantly contribute to the multidisciplinary training of the next generation of heritage-related early-stage (Ph.D. candidates) as well as experienced researchers (post-docs) and heritage professionals. This book follows a pedagogic approach based on the secondments, training, conferences, workshops, and summer schools that the ITN-DCH fellows have been following. The book also contains an introduction from digital humanities (including the activities of the London and Seville Charters, as well as the *EU DARIAH ERIC European Research Infrastructure Consortium on Digital Humanities*: www.dariah.eu) and their relationship with latest 3D multimedia disciplines.

In closing, this book was conceived to be a catalyst for debate in the area of computer graphics documentation and knowledge engineering in cultural heritage by focusing on MR and gamification 3D interactive computer technologies used in a manner whereby, for instance, computer scientists/engineers, digital humanities researchers, creative industries-heritage professionals, museum specialists, human-computer interaction practitioners, and creative industries professionals are encouraged to communicate with each other. From this position, we anticipate your reading and reactions to these chapters as a step in furthering this goal, as well as to contribute to formalizing the diverse training of early-stage and experienced researchers and professionals in these exciting fields.

Limassol, Cyprus Marinos Ioannides
Carouge, Switzerland Nadia Magnenat-Thalmann
Heraklion, Greece George Papagiannakis

Contents

List of Contributors

Martine Adda-Decker CERTH, Thermi, Greece

Panagiotis Agrafiotis NTUA, Zografou, Greece

Amin Ahmadi CERTH, Thermi, Greece

Samer Al Kork CERTH, Thermi, Greece

Emmanouil Alexakis NTUA, Zografou, Greece

Marilena Alivizatou-Barakou University College of London, London, UK

Daniel Andrews Aston University, Birmingham, UK

Margherita Antona FORTH, Heraklion, Greece

Maria Apostolopoulou NTUA, Zografou, Greece

Marlene Arevalo MIRALab, University of Geneva, Geneva, Switzerland

Vasilis Athanasiou CUT, Limassol, Cyprus

Asterios Bakolas NTUA, Zografou, Greece

Marcello Balzani University of Ferrara, Ferrara, Italy

Fabrizio Banfi Politecnico di Milano, Milan, Italy

Luigi Barazzetti Politecnico di Milano, Milan, Italy

Victor Manuel López-Menchero Bendicho University of Murcia, Murcia, Spain

Lise Buchman CERTH, Thermi, Greece

Nedjma Cadi-Yazli MIRALab, University of Geneva, Geneva, Switzerland

Alan Chalmers University of Warwick, Coventry, UK

Vasileios Charisis CERTH, Thermi, Greece

Pavlos Chatzigrigoriou CUT, Limassol, Cyprus

Alexandros Chortaras NTUA, Zografou, Greece

Marius Cotescu CERTH, Thermi, Greece

Petros Daras CERTH, Thermi, Greece

Rob Davies CUT, Limassol, Cyprus

Sara de Freitas Murdoch University, Murdoch, WA, Australia

Ekaterini T. Delegou NTUA, Zografou, Greece

Bruce Denby CERTH, Thermi, Greece

Roberto Di Giulio University of Ferrara, Ferrara, Italy

Kosmas Dimitropoulos CERTH, Thermi, Greece

Matevz Domajnko Fraunhofer, IGD, Darmstadt, Germany

Anastasios Doulamis NTUA, Zografou, Greece

Nikos Doulamis NTUA, Zografou, Greece

Giannis Drossis FORTH, Heraklion, Greece

Yilmaz Erdal CERTH, Thermi, Greece

Dieter Fellner GRIS/TU-Darmstadt, Darmstadt, Germany

Federico Ferrari University of Ferrara, Ferrara, Italy

Philipp Franck Deutsches Archäologisches Institut, Berlin, Germany

Constanze Fuhrmann Fraunhofer, IGD, Darmstadt, Germany

Andreas Gebhard Aachen University of Applied Sciences, Aachen, Germany

Andreas Georgopoulos NTUA, Zografou, Greece

Chantas Giannis CERTH, Thermi, Greece

Nikos Grammalidis CERTH, Thermi, Greece

Dimitris Grammenos FORTH, Heraklion, Greece

Mariano Flores Gutiérrez University of Murcia, Murcia, Spain

Stelios Hadjidimitriou CERTH, Thermi, Greece

Leontios Hadjileontiadis CERTH, Thermi, Greece

Susan Hazan The Israel Museum, Jerusalem, Israel

Marinos Ioannides Digital Heritage Research Lab, Cyprus University of Technology, Limassol, Cyprus

Charalabos Ioannidis NTUA, Zografou, Greece

Anna Lobovikov Katz Technion Israel University of Technology, Haifa, Israel

Alexandros Kitsikidis School of Electrical and Computer Engineering, National Technical University of Athens, Zografou, Greece

Michael Klein 7Reasons, Absdorf, Austria

Martin Knuth Fraunhofer, IGD, Darmstadt, Germany

Stefanos Kollias School of Electrical and Computer Engineering, National Technical University of Athens, Zografou, Greece

Manolis Korres NTUA, Zografou, Greece

Lydia Kotoula NTUA, Zografou, Greece

Cindy Kröber Dresden University of Technology, Dresden, Germany

Kyriakos Labropoulos NTUA, Zografou, Greece

Evangelia Lambrou NTUA, Zografou, Greece

Alfredo Grande León University of Murcia, Murcia, Spain

Asterios Leonidis FORTH, Heraklion, Greece

Georgios Leventis CUT, Limassol, Cyprus

Fotis Liarokapis Masaryk University, Brno, Czech Republic

Maria T. Linaza CERTH, Thermi, Greece

Pietro Maria Liuzzo Hamburg University, Hamburg, Germany

Nadia Magnenat-Thalmann MIRALab, University of Geneva, Geneva, Switzerland

Federica Maietti University of Ferrara, Ferrara, Italy

Francesco Mambrini Deutsches Archäologisches Institut, Berlin, Germany

Athanasios Manitsaris CERTH, Thermi, Greece

Sotiris Manitsaris CERTH, Thermi, Greece

George Margetis FORTH, Heraklion, Greece

Marco Medici University of Ferrara, Ferrara, Italy

George Metaxakis FORTH, Heraklion, Greece

Rafael Monroy Fraunhofer, IGD, Darmstadt, Germany

Antonia Moropoulou NTUA, Zografou, Greece

Petros Moundoulas NTUA, Zografou, Greece

Sander Münster Dresden University of Technology, Dresden, Germany

Vasiliki Nikolakopoulou CUT, Limassol, Cyprus

Spiros Nikolopoulos CERTH, Thermi, Greece

Noel E. O'Connor CERTH, Thermi, Greece

Michela Ott CERTH, Thermi, Greece

George Pantazis NTUA, Zografou, Greece

Alexandra Papadaki NTUA, Zografou, Greece

Margarita Papaefthymiou Institute of Computer Science, Foundation for Research and Technology—Hellas, Heraklion, Greece

Eirini Papageorgiou CUT, Limassol, Cyprus

George Papagiannakis Institute of Computer Science, Foundation for Research and Technology—Hellas, Heraklion, Greece

Nikolaos Partarakis FORTH, Heraklion, Greece

Maria Pateraki FORTH, Heraklion, Greece

University of Crete, Crete, Greece

Panagiotis Petridis Aston University, Birmingham, UK

Emanuele Piaia University of Ferrara, Ferrara, Italy

Benjamin Picart CERTH, Thermi, Greece

Claire Pillot-Loiseau CERTH, Thermi, Greece

Francesca Pozzi CERTH, Thermi, Greece

Nikolas Prechtel Dresden University of Technology, Dresden, Germany

Marc Proesmans KU Leuven, Leuven, Belgium

Martin Ritz Fraunhofer, IGD, Darmstadt, Germany

Pedro Santos Fraunhofer, IGD, Darmstadt, Germany

Hendrik Schmedt Fraunhofer, IGD, Darmstadt, Germany

Simon Sénécal MIRALab, University of Geneva, Geneva, Switzerland

Nikolaos Simou School of Electrical and Computer Engineering, National Technical University of Athens, Zografou, Greece

Giorgos Stamou School of Electrical and Computer Engineering, National Technical University of Athens, Zografou, Greece

Constantine Stephanidis FORTH, Heraklion, Greece

University of Crete, Crete, Greece

Reimar Tausch Fraunhofer, IGD, Darmstadt, Germany

Joëlle Tillmane CERTH, Thermi, Greece

Yvain Tisserand MIRALab, University of Geneva, Geneva, Switzerland

Panos Trahanias FORTH, Heraklion, Greece

University of Crete, Crete, Greece

Filareti Tsalakanidou CERTH, Thermi, Greece

Luis Unzueta CERTH, Thermi, Greece

Luc Van Gool KU Leuven, Leuven, Belgium

Frank Verbiest KU Leuven, Leuven, Belgium

Matthew L. Vincent University of Murcia, Murcia, Spain

Rajcic Vlatka University of Zagreb, Zagreb, Croatia

Barbara Vodopivec Research Centre of the Slovenian Academy of Science and Arts, Ljubljana, Slovenia

Christina Volioti CERTH, Thermi, Greece

Heide Weller Dresden University of Technology, Dresden, Germany

Roko Zarnic University of Ljubljana, Ljubljana, Slovenia

Dimitrios Zarpalas CERTH, Thermi, Greece

Emmanouil Zidianakis FORTH, Heraklion, Greece

Nikolaos Zioulis CERTH, Thermi, Greece

Part I
Introduction

Chapter 1
Digital Heritage and Virtual Archaeology: An Approach Through the Framework of International Recommendations

Víctor Manuel López-Menchero Bendicho, Mariano Flores Gutiérrez, Matthew L. Vincent, and Alfredo Grande León

Abstract Undoubtedly today, 3D technology (either virtual reality, augmented reality or mixed reality) helps us in the representation and interpretation of reality, present and past, so it has become a powerful ally of the social sciences and humanities, especially cultural heritage and archaeology. The digital 3D representation of reality around us has opened a world of possibilities—possibilities which grow each day with the emergence of new challenges and concepts such as 4D or 5D. Emerging technologies applied to the field of cultural and archaeological heritage have resulted in the emergence of new concepts such as virtual heritage, digital heritage, digital archaeology, virtual museums, cyberarchaeology or virtual archaeology, amongst others. New concepts to describe new realities, which in turn generate new challenges.

In this scenario, we are witnessing the first steps of what may soon be a new discipline, for which there is still no consensus on its name. This new field of knowledge demands a theoretical corpus to support it but also new recommendations and guidelines, internationally accepted and able to guide research and ensure the quality of new projects.

Keywords Cultural heritage • Virtual archaeology • Standards • Professional guidelines • Digital heritage

1.1 International Recommendations in Cultural Heritage

Since the mid-twentieth century, a number of charters, conventions, principles, recommendations, protocols, standards and other documents have been adopted in parallel to the creation of various international organisations linked to cultural heritage [1–3]. Those documents form an interesting theoretical corpus, and

V.M. López-Menchero Bendicho (✉) • M. Flores Gutiérrez • M.L. Vincent • A. Grande León
Centro de Estudios de Arqueología Virtual, Universidad de Murcia, Murcia, Spain
e-mail: victor.lopezmenchero@gmail.com; ocytsim@um.es

M. Ioannides et al. (eds.), *Mixed Reality and Gamification for Cultural Heritage*,
DOI 10.1007/978-3-319-49607-8_1

knowing more about them can be very useful to those professionals who work in the new field of digital cultural heritage. The origins of these documents are as diverse as the people and the institutions behind them (from international organisations to teams of professionals).

1.1.1 The First Steps

One of the first legal documents to lay the foundations for the management of archaeological and cultural heritage in modern times was the Antiquities Act passed by the US Congress and signed into law by President Theodore Roosevelt in 1906. This pioneering document was used to protect not only monuments but also historic and prehistoric sites. In fact, one of the main reasons for its creation was the US Congress's desire to protect a number of very significant archaeological sites in the southwest of the country. One of the ways to do this was to create the figure of "national monuments" (subsequently made into national parks) to protect vast extensions of land. This helped promote the preservation of archaeological heritage (both fixed and movable assets). The Antiquities Act was an interesting and relevant document at the time, but it was not until 1931 that a truly international document was born: the Athens Charter.

The idea for the Athens Charter for the Restoration of Historic Monuments emerged a decade after the end of World War I, during which many historic monuments throughout Europe had been destroyed or damaged. The restoration or reconstruction of those monuments prompted a serious debate amongst the specialists: what were the most appropriate methods and techniques to be used for the reconstruction work? It was in that context that the Athens Charter was written and approved during the First International Congress of Architects and Technicians of Historic Monuments in Athens in 1931. Its main goal was to unify criteria for interventions on architectural heritage. Although architectural heritage is discussed, throughout the document there is a strong focus on archaeological heritage. This would become even more evident later on in the Venice Charter, with ten articles covering different topics, from guidelines for intervention to the importance of conservation and education and avenues for international cooperation. Its main contribution was the rejection of physical reconstruction as a type of restoration and the emphasis on a minimum degree of intervention on the original remains. Although the final version of the document was not ratified by any countries, the Athens Charter contributed to the development of a vast international movement for the protection and conservation of cultural heritage and laid the foundations for all the national and international documents that subsequently appeared, such as the Italian Carta del Restauro of 1932. It has had such an impact that even today, more than 80 years later, many professionals in the field of cultural heritage back their actions by referring to the principles of the Athens Charter.

1.1.2 ICOMOS's Major International Charters

The success of the Athens Charter led a large number of heritage professionals to organise the Second International Congress of Architects and Technicians of Historic Monuments, similar to the one held in Athens 30 years earlier. This second congress set out as one of its fundamental goals to update the Athens Charter by drawing up a new document which not only would lay the foundations for the modern practice of cultural heritage conservation but would also herald the birth of ICOMOS exactly one year after, in 1965. And so in 1964, the Venice Charter came to life. Its principles are still very much valid today, as Piero Gazzola, one of the authors of the charter, predicted back in 1971, seven years after the document was published and officially adopted. Gazzola wrote that “the Venice Charter is a piece of work that nobody will ignore in the future and all specialists will need to follow its spirit if they do not want to be considered as cultural outlaws”. The Venice Charter emphasised the need to respect the original monuments and remains and reiterated the objections to any physical reconstructions. It also included relatively detailed guidelines for the restoration of monuments. As regards archaeological heritage, it included an article specifically dedicated to archaeological excavations which was very much in line with the recommendation adopted by UNESCO in 1956. All in all, the charter has a strong focus on archaeology, as is evident throughout the document.

Fast-paced changes in the world of heritage during the 1960s and 1970s and the work of researchers and experts from very diverse areas (both geographically and culturally speaking) led to new documents being drawn up with much more innovative approaches than that of the Venice Charter. In 1979, the Australian National Committee of ICOMOS, during a meeting in the town of Burra, approved the ICOMOS Charter for Places of Cultural Significance. In it, the notion of the importance of monuments was replaced by a new one: the importance of places or sites. This concept is much more relevant for, say, archaeological sites whose sheer dimension means it is more appropriate to think in terms of sites, not monuments. The Burra Charter overruled the hitherto prevalent Eurocentric approach to cultural heritage by introducing a completely new idea: significance is more important than fabric. In other words, a historic site is not historic just because of the material remains in it but also because of the meaning it holds, because of the history (or histories) kept in it and because of the intangible heritage that is hidden behind the material remains. The Burra Charter also included a whole series of definitions in its first article. This was a very interesting development, as the meaning of some words can vary between different countries and even between different professionals. This contributed to create a more objective, clear and precise text. The introduction of the concept of cultural significance meant this charter is much more tolerant on the subject of physical reconstructions and attributed much more importance to the question of use and public enjoyment of heritage. In Article 25, the notion of heritage interpretation is introduced:

> The cultural significance of many places is not readily apparent, and should be explained by interpretation. Interpretation should enhance understanding and enjoyment, and be culturally appropriate.

The Burra Charter also helped to emphasise the importance of the actual applicability of international documents, as evinced by the fact that, towards the end of the text, a chart was included with proposals for developing decision-making processes about cultural heritage. This eminently practical approach in a theoretical document opened a debate about the need to do more work on the applicability of all international recommendations, both past and future.

In the 1980s, two new ICOMOS charters were approved, although neither of them was particularly relevant in terms of archaeological heritage, as they dealt with the subject in a tangential and non-explicit way. This trend changed in 1990, when the Charter for the Protection and Management of the Archaeological Heritage was approved in the city of Lausanne. All professionals in the fields of archaeology and related disciplines are expected to be familiar with this charter and implement its criteria. One of the many aspects worth highlighting in connection with the document is that it is a staunch advocate of on-site conservation and presentation. In other words, archaeological heritage must be preserved and displayed in its original location, as described in Article 6:

> The overall objective of archaeological heritage management should be the preservation of monuments and sites in situ, including proper long-term conservation and curation of all related records and collections etc. Any transfer of elements of the heritage to new locations represents a violation of the principle of preserving the heritage in its original context. This principle stresses the need for proper maintenance, conservation and management. It also asserts the principle that the archaeological heritage should not be exposed by excavation or left exposed after excavation if provision for its proper maintenance and management after excavation cannot be guaranteed.

Another valuable piece of content can be found in Article 7 ("Presentation, Information, Reconstruction"), which introduces a key recommendation in order to understand the latest developments in the management of archaeological heritage:

> The presentation of the archaeological heritage to the general public is an essential method of promoting an understanding of the origins and development of modern societies. At the same time it is the most important means of promoting an understanding of the need for its protection. Presentation and information should be conceived as a popular interpretation of the current state of knowledge, and it must therefore be revised frequently. It should take account of the multifaceted approaches to an understanding of the past. Reconstructions serve two important functions: experimental research and interpretation. They should, however, be carried out with great caution, so as to avoid disturbing any surviving archaeological evidence, and they should take account of evidence from all sources in order to achieve authenticity. Where possible and appropriate, reconstructions should not be built immediately on the archaeological remains, and should be identifiable as such.

Although underwater heritage is de facto considered an integral part of archaeological heritage, the truth is that its peculiar characteristics made it necessary to treat it in a different and specific way. This was done by means of a specific charter: the International Charter on the Protection and Management of the Underwater Cultural Heritage, initially designed as a supplement to the Lausanne Charter and published 6 years later, in 1996. It focuses on the need to protect a type of heritage which is seriously under threat due to the fact that it is in unguarded or international waters. As in the Lausanne Charter, there is an emphasis on the importance of on-site conservation (Articles 1 and 10) and the promotion of, and public access to, underwater heritage (Articles 1, 10 and 14).

Another ICOMOS Charter that can be considered as directly related to archaeological heritage is the Cultural Tourism Charter. It was approved in 1999 and, although it does not mention archaeological heritage explicitly, virtually all its principles are applicable to archaeological sites that are open to tourism. In line with the growing diversification process in the tourism industry, some authors have detected an emerging trend within the field of cultural tourism which has been named "archaeotourism" or "archaeological tourism". In this case, the visitor's main motivation, or at least one of them, would be an interest in finding out about the archaeological offer in a given area. The emergence of this new type of tourist explains to a certain extent the phenomenal growth experienced in accessible sites throughout the world. These places have become a preferred destination for a massive number of tourists who bump up the visitor figures in those cultural sites. Precisely for that reason, the International Cultural Tourism Charter must necessarily be included amongst the international documents used as a reference when working with archaeological heritage.

In 2008, a new document with close links to cultural tourism was approved: the Charter on Cultural Routes, which aims to go beyond concepts such as those of touristic route and historic/archaeological site. Cultural routes do in fact help to illustrate the modern social concept of cultural heritage values as a resource for sustainable social and economic development.

It is evident that modern notions of cultural heritage demand new approaches from a much wider perspective in order to explain and preserve all significant relations directly associated with the historic and cultural environment, as well as with the physical environment (whether natural or man-made). Aside from the progress achieved on the conceptual front, cultural routes have a complex, innovative and multidimensional nature, as they provide a significant contribution to the theory and practice of heritage conservation and dissemination.

Cultural routes, however, cannot be seen as mere tourist routes connecting heritage sites: because of their very nature, they are historic events which cannot be created out of thin air or out of a desire to fabricate cultural ensembles in present times. Because they correspond to past historic realities and are entities in their own right, in-depth research is required to properly comprehend them. In a way, we could say that a cultural route cannot be invented, but it can be brought back to life by respecting the individual value of all its elements as substantive parts of an ensemble. If this is done, the end result will ultimately be of far greater value and significance than the sum of its elements.

The ICOMOS Charter on the Interpretation and Presentation of Cultural Heritage Sites, approved in 2008 and very much related to the International Cultural Tourism Charter, is also of interest as a new document dealing with the dissemination of cultural and archaeological heritage and its accessibility by the public.

Finally, it would be interesting to draw attention to a set of principles regarding different material elements. These include the Principles for the Preservation and Conservation-Restoration of Wall Paintings (which can be applied, for instance, to fresco wall paintings found in many Roman archaeological sites), the Principles for the Preservation of Historic Timber Structures (which can be applied to numerous cases involving underwater archaeology or extremely humid or dry environments) and the Principles for the Analysis, Conservation and Structural Restoration of Architectural Heritage (which can be applied, amongst others, to the archaeological study of architecture).

1.1.3 The UNESCO Conventions

The United Nations Organization for Education, Science and Culture (UNESCO) is a United Nations agency founded in 1945 to contribute to peace and security in the world by means of education, science, culture and dialogue.

Over the course of its extensive existence, the UNESCO has promoted the approval of numerous international conventions. These conventions, synonymous with treaties, designate any agreement reached between two or more states and represent the parties' shared desire for the agreement to yield legally binding agreements. With the adoption of the Convention on the Protection and Promotion of the Diversity of Cultural Expressions, the UNESCO today already possesses, in the area of culture, a "complete set of regulatory instruments made up of seven Conventions".

Amongst all these conventions approved by UNESCO one is of special note: "Convention Concerning the Protection of the World Cultural and Natural Heritage", approved by UNESCO General Conference on 16 November 1972. This agreement would mark the culmination of a process initiated several years prior and, at the same time, the starting point for a new phase in the identification, protection and conservation of heritage elements, both natural and cultural. The 1972 Convention included important advances and contributions in the field of heritage, managing to encompass in one document the conservation and preservation of both cultural and natural heritage, which until that time always had been addressed in a differentiated way. The idea was also firmly established that there are assets whose meaning and value transcend the borders of the country in which they are located and whose disappearance or deterioration would represent an irreparable loss for humanity as a whole. Following the recognition of the importance of an asset, to ultimately be considered world heritage requires an awareness of a shared inheritance and a common commitment to its conservation and legacy for future generations. In this regard, the Convention can be considered an instrument to promote respect for cultural diversity, international cooperation, understanding and peace between nations.

The World Heritage Convention is considered to be the most successful of all those approved by UNESCO, as demonstrated by the fact that it was ratified by

188 member states. Its most significant contribution was the creation of the World Heritage List, which currently includes 1031 sites located in 163 member states, including 802 cultural sites, 197 natural sites and 32 sites of a mixed nature. ICOMOS has played a key role in the application of the Convention, along with the UICN and the ICCROM. These three entities make up the consultative organs of the World Heritage Committee, a body formed by 21 member states charged with applying the Convention.

As defined in Article 11, the World Heritage List includes cultural, natural or mixed assets possessing exceptional universal value, in accordance with the criteria adopted by the World Heritage Committee. ICOMOS is the consultative organisation responsible for evaluating proposals for cultural and mixed assets (in this case, along with the UICN), to later make the appropriate recommendations to the World Heritage Committee, which ultimately makes the final decisions.

Once the sites are placed on the list, ICOMOS participates in the process, following up on its state of conservation and management. ICOMOS also contributes through the execution of comparative and thematic studies on specific heritage categories for the purpose of providing a context for evaluations. In recent years, ICOMOS actively participated in the creation of tools and specialised manuals, such as "Managing Disaster Risks for World Heritage", "Preparing World Heritage Nominations" (2010) and the "Guidance on Heritage Impact Assets for World Heritage" (2011).

Although the Convention's best-known aspect is the World Heritage List, the document also encompasses all of the cultural and natural heritage located in the territories of the States Parties, as established in its Article 5: "Each one of the States Parties to this Convention shall strive, whenever possible: (a) to adopt a general policy aimed at attributing cultural and natural heritage a function in the collective life and to integrate the protection of that heritage into general planning programs; [...] (d) to adopt the adequate legal, scientific, technical, administrative and financial measures to identify, protect, conserve, value and rehabilitate that heritage".

Of great interest was the approval of the Convention for the protection of underwater cultural heritage in 2001. A long and detailed text that served to improve and fortify the validity of the ICOMOS Charter on the protection and management of underwater cultural heritage approved in 1996.

1.1.4 Other International Documents

Along with the main ICOMOS charters and the UNESCO conventions, there have arisen, over the course of the twentieth century and the start of the twenty-first century, a set of regulations, recommendations, principles, protocols, declarations, codes, etc. which, although considered in many cases to be secondary to the charters, contribute interesting new features and ideas.

With regard to archaeological heritage, we have at least three European and one American document totally dedicated to this area. This involves, first, the European Convention for the Protection of the Archaeological Heritage, signed in London on 6 May 1969, which served as the basis for the drafting, 20 years later, of the European Convention on the Protection of the Archaeological Heritage signed at Valetta (1992). Between the elaborations of both documents stands the Recommendation of the Committee of Ministers to the Member States Concerning the Protection and Enhancement of Archaeological Heritage in the Context of Town and Country Planning Operations. During these years, outside of Europe, worthy of note is the Convention on the Defense of the Archaeological, Historical and Artistic Heritage of the American Nations, also known as the San Salvador Convention, although this document was actually approved in Santiago de Chile via an Organization of the American States (OAS) resolution on 16 June 1976 in the sixth ordinary period of General Assembly sessions.

Another set of documents of great interest for its connection to the world of archaeological heritage and reconstructions is that which arose in the middle of the 1990s regarding the question of authenticity—a concept that until that time, in accord with clearly Eurocentric viewpoints, had been very restricted to a purely material plane and scope. Thus, on 1–5 November 1994, 45 experts from 28 different countries were convened in the town of Nara by Japanese authorities. The conference there made it possible to analyse in depth the concept of authenticity based on cultural diversities and the different categories of properties. A result of that conference was the drafting of the Nara Document on authenticity, also known as the Nara Charter, which would lead to the elaboration of new documents, including regional Southern Cone Document on Authenticity (Brasilia Charter), fruit of the fifth ICOMOS regional meeting, held in Brazil in 1995. One year later, in 1996, came the San Antonio Declaration at the Inter-American Symposium on authenticity in the conservation and handling of cultural heritage in America.

Also of great interest is the European Landscape Convention, also known as the Florence Convention, which, though drafted in the year 2000, would not take effect until 2004. This agreement has a clear connection and utility in the field of cultural landscape.

From that same year dates the Charter of Krakow, Principles for the Conservation and Restoration of Built Heritage. An effort was made to update the latter by means of the Venice Charter, though without obtaining ICOMOS support. Despite this it is a document of great interest that essentially takes the terms of the Venice Charter one step further.

Although of a more generic nature, the 1997 UNESCO Declaration on the Responsibilities of Present Generations Towards Future Generations includes two noteworthy articles that merit study, as they represent the ultimate expression of the ethical code that should guide the actions of all professionals in the field of heritage. Its Article 7, on cultural diversity and cultural heritage, states: "With due respect for human rights and fundamental freedoms, the present generations should take care to preserve the cultural diversity of humankind. The present generations have the responsibility to identify, protect and safeguard the tangible and intangible cultural heritage and to transmit this common heritage to future generations". Article 8, meanwhile, addressing humanity's shared heritage, states that: "The present generations may use the common heritage of humankind, as defined in international law, provided that this does not entail compromising it irreversibly".

In relation to the field of the Cultural Heritage and Information and Communication Technologies (ICTs) we could say that arrives on the scene at the dawn of the new millennium. More specifically, thanks to the inclusion of Article 5 of the Krakow Charter 2000: Principles for the Conservation and Restoration of Built Heritage that indicates: "In the protection and public presentation of archaeological sites, the use of modern technologies, databanks, information system and virtual presentation techniques should be promoted". This reference, never seen before in other previous charters, marked an important turning point in the use of computers as one more tool in the regular work to conserve and present archaeological heritage. In fact, the Krakow Charter would pave the way for the writing of new international texts aimed at regulating the use of new technologies in the field of cultural heritage. For example, in 2003 UNESCO approved the Charter on the Preservation of Digital Heritage, with the objective of protecting, conserving and improving access to products "of digital origin". This UNESCO declaration came about in the face of the real danger of losing of an immense wealth of cultural heritage existing in electronic format. This heritage includes virtual reconstructions, 3D digitisations and a whole set of products derived from the practice of virtual archaeology, rendering this document of great interest. Less momentous with regard to new technologies, although also of interest, would be the approval on 4 October 2008 of a new international charter officially named the ICOMOS Charter for the Interpretation and Presentation of Cultural Heritage Sites, also known as the Ename Charter. Article 2.4 of this new international text would feature the following recommendation: "Visual reconstructions, whether by artists, architects, or computer modellers, should be based upon detailed and systematic analysis of environmental, archaeological, architectural, and historical data, including analysis of written, oral and icon-graphic sources, and photography. The information sources on which such visual renderings are based should be clearly documented and alternative reconstructions based on the same evidence, when available, should be provided for comparison".

These three previous recommendations would serve as both the foundations and reference points for the documents that thus far constitute the most important theoretical texts on Cultural Heritage and ICTs: the London Charter and the Seville Principles.

1.2 London Charter

The London Charter for the computer-based Visualisation of Cultural Heritage seeks to establish the requirements necessary to verify that a 3D visualisation of cultural heritage is intellectually responsible and solid, as would be incumbent upon any other research method [4–8].

This initiative was born in an international scientific context in which the question of the transparency of the different 3D visualisation applications for cultural heritage became a highly charged and vital issue, in as much as scientific transparency is a fundamental requirement in the process of these applications' development as a research method, that is, to say, as a scientific discipline.

Logically, it is necessary for this research method to enjoy widespread acceptance amongst the international scientific community, which is why the London Charter features, in addition to an Advisory Board, an Interest Group made up of researchers hailing from a range of different countries.

The main objective and accomplishment of the London Charter was to overturn the principle of authority in the creation of virtual models according to which, depending on the inventor of a given model, it enjoyed more or less scientific standing. The authority principle has been replaced by the scientific method, according to which all virtual models must feature a set of data and information (metadata and paradata) facilitating their verification and evaluation by independent experts.

1.2.1 The Scope of the London Charter

It is important to point out that the London Charter is not limited to a specific discipline but rather aims to serve a whole range of disciplines and branches of knowledge, spanning the Arts, the Humanities and Cultural Heritage, provided that they employ 3D visualisation in the development of their respective research and diffusion projects. To this end, the London Charter adopts the format and style of the Ename Charter (ICOMOS Charter for the Interpretation and Presentation of Cultural Heritage Sites) in both its internal structure and its dimensions, while also adopting a very broad definition of the concept of "cultural heritage," encompassing all areas of human activity related to understanding and conveying material and immaterial culture. Such areas would include, but would not be limited to, museums, art galleries, monuments, interpretation centres, archaeological sites, research institutes in the field of cultural heritage, educational institutions of all kinds and tourism.

The London Charter was not undertaken to launch new and radical proposals but rather to consolidate the main principles already advanced in publications by numerous authors, but which still have not been fully assimilated by a large portion of the international scientific community. This is the reason why the "Charter" format was used, rather than drafting a new article, as it seemed the most suitable instrument to guarantee its diffusion and discussion amongst the numerous communities of experts who use 3D visualisations in their daily work.

Although, as was already made clear in our discussion of this issue above, the term "Charters" is reserved for those documents officially approved by ICOMOS, the importance and breadth of the subject addressed in the London Charter is such that the use of the term seems reasonable—even though it has not been ratified by the ICOMOS General Assembly. In fact, we are probably dealing with a visionary document here, one that is ahead its time, as the use of new technologies in the area of cultural heritage is still viewed by many as a secondary issue in traditional discussions pertaining to this field. Nevertheless, it is evident that the growing impact and interest in the 3D visualisation of cultural heritage seem to augur the ratification of this document (or one very similar to it) by ICOMOS, as it is becoming increasingly necessary to have recommendations and guidelines governing this new field of knowledge.

1.2.2 The Charter Principles

All the principles behind the London Charter aim at improving the levels of scientific transparency present in 3D visualisations of cultural heritage, since improving the levels of scientific transparency of such models is an imperative step prior to reaching a greater level of academic recognition that will propel more consolidated and ample research and studies.

1.2.2.1 Principle 1: Implementation

"The principles of the London Charter are valid wherever computer-based visualisation is applied to the research or dissemination of cultural heritage". The chances of implementation of the London Charter are directly conditioned by the development of more specific guidelines and recommendations based on the fields of knowledge: Such is the case with virtual archaeology, for example, where the application of the London Charter is totally impossible since it has been designed to be too general and therefore makes its applicability too difficult. It therefore needs to be adapted for more specific fields of knowledge (Principle 1.1).

While the mentioned guides or more specific recommendations that will allow for the standardisation of work methodologies are developed, "Every computer-based visualisation heritage activity should develop, and monitor the application of, a London Charter Implementation Strategy" (1.2); in other words, every 3D visualisation of cultural heritage should foresee the specific manner in which the recommendations established by the London Charter will be complied with.

"In collaborative activities, all participants whose role involves either directly or indirectly contributing to the visualisation process should be made aware of the principles of the London Charter, together with relevant Charter Implementation Guidelines, and to assess their implications for the planning, documentation and dissemination of the project as a whole" (1.3). In this sense, all parties involved in 3D visualisation projects for cultural heritage must bear in mind the importance of the development, in a practical and efficient manner, of the principles derived from the London Charter. These principles must not be considered as an appendix to the project or as a source of reference at a particular stage of the project.

It would obviously be less expensive and more practical to obviate the principles from the London Charter, since complying with them means an extra expense due to the time needed to develop the paradata and metadata, amongst others. However, the implementation costs for this strategy must be justified in relation to the added intellectual, explanatory and/or economic value resulting from producing results with a high level of intellectual integrity; in other words, scientific quality (Principle 1.4), in this case, should be enough to justify the increase in production costs of the 3D models, though as we have previously mentioned, it is now important to develop mechanisms that would allow the certification of such quality, since the sources requesting this 3D visualisations (generally public institutions) lack the necessary knowledge to undertake this task.

1.2.2.2 Principle 2: Aims and Methods

"A computer-based visualisation method should normally be used only when it is the most appropriate available method for that purpose". In this sense "It should not be assumed that computer-based visualisation is the most appropriate means of addressing all cultural heritage research or communication aims" (2.1) since other conventional methods can turn out to be more effective, from the financial, temporal or qualitative point of view, than 3D visualisations when it comes to achieving specific objectives. This is why "A systematic, documented evaluation of the suitability of each method to each aim should be carried out, in order to ascertain what, if any, type of computer-based visualisation is likely to prove most appropriate" (2.2). It makes no sense to develop complex and expensive 3D visualisations if their final use and location is in standard panels where, obviously, it will not be possible for the end user to manage or handle 3D models. In such cases, a simple traditional drawing or a computer-generated photograph can be more than enough.

"While it is recognised that, particularly in innovative or complex activities, it may not always be possible to determine, a priori, the most appropriate method, the choice of computer-based visualisation method (e.g. more or less photo-realistic, impressionistic or schematic; representation of hypotheses or of the available evidence; dynamic or static) or the decision to develop a new method, should be based on an evaluation of the likely success of each approach in addressing each aim" (2.3). Or in other words, the first step to be taken in any 3D visualisation project for cultural heritage should be to set the objectives to be achieved in a clear and concise way. That done, one can choose the best methodology to develop and achieve those mentioned aims.

1.2.2.3 Principle 3: Research Sources

"In order to ensure the intellectual integrity of computer-based visualisation methods and outcomes, relevant research sources should be identified and evaluated in a structured and documented way". "In the context of the Charter, research sources are defined as all information, digital and non-digital, considered during, or directly influencing, the creation of computer-based visualisation outcomes" (3.1). As such, for example, good source of information would be scientific articles or books used to give shape to the model, other projects and other 3D models used as examples, archaeological data retrieved directly from the field, available historical documents, old photographs, audio or audiovisual archives, oral or written testimonies, etc.

"Research sources should be selected, analysed and evaluated with reference to current understandings and best practice within communities of practice" (3.2). That is why it would be useful to fit the project within a consolidated field of knowledge such as contemporary history, mediaeval history, anthropology, etc., since these disciplines already have soundly developed classifications of research resources.

Finally, "Particular attention should be given to the way in which visual sources may be affected by ideological, historical, social, religious and aesthetic and other such factors" (3.3), since the intellectual integrity of any model can only be guaranteed when there is an attempt to provide objective information free of any sort of manipulation. In the cases where, due to ideological or other interests of the hiring institution, it is not possible to offer an objective final product, the aim should be to at least keep such objectivity in the information sources (meta- and paradata).

1.2.2.4 Principle 4: Documentation

"Sufficient information should be documented and disseminated to allow computer-based visualisation methods and outcomes to be understood and evaluated in relation to the contexts and purposes for which they are deployed". Generally speaking, "Documentation strategies should be designed and resourced in such a way that they actively enhance the visualisation activity by encouraging, and helping to structure, thoughtful practice" (4.1). Along the same lines, "Documentation strategies should be designed to enable rigorous, comparative analysis and evaluation of computer-based visualisations and to facilitate the recognition and addressing of issues that visualisation activities reveal" (4.2). The utilisation of a single documentation system for all cultural heritage 3D visualisation projects would help to perform objective comparisons and evaluate models; it would also help avoid having to reinvent the wheel over and over again. Unfortunately, such a system is, to date, a utopia, and therefore it is necessary to continue working in the design of such documentation systems.

"Documentation strategies may assist in the management of Intellectual Property Rights or privileged information" (4.3). This topic is capital, particularly in regard to the copyrights, where there are legal loopholes that are having negative effects.

The end users of cultural heritage 3D visualisation projects usually see how their rights to information are limited, that is, the right to know the degree of reality or objectiveness shown in the 3D models, since in general no project pays attention to those particular aspects. This is why "It should be made clear to users what a computer-based visualisation seeks to represent, for example the existing state, an evidence-based restoration or an hypothetical reconstruction of a cultural heritage object or site, and the extent and nature of any factual uncertainty" (4.4). End users have the right to know what is hidden behind a 3D visualisation, since this information is key in guaranteeing that they will be able to reach their own conclusions and have their own opinions.

On the other hand and for the sake of scientific transparency and to favour the right to information, not so much that of the conventional users but that of those in research, "a complete list of research sources used and their provenance should be disseminated" (4.5). Additionally "Documentation of the evaluative, analytical, deductive, interpretative and creative decisions made in the course of computer-based visualisation should be disseminated in such a way that the relationship between research sources, implicit knowledge, explicit reasoning, and visualisation-based outcomes can be understood" (4.6); in other words, the dissemination of the documentation or paradata processes must be promoted. As such, "The rationale for choosing a computer-based visualisation method, and for rejecting other methods, should be documented and disseminated to allow the activity's methodology to be evaluated and to inform subsequent activities" (4.7). "A description of the visualisation methods should be disseminated if these are not likely to be widely understood within relevant communities of practice" (4.8). "Where computer-based visualisation methods are used in interdisciplinary contexts that lack a common set of understandings about the nature of research questions, methods and outcomes, project documentation should be undertaken in such a way that it assists in articulating such implicit knowledge and in identifying the different lexica of participating members from diverse subject communities" (4.9).

Apart from disseminating documentation processes and methodologies, there should also be importance given to dependency relationships. In this sense "Computer-based visualisation outcomes should be disseminated in such a way that the nature and importance of significant, hypothetical dependency relationships between elements can be clearly identified by users and the reasoning underlying such hypotheses understood" (4.10).

Finally, when carrying out the dissemination of all documentation used and generated during a cultural heritage 3D visualisation project, it is important that "Documentation should be disseminated using the most effective available media, including graphical, textual, video, audio, numerical or combinations of the above" (4.11). Bearing in mind the number and diversity of the professionals that participate in cultural heritage 3D visualisation projects, "documentation should be disseminated sustainably with reference to relevant standards and ontologies according to best practice in relevant communities of practice and in such a way that facilitates its inclusion in relevant citation indexes" (4.12). One must not forget that every cultural heritage 3D visualisation project performed in a professional manner constitutes in itself a valuable contribution to scientific knowledge of our heritage, and therefore its dissemination must also be performed using scientific means and formats.

1.2.2.5 Principle 5: Sustainability

"Strategies should be planned and implemented to ensure the long-term sustainability of cultural heritage-related computer-based visualisation outcomes and documentation, in order to avoid loss of this growing part of human intellectual, social, economic and cultural heritage". This principle has become one of the main priorities of the European Union in the last few years, under the name of "long-term preservation". The EU is financing new projects within the field of Information and Communication Technologies. The concerns regarding sustainability in cultural heritage 3D visualisation projects has its roots in the continuous loss of useful and valuable information that has been taking place over the last few years. Such is the case of temporary exhibitions, so common at present that once finalised do not normally have a preservation plan, whereby the digital models or 3D visualisations can be reused, even though a great deal of money and resources have been dedicated to their design and implementation. It would only require a small amount of organisation to guarantee that that information would continue being useful in interpretation centres, museums or websites.

On the other hand, it is important that "The most reliable and sustainable available form of archiving computer-based visualisation outcomes, whether analogue or digital, should be identified and implemented" (5.1). "Digital preservation strategies should aim to preserve the computer-based visualisation data, rather than the medium on which they were originally stored, and also information sufficient to enable their use in the future, for example through migration to different formats or software emulation" (5.2). However, experience shows that to date digital preservation is still a risky way of preserving digital content, and therefore even though it is less precise and it can only safeguard a part of it, preservation in conventional formats such as paper or physical replicas (2D or 3D) is more suitable; "where digital archiving is not the most reliable means of ensuring the long-term survival of a computer-based visualisation outcome, a partial, two-dimensional record of a computer-based visualisation output, evoking as far as possible the scope and properties of the original output, should be preferred to the absence of a record" (5.3).

Likewise, it is recommended that "Documentation strategies should be designed to be sustainable in relation to available resources and prevailing working practices" (5.4), since it would be absurd to establish expensive or complex digital preservation strategies, especially when dealing with low cost or limited budget projects.

1.2.2.6 Principle 6: Access

"The creation and dissemination of computer-based visualisation should be planned in such a way as to ensure that maximum possible benefits are achieved for the study, understanding, interpretation, preservation and management of cultural heritage"; in other words, these should be oriented, in as much as possible, to improving research, preservation and dissemination of cultural heritage, particularly when they are financed with public funds. Therefore, "The aims, methods and dissemination plans of computer-based visualisation should reflect consideration of how such work can enhance access to cultural heritage that is otherwise inaccessible due to health and safety, disability, economic, political, or environmental reasons, or because the object of the visualisation is lost, endangered, dispersed, or has been destroyed, restored or reconstructed" (6.1). There are many cases in which access to cultural heritage is impossible for both researchers and the public in general. For such cases, the creation of virtual replicas can play an important role in the work carried out by research, preservation and dissemination, since the said replicas can be consulted and enjoyed by experts and users from anywhere in the planet, provided they are accessible via the Internet.

"Projects should take cognizance of the types and degrees of access that computer-based visualisation can uniquely provide to cultural heritage stakeholders, including the study of change over time, magnification, modification, manipulation of virtual objects, embedding of datasets, instantaneous global distribution" (6.2). Thanks fundamentally to the use of Internet. Logically, this potential can only be developed when the 3D visualisation projects are prepared with time and with suitable strategies that will put no barriers to the access to their information; the use of 3D models through the Internet would usually require a reduction of the geometric complexity of the models or an adaptation of the contents to be more useful and attractive to the general public and researchers. Adopting policies and strategies that facilitate the access to cultural heritage 3D visualisations through the Internet can generate important economic and social benefits thanks to its ties with other industries such as education and tourism.

1.3 The Seville Principles

The International Principles of Virtual Archaeology, also known as the Seville Principles from the city where they were forged, represent a specification of the London Charter [9–11]. While the London Charter includes a set of recommendations applicable to cultural heritage in general, the Seville Principles focus their attention solely on archaeological heritage, as a specific part of cultural heritage. Thus, the London Charter maintains its "charter" designation, and the Seville Principles fall into the category of "principles", a level below charter, following the nomenclature commonly used by ICOMOS. Despite following the structure and common nomenclature used by ICOMOS, it is important to note that neither the London Charter nor the Seville Principles have been approved so far by the organisation, though these are the only recommendations available at the international level in this area.

From a formal point of view, the Seville Principles are structured following the same pattern as the London Charter, which has four main sections: preamble, objectives, principles and definitions.

The heart of the document is made up of principles, a set of recommendations that seek to improve the applicability of the London Charter in the field of archaeological heritage. In total there are eight principles that follow a logical sequence structured according to the phases of development and implementation of a project of virtual archaeology. This structure aims to facilitate the implementation of the principles in actual projects.

1.3.1 Principle 1: Interdisciplinarity

"Any project involving the use of new technologies, linked to computer-based visualisation in the field of archaeological heritage, whether for research, documentation, conservation or dissemination, must be supported by a team of professionals from different branches of knowledge". "Given the complex nature of computer-based visualisation of archaeological heritage, it can not be addressed only by a single type of expert but needs the cooperation of a large number of specialists (archaeologists, computer scientists, historians, architects, engineers etc.)" (1.1). Logically, this recommendation is limited by the available budget for each project. In some cases, there are sufficient specialised publications on a monument or archaeological site to deal with security a virtual reconstruction or a digitalization without having to add to the team to all specialists. However, whenever possible, the participation of various experts will help to get results with higher scientific quality. Such participation should be active insomuch as "a truly interdisciplinary work involves the regular and fluid exchange of ideas and views among specialists from different fields. Work divided into watertight compartments can never be considered interdisciplinary even with the participation of experts from different disciplines" (1.2).

Given that virtual archaeology is archaeology or is nothing at all, "among the experts who must collaborate in this interdisciplinary model, it is essential to ensure the specific presence of archaeologists and historians, preferably those who are or were responsible for the scientific management of the excavation work or archaeological remains to be reconstructed" (1.3). In the case of 3D digitisation of an archaeological site, only the archaeologist who has excavated or knows in depth the site can tell which areas should be scanned with greater precision and which have a secondary character. This information will be crucial to conduct a thorough and efficient work; otherwise we run the risk of insufficiently documenting areas of high historical interest or spending too much time and resources on areas that lack scientific interest. On the other hand, many archaeological sites that have been excavated have no visible structures for the public, having been reburied for conservation reasons. Before scanning, a site should be evaluated in collaboration with the archaeologist responsible for the uncovering of those areas. Obviously, this work can only be done by a professional archaeologist.

1.3.2 Principle 2: Purpose

"Prior to the development of any computer-based visualisation, the ultimate purpose or goal of our work must always be completely clear. Therefore, different levels of detail, resolutions and accuracies might be required". Given the limited nature of virtual archaeology budgets, it is very important to set clear objectives to pursue. Funders or contracting entities, generally public administrations, rarely are able to set such targets. However, the researcher should have the responsibility to find a proper balance between the objective and the means necessary to achieve it.

"Any proposed computer-based visualisation will always aim to improve aspects related to the research, conservation or dissemination of archaeological heritage. The overall aim of the project must be encompassed within one of these categories (research, conservation and/or dissemination). The category concerning dissemination includes both educational projects, whether formal or informal education, and recreational projects (cultural tourism)" (2.1). However, sometimes some projects do not pursue a specific purpose but a global objective, such as the case of some 3D scanning projects whose results can be useful for any category (research, conservation or dissemination). After all, the documentation of heritage forms the foundation on which the building of comprehensive management is constructed.

"In addition to clarifying the main purpose of computer-based visualisation, more specific objectives must always be defined in order to obtain more precise knowledge of the problem or problems to be resolved" (2.2). "Computer-based visualisation must be always at the service of archaeological heritage rather than archaeological heritage being at the service of computer-based visualisation. The main objective of applying new technologies in the comprehensive management of archaeological heritage must be to satisfy the real needs of archaeologists, curators, restorers, museographers, managers and/or other professionals in the field of heritage and not vice versa" (2.3). It seems unreasonable that large amounts of public money should be invested in solving problems that no one has raised, while key issues in the management of archaeological heritage remain unanswered.

"Ultimately, the main purpose of virtual archaeology will always be to serve society as a whole and contribute to increase the human knowledge" (2.4). Precisely for this reason, as far as possible, it should promote open access to all content generated by virtual archaeology projects, whether virtual reconstructions or 3D scans. The democratisation of culture is also an objective of virtual archaeology.

1.3.3 Principle 3: Complementarity

"The application of computer-based visualisation for the comprehensive management of archaeological heritage must be treated as a complementary and not alternative tool to other more traditional but equally effective management instruments". To this effect, "Computer-based visualisation should not aspire to replace other methods and techniques employed for the comprehensive management of archaeological heritage (e.g. virtual restoration should not aspire to replace real restoration, just as virtual visits should not aspire to replace real visits)" (3.1). The clashes and controversies that have sometimes arisen between supporters and opponents of the use of new technologies in cultural heritage have their origin in this point. The most classically oriented heritage experts have seen in new technology an enemy whose purpose is to replace time-tested traditional systems. Far from that vision, reality shows that virtual archaeology is complemented by classical techniques and methods, which often remain much more useful in the relationship between value, time and money.

"Computer-based visualisation should seek forms of collaboration with other methods and techniques of a different nature to help improve current archaeological heritage research, conservation and dissemination processes. To do so, compliance with 'Principle 1: Interdisciplinarity' will be fundamental" (3.2). "Nevertheless, computer-based visualisations might be an alternative approach when original archaeological remains have been destroyed (e.g. due to the construction of large infrastructures), are placed in areas with difficult accessibility (e.g. without roads) or at risk of deterioration due to the huge influx of tourists (e.g. rock paintings)" (3.3).

1.3.4 Principle 4: Authenticity

"Computer-based visualisation normally reconstructs or recreates historical buildings, artifacts and environments as we believe they were in the past. For that reason, it should always be possible to distinguish what is real, genuine or authentic from what is not. In this sense, authenticity must be a permanent operational concept in any virtual archaeology project". This principle does not only affect virtual reconstructions but also the 3D digitisation. For example, in 3D digitisation projects, it is often the case that occlusions occur, which must be filled artificially using various algorithms. However, it is rarely possible to know which areas have been artificially filled. This information is key to determining the authenticity of a 3D model. A small occlusion may be hiding an important detail for an investigation on a particular type of object or monument.

"Since archaeology is complex and not an exact and irrefutable science, it must be openly committed to making alternative virtual interpretations provided they afford the same scientific validity. When that equality does not exist, only the main hypothesis will be endorsed" (4.1). "When performing virtual restorations or reconstructions, these must explicitly or through additional interpretations show the different levels of accuracy on which the restoration or reconstruction is based" (4.2). Unfortunately, there is no internationally accepted system. The representation of uncertainty in visualisations is one of the great challenges that face virtual archaeology. Nevertheless, there are few publications and projects that have attempted to address this issue. Generally, the solutions proposed to date have used colour, transparency or texture to show levels of uncertainty.

"In so far as many archaeological remains have been and are being restored or reconstructed, computer-based visualisation should really help both professionals and public to differentiate clearly among: remains that have been conserved "in situ"; remains that have been returned to their original position (real anastylosis); areas that have been partially or completely rebuilt on the original remains; and finally, areas that have been virtually restored or reconstructed" (4.3). This principle not only applies to virtual reconstructions but also to 3D digitisations. Many buildings and objects that are digitised today have been subjected to various restorations and physical reconstructions over time. Being able to know the areas, on the 3D model, that have been affected by these interventions means moving forward on the path of authenticity.

1.3.5 Principle 5: Historical Rigour

"To achieve optimum levels of historical rigour and veracity, any form of computer-based visualisation of the past must be supported by solid research, and historical and archaeological documentation". We must not forget that virtual archaeology is a scientific discipline that has its base and meaning in historical science and archaeological practice. Its social significance is greater than we might think as it helps to set images and feelings about the past. The way we understand our past affects our present and often justifies our actions in the future. Precisely for this reason, historical accuracy is essential in creating these images, especially when we talk about virtual reconstructions.

"The historical rigour of any computer-based visualisation of the past will depend on both the rigour with which prior archaeological research has been performed and the rigour with which that information is used to create the virtual model" (5.1). "All historical phases recorded during archaeological research are extremely valuable. Thus, a rigorous approach would not be one that shows only the time of splendour of reconstructed or recreated archaeological remains but rather one that shows all the phases, including periods of decline. Nor should it display an idyllic image of the past with seemingly newly constructed buildings, people who look like models, etc., but rather a real image, i.e. with buildings in varying states of conservation, people of different sizes and weights, etc". (5.2). Generally, it should pay close attention to details because one thing is what we want to convey and quite another what we actually convey.

"The environment, landscape or context associated with archaeological remains is as important as the ruin itself. Charcoal, paleobotanical, paleozoological and physical paleoanthropological research must serve as a basis for conducting rigorous virtual recreations of landscape and context. They cannot systematically show lifeless cities, lonely buildings or dead landscapes, because this is an historical falsehood" (5.3). The incorporation of human figures to 3D models probably is one of the most recurrent issues. Different researchers have different solutions ranging from the incorporation of figures in a cartoon style to the incorporation of real actors using the technique of chroma keying. Intermediate solutions have also been used as dark silhouettes of real actors or dark silhouettes of human figures modelled in 3D. Anyway, the humanization of digital spaces helps increase historical accuracy; for that reason this issue should be the subject of a much deeper debate.

"Archaeological heritage recording is extremely important not only for archiving, documentation, analyses and dissemination but for management. New techniques such as photogrammetry or laser scanners can be used to increase the quality of the scientific documentation. In the way that better metric documentation of archaeological heritage is carried out higher will be the chance to monitor and obtain historically and valuable replicas" (5.4). However, at this point it should be to reflect on the digitisation policy that continues today, with some monuments and archaeological sites that have been the subject of countless digitisations, while others remain forgotten and untouched.

1.3.6 Principle 6: Efficiency

"The concept of efficiency applied to the field of virtual archaeology depends inexorably on achieving appropriate economic and technological sustainability. Using fewer resources to achieve steadily more and better results is the key to efficiency". "Any project that involves the use of computer-based visualisation in the field of archaeological heritage must pre-screen the economic and technological maintenance needs that will be generated once installed and operative" (6.1). "Priority must be given to systems that may initially require high investments but long term profit, with minimum maintenance cost and high veracity, i.e. low-consumption resistant, easy to repair or modify systems will be preferred" (6.2). "Whenever possible, draw on the results obtained by previous visualisation projects, avoiding duplicity, i.e. performing the same work twice" (6.3). The results achieved by some projects should be the basis for future work, as starting from scratch is a poor use of already scarce resources. For that reason, it is essential to move forward in creating global databases (Principle 7), incorporating a clear policy of access and use of information stored by using, for example, the creative commons system.

1.3.7 Principle 7: Scientific Transparency

"All computer-based visualisation must be essentially transparent, i.e. testable by other researchers or professionals, since the validity, and therefore the scope, of the conclusions produced by such visualisation will depend largely on the ability of others to confirm or refute the results obtained".

"It is clear that all computer-based visualisation involves a large amount of scientific research. Consequently, to achieve scientific and academic rigour in virtual archaeology projects it is essential to prepare documentary bases in which to gather and present transparently the entire work process: objectives, methodology, techniques, reasoning, origin and characteristics of the sources of research, results and conclusions" (7.1). They should logically be public authorities responsible for promoting and sustaining these databases through their respective ministries or directorates of culture.

"Without prejudice to the creation of such databases it is essential to promote the publication of the results of virtual archaeological projects in journals, books, reports and editorial media, both scientific and popular science, for information, review and consultation of the international scientific community and society in general" (7.2). Unfortunately, many virtual archaeology projects remain unpublished, especially those that have been developed by private companies, whose interests are usually different from the interests of academic researchers. Greater effort should be made to bring the publishing of field work closer to private companies, facilitating publication channels adapted to their abilities and interests.

"The incorporation of metadata and paradata is crucial to ensure scientific transparency of any virtual archaeology project. Paradata and metadata should be clear, concise and easily available. In addition, it should provide as much information as possible. The scientific community should contribute with international standardization of metadata and paradata" (7.3). Undoubtedly, metadata and paradata standardisation systems are one of the great unfinished tasks of the international scientific community. The challenge is to achieve a system that will be not overly complex or costly.

"In general, the registration and organisation of all documentation relating to virtual archaeological projects will be based on the Principles for the recording of monuments, groups of buildings and sites ratified by the 11th ICOMOS General Assembly in 1996" (7.4). "In the interests of scientific transparency, it is necessary to create a large globally-accessible database with projects that offer optimum levels of quality (Art 8.4), without undermining the creation of national or regional databases of this type" (7.5). These databases should store all kinds of 3D models as virtual reconstructions or 3D digitisations. Sometimes it would be advisable to have databases that, in addition to storing the final results of the projects, also include raw data. For example, in the case of photogrammetry, it would be especially useful to store not only the final 3D model but the photographs used to obtain the 3D model, as the algorithms currently used to process these images certainly will be improved in the future. With new algorithms, one will be able to obtain much better results with the same data. On the other hand, we cannot forget that the archaeological heritage is seriously threatened by whether the documentation obtained in the field can be invaluable in the future against the risk of destruction of the documented asset.

1.3.8 Principle 8: Training and Evaluation

"Virtual archaeology is a scientific discipline related to the comprehensive management of archaeological heritage that has its own specific language and techniques. Like any other academic discipline, it requires specific training and evaluation programmes". "High-level postgraduate training programmes must be promoted to strengthen training and specialisation of a sufficient number of qualified professionals in this field" (8.1). The future of this discipline is inexorably joined to formal university education. The higher the education, the better the results obtained by the projects of virtual archaeology. "When computer-based visualisations are designed as instruments for edutainment and knowledge of the general public, the most appropriate method of evaluation will be visitor's studies" (8.2). "When computer-based visualisations are intended to serve as an instrument for archaeological research and conservation, the most appropriate archaeological evaluation method will be testing by a representative number of end users, i.e. professionals" (8.3). "The final quality of any computer-based visualisation must be evaluated based on the rigour of the measures and not the spectacularity of its results. Compliance with all the principles will determine whether the end result of a computer-based visualisation can be considered or not 'top quality'" (8.4).

1.4 Conclusion

Despite the efforts made so far by researchers, many challenges remain to be addressed in the field of international recommendations applied to cultural heritage and ICT. The largest challenge is to have ICOMOS write or approve an international charter on digital heritage. The London Charter should serve as a basis for drafting such a document, because it has the scientific strength and sufficient consensus to fulfil that mission.

For its part, the Seville Principles, born originally to meet the demands of scientific rigour of virtual reconstructions, need to incorporate a greater number of case studies intended for the field of 3D digitization. A more solid and sustained collaboration with CIPA-ICOMOS would guarantee the successful revision of the document.

Meanwhile, the community of experts should work on drafting new principles to address the needs of the emerging fields of knowledge, such as virtual museums or industrial digital heritage.

This is a challenge that will only be possible to achieve with the collaboration and generosity of all those who work to build the future of cultural heritage.

Acknowledgements The research leading to these results is partly funded by the EU Community's FP7 PEOPLE under the ITN-DCH Project (Grant Agreement 608013). The publication reflects only the authors' views, and the Community is not liable for any use that may be made of the information contained therein. Neither the ITN-DCH consortium as a whole nor a certain participant of the ITN-DCH consortium warrants that the information contained in this document is capable of use nor that the use of the information is free from risk and accepts no liability for loss or damage suffered by any person using this information.

References

1. Y. Abdulqawi, *Standard-Setting in UNESCO: Conventions, Recommendations, Declarations, and Charters Adopted by UNESCO (1948–2006)* (UNESCO, Leiden, 2007)
2. P.J. O'Keefe, L.V. Prott, *Cultural Heritage Conventions and Other Instruments: A Compendium with Commentaries*. Institute of Art and Law (2011)
3. M. Petzet, J. Ziesemer, *International Charters for Conservation and Restoration = Chartes Internationales sur la Conservation et la Restauration = Cartas Internacionales sobre la Conservación y la Restauración. Documentation* (ICOMOS, München, 2004)
4. R. Beacham, H. Denard, F. Niccolucci, An introduction to the London charter, in *The Evolution of Information Communication Technology in Cultural Heritage: Where Hi-tech Touches the Past: Risks and Challenges for the 21st Century (Short papers from the joint event CIPA/VAST/EG/EuroMed)*, ed. by M. Ioannides et al. (Archaeolingua, Budapest, 2006)
5. S. Hermon, G. Sugimoto, H. Mara, D. Arnold, A. Chalmers, F. Niccolucci, The London charter and its applicability, in *VAST 2007. The 8th International Symposium on Virtual Reality, Archaeology and Cultural Heritage*, Brighton, 26–30 Nov 2007 (Short and Project Papers, ed. Archaeolingua), pp. 11–14
6. R. Georgiou, S. Hermon, A London charter's visualization: the ancient Hellenistic-Roman theatre in Paphos, in *The 12th International Symposium on Virtual Reality, Archaeology and Cultural Heritage VAST (2011)*, eds by M. Dellepiane, F. Niccolucci, S. Pena Serna, H. Rushmeier, L. Van Gool, pp. 1–4 (2011)
7. A. Bentkowska-Kafel, H. Denard, D. Baker (eds.), *Paradata and Transparency in Virtual Heritage* (Ashgate, Farnham, 2012)
8. H. Denard, Implementing best practice in cultural heritage visualisation: the London charter, in *Good Practice in Archaeological Diagnostics*, eds by C. Corsi, B. Slapšak, F. Vermeulen. Springer, pp 255–268 (2013)
9. V.M. López-Menchero, Propuesta para profundizar en la Carta de Londres y mejorar su aplicabilidad en el campo del patrimonio arqueológico. Virtual Archaeol. Rev. **4**, 65–69 (2011)
10. V.M. López-Menchero, A. Grande, Hacia una carta internacional de arqueología virtual. El borrador SEAV. Virtual Archaeol. Rev. **4**, 71–75 (2011)
11. V.M. López-Menchero Bendicho, International guidelines for virtual archaeology: the seville principles, in *Good Practice in Archaeological Diagnostics*, eds by C. Corsi, B. Slapšak, F. Vermeulen. Springer, pp. 269–284 (2013)

Part II
Digitization and Visualization

Chapter 2
Data Acquisition for the Geometric Documentation of Cultural Heritage

Andreas Georgopoulos

Abstract This chapter is divided into five sections. In the first introductory section, the geometric documentation of cultural heritage is defined, while its necessity is also stressed. In addition, the various products which could be included in a geometric documentation are also presented. Moreover, the standards and specifications accepted nowadays are mentioned. In the second section, the passive data acquisition methods are presented. They include those sensors and methodologies which collect data based on the radiation emitted from the objects and have an external—usually natural—source, e.g. the sun. In the third section, the active methods are presented. They include sensors and devices that emit their own radiation and record the part radiating back from the objects of interest. In the fourth section, the contemporary processing methods of the acquired data are presented. They include processing of all kinds of raw data, irrespective of their origin or method of acquisition. Finally, in the last section, three examples are presented in order to enlighten the readers with the various methodologies of acquisition and processing of the data for three representative cultural heritage objects of varying size and properties.

Keywords Geometric documentation • Digital image • Terrestrial laser scanners

2.1 Geometric Documentation

2.1.1 Necessity

Monuments, including immovable structures of any kind and movable artefacts, are undeniable documents of world history. Their thorough study is an obligation of our era to mankind's past and future. Respect towards cultural heritage already had its roots in the era of the Renaissance. During the nineteenth century, archaeological excavations became common practice, maturing further in the twentieth century.

A. Georgopoulos (✉)
Laboratory of Photogrammetry, School of Rural and Surveying Engineering, National Technical University of Athens (NTUA), 9, Iroon Polytechniou, 15780 Athens, Greece
e-mail: drag@central.ntua.gr

M. Ioannides et al. (eds.), *Mixed Reality and Gamification for Cultural Heritage*,
DOI 10.1007/978-3-319-49607-8_2

Over the recent decades, international bodies and agencies have passed resolutions concerning the obligation to protect, conserve and restore monuments. The Athens Convention (1931), the Hague Agreement (1954), the Venice Charter (1964) and the Granada Agreement (1985) are some of the resolutions in which the need for the full documentation of the monuments is also stressed, as part of their protection, study and conservation. Nowadays, all countries in the civilized world are focussing their scientific and technological efforts towards protecting and conserving the monuments within or even outside their borders to assist other countries. These general tasks include geometric recording, risk assessment, monitoring, restoring, reconstructing and managing cultural heritage.

UNESCO (1946) and the Council of Europe have formed specialized organizations for this goal. The International Council for Monuments and Sites (ICOMOS) is the most important. The International Committee for Architectural Photogrammetry (CIPA), the International Society for Photogrammetry and Remote Sensing (ISPRS), the International Council for Museums (ICOM), the International Centre for the Conservation and Restoration of Monuments (ICCROM) and the International Union of Architects (UIA) are all involved in this task. However, all countries of the civilized world are putting their scientific and technological efforts towards protecting and conserving the monuments, either within or outside their borders.

In this context, the integrated documentation of monuments includes the acquisition of all possible data concerning the monument that may contribute to its safeguarding in the future. Such data may include historic, archaeological, architectural information, as well as administrative data and past drawings, sketches, photos, etc. Moreover, these data also include metric information that define the size, form and location of the monument in 3D space, documenting the monument geometrically.

2.1.2 Definition

It was in the Venice Charter (1964) that, before any other form of intervention, the absolute necessity of geometric documentation of a monument was first stressed upon. The geometric documentation of a monument, which should be considered as an integral part of the greater action, the Integrated Documentation of Cultural Heritage, may be defined as [1]:

- The action of acquiring, processing, presenting and recording the necessary data for the determination of the position and the actual existing form, shape and size of a monument in three-dimensional space at a particular given moment in time.
- The geometric documentation records the present of the monuments as they have been shaped in the course of time and is the necessary background to study their past, as well as preserve them for the future.

The geometric documentation of a monument consists of a series of necessary measurements, from which visual products such as vector drawings, raster images and 3D visualizations may be produced at small or large scales. These products usually have metric properties, especially those being in suitable orthographic projections. Hence, one could expect from the geometric documentation a series of drawings that actually present the orthoprojections of the monument on suitably selected horizontal or vertical planes (Fig. 2.1). Two very important properties of these products are their scale and accuracy. These should be carefully defined at the outset before any action on the monument is begun. Depending on the usage of the final product, the scale may be small (e.g. 1:200 or 1:100) or large (e.g. 1:50, 1:20). Accuracy is directly related to the scale factor and could be defined according to the following simple relationship:

$$\text{Drawing Accuracy} = 0.25\,\text{mm} \times \text{Scale Coefficient}.$$

This is based on the fact that the resolution of the human eye on a printed document is approximately ¼ of a millimetre. In the case of digital products, this limit may become more strict, i.e. 0.1 of a mm.

Another important issue is the level of detail which should be present in the final product. For a justified decision on that matter, the contribution of the expert who is going to be the user is indispensable. A survey product, a line drawing or an image implies generalization to a certain degree, depending on the scale. Hence, the requirements or the limits of this generalization should be set very carefully and always in cooperation with the architect or the relevant conservationist, who already has deep knowledge of the monument [2].

In essence, the geometric documentation products are orthogonal projections of a carefully selected set of points. After all, the main data acquisition methods for

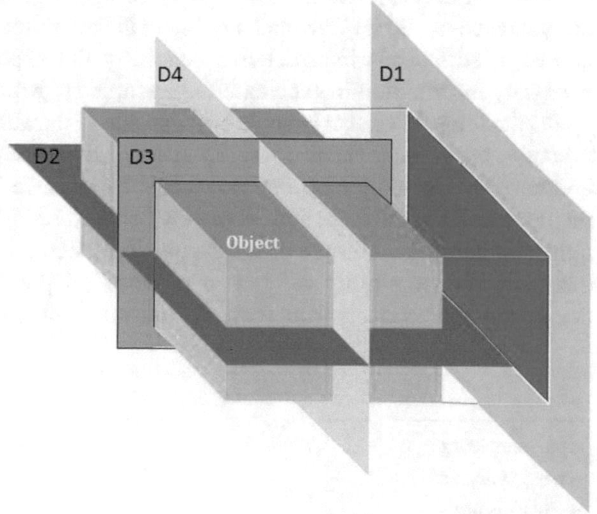

Fig. 2.1 The possible drawings (Di) for the geometric documentation of a monument, horizontal (D2) and vertical (D3, D4) sections and facades (D1)

geometric recording are all point based. The selection of these points requires knowledge, experience and skill. The tools to be used for the determination of these points in space are many and vary in speed, accuracy and efficiency; however, they should all be available to the user.

In any case, the geometric documentation of monuments should serve the needs of conservators and users in general. Hence, it should document those properties of the monument which are necessary to support the right decisions for its conservation. Consequently the monument should be carefully "read" and understood by the documenters as far as its construction, state of conservation and pathologies are concerned. This action calls for an interdisciplinary approach for the geometric documentation of cultural heritage. CIPA,[1] the International Scientific Committee of ICOMOS[2] and ISPRS[3] for heritage documentation, has been striving for many decades to bridge the gap between "users" and "providers" of the documentation products.

2.1.3 Geometric Documentation Products (2D–3D)

These documentation products have traditionally been two-dimensional vector drawings as already mentioned in Sect. 2.2. For many years, users, i.e. architects, archaeologists and conservators were used to working with such geometric documentation products and based their conservation and restoration studies on these.

Technological advances have offered experts the opportunity to produce two-dimensional drawings containing raster images. These images are orthogonal projections of suitably taken digital images and have all the metric properties of conventional drawings. They are referred to as orthophotos or orthoimages. Consequently 2D raster documentation material has come into play, but it needed, and perhaps still needs, some time to be fully accepted by the users, as acceptance has not yet reached 100 %. The main argument is that although the information content is vast, it still needs interpretative action by the experts in order to isolate the necessary information in each case (e.g. geometry, pathology).

3D drawings have also become possible due to the ability of the CAD software to process and present vectors in 3D space. However the latest development is undoubtedly the ability offered nowadays to produce 3D point clouds and from them meshes and surfaces and ultimately 3D textured models. This can be realized quite fast using a multitude of data acquisition techniques. The great advantage is definitely the possibility offered to produce all previously accepted geometric documentation products from these 3D models. Moreover, it is possible to perform

[1] cipa.icomos.org

[2] www.icomos.org

[3] www.isprs.org

3D measurements directly on these 3D models and set up virtual visits and visualizations, thus serving a multitude of other purposes.

2.1.4 Documentation Methods

For the geometric recording, several measurement methods may be applied, ranging from the conventional, simple, topometric methods for partially or totally uncontrolled surveys to the elaborated contemporary surveying and photogrammetric ones for completely controlled surveys. The simple topometric methods are applied only when the small dimensions and simplicity of the monument may allow it, when an uncontrolled survey is adequate or in cases when a small completion of the fully controlled methods is required.

Surveying and photogrammetric methods are based on direct measurements of lengths and angles, either on the monument or on images thereof. They determine three-dimensional point coordinates in a common reference system and ensure uniform and specified accuracy. Moreover, they provide adaptability, flexibility, speed, security and efficiency. All in all, they present undisputed financial merits, in the sense that they are the only methods that may surely meet any requirements with the least possible total cost and the biggest total profit. To this measurement group belong the terrestrial laser scanners (TLS). They manage to collect a huge number of points in 3D space, usually called point cloud, in a very limited time frame.

It should, however, be stressed that since till date there is no generally acceptable framework for specifying the level of detail and the accuracy requirements for the various kinds of geometric recordings of monuments, every single monument is geometrically documented on the basis of its own accuracy and cost specifications. Therefore it is imperative that all disciplines involved should cooperate closely, exchange ideas and formulate the geometric documentation requirements in common, as well as deeply understand the monument itself and each other's needs.

As it has already been established, the geometric documentation of monuments requires the acquisition of a carefully selected set of points and the determination of their position in space. Hence, all data acquisition methodologies have been developed to serve this exact purpose. Nowadays, there are many available methods for this purpose, and none of them can be considered obsolete. All have a role to play and contribute their share to the final product.

Boehler and Heinz [3] first attempted to illustrate the implementation range of these methods. Today their approach may be adopted to include the newly developed methodologies. In this, the implementation range of each method is characterized in terms both of number of points and object size. More traditional methods include hand and tactile measurements, which are always useful for important details or small objects. Geodetic and tacheometric measurements, i.e. using an electronic total station, although accurate, can only record a limited number of points at a considerable range. Photogrammetry, terrestrial or aerial, is a passive image-based methodology for massive point acquisition from considerable ranges.

Laser scanning or LiDAR, terrestrial or airborne, on the other hand, allows for massive point acquisition using active techniques. For the geometric documentation of monuments, the range of object sizes up to a couple of thousand metres applies, while the number of acquired points should practically have no limit. It should be noted that all methodologies measure angles and distances and indirectly determine the position of the required points in space.

These documentation methods may be grouped in several ways. Firstly, to those involving light recording and those that do not. However, their main distinction is whether they are passive or active. Passive methods record radiation reflected by the objects of interest, while active methods emit their own radiation and measure the returned portion. Image-based measuring techniques are considered passive, and terrestrial laser scanning is active.

2.2 Specifications and Standards

The geometric documentation products are usually used as base material for restoration or conservation studies, where increased accuracy and detail are required. Unfortunately worldwide there are no complete, systematic and accepted specifications recognized as a standard. Moreover, those existing fail to evolve in parallel to and incorporate the rapid technological advances. Consequently, specifications are formed almost ad hoc, especially for each geometric documentation project, which results in a non-systematic approach to this very serious task, and every time the qualities of the documentation products depend on the experience of the experts involved in the compilation of these specifications and not on the particular needs of each case. In addition, the non-existence of specifications causes problems among those who carry out the documentation, those who supervise it and those who are going to finally use it.

Moreover, it would be very useful if the experience gathered from similar projects could be exploited and incorporated into the existing specifications in some form, for the benefit of future projects worldwide. This would only be possible through standardization and specification of the procedures and products. This would also be useful for agencies which are involved with many geometric documentation projects every year [4].

The International Council of Monuments and Sites (ICOMOS) in cooperation with the Getty Conservation Institute (GCI) and CIPA-Heritage Documentation have formed the RecorDIM Initiative, a "Partnership for Heritage Recording, Documentation and Information Management," aiming to cover the gaps between "users" and "providers" of the information concerning cultural heritage. This would be achieved via the development of strategies and the formation of an action framework. Several task groups were formed, of which TG16 International Heritage Documentation Standards was concerned with studying and analysing international standards and specifications for cultural heritage and compiled a technical report with practical recommendations, technical specifications and standards (RecorDIM TG16, 2007).

English Heritage, now Historic England, on the other hand is using specifications especially developed for the documentation of English monuments [5]. In the USA and within Heritage Documentation Programs of the Department of the Interior and the National Park Service, standards and guidelines were compiled, which to a certain extent cover pertinent needs [6].

In countries with rich cultural heritage, e.g. Greece and Italy, the issue of standards and specifications becomes even more critical. In particular the Hellenic Ministry of Culture (Directorate of Byzantine and Post-Byzantine Monuments Restoration) has compiled specifications, which refer to the requirements of the geometric documentation, but unfortunately enforcing outdated methods [7]. In addition, the Technical Chamber of Greece has attempted to compile technical specifications for restoration and conservation studies, whose main weight however was not on the documentation actions [8].

Consequently, this need should be fulfilled. International organizations like UNESCO and ICOMOS should undertake the initiative, and CIPA is the executive committee to actually compile widely accepted standards and specifications. UNESCO can also offer a great contribution in this area. It can initiate standards and have them implemented by all member countries in the area of cultural heritage. It is then possible to imagine a world database having a uniform format/data structure and guidelines for the documentation of different cultural heritage objects/monuments/sites. With this initiative UNESCO can create a world cultural heritage website "using a common albeit technological language" accessible to the universal public. ICOMOS and CIPA are two professional organizations working together in the area of cultural heritage. ICOMOS has developed and is currently working in the area of e-documentation while CIPA developed the 3-by-3 rules for photogrammetry that are widely used throughout the world today (cipa.icomos.org). These organizations need to be encouraged to continue in this area with common goals and initiatives.

Consequently, surveying and photogrammetric methodology are highly recommended to be the methodologies of choice for cultural heritage documentation. As already described, they are based on direct measurements of lengths and angles on the object or on images thereof, thus resulting to 3D coordinates of the selected points in a common reference system. Their advantages, compared to the conventional methods, can be summarized as follows:

- They achieve the prescribed accuracy for all documentation products.
- They are flexible and adaptable to the particular needs for each object.
- They are characterized by speed, security and efficiency.
- They have the possibility of producing multiple alternative products, such as orthophotos, 3D models and rendered reconstructions.
- They are economical in the sense that they achieve the prescribed result with the least possible effort and cost.

2.3 Passive Data Acquisition Methods

2.3.1 Geodetic Data Acquisition

The contemporary geodetic methodology of data acquisition is mainly employing electronic total stations and is based on the direct measurement of angles and distances in the object space and the indirect determination of the point positions in space. The advantage of this methodology is the possibility for the measurement of specific points with increased accuracy. Obviously, the main disadvantage is the time needed to acquire a large number of points. Technological advances on the other hand are promising that measuring speed will increase in the near future. One such example is the Leica Nova MS50 total station with scanning and imaging capabilities.

Conventional surveying measurements determine a rigid network of well-determined points in 3D space, in order to reference all the subsequent geometric documentation data acquisition methods. Hence, surveying measurements and network establishment should always be performed before any images or point clouds are acquired. Distance measurements with the help of total stations may be performed with or without a reflector. In the case of monument recording, accuracy requirements are increased. In order to meet these accuracy requirements, a very careful setup of the instruments is required and also the manufacturer's specifications for angle and distance measurement should be taken into account. Needless to add that a recent instrument calibration is also required in cases of geometric documentation with increased accuracy requirements.

For the use and measurement performance with a total station, prior knowledge of simple surveying techniques is required. It is absolutely necessary for the user to be familiar with (a) setting up an instrument on a tripod (b) to setting out and measuring a surveying traverse, which is actually defining the desired coordinate system, and (c) handling the total station menu both for the measurements and the downloading of the stored data. To calculate the point coordinates and transform them to the proper system requires basic knowledge of analytical geometry.

2.3.2 *Image-Based Data Acquisition*

When a large amount of points are required to document the geometry of an object, which is the case for cultural heritage monuments, photogrammetric techniques come to the rescue!! The main task of the various mapping tools, like photogrammetry, is the determination of the shape, size and position of objects in 3D space. Usually these objects are parts of the earth's surface. However, one should not overlook the fact that very often these tools are implemented for "mapping" different kinds of objects, like buildings, monuments—movable or not—and in general objects of different sizes for which the determination of shape, size and position in 3D space is required.

The photogrammetric technique is based on the fact that an image is indirectly recording the directions to all points imaged. Special algorithms are employed in order to "reverse" the process and determine the position of the points imaged on adjacent images in 3D space. According to the International Society for Photogrammetry and Remote Sensing [9], photogrammetry is defined as "The Art, Science and Technique for acquiring reliable information about physical objects and the environment through recording, measuring and interpreting photographic images and patterns of electromagnetic radiation and other phenomena".

It is obvious that this definition by no means confines photogrammetry to a specific kind of image (e.g. aerial image) or to a specific application (e.g. mapping). Photogrammetry in general is a methodology, a tool actually, to perform measurements in 3D space, i.e. measurements of geometric dimensions, such as length, volume, size, form, position and direction, as opposed to pressure, voltage and speed. Very often, however, these measurements are correlated with the determination of other variables, such as the determination of speed through measurement of distance and time. Based on the above, photogrammetry may be characterized as a measuring tool for everything that can be imaged. More specifically what is measured is a 3D copy, a model of the real object. This model may be optical or digital and is conceived by computers or humans. Photogrammetry is in essence an analogue procedure. Under this term it is meant that the object under examination is replaced by a related copy, just like the use of mechanical, hydraulic or electrical analogues in engineering practice.

Photogrammetry is advantageous in cases where the direct measurement of the object is rather impossible, difficult or costly. Naturally an object may belong to more than one of these cases. In addition, one should also mention some other cases which are not concerned with the nature of the object but with the needs which arise during the study of a technical problem. Hence, photogrammetry is also recommended when:

- Large amounts of detail are required from the object's measurements.
- Contours of the object's surface are required.
- It is not certain whether the measurements are going to be needed or not.
- It is not certain beforehand which measurements are going to be necessary and when.

Today photogrammetry is mostly implemented in aerial mapping using airborne or satellite imagery. However, by the end of the nineteenth and the beginning of the twentieth century, the implementation of photogrammetry—with the camera axis mostly horizontal and close to the object—was already developed. The German architect and engineer Albrecht Meydenbauer is considered to be the inventor of architectural photogrammetry as a result of the difficulties he had in documenting high buildings. Since then, the implementation of photogrammetry in cultural heritage documentation has been constantly increasing at the international level.

Most of the international conventions concerned with cultural heritage (e.g. Venice Charter, Granada Convention) specifically mention the absolute necessity of a thorough geometric documentation before any kind of intervention to the monuments. Photogrammetry is an ideal tool for providing a reliable metric base document, which is indispensable for any study. In the interdisciplinary approach, the photogrammetry expert has an important role to play. Needless to say that a complete photogrammetric record of a monument actually constitutes a preservation record, which may be exploited only when needed.

As already mentioned, photogrammetry is a methodology for determining the shape, size, position and also the details of an object in 3D space with the help of images. As a consequence, an important advantage is the fact that at the same time quantitative and qualitative information are recorded in an image. Information about the material, the state, the colour, etc. of the object may be later extracted through suitable interpretation of the image. This record is performed at a given moment in time, which enables the recording of time, as the fourth dimension, thus enabling the monitoring of objects and phenomena variating with time. Additional advantages of the methodology are:

- Most of the processing is performed in the laboratory, thus contributing to lower labour costs and minimizing the work on site.
- Storing and archiving of all information recorded in images is easy and economical.
- Photogrammetry in general is a non-contact method, which is very important for recording and measuring sensitive or hazardous objects.
- Fieldwork is rather independent from weather conditions.

Perhaps the most important step for implementing photogrammetric techniques is the data acquisition. Taking the correct images is essential for extracting the required information from them later. Special care should be taken as to what camera or cameras to use, while the lenses used and the placements (of camera) play an equally important role.

Nowadays, digital cameras are mostly used for photogrammetric applications. However, there are still some implementations of analogue cameras, especially in the field of aerial mapping. Since metric information is to be extracted from the images, the geometric properties of these images and, of course, of the cameras used to acquire them should be controlled and known. Hence, for many decades during the analogue and analytical era of photogrammetry, special cameras were built specifically for metric information extraction with very accurately known geometric properties. These cameras were characterized as metric cameras and presented the following basic properties:

- Stable and known geometry, to increase metric accuracy
- Fiducial marks, to define a reference system for image coordinate measurements
- Low radial distortion, to minimize geometric errors
- Film-flattening devices (mechanical, pneumatic, etc.)
- Fixed focusing distance, to avoid moving lens elements and enhance camera geometry

Metric camera manufacturers provided their clients with a calibration certificate, which describes in detail the camera geometry. Several procedures for calibrating the cameras have been developed as cameras ought to be recalibrated every 2 years or so [10]. Special metric cameras for terrestrial use were also produced by large camera manufacturers, such as Wild, Zeiss, Zeiss Jena, etc. Today digital airborne cameras are the standard for aerial photography. They still have the drawback of the small image size, as technology is still unable to compete with the $230 \times 230\ \text{mm}^2$ negative size of the analogue film cameras. Hence, several techniques are being employed in order to overcome this obstacle, such as implementation of the three-line scanning method (e.g. Leica ADS series) and the composition of a larger image size by stitching together smaller images from the same perspective centre (e.g. Z/I DMC series or Microsoft Vexcel Ultracam series). Today a lot of manufacturers produce digital cameras for aerial images. Aerial imaging is rather outside the scope of this chapter, and for further information the reader is advised to visit the web pages of the manufacturers.

Non-metric cameras were also used for photogrammetric purposes, mainly for their versatility, low weight, interchangeable lenses and, of course, low cost. Initially, they were seen as angle-recording instruments of lower accuracy, suitable for less-demanding applications. With the advancement of computer power and the development of suitable software able to perform camera calibration of high standard, non-metric cameras became more attractive and, nowadays, all digital cameras used for terrestrial applications are non-metric. For cultural heritage documentation, commercial digital cameras are used today. They may be either high-end DSLRs or compact cameras. Each category has its pros and cons. The DSLRs have large sensor sizes and consequently bigger pixel pitch, extremely important for metric imaging. Moreover they have the undeniable advantage of interchangeable lenses, which makes them highly versatile. On the other hand, they are heavier and more expensive. The compact cameras are light and of low cost, but their small sensor size and unstable internal geometry are disadvantages that cannot be overlooked.

2.3.2.1 Digital Cameras and Their Operation

Digital optical cameras have nowadays replaced analogue cameras almost completely. They are the result of the development of the digital sensors, which started in the 1960s. Digital sensors are based on the property of silicon dioxide to generate electric current when exposed to light. Thus two similar technologies have been developed over the years for constructing and operating digital sensors. These are the charge-coupled device (CCD) and the complementary metal–oxide–semiconductor (CMOS). Essentially they differ in the way the intensities at each sensor element are read and converted to digital information.

2.3.2.2 Characteristics

Colour is attributed to each registered sensor element intensity using the Beyer principle by which each sensor element (sel) has a filter in front and registers the intensity of the respective colour band, i.e. red, green or blue. The green "sensitive" sels are double in number compared to the red or the blue ones to exactly simulate the way the human eye perceives colour. Of course there are other systems to attribute colour to the digital image, but they are used by very few manufacturers, e.g. the FOVEON system used by Sigma[4] and the Multi-Shot system employed mainly by Hasselblad.[5]

Another very important, but often overlooked, property of the digital sensors is their size, especially the size of the sensor elements, also known as pixel pitch. As the sensor elements vary in physical size and the number of sensor elements—which will later become pixels in the digital image—it would be useful to pay attention to the following parameters. For a sensor element to register reliably the intensity of light, it should have a size of more than 4 μm, i.e. 0.004 mm. Hence, the combination of the physical sensor size and the resolution, usually given in megapixels (MP), is of utmost importance in order to ensure reliable digital image registration.

Digital sensor sizes can vary from a few mm^2 up to the "full frame" for the commercial compact and DSLR cameras and even bigger for specially developed digital systems.

2.3.3 *The Digital Image*

The replacement of analogue film with electronic chips has introduced a new reality as far as the internal geometry of the camera is concerned. On one hand the imaging plane

[4]http://www.foveon.com/article.php?a=67

[5]http://www.hasselblad.com/digital-backs/multi-shot-digital-back

is almost by definition planar, but on the other hand the size and shape of the pixel are introduced as new parameters. On the other hand, digital recording has also introduced some problems and defects as far as radiometry of digital images is concerned, such as dark current, blooming, smear, traps and blemishes to name but a few. All these contribute to the final quality of the digital image and, consequently, to the final accuracy of the measurements and reliability of imagery products.

One of the most important problems caused by digital recording is noise. By that all useless radiation recorded is meant, which is caused by a number of sources, such as the ambient conditions and the electronic chip itself. The ratio of useless radiation recorded to the useful signal is the measure of noise, and it is called the signal-to-noise (SnR) ratio and is measured in dB (Fig. 2.2).

Digital recording has clear advantages over the obsolete analogue film, some of which are the following:

- Lower cost
- Lower noise

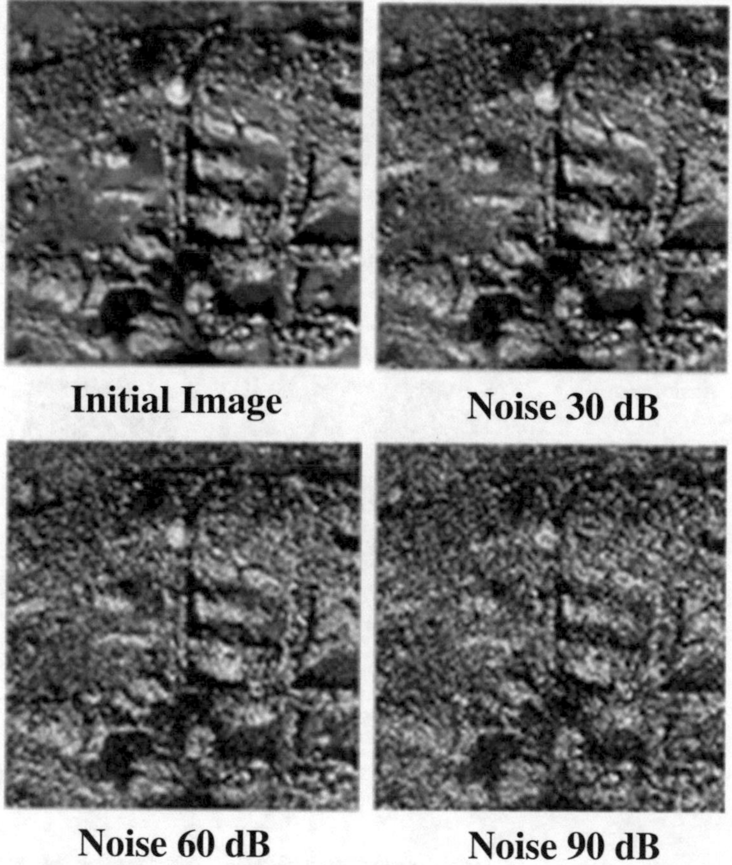

Fig. 2.2 Noise in digital images

- High dynamic range
- Reliability
- Stable geometry
- No processing—developing—time
- Possibility for real-time processing

Today digital cameras are in their phase of maturity, after almost three decades of existence. In this section, some principles of digital image processing will be presented for the benefit of understanding the photogrammetric processing of digital images.

A digital image is defined as the depiction of the object of interest on a planar surface using a finite number of picture elements (pixels) for which their position (i, j) and grey tone (or colour) value $(f(i, j))$ are known. This implies that the image is actually a set of numbers; hence, it may be stored and handled by a computer. On the other hand, it is a discrete imaging function as opposed to the analogue image, which is considered to be a continuous one (Fig. 2.3).

This set of numbers, which forms the image and actually only the colour values, has some interesting statistical properties, which are characteristic of the digital image itself. Let us suppose that there is a digital image of C columns and R rows (Fig. 2.4). The mean value m of the set of colour values is determined as:

$$m = \bar{f}(x, y) = \frac{1}{CR} \sum_{x=0}^{C-1} \sum_{y=0}^{R-1} f(x, y).$$

This mean value is indicative of the brightness of the image. The bigger the value, the brighter the image. The variance var of the set of colour values is determined by:

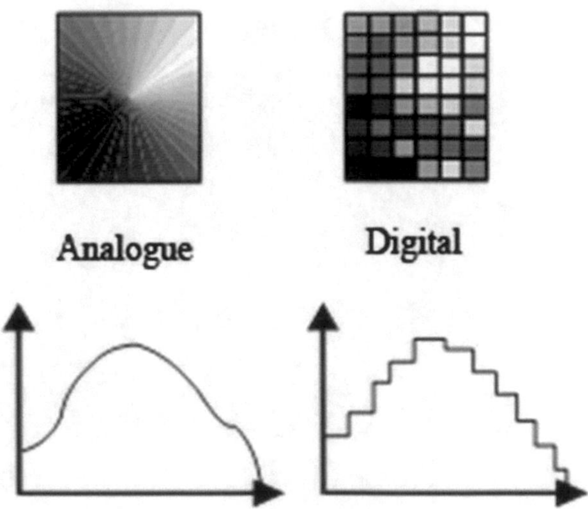

Fig. 2.3 Analogue and digital image

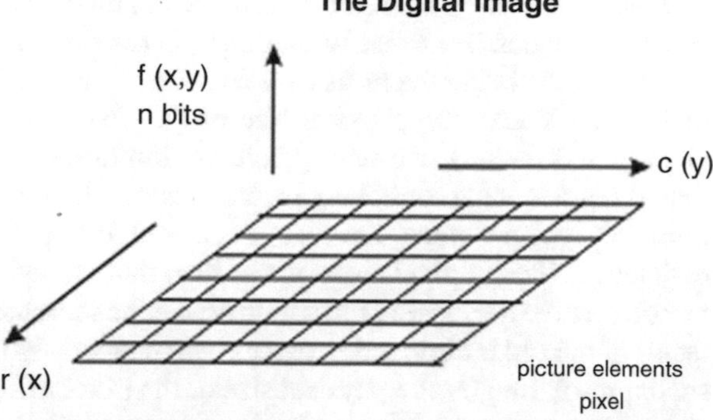

Fig. 2.4 Structure of a digital image

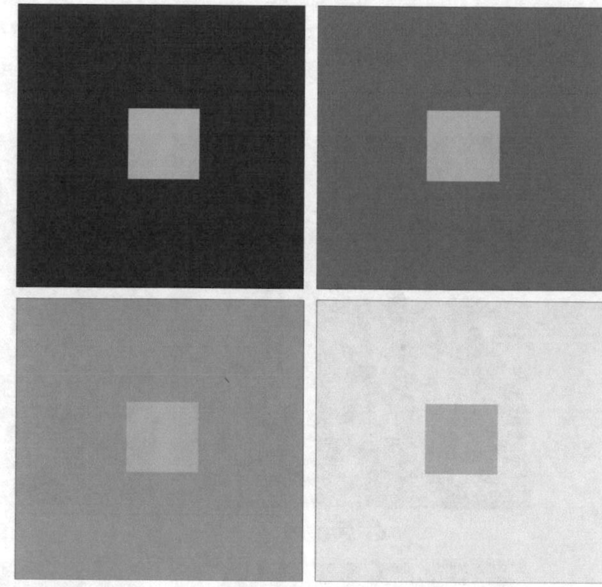

Fig. 2.5 The relativity of the contrast

$$var = \frac{1}{CR} \sum_{x=0}^{C-1} \sum_{y=0}^{R-1} (f(x,y) - m)^2$$

The variance is expressing the contrast of the image. The bigger the value of var, the more contrast is present in the digital image. It should be noted that contrast is rather a subjective property, as it is dependent on the background and surrounding colours (or grey tones). In Fig. 2.5 this relativity is depicted as the squares in the middle have exactly the same colour value, but they seem different to the observer.

Finally, the histogram of the digital image, i.e. of the grey (or colour) values, is actually the frequency of appearance for each value in the image and is indicative of the quality of the digital image. The wider the value range is, the better the quality of the image, as it stretches over the whole range of the available grey tone (or colour) values.

Spatial resolution of an image is related to the physical size of each pixel and, of course, their number in the digital image. It is obvious that the smaller the size of each pixel, the better the measurement accuracy on the image but the bigger the size of the file. Today the physical size of the pixels is down to a few micrometres (1 μm = 0.001 mm). However, there are limitations, since a pixel of size smaller than 4 μm is unable to reliably record enough photons in order to register the grey tone (or colour) value for that pixel, and interpolation is used to cover this deficiency. Hence, pixel sizes of less than that value in size should be avoided for metric use. Earlier, spatial resolution used to be measured in dots per inch (DPI) as a result of the older digitization process on scanners. Nowadays, we tend to measure spatial resolution by the physical size of the pixel in conjunction with the physical size of the sensor. This last value is not very easily known by the manufacturers, who tend to promote the amount of pixels (MP) for obvious commercial reasons. Alternatively, we tend to use the GSD (ground sampling distance), which is the size of the object imaged in a pixel of a digital image at a given scale. In Fig. 2.6 the

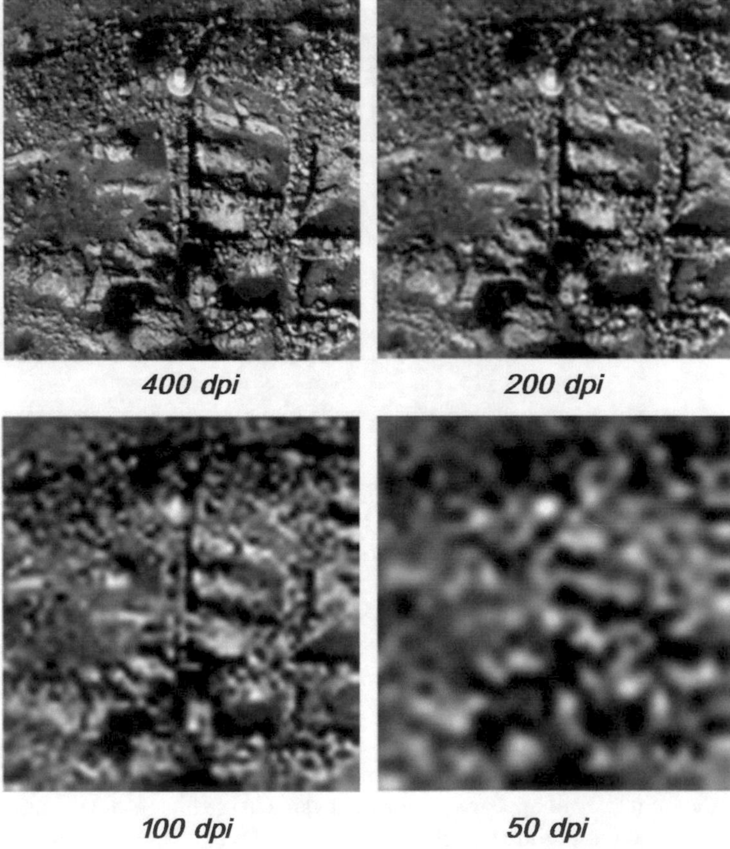

Fig. 2.6 Image spatial resolution

Table 2.1 File size and spatial resolution of an aerial B&W image

Spatial resolution	1000	600	300	100	dpi
Size of image file (23 × 23 cm^2)	80.1	28.8	7.2	0.8	MB
Pixel size	25.4	42.3	84.7	254	μm
GSD for image scale 1:8000	0.20	0.34	0.68	2.00	m

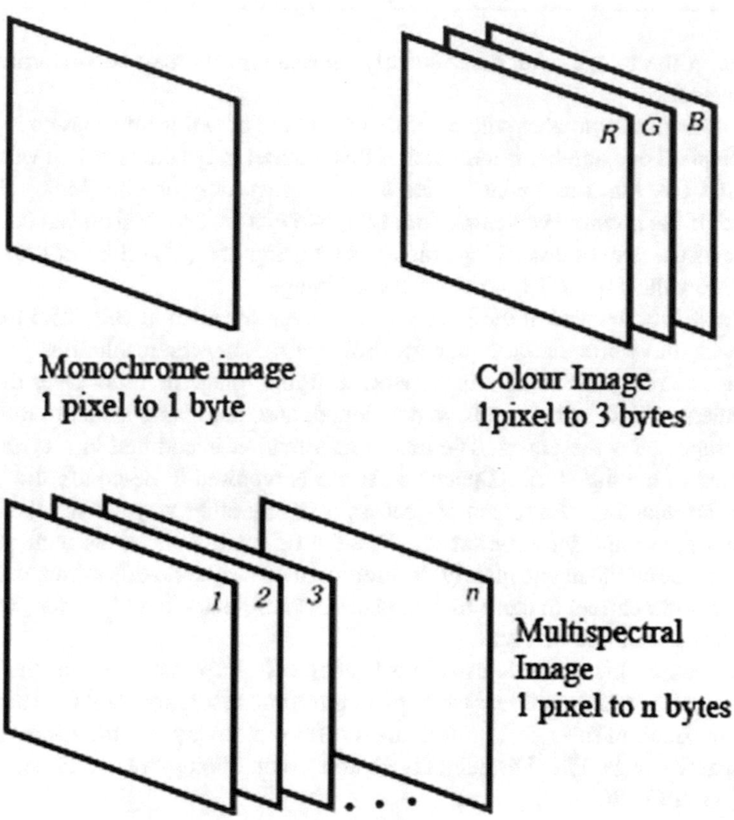

Fig. 2.7 Colour depth of a digital image

same image is shown with different spatial resolutions, and in Table 2.1 the size of an analogue aerial image (negative size of 23 × 23 cm^2) digitized for different spatial resolutions is presented.

Radiometric resolution, on the other hand, is related to the number of grey values (or colours) that are used in the available palette to describe the image. If the image is black and white, only grey values are used. If it is coloured, which is the most common case nowadays, a combination of the basic colours, i.e. red, green and blue (RGB), is required to assign colour to each pixel (Fig. 2.7). It is interesting to note that the multispectral satellite images also use the same principle. The number of available colours has a direct effect on the size of the image file and on the amount of the imaged detail. The more colour values are available, the more details are

Table 2.2 File size and radiometric resolution of an aerial B&W image

Radiometric resolution Number of values	Black	White	Bit	Pixel/byte	MB
2	0	1	1	8	10
4	0	3	2	4	20
16	0	15	4	2	40
256	0	255	8	1	80

depicted in the image, and, consequently, measurements may be performed with more accuracy.

The amount of available colours is also related to how this information is stored. For each pixel one number is assigned. If this number may take only two values (2^1, e.g. 0 and 1 or black and white), then for its storage only one bit (binary digit) is required. If the possible values are four (2^2), two bits are required and so on. Today the most usual way of describing colours is by using 256 (2^8) different grey values or 3×256 values for RGB, i.e. for a colour image.

In Table 2.2, the size of the image files is given for a 1,000 DPI (25.4 μm pixel size) black and white digital image for different radiometric resolutions.

There are many different ways to store a digital image in a file. Over the years many image file formats have been developed, and there is no standard today that clearly supersedes the others. The image information is codified in a certain way and stored in the digital file. Special software is required to de-codify the file and present the image on the screen or process it in any other way. Some file formats compress the image information for the sake of smaller file sizes with negative consequences on the image quality. In addition there are standards introduced by all camera manufacturers to store their images in proprietary RAW format, which is different for each one of them.

In the image file, there is usually a header with information about the image, such as number of columns and rows, pixel pitch and resolution, and then the actual image information follows. The formats mostly used today to store digital images are Tagged Image File Format (TIFF) and Joint Photographers Expert Group (JPEG) or JPEG 2000.

2.3.4 Good Practice for Digital Imaging

The geometric recording of cultural heritage assets implies in essence the projection of a carefully selected set of points on horizontal or vertical planes, thus forming the required 2D drawings, which traditionally form the basis of all intervention studies. The fact that nowadays 3D models have also undertaken a significant role in these actions has not affected this principle, as 3D models are actually a set of millions of points, not carefully selected this time. Terrestrial image-based techniques for recording and documentation are based on the fact that through the camera an infinite number of angles from the camera station to the points of the object imaged are recorded. The photogrammetric procedure is then responsible to extract metric information, i.e. to determine the position in space of the selected or all of these points. This may be achieved using two different but similar pathways: the typical photogrammetric pipeline or the automated approach using the structure-from-motion (SfM) algorithm.

2.3.5 Platforms for Data Acquisition

Positioning the camera for metric photography is most of the times crucial. The images have to be taken from specific positions with certain orientation. These parameters contribute to the correct image scale and GSD, to the required coverage and, most importantly, to the correct orientation of the camera axis. Consequently, it is often necessary to employ special means to position the camera to the desired position. The platforms employed for that purpose may be limited only by imagination.

Tripods, scaffolding and cranes are perhaps some obvious solutions. However, kite systems and balloons, manned or unmanned, have also been employed in the past. Of course, helicopters, airplanes and satellites are also common practice (Fig. 2.8). Kites, tethered balloons, airships, remote controlled airplanes and

Fig. 2.8 Platforms for aerial photography

helicopters and multirotor and fixed-wing systems are unmanned aerial vehicles appropriate for large-scale mapping [11].

All these different platforms present advantages and disadvantages, which are summarized in Table 2.3. This table also includes the more recently used platforms, namely, the unmanned aircraft systems (UAS). These systems, no matter which kind, have experienced an incredible boom for large-scale mapping and in the geospatial domain in general [13].

Over a short period of time, a plethora of UAS platform types and, most importantly, a multitude of cameras and other sensors have been made available and are being implemented with different and often uncontrollable results. Sometimes their combinations also challenge the implementation of conventional aerial photography for certain applications [14]. Legislation is another critical issue when unmanned aerial platforms are involved, as it varies a lot from country to country, if rules apply at all. Gradually, however, most of the countries pass pertinent laws governing the flight and use of these UAS.

UAS can be remotely controlled, semi-autonomous, autonomous or be driven by a combination of these capabilities. The flight trajectory of a UAS depends on flight dynamics and flight management systems and displays larger off-nadir deviations in contrast with the traditional airborne blocks.

Multirotor and fixed-wing aircraft stand out from the others because of their recent upgrade to assisted or fully autonomous systems. Furthermore, the acquisition accuracy is increasing with these systems, and they are becoming less weather dependent. Multirotor UAS are widely used for surveying smaller areas due to the fact that they can fly in lower flying heights but have shorter flying autonomy. They display greater stability in the wind, and therefore the obtained images are suitable for photogrammetric use. Fixed-wing systems stand out for their increased autonomy and the capability of covering wider areas, as a result of the larger flying height and the greater flying speed they can achieve. However, enough space is usually required for their takeoff and landing. A significant difference between these two groups of systems is the capability of multirotor systems to obtain oblique imagery.

Simple compact digital cameras are usually attached on a UAS. However, they can also be equipped with thermal or infrared camera systems, airborne LiDAR systems, SAR or a combination thereof. In order to define the position and the orientation of the acquisition platform, other navigation sensors are used, such as miniature global positioning systems (GNSS) and inertial measurement units (IMU), compasses and barometers.

Relative recent literature includes studies about the usability of UAS in cultural heritage mapping or surface measurement [15–17], using different UAS acquisition platforms [18], combination of terrestrial and aerial UAS data for 3D reconstruction evaluation [19] or assessments on UAS data dense matching [20].

For close-range applications, which mostly concern the documentation of cultural heritage and especially for taking close-range vertical images from a height greater than the human abilities but smaller than the normal and allowed flying heights of aircraft and helicopters, there was always a desperate need for platforms capable of flying at low altitudes [11]. Nowadays, technological advances have

Table 2.3 Rough evaluation of aerial photography platforms [12]

	Cost	Maintenance and running costs	Deployment time	Experience needed	Time of flight	Weather dependency	Acquisition speed	Acquisition accuracy
Kite	3	3	1	1	2	1	2	0
Balloon	2	2	1	3	3	0	0	2
Airships	1	2	1	3	3	1	0	2
RC single and multicopter	1–0	2–0	3	0	0	2	1–2	3
RC plane	1–0	2–1	2–3	0	1–2	1	3	3
UAV multicopter	1–0	2–0	3	2	0	2	1–2	3
UAV fixed wing	0	2–1	1–3	2	1–2	1	3	3

enabled the manufacturing of a variety of autonomous aerial platforms, which are capable of carrying a digital camera and perform aerial imaging from a few meters to a few hundred meters.

The use of UAVs or UAS or RPAS or drones as they are more popularly known is usually and almost associated with surveillance projects and military action. As the request for timely, accurate, high-resolution data for documentation, surveying, mapping and monitoring natural resources and man-made objects becomes more and more demanding, the UAVs are becoming more and more promising. Nowadays, UAVs can carry not only imaging but also non-imaging sensors, but such a platform for collecting imagery data are in a niche in geospatial technologies. The hardware costs are going down and down, while the advances in sensor and camera technologies, along with the availability of light and lifelong batteries, have made the mass production of UAVs possible.

UAVs for mapping purposes are nowadays mainly categorized as "fixed-wing" and "multirotor" devices. There are also helicopter-based UAVs. Fixed-wing UAVs fly faster and are suitable for covering larger areas but at smaller image scales. They usually have lower payload capabilities than the multirotor ones and, obviously, cannot hover over a target. In addition, they need some plane area for takeoff and landing. On the other hand, multirotor UAVs can usually have four to eight rotors and are capable of hovering and thus performing pinpoint photography. They are also capable of flying lower, thus allowing for larger image scales. With their increased payload capability, they may also be equipped with bigger DSLRs and, even, with small LiDAR systems. Multirotor UAVs are more complicated platforms than their fixed-wing counterparts, and consequently, are more demanding as far as their navigation and control are concerned.

All imaging UAVs are equipped with a GNSS receiver and an INS system in order to provide orientation and control while airborne. These devices also enable the UAVs to perform preprogrammed flights and take images at designated points in space. This flight planning may be performed in specialized software which usually accompanies the UAVs and may be run on a simple computer. The flight plan may even be realized on Google Earth, which is very convenient. Legislation on the other hand is very fuzzy and it varies from country to country, if there is one established. In the USA, drone-flying regulations vary from state to state. In the EU there is currently an effort to accept common rules for flying UAVs. In any case, the local authorities should always be informed about an imminent flight, which should under no circumstances interfere with normal air traffic.

2.4 Active Data Acquisition Methods

Accurate representation of objects, large and small, has been in the forefront of scientific interest for as long as the specialists felt the need for studying those objects. Two-dimensional representations using rules and techniques of projective and descriptive geometry have been common practice for centuries. It was from these 2D representations that three-dimensional information ought to be extracted. This task required special education, hard practice, skill and imagination. Nowadays these techniques have been largely replaced by digital scanning which is achieved using 3D scanners.

A 3D scanner is a device that records a real-world object or the environment to collect data on its shape and possibly its appearance (i.e. colour, material). The collected data can then be used to construct digital, three-dimensional models useful for a wide variety of applications. Digital scanning of objects has been common practice for more than two decades. Laser technology has been the flagship of this activity, but other means of acquiring 3D information of an object's surface have also been used widely. Modulated light scanners, non-contact passive scanners, photometric systems and silhouette scanners are the most known kinds of systems acquiring vast numbers of points describing the surface of interest. All these systems work at different rates, achieving various densities and providing different accuracies; hence, each one serves special needs in the market.

The final products of digital scanning methods are, of course, point clouds of varying densities and accuracies. Processing of these point clouds involves the implementation of a multitude of software and techniques, in order to produce 3D meshes, 3D surface models and, finally, 3D-rendered models of varying resolutions. Digital scanning has been used extensively in many applications, such as cultural heritage documentation, industrial applications and design, automotive industry, orthodontics and prosthetics, reverse engineering and prototyping, quality control and inspection and—of course—in the entertainment industry for the production of movies and video games (e.g. [21, 22]).

2.4.1 Scanners

2.4.1.1 Terrestrial Laser Scanners

Terrestrial laser scanners are devices that emit laser radiation and detect its reflection in order to probe an object or environment. Active scanners may use any kind of radiation, which may include light, ultrasound or X-ray. Laser scanners are also referred to as LiDAR scanners, from the acronym Light Detection and Ranging. These LiDAR scanners may be used to scan buildings, rock formations, etc. in order to produce a point cloud, i.e. millions of points in 3D space and from that a 3D model.

The device can aim its laser beam in a wide range: its head rotates horizontally, a mirror flips vertically. The laser beam is used to measure the distance to the first object on its path. Terrestrial laser scanners are distinguished into three main categories: time-of-flight scanners, which may use the pulse; phase-shift technique to measure the distance; and triangulation scanners.

Time-of-flight 3D laser scanners are active devices that use laser light to probe the subject. At the heart of this type of scanner is a time-of-flight laser source and a rangefinder. The device determines the distance of a point by timing the round-trip time of a pulse of light. Since the speed of light c is known, the round-trip time determines the travel distance of the laser beam, which is twice the distance between the scanner and the point which reflected it. If t is the round-trip time, then distance is equal to:

$$(c \cdot t)/2.$$

The accuracy of a time-of-flight 3D laser scanner depends on how precisely it can measure the t time. Highly accurate clocks are operating in today's laser scanners, which are able to measure time to a few picoseconds. It is pointed out that the time taken for light to travel 1 mm is 3.3 picoseconds.

The laser rangefinder only detects the distance of one point in its direction of view. Thus, the scanner scans its entire field of view one point at a time by changing the rangefinder's direction of view to scan different points. The view direction of the laser rangefinder can be changed by either rotating the rangefinder itself or by using a system of rotating mirrors. The latter method is commonly used because mirrors are much lighter and can thus be rotated much faster and with greater accuracy. Typical time-of-flight 3D laser scanners can measure the distance of 10,000–100,000 points every second. Pulse scanners can achieve an accuracy of 3–5 mm and may have a range of a few hundred metres up to a couple of kilometres, depending on the power of the laser source.

Phase-shift technology is a variation of the above described pulse method, by which the phase difference between the emitted and the returned radiation is determined. In this way the device is able to determine the distance to each measured point to an accuracy of 2–3 mm and collects far more points per second. Today's phase-shift scanners may reach a recording rate of one million points per second, but their range is confined to a couple of hundred metres.

Triangulation laser scanners use a slightly different method for determining the relative position of the collected points in 3D space. The triangulation laser scanner casts a laser beam on the object and exploits a camera to look for the location of the laser dot. Depending on how far away the laser strikes a surface, the laser dot appears at different places in the camera's field of view. This technique is called triangulation because the laser dot, the camera and the laser emitter form a triangle. The length of one side of the triangle—the distance between the camera and the laser emitter—is known. The angle of the laser emitter corner is also known. The angle of the camera corner can be determined by looking at the location of the laser dot in the camera's field of view. These three pieces of information fully determine the shape and size of the triangle and gives the location of the laser dot corner of the triangle. In most cases, a laser stripe, instead of a single laser dot, is swept across the object to speed up the acquisition process. Triangulation laser scanners have very limited range capability, i.e. at the order of a few metres, but they are very accurate in determining the points in space. They may provide accuracies to the order of micrometres.

The time-of-flight scanner's accuracy can be disrupted when the laser hits the edge of an object because the information that is sent back to the scanner is from two different locations for one laser pulse. The coordinate relative to the scanner's position for a point that has hit the edge of an object will be calculated based on an average and therefore will put the point in the wrong place. When using a high-resolution scan on an object, the chances of the beam hitting an edge are increased, and the resulting data will show noise just behind the edges of the object. Scanners with a smaller beam width will help to solve this problem but will be limited by range as the beam width will increase over distance. Software can also help by determining that the first object to be hit by the laser beam should cancel out the second.

At a rate of 10,000 sample points per second, low-resolution scans can take less than a second, but high-resolution scans, requiring millions of samples, can take minutes for some time-of-flight scanners. The problem this creates is distortion from motion. Since each point is sampled at a different time, any motion in the subject or the scanner will distort the collected data. Thus, it is usually necessary to mount both the subject and the scanner on stable platforms and minimize vibration. Using these scanners to scan objects in motion is very difficult. When scanning in one position for any length of time, a slight movement can occur in the scanner position due to changes in temperature. If the scanner is set on a tripod and there is strong sunlight on one side of the scanner, then that side of the tripod will expand and slowly distort the scan data from one side to another. Some laser scanners have a level compensator built into them to counteract any movement of the scanner during the scan process [23, 24].

2.4.1.2 Structured Light Scanners

An alternative to the mostly known and market-dominating laser scanners are structured light scanners. Structured light 3D scanners project a pattern of light on the object and detect the deformation of the pattern on the object. They are basically non-contact optical systems, based almost entirely on the principles of photogrammetry in order to transform image pairs to surface information. They are able to achieve information of very high density and of very high accuracy.

Several practical applications of the system are presented, in order to demonstrate its range of applicability. Special interest is given in processing aspects for the creation and visualization of detailed photorealistic 3D models. Various well-known open issues in the related processes are identified, and the respective solutions and improvements in the workflow pipeline brought by the employment of this technology are highlighted. The software used for processing the data acquired by structured light scanners is briefly described, and high-resolution visualizations of submillimetre accuracy for each case study are presented and assessed based on completeness, accuracy and ease of processing. The practical results are discussed and evaluated based on the experience gained through these applications.

As already mentioned, structured light 3D scanners project a pattern of light on the subject and detect the deformation of the pattern on the object's surface. The pattern may be one dimensional or two dimensional. An example of a one-dimensional pattern is a line. The line is projected onto the subject using either an LCD projector or a sweeping laser. A camera, offset slightly from the pattern projector, records the shape of the line at an angle α, and a technique similar to the triangulation principle is used to calculate the distance of every point on the line. In the case of a single-line pattern, the line is swept across the field of view to gather distance information one strip at a time.

An example of a two-dimensional pattern is a grid or a line strip pattern [21]. A camera is used to record the deformation of the pattern, and a fairly complex algorithm is used to calculate the distance at each point in the pattern. One reason for this complexity is ambiguity. The advantage of structured light 3D scanners is speed. Instead of scanning one point at a time, structured light scanners scan multiple points or the entire field of view at once. This reduces or eliminates the problem of distortion from motion. Some systems that employ such methods enable the scanning of moving objects in real time. In most cases such systems have a relatively narrow field of view that may range from a few centimetres to a couple of metres, based on the components of the system and the calibration process.

Zhang and Huang [25] developed a real-time scanner using digital fringe projection and phase-shift technique, a somewhat different structured light method. The system is able to capture, reconstruct and render the high-density details of the dynamically deformable objects, such as facial expressions, at 40 frames per second.

A typical structured light scanner system comprises low-cost off-the-shelf hardware. Two digital SLR cameras of 12 MP or alternatively two machine vision cameras mounted on a rigid base take up the role of image pair acquisition. A DLP projector is used to project the necessary structured light alternations, and the whole system, including supportive tripods, is operated through a standard laptop running the usually proprietary software. The distance between the cameras, i.e. the base, may be varied, according to the size of the object of interest and to its distance from the cameras. The system is driven via a laptop with proprietary software that carries out the required processing for the structured light data (Fig. 2.9). This software takes care of the camera and projector's smooth coordination. It provides for the necessary setup calibration, which includes both camera geometry parameters and also relative positioning of the image acquisition set with the help of a suitable test field, most usually a checkerboard.

The fact that some of these systems employ two cameras is clearly an advantage. The workflow usually requires a calibration sequence, and after that it is ready to acquire the data for producing the 3D information. The calibration procedure determines both the interior orientation parameters of the camera(s) and their relative positions and the scale of acquisition. For this purpose, a custom calibration board, a simple chequered board, is imaged at various angles by both cameras

Fig. 2.9 The main components of the SL2 scanner

Fig. 2.10 SL2 scanner calibration

(Fig. 2.10). The software then calculates the various parameters and the system is ready for use. A series of calibration boards with different physical and square sizes is usually provided, in order to cover various taking distances. The larger the distance, the bigger the calibration board obviously necessary. The calibration procedure theoretically needs a few minutes to be completed, but in practice it is proven that it takes something between 20 and 40 min for each new setup, depending on the ambient conditions, i.e. taking distance and lighting. After the setup calibration, the software drives the cameras for the main data acquisition phase.

Fig. 2.11 Projected structured light during data acquisition

Scanning with such systems actually involves the acquisition of several consecutive image pairs; alternating patterns of light are projected onto the object in sequence (Fig. 2.11). These patterns are alternating black and white stripes with decreasing width. Based on the distortion of these stripes on the object as they are imaged on both images of the stereopair, the software later calculates a triangular mesh of the object's surface, on which the texture may be projected. The system calculates depth by the exploitation of the distortion of these patterns on the surface of the object, following the triangulation principle, only in this case two cameras are employed. The result is a dense (up to 150 μm) mesh of triangles, with points on the objects surface (Fig. 2.12).

Once the system has been calibrated, scanning is fast and reliable. However, the results are highly dependent on the behaviour of light on the surface of the object, and great care should be given to the imaging parameters of the cameras. The use of suitable polarizing filters both for the projector and for the cameras is often recommended.

Depending on the complexity of the object's surface, on its size and on the required density and final accuracy, a considerable number of individual scans may be necessary to cover the object. Using 3D processing software that is usually included in the bundled software, mesh registration is very fast, precise and easy. However, further processing for visualization or rendering requires use of other more specific software, such as 3D Studio Max, Geomagic and Maya.

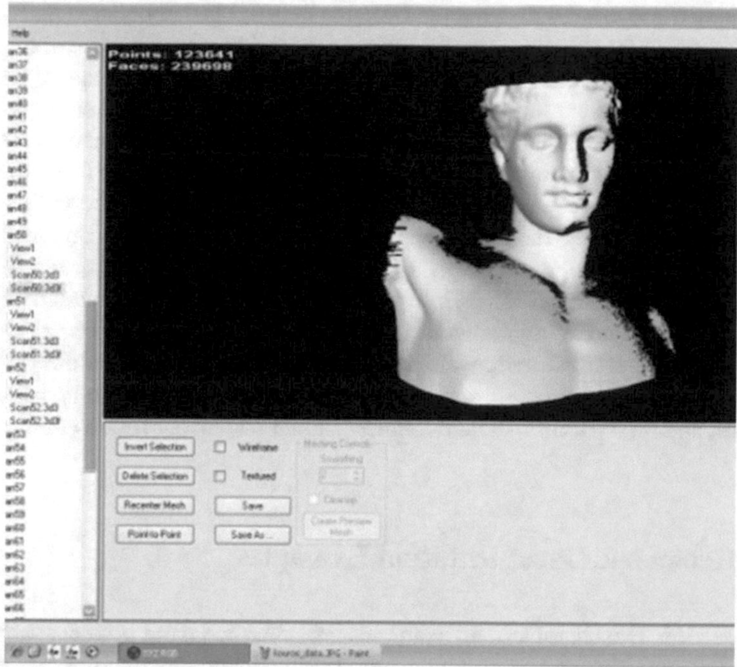

Fig. 2.12 The resulting 3D mesh

2.4.1.3 Range Cameras

A time-of-flight (TOF) camera, usually referred to as a range camera, is a range-imaging camera that basically measures the TOF of a light signal between the camera and each point of the object and thus actually resolves the distance based on the known speed of light. Such a device measures the direct TOF required for a single laser pulse to leave the camera and come back into the focal plane. In the "trigger mode", the 3D images captured, image complete spatial and temporal data, recording full 3D scenes with single laser pulse.

Nowadays, several different technologies for range-imaging flight cameras have been developed. A TOF camera delivers a range image and an amplitude image with infrared modulation intensities at video frame rates. As reported in different studies [26–28], the distance measurements of range-imaging cameras are influenced by some systematic errors, which can be managed by using different distance error models.

On the other hand, in the area of cultural heritage, Rinaudo et al. [29] used SR-4000 camera (Fig. 2.25, first from left) in a standard survey procedure to generate a realistic 3D model, applying at the same time a self-calibration model on the captured point clouds they had to compare. In addition, a high-resolution digital image from a calibrated camera was used to colour the 3D model by using the radiometric information extracted from the image. They concluded that the high sampling rate of the SR-4000 camera allows conceiving a possible use of the range-imaging camera to record data on objects like windows, rooms or statues. The same authors, Chiabrando et al. [27] perform a relevant work for metric surveys. In this work a systematic investigation of the influence of object reflectivity on the range camera distance measurement accuracy and precision was performed, which outlined that the object reflectivity strongly influences the distance measurement precision. Nevertheless, the worse measurement precision of 5 mm obtained is still acceptable for specific applications. Considering a comparison between SR-4000 data and LiDAR data on an architectural element, they demonstrated the high potential of range-imaging cameras for metric surveys of architectural elements and for 3D object reconstruction. These sensors do not seem to be mature yet for use in high-accuracy, demanding applications. However, they definitely have some potential, and their technological evolution should be closely followed.

2.5 Geometric Documentation Examples

In this section, two characteristic examples are presented from projects carried out by the authors. The aim is to show real practical implementations of the data acquisition methods presented in this chapter. It is not important to present details but to show the results and what may be done with them.

The first example refers to the geometric documentation of four historic buildings, namely, the Byzantine churches of Mount Troodos in Cyprus. They are complex and challenging structures, especially as far as their interior decoration with frescoes is concerned. The second example refers to smaller cultural heritage objects, namely, two ancient vessels displayed in the archaeological museum in Athens. The challenge, in this case, is their size and the fact that they should be handled with utmost care.

2.5.1 The Geometric Documentation of Byzantine Churches in Cyprus

In this section some characteristic applications of ICT for cultural heritage will be presented in order to show their contribution and also their evolution. All examples are concerned with the documentation of the Byzantine churches of Mount Troodos in Cyprus.

In the central area of Mount Troodos in Cyprus (Fig. 2.13), there are ten Byzantine churches, unique specimens of Byzantine architecture and religious art dating from the eleventh to the fourteenth century. These ten churches (Fig. 2.14) have been inscribed in the WHL of UNESCO since 1985. The criteria for that were their unique architecture and also their wonderful frescoes (Fig. 2.15), which constitute a "special document of cultural tradition". About one million visitors are attracted each year to these churches. They are:

Saint Nikolas of Stegi in Kakopetria
Saint John the Lambadistis in Kalopanagiotis
Lady Mary Forviotissa of Asinou in Nikitari
Lady Mary of Arakas in Lagoudera
Lady Mary of Moutoullas
Archangel Michael in Pedhoulas
The Holy Cross in Pelendri
Lady Mary of Podithou in Galata
The Cross of Agiasmati in Platanistasa
The Transfiguration of the Saviour in Paliochori

The Geometric Documentation of the Troodos Churches is already underway since 2005 as an effort in collaboration between the Laboratory of Photogrammetry of National Technical University of Athens and the HTI of Nicosia, initially, and later with Cyprus University of Technology.

During the past 11 years, four out of the ten churches have been geometrically documented. Every time with different methodology and always with the latest and most advanced instrumentation for collecting and processing the data [30–33]. In Table 2.4 all important details of these projects can be seen.

By studying Table 2.4, it is apparent how the evolution of the methods has influenced the instrumentation as well as the time necessary for collecting and processing the raw data. The geodetic instrumentation has not experienced a dramatic progress. The use of the imaging total station has perhaps enabled the correct identification of the measured points, thus avoiding gross errors. During these last 10 years, the 3D scanning technology has advanced a lot. However, the high cost of the newer and more modern scanners is prohibiting the constant update of the related instrumentation. Hence, the most important change is identified in the photographic instrumentation. The resolution increase becomes apparent, but the sensor size also plays an important role for the final quality of the products. In parallel, the modernization of the software is perhaps the main source of improving the results and saving processing time. This modernization is based on the overwhelming progress of computer power and on the development of more efficient algorithms. The main algorithm which brought a big change is the incorporation of the structure-from-motion (SfM) procedure, which makes use of the computer power of newer processors in order to determine the orientation of the images and also to achieve the object reconstruction imaged in a series of densely overlapping digital images. The result of these algorithms is equivalent, if not better, to the one from terrestrial laser scanners. In addition, these pieces of software are in a position to produce textured 3D models using colour from the digital images.

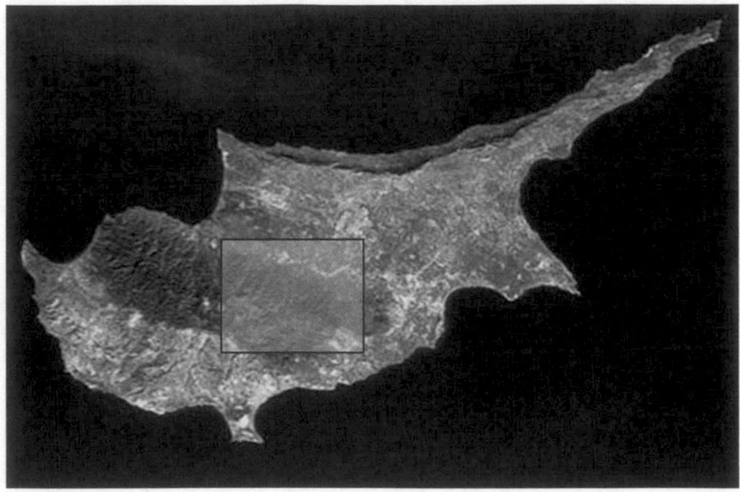

Fig. 2.13 The area on Troodos mountain where the ten Byzantine churches included in the UNESCO WHL are situated (Source: Google Earth)

Fig. 2.14 Specimens of the architecture of the Byzantine churches of Troodos Mountain

Fig. 2.15 Specimens of the frescoes of the Byzantine churches of Troodos Mountain

Table 2.4 Comparative presentation of the basic characteristics of the geometric documentation methods

	Lady Mary of Asinou	Lady Mary of Podithou	Holy Cross	Archangel Michael
Date	2005	2008	2011	2014
Instrumentation				
Geodetic	Topcon GPT-3003 reflectorless total station	Pentax R-323NX reflectorless total station	Leica TPS 1200 reflectorless total station	Topcon 7003i Imaging station
3D scanner	HDS/Cyrax 2500	HDS/Cyrax 2500	Scanstation 2	Scanstation 2
Image acquisition	Canon MII 8M pixel	Canon MII 8M pixel	Canon M III—21Mp full frame	Canon M III—21Mp full frame
Other			Z-scan, TheoLT	
Software	ARCHIS by SISCAM SSK of Z/I Imaging	PhotoModeler	RDF Image Master	Image Master, PhotoScan
Members of the team	3	4	4	3
Duration of works				
Fieldwork (days)	14	10	7	5
Processing (months)	8	7	6	5
Results	Plan, roof plan, outside facades, sections (with orthophotos)	Plan, roof plan, outside facades, sections (with orthophotos)	Plan, roof plan, outside facades, sections (with orthophotos)	Plan, roof plan, outside facades, sections (with orthophotos)
Documentation products	3D model	3D model	3D model	3D model

The production procedure of the contemporary geometric documentation products follows some basic steps, which in brief are the measurements of three-dimensional points in space. This may be done in three ways:

- Using geodetic methods, which collect specifically selected points with great accuracy
- Using scanning methods, usually based on laser technology, which collect a huge number of non-controlled points with lower accuracy but in certain cases with the ability of assigning colour information to them
- Using dense image matching methods on digital images, which determine a large number of points with high accuracy including colour information

From these points, and also from the point cloud, there is the possibility of producing the section lines of various vertical and horizontal sections, which were decided to be the geometric documentation products of the monument. However, the details, and those in image form in particular, demand the production procedure of an orthophoto (Fig. 2.16). This may be done the classic way from the images and the description of the surface, i.e. the point cloud, and also directly from the point cloud using specialized software [34, 35].

The production of the 3D model is rather complicated and demands a time-consuming procedure. From the point cloud points, a triangular mesh should be produced and from that the surface of the object. In this procedure one should make sure that there are no residual errors on the surface, such as holes, wrongly oriented triangles, which occurs very often. Afterwards, the texture information should be identified on the digital images available. This action is in essence a mapping of the desired information on the object's surface. This results in a realistic 3D model with texture and colour, which may serve different needs (Fig. 2.17).

The use of these 3D models is not completely clear yet. Other researchers desire to have the 3D model just for visualization purposes, others desire to publish it online, others use them for educational and touristic purposes, while others would like to use them for metric purposes, i.e. they extract metric information from them. It is obvious that all these uses demand 3D models of different specifications. Hence, the provider and technology expert should understand the user's needs, in order to provide him with the suitable 3D model each time.

It becomes apparent from the above that the implementation of contemporary information and communication technologies (ICT) during the last decades has had a positive influence on the curation of cultural heritage. This positive influence is identified both on the required time, on the accuracy of the final products and also on the multitude of alternative products which are possible nowadays. The final users are still a little reluctant to accept new technologies and sometimes understand their usefulness. Hence, it is imperative that the users get acquainted with them, but, at the same time, the providers should show patience for understanding the needs of the users in order to provide the most suitable product each time. This mutual effort requires interdisciplinary approach to the problem.

2.5.2 The Geometric Documentation of Ancient Vessels

Besides the display of the findings, modern museums organize educational programmes which aim to experience and knowledge sharing combined with entertainment rather than to pure learning. Towards that effort, 2D and 3D digital representations are gradually replacing the traditional recording of the findings through photos or drawings. This example refers to a project that aims to create 3D textured models of two lekythoi that are exhibited in the National Archaeological Museum of Athens in Greece; on the surfaces of these lekythoi scenes, the adventures of Odysseus are depicted. The creation of accurate developments of the paintings and of accurate 3D models is the basis for the visualization of the adventures of the mythical hero.

The data collection was performed by using a structured light scanner consisting of two machine vision cameras used for the determination of the geometry of the

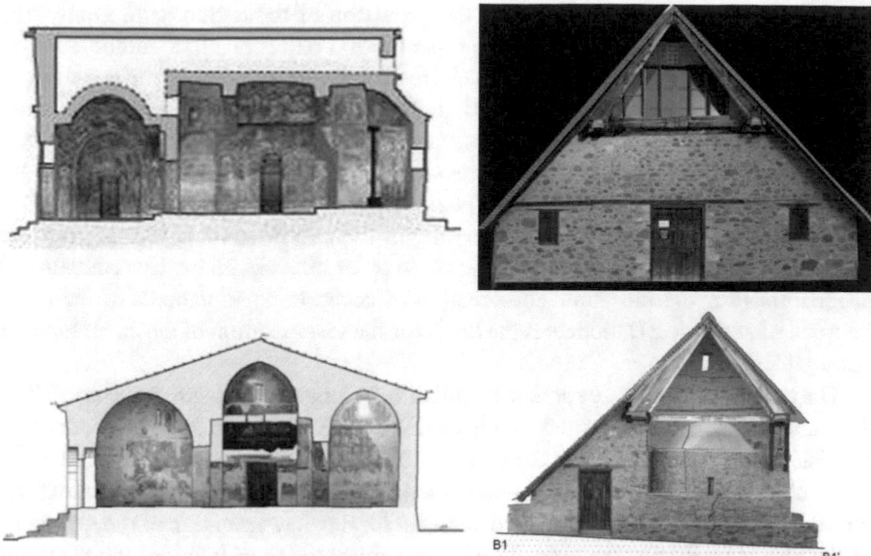

Fig. 2.16 Selected sections with orthophotos of the four Byzantine churches

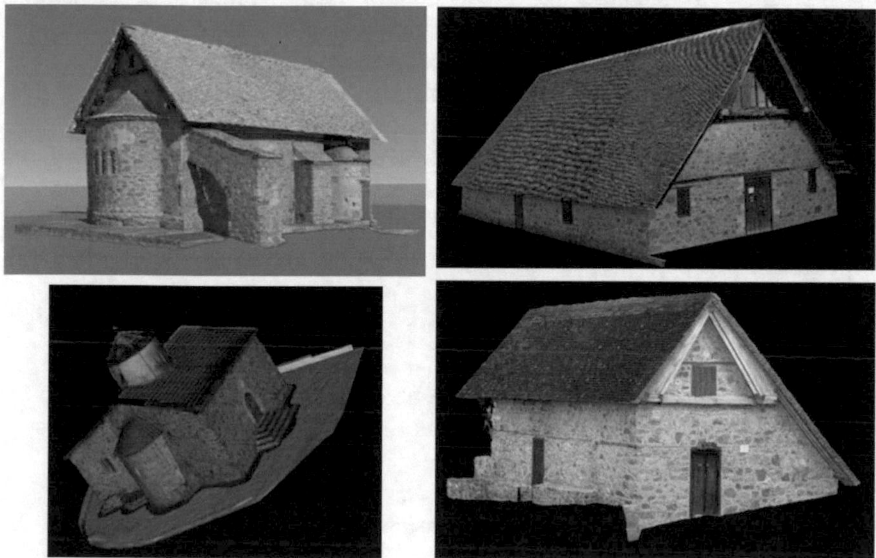

Fig. 2.17 3D models of the four Byzantine churches

object, a high-resolution camera for the recording of the texture and a DLP projector. The creation of the final accurate 3D-textured model is a complicated and tiring procedure which includes the collection of geometric data, the creation of the surface, the noise filtering, the merging of individual surfaces, the creation of a *c*-mesh, the creation of the UV map, the provision of the texture and, finally, the general processing of the 3D-textured object. For a better result, a combination of commercial and in-house software developed for the automation of various steps of the procedure was used. The results derived from the above procedure were especially satisfactory in terms of accuracy and quality of the model. However, the procedure was proved to be time consuming, while the use of various software packages presumes the services of a specialist [36].

The 3D recording and digital processing of the two lekythoi aim to support the production of an educational movie and some other relevant interactive educational programmes for the museum. The creation of accurate developments of the carvings and of accurate 3D models is the basis for the visualization of the adventures of the mythical hero.

The technique used here for data acquisition belongs to the passive methods. The data collection was performed using an XYZRGB® structured light scanner. It consists of two machine vision cameras, used for the determination of the geometry of the object, and of a high-resolution camera, used for the recording of the texture, plus a DLP projector. The use of two cameras for the determination of the geometry of the object facilitates the procedure since neither the correlation of the pixels of the projector with the pixels of the camera nor the knowledge of interior orientation is required. The representations need to be of good quality and the data need to be of high accuracy to facilitate the production of further product representations (e.g. developments), which help in a better understanding of the story that is painted or carved on a finding (e.g. a vessel or a decorative part of an object).

Two lekythoi (cosmetic vessels) exhibited at the National Archaeological Museum of Athens were selected: a bigger one with a height approximately up to 30 cm (Fig. 2.18, left) and a smaller one with a height approximately up to 20 cm (Fig. 2.18, right). On the surface of these two vessels, scenes of the adventures of Odysseus are depicted. These vessels are dated back to the fifth century BC and were discovered in the region of Athens, Greece. They are painted in dull red and black colours.

For the acquisition of the 3D data, the SL2 model of XYZRGB structured light scanner was used (Fig. 2.19). It consists of the following components:

- A Canon 450D digital SLR 12MP high-definition camera
- Two uEye 5MP machine vision cameras
- An InFocus IN35W DLP projector
- A laptop running the appropriate software
- A calibration board, with known dimensions

The three cameras are mounted on a rigid base. The distance between the cameras may vary according to the object scanned, and it is usually set up to 1/3 of the scanning distance. The maximum density capability equals to 150 μm and the maximum precision to 50 μm, according to the manufacturer.

The calibration affects the precision of the extracted point cloud. The calibration board is set in approximately 11 different positions, including change in position

Fig. 2.18 The two lekythoi, with the adventures of Odysseus depicted on their surface

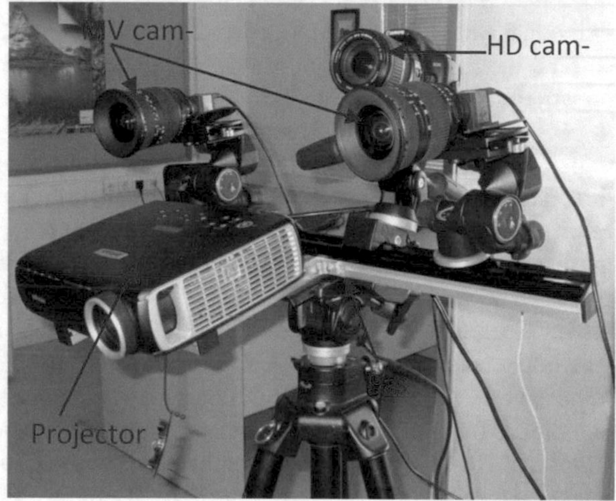

Fig. 2.19 The SL2 model of XYZRGB structured light scanner

and rotation. Performing plane-based calibration, the interior orientations of the three cameras and the relative (scaled) orientations between them are computed.

During the procedure of scanning, the relative position between the three cameras has to remain unchanged. The scanning procedure is fast and reliable. However, for a successful result, the imaging parameters of the cameras have to be set correctly in the scanning software, according to object's colour, material and lighting conditions.

The uEye software is responsible for the determination of the suitable imaging parameters of the cameras, so as to acquire data with best quality. Some of these well-known parameters are pixel clock and exposure, which are related to the refresh rate of the pixels on the screen and the amount of light allowed to fall on the photographic sensor.

For the scanning procedure, the software provided by the company XYZRGB® is used. The ideal number of scans varies according to the size and complexity of the object and also according to the desirable accuracy and density of the final product. Attention should be paid so that the scans will have adequate overlap. In this application, 41 scans were necessary for the first vessel and 39 scans for the second one. The result of each scan is a point cloud. The software gives the opportunity to test the quality of the data that will be acquired before each scan. Each point cloud is triangulated into a mesh, which is easier to handle, using Delaunay triangulation. The image from the high-resolution camera ensures that the mesh is textured. The results from each individual scan are the mesh, which is exported in OBJ format for further processing, and an image in JPG format, which is responsible for the texture information.

The products of the scanning procedure were processed using various software packages for the production of the final accurate 3D-textured model of the vessel. For a better result and automation of various steps of the procedure, a combination of (commercial and in some cases in-house) software is made. In the following, the individual steps of this procedure and the used software are given.

First the meshes were inserted in Geomagic Studio for the hole filling and the registration (merging) of the individual meshes for the creation of the final surface, as each mesh refers to a different local system. The most popular algorithm for the registration of the meshes, which was also used here, is the ICP. Selecting at least three common points between the two meshes, initial values are calculated for the transformation, which are then optimized. Having completed the registration of all meshes, the final surface is processed as a whole, and all the individual meshes are extracted separately in OBJ format,[6] so as to be georeferenced (Fig. 2.20).

The texture of the final 3D model relies on the procedure of texture mapping. To generate a texture map, the 3D model has to be simple enough due to restrictions imposed by computer memory limitations. As the surface of the lekythoi is really complex and the 3D model is detailed and precise, it is absolutely necessary to be simplified. Thus, a new surface is created, called constrained mesh (c-mesh). This surface is composed of quadrangles or triangles. The specific procedure was implemented in the GSI Studio software (a product of the XYZRGB Company).

The UV map, that is actually offering the texture to the 3D model, is a kind of development of the created constrained mesh. Each vertex of the 3D model, defined by X, Y, Z coordinates, is projected onto this two-dimensional image (texture map)

[6]http://en.wikipedia.org/wiki/Wavefront_.obj_file

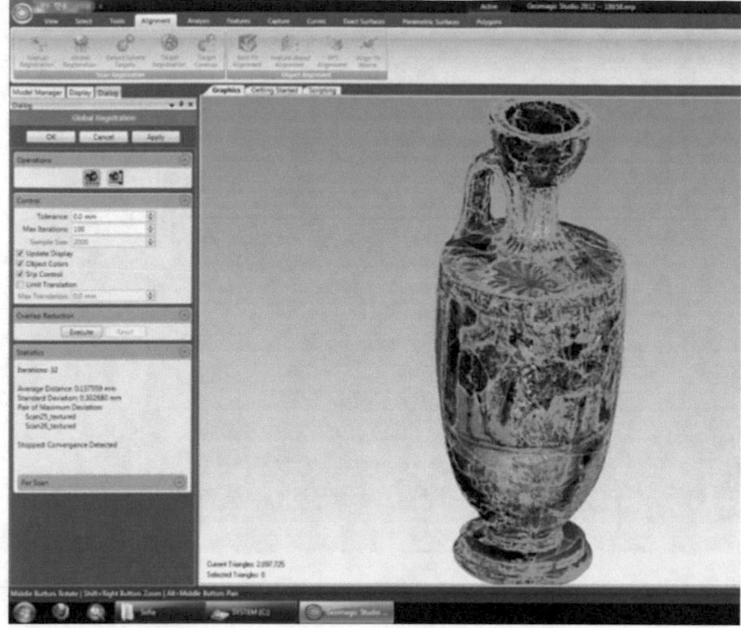

Fig. 2.20 The surface of a lekythos after the registration of all individual meshes

and is now defined by *U*, *V* coordinates.[7] The creation of the UV map was performed in the Deep UV software of Right Hemisphere®. This procedure may be done either automatically or manually. The shape of the vessels does not comply with any developable surface, and thus the automated procedure has created a complicated texture map hard to use (Fig. 2.21). Thus, the texture map was extracted manually, by selecting parts of the surface with common characteristics (complexity, curvature) and deciding in which developable surface it adjusts better (cone, cylinder).

The next step is to provide the texture map with the right colours. For this procedure, the georeferenced meshes and the image of each scan and the constrained mesh were inserted in the 3D Studio Max software by Autodesk. The result is a texture map with colour, containing the information from each scan. This step results in many texture maps; the number of texture maps equals the number of individual scans, acquired during the field work. However, for the texture of the final surface, only one texture map must be used. Thus, all the individual texture maps are composed and turned into the final texture map using the Photoshop CS5® software (Fig. 2.22).

For the visualization of the final product in any software capable of managing 3D information, the OBJ file of the constrained mesh, the final texture map (a JPG file)

[7] http://en.wikipedia.org/wiki/UV_mapping

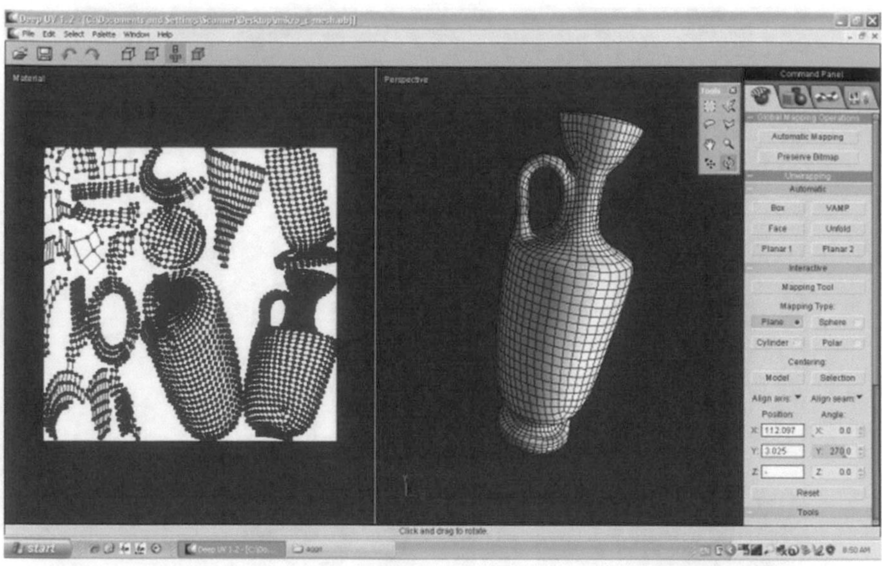

Fig. 2.21 Automated creation of UV map (2D texture map) through the algorithms of the Deep UV software

Fig. 2.22 The final texture map of the smaller lekythos

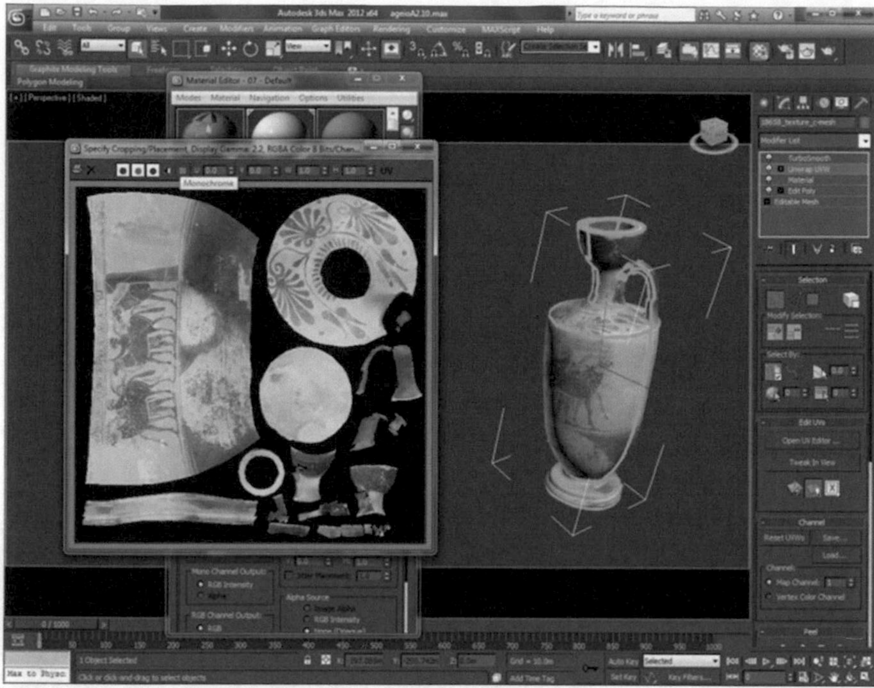

Fig. 2.23 Final processing of the bigger lekythos, a 3D-textured model

and an MTL file are needed. The MTL file contains the name of the material (in this case the texture map) and its properties.[8] In this project, the final optimization of the 3D-textured model was implemented in 3D Studio Max software, where radiometric and smoothing interventions were made (Fig. 2.23).

In addition, as a by-product of the processing, the development of the main body of each lekythos is created, the surface of which is close to a cylinder, and it shows the representation of an adventure of Odysseus. The developments are shown at the lower part of Figs. 2.24 and 2.25 for both lekythoi. This product is very useful for the visualization of the story of each myth as it represents in an easily understandable way (2D image) the scene that decorates all the (almost cylindrical) surface of the vessel.

For the processing of the scanned data, a combination of software was used; each step of the procedure was done using different software (XYZRGB, Geomagic Studio, GSI Studio, Deep UV, Photoshop, 3D Studio Max). The selection was made after several thorough trials using various software that can execute each individual step of the process and by determining the appropriate parameters for their best operation. Many of the above procedures were repeated several times in order to

[8]http://people.sc.fsu.edu/~jburkardt/data/mtl/mtl.html

Fig. 2.24 The final 3D model (*up*) and the development of the texture map of the carving (*bottom*) of the bigger lekythos

have an acceptable result. That way, some very good results have been obtained in terms of accuracy and quality of the final products (developments and 3D-textured models), but the process is time consuming, and the quality of the results is up to the user's experience. In addition, particular attention should be given to fieldwork, where the definition of the scan parameters play a crucial role for proper collection of data, which facilitates continuity and correct processing and workflow.

In general, the hardware and the processing of the selected 3D data provide satisfactory results regarding the geometry of the final product, making good use of the capabilities of the structured light scanner.

A disadvantage of the used method is the step of simplifying the surface, so as a suitable texture can be attributed to the 3D model. It is advisable that this step be carried out manually, so the user can decide the rate of simplification. The final results seem to depict the object with high fidelity, but the problem is the lack of a quantitative criterion for checking the rendering texture.

The procedure followed in this project proved to be the most appropriate method for the creation of the 3D-textured models of archaeological findings. Its

Fig. 2.25 The final 3D model (*up*) and the development of the texture map of the carving (*bottom*) of the smaller lekythos

application on the two lekythoi gave very good results both in terms of accuracy and quality. However the low degree of automation of the process may create a problem as the final product depends on the experience and the knowledge of the user.

Also, a general conclusion is that each geometric documentation process of an archaeological object has different requirements, and the most appropriate method to be followed must be studied examining numerous factors. The creation of accurate 3D-textured models is a field with many opportunities for future research.

However, the three-dimensional-textured models and their 2D developments are an attractive solution to the presentation of archaeological findings in an effort to create an attractive educational tool, which may help kids and students to participate actively during their visit to an archaeological museum. The museum becomes a cosy and intimate space, a place of learning through play. Children are encouraged to observe, to think, to express themselves and to act. Also the ability to view 3D models via Internet is another important area of action to be developed in museums. An interactive museum visit converts visitors to active participants of the museum process. The hidden information is the additional material that is stored on the computer, which is revealed and activated through an interactive application, stimulates interest and activates the processes of participation and guest's choice.

References

1. UNESCO, Photogrammetry applied to the survey of Historic Monuments, of Sites and to Archaeology. UNESCO editions (1972)
2. C. Ioannidis, A. Georgopoulos, Innovative techniques for the acquisition and processing of multisource data for the geometric documentation of monuments. Int. J. Archit. Comput. (IJAC) **5**(2), 179–198 (2007)
3. W. Böehler, G. Heinz, *Documentation, Surveying, Photogrammetry*. Paper presented at the XVII CIPA International Symposium, Olinda (1999)
4. D. Barber, J. Mills, P. Bryan, Towards a standard specification for terrestrial laser scanning of cultural heritage, in *Proceedings of CIPA XIX International Symposium*. Antalya (2003). http://cipa.icomos.org/index.php?id=357. Last accessed 18 June 2008
5. P. Bryan, B. Blake, *Metric Survey Specifications for English Heritage*, English Heritage, York and Swidon, 111 σελίδες (2000)
6. National Park Service (2008) http://www.nps.gov/history/hdp/standards/index.htm. Last accessed 18 June 2008
7. Hellenic Minstry of Culture, "General Specifications for Studies of Byzantine and Post-Byzantine Monuments", Directorate of Restoration of Byzantine and Post-Byzantine Monuments (1998) 90 pp. (in Greek)
8. Technical Chamber of Greece, "Specifications for the Studies of Architectural documentation, restoration and support for Monuments and Monumental Complexes", Technical Chamber of Greece No 1694, 07/01/1992 (1992) (in Greek)
9. C. Slama, *Manual of photogrammetry*, 4th edn. (American Society of Photogrammetry, Falls Church, 1980)
10. T.A. Clarke, J.G. Fryer, The development of camera calibration methods and models. Photogram. Record **16**(91), 51–66 (1998)
11. A. Georgopoulos, Low altitude non-metric photography in surveying, Doctoral dissertation, University College London, University of London (1981)
12. D. Skarlatos, Autonomous platforms for aerial photography and their applications for mapping. Open lecture in Cyprus University of Technology (2012)
13. A. Eltner, D. Schneider, Analysis of different methods for 3D reconstruction of natural surfaces from parallel-axes UAV images. Photogram. Record **30**(151), 279–299 (2015)
14. I. Colomina, P. Molina, Unmanned aerial systems for photogrammetry and remote sensing: a review. ISPRS J. Photogram. Rem. Sens. **92**, 79–97 (2014)
15. M. Sauerbier, H. Eisenbeiss, UAVs for the documentation of archaeological excavations, in *International Archives of Photogrammetry, Remote Sensing and Spatial Information Sciences*, Newcastle upon Tyne, Vol. XXXVIII, Part 5, (2010), pp. 526–531
16. F. Remondino, L. Barazzetti, F. Nex, M. Scaioni, D. Sarazzi, UAV photogrammetry for mapping and 3D modeling–current status and future perspectives. Int. Arch. Photogram. Rem. Sens. Spatial Inf. Sci. **38**(1), C22 (2011)
17. F. Neitzel, J. Klonowski, S. Siebert, J.P. Deshbach, Mobile 3D mapping with a low-cost UAV system on example of a landfill survey. Int. Arch. Photogram. Rem. Sens. Spatial Inf. Sci. **38** (1/C22) (2011)
18. M. Lo Brutto, A. Garraffa, P. Meli, UAV Platforms for Cultural Heritage Survey: First results, ISPRS Annals of the Photogrammetry, Remote Sensing and Spatial Information Sciences, Volume II-5, pp. 227–234, 2014 – ISPRS Technical Commission V Symposium, 23 – 25 June 2014, Riva del Garda, 2014

19. A. Koutsoudis, B. Vidmar, G. Ioannakis, F. Arnaoutoglou, G. Pavlidis, C. Chamzas, Multi-image 3D reconstruction data evaluation. J. Cult. Herit. **15**(1), 73–79 (2014)
20. N. Haala, M. Rothermel, Dense multiple stereo matching of highly overlapping uav imagery, in *ISPRS – International Archives of the Photogrammetry, Remote Sensing and Spatial Information Sciences*, Vol. XXXIX-B1, (2012), pp. 387–392
21. C. Teutsch, Model-based Analysis and Evaluation of Point Sets from optical 3D Laser Scanners. PhD Thesis. Magdeburger Schriften zur Visualisierung, Shaker, 2007, 145 pp
22. C. Rocchini, P. Cignoni, C. Montani, P. Pingi, R. Scopigno, A low cost 3D scanner based on structured light. Comput. Graph. Forum **20**(3), 299–308 (2002)
23. F. Bernardini, H.E. Rushmeier, The 3D model acquisition pipeline. Comput. Graph. Forum **21** (2), 149–172 (2002)
24. R. Mayer, *Scientific Canadian: Invention and Innovation From Canada's National Research Council* (Raincoast Books, Vancouver, 1999)
25. S. Zhang, P. Huang, High-resolution, real-time 3-D shape measurement. Opt. Eng. **45**, 123601-1–8, 2006
26. M. Lindner, A. Kolb, Lateral and depth calibration of PMD-distance sensors, in *Proceedings of ISVC*, Lake Tahoe, 2006, pp. 524–533
27. D. Falie, V. Buzuloiu, Noise characteristics of 3D Time-of-Flight cameras, in *Proceedings of IEEE Symposium on Signals Circuits & Systems (ISSCS)*, Iasi, 2007, pp. 229–232
28. F. Chiabrando, R. Chiabrando, D. Piatti, F. Rinaudo, Sensors for 3D imaging: metric evaluation and calibration of a CCD/CMOS Time-of-Flight camera. Sensors **9**, 10080–10096 (2009)
29. F. Rinaudo, F. Chiabrando, F. Nex, D. Piatti, in *New Instruments and Technologies for Cultural Heritage Survey: Full Integration between Point Clouds and Digital Photogrammetry*, eds by M. Ioannides, D.W. Fellner, A. Georgopoulos, & D.G. Hadjimitsis (EuroMed, Springer, 2010), ISBN: 978-3-642-16872-7, pp. 56–70
30. E. Sofocleous, A. Georgopoulos, M. Ioannides, Ch. Ioannidis, The Geometric Documentation of the Asinou Church in Cyprus. VAST 2006, Lefkosia Cyprus, Oct–Nov 2006, in *The Evolution of Information Communication Technology in Cultural Heritage*, eds. by M. Ioannides et al. (2006), pp. 138–144, ISBN-10: 963-8046-75-9
31. Ch. Chrysostomou, S. Ioakim, N. Shieittanis, A. Georgopoulos, Ch. Ioannidis, Contemporary digital methods for the Geometric Documentation of Churches in Cyprus, in *VSMM 2008 – Conference on Virtual Systems and MultiMedia Dedicated to Digital Heritage*, 20–25 Oct 2008, Project Paper Volume, 2008, pp. 24–28
32. A. Georgopoulos, C. Ioannidis, C. Crysostomou, S. Ioakim, N. Shieittanis, M. Ioannides, Contemporary digital methods for the geometric documentation of Churches in Cyprus. Int. J. Archit. Comput. **7**(1), 21–37 (2009)
33. G. Bariami, M. Faka, A. Georgopoulos, M. Ioannides, D. Skarlatos, Documenting a UNESCO WH Site in Cyprus with Complementary Techniques. Project paper in "Lecture Notes in Computer Science (LNCS)", Springer. 4th International Euro-Mediterranean Conference (EUROMED), 29/10 – 03/11 2012 Limassol Cyprus (2012)
34. A. Georgopoulos, S. Natsis, A simpler method for large scale orthophoto production, in *IAPRS, International ISPRS Congress* (Beijing, 2008a)
35. A. Georgopoulos, S. Natsis, Evaluation of a simpler method for large scale orthophoto production. VSMM 2008 (Lemessos, 2008b)
36. S. Soile, K. Adam, C. Ioannidis, A. Georgopoulos, Accurate 3D textured models of vessels for the improvement of the educational tools of a museum, in *Proceedings of 3D-ARCH 2013, International Archives of the Photogrammetry, Remote Sensing and Spatial Information Sciences,* Trento, Vol. XL-5/W1 (2013), pp. 219–226

Chapter 3
Autonomous Mapping of the Priscilla Catacombs

Frank Verbiest, Marc Proesmans, and Luc Van Gool

Abstract This chapter describes the image-based 3D reconstruction of the Priscilla catacombs in Rome, as carried out in the European ROVINA project. The 3D reconstruction system was mounted on a small mobile robot, which could autonomously roam the labyrinth of the catacombs' corridors. The 3D reconstruction system was designed to cope with the specific challenges posed by the narrow passages found there. It consists of multiple cameras and light sources, mounted on spherical arcs. Also the structure-from-motion (SfM) software needed adaptation to optimally cope with the particular circumstances. Firstly, the information coming from the different cameras is handled jointly. Secondly, the feature matching needs to withstand the negative effects of the strongly changing illumination between different robot positions—moreover the environment is mostly dark and humid. Thirdly, for the same reasons, the usual texture mapping techniques would cause strong seams between the textures taken from different robot positions, and these were avoided through a more sophisticated analysis of surface reflectance characteristics. The chapter includes visual examples for parts of the 3D reconstruction.

Keywords Autonomous mapping • 3D reconstruction • Structure from motion • Mobile robot

3.1 Introduction

3.1.1 Background

Mapping and digitizing archeological sites is an important task to preserve cultural heritage. Systems used for digitizing archeological sites typically build upon static 3D laser scanning technology that has to be brought onto archeological sites by humans. While this is acceptable for accessible sites, it prevents the digitization of

---

F. Verbiest (✉) • M. Proesmans • L. Van Gool
Department of Electrical Engineering-ESAT/PSI, KU Leuven, Kasteelpark Arenberg 10, 3001 Leuven, Belgium
e-mail: frank.verbiest@esat.kuleuven.be; marc.proesmans@esat.kuleuven.be; luc.vangool@esat.kuleuven.be

M. Ioannides et al. (eds.), *Mixed Reality and Gamification for Cultural Heritage*,
DOI 10.1007/978-3-319-49607-8_3

sites that are inaccessible to humans. Such areas call for the use of autonomous robots. Even if there has been tremendous progress in their development, the task of autonomously exploring three-dimensional underground environments such as caves remains challenging. The reasons for this are manifold: problematic perception (no/poor lighting, unpredictable situations, difficult scene interpretation, complex traversability analysis, etc.) paired with limited communication capabilities, which restrict the continuous supervision and tele-operation by human users.

The particular scenario of the European project ROVINA has been to develop novel techniques that allow a robotic system to autonomously explore catacomb-like environments and to build highly accurate, textured 3D models of large environments including object annotations and semantic information from sensor data collected by the robot. This chapter focuses on the construction of the detailed 3D model.

3.1.2 Application Scenario: Exploration of the Catacombs of Rome

The ROVINA consortium was given the opportunity to digitize the Priscilla catacombs in Rome. Large parts are quite inaccessible to humans due to their hazardous nature; therefore they offer a well-suited test bed.

The Priscilla catacombs considered here are belowground, collective Christian burial areas used from the late second century through the fourth century. They became increasingly popular starting second century AD, as burials became more popular than cremations. This was also very much the case among Christians, because of their belief in bodily resurrection. As the price of tombs was calculated on the basis of the square meters they took, they were often stacked on top of each other, yielding the typical patterns found in Roman catacombs. Moreover, they were organized along galleries at different levels, like six in the case of the Priscilla catacombs. The rapid development of some catacombs was also due to the cult of the martyrs buried there. Many Christians wanted a tomb close to their graves. Today, the catacombs are visited by thousands of tourists every year. With their early Christian paintings, inscriptions, sculptures, etc., they are true archives of the early church. They document the customs, rites, and beliefs of the first Christians. The Roman catacombs are entrusted to the Pontifical Commission of Sacred Archeology, which carries out the excavations, explorations, and restorations. It also edits studies and other publications.

Operating in such environments requires solving several problems simultaneously. This includes the need for (1) robust hardware and software due to the inaccessibility of most catacombs, (2) online methods to provide autonomy, (3) sophisticated navigation techniques due to the complexity of the environment (including debris and dangerous passages), (4) mapping, reconstruction, and detection algorithms that can deal with a high degree of repetitive structures in such large-scale environments, (5) user interfaces with a high degree of situation awareness, and (6) postprocessing of the acquired data to allow for the detection of differences over time, etc. Within the ROVINA project, tasks have been defined to address and meet all these requirements [1, 2]. The core tasks described here are to build a 3D reconstruction of the catacombs and to provide this information to archeologists as well as virtual tourists.

Figure 3.1 (left) illustrates typical scenes encountered in the catacombs. The instability of the structure and the potential presence of gases (depending on where in the catacomb and the corresponding airflow) render the exploration of part of the catacombs hazardous to humans. Therefore, several parts of the catacombs have not been explored yet. So far, maps of catacombs have often been built manually. Providing virtual 3D models instead, archeologists could safely perform a large part of their investigations offline. For the remainder, a prior, high-quality 3D reconstruction allows the archeologists to better direct their on-site missions. Furthermore, these models could be used for applications like virtual tourism or for teaching purposes.

Generating useful models of these environments still poses a challenge. First of all, the potentially large regions (up to 10 km of tunnels) covered by the catacombs might be critical for state-of-the-art modeling systems. Second, the highly recurring labyrinth-like layout of the catacombs makes it hard to choose proper viewpoints and poses additional challenges for the robot platform to localize. In traditional structure-from-motion applications, one usually has the flexibility to keep a comfortable distance from the objects and to take images from good viewpoints to arrive at a good 3D model. Another challenge is to generate models and textures of sufficiently high resolution to study structures of interest. Figure 3.1 (right) illustrates some of these areas, typically decorative paintings, frescoes, or marble pieces, where additional focus is needed.

Fig. 3.1 *Left*: typical scenes encountered at the Catacombs of Priscilla in Rome. *Right*: examples of fine structures and paintings (© 2016 Catacombe Priscilla, reprinted with permission)

3.2 State of the Art in 3D Reconstruction

The creation of 3D reconstructions has undergone an impressive evolution over the past decades. For a long time, the field had been dominated by interactive, photogrammetric approaches, starting from images (see [3] for an excellent review) and theodolitic measurements. Many successful archeology-related projects have been carried out based on this kind of approach, but in the 1990s, the area of mapping larger sites started changing dramatically because of two major, technological advances.

On the one hand, the market saw the introduction of the first, practical ground-level light detection and ranging (LIDAR) systems that automatically scan large portions of a 3D scene with a laser, using time-of-flight principles. LIDAR is a useful tool for archeology, as also documented in [4], since it can help with the planning of field campaigns and the mapping of large sites. Mounting a laser scanner system on a robot may not be practical however, since the platform should remain still during the acquisition and because of its size and weight.

On the other hand, the typically strongly interactive approaches of traditional, image-based photogrammetry were increasingly replaced by far more automated, self-calibrating structure-from-motion (SfM) approaches. Crucial were mainly some algorithmic advances. First of all, correspondence search got a lot more robust, to the point where corresponding features could also be matched between images taken from viewpoints that are far apart [5]. A second major advance was the theoretical underpinning of 3D reconstruction from uncalibrated images [6, 7]. Supposing that sufficient corresponding features between views can be detected, it was shown that the intrinsic and extrinsic parameters for the different views can be extracted purely from image data [8]. Hence, from a single, moving camera, already rich 3D data can be recovered [9]. Uncalibrated structure from motion also has a strong history in archeology (e.g., [10]). Online web services like ARC3D (www.arc3d.be; implemented by KULeuven) have a substantial user base in the cultural heritage community [11]. Documenting excavations and sites with photographs is part of the archeological practice anyway. Thus it is not surprising that both open-source and commercial packages [12, 13] have found their way to this community to turn these photos also into 3D representations.

Of course, other methods exist to recover 3D information such as the projection of structured light patterns. For example, the Kinect system by Microsoft [14] has already been shown that good results can be achieved within a limited distance range and indoors (although the Kinect is not the first such system—see, e.g., the early system of [15, 16]). Its one-shot character is a nice property (a single pattern projection suffices), so that movement during data capture is not a problem. For the autonomous navigation of the robot, these 3D sensors have proven to be very valuable, as in this context [1, 2]. This said, they are not meant to capture the environment at high resolution and it can become problematic to let several such devices capture the same environment at the same time, as interference between the projected patterns could jeopardize the result. Therefore, the importance of structured light systems in archeology for 3D modeling has been mainly limited to building 3D models for smaller objects (e.g., [17]).

3.3 Recording Constraints/Hardware Setup

In order to build a detailed 3D reconstruction, a proper image acquisition setup needs to be chosen that takes into account the environmental circumstances but also the constraints resulting from the design of the robot. Exploring catacombs by means of a robotic system imposes several challenges. There is a substantial variation in surface shape, width, and curvature of the galleries; the surface is uneven, possibly holding pieces of debris, and there are occasionally stairs. All this is performed in unknown environments and under potentially unreliable communication links.

The final robot design, as shown in Fig. 3.2, addresses the mobility requirements through the choice of an off-the-shelf robotic platform: the Mesa Robotics Element, which is based on a caterpillar driving mechanism. This robot is agile enough to overcome most of the obstacles encountered in the catacombs and is small enough to navigate through narrow corridors. On top of the Element, an aluminum and polycarbonate case is built that houses all the additional computational units and sensors. The housing has been made shockproof where necessary.

On the sensor side, the robot is equipped with a laser scanner, to create ground truth during stationary phases, and a set of 3D depth sensors of the type ASUS Xtion. Just like the Kinect, the latter are infrared structured light depth sensors. They work best in dark environments and are mainly used for navigation and the determination of scene transversability. Even if these sensors come with color cameras, their image quality (contrast) proved insufficient to base the uncalibrated structure-from-motion on, even with powerful LED matrix lights—hence the need

Fig. 3.2 ROVINA robot design, here shown with laser scanner and a set of 3D sensors (ASUS Xtions) for autonomous navigation (© 2016 EC FP7 ROVINA project, reprinted with permission)

for a dedicated imaging setup. In the same vein, not any off-the-shelf omnidirectional or panoramic imaging setup is suited, because of motion blur and low dynamic range and contrast. The research has led to the development of a dedicated camera arc:

- Seven cameras are mounted in an arc configuration looking at the surrounding walls, orthogonal to the direction of motion. This is not to say that any viewing along the direction of motion would be irrelevant, but such viewpoints are oblique to the surface and are less suited for structure from motion. An additional argument for this configuration is that the camera fields of view do not interfere with the ASUS Xtions or the 3D laser scanner.
- Compared to traditional omnidirectional cameras, the cameras in the current setup are not mounted on a traditional arc, but instead the arc is inversed and the cameras are mounted opposite to the direction they are facing (Fig. 3.3). This ensures that the distance to the walls of the galleries (which may be very narrow) is not too small and that the images are in focus. In the proposed setup, one therefore has better control options on depth of field, shutter speed, integration time, etc.
- Finally, the cameras are oriented to show overlap between the images (of about half the image height between successive camera views along the arc). For a traditional omnidirectional setup, the focal points would nearly coincide, rendering the setup similar to a single, wide-angle pinhole camera. In our case, the baselines between the cameras of our inverse arc allow to instantiate scene structure from feature correspondences that can be used as additional constraints to the structure-from-motion pipeline, especially in case of ambiguities, as we will see.

To deal with the dark recording circumstances in the catacombs, the chosen cameras have onboard gamma correction to increase the dynamic range in the lower bit range. Initially, when using only extra LED lighting on the sides, the results still suffered from a motion blur and a lack of contrast. Therefore, an additional light arc

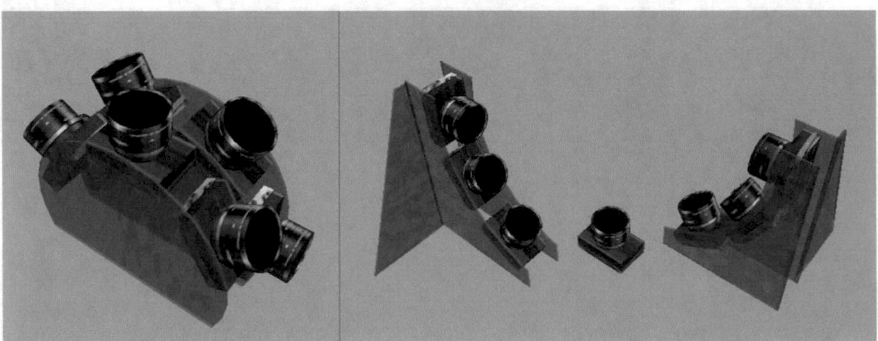

Fig. 3.3 Instead of using a traditional omnidirectional camera approach (*left*), the arc is inversed to guarantee better depth of field, parallax, and contrast (© 2016 EC FP7 ROVINA project, reprinted with permission)

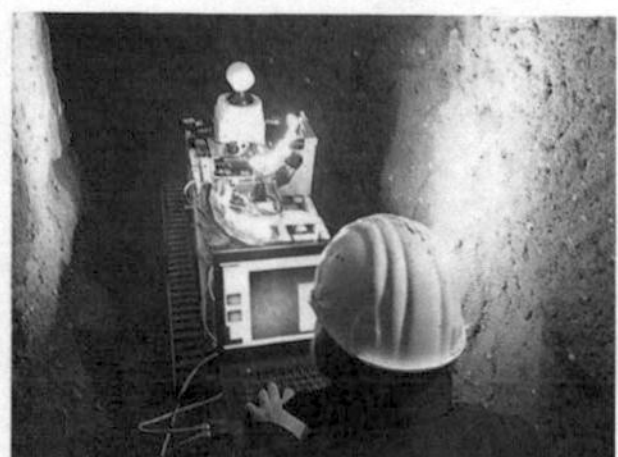

Fig. 3.4 *Left*: final design of the camera and light arc, here shown on a test trolley. *Middle* and *right*: robot carrying camera and light arcs in operation. Note illumination stripe projected on the walls (© 2016 EC FP7 ROVINA project, reprinted with permission)

is mounted next to the camera arc, in order to create a more intense and quasi-uniform light strip on the walls. It consists of ten power LED light bulbs, five on each side of the camera arc, as shown in Fig. 3.4. The methodologies to cope with the effects of the lighting are discussed in the next sections.

3.4 SfM-Based 3D Reconstruction

Creating a 3D textured model of the Priscilla catacombs is a central goal in ROVINA project. The overlapping images taken with the arc, and the progression of such image capture over time, allow for the combination of stereo reconstruction and structure-from-motion (SfM) techniques. In particular, the matching should be sufficiently robust to deal with the widely time-varying illumination. In the same vein, textures acquired at different times should be normalized before they can be merged onto the 3D model.

3.4.1 Initial Structure from Motion

Traditional SfM pipelines operate on image sequences, typically under fixed ambient lighting. Not so here. Thus, as initial step, the feature detection and matching procedures are investigated in order to exploit the nature of the camera arc and the recording circumstances within the catacombs.

3.4.1.1 Feature Detection

First, the sensitivity of the feature detection had to be verified under these circumstances. For instance, when using SIFT- or SURF-like features for matching, it may happen that some contrast polarities are reversed due to light hitting the surface from different directions.

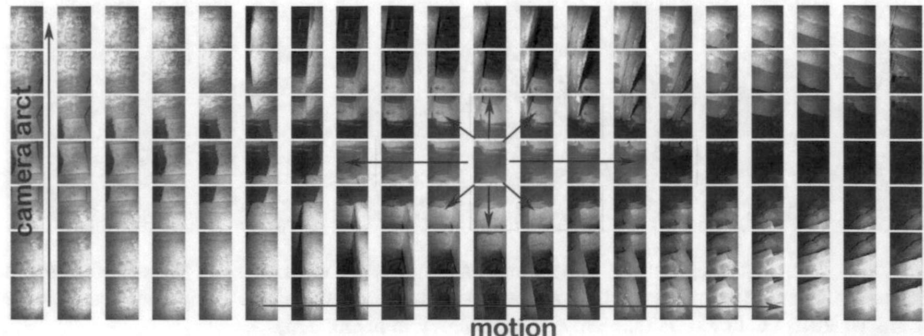

Fig. 3.5 SfM on a grid structure. The *vertical axis* refers to the viewpoints of the seven cameras along the arc. Along the *horizontal axis*, the images are shown when the robot moves through the galleries (© 2016 EC FP7 ROVINA project, reprinted with permission)

In order to verify the effects of nonuniform lighting on feature detection, we used a traditional SfM pipeline using flash-based photography. In such a scenario, the built-in flash of a commercial camera is used as the main light source, thus sharing the special property that the light sources move with the camera. For feature detection, we use a SURF-like [18] implementation based on the ARC3D SfM pipeline [11]. For diffuse scenes, the features prove reasonably robust against the illumination changes. The pictures in Fig. 3.5 have been recorded in the catacombs using flash-based photography, for some parts already shown in Fig. 3.1. After determining the camera positions and feature correspondences, dense matching is applied between the camera/image pairs that have sufficient amount of overlap. Using the known camera parameters, the disparities are converted into partial point cloud as seen from the selected image pairs (the ARC3D way). The final 3D meshes are generated using a Poisson-based 3D reconstruction scheme on the merged point clouds.

As these illustrations show, the reflectance as observed from subsequent robot and therefore illumination positions changes quite dramatically indeed. Such changes would show up as clearly visible texture seams under regular texture projection. This chapter proposes a bidirectional reflectance distribution function (BRDF)-based measurement/clustering method to compensate for those intensity changes and to create a consistent final texture map.

3.4.1.2 Initial Feature Matching and Bundling for the Camera Arc

Traditional SfM pipelines operate on single-camera image sequences. With our camera arc, assuming the differences in camera intrinsics between the seven cameras are negligible, the recorded images can be viewed as if obtained from a single camera moving both along the arc and the direction of motion of the robot. Features are matched on a grid, where the vertical axis represents inter-camera observations, which arise from correspondences between different cameras, and the horizontal axis represents intra-camera observations, which arise from movement of points in

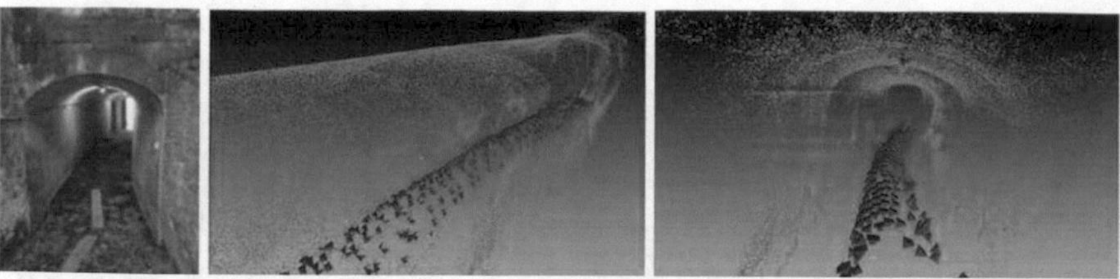

Fig. 3.6 Initial SfM: results for a test tunnel sequence. *Left*: example image. *Middle*, *right*: 3D point clouds (*gray*) and recovered camera positions (*purple pyramids*) derived from feature correspondences on a relatively small track (© 2016 EC FP7 ROVINA project, reprinted with permission)

the same camera. Figure 3.5 shows a graphical representation of the layout using actual input data. These matches are used by the self-calibrating ARC3D SfM pipeline to determine the unknown camera calibration and scene structure.

In Fig. 3.6 this approach is evaluated on a small piece of tunnel. The purple pyramids represent the recovered camera positions and fields of view, and the gray points correspond to the triangulated 3D positions of matched SURF features.

Although the result appears convincing overall, closer inspection shows that some cameras are not well positioned or recovered at all due to ambiguities in motion and/or lack of general scene structure. Another reason is to be found in the fact that this approach does not exploit the fixed relative poses of the seven cameras. Nevertheless, this method is useful for providing an initial estimate for the intrinsics and (relative) extrinsics of the cameras on the arc.

3.4.2 Large-Scale Bundling

A number of additional measures have to be taken to better calibrate the cameras, including the determination of their tracks, and to cope with several ambiguities and degeneracies [19–23].

3.4.2.1 Generalized Camera Model

Using a multiple-camera rig for 3D reconstruction and motion estimation has received a lot of attention over the last years. A common case is a set of cameras, often with nonoverlapping views, attached to a vehicle. It has been shown that such a set can be considered as a single generalized camera for which SfM equations can be derived, as well as a generalized epipolar constraint (e.g., the 17-point algorithm).

For the camera arc, the generalized approach considers one single pose for the fixed setup of seven cameras. After motion, the new recordings are related to the previous ones by a rigid transformation (cf. Fig. 3.7). Similar to traditional SfM, the features matched across two views of the generalized camera constrain the motion and can be expressed in terms of a generalized epipolar constraint. Figure 3.8 shows

Fig. 3.7 SfM using a generalized camera model. The *vertical axis* shows the seven viewpoints of the camera arc which have a fixed configuration. The feature correspondences with the consecutive recordings define the rigid motion of the robot as a rotation and translation (© 2016 EC FP7 ROVINA project, reprinted with permission)

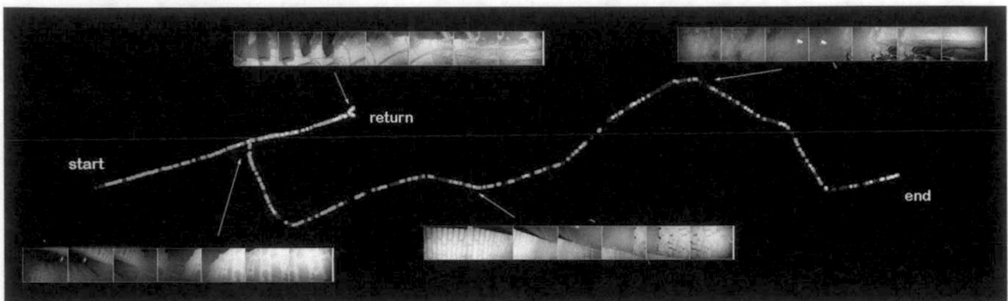

Fig. 3.8 The robot tracks for the Priscilla catacombs (© 2016 EC FP7 ROVINA project, reprinted with permission)

the tracks of the robot resulting from such generalized approach. The robot went straight ahead from the start, ended up in a small niche with fresco paintings, returned, and halfway turned into a longer section which it followed until the end. A few locations are illustrated with the seven separate arc images. The following paragraphs explain the strategy.

3.4.2.2 Initial Camera Calibration

To set up a generalized camera model, we estimate the initial camera intrinsics and relative positions. It is reasonable to assume that the seven arc cameras have similar—not to say identical—intrinsics, since they are based on the same sensors and lenses. Therefore the arc can be seen as a single camera moving along the arc. To find an initial estimate for the camera configuration, a feature-rich section of the catacombs is chosen, and for this area, the grid-based SfM of the previous section is applied. Figure 3.9 shows the resulting camera configuration (note: there is a slight asymmetry that is solved in a later stage).

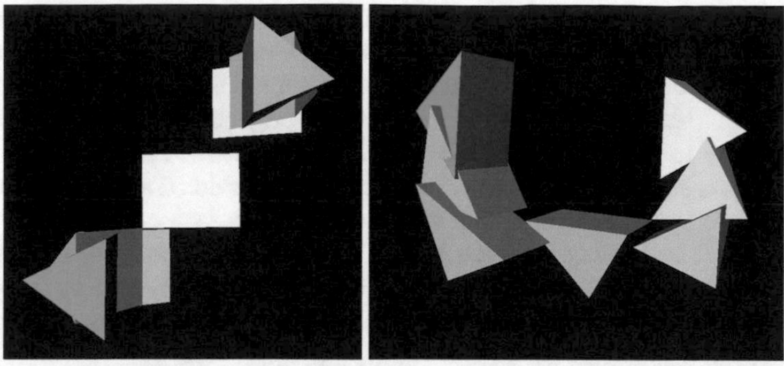

Fig. 3.9 Camera configuration of the arc found after initial SfM, *top* and *side* view (© 2016 EC FP7 ROVINA project, reprinted with permission)

3.4.2.3 Degeneracies

Although the generalized camera model is quite appealing for handling multi-camera setups, it has been hinted quite early since its introduction that the generalized epipolar constraint may accept multiple or ambiguous solutions. For a given set of feature correspondences, the SfM equation may have one, several, or an infinite number of solutions depending on camera geometry, motion, and scene structure. This remains an active research area.

It is not our purpose to list all possible cases and solutions; we refer the reader to the references [19–23]. Yet, also the specific circumstances in which the camera arc is observing and moving through the catacombs cause certain ambiguities or instabilities. Below we list some of the effects that have been observed, and it is their joint influence that had to be iteratively solved.

- The parallax between consecutive frames from the arc's data stream should not be too large, since there is a need for a minimum amount of feature correspondences to solve the SfM equations. On the other hand, the parallax should not be too small; otherwise the SfM equations become unstable. Especially at times when the robot is moving slowly or standing still, superfluous frames need to be eliminated. Therefore, key frames are selected automatically based on the median disparity of matched (Harris) features between frames, so that the baseline in between allows for accurate 3D triangulation. Also, this selection reduces the amount of data to be processed.
- SfM needs depth variations to guarantee a stable solution, but with cameras facing the gallery walls perpendicularly, many structures appear locally planar. Assuming any pair of images, it is known that if the 3D points in view are coplanar, the fundamental matrix cannot be determined uniquely from feature correspondences alone. Given an estimate of the camera intrinsics, the essential matrix, which is a representation of the relative pose between views, has two

discrete solutions for the planar case. This is shown in Fig. 3.10, where the two possible epipolar geometries can be found between two cameras on the arc. Note that these problems also occur for scenes that are close to planar.

- For a multi-camera rig with locally central projection, as in our case, it is impossible to determine the scale of the translation when the motion is a pure translation, and the only point correspondences considered are correspondences which are seen by the same camera over two consecutive key frames [21, 24]. Here, correspondences between different cameras are available, see diagonal arrows in Fig. 3.7, so in principle it should be possible to recover the scale. However, the short baselines between cameras cause their effect to be limited, so that at least numerically some ambiguity remains.

This situation is not uncommon in catacombs, since in various sections, the robot is moving straight ahead, and the rotation is relatively small. If the generalized approach is used to track the motion of the robot (translation/rotation) using a RANSAC procedure [25] applied to possible feature correspondences, one observes the results shown in Fig. 3.11. It shows the tracks for three different seeds for the RANSAC procedure. Not only is there quite a difference in drift for the different

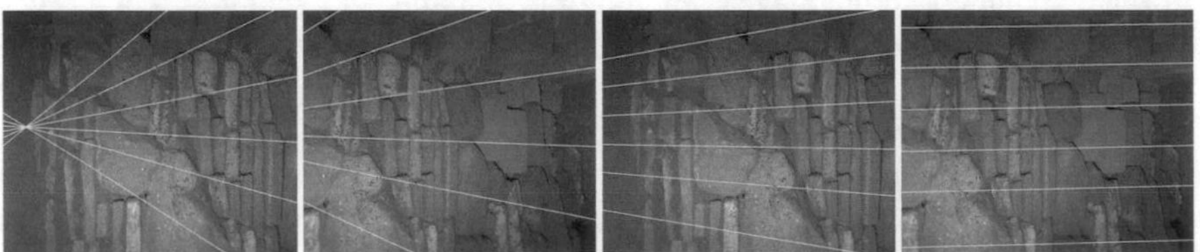

Fig. 3.10 Epipolar ambiguity: two neighboring cameras of the arc looking at the wall. The *right* pair is the correct solution, consistent with other image pairs. The *left* image pair shows the alternative solution that is due to local ambiguities (© 2016 EC FP7 ROVINA project, reprinted with permission)

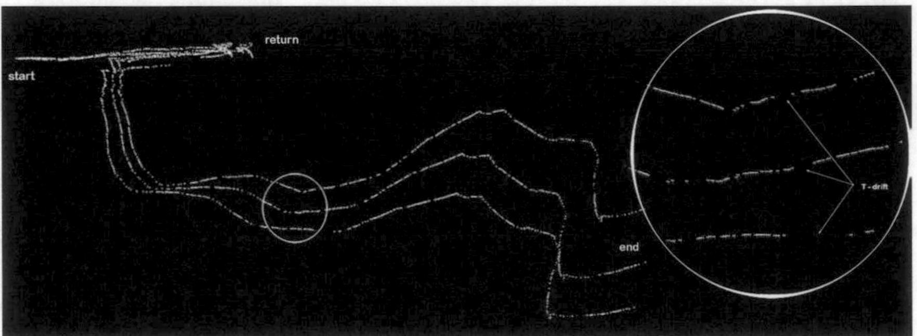

Fig. 3.11 Default motion tracking or pose detection using a generalized camera model, based on feature correspondences. Given three different random seed initializations, the ambiguity is substantial (© 2016 EC FP7 ROVINA project, reprinted with permission)

initializations, the zoomed area also shows that the estimated translation differs for each trajectory.

3.4.2.4 Overall Strategy

To avoid degeneracies, we exploit the baseline between the inter-camera feature correspondences. Given an initial calibration for the multi-camera, as described in the previous section, feature correspondences are proposed (1) between different cameras at the same time step, (2) for the same camera, with the next time step, and finally, (3) between neighboring cameras at subsequent time steps as indicated by the diagonal arrows in Fig. 3.7. For the inter-camera feature correspondences, 3D positions are determined by triangulation and verified by projection onto the camera viewpoints at the next time step. The additional constraints allow to more robustly solve for the robot pose at each time step. The result is shown in Fig. 3.12. Again, it shows the tracks for three different seeds for the RANSAC procedure. Now, freed from ambiguity, the differences in outcome are drastically reduced and only due to regular drift. In the zoomed area, one can observe that the estimated relative motions for each trajectory are quite consistent for different initializations. For a single trajectory, the irregularity of the relative motions over time can be explained by local speed.

In the next stage, the multi-camera calibration is further refined using a bundle adjustment procedure that jointly optimizes both the calibration parameters and the trajectory poses. Here, we relax the assumption that the camera intrinsics for each individual camera should be identical. The effect of the rebundling is twofold. Firstly, the estimated camera arc configuration is more accurate and can be treated as known for further reconstructions. As shown in Fig. 3.13, the asymmetries and slight misalignments in the original arc configuration are largely gone in the newly estimated configuration. Secondly, because of the more accurate camera

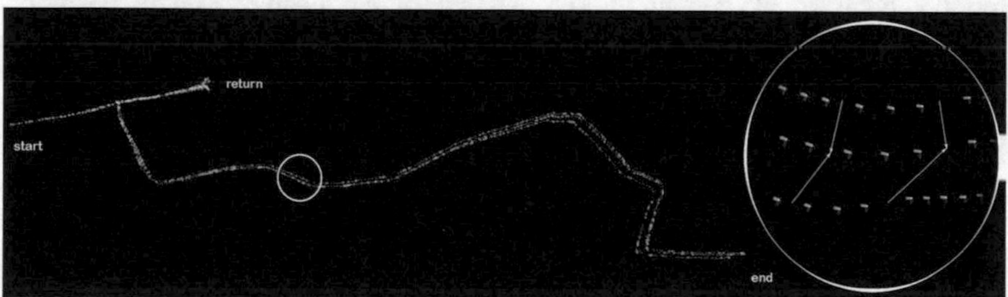

Fig. 3.12 Motion tracking or pose detection using a generalized camera model, exploiting 3D triangulation between overlapping camera viewpoints. Given three different random seed initializations, the differences in the trajectories are largely reduced (© 2016 EC FP7 ROVINA project, reprinted with permission)

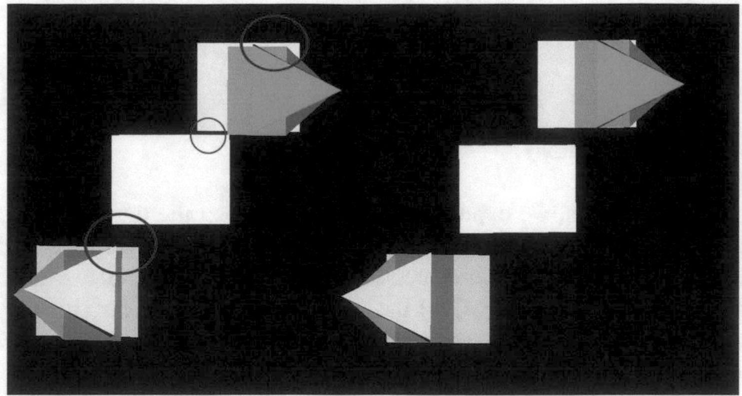

Fig. 3.13 After final rebundling the camera arc configuration is more accurate. The asymmetries and misalignments in the original (*left*) are largely gone in the newly estimated configuration (*right*) (© 2016 EC FP7 ROVINA project, reprinted with permission)

calibration, the amount of accepted point correspondences increases as well. Figure 3.14 shows the point cloud for two sections of the catacombs, built from the 3D positions of all feature points found across inter- and intra-camera viewpoints. Three close-ups show the detail that one can already observe in the point distribution.

3.4.2.5 Mesh Generation

In order to generate a 3D mesh structure, we use a similar approach as for the single examples of Fig. 3.15. Yet, for larger structures such as these tunnels, the approach would reach its limits in terms of computing power and memory. We therefore applied the strategy of processing different overlapping chunks along the path of motion. Each chunk contains a selected set of consecutive camera positions, together with their recovered feature point clouds and depth maps, on which the Poisson reconstruction is executed separately.

On the overlapping parts, the geometry is cut along a plane, to create a clean boundary and make sure that subsequent chunks concatenate smoothly. An additional advantage of the resulting mesh chunks is that for visualization purposes the visualization tool can automatically select the chunks which are in the vicinity of the virtual camera viewpoint, thus reducing demands on the graphics engine.

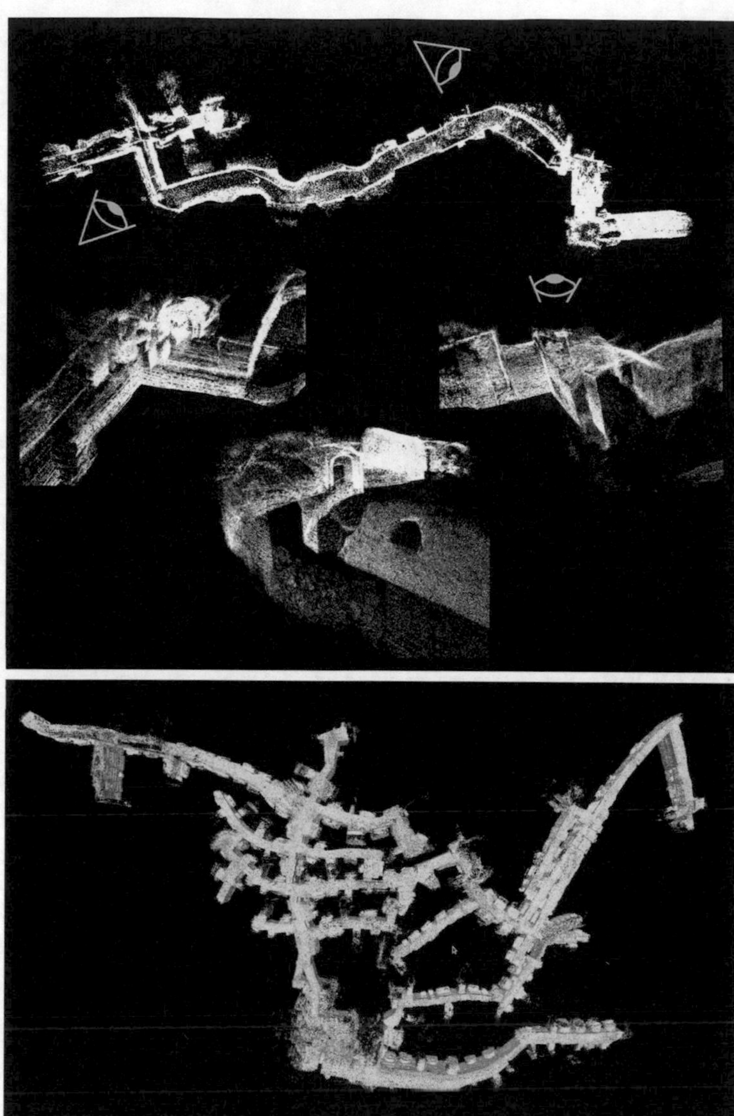

Fig. 3.14 *Top*: Point cloud built from the 3D positions of all validated feature points for the entrance of the Priscilla catacombs; three additional close-ups to illustrate the detail. *Bottom*: 3D feature point cloud for a larger-scale area underneath Priscilla's church (© 2016 EC FP7 ROVINA project, reprinted with permission)

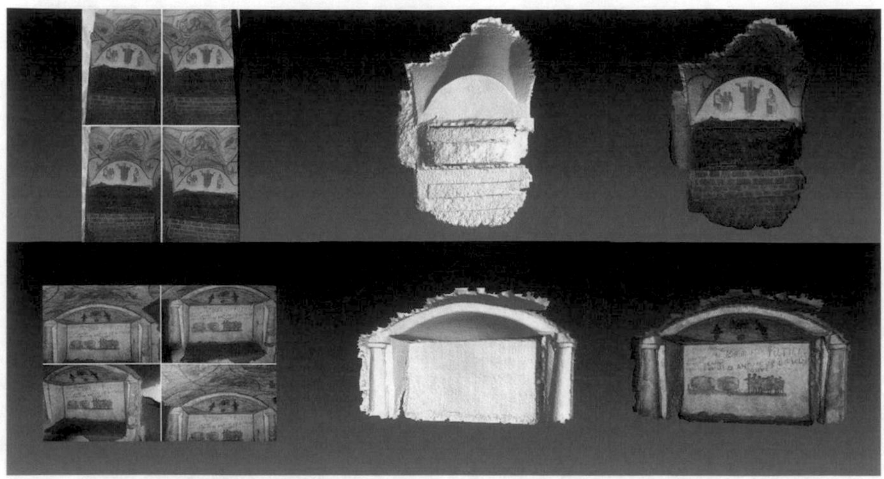

Fig. 3.15 Some results of structure from motion using flash-based photography in the catacombs of Rome. *Left*: a few input images. *Middle*: the recovered shape. *Right*: a texture-mapped 3D model (© 2016 EC FP7 ROVINA project, reprinted with permission)

3.5 Texturing

As the ROVINA robot had to move through dark underground areas, all visual processing had to rely on mobile lighting from the robot. Brightness and color of the surfaces are therefore affected by their positions, distances, and angles to the active light sources, as well as by the light sources' colors. The differences in brightness and color inevitably show up in the final texture map of the 3D model.

It is important to compensate for those effects in order to create a reconstruction that is visually pleasing (for the general public) and photometrically reliable (for scholars). As real surfaces hardly ever are purely Lambertian, one has to go beyond albedo and to specularity estimation to add vividness to the 3D models.

3.5.1 Texturing by BRDF Clustering and Inference

The appearance properties of opaque materials are effectively encoded by the bidirectional reflectance distribution function (BRDF), which for illumination under an incoming direction gives the fraction reflected in an outgoing direction. Typically, such BRDF has to be recorded with sophisticated hardware setups that independently drive a light source and a sensor to many different positions around the object. These setups are expensive, time-consuming, and inaccessible to most researchers.

Because of the specific nature of mobile lighting (directional lighting, flash-based or onboard lighting on the robot), the sampling is by definition quite low, and full BRDF measurement is hardly possible. Inspired by [26, 27], it is possible to infer an entire BRDF from a minor part, by exploiting statistical information on the BRDFs of real-world materials (e.g., databases such as MERL [28]). Figure 3.16 shows a number of representative cases. Our starting point is introduced by [29], where the 4D BRDF is reduced to 2D, because it can efficiently capture the behavior of the majority of real materials (Fig. 3.16, left). In the case of head-on flash-based photography, where the angle between the viewing and lighting direction is zero, only the first column of the 2D BRDF can be sampled. For situations where the light source shows an angle with the viewing direction, the 1D slice is shifted. In a more general case, the sampling is more random. In our case, flash-like photography is used if the lamps on the illumination arc are lit for the corresponding camera only, with these light sources close to the cameras (compared to the distance to the gallery surface). Given the surface geometry from SfM, we can fill the column slice. The rest of the BRDF is inferred, using a Gaussian process latent variable model. For details we refer the reader to the references [19–23].

The BRDF sampling and inference described above assume that the observations are the result of a single material. For complex scenes, it can be assumed that the material description at a surface point can be expressed as a linear combination of base materials. While jointly refining the 3D structure and BRDF reflectance model, the base materials are determined by clustering the BRDF information. Like so, realistic visualizations can be achieved that also reflect the actual material characteristics.

The models in Fig. 3.17 show how the approach can be used for realistic texturing. The two models on the left are the same ones as shown in Fig. 3.5, but now the derived BRDFs are used for texturing, where the effects of changing lighting and reflectance can be eliminated. The final renderings are shown at the bottom. The material labeling/weighting is indicated by a green-bluish colors in the middle. The strength of this approach can be demonstrated especially for more complicated material characteristics such as marble. The marble piece in Fig. 3.17 is found on the entrance wall of the Priscilla catacombs. In the renderings, the changes in reflections, while changing the virtual viewpoint, give a vivid impression of a shiny, marble material.

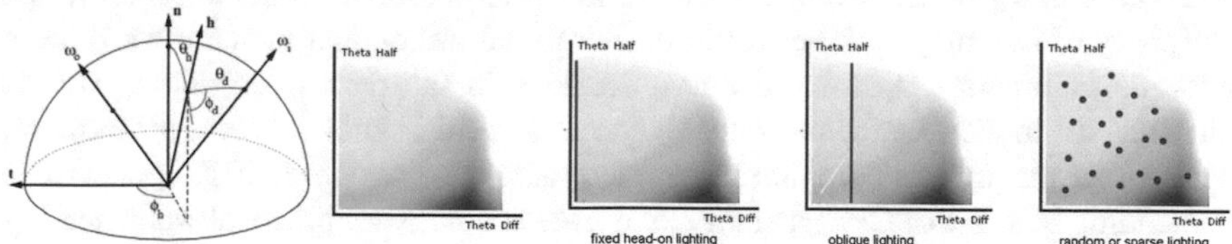

Fig. 3.16 *Left*: a BRDF relates incoming and outgoing directions of light transport. *Right*: in practice, only a fraction of the BRDF can be sampled. The figures show the sampled slices for head-on lighting, oblique lighting, and random/sparse sampled lighting, respectively (© 2016 EC FP7 ROVINA project, reprinted with permission)

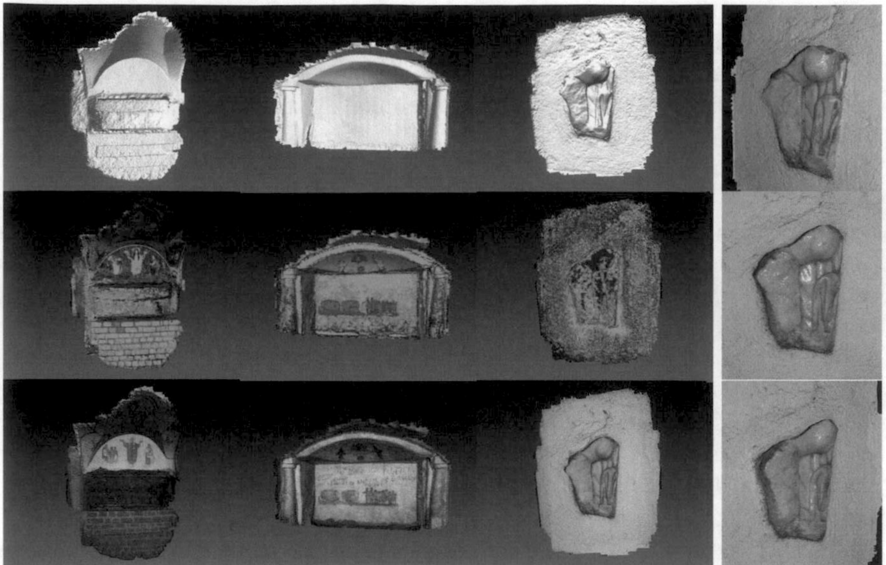

Fig. 3.17 Texture BRDF clustering on catacomb samples. From *top* to *bottom*, *shaded* view, BRDF labeling, and textured view. *Right* column: virtual rendering, showing the specular nature of the marble material (© 2016 EC FP7 ROVINA project, reprinted with permission)

3.5.2 Large-Scale Texturing

Whereas BRDF inference is quite promising for uniform point light sources, the lighting circumstances on the robot are more complex. In order to provide imagery with sufficient dynamic range, and minimize motion blur, all lights on the illumination arc had to be lit jointly. Like that, the arc creates a more-or-less uniform light strip on the walls and allows for shorter camera shutter opening times to create sharper images.

The effect of the light arc is much more complex than that of a single point light source such as a flash. Not only are there more overlapping light sources at the same time, but also the spatial light distribution of each individual LED light source is noticeable as a gradual fade-out of the lightness as we move from the center to the periphery of the image. The effect is similar to natural optical vignetting but more intricate in practice because of interreflections in the narrow corridors. This is difficult to model mathematically without a priori knowledge. Furthermore, because of its inherent nonlinear characteristic, the above BRDF approach is demanding in terms of CPU, memory, and time and not very practical when dealing with large-scale 3D models.

On the other hand, using the BRDF approach described above, we have observed that most of the structures in the catacombs exhibit a very Lambertian, i.e., diffuse behavior. We therefore can reasonably assume that the lightness changes can be reformulated in a linear way. Furthermore, since the reflectance changes across the images are very smooth, we model these changes only using the sparse inter- and intra-camera feature correspondences, as explained below, instead of the dense formulation in [26, 27]. We refer to this principle as an affine texture correction; the principle is shown in Fig. 3.18.

- Consider a reconstructed 3D point p and the corresponding intensity observations in the images for which it is visible. For each such observation i, we assume that it can be expressed as an affine weighted combination of its true underlying color I, where different weights are used for different observations.
- In order to guarantee a unique solution, the weights are subjected to a smoothness constraint, meaning that neighboring observations should have similar weights. Neighbors are defined by the edges of a Delaunay triangulation between the extracted feature points.
- The problem statement is nonlinear in a, b, and I. A linear implementation is proposed by alternatively solving for I and a, b, respectively, till convergence.
- For arbitrary pixels in the image textures, the affine weights are defined by barycentric interpolation between the three feature points of the closest triangle within the Delaunay triangulation.

In Fig. 3.18, the original images clearly show the intensity falloff from the center to the boundaries, which affects the texturing of the 3D model. A model's texture map is built as a mosaic of image parts originating from the original camera viewpoints. For each local mesh neighborhood, one chooses the texture from the camera viewpoint for which the projection of the mesh area is maximized. This

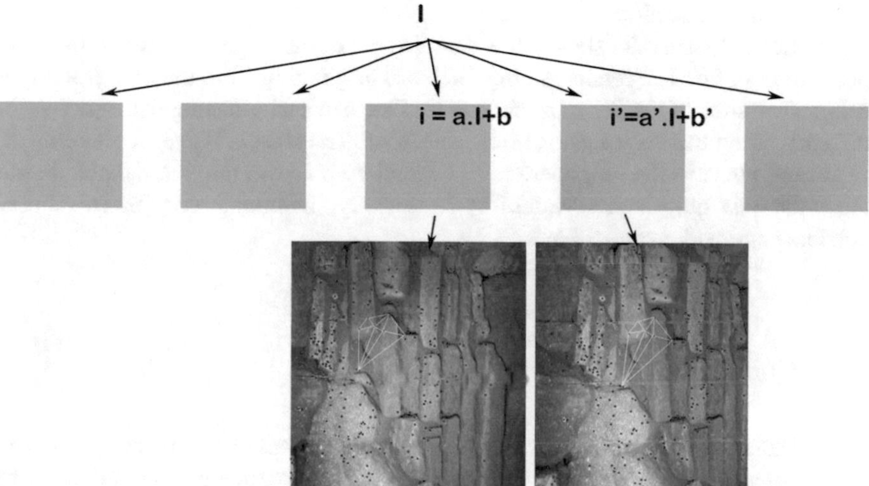

Fig. 3.18 The images show intensity falloff from the center to the outer boundaries. In order to compensate for this effect, the real color I of a certain point on the surface is expressed as an affine transformation of its observations in the images where it is observed (© 2016 EC FP7 ROVINA project, reprinted with permission)

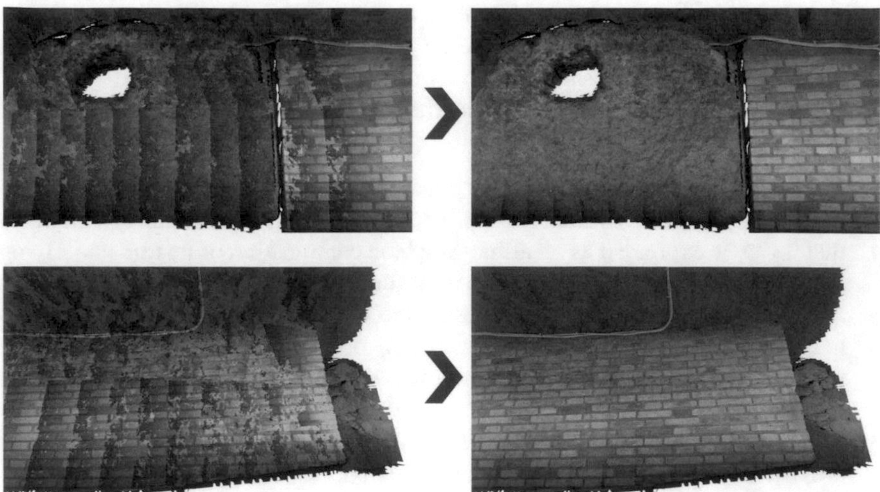

Fig. 3.19 Large-scale texturing results. Two close-ups showing the result before (*left*) and after (*right*) affine texture correction (© 2016 EC FP7 ROVINA project, reprinted with permission)

means that along the mesh there are so-called UV boundaries where the chosen viewpoint changes from one camera to another. If the original images are not corrected, there is a clear distinct discontinuity in the texturing. After correction though, the transitions in UV space are substantially reduced, and the texturing gives a much smoother impression. Figure 3.19 shows a close-up on the result of large-scale texturing on the resulting mesh, with and without the aforementioned affine texture correction.

Figures 3.20 and 3.21 show a few samples out of the large-scale reconstructions performed so far. The renders in Fig. 3.20 are originating from the area around the official entrance of the Priscilla catacombs. One can easily distinguish between the different structures such as tufa, brick, and stone. The ones in Fig. 3.21 are referring to several areas in the neighborhood of the church across the Via Salaria. In this area, there is quite some variability in scenery, including very narrow burial corridors and wider chapel areas.

3.6 Conclusion

This chapter proposed a novel approach for image-based 3D reconstruction of underground, catacomb-like environments, which is particularly complicated by the variability in depth and the necessary moving light sources on the robot causing changing illumination.

The research resulted in the design of a dedicated joint camera/light arc as a hardware option and a custom structure-from-motion pipeline to create texture-

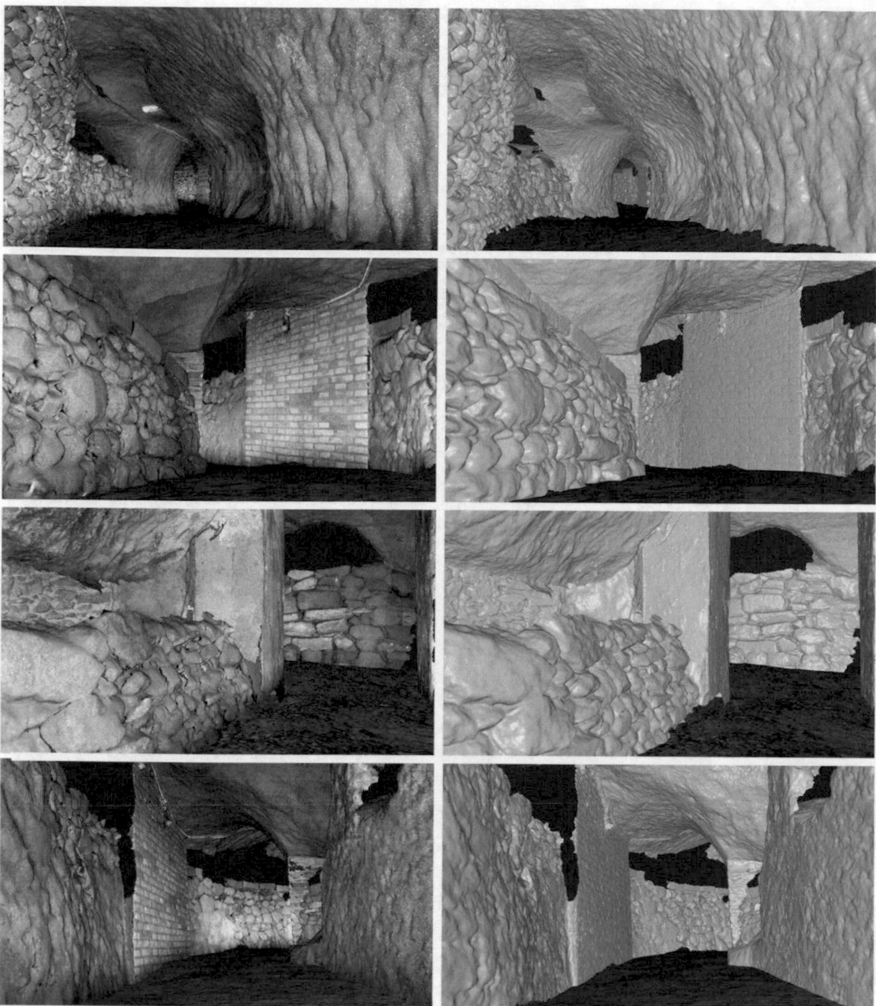

Fig. 3.20 Selection of renders from the texture-mapped 3D models from the entrance of the Priscilla catacombs. *Left*: textured, *right*: *shaded* (© 2016 EC FP7 ROVINA project, reprinted with permission)

mapped 3D geometry of the environment. In the treatment of changing illumination, we have demonstrated the potential of BRDF inference for the simultaneous extraction of shape and complex material properties. For large-scale texturing of 3D reconstructions, a more pragmatic approach was proposed where the original images are corrected so that afterward corresponding feature points in different images will have the same color.

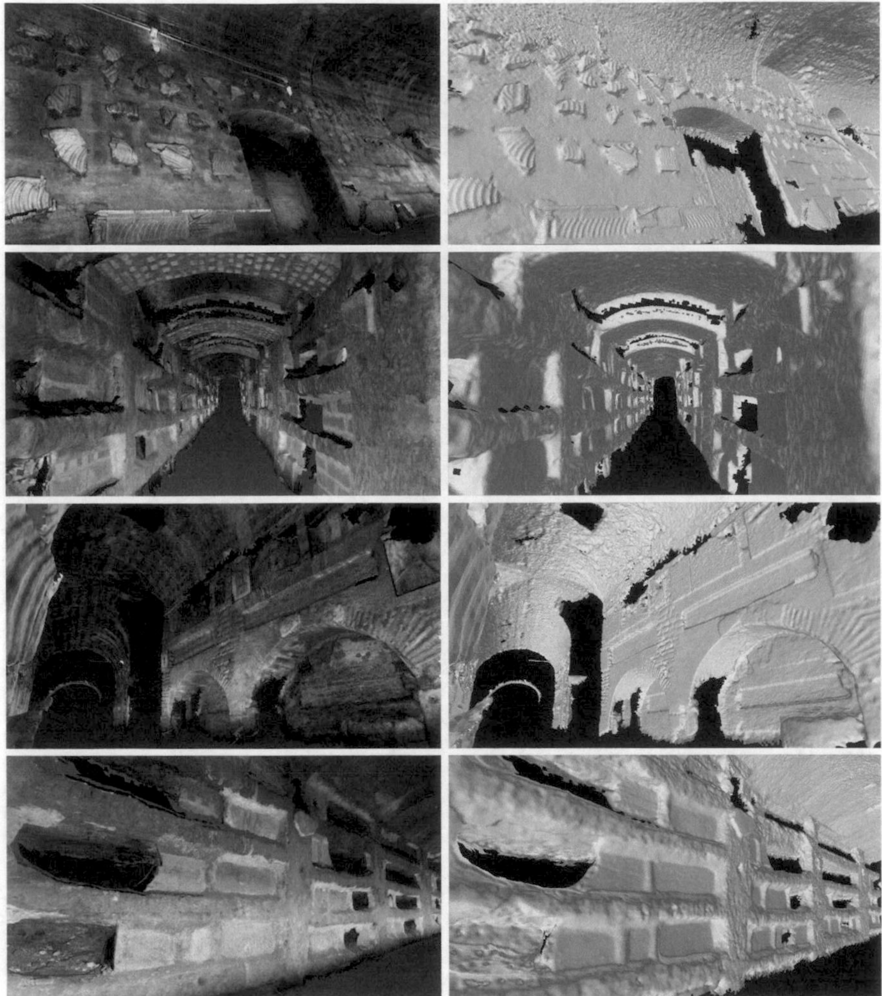

Fig. 3.21 Selection of renders from Priscilla catacomb sections located underneath the church on the opposite side of the entrance on the Via Salaria. *Left*: textured, *right*: *shaded* (© 2016 EC FP7 ROVINA project, reprinted with permission)

The net result is a visualization of large-scale texture-mapped 3D model, based on the improved local reflectance characteristics and shapes, useful for further semantic analysis and classification.

Acknowledgments The authors gratefully acknowledge support by the EC FP7 project ROVINA.

References

1. V.A. Ziparo, G. Castelli, L. Van Gool, G. Grisetti, B. Leibe, M. Proesmans, C. Stachniss, The rovina project. Robots for exploration, digital preservation and visualization of archeological sites, in *Proceedings of the 18th ICOMOS General Assembly and Scientific Symposium 'Heritage and Landscape as Human Values'* (2014)
2. V.A. Ziparo, M. Zaratti, G. Grisetti, T.M. Bonanni, J. Serafin, M. Di Cicco, M. Proesmans, L. van Gool, O. Vysotska, I. Bogoslavskyi, C. Stachniss, Exploration and mapping of catacombs with mobile robots, in *Safety, Security, and Rescue Robotics (SSRR)* (2013)
3. A. Gruen, Digital close-range photogrammetry, in invited paper to G. Togliatti Memorial '*Modern Trends in Photogrammetry*', XVII. ISPRS Congress, Washington, DC, August 1992
4. LIDAR. http://en.wikipedia.org/wiki/LIDAR
5. T. Tuytelaars, L. van Gool, Matching widely separated views based on affinely invariant neighbourhoods. Int. J. Comput. Vis. **59**(1), 61–85 (2004)
6. R. Hartley, A. Zisserman, *Multiple view geometry in computer vision* (Cambridge University Press, New York, 2000)
7. T. Moons, L. Van Gool, M. Vergauwen, 3D reconstruction from multiple images: Part 1 – principles. Found. Trends Comput. Graph. Vis. **4**(4), 287–404 (2009)
8. M. Pollefeys, R. Koch, L. Van Gool, Self-calibration and metric reconstruction inspite of varying and unknown intrinsic camera parameters. Int. J. Comput. Vis. **32**(1), 7–25 (1999)
9. M. Pollefeys, L. Van Gool, M. Vergauwen, F. Verbiest, K. Cornelis, J. Tops, R. Klein, Visual modeling with a hand-held camera. Int. J. Comput. Vis. **59**(3), 207–232 (2004)
10. P. Mueller, T. Vereenooghe, A. Ulmer, L. Van Gool, Automatic reconstruction of Roman housing architecture. Recording, Modeling and Visualization of Cultural Heritage (2005)
11. M. Vergauwen, L. Van Gool, Web-based 3D Reconstruction Service. Mach. Vis. Appl. **17**(6), 411–426 (2006)
12. Bundler: http://www.cs.cornell.edu/~snavely/bundler/
13. Agisoft Photoscan: http://www.agisoft.com/
14. Microsoft Corporation. Kinect for XBOX 360
15. P. Vuylsteke, A. Oosterlinck, Single binary-encoded light pattern. IEEE Trans. Pattern Anal. Mach. Intell. **12**(2), 148–164 (1990)
16. M. Proesmans, L. Van Gool, A. Oosterlinck, One-shot active 3D shape acquisition, in *IEEE International Conference on pattern Recognition* (1996)
17. P. Cignoni, R. Scopigno, Sampled 3D models for CH applications: a viable and enabling new medium or just a technological exercise? J. Comput. Cult. Herit. **1**(1), 1–23 (2008)
18. H. Bay, A. Ess, T. Tuytelaars, L. Van Gool, Speeded-up Robust features (SURF). Comput. Vis. Image Underst. **110**(3), 346–359 (2008)
19. R. Pless, Using many cameras as one, in *Computer Vision and Pattern Recognition* (2003)
20. M.D. Grossberg, S.K. Nayar, A general imaging model and a method for finding its parameters, in *International Conference on Computer Vision* (2001)
21. L. Hongdong, R. Hartley, K. Jae-Hak, A linear approach to motion estimation using generalized camera models, in *Conference on Computer Vision and Pattern Recognition, (CVPR)* (2008)
22. L. Kneip, H. Li, Efficient computation of relative pose for multi-camera systems, in *Conference on Computer Vision and Pattern Recognition (CVPR)* (2014)
23. J. Ventura, C. Arth, V. Lepetit, An efficient minimal solution for multi-camera motion, in *International Conference on Computer Vision (ICCV)* (2015)
24. G.H. Lee, F. Faundorfer, M. Pollefeys, Motion estimation for self-driving cars with a generalized camera, in *Conference on Computer Vision and Pattern Recognition* (CVPR) (2013)
25. M.A. Fischler, R.C. Bolles, Random sample consensus: a paradigm for model fitting with applications to image analysis and automated cartography. Commun. ACM **24**(6), 381–395 (1981)

26. S. Georgoulis, M. Proesmans, L. Van Gool, Head-on analysis of shape and reflectance, in *International Conference on 3D Vision (3DV)*, Tokyo, 8–11 Dec 2014
27. S. Georgoulis, V. Vanweddingen, M. Proesmans, L. Van Gool, A gaussian process latent variable model for brdf inference, in *International conference on Computer Vision, ICCV* (2015)
28. W. Matusik, H. Pfister, M. Brand, L. McMillan, A data-driven reflectance model, in *SIGGRAPH* (2003)
29. F. Romeiro, Y. Vasilyev, T. Zickler, Passive reflectometry, in *European Conference on Computer Vision (ECCV)* (2008)

Chapter 4
Acceleration of 3D Mass Digitization Processes: Recent Advances and Challenges

Pedro Santos, Martin Ritz, Constanze Fuhrmann, Rafael Monroy, Hendrik Schmedt, Reimar Tausch, Matevz Domajnko, Martin Knuth, and Dieter Fellner

Abstract In the heritage field, the demand for fast and efficient 3D digitization technologies for historic remains is increasing. Besides, 3D has proven to be a promising approach to enable precise reconstructions of cultural heritage objects. Even though 3D technologies and postprocessing tools are widespread and approaches to semantic enrichment and storage of 3D models are just emerging, only few approaches enable mass capture and computation of 3D virtual models from zoological and archeological findings. To illustrate how future 3D mass digitization systems may look like, we introduce *CultLab3D*, a recent approach to 3D mass digitization, annotation, and archival storage by the *Competence Center for Cultural Heritage Digitization* at the *Fraunhofer Institute for Computer Graphics Research IGD*. *CultLab3D* can be regarded as one of the first feasible approaches worldwide to enable fast, efficient, and cost-effective 3D digitization. It is specifically designed to automate the entire process and thus allows to scan and archive large amounts of heritage objects for documentation and preservation in the best possible quality, taking advantage of integrated 3D visualization and annotation within regular Web browsers using technologies such as WebGl and X3D.

Keywords Fast and economic 3D digitization • Cultural heritage • Documentation methods • Technological innovation • Industrialization • Automation • 3D reconstruction • Photorealistic rendering • Virtual replica

---

P. Santos (✉) • M. Ritz • C. Fuhrmann • R. Monroy • H. Schmedt • R. Tausch • M. Domajnko • M. Knuth
Fraunhofer IGD, Fraunhoferstr. 5, 64283 Darmstadt, Germany
e-mail: pedro.santos@igd.fraunhofer.de; martin.ritz@igd.fraunhofer.de; constanze.fuhrmann@igd.fraunhofer.de; rafael.monroy@igd.fraunhofer.de; hendrik.schmedt@igd.fraunhofer.de; reimar.tausch@igd.fraunhofer.de; matevz.domajnko@igd.fraunhofer.de; martin.knuth@igd.fraunhofer.de

D. Fellner
GRIS/TU-Darmstadt, Fraunhoferstr. 5, 64283 Darmstadt, Germany
e-mail: dieter.fellner@gris.tu-darmstadt.de

M. Ioannides et al. (eds.), *Mixed Reality and Gamification for Cultural Heritage*,
DOI 10.1007/978-3-319-49607-8_4

4.1 Introduction

In order to optimize the preservation and documentation of cultural heritage in the best possible way, digital strategies have been formally established at the political level worldwide. New initiatives in the USA, for example, foster advanced digitization of biological collections such as the *iDigBio Infrastructure* or the *Thematic Collections Networks*. Also, the EU Member States are called upon for increased digitization efforts by the *European Commission*. Accordingly, this executive body of the EU advises on the necessity of digitization and online accessibility of historic inventories as part of the *Digital Agenda* for Europe, among other points the request for improved conditions underpinning large-scale digitization [1]. As one of the flagship initiatives of the *Europe 2020 Strategy*, the *Digital Agenda* further defines the long-term preservation of cultural heritage for better access to culture and knowledge through better use of information and communication technologies as one of the key areas [2]. These measures are therefore connected with article 3.3 of the *European Union Lisbon Treaty*, which stipulates that "Europe's cultural heritage is safeguarded and enhanced" [3] for future generations.

Despite these legal frameworks and the political acknowledgment of the important role cultural heritage plays in society, damaging risks of different types may impact its integrity and compromise its values. How fragile it really is has been made apparent by several natural and man-made disasters. Incidents such as the recent intentional destruction of the ancient Semitic city Palmyra, Syria, and the archeological finds at the museum in Mosul, Iraq, underline the need for new documentation methods and have led to a reevaluation of the importance of high-resolution facsimiles. Furthermore, the fact that merely a small amount of all the artifacts in collecting institutions is publicly available indicates the need for improved accessibility to cultural heritage information in accordance with modern requirements [4]. Therefore, innovative documentation methods for heritage remains are becoming increasingly important. This heightened relevance results from both the desire to provide better access to unique objects, for example, to make collections more easily available for research or to a wider audience, and the looming threat of losing them due to disasters and other environmental influences.

Against this background, numerous research activities have led to innovative technologies for digitization, including also the significant aspect of mass scanning for large inventories. However, the latter remains mostly limited to two-dimensional objects such as books and paintings or focus on digital items such as videos, films, photographs, or audio recordings [5]. A notable example among many is the *Herbarium Digistreet*, developed by the Dutch company *Picturae* for the *Naturalis Biodiversity Center* for comprehensive 2D digitization. Focused on digital photography, its automated conveyor belt setup successfully allows to scan heritage material such as herbarium sheets on a large scale and at high speed [6]. Besides, the *Smithsonian Institution*, the world's largest museum and research complex, launched its *Mass Digitization Program* in order to support its 19 museums and 9 research centers in their efforts to digitize their collections in high speed and high quality. This approach to integrate mass digitization into daily operations in order to provide global access to its collections is based on the *Smithsonian Strategic Plan* [7].

While digitization in 2D is already highly efficient and thus implemented on a wide scale, 3D acquisition [8] still remains costly in terms of time and money. Because of the still slow and highly manual process, digitizing objects in 3D continues to be a tedious task, in particular, if it targets a faithful reproduction of its geometric complexity and its optical material properties [9]. 3D digitization technologies and postprocessing tools are widespread [10, 11]. However, only few approaches enable mass capture and computation of 3D virtual models from zoological and archeological findings [12]. In addition, no commercially available 3D technology for large-scale scanning has been developed until now, resulting in the growing need for cost-effective and fast-scanning solutions with high output. At the same time, the demand to capture 3D artifacts has grown.

Recognizing the value added by 3D, cultural heritage institutions have begun to leverage and understand its potential for stimulating innovation. Having proved to be promising and innovative, 3D digitization not only enables a precise reconstruction of heritage objects for documentation and preservation, it also offers new ways of presentation that will change the cultural heritage domain: new visualization and interaction technologies allow heritage experts or curators to display and share collections or research results in novel ways both on-site in a museum setting as well as online. Especially the ways afforded to better present artifacts online gives institutions the chance to achieve greater visibility for their collections and engage with a wider audience.

3D digitization offers a range of benefits and can therefore add value in the cultural heritage sector by enabling new forms of participation and a broad range of new applications, services, and business models in areas such as education, tourism, or gaming to attract new audiences:

Accessibility
3D replicas allow for global digital access to collections and research results. Numerous objects, of which only a fraction is displayed in museums, for example, can be scanned, classified, and documented in online catalogs, making them accessible to education and the public at large. 3D replicas can be made available easily and therefore accessed by several researchers at once. Also, they pave the way for new research methodologies. For example, fragments of complex fossils can be reassembled correctly with the aid of 3D models or archeologic objects scanned in situ and analyzed immediately.

Conservation
High-quality 3D virtual models can be used by conservators as a reference for conservation and restoration measures on damaged goods and serve as a basis to generate physical replicas. Furthermore, a 3D model can help to precisely visualize damage patterns or worn areas and thus support better restoration decisions. In addition, high-quality virtual exhibits can in many cases replace the shipping and loaning of originals to exhibitions, eliminating the risk of further deterioration due

to accidental damages or detrimental environmental conditions and high insurance costs.

Documentation
Significant pieces of art, which are endangered by environmental influences or even irrevocably destroyed by disastrous events, may at least be secured in their current state of conservation and made accessible for research around the world. In case of the loss of an original, the image, form, and context are still available for scientists and interested parties due to photorealistic 3D models. With the aid of such digital "3D conservation," objects remain accessible for subsequent generations.

New Exhibition Formats
3D models enable new ways of exhibition planning and implementation. Collections spreading over multiple museums can be showcased concurrently at different geographic locations. Virtual reproductions can be used in hybrid exhibitions and create innovative and interactive visitor experiences. Collections and exhibits become accessible for visitors from anywhere in the world and enable new ways of interaction with collections. 3D models can also be presented through purely virtual museum experiences and even allow for customized "digital exhibitions at home."

New Applications and Services
3D replicas can be used for the development of apps, games, documentaries, tourism services, and educational content and can thus ensure a more intense visitor experience, new forms of participations, and additional revenue streams.

3D Print
3D replicas can be used in printed form as exhibition and loan objects for various purposes (i.e., to avoid damages and insurance costs or legal uncertainty relating to ownership). Not only delicate or particularly fragile artifacts but also those too valuable for transport or loan lend themselves to the creation of copies true to the original. High-precision printing models developed from the collected 3D data can serve the physical reproduction of destroyed or fragmented cultural heritage goods.

To enable collecting institutions to reap these benefits, the need is for efficient 3D scanning processes that can be used in a wide array of settings and allow for swift high-quality scanning of even entire collections.

4.2 A First Approach to 3D Mass Digitization

To make 3D more widely available to heritage institutions, a recent approach to 3D mass digitization, annotation, and archival storage is introduced by the *Competence Center for Cultural Heritage Digitization* at the *Fraunhofer Institute for Computer Graphics Research IGD*. The scanning facility named *CultLab3D* can be regarded as one of the first feasible approaches worldwide to enable fast, efficient, and cost-effective 3D digitization. It is specifically designed to automate the entire process and thus allows to scan and archive large amounts of heritage objects for documentation and preservation in the best possible quality. Moreover, scanning and lighting technologies are combined to capture the exact geometry, texture, and optical material properties of artifacts to produce highly accurate photorealistic representations. The final digitization result is a fused and consolidated 3D model of the artifact.

Objective 1: High-Speed Capture and Low Cost per Artifact
Given the often time-consuming nature of current 3D scanning technologies, the core objective of the *CultLab3D* technology is to significantly increase the speed at which heritage material can be scanned in 3D by automating the process to the greatest extent possible while ensuring high quality of the scans. Most existing 3D scanning technologies require significant manual intervention and postprocessing, while *CultLab3D* is designed to reduce it to a minimum. It aims at shortening the time required for scanning to only several minutes per artifact (depending on its geometric complexity), compared to several hours with conventional 3D scanning methods. This increase in speed is expected to allow for a 10- to 20-fold cost reduction for 3D scans.

Objective 2: Flexibility, Extendibility, and Sustainability by Design
As opposed to many industrial applications, there is no rule for how cultural heritage artifacts look like, which sizes they come in, and which combination of materials they are made of. Currently, there is not a single scanning technology that can capture artifacts made of any material. In fact, for some materials, there are no appropriate scanning technologies as of now, and research is being undertaken to capture, for example, the geometry of translucent and very shiny objects without tampering with their surfaces. The scanning technology *CultLab3D* is therefore designed as a multimodular scanning system where objects are placed on transparent glass trays once and pass a battery of various scanning modules connected by a conveyor belt. Therefore, no scanning station ever becomes obsolete, and not all of them have to be assembled into a pipeline and used for a specific collection. Instead, they can be combined to match the specific, individual requirements. *CultLab3D* is designed from the ground up to be continuously extended by additional scanning stations that can handle additional types of materials and sizes of artifacts or increase the throughput of the overall system. Furthermore, additional scanning modules can contribute with complementary information, such as volumetric data stemming from ultrasound or CT technologies and much more. While *CultLab3D* is currently generating surface models, in the long-term, *CultLab3D* is supposed to generate consolidated 3D models fusing data from a variety of capture sources.

Objective 3: High Quality and Accuracy
Producing precise replicas of cultural heritage is essential to reap the many benefits of 3D scanning. Only high-quality 3D models will suffice to meet the demands of experts and researchers. To achieve the best possible scanning results, *CultLab3D* combines innovative scanning and lighting technologies to capture the exact

geometry, texture, and optical material properties above and below their surface to allow for a faithful, photorealistic virtual reproduction of heritage objects. To compute the geometry and texture of an artifact, *CultLab3D* uses photogrammetric 3D reconstruction technologies where multiple images of an object, taken from a variety of angles, serve as a basis to extract information regarding its depth and the color of its surface. The resolution of the resulting virtual models is in the range of 200–300 μm.

Objective 4: Semantic Enrichment for Inventory
A 3D replica model is most useful when annotated with context information. The annotation of a digital replica with semantic information linked to related documents, photographs, videos, and other materials allows leverage of its full potential for education and research. Therefore, *CultLab3D* also developed a Web-based, 3D-centered annotation system for object classification and metadata enrichment as part of the research (see Sect. 4.3). With this system, 3D replicas can be linked to additional information such as the object's origin, artist, or details of prior restoration measures. To date, most collection management systems are text centric and only allow for managing text, pictures, and videos linked to individual artifacts. Eventually, they allow uploading and linking to 3D models. However, hardly any system can directly integrate and annotate 3D models. *CultLab3D* proposes a paradigm shift by developing a 3D-centered Web-based annotation tool called *the Integrated Viewer Browser (IVB)*, allowing to directly create annotations on the 3D object surface. On the end-user side, the tool only requires an Internet connection, can be run on any platform featuring a recent Web browser, and supports a variety of metadata formats such as the one used by Europe's digital library portal *Europeana*.

4.2.1 Automated Photogrammetry

This section describes in more detail the current development status of *CultLab3D*, its first two scanning units, the *CultArc3D*, and the *CultArm3D*, as well as the underlying *CultLab3D platform*.

4.2.1.1 CultLab3D Platform

As described above, the *CultLab3D platform* was developed in a way to enable a fully automated operation of the scanning. It is tasked with monitoring and triggering all the processes involved while scanning. The *CultLab3D* interface is also the single entry point to control the entire pipeline and initiate a scan. The software is currently installed on a tablet PC for ease of use.

In the current setup, CultLab3D controls

- Four conveyor belts used to move objects throughout the pipeline

- Two scanning stations (*CultArc3D*)
- A so-called *Reconstruction Service* that oversees the reconstruction process running on two powerful workstations

It is capable of handling up to two objects at the same time, while avoiding conflicting situations and preventing potential problems, for example, placing a new object when the system is not yet ready will stop the workflow and alert the operator about it. A regular scan starts when the operator places an object at the beginning of the pipeline. This action is immediately detected, and the user is then asked to introduce some information about the object. The information required to be entered for every object is the following:

- Project name: User-friendly name used to identify the object.
- Universally Unique Identifier (UUID): Identifier used by all the different systems involved. Together with the project's creation timestamp, it uniquely identifies a scan process.
- Bounding cylinder: Diameter and height in millimeters of the bounding cylinder that encloses the object.

The operator can enter this information manually by typing the details. In case of the *UUID*, it can be randomly generated. Alternatively, if the data was added into the platform's database, a *Quick Response Code* (commonly called QR code) [13] can be presented to the tablet's frontal camera. When detected, all related information will automatically be filled in. Once the object's information has been made available to the system and all the required systems are ready, the operator is allowed to initiate a scan. From that point on, all the remaining processes are taken care of automatically by the *CultLab3D platform*. Human intervention will only be required when the object has been successfully scanned at the pipeline and needs to be retrieved or if a problem was detected.

At present, we work on a set of specialized scanners for flat objects that will be added to the modular scanning pipeline upon completion.

4.2.1.2 CultArc3D

CultArc3D is a modular mechanism, designed to be either self-sufficient or fully integrated into *CultLab3D*. Both 3D geometry and optical material properties are the acquisition specialties of the module. During the digitization process, artifacts are transported on glass carrier disks into the scanning station by means of a conveyor belt system, thus achieving full automation.

Not only does *CultArc3D* allow for geometry and texture capture, it also allows to measure optical material properties by design, mimicking a material acquisition dome. Early works by Weyrich et al. [14] showed how BRDFS can be captured to retrieve spatially and directionally varying reflectance and subsurface scattering of complex materials. Also Holroyd et al. [15] used two identical setups of a coaxial setup of a camera and a light source looking from the side and from the top on an artifact. Schwartz et al. [16] built a setup called the DOME with 151 consumer cameras and LED lights to capture form and appearance of an artifact's surface. An improved construction [11, 17] uses industrial high-resolution video cameras mounted on a vertical quarter arc rotating inside the DOME, with LED lights replacing the consumer camera's flashlights. The ORCAM [18] built at DFKI by Koehler et al. [19] comprises a full sphere as opposed to the DOME, allowing to also capture the bottom of artifacts by placing them on a transparent, rotational, antireflective glass carrier, pivo-mounted on a steel ring. They use high-resolution DSLR photo cameras and a structured light projector revolving around the sphere, capturing geometry, texture, and optical material properties.

CultLab3D's setup consists of two coaxial, semicircular arcs that rotate around a common axis, coplanar with the surface of the carrier disks passing through it. The two arcs that lend the system its name cover a hemisphere around the center of the glass carrier disks. The reason why disks are used is to limit human contact with the often sensitive artifacts to the actions of placing artifacts onto and removing them from the disks after digitization, and since perspectives from below the artifact are captured through the disks, glass was chosen as material. Each arc is driven by its own actuator, allowing for a discrete number of stop positions. The radii of the arcs differ to allow for independent movement. The outer arc, subsequently referred to as the camera arc, holds nine equiangular cameras, mounted at the same distance to the center of the hemisphere. Any image sensor can be used. Currently, we use nine industrial 10 MP video cameras in equiangular distribution along the camera arc, plus nine statically mounted cameras for acquisition of the bottom side of artifacts, capturing the visible spectrum of light. Multispectral sensors can be easily integrated into the system, and laser planes can be mounted on the arcs to exploit the possibilities of movement around the artifact through alternative methods of geometry acquisition. Even volumetric data capturing sensors using X-ray or MRT could be added, either on the camera arc or as additional data capturing arcs or as separate modules along the *CultLab3D* digitization pipeline. In analogy to the outer camera arc, the inner arc (subsequently referred to as light arc) holds nine equiangular light sources. The light sources currently used emit light in the visual spectrum. However, multispectral lighting is considered as a possible enhancement. For example, ultraviolet illumination can be used to visualize traces left by chisels when carving wooden sculptures.

If N is the number of camera positions on the camera arc and analogously the number of light positions on the light arc, then the virtual hemisphere is divided into $N + 1$ longitudinal divisions in one dimension. The discrete stopping positions of each arc divide the virtual hemisphere into $N + 1$ latitudinal divisions. The result is an equiangular spacing in two dimensions of reachable camera and light poses (positions and directions) on the virtual hemisphere. There are N cases where the position of the two arcs around their common rotation axis is identical due to equal angle (motor position). In order to prevent the light sources or parts of the light arc (inner arc) from blocking the camera views, the light sources are designed as ring lights with inner diameters large enough to avoid intersection with the camera viewing frustums. Light arc and camera arc are driven such that the center points of the ring light sources are positioned on the optical axis of the respective camera whenever both arcs are in the same stopping position. The result of this design concept is the capability to achieve any combination of an arbitrary light direction, limited to a discrete homogeneous spacing over the virtual hemisphere at $N \times N$ light positions, with an arbitrary camera angle, again limited to the same discrete homogeneous spacing over the virtual hemisphere at $N \times N$ camera positions. This leads to a combinatory space of N^4 possible combinations of any given camera view with a light direction (see Fig. 4.1).

Versatility of Acquisition Modes

Currently, *CultArc3D* allows for two distinct modes of digitizing an artifact in the center of the capturing hemisphere described by the camera and light arcs. When acquiring 3D geometry and texture only, both arcs move in synchrony and stop at nine equiangular positions on the upper hemisphere around their joint rotating axis, resulting in $9^2 = 81$ images being taken, which can be used for photogrammetric 3D reconstruction of the artifact. When 3D geometry, texture, and optical material properties are acquired, both arcs are moved independently such that all discrete combinations of evenly displaced camera and light positions on the upper hemisphere around an artifact are captured, resulting in $9^4 = 6561$ images being taken. The acquired image set can be used for both photogrammetric 3D reconstruction of an artifact and to compute its optical material properties. After completion of each mode, the arcs move into the upright position, and the artifact is moved out of the

Fig. 4.1 CultArc3D: Two hemispherical rotating arcs, one equipped with cameras, one with ring light sources. Norbert Miguletz © 2014, Liebieghaus Skulpturensammlung, reprinted with permission

CultArc3D module. There is one more specialty of the design: the length of artifacts is theoretically unlimited. Front and back of an object can be acquired by a quarter sphere of perspectives each, while the middle part is acquired by moving the object through the arcs while they are resting in vertical position, capturing image data.

3D Geometry and Texture Acquisition
The *CultArc3D* setup provides an ideal basis for controlling incident light angles of one or many simultaneous light sources and capturing from one or many different angles using an equidistant distribution of viewing directions over a hemisphere. Many approaches to surface reconstruction can easily be realized; some examples are:

Multi-view Stereo (MVS)
The well-known method of *Multi-view Stereo (MVS)* [20], drawing from a set of multiple images, shot from several different directions with sufficient overlap, and centered on the target artifact under a corresponding lighting situation, is used to generate a 3D reconstruction of the artifact's surface points, based on a previous registration of all camera coordinate systems into one world coordinate system and sparse reconstruction of 3D points using image-space features. A surface is then generated based on the reconstruction results and the information on the image point topology.

Photometric Stereo (PS)
The method of *Photometric Stereo (PS)* [21], somewhat complementary to MVS due to its exploitation of visual depth cues from a set of multiple images shot from a single perspective centered on the target artifact under different incident light angles, is used to generate a normal map of the artifact's surface. This is then repeated for different camera views and the results merged. A depth map is generated by interpolating the normal map, and analogously, as for MVS reconstruction, a surface can be generated.

Laser-Based Line Scanning
For yet higher accuracies, one or more light sources on the light arc can be complemented or replaced by laser lines in order to be able to optically codify the surface of the target artifact and derive 3D positions of the surface by plane-ray intersection.

4.2.1.3 CultArm3D

In the cultural heritage domain, artifacts come in high variety and uniqueness. To ensure complete and accurate 3D reconstruction of arbitrary objects, it is important to carefully position scanners with respect to the object's surface geometry as well as the scanner's measurement volume. The *CultArm3D* is a robotic system for automated 3D reconstruction consisting of a lightweight compliant robotic arm [22] with a mounted camera and a turntable for the object to be scanned. In a virtual 3D environment, all relevant parts of the system are modeled and monitored. This allows for planning and almost arbitrary positioning of the camera around the object of interest with respect to safety and workspace constraints.

The applied robot arm consists of 5° of freedom with all rotational joints and can accurately move payloads up to 2 kg. This robot arm is collaborative and can safely operate next to humans with a quasi-hemispheric of around 80 cm. The turntable is capable to precisely and smoothly rotate, clockwise and counterclockwise, around its vertical axis with infinite 360° rotations and is designed for object weights up to 50 kg. A high-resolution camera (10–20 MP) is mounted on the tip of the robot arm and synchronized with a lighting setup that can be either a mounted ring light or an external static soft box setup. The robot arm is restricted to operate only on one side of the turntable, while the other side is shielded against the background in either black light absorbing or white reflective panels, depending on the desired illumination setup.

CultArm3D complements the *CultLab3D* photogrammetric digitization pipeline assemblage as the second scanning station, *CultArc3D* as the first scanning station at the conveyor system [23]. Unlike the first station, where camera views with a large field of view are achieved on a fixed hemisphere around the object, the camera optics of the *CultArm3D* system is more focused, aiming for adaptive detailed close-up views on the object. These views are then planned based on the result of the first scan pass at the *CultArc3D* scanning station in such a way that additional object features are captured to resolve remaining occlusions and locally enhance the quality and completeness of the scan. The number of additionally planned views needed to fulfill certain quality criteria is strongly dependent on the object's surface and texture complexity. Automatically planning a different number of views and thus dynamically allocating scanning time dependent on the objects complexity contributes to the high throughput of the *CultLab3D* digitization pipeline. When operating the *CultArm3D* scanning station in stand-alone mode outside the *CultLab3D* assemblage, the first scan pass is conducted with generic camera views planned with respect only to the object's cylindrical outer dimension, such as the height and diameter (see Fig. 4.2).

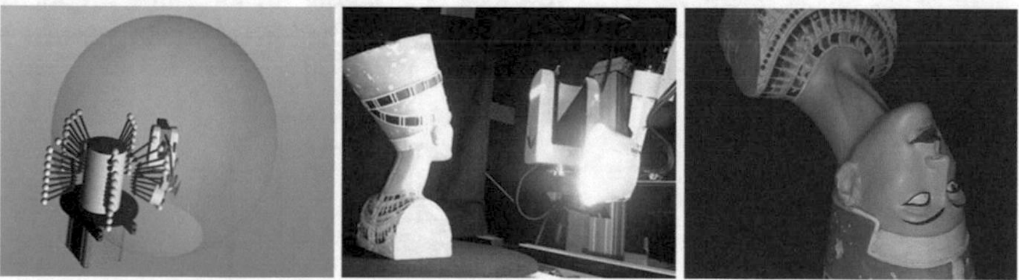

Fig. 4.2 *Left*: A virtual simplified representation of the *CultArm3D* system with a set of planned views for the first scan pass based on the cylindrical dimensions of the object. *Middle*: The real system in action illuminating and capturing the object with a mounted diffuse ring light around the camera. *Right*: Acquired object image. © Fraunhofer IGD, Germany, 2016, reprinted with permission

Considering the limited workspace [24] of the applied light-weight robotic arm, the task of capturing arbitrary objects up to a size of 60 cm in height and diameter becomes challenging. In some cases, planned camera views that are optimal in terms of scan coverage/quality cannot be exactly achieved due to safety or reachability constraints. However, in most cases a slightly modified and feasible view (or set of views) can be found that equally contributes to the scan quality as the original one. To address this problem, we use an iterative approach [25]. Given a desired camera view x_d to the object, we adopt the closed-loop inverse kinematics (*CLIK*) algorithm [26] to retrieve possible angle combinations q of the robot arm and the turntable. Figure 4.3 shows the *CLIK* scheme with the direct kinematic expression $k(\cdot)$ that transforms a robot joint configuration q into a camera view x_e. The goal is to minimize the error term e that is iteratively evaluated based on the desired view x_d and the updated feasible view x_e. The gain matrix K weights specific elements of the error term and can be chosen depending on the camera model or measurement volume. For example, for camera optics with a very limited depth of field, a translation along the view vector should lead to a higher error compared to slightly changing the angle of incidence, because the focus distance is more crucial to the setup.

Desired camera view candidates are calculated based on the result of a fast preview scan. In less than 5 min, a first 3D model is reconstructed using a generic set of downscaled images around this object. The local point cloud density and surface normal vector distribution is then analyzed using a volumetric representation of the preview scan (see Fig. 4.4). The green voxels indicate sufficient local quality of the scan. Yellow- to red-colored voxels can be found in areas of the preview scan with a bad local quality estimate, such as partially occluded regions with low image coverage or poorly textured surfaces where not enough features could be retrieved with the applied camera resolution. These bad areas are then clustered, and principle view candidates are retrieved, indicated by the green arrows in Fig. 4.4. These candidates are already checked against occlusion and visibility using rendering and ray-tracing methods and are considered optimal with respect to the 3D model.

However, as mentioned before, in some cases views are readjusted by the *CLIK* algorithm in order to be reachable by the robotic system. During this refinement process, a single principle view candidate that is not directly feasible can lead to multiple feasible camera views all together contributing to the same originally targeted object area. For photogrammetric reconstruction methods based on

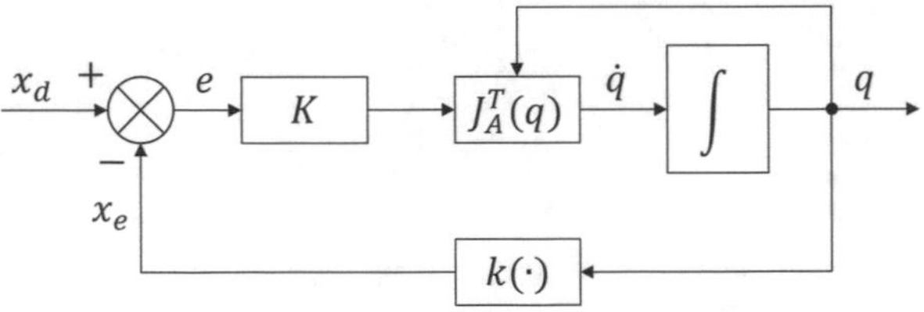

Fig. 4.3 Scheme for closed-loop inverse kinematics (CLIK) showing the iterative refinement of the Jacobian transpose J^T and the resulting robot arm and turntable joint angles q. © Fraunhofer IGD, Germany, 2016, reprinted with permission

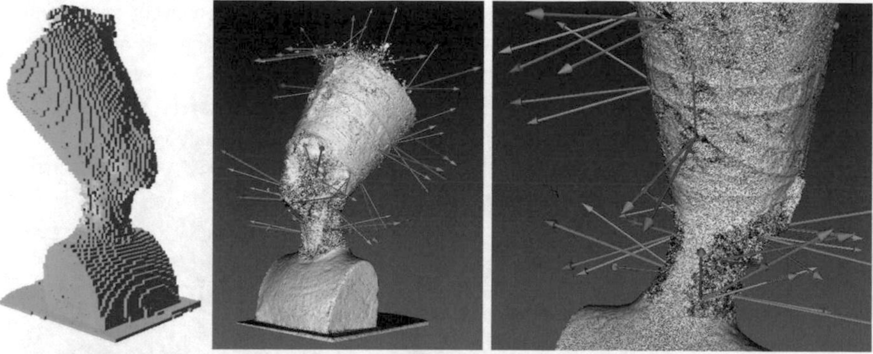

Fig. 4.4 *Left*: The voxel model of an incomplete preview scan with the voxel color representing the local model quality. *Middle* and *right*: The corresponding point cloud with retrieved and refined view candidates visualized in *green color*. © Fraunhofer IGD, Germany, 2016, reprinted with permission

multi-view stereo, it is important to capture the same areas multiple times with the same camera optics. Figure 4.5 shows a set of finally solved camera views pointing toward the orange safety hull cylinder of the object. With the current robotic system, the turntable rotations are less time consuming and more stable than positioning the camera with the compliant robot arm. For this reason, additional neighboring views are here introduced by just slightly rotating the turntable.

Compared to view planning with depth image scanners [27], such as structured light, photogrammetric view planning is more challenging when establishing it as incremental online process rather than using a fixed number of scan passes. This is because, unlike with depth image scanners, for photogrammetry the knowledge of a 3D surface is not immediately available after acquiring a single image. On the contrary, several images from different angles must be captured for the reconstruction of a 3D surface part.

Another challenge is the relatively computationally expensive photogrammetric reconstruction process that becomes even more expensive with every image added to the set. Appropriate clustering and selection of images becomes important when focusing on certain surface regions, as well as parallel processing techniques, in order to make photogrammetry a more incremental process. In the future we want to address this issue and directly integrate a photogrammetric online feedback into the current *CLIK* process. This will allow for more reactive view planning that can reduce the overall scanning time and improve the surface quality criteria.

4.2.1.4 Reconstruction

The crucial step for successful photogrammetric reconstruction is image acquisition on the calibrated system, which is established by geometric and radiometric calibration and by the definition of the reference system. The current version of the

Fig. 4.5 Refined view candidates achievable by the *CultArm3D* robotic system. © Fraunhofer IGD, Germany, 2016, reprinted with permission

CultLab3D system acquires images of objects on two stations with 19 cameras in total (18 cameras on the *CultArc* and 1 camera on the *CultArm*). It is essential that each single camera is radiometrically and geometrically calibrated. Color calibration is described in Sect. 4.2.3, while geometric calibration of multiple cameras is described below. Furthermore, this chapter focuses on two reconstruction procedures that are necessary for automated photogrammetry (so-called quick reconstruction and final reconstruction). Quick reconstruction provides a draft dense point cloud, which serves as input for next-best-view planning algorithm, and final reconstruction, which calculates the final textured 3D model from all acquired images.

With recent advances in photogrammetry, geometric calibration (estimation of interior and exterior parameters of cameras) can be a fully automatic procedure [28]. However, for systems with multiple cameras, it is still important to estimate the interior parameters of each camera before image acquisition in order to get the best possible results of a photogrammetric reconstruction. For calibration of the cameras at the *CultArc system*, a ring pattern calibration board mounted on a motorized arm is used. The motorized calibration system allows the calibration board to be moved and rotated in all directions in order to capture sufficient number of images of the ring pattern for successful calibration.

Quick Reconstruction

The *CultLab3D system* is designed in a way that the second station, the *CultArm3D*, acquires images of occluded parts of an object. Occlusions are calculated by the next-best-view planning algorithm based on input dense point cloud obtained from images from the first station, *CultArc3D*. For convenient automatic workflow of the whole pipeline, it is crucial that the dense point cloud is computed in less than 5 min. In order to get a dense cloud of entire object in a short period, some adjustments are made on a typical photogrammetric reconstruction. First, only the most important images from the *CultArc3D* are used in the reconstruction process together with their predefined interior and exterior parameters. In this way, few algorithms can be skipped in order to speed up the total computational time. Additionally, irrelevant parts of the images are masked out; hence, feature detection is performed only on the relevant part of images (see Fig. 4.6). All the computations are made on a powerful workstation (*CPU: 2× Intel Xeon E52699v3 HaswellEP; RAM: 512 GB DDR4 2133 MHz; SSD: 2× Sandisk Cloudspeed Ascend SSD 2,5 960GB SATA*). The described quick reconstruction provides a resulting dense point cloud for next-best-view planning in an average time of 4 min 30 s.

Final Reconstruction

Final reconstruction refers to the photogrammetric reconstruction procedure at the end of the *CultLab3D pipeline*. All images from both stations are color corrected, and camera interior parameters are assigned to them. Additionally, local coordinates of four images (*acquired at the CultArc3D*) are estimated in order to define a local reference system and consequently get the scale of the final 3D model. The abovementioned elements are input for the final image-based 3D reconstruction, which provides a complete 3D model with color-corrected textures (see Fig. 4.7).

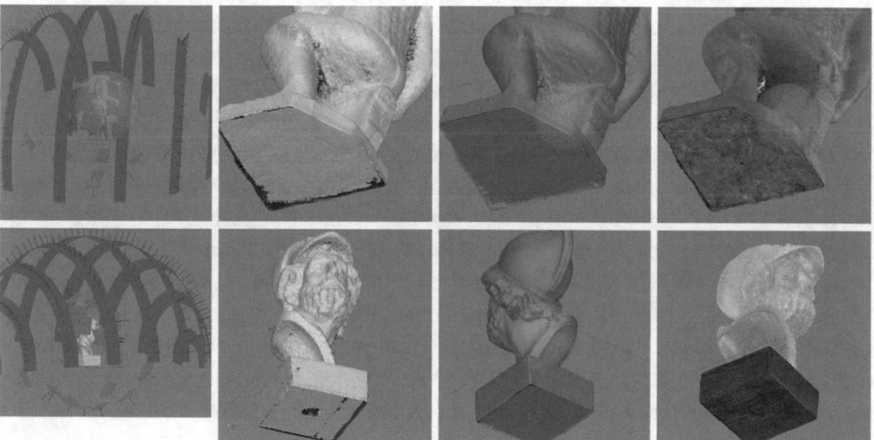

Fig. 4.6 *Left* to *right*: Consolidated input images from *CultArc3D* and *CultArm3D*: Camera alignment, Dense cloud, Mesh, Textured mesh—all including masking. © Fraunhofer IGD, Germany, 2016, reprinted with permission

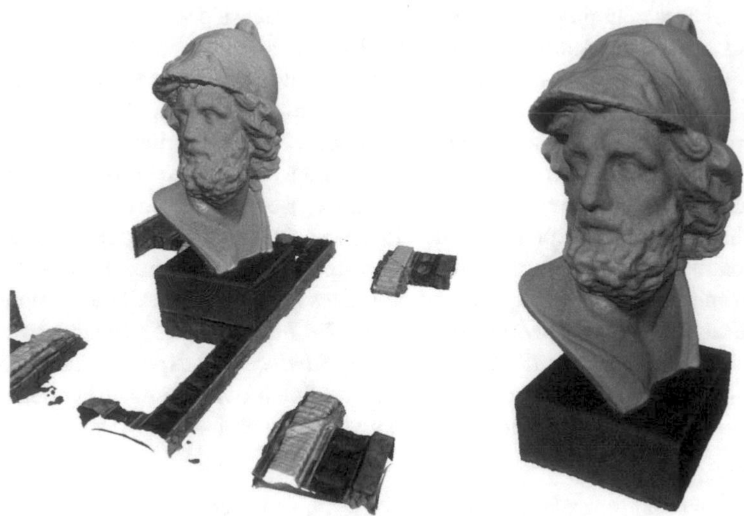

Fig. 4.7 *Left* to *right*: color-corrected 3D preview model to identify remaining holes and occlusions; final reconstruction based on consolidated input images from *CultArc3D* and *CultArm3D*. © Fraunhofer IGD, Germany, 2016, reprinted with permission

4.2.2 Automated Structured Light

Our real-time scanner is a fast structured-light 3D scanner that uses the principle of light sectioning. The approach is loosely based on the Flying Triangulation project [29]. While many other scanning approaches require a time-intensive stop-and-go approach, this setup can be used handheld or mounted on a light weight compliant robot arm as shown in Fig. 4.8. The reconstructed point cloud is directly available and visible while scanning, in contrast to other methods that require expensive post processing. This property makes it possible to give an online feedback to the user or the view-planning algorithm about the current scan quality and completeness. In this way, missing surface parts can be immediately addressed and filled.

The system consists of two cameras and two custom pattern projectors. While both projectors use a static pattern mask with multiple stripes, one is tilted by 90° such that vertical and horizontal lines can be projected crossing each other on the object. During the scan, the vertical and horizontal patterns are projected alternating at a frequency of 20 Hz. Every time one of the projectors is active, both cameras are triggered. The captured images are processed in real time for depth estimation using GPGPU techniques. Parallel to the acquisition process, the resulting depth images are continuously registered and aligned to each other, forming a dense successively updated 3D point cloud. In a final step, this point cloud is cleaned and exported as a 3D mesh.

For the actual reconstruction process, it is necessary to have a fast mapping from line coordinates to depth values. More formally, one function $Z\_i\ (u,\ v)$ per projected line i, where u and v are the coordinates at which the line was detected.

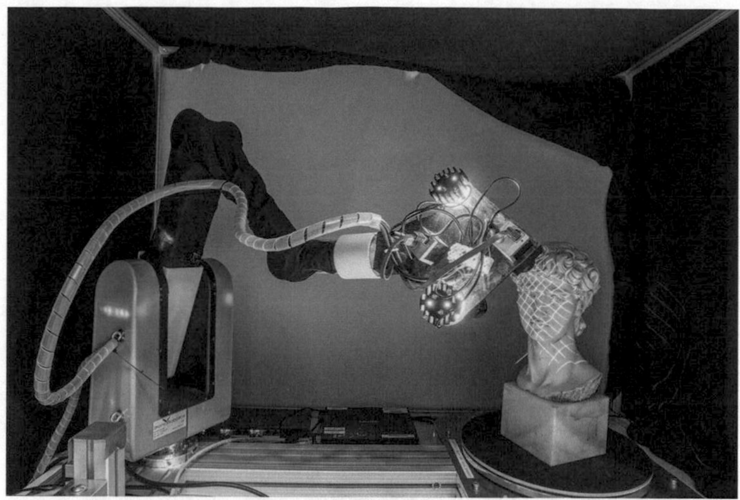

Fig. 4.8 Real-time scanner mounted on a light-weight robot arm while scanning an object. © Fraunhofer IGD, Germany, 2016, reprinted with permission

Those depth functions are estimated beforehand in a special calibration procedure, which works similar to a common camera calibration [30] except that for each pose of the calibration pattern, three images are captured: one image with full illumination, in which only physical pattern of a calibration board itself is visible, and two additional images capturing the vertical and horizontal projections on the board. Altogether, this data allows for optimizing a depth function of every horizontal and vertical line. In general, there are very different ways to define the form of a depth function for structured light systems. Distinctive properties of depth functions are:

- The number of free parameters, which need to be fitted,
- The robustness against imperfections of the relative position of cameras and projectors to each other,
- The ability to model lens distortion of the projectors,
- The run time cost to evaluate the function.

We successfully reduced the parameter space to enable fast real-time processing, while maintaining a necessary amount of robustness and handling the lens distortion of cameras and projectors. A successful sensor calibration then leads to one depth function per projected line. In Fig. 4.9, the exemplary result is shown for all vertical stripes.

With the calibration result at hand, it is possible to start the actual scanning. On each camera image captured during the scanning process, the multiple projected stripes have to be localized and assigned to the corresponding depth function. We first perform the stripe localization in subpixel precision [31]. The result is a set of 2D line coordinates (u, v), which can then be put into the $Z\_i\ (u, v)$ functions. However, it is not yet clear which depth function Z_i corresponds to the found

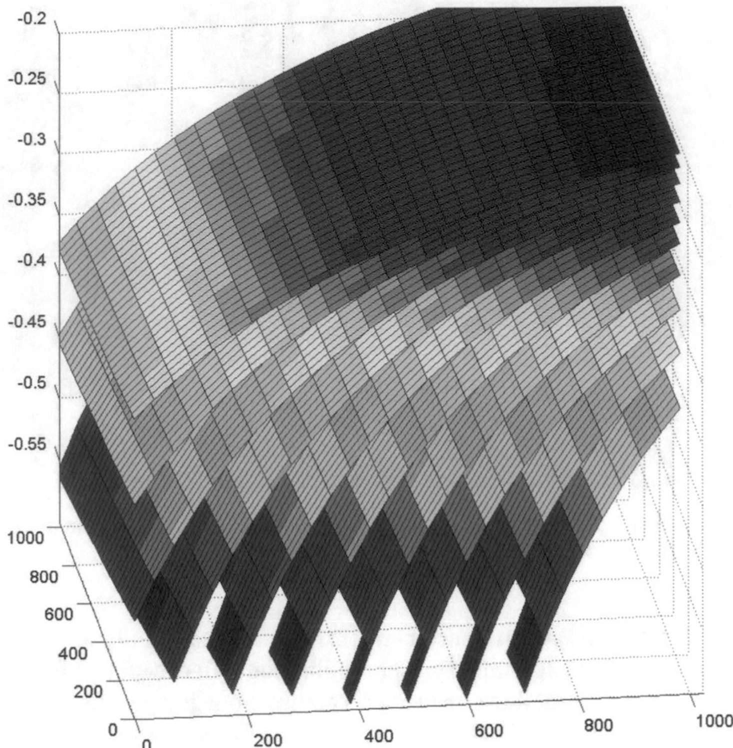

Fig. 4.9 Result of the calibration procedure for all vertical lines in the static projection pattern. Every surface represents a depth function $Z\_i\ (u, v)$ corresponding to a project line i. The depth value Z is assigned to the vertical axis. © Fraunhofer IGD, Germany, 2016, reprinted with permission

coordinates, because the fine lines of the applied static projection pattern do not contain any additional encoded numbering for i. To resolve this problem, we evaluate the coordinate with all depth functions in parallel. In a subsequent verification step, the estimated 3D points are projected back into the contemporaneously captured image of the second camera and then rejected if there is no line visible at this position. Thus, only the valid 3D points remain.

At this point, a sparse reconstruction for a single view is available. In order to construct a complete model, all views need to be aligned and transformed into a global coordinate system, which requires an estimation of the sensor pose for every frame. Since we do not want to rely on external sensor tracking devices, we achieve the registration of subsequent frames using a modified iterative closest point *(ICP)* method. The underlying idea is to optimize the pose estimation in an iterative way such that the distance between the measured depth maps is close to zero. One important and time-consuming step in this method is the search for point correspondences, which are used to estimate a new pose. These correspondences are only reliably found between the alternating subsequent vertically and horizontally projected stripes. For example, if only vertical lines would be projected, a slight lateral motion of sensor in orthogonal direction to the stripes would result in finding no correspondences and losing the sensor track. On the other hand, it is very likely to find correspondences in the crossings of subsequent vertical and horizontal lines. However, the sparsity of the data can make it challenging to achieve robust pose estimation. We solve this issue by performing a more stable frame-to-cluster registration rather than a simple frame-to-frame registration. Thus, a view is not only registered to its direct but to multiple predecessor views. Small errors in the pose estimation can lead to an error accumulation that becomes obvious when a circular trajectory is completed. This is called the loop-closing problem because of the accumulated gap between the first and the last view. We address this problem with a global registration method that runs in background parallel to the scanning and corrects the accumulated errors using message-passing techniques on a clustered view graph. This works similar to the initial local registration, but instead of registering only with direct predecessors, it is possible to match views that were captured at completely different angles and points in time.

To evaluate the reconstruction quality, a bust replica of Michelangelo's famous *David* was scanned as shown in Fig. 4.9. The whole process took 175 s which is relatively fast compared to other scanning methods. Additionally, the same object was scanned using a high-quality phase-shifting scanner and used as ground truth reference model. Using both models it is possible to register and compare them against each other, as shown in Fig. 4.10. The histogram on the left side of the color scale indicates the distribution of measurement errors. It is clearly visible that the distance to the reference model is below 0.5 mm for the vast majority of surface points. For a lot of use cases, this is already an acceptable reconstruction quality. However, we are confident to further improve the accuracy and speed of this prototype scanner by increasing the precision and illumination of the custom-built pattern projectors as well as adopting faster high-resolution cameras.

Fig. 4.10 Real-time scanner reconstruction compared to reference mesh. © Fraunhofer IGD, Germany, 2016, reprinted with permission

4.2.3 Color Calibration

Color calibration refers to the processes involved in making sure the colors seen on, for example, a computer screen match as close as possible the ones seen through the human eye. Particularly in the cultural heritage domain, color accuracy is paramount [32]. In the digital photography field, standard practices and workflows are already in place to ensure color consistency across different mediums, for example, computer monitors, printed material.

It can be argued that the most accurate method for digital photography is the spectral characterization of the camera and light source. However, it usually involves expensive equipment and a complex setup. Most photographers prefer to use color patterns instead. They offer an easier and quicker method for characterizing a camera and lighting condition.

As an exploratory investigation, we introduced a pattern-based color management workflow to the pipeline using a *ColorChecker SG*. The color chart is shown to all the cameras used in the pipeline under the same illumination conditions that will be used while capturing the images. These images are then collected to obtain an *ICC profile* [33] per camera, which is used to convert the images to a device-independent color space.

The color seen in the resulting 3D models is usually described using one or more texture files, which are simple image files. In all likelihood, the 3D viewer used to analyze the models will not be color managed, which means that even if the textures have a specific *ICC profile* attached, it will be ignored and an *sRGB* color space will be assumed. It then makes sense to ensure that the textures already describe colors in this color space. The *sRGB color space* has a very restricted gamut when compared to that of *Adobe RGB* or *ProPhoto RGB*, but it is the most widely adopted when transmitting images to the public [34]. This motivated us to transform all of our images to the *sRGB color space* and guarantee that the colors in the 3D models can be seen accurately, albeit in a reduced gamut, in most display devices as long as they are calibrated.

4.2.4 Optical Material Capture

The term *optical material properties* describes a class of manifold characters of materials, leading to different visible effects. The goal of material acquisition is to record these effects as accurately as necessary and reproduce them as close to reality as possible. There are different models to capture these effects that can be acquired with the acquisition modes currently available for *CultArc3D* (see Sect. 4.2.1.2):

BTF

"Material" acquisition is a term used for the acquisition of material behavior in response to incident light from a certain direction, reflected into a certain outgoing angle. Its explanation is straightforward: every possible combination of incoming light directions and outgoing observer (camera) directions within the discrete set of combinations defined by a discrete homogeneous spacing over a virtual hemisphere is simulated. This is achieved by lighting the respective light, while the resulting light-surface interaction is captured by the respective camera, implicitly including texture due to the color array (camera) sensor. Rendering using a *Bidirectional Texture Function (BTF)* exploits the data acquired in the material behavior simulation, in that for each surface point to be rendered under a virtual observer (rendering view) and light positions defined by the scene illumination, the corresponding simulation data defined by the angle toward the camera and the light source(s) are used for surface point shading, according to the material response recorded in the acquisition phase. In addition, the position to be used within the measured arrays is determined by a texture-like mapping of the measured material representation on the target geometry.

SVBRDF

The representation of BTFs as *Spatially Varying Bidirectional Reflectance Distribution Functions (SVBRDF)* can be derived using the approach of *Massively Parallel SVBRDF-Fitting BTF* data [35]. Using this technique, the vast amount of data needed by the BTF representation is parameterized by fitting a parametric model to the data such that it represents the optical material behavior sufficiently well, with the advantages over BTF that the model then is controllable, and requires a fraction of the space needed by a BTF (up to several terabytes), making real-time rendering possible with standard hardware.

BRDF

This method is a special case of BTFs, where instead of a matrix of measurements of the material, only one intensity measure is taken, for example, by averaging over the sensor matrix for each camera position and abstracting to obtain two different measures using filters: first, the reflected light intensity, which is proportional to the specularity of the material for the given light and observer direction, and second, the hue of the material, which basically is the color averaged over the sensor matrix or over subregions of the sensor matrix. The result is a material measurement that expresses both reflectivity of the material and hue for a hemispherical, discrete set of combinations of incident light and outgoing view directions. Rendering is done by omitting the step of deciding for a specific position within the measured arrays, as this is already accounted for by averaging as described above, since a BRDF is not spatially varying but is applied to the whole surface as a function of incoming and outgoing light directions.

The sets of camera and light positions required by the methods for 3D geometry and texture acquisition on one side, and for optical material properties acquisition on the other side, have a nonempty set of intersection, which means that in subsequent runs of the methods mentioned above, there would be a high number of redundant positions. As a consequence, the acquisition of optical material properties in the form of BTFs results in the super-set of camera-light combinations required by any of the other methods mentioned. Thus, subsets of the acquired data lead to BRDF and SVBRDF, as well as 3D geometry and texture, while only performing the acquisition process once.

4.3 3D-Centered Annotation and Visualization

Current content management systems used in the museum domain are very text centric, such as Adlib Museum [36] or Museum Index [37], which are used with large collections (e.g., *British Film Institute, the State Museums of Berlin, Louvre, Victoria and Albert Museum, Europeana*). They provide support for a variety of metadata schemata such *as CIDOC CRM, LIDO, METS*, and a range of document and image and media formats. However, native support of 3D formats to annotate, store, and display virtual 3D/4D models is poor or nonexistent, which is even more true for the visualization and analysis of 3D/4D information. The workaround mostly used is to store the 3D data and then link to external tools to open, visualize, and work with it, which means the data is not natively integrated in the museum content management system and that there are no native tools to further explore, annotate, or work with the virtual 3D/4D models. A good overview of current content management systems can be found with the *Collections Trust*, UK [38]. There have been some projects focusing on 3D-centered interaction such as *3DSA* [39] from the University of Queensland in which annotations could be placed directly on the surface of objects and connected to metadata, or measurements could be taken. Also, some scanner companies such as *Artec* are starting to include basic annotation functionality to work with 3D models in their products. Other examples include the *Smithsonian Explorer* in collaboration with *Autodesk* using proprietary technology to showcase items on the Web in 3D but not integrated into their database backend. It allows to explore, measure, and light objects and present narrative stories centered on the 3D artifact. With the advent of 3D mass digitization, annotation with provenance and metadata is centered around the 3D Model with the possibility to create annotations using drag and drop, connecting them to the surface of an object or marking surface areas or regions of interest and connecting them to documents, pictures, or other 3D models. The frontend consisting of the Integrated Viewer Browser (IVB) [40] and the backend consisting of a *CIDOC-CRM* [41] and *CRMdig* [42] conform metadata repository [43] and object data repositories at the corresponding museums.

New and improved technologies for mass digitization like *Cultlab3D* lead to a rapid increase of digitized cultural heritage objects. Once the digitized cultural heritage assets and their metadata are available, an appropriate storage solution is needed. But only storing the data is not enough; the system should include a complete digital library service handling, for example, indexing, retrieval, and permission management.

The *Repository Infrastructure* (RI), first developed as part of the *3D-COFORM* project, is able to accomplish the demands on a storage system for cultural heritage assets. Many different tools for users and specific use-cases were developed, but an integrated, flexible, and easy-to-use graphical user interface (GUI) had still been missing.

In contrast to state-of-the-art museum annotation databases, the newly developed *Cultural Heritage Repository* (CHR), which is based on the ideas of the RI, puts the 3D consolidated model at the center of all activities (see Fig. 4.11). It uses *X3D* by the *Web3D* consortium, which is an integral part of all current browsers supporting at least *HTML5*. The latest state-of-the-art 3D Web technology enables platform-independent single-page Web applications allowing presentation, processing, and annotation of 3D content. This immensely reduces hardware requirements for museums and curators. They can use almost any Web-capable device able to access the Internet from almost anywhere at any time. At the same time, this approach opens the door to community participation in the process of annotating artifacts through the Web, democratizing access to cultural heritage.

In addition, new technologies like geometric *3D-HOG* feature search over already existing 3D consolidated models in the database as well as over available Web databases and simplify annotation of similar provenance data and identification of similar artwork across museums and databases. Curators shall be empowered to semiautomatically annotate newly scanned artifacts that are stored in the repository database in various mesh resolutions with their corresponding similarity descriptors ready to be queried. Once a query is successful, the curator will be given an expectation list of possible corresponding and already annotated artifacts. Then he can choose to apply some of the corresponding annotations to the current artifact.

While the user tools are implemented with *HTML5*, *JavaScript*, and *CSS3*, a *REST*-based common server interface (*CHRBackendAPI*) is used for communication with the backend. The *CHRBackendAPI* (see Fig. 4.12) is a flexible solution

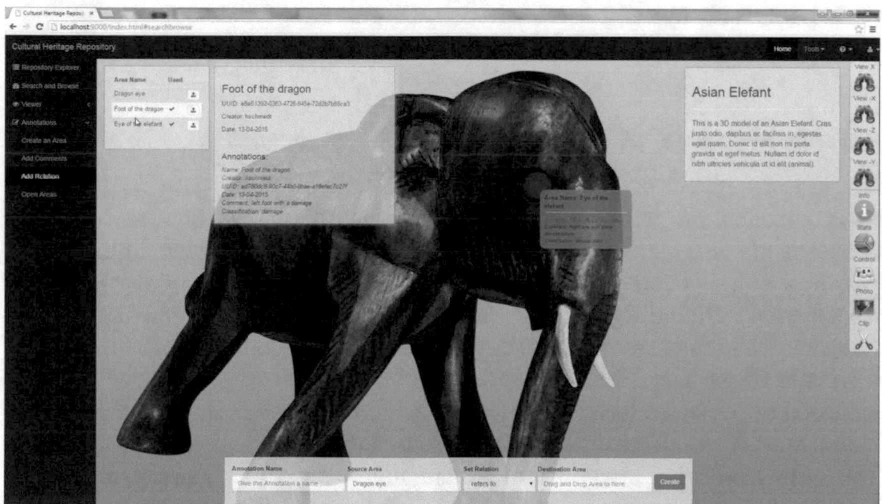

Fig. 4.11 Web-based 3D-centered annotation browser: Query interface and annotation tool. © Fraunhofer IGD, Germany, 2016, reprinted with permission

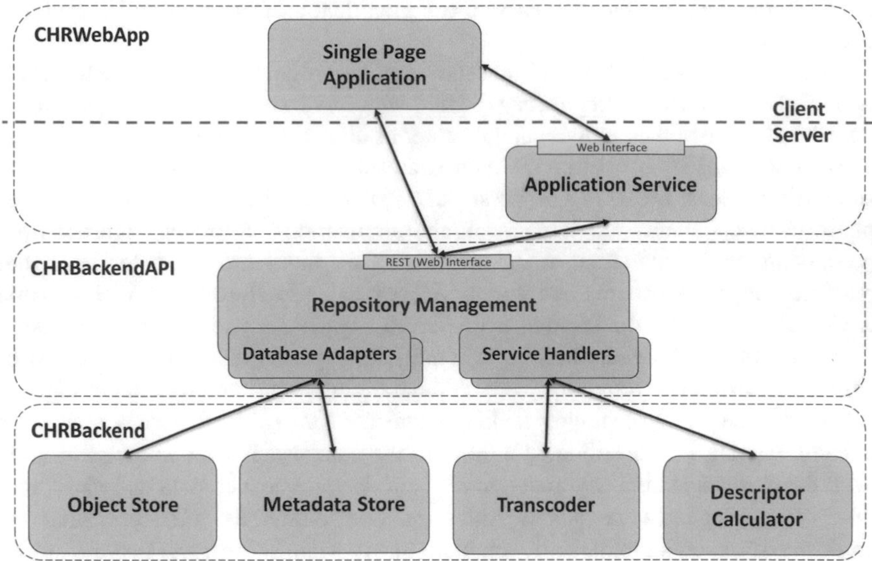

Fig. 4.12 Schematic representation of the CHR. © Fraunhofer IGD, Germany, 2016, reprinted with permission

supporting any kind of ontology and database. It supports *CIDOC-CRM/CRDig* as well as *Dublin Core* and *EDM* (*Europeana Database Model*) and databases such as *MySQL*, *MSSQL*, and others as needed. It includes user, permission, data and metadata management, and service handlers for data services. Modules such as the 3D-HOG feature descriptor generator are integrated as a service connected to the service handler.

4.4 Summary and Outlook

In this section we presented *CultLab3D* as an example of how to tackle the challenge of automated 3D mass digitization and annotation for the digital preservation of entire collections. In line with the overall objective of the *European Commission's Digital Agenda* for Europe, the scanning facility provides a solid foundation for future research and development of 3D technologies in the realm of cultural heritage. The system serves as a platform for future improvements and the inclusion of advanced technologies and therefore represents an important contribution to leveraging innovative digital technologies for the cultural heritage sector. The work conducted marks an important milestone in the journey of cultural heritage research toward a connected and digital future, allowing for various new applications. The high-quality 3D models enable from better visitor experiences in museums by innovative exhibition concepts based around 3D replicas to new business models such as "virtual loans" of 3D models or educational applications. *CultLab3D* therefore offers the chance for cultural institutions to tap into additional revenue streams and secure their funding with complementary business models.

Besides, we envisage future challenges and potential technical solutions for consolidated 3D models in order to go beyond visualization and to expand knowledge for computer-aided restoration. Fusing external surface with internal structure information, consolidated 3D models can prove to be an efficient way to enhance the perception of the respective artifact and to overcome limitations of traditional documentary and diagnostics methods for improved conservation practice.

Recognizing the potential of 3D for cultural heritage analysis, research has focused on 3D acquisition and the visual processing of data for around 30 years now [44]. Since then, computer graphics techniques are widely used for cultural heritage applications and to support the work of heritage experts, be it for detecting geometrical changes as holes and cracks, for reconstructing archeological fragments, or for visually reconstructing polychrome layers of sculptures [10, 11]. Significant advances have also been made regarding the physically correct reconstruction of the geometry and texture of an object's surface. Additionally, initial approaches toward capturing the reflection of various materials are developed [45, 46].

However, for a comprehensive analysis of historic artifacts, data regarding their inside, their material composition, and their properties need to be acquired as well and potential damages identified. Invaluable for assessing the conservation status, and thus for the restoration purpose, is therefore a thorough investigation of both the external and internal structure of an artifact, stemming from a variety of diagnostic analysis tools that allow for sound prediction and careful documentation.

To support restoration work, a wide range of diagnostic technologies have long been deployed in conservation science in order to examine objects' microstructure and composition or the aging and deterioration process. Scientific imaging techniques are routinely applied to reveal underlying details not visible to the naked eye or to discover later changes by the artist and restorers. By way of example, computed tomography (CT) is being used extensively for the study of artifacts and finds in order to gain in-depth information about the making process, the level of degradation, or the internal structure of a wooden sculpture, for example. On the basis of the acquisition of digital X-rays at different angles, CT allows to reconstruct a 3D structure of the respective artifact volumetrically. Also, spectrometric methods have found wide application in the study of heritage materials; among them are X-ray-, UV-visible, or infrared spectroscopy as the most widely used spectroscopic technique for analyzing a wide range of organic and inorganic materials, natural substances, and pigments.

Despite the widespread use of these diagnostic tools and computer-assisted technologies in the cultural heritage domain, methods are often used independently. There is still a lack of combining different data sets in one single 3D model, although they collect complementary information. Consolidated 3D models, created by photogrammetric and close-range multi-image systems and enriched with additional information from diagnostic methods, can provide new ways for analyzing the conservation status or implementing restoration. They are a comprehensive documentation tool for in-depth understanding of the complex coherence of object degradation and restoration needs. Further advantages include a complete and continuous inspection of an object and the recording of results in one single file: any kind of object information concerning the state of preservation, deterioration aspects, previous conservative interventions, or the use of pigments can thus be documented digitally at once. A digital 3D model can also facilitate the indexing of knowledge gathered from different methods by allowing for annotations and storing of additional information and thus enabling easier indexing and retrieval.

First initial steps toward a complete virtual asset analysis have been taken within the pilot project *Fraunhofer Innovations for Cultural Heritage* [47]. Its subproject *Sculptures: Novel damage and material analysis in 3D* aims at combining for the first time contact-free and nondestructive technologies in order to create consolidated 3D models from surface and volumetric scanning data. They range from optical, electromagnetic, and acoustic methods and include:

- 3D digitization,
- Kommata after 3D digitization Confocal microscopy,
- Terahertz technology,
- Mobile ultrasonic tomography.

The final consolidated 3D visualization consists of information on the objects' surface, such as their geometry, texture, and optical material properties, as well as the objects' inside. The sculptures' surfaces are captured in micron accuracy, using the digitization setup *CultLab3D* among others. Furthermore, confocal microscopy, with its high-resolution recordings reaching nanometer range, is employed for analyzing the objects' surface structure. Information on the inside is acquired with the aid of mobile ultrasonic tomography and nondestructive terahertz technology which reveal information on the object's degree of damage such as pulverization, corrosion, or biocide load. The results generated in this way are brought together in a final consolidated 3D model that allows for optimized data processing and presentation in a 3D-centered annotation and analysis system (see Sect. 4.3).

With consolidated 3D models, improved object monitoring is made possible by aiming at the virtual presentation of the artifacts including their intrinsic properties. The 3D model allows for a sound damage and material analysis for further works that require knowledge on the object's condition and thereby contribute significantly to decisions regarding conservation. Furthermore, the Web-based visualizations offer new ways of presenting objects virtually for purposes of documentation, research, and education. In addition, the 3D content could also be visualized in real space on a so-called floating image display for interactive presentation purpose. By this means, the annotated 3D model will appear in front of the screen and can be controlled interactively.

CultLab3D is currently generating surface models. But in the long term, it is supposed to accomplish consolidated 3D models fusing data from a variety of capture sources, ranging from surface-scanning methods such as photogrammetry, structured light or time of flight, to volumetric scanning technologies such as ultrasound, MRI, and CT. In addition to the inside and outside geometry and the appearance of artifacts, information on the conservation state can be gathered through mass spectroscopy or chemical analysis. Decimated variants of the final results can then be used for a variety of purposes, ranging from scientific work to commercial purposes, fostering new levels of information accessibility, and revenue streams for cultural heritage institutions to preserve our past for future generations.

Acknowledgments *CultLab3D* is funded by the *German Federal Ministry for Economic Affairs and Energy* under grant agreement 01MT12022E with support of strategic funds of the *Fraunhofer-Gesellschaft*.

References

1. European Commission: Commission recommendation of 27 October 2011 on the digitisation and online accessibility of cultural material and digital preservation (2011/711/EU) [online], available from: http://eur-lex.europa.eu/LexUriServ/LexUriServ.do?uri=OJ:L:2011:283:0039:0045:EN:PDF. Accessed 5 June 2016
2. European Commission: Communication from the Commission to the European Parliament, the Council, the European Economic and Social Committee and the Committee of the Regions. A Digital Agenda for Europe (COM(2010)245 final) [online], available from: http://eur-lex.europa.eu/legal-content/EN/TXT/HTML/?uri=CELEX:52010DC0245&from=en. Accessed 5 July 2016
3. Article 3.3 of the Treaty of Lisbon, Treaty of Lisbon, Amending the Treaty on European Union and the Treaty Establishing the European Community, 17.12.2007 (2007/C 306/01). Official Journal of the European Union, C 306/1 [online], available from: http://eur-lex.europa.eu/legal-content/EN/TXT/?uri=OJ:C:2007:306:TOC. Accessed 10 Sept 2015
4. S. Keene (ed.), *Collections for People. Museums' stored Collections as a Public Resource* (London 2008) [online], available from: discovery.ucl.ac.uk/13886/1/13886.pdf. Accessed 29 June 2016
5. To mention are the *Google Books Library Project*, the *Google Art Project*, the *German Digital Library* (German: *Deutsche Digitale Bibliothek*) or *Europeana*. This cultural platform and, at the same time, digital library, archive and museum was launched in 2008 with the aim to consolidate all national digital libraries under one roof and to make historic inventories and collections in digital form widely available to the public
6. See company website *Picturae* [online], available from: https://picturae.com/uk/digitising/herbarium-sheets. Accessed 28 June 2016
7. Smithsonian Strategic Plan [online], available from: http://www.si.edu/Content/Pdf/About/SI_Strategic_Plan_2010-2015.pdf. Accessed 29 June 2016
8. In this context, the term '3D digitization' refers to the digital capture of a three-dimensional object with its shape and its visual appearance from all possible angles. For this reason, a digital replication in 3D is different to a photograph, "seeking to map the complete geometry of an object, its surface texture and where possible its visual material characteristics, and combining these to produce an integrated digital 3D model that depicts the object as accurately as possible". Contrary to a 3D replica, which can be viewed from any angle, a photograph is a static image of an object taken from only one specific perspective. See DFG Practical Guidelines on Digitisation (2013), DFG form 12.151 – 02/13, p. 20

9. P. Santos, S. Peña Serna, A. Stork, D. Fellner, The potential of 3D internet in the cultural heritage domain, in *3D Research Challenges in Cultural Heritage – A Roadmap in Digital Heritage Preservation*, eds. by M. Ioannides, E. Quak. Lecture Notes in Computer Science 8355, (2014), pp. 1–17
10. R. Pintus, K. Pal, Y. Yang, T. Weyrich, E. Gobbetti, H. Rushmeier, A survey of geometric analysis in cultural heritage. Comput. Graph. Forum **35**(1), 4–31 (2015)
11. R. Scopigno, Sampled 3D models for cultural heritage: which uses beyond visualization? VAR **3**(5), 109–125 (2012)
12. Digital acquisition in 3D on a broader scale is offered by the company Witikon. A large amount of collection artifacts were already digitized in high resolution with *Phase One* cameras as object panoramas. 3D reconstruction from object panoramas is now being offered as well. See company website Witikon [online], available from: http://www.witikon.eu/. Accessed 29 June 2016
13. ISO/IEC 18004:2000: Information Technology. Automatic identification and data capture techniques. Bar code symbology. QR Code. International Organization for Standardization, Geneva
14. T. Weyrich, J. Lawrence, H. Lensch, S. Rusinkiewicz, T. Zickler, Principles of appearance acquisition and representation, in *ACM SIGGRAPH 2008 Classes* (ACM, New York, 2008), pp. 80:1–80:119
15. M. Holroyd, J. Lawrence, T. Zickler, A coaxial optical scanner for synchronous acquisition of 3D geometry and surface reflectance, in *ACM SIGGRAPH 2010 Papers* (ACM, New York, 2010), pp. 99:1–99:12
16. C. Schwartz, R. Klein, Acquisition and presentation of virtual surrogates for cultural heritage artefacts, in Gesellschaft zur Förderung angewandter Informatik e.V., *Proceedings of EVA 2012* Berlin, pp. 50–57
17. C. Schwartz, M. Weinmann, R. Ruiters, R. Klein, Integrated high-quality acquisition of geometry and appearance for cultural heritage, in *The 12th International Symposium on Virtual Reality, Archeology and Cultural Heritage VAST 2011* (Eurographics Association, 2011), pp. 25–32
18. T. Noell, J. Koehler, R. Reis, D. Stricker, Fully automatic, omnidirectional acquisition of geometry and appearance in the context of cultural heritage preservation. J. Comput. Cult. Herit. (Special Issue on Best Papers from Digital Heritage 2013 JOCCH Homepage archive), **8** (1), Article No. 2
19. J. Kohler, T. Noell, G. Reis, D. Stricker, A full-spherical device for simultaneous geometry and reflectance acquisition, in *Applications of Computer Vision (WACV)*, 2013 I.E. Workshop (2013), pp. 355–362
20. M. Goesele, J. Ackermann, S. Fuhrmann, R. Klowsky, F. Langguth, P. Muecke, M. Ritz, Scene reconstruction from community photo collections. Computer **43**(6), 48–53 (2010)
21. A. Hertzmann, S. Seitz, Example-based photometric stereo: shape reconstruction with general, varying BRDFs. IEEE Trans. Pattern Anal. Mach. Intell. **27**(8), 1254–1264 (2005)
22. T. Lens, J. Kunz, C. Trommer, A. Karguth, O. von Stryk, *BioRob-Arm. A Quickly Deployable and Intrinsically Safe, Light- Weight Robot Arm for Service Robotics Applications.* 41st International Symposium on Robotics (ISR 2010), 6th German Conference on Robotics (ROBOTIK 2010) pp. 905–910
23. P. Santos, M. Ritz, R. Tausch, H. Schmedt, R. Monroy, A. De Stefano, D. Fellner, CultLab3D – On the Verge of 3D Mass Digitization, in *GCH 2014, Eurographics Workshop on Graphics and Cultural Heritage*, eds. by R. Klein et al. (Eurographics Association, Goslar, 2014), pp. 65–73
24. T. Lens, J. Kunz, O. von Stryk, Dynamic modeling of the 4 DoF BioRob series elastic robot arm for simulation and control, in *Simulation, Modeling, and Programming for Autonomous Robots (SIMPAR 2010)*, vol. 6472 (Springer, 2010), pp. 411–422

25. A. De Stefano, R. Tausch, P. Santos, A. Kuijper, G. Di Gironimo, D.W. Fellner, B. Siciliano, Modeling a virtual robotic system for automated 3D digitization of cultural heritage artifacts. J. Cult. Herit. **19**, 531–537 (2016)
26. B. Siciliano, L. Sciavicco, L. Villani, G. Oriolo, *Robotics. Modelling, Planning and Control* (Springer, London, 2009)
27. M. Karaszewski, R. Sitnik, E. Bunsch, On-line, collision-free positioning of a scanner during fully automated three-dimensional measurement of cultural heritage objects. Robot. Auton. Syst. **60**, 1205–1219 (2012)
28. F. Remondino, C. Fraser, *Digital Camera Calibration Methods: Considerations and Comparisons*. ISPRS (2006)
29. E.W. Arold, Hand-guided 3D surface acquisition by combining simple light sectioning with real-time algorithms. arXiv: 1401.1946 (2014)
30. Z. Zhang, A flexible new technique for camera calibration. IEEE Trans. Pattern Anal. Mach. Intell. **22**(11), 1330–1334 (2000)
31. N. Fisher, A comparison of algorithms for subpixel peak detection, in *Image Technology*, ed. by J.L.C. Sanz (Springer, Berlin, 1996), pp. 385–404
32. S.R. Berns, The Science of digitizing paintings for color-accurate image archives: a review. J. Imaging Sci. Technol. **45**(4), 305–325 (2001)
33. ISO 15076-1:2010: Image technology colour management. Architecture, profile format, and data structure based on ICC.1:2010
34. IEC61966-2-1:1999: Multimedia systems and equipment. Colour measurement and management. Part 2-1: Color management-Default RGB color space. sRGB. International Electrotechnical Commission, Geneva
35. M. Schnoes, M.D. Goesele, Massively parallel SVBRDF fitting BTF data, bachelor thesis, TU Darmstadt, 2010
36. See company website Adlibsof [online], available from: http://www.adlibsoft.com. Accessed 28 June 2016
37. See company website System Simulation [online], available from: http://www.ssl.co.uk. Accessed 28 June 2016
38. Collections Trust, [online], available from: http://www.collectionstrust.org.uk/collections-link/collections-management/spectrum/choose-a-cms. Accessed 29 June 2016
39. J.H.C.H. Yu, Assessing the value of semantic annotation services for 3d museum artefacts. Sustainable Data from the Digital Research Conference (SDDR 2011) (2011)
40. S.P. Serna, H. Schmedt, M. Ritz, A. Stork, Interactive semantic enrichment of 3D cultural heritage collections, in *VAST: International Symposium on Virtual Reality, Archaeology and Intelligent Cultural Heritage*, eds. by D. Arnold, J. Kaminski, F. Niccolucci, A. Stork, Eurographics Symposium Proceedings, The 10th Eurographics Workshop on Graphics and Cultural Heritage (Brighton, 2012). The Eurographics Association 2012, pp. 33–40
41. N. Crofts, M. Doerr, T. Gill, S. Stead, M. Stiff, Definition of the cidoc conceptual reference model. ICOM/CIDOC CRM Special Interest Group (2006)
42. M. Doerr, M. Theodoridou, Crmdig. A generic digital provenance model for scientific observation, in: 3rd Workshop on the Theory and Practice of Provenance, TaPP'11, Heraklion, Crete, Greece, June 20–21, available from: https://www.usenix.org/conference/tapp11/crmdig-generic-digital-provenance-model-scientific-observation. Accessed 29 June 2016
43. X. Pan, M. Schröttner, S. Havemann, T. Schiffer, R. Berndt, M. Hecher, D.W. Fellner, A repository infrastructure for working with 3D assets in cultural heritage. Int. J. Herit. Dig. Era **2** (1), 144–166 (2013)
44. P. Boulanger, M. Rioux, J. Taylor, F. Livingstone, Automatic replication and recording of museum artifacts, in *Analysis and Examination of an Art Object by Imaging Technique* (Tokyo National Research Institute of Cultural Properties, 1988), pp. 131–147
45. T. Noell, J. Koehler, R. Reis, D. Stricker, Fully automatic, omnidirectional acquisition of geometry and appearance in the context of cultural heritage preservation. J. Comput. Cult. Herit. (Special Issue on Best Papers from Digital Heritage) **8**(1), 2 (2013)

46. C. Schwartz, M. Weinmann, R. Ruiters, R. Klein, *Integrated high-quality acquisition of geometry and appearance for cultural heritage*. The 12th International Symposium on Virtual Reality, Archeology and Cultural Heritage VAST 2011 (Eurographics Association, 2011), pp. 25–32
47. See project website *Fraunhofer innovations for cultural heritage* [online], available from: https://www.igd.fraunhofer.de/en/Institut/Abteilungen/CHD/Projekte/Pilot-project-Saving-our-cultural-heritage-Fraunhofer-innovations. Accessed 8 June 2016. The project is funded by the *Fraunhofer-Gesellschaft* and being carried out in cooperation with the *Dresden State Art Collections* (*Staatliche Kunstsammlungen Dresden*), and the *Saxon State and University Library Dresden* (*Sächsische Landesbibliothek, Staats- und Universitätsbibliothek Dresden*)

Chapter 5
Intangible Cultural Heritage and New Technologies: Challenges and Opportunities for Cultural Preservation and Development

Marilena Alivizatou-Barakou, Alexandros Kitsikidis, Filareti Tsalakanidou, Kosmas Dimitropoulos, Chantas Giannis, Spiros Nikolopoulos, Samer Al Kork, Bruce Denby, Lise Buchman, Martine Adda-Decker, Claire Pillot-Loiseau, Joëlle Tillmane, S. Dupont, Benjamin Picart, Francesca Pozzi, Michela Ott, Yilmaz Erdal, Vasileios Charisis, Stelios Hadjidimitriou, Leontios Hadjileontiadis, Marius Cotescu, Christina Volioti, Athanasios Manitsaris, Sotiris Manitsaris, and Nikos Grammalidis

Abstract Intangible cultural heritage (ICH) is a relatively recent term coined to represent living cultural expressions and practices, which are recognised by communities as distinct aspects of identity. The safeguarding of ICH has become a topic of international concern primarily through the work of United Nations Educational, Scientific and Cultural Organization (UNESCO). However, little research has been done on the role of new technologies in the preservation and transmission of intangible heritage. This chapter examines resources, projects and technologies providing access to ICH and identifies gaps and constraints. It draws on research conducted within the scope of the collaborative research project, i-Treasures. In doing so, it covers the state of the art in technologies that could be employed for access, capture and analysis of ICH in order to highlight how specific new technologies can contribute to the transmission and safeguarding of ICH.

Keywords Intangible cultural heritage • ICT • Safeguarding • Transmission • Semantic analysis • 3D visualisation • Game-like educational applications

---

M. Alivizatou-Barakou
UCL Institute of Archaeology, London WC1H 0PY, UK
e-mail: m.alivizatou@ucl.ac.uk

A. Kitsikidis • F. Tsalakanidou • K. Dimitropoulos • C. Giannis • S. Nikolopoulos • S. Al Kork • B. Denby • L. Buchman • M. Adda-Decker • C. Pillot-Loiseau • J. Tillmane • S. Dupont • B. Picart • F. Pozzi • M. Ott • Y. Erdal • V. Charisis • S. Hadjidimitriou • L. Hadjileontiadis • M. Cotescu • C. Volioti • A. Manitsaris • S. Manitsaris • N. Grammalidis (✉)
Information Technologies Institute, CERTH, 57001 Thessaloniki, Greece
e-mail: ngramm@iti.gr

M. Ioannides et al. (eds.), *Mixed Reality and Gamification for Cultural Heritage*,
DOI 10.1007/978-3-319-49607-8_5

5.1 Introduction

In the last decades, the protection and promotion of cultural heritage (primarily in the form of monuments, historic sites, artefacts and more recently cultural expressions) has become a central topic of European and international cultural policy. Since the end of World War II, UNESCO has been a key organisation in defining cultural heritage and ensuring its protection through the adoption of a series of conventions and financial and administrative measures. Parallel to the work of UNESCO, governmental and non-governmental organisations, professional associations and academic institutions around Europe have been involved with documenting and providing access to different forms of cultural heritage (ranging from archaeological sites and natural parks to museum collections and folk traditions). In this process, a significant body of resources dealing with the documentation and promotion of cultural heritage through different technologies has been developed. There is little doubt that digital technologies have revolutionised scientific and public access to cultural heritage [1, 2].

Following the adoption of the UNESCO Convention for the Safeguarding of Intangible Cultural Heritage in 2003, the protection of cultural traditions has become prominent on an international level. One of the key arguments in this area is that humanity's intangible heritage is threatened by processes of globalisation. Modern technologies and mass culture are often regarded as a threat to the survival of traditional expressions. According to the Convention, it falls upon national governments, cultural organisations and practising communities to transmit these vulnerable cultural expressions to the next generations. Safeguarding activities vary according to local and national contexts. Interestingly, although modern technologies are often identified as a threat to traditional expressions, it is these very technological innovations that frequently play a key part in the preservation and dissemination of ICH.

Drawing on the existing literature and body of research, this chapter will provide an overview of current safeguarding programmes with a particular focus on specific technological methods and how they contribute to the documentation and transmission of intangible heritage. What we argue is that new technologies can provide innovative approaches to the transmission and dissemination of intangible heritage by supporting human interaction and communication.

More precisely, this chapter offers an overview of the literature, resources, projects and technologies providing access to ICH. It aims to identify gaps and constraints of existing projects in the area. It covers the state of the art in technologies that could be employed for access, capture and analysis of ICH in order to highlight how specific new technologies can contribute to the transmission and safeguarding of ICH.

Section 5.2 looks at previous work, including the broad scope of safeguarding activities supported by UNESCO, which mainly consist of national and international inventories and rely mostly on archival approaches. Furthermore, projects run by museums, cultural organisations and grassroots initiatives, which are driven by community participation, are examined. Section 5.3 takes a closer look at specific technological methods (facial expression analysis and modelling, vocal tract sensing and modelling, body motion and gesture recognition, semantic multimedia analysis, 3D visualisation and text to song) that relate to the documentation and transmission of ICH. Finally, Sect. 5.4 draws conclusions and discusses future work.

5.2 Previous Work

In the 2003 Convention for the Safeguarding of Intangible Cultural Heritage, UNESCO defines safeguarding as 'measures aimed at ensuring the viability of intangible heritage, including the identification, documentation, research, preservation, protection, promotion, enhancement, transmission, particularly through formal and informal education and revitalisation of the various aspects of such heritage'. Although their role in safeguarding intangible heritage is not directly addressed in the Convention, new technologies can play an important part in areas of identification, documentation, preservation, promotion and education. Audio-visual documentation and digital and multimedia resources from the areas of information and communication technologies can provide useful tools for recording and collecting information about expressions of intangible heritage.

Taking forward this idea, i-Treasures project [3] attempts to explore the challenges and opportunities that emerge when considering the safeguarding of intangible heritage from a technological perspective. More specifically, its overall goal is to develop an open and extendable platform to provide access to intangible cultural heritage resources for research and education. The core of the system lies in the identification of specific features or patterns (e.g. postures, audio patterns, etc.) using multisensor technology (e.g. cameras, microphones, EEG, etc.) from different ICH forms. Subsequently, data fusion analysis is applied to exploit information across different modalities, while context and content are integrated for mapping the set of low- or medium-level multimedia features to high-level concepts using probabilistic inference, i.e. transforming the extracted data into a level of interpretation that is understandable by humans. This information, coupled with other cultural resources, is accessible via the i-Treasures platform (an open-source CMS), in order to enable the widest possible participation of communities, groups and individuals in the safeguarding of ICH. The platform gives access to different types of content (e.g. text, audio, images, video, 3D graphics) from different types of heritage or educational institutions. Furthermore, using the latest advances in web-based game engines, a learning environment is developed to enhance the training and evaluation of the learner's performance by means of sensorimotor learning. Finally, a text-to-song system can also be used, allowing the user to enter text and/or notes and produce the equivalent singing voice. An overview of the system is presented in Fig. 5.1.

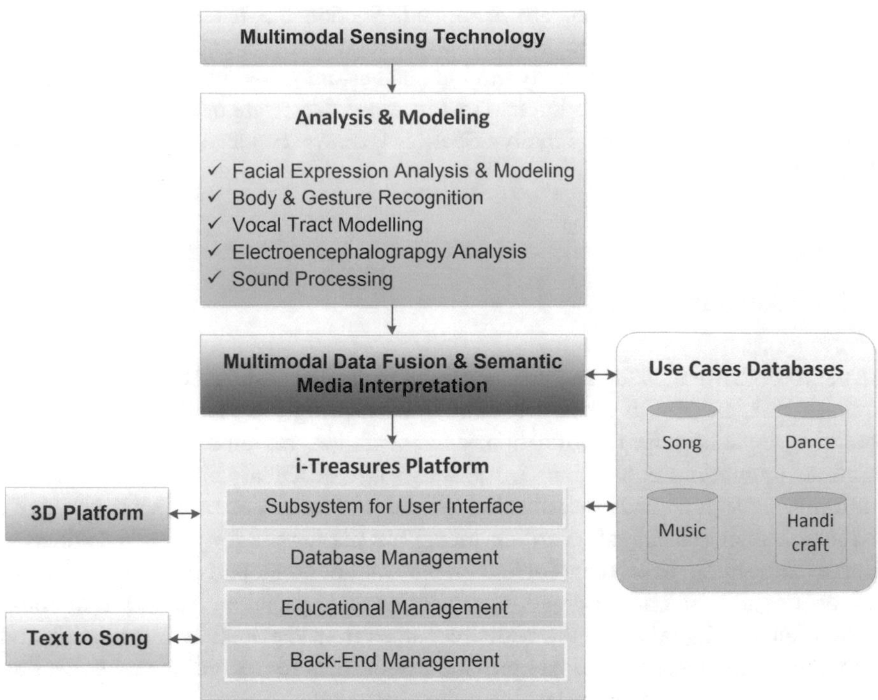

Fig. 5.1 Overview of i-Treasures system (© 2015 EC FP7 i-Treasures project, reprinted with permission)

As shown in the cases discussed below, the first attempts at using documentation technologies for safeguarding expressions of intangible heritage have had a primarily archival and encyclopaedic orientation.

Even before the adoption of the 2003 Convention, UNESCO supported projects aimed at the safeguarding of intangible heritage. For example, the Red Book of Endangered Languages (subsequently known as Atlas of Endangered Languages) is a publication and online resource that provides basic information on more than 2000 languages. It has taken the form of an online map and archival *resource* and provides an encyclopaedic list of world languages ranging from vulnerable to extinct. However, the information available online is limited, and there are limited learning possibilities available.

Another example has been the Traditional Music of the World, a project that includes recordings of traditional music [4]. The recordings have been made by ethnomusicologists in situ and then copied on vinyl and CD format. Relevant photographs accompany the audio recordings. The project has made available these recordings to an international audience and raising awareness about traditional music. However, it seems to act primarily as an archival resource and has limited educational application. Moreover, there is no online access to the recordings.

The 2003 Convention has put in place two lists that act as mechanisms for identifying intangible heritage on a global level: the International List of the Intangible Cultural Heritage of Humanity and the List of Intangible Cultural Heritage in Need of Urgent Safeguarding. These are international inventories of traditional expressions which are accessible online and include photographs and audio-visual recordings of cultural expressions. Their primary function is that of an archival resource that raises awareness about the listed expressions and their communities. The drawback of the lists is that they seem to be serving primarily promotional objectives rather than activities that have a direct impact on local communities [5]. Moreover, the amount of documentation available online is relatively limited. Prior to these lists, UNESCO supported the programme for the Proclamation of Masterpieces of the Oral and Intangible Heritage of Humanity [6, 7]. This was the first international project to raise major awareness at a governmental level and influence the adoption of the 2003 Convention. The database of selected masterpieces of intangible heritage is available online and includes audio-visual and photo material but has a relatively limited educational scope.

UNESCO has also supported national inventories of intangible heritage in several countries. Some examples with information available on the Internet are the national inventories and/or registers of Japan, Brazil, Portugal, Bulgaria and Venezuela. Different methodologies have been used for the creation of these inventories. In Bulgaria, catalogues were set up drawing on information collected through questionnaires distributed to local communities via cultural centres. In Japan and Brazil, inventories were drawn mostly through ethnographic research. The national inventories have raised awareness about the importance of intangible heritage among local communities. However, the amount of documentation available seems to be relatively limited. An innovative methodology has been used for the documentation of intangible heritage in Scotland. The UK Commission of UNESCO in collaboration with the Scottish Arts Council funds this project. It consists of an online archive of Scottish intangible heritage that is open to the public in the form of a wiki. It contains photographic and audio-visual documentation and uses participatory approaches.

In terms of the transmission and revitalisation of cultural expressions of intangible heritage, UNESCO collaborates with relevant organisations for their promotion and enhancement. In this process, UNESCO has proposed a group of accredited NGOs and INGOs to provide advice and support in the nomination of elements of intangible heritage for the International List. For the case of traditional dance, the International Council of Organizations of Folklore Festivals and Folk Arts (http://www.cioff.org) and the European Association of Folklore Festivals (http://www.eaff.eu/en) are relevant cases to consider. Their work has allowed for a more direct contact between UNESCO and cultural practitioners and the enhanced visibility of traditional expressions.

Further uses of new technologies in the safeguarding of intangible heritage have been made by local community centres, museums and EU-funded research networks.

The EU has supported projects relating directly and indirectly to the transmission of intangible heritage. For example, the I-MAESTRO project aims to build a multimedia environment for technology-enhanced music education. This employs self-learning environments, gestural interfaces and augmented instruments promoting new methods for music training. The question that is raised, however (and is also relevant for i-Treasures), is whether technology risks replacing human interaction as a process of transmission.

More directly related to intangible heritage and local development is the EU-funded project entitled Cultural Capital Counts. The project aims to enable a positive development of six regions in Central Europe by focusing on intangible heritage resources like living traditions, knowledge and talents. By developing a strategy that is based on intangible cultural resources, the project aims to enable a sustainable regional development in order to increase the region's attractiveness for enterprises. The project appears to develop around a website that contains a list of various traditions and expressions of intangible heritage in the six regions. It proposes strategies for local, sustainable development and collaborative research. But the focus seems to be more on the commercialisation of intangible heritage than on how these practices and traditions can be transmitted to the next generations.

Europeana (http://www.europeana.eu/) is a well-known EU portal for exploring the digital resources of Europe's museums, libraries, archives and audio-visual collections, thus offering direct access to millions of books, manuscripts, paintings, films, museum objects and archival records that have been digitised throughout Europe. Europeana's collection includes more than 53 million items and has released all metadata under a CC0 waiver, making it freely available for reuse. However, until now, Europeana includes just a small number of 3D tangible objects and no 3D representations of ICH.

Indigenous groups and communities have made innovative uses of new technologies in local attempts at safeguarding intangible heritage. The Oral Traditions Project of the Vanuatu Cultural Centre is a useful case to consider. The national museum and cultural centre runs a project [8] through a network of volunteers, called fieldworkers. These are representatives of different communities who conduct research on traditional customs and cultural expressions. The fieldworkers have been trained in ethnographic research methods and photographic and audio-visual documentation. The material collected during their research is kept in a specifically designated room of the national museum. The project has been instrumental in raising awareness about the importance of traditional culture. Its primary function is to create a 'memory bank' of traditional culture and languages, but the collected material are not only kept for posterity but used in educational programmes for schools, the museum and the radio and community development. A key theme is the idea of 'heritage for development' translated in eco- and cultural tourism projects. The project is active since the early 1970s, and some of the issues raised relate to the limited budget, the engagement of fieldworkers and how best to protect traditional culture from commercialisation [9].

Online learning resources constitute another area of intangible heritage preservation. For instance, many indigenous groups in partnership with museums have created online heritage resources with a pedagogical focus. One example is the online resource created by the U'mista Cultural Centre for the interpretation of ceremonial masks. The resource, entitled 'The Story of the Masks', presents stories related to the masks, which are narrated by tribe members. The specific project involves the digitisation of relevant content, the use of audio-visual technology and the creation of a website. Through the project, community members are empowered to share their stories and memories.

Interestingly, the above projects are driven and managed by local communities. As such, they are not only about documenting and archiving intangible heritage but also making the information available to cultural practitioners and the new generations and using it in educational programmes and activities. However, the technologies discussed so far are primarily archival, and their potential for transmission and education relies primarily on how they can be used further by local agents and documentation institutions, like museums and cultural centres.

Taking the idea of participatory methods forward, i-Treasures project aims to make a contribution to collaborations between researchers and local communities by employing technologies that allow for a more direct interaction in terms of learning and transmission. The idea is to empower local actors to use new technologies as a new learning tool by bringing into the discussion a different range of technologies that are discussed in more detail below. One of the central arguments of the project is that although modern technologies cannot replace human interaction in the transmission of intangible heritage, they can contribute significantly to processes of dissemination, especially among younger generations. For this reason, the project proposes the development of territorial schools acting as local hubs for the transmission of local intangible heritage expressions.

5.3 Modern Technologies in the Transmission and Documentation of Intangible Heritage

This section looks more closely at the technological methods that could be employed for safeguarding and transmission of intangible heritage. New technology can be used not only for the digitisation and archiving of cultural expressions but also in terms of cultural transmission, education and community development. Although technology cannot replace human interaction, it can nevertheless support cultural transmission in new and innovative ways.

To this end, this chapter provides a detailed analysis of the state of the art in some of the main technologies for capture, preservation and transmission of the ICH (Fig. 5.2), namely: (1) facial expression analysis and modelling, (2) vocal tract sensing and modelling, (3) body motion and gesture recognition, (4) encephalography analysis, (5) semantic multimedia analysis, (6) 3D visualisation and (7) text-to-song synthesis.

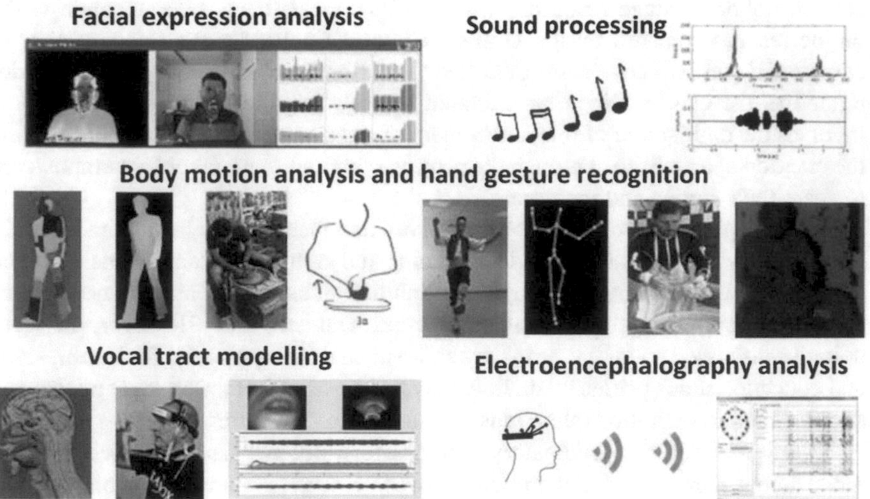

Fig. 5.2 Overview of main capture technologies for ICH (© 2015 EC FP7 i-Treasures project, reprinted with permission)

For each of the above, some key developments in each specific field are presented, and the potential use and contribution of each technology in the preservation of intangible heritage are discussed.

5.3.1 Facial Expression Analysis and Modelling

Facial expressions are one of the most cogent, naturally pre-eminent means for human beings to communicate emotions and affective states; to clarify and stress what is said; to signal comprehension, disagreement and intentions; and in brief to regulate interactions with the environment and other persons in the vicinity [10]. Facial expressions are generated by facial muscle contractions, which result in temporary facial deformations of facial geometry and texture. Human faces are estimated to be capable of more than 10,000 different expressions. This versatility makes non-verbal expressions of the face extremely efficient and honest, unless deliberately manipulated. Many of these expressions are directly associated with emotions and affective states such as happiness, sadness, anger, fear, surprise, disgust, shame, anguish and interest, which are universally recognised [11].

This natural means of communication becomes even more important in the case of artistic expressions like singing or acting where the face and body are the main tools used by the performer to communicate the emotional aspects of their role. A great singing performance is not only the result of a great voice but also reflects the emotional involvement of the performer who expresses what he feels through his voice and body.

The performer's facial expressions could be analysed in terms of facial actions, which can be used either as a means of extracting facial muscle movements useful for describing the performer's technique or as a means for decoding the performer's emotional state.

The preservation and transmission of this expression involves more than analysing voice and music patterns and decoding voice articulation. It should also involve analysing and preserving the expressive and emotional aspects revealed by the performer's face, since the performance is more than correct voice articulation: it is also emotion revealed through voice and face. This is also very important for educational purposes. New singers will not only be taught how to use their vocal tract to sing different types of songs but can also learn how to give a complete performance.

Besides the emotional aspect, facial expressions can also be used to reveal details of the performer's technique, e.g. how much he/she opens the mouth while singing.

5.3.2 Vocal Tract Sensing and Modelling

Since the dawn of human communication, man has been curious about the speech production mechanism and has sought to model and exploit it in a variety of useful applications. The first vocal tract models were physical models, constructed of tubes and valves and resonators, which sought to duplicate the intricate process by which speech is produced in the human vocal tract via the articulators: the larynx (vocal folds), tongue, lips, teeth, jaw and nasal cavity. With the advent of powerful digital computers, it became possible to produce 2D and 3D vocal tract models of surprising realism in software, often referred to as 'talking heads' [12–14] which, when coupled with an appropriate acoustic simulation, allow to synthesise speech in a way totally analogous to actual human speech production. Although such so-called articulatory synthesis systems have been claimed by some researchers for having poorer performance than the codebook-style vocoder synthesisers, articulatory synthesis remains an active area of research, as many researchers believe it will ultimately lead to the most effective means of communication between man and machines.

To model the vocal tract effectively, it is necessary to study and understand its physical characteristics. Early studies on cadavers were the first sources of such information, followed by various types of endoscopic investigations, many of which are still in use today, but in the twentieth century, the non-invasive nature of real-time medical imaging techniques led to significant breakthroughs in vocal tract sensing. Very high-resolution real-time imaging of the entire vocal tract is possible using cineradiography (X-rays) and magnetic resonance imaging (MRI). As the use of X-rays on living subjects is regulated by strict radiation exposure limits, its use as a research tool is rather limited, although a number of studies have been carried out [15, 16]. Concerning MRI, although real-time studies of the vocal tract have been carried out [15, 17, 18], the procedure requires the subject to recline within the confines of a very constrained volume containing a strong magnetic field. Time on an MRI machine is also very expensive, and, finally, the repetition rate of MRI, at best several hertz, is insufficient for a delicate, real-time physioacoustic study of speech production.

The routine availability of inexpensive, powerful computing resources is today beginning to make unexpected inroads into a variety of new fields.

In addition, the combination of instruments might enhance the level of knowledge. For example, in the Sardinian Canto a Tenore, some singers use a traditional laryngeal phonation, while others use a method that pitch-doubles the fundamental frequency [19, 20]. It is not clear if this is done by vibrating both the vocal folds and the ventricular folds as is found in diplophonia or whether this is done by amplifying an overtone as is done in Tuvan throat singing. The combination of ultrasound and EGG could allow the recording of the tongue, anterior pharyngeal wall and vocal folds in both methods. Between them, all the structures and behaviours of interest could be recorded and allow visual and auditory documentation of the technique for purposes of archiving and future teaching. As stated in [21], it is possible to assess changing true vocal fold length with ultrasonography and to observe vowel tongue shapes in untrained and trained singers [22].

Sensors that can be considered for data collection include microphone, external photoglottography (ePGG), electroglottography (EGG) (for vocal cords), ultrasound (for tongue contour detection), RGB or RGB-D cameras (for lip/mouth movement), piezoelectric accelerometer and breathing belt.

Data from these sensors may be used for studies such as (a) pharyngeal or labial embellishment (soloists), (b) nature of tiling, (c) position of tongue and lips, (d) vocal quality tessitura of voice alone and ornamentations, (e) comparison of voice alone/accompanied and (f) correlation between body gestures and laryngeal gestures.

5.3.3 Body Motion and Gesture Recognition

The study of human body motion is central in different scientific fields and applications. In the last decade, 3D motion capture systems have known a rapid evolution and substantial improvements, which have attracted the attention of many application fields, such as medicine, sports, entertainment, etc.

The applications of motion capture are numerous in different application fields, and the related research directions can be categorised as follows:

- Motion capture system design: motion capture technologies, developing new approaches for motion capture, or improving the current motion capture tools
- Motion capture for motion analysis: gesture recognition, extracting information from motion capture sequences, analysing similarities and differences between

motions, characterising the motion and recognising specific information (identity, style, activity, etc.) from the motion capture sequence, etc.
- Motion capture for animation: the use of motion capture, performed either in real time or offline, to animate virtual characters using motions recorded from human subjects

Motion capture (or *mocap*) systems can be divided into two main categories: marker-based and markerless technologies. Even if some very important improvements have been made in the last years, no perfect system exists, each one having its own advantages and drawbacks.

Marker-based systems include optical systems and inertial systems (accelerometers, gyroscopes, etc.). The optical motion capture systems are based on a set of cameras around the capture scene and on markers, reflecting or emitting light, placed on the body of the performer. Various types of sensors [23, 24] or commercial interfaces (e.g. Wii joystick, MotionPod or the IGS-190 inertial motion capture suits from Animazoo) can easily provide real-time access to motion information. On the contrary, markerless technologies do not require subjects to wear specific equipment for tracking and are usually based on computer vision approaches. Even if the accuracy and sensitivity of the tracking results do not yet meet the needs of the industry for the usual use of motion capture for animation, markerless systems are the future of the field. Nonetheless, markerless systems still suffer from a lack of precision and cannot compete with marker-based technologies that now reach submillimetre precision in real time. On the other hand, marker-based systems are often very expensive and need a more complicated setup.

Markerless motion capture technologies based on real-time depth sensing systems have taken a huge step ahead with the release of Microsoft Kinect and its accompanying skeleton tracking software (Kinect for Windows) and other affordable depth cameras (ASUS Xtion, PMD nano). These sensors are relatively cheap and offer a balance in usability and cost compared to optical and inertial motion capture systems. Kinect produces a depth-map stream at 30 frames per second with subsequent real-time human skeleton tracking. Estimation of the positions of 20 predefined joints that constitute a skeleton of a person is provided by software SDKs (Microsoft Kinect SDK, OpenNI) together with the rotational data of bones. Subsequent algorithmic processing can then be applied in order to detect the actions of the tracked person. The estimated 3D joint positions are noisy and may have significant errors when there are occlusions, which pose an additional challenge to action detection problem. Multi-Kinect setups with subsequent skeleton fusion techniques have been employed to combat the occlusion problems [25].

In conclusion, we can say that no perfect motion capture system exists. All systems have their advantages and drawbacks and must be carefully chosen according to the use case scenarios in which they are to be used. A compromise must be found between motion capture precision, the need for burdensome sensors and other external constraints like the motion capture area, the lighting environments, the portability of the system, etc.

5.3.3.1 Motion Capture Technologies for Dance Applications

As the interdisciplinary artist Marc Boucher says in [26], 'Motion-capture is the most objective form of dance notation insofar as it does not rely on subjective appreciation and verbal descriptions of individuals but rather on predetermined mathematical means of specifying spatial coordinates along x, y and z axes at given moments for each marker. These data can be interpreted (inscribed, 'read,' and 'performed') cybernetically (human-machine communication) while previous dance notation methods are based on symbolic representations, written and read by humans alone'. However, as discussed above, all motion capture solutions have advantages and drawbacks, and even though motion capture is the most informative tool for recording dance, issues like obtrusiveness of markers, need to wear specific costumes and motion recoding precision are different subjects that require further investigation and appropriate solutions. Furthermore, motion capture is not yet widely known, and its costs and complexity have also prevented this technology to reach most artists and dancers. A wide adoption of these technologies needs adapted and usable tools and convincing system demonstrations.

Although motion capture technologies are most often designed and developed in generic application purposes, we have identified several studies where new sensors were designed or adapted to be used in the specific use case of dance motion capture. The SENSEMBLE project [27] designed a system of compact, wireless sensor modules worn at the wrist or ankles of dancers and meant to capture expressive motions in dance ensembles. The collected data enabled them to study if the dancers of the ensemble were moving together, if some were leading or lagging, or if they were responding to one another with complementary movements. However, this sensor is aimed to be worn at the wrists and ankles of a dancer, not at every body segment, and thus does not consist of a true motion capture system since the whole body is not captured, and the dance motion cannot be reconstructed based on the recorded information. The sensor captures some information about the motion but not the 3D motion itself.

Saltate! [28] is a wireless force sensor system mounted under the dancers' feet which is used to detect synchronisation mistakes and emphasise the beats in the music when mistakes are detected in order to help the dancer stay synchronised with the music. Once again, the sensor records some information about the dance moves and more especially about the feet interactions with the ground, but the whole body motion is not captured at all.

Other approaches consist in capturing the dancer's motion through motion capture in order to control the soundtrack through the gesture to music mapping. This is, for instance, the approach followed in [29, 30], whose goal is mainly to explore possible relationships between gesture and music using the optical motion capture Vicon 8 system.

Detection, classification and evaluation of dance gestures and performances are research fields, in which existing commercial products have been often employed [31]. Experiences such as Harmonix' Dance Central video game series, where a player repeats the motion posed by an animated character, are becoming commonplace. Research is being conducted on automatic evaluation of dance performance against the performance of a professional, within 3D virtual environments or virtual classes for dance learning [32, 33].

Numerous research studies have addressed the issue of synthesising new dance motion sequences. They often base their synthesis model on existing dance motion capture databases [34]. Although their aim is not to preserve cultural heritage of the dance content, these studies have developed interesting approaches and tools, which can be used in order to analyse dance motions and the synchronised music track. For instance, Alankus et al. [34] have developed a dance move detection algorithm based on the curvature of the limbs' path, while Brand and Hertzmann [35] have developed an unsupervised dance-modelling approach based on hidden Markov models.

Laban Movement Analysis (LMA) is a method developed originally by Rudolf Laban, which aims at building a language capable of describing and documenting precisely all varieties of human movements. The Laban Movement Analysis describes movements through six main characteristics of the motion: body, effort, shape, space, relationship and phrasing. Even though this method has its drawbacks and requires a long training, it is one of the very few attempts at building a vocabulary or dictionary of motions that have been adopted quite widely. Bouchard and Badler [36] use Laban Movement Analysis (LMA) to extract movement qualities, which are used to automatically segment motion capture data of any kind. They hence use concepts initially developed for dance and apply them to general motions. Kahol et al. [37] implement an automated gesture segmentation dedicated to dance sequences.

Dance motion capture has also been attracting great interest recently in the performing arts for its use in interactive dance performances [38].

5.3.3.2 Hand and Finger Motion Recognition

Hand motion recognition and particularly finger motion recognition are very different from the usual motion capture approaches, which are generally designed for full body motion capture. Although special gloves for capturing finger motion are commercially available, the above motion capture methods are usually not suitable for finger gesture recognition. In [39], recognition of the musical effect of the guitarist's finger motions on discrete time events is proposed, using static finger gesture recognition based on a specific computer vision web platform. The approach does not take into consideration the stochastic nature of the gestures, and this method cannot be applied in the human–robot collaboration. Recently, a new method for dynamic finger gesture recognition in human computer interaction has been introduced in [40]. This method, based on a low-cost webcam, recognises the entire finger gesture individually, and it is non-obtrusive since it does not put any limit on finger motions.

When considering gesture analysis and more specifically fingering analysis in music interaction, there are four main approaches. These are (a) the preprocessing using score analysis based on an acyclic graph (this approach does not take into consideration all the factors influencing the choice of specific fingering, such as physical and biomechanical constraints [41]), (b) the real time using MIDI technology (this approach does not concern classical musical instruments [42]), (c) the post-processing using sound analysis that works only when one note is played at a time [43] and (d) the computer vision methods for the guitarist fingering retrieval [39]. The existing computer vision (CV) methods are of a low cost, but they presuppose painted fingers with a full-extended palm in order to identify the guitarist fingers in the image and specific recognition platforms, such as EyesWeb. Another great example of fingering recognition is the system of Yoshinari Takegawa, who used colour markers on the fingertips in order to develop a real-time fingering detection system for piano performance [44]. This system is restricted in electronic keyboards, such as synthesisers, and it cannot be applied for classical music instruments neither for the finger gesture recognition and mapping with sounds in space. Moreover, MacRitchie used Vicon System and Vicon Markers modelling in order to visualise musical structures. His method requires the music score in advance [45]. None of the above methods can be extended towards a dynamic gesture recognition taking into consideration the stochastic nature of gestures. They all recognise the musical effect of finger motions on discrete time events.

The study of the above categories for gesture analysis in music interaction can lead to the conclusions that (a) the gesture measurement approaches are based on rather expensive commercial systems, they are suitable for offline analysis and not for live performances and they cannot be applied on finger gestures; (b) gesture recognition via WSBN or CV does not cost a lot and has many important paradigms of live performance applications, while on the other hand, sensors cannot be applied for finger gestures performed on the piano keyboard or on woodwind musical instruments; (c) fingerings can be retrieved with low-cost technologies but the information acquired is related to discrete time events without taking into consideration the stochastic nature of the gestures; and (d) new paradigms for the recognition of the musician gestures performed on surface or keyboards, with a semi-extended palm, can only be based on CV.

5.3.3.3 Intangible Heritage Preservation and Transmission

Very few attempts at using body and gesture recognition for intangible heritage preservation can be found in the literature. To our knowledge, past attempts for preserving the ICH of the traditional dances were mainly based on informal interviews of the people practising these dances. The results of these interviews were then summarised in books such as [46]. According to Calvert et al. [47], dance has probably been the slowest art form to adopt technology, partially because useful tools have been slow to develop because of the limited commercial opportunities brought by dance applications. In their article, they describe applications such as animate and visualise dance, plan choreography, edit and animate notation, and enhance performance, but they do not cover intangible performance preservation. However, they interestingly underline a recurring issue of such applications, i.e. the need for a unique, unambiguous way to represent human movement and dance in particular.

In [48], the concept of using motion capture technology is introduced for protecting national dances in China. However, their report lacks basic details and information. In [49], the creation of a motion capture database of 183 Jamaican dancers is reported. Their study aimed at evaluating if dance revealed something about the phenotypic or genotypic quality of the dancers and showed that there are strong positive associations between symmetry (one measure of quality in evolutionary studies) and dancing abilities. However, the aim of this research is not to preserve the dance but rather to study it, here at a very fundamental level.

For contemporary dance, the DANCERS! project [50] aimed at collecting a database of dancers. The recording setup consisted of a formatted space, videos recorded from the front and top of the scene and metadata describing the dancer. No motion capture was performed, and no precise motion information is hence available; the only possible views of the scene are the ones originally recorded by the videos since the scene was not captured in 3D.

Some research projects have shown that dance-training systems based on motion capture technologies could successfully guide students to improve their dance skills [51] and have evaluated different kinds of augmented feedback modalities (tactile, video, sound) for learning basic dance choreographies.

5.3.4 Encephalography Analysis and Emotion Recognition

Emotion recognition (ER) is the first and one of the most important issues affecting computing (AC) brings forward and plays a dominant role in the effort to incorporate computers, and generally machines, with the ability to interact with humans by expressing cues that postulate and demonstrate emotional intelligence-related attitude. Successful ER enables machines to recognise the affective state of the user and collect emotional data for processing in order to proceed towards the terminus of emotion-based human machine interface, the emotional-like response. Towards effective ER, a large variety of methods and devices have been implemented, mostly concerning ER from face [52, 53], speech [54, 55] and signals from the autonomous nervous system (ANS), i.e. heart rate and galvanic skin response (GSR) [56–58].

A relatively new field in the ER area is the EEG-based ER (EEG-ER), which overcomes some of the fundamental reliability issues that arise with ER from face, voice or ANS-related signals. For instance, a facial expression recognition approach would be useless for people with the inability to express emotions via face, even if they really feel them, such as patients within the autism spectrum [59], or for situations of human social masking, for example, when smiling though feeling angry. Moreover, voice and ANS signals are vulnerable to 'noise' related to the activity that does not derive from emotional experience, i.e. GSR signals are highly influenced by inspiration, which may be caused from physical and not emotional activity. On the other hand, signals from the central nervous system (CNS), such as EEG, magnetoencephalogram (MEG), positron emission tomography (PET) or functional magnetic resonance imaging (fMRI), are not influenced by the aforementioned factors as they capture the expression of emotional experience from its origin. Towards such a more reliable ER procedure, EEG appears to be the less intrusive and the one with the best time resolution than the other three (MEG, PET and fMRI). Motivated by the latter, a number of EEG-ER research efforts have been proposed in the literature.

There are important cultural differences in emotions that can be predicted, understood and connected to each other in the light of cultural expressions. The main cultural differences reflected at the affective space are expressed through initial response tendencies of appraisal, action readiness, expression and instrumental behaviour but also in regulation strategies. Moreover, the ecologies of emotion and contexts, as well as their mutual reinforcement, are different across cultures. By capturing the emotions, and even better their dynamic character using EEG signals during cultural activities, the response selection at the levels of different emotional components, the relative priorities of initial response selection and effortful regulation, the sensitivity to certain contexts, the plans that are entailed by the emotions and the likely means to achieve them could be identified and used as dominant sources of information to acquire ICH elements. Consequently, the ways in which the potential of emotions is realised could reveal cultural facets that are intangible in character but form tangible measures at the affective space, contributing to their categorisation and preservation, as knowledge-based cultural/emotional models.

Moreover, most folklore/popular culture is shaped by a logic of emotional intensification. It is less interested in making people think than it is in making people feel. Yet that distinction is too simple: folklore/popular culture, at its best, makes people think by making them feel. In this context, the emotions generated by folklore/popular culture are rarely personal; rather, to be traditional or popular, it has to evoke broadly shared feelings. The most emotional moments are often the ones that hit on conflicts, anxieties, fantasies and fears that are central to the culture. In this perspective, folklore/cultural expressions try to use every device their medium offers in order to maximise the emotional response of their audience. Insofar as these folklore/popular artists and performers think about their craft, they are also thinking about how to achieve an emotional impact. By using EEG-based emotion acquisition of the performers of rare singing, and the corresponding audience, the difference in contexts within these works could be identified at the affective space, contributing to the exploration of the ways intangible cultural hierarchies respect or dismiss the affective dimensions, operating differently within different folklore cultures.

5.3.5 Semantic Multimedia Analysis

Semantic multimedia analysis is essentially the process of mapping low-level features to high-level concepts, an issue addressed as bridging the 'semantic gap' and extracting a set of metadata that can be used to index the multimedia content in a manner coherent with human perception. The challenging aspect of this process derives from the high number of different instantiations exhibited by the vast majority of semantic concepts, which is difficult to capture using a finite number of patterns. If we consider concept detection as the result of a continuous process where the learner interacts with a set of examples and his teacher to gradually develop his system of visual perception, we may identify the following interrelations. The grounding of concepts is primarily achieved through indicative examples that are followed by the description of the teacher (i.e. annotations). Based on these samples, the learner uses his senses to build models that are able to ground the annotated concepts, either by relying on the discriminative power of the received stimuli (i.e. discriminative models) or by shaping a model that could potentially generate these stimuli (i.e. generative models). However, these models are typically weak in generalisation, at least at their early stages of development. This fact prevents them from successfully recognising new, unseen instantiations of the modelled concepts that are likely to differ in form and appearance (i.e. semantic gap). This is where the teacher once again comes into play to provide the learner with a set of logic-based rules or probabilistic dependencies that will offer him an additional path to visual perception through inference. These rules and dependencies are essentially filters that can be applied to reduce the uncertainty of the stimuli-based models or to generate higher forms of knowledge through reasoning. Finally, when this knowledge accumulates over time, it takes the form of experience, which is a kind of information that can be sometimes transferred directly from the teacher to the learner and help him to make rough approximations of the required models.

In the cultural heritage domain, multimedia analysis has been extensively used in the last decades for automatic indexing of multimedia cultural content. This necessity grows even more these days considering the popularity of digitising cultural content for purposes such as safeguarding, capturing, visualising and presenting both tangible and intangible resources that broadly define that heritage. When it comes to ICH, the task of semantic analysis becomes even more challenging, since the significance of heritage artefacts is implied in their context and the scope of the preservation extends also to the preservation of the background knowledge that puts these artefacts in proper perspective. These intangible assets may, for instance, derive from performing arts (e.g. singing, dancing, etc.), and semantic multimedia analysis is essential for mapping the low-level features originating from the signal of the utilised sensors (e.g. sound, image, EEG) to important aspects that define the examined art (e.g. singing or dancing style). In the typical case, semantic multimedia analysis consists of the following four components: (1) pattern recognition, (2) data fusion, (3) knowledge-assisted semantic analysis and (4) schema alignment. Next, further details are provided for each of the above four cases.

1. Pattern recognition
   In an effort to simulate the human learning techniques, researchers have developed algorithms to teach the machine how to recognise patterns, hence, the name pattern recognition, by using annotated examples that relate to the pattern (positive examples) and examples that are not (negative examples). The aim of this procedure is to create a general model that maps the input signals/features to the desired annotations and, in parallel, generalise from the presented data to future, unseen data.
   Pattern recognition techniques have been used in the cultural domain for various cultural heritage categories. In [60], a method that processes historical documents and transforms them to metadata is proposed. In [61], SVM-based classification of traditional Indian dance actions using multimedia data is performed. In [62] and [63], computer vision techniques are employed in order to automatically classify archaeological pottery sherds. Lastly, a computer vision technique is also used in [64] where the authors present a search engine for retrieving cultural heritage multimedia content.
2. Data fusion
   Fusion [65] is the process of combining the information of multiple sources in order to produce a single outcome. In general, fusion is formulated as the problem of deducing the unknown but common information existing in all sources that lead to the observed data by using all the observations coming from the multiple sources. Thus, fusion can be seen as an inverse problem that can be naturally formulated in a Bayesian framework [66]. For example, in [67], heterogeneous media sources are combined in the context of Bayesian inference, in order to analyse the semantic meaning. Also, in [68], semantic analysis of audio-visual content is performed, by employing multimodal fusion based on Bayesian models. In [69], naive Bayesian fusion was used for ancient coin identification. In [70], a dynamic Bayesian network (DBN) is employed in order to fuse the audio and visual information of audio-visual content and provide an emotion recognition algorithm.
3. Knowledge-assisted semantic analysis
   Research has shown that, in general, expert knowledge can augment the efficiency of the semantic analysis task when applied to a domain. Particularly, in [71], it is shown that the accuracy of retrieving cultural objects is increased when the data are appropriately structured, using knowledge about the objects. In [72], a video semantic content analysis framework is proposed, where an ontology is used in combination with the MPEG-7 multimedia metadata standard. In [73], an approach to knowledge-assisted semantic video object detection is presented where Semantic Web technologies are used for knowledge representation. Another example of an ontology framework used in order to facilitate ontology-based mapping of cultural heritage content to corresponding concepts is proposed in [61]. Towards the same direction, the authors of [74] perform

ontology-based semantic analysis with a view to link media, contexts, objects, events and people.
An interesting work is that presented in [75], developed in the framework of the DECIPHER project, which proposes a methodology for the description of museum narratives (i.e. the structure of the exhibits). Narratives automate the presentation of the exhibits to the public in a coherent manner and by including the context of the exhibit in which the latter was created and being used.

4. Schema alignment
A vast number of Europe's cultural heritage objects are digitised by a wide range of data providers from the library, museum, archive and audio-visual sectors, and they all use different metadata standards. This heterogeneous data needs to appear in a common context. Thus, given the large variety of existing metadata schemas, ensuring the interoperability across diverse cultural collections is another challenge that has received a lot of research attention.

Europeana data model (EDM), which was developed for the implementation of the Europeana digital library, was designed with the purpose of enforcing interoperability between various content providers and the library. EDM transcends metadata standards, without compromising the range and richness of the standards. Also, it facilitates Europeana's participation in the Semantic Web. Finally, the EDM semantic approach is expected to promote richer resource discovery and improved display of more complex data. It is worth to note that the work in [76] provides a methodology to map semantic analysis results to the EMD metadata schema. In this way, metadata are made available and reusable by end users and heterogeneous applications.

The PREMIS Data Dictionary for Preservation Metadata is an international standard for metadata that was developed to support the preservation of digital objects/assets and ensure their long-term usability. PREMIS metadata standard has been adopted globally in various projects related to digital preservation. It supports numerous digital preservation software tools and systems. The CIDOC Conceptual Reference Model (CRM), an official standard since 9/12/2006, provides the ability to describe the implicit and explicit relationships of cultural heritage concepts in a formalised manner. Thus, CIDOC CRM is intended to promote a common understanding of cultural heritage information by providing a common and extensible semantic framework that can represent any cultural heritage information. It is intended to be a common language for cultural knowledge domain experts to formulate user requirements for information systems and, thus, facilitating in this way the interoperability between different sources of cultural heritage information in a semantic level.

Due to the multimodal nature of the content that is to be analysed semantically in i-Treasures, a common metadata schema was designed and implemented for the interoperability between the elementary concept detection and the semantic analysis tasks. More specifically, the results of both of the above tasks are stored in an XML file, with a structure a priori specified. The XML file of the first task is, first, embedded with metadata containing general info (similarly to the EMD metadata schema), and, after the basic concepts are also stored in the file, it is deposited in a central repository (i.e. the i-Treasures web platform). Next, the file is given as input to the semantic analysis task. The results of this task are to be also deposited in the repository by storing an XML with a structure a priori defined. Finally, a user, by using the repository access providing facilities, can conveniently obtain and access the above information.

5.3.6 3D Visualisation of Intangible Heritage

Intangible culture is quite different from tangible culture, since intangible culture such as skills, crafts, music, song, drama and the other recordable culture cannot be simply touched and interacted with or without the use of other means. In real life, tangible cultural heritage can be demonstrated in an environment like museums and related exhibitions. A cultural heritage structure which is totally destroyed such as a temple can be even reproduced as a replica, so that audience can personally wander inside. On the other hand, due to its nonphysical nature, ICH is more restricted and hard to demonstrate in real life which is a real challenge to prevent it from disappearing. This is where 3D visualisation and interaction technology comes into play.

Thanks to the recent advances in computer graphics, it is now possible to visualise almost anything, either tangible [77] or intangible. What can be done is limited only by imagination and allows reaching new larger audiences via the Internet. It is certain that 3D visualisation and interaction will hardly be on par with the real thing, and instruction system in a computer application and simulation cannot possibly match a real-life master's tutoring. Obviously, the degree of reality in interaction, visualisation and physics simulation becomes a very important concern for users to become well accustomed to the culture and encourage others to do so.

ICT technologies are increasingly becoming one of the pillars of Cultural Heritage Education [78–80]. Virtual worlds are often used in the field of Cultural Heritage Education in order to broaden the opportunity to appreciate cultural contents that are remote in space and/or time. Even though they should be considered very helpful for widening access to cultural contents, these applications, for example, virtual museums, often are not intrinsically engaging and, sometimes, fail in supporting active learning, just giving the opportunity to access information [81].

Digital games support learning in a more active and engaging way, and, from the pedagogical viewpoint, they offer advanced interaction, such as the possibility of customising the learning paths and of keeping track of the learners' behaviour and successes/failures, and are more adaptive to meet the specific users' learning needs.

As to the digital games available in the cultural heritage (CH) area, Anderson et al. [82] and afterwards Mortara et al. [81] carried out interesting state-of-the-art reviews. While the first focuses more on technical aspects, the second sketches a panorama of the actual use of SGs in CH education. According to Mortara et al. [81]

in the field of CH, SGs of different kinds are adopted: from trivia, puzzle and mini-games to mobile applications for museums or touristic visits (e.g. Muse-US,[1] Tidy City[2]), to simulations (e.g. the Battle of Waterloo[3]) and to adventures and role playing games (the Priory Undercroft,[4] Revolution[5]).

As it could be expected, games are more widespread in the tangible cultural heritage (TCH) area, where several different examples can be found [83]. Among these are Thiatro,[6] a 3D virtual environment where the player acts as a museum curator or a curator of other digital artefacts; My Culture Quest,[7] which aims at advertising real collections; or even the History of a Place,[8] which is an integral part of a museum experience at the Archaeological Museum of Messenia in Greece.

A number of games for smartphones also exist, like Tate Trumps[9] and YouTell,[10] which, for instance, allow museum visitors to create and share through smartphones their own media and stories.

Many games also exist in the area of historical reconstruction, for instance, the Battle of Thermopylae[11] and the Playing History,[12] which are mainly based on 3D technology, to closely recreate the environment in which each event happened.

Although to a lesser extent, a number of promising games have been developed in the field of ICH [30]. Some examples are:

- Icura,[13] a 3D realistic environment to teach about Japanese culture and etiquette, which can raise cultural interest and support a real pre-trip planning.

---

[1]Coenen T.(2013). Muse-US: case study of a pervasive cultural heritage serious game. Journal on Computing and Cultural Heritage (JOCCH), 6(2), 8:2–8:19.

[2]http://totem.fit.fraunhofer.de/tidycity The game consists in solving riddles about a specific city, which might require the player to explore places never seen before while learning about the city's cultural heritage.

[3]http://www.bbc.co.uk/history/british/empire_seapower/launch_gms_battle_waterloo.shtml, a strategy game reconstructing the famous battle.

[4]A. Doulamis et al. (2011). Serious games for cultural applications. In D. Plemenos, G. Miaoulis (Eds.), Artificial Intelligence Techniques for Computer Graphics, Springer (2011). The game is a reconstruction of the Benedictine monastery in Coventry, dissolved by Henry VIII.

[5]Francis R. (2006). Revolution, learning about history through situated role play in a virtual environment. Proc. of the American educational research association conference. The game is a role-playing game in the town of colonial Williamsburg during the American Revolution.

[6]http://www.thiatro.info/

[7]http://www.mylearning.org/interactive.asp?journeyid=238&resourceid=587

[8]http://www.makebelieve.gr/mb/www/en/portfolio/museums-culture/54-amm.html

[9]http://www.hideandseek.net/tate-trumps/

[10]Cao, Y.et al (2011). The Hero's Journey – template-based storytelling for ubiquitous multimedia management. Journal Multimedia, 6 (2) 156–169.

[11]Christopoulos, D. et al (2011). Using virtual environments to tell the story: The battle of Thermopylae. Proceedings of VS-Games 2011.

[12]http://www.playinghistory.eu

[13]Froschauer, J., et al. (2010). 'Design and evaluation of a serious game for immersive cultural training'. Proceedings of the 16th International Conference on Virtual Systems and Multimedia (VSMM) 253–260.

- Discover Babylon,[14] Roma Nova[15] and Remembering 7th Street,[16] which are aimed at raising awareness about ancient Mesopotamia's contribution to modern culture, ancient Rome and West Oakland in the time period post-World War II
- Africa Trail[17] and Real Lives 2010[18] simulate a 12,000 mile travel by bicycle through Africa or a different life in any country of the world (e.g. a peasant farmer in Bangladesh or a computer operator in Poland), respectively.
- Papakwaqa,[19] a serious game about the Atayal minority in Taiwan, particularly focused on ICH assets like tribal beliefs, customs and ceremonies.

Game-like applications are also a powerful tool for ICH transmission, following a well-consolidated trend in the technology-enhanced learning field, which promotes the adoption of digital games to sustain learning and training in a variety of educational fields aiming to empower constructive, experiential, self-regulated learning and increase the user's engagement and motivation.

For instance, within i-Treasures project, seven prototype educational game-like applications for sensorimotor learning have been implemented for selected ICH sub-use cases (Tsamiko dance, Walloon dance, Calus dance, Human Beat Box singing, Byzantine music, pottery and contemporary music composition). These games (Fig. 5.3) are designed to get input from various sensors and game devices, such as the prototype hyper-helmet or off-the-shelf commercial sensors like Kinect. The system allows the user to (a) observe the expert performance and (b) practice

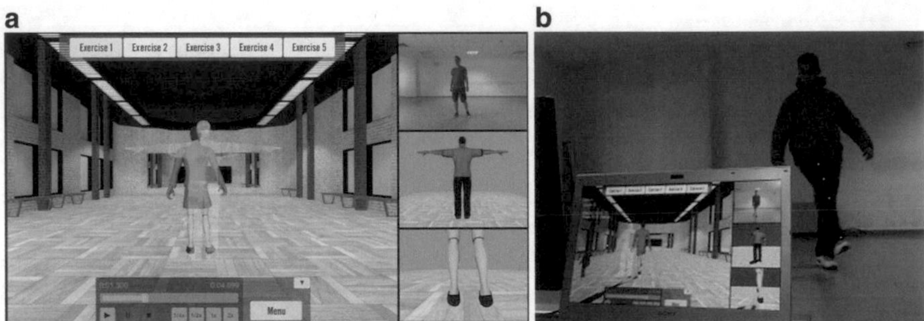

Fig. 5.3 Screenshot from the game-like application for Tsamiko dance. It presents the ghost avatar implementation, which allows the user to see his/her own character 'superposed' with the expert's one so as to be able to visually detect where she/he is making a mistake (© 2016 EC FP7 i-Treasures project, reprinted with permission)

[14]http://www.fas.org/babylon/

[15]http://www.seriousgamesinstitute.co.uk/applied-research/Roma-Nova.aspx

[16]http://7thstreet.org/

[17]http://www.mobygames.com/game/africa-trail

[18]http://www.educationalsimulations.com/products.html

[19]Huang, C. & Huang, Y. (2013). Annales school-based serious game creation framework for Taiwan indigenous cultural heritage. Journal of Computing in Cultural Heritage, 6 (2).

by trying to reproduce the expert performance and then getting an evaluation and additional feedback about his/her performance.

5.3.7 Text-to-Song Synthesis

Singing voice synthesis (SVS) is a branch of the text-to-speech (TTS) technology that deals with generating a synthetic interpretation of a song, given its text and musical score. Synthesis of singing voice has been a research area for a long time, and for each decade a major technology improvement has been achieved.

The beginnings of the synthetic voice in musical representations in the artistic domain date back to the beginning of the 1980s, with the 'Chant' project developed at IRCAM and used by composers of contemporary classical music [84]. 'Chant' is based on the synthesis by formants (by rules), like other well-known systems, as those developed at KTH in Stockholm [85] or CCRM Stanford [86]. A state-of-the-art description can be found in [87] or in [88]. Such systems were capable of synthesising realistically vocal vowels (vocals), at the price of a big studio work to analyse and adjust the settings of the systems.

For singing, as for speech, the 1990s are marked by the generalisation of concatenative synthesis, driven by the impressive increase in size of the speech corpora. An alternative approach to singing synthesis that found its way in professional quality productions is based on voice conversion. The first example was the merger of two voices, a male alto and a soprano voice from a woman to 'create' the voice of a castrate (male soprano) in the film 'Farinelli'; examples can be found on YouTube and in [88]. The voice was capable of high-quality articulate speech; however, it was not synthesis but just voice transformation.

The 2000s were marked by the appearance of Vocaloid [89]. It is the first software for singing voice synthesis with articulate lyrics which had a very important mainstream development. Vocaloid is marketed by Yamaha since 2003. During this period, concatenative synthesis is being generalised, and statistical parametric synthesis systems appeared for speech and more marginally for singing.

Recently, there is a revival of interest for singing voice synthesis. The request is coming from both the composers, the audio-visual and public games industries. Recent innovations include real-time control speech synthesis, both in the sphere of mobile orchestras (project Chorus Digitalis, Vox Tactum, meta-orchestra, laptop orchestra) and the use of various sensors in conjunction with a synthesiser.

5.4 Discussion and Future Challenges

From the above, it becomes obvious that the advanced technological methods discussed earlier have not been thoroughly applied in the preservation or transmission of intangible heritage. Yet previous projects and studies would suggest that there are several opportunities to employ the specific technologies in cultural heritage preservation with a particular focus on transmission and education. Although technology cannot replace human interaction, there is significant scope to develop activities that on the one hand document and preserve the knowledge of rare songs, dances, composition and craftsmanship but also ensure the transmission of this knowledge to younger generations. In this sense, technology can help sustain the knowledge of the past and enable its transmission to future generations. For this reason, it is important to ensure the active involvement of cultural practitioners in all related research and development efforts. Rather than a threat, new technologies constitute a great opportunity for the documentation and dissemination of intangible heritage. Instead of only focusing on the documentation of intangible heritage, the combination of the technologies discussed above can create a novel approach for the safeguarding of intangible heritage that is primarily focused on education, training and pedagogical interaction.

In the case of rare traditional singing, the combination of these technologies can contribute significantly not only to the documentation of the knowledge of singing but also to its dissemination to a broader audience. Facial expression analysis technologies could therefore enable the detailed recording of the singers' expression and singing technique, and EEG analysis could provide information about the performers' emotional state. Vocal tract sensing technologies could be used to document the various changes of the vocal tract, and motion capture technologies could give an indication of the performers' body movements. Text-to-song technology could provide sophisticated software for the creation of an educational tool to be used in educational scenarios and a 'performative tool' that can be used as a traditional musical instrument.

With respect to the case of dance, motion capture technologies can provide a detailed representation of the movement of the human body in performance bringing new insights to motional and gestural aspects whose examination is not always possible due to complex outfits and costumes. Recent studies [90] report promising results on recognising predefined dance motion patterns from skeletal animation data captured by multiple Kinect sensors. However, the recognition of different dance styles and analysis of more complex dance patterns and variations are still a challenging problem for the future. EEG analysis and facial expression analysis can contribute to the examination of the emotional state of the dancers when performing. Moreover, 3D visualisation can enable the representation of dance movements in a 3D and sensorimotor learning context.

Regarding the case of craftsmanship and pottery, motion capture can be used again for the detailed documentation of hand and finger movement during the creation process. As discussed earlier, 3D visualisation can provide educational opportunities for virtual learning scenarios.

Concerning contemporary music composition, technologies such as motion capture and EEG could potentially provide combined information on finger movement and emotional condition. In addition, facial expression analysis could give insight as to how the creative process is mirrored in the composer's face.

Finally, in all use cases, multimodal semantic analysis enables, first, the combination of different levels of information and data for documentation and, second, the detection of high-level concepts in the data in an automatic manner. The former is very useful for the system integration, since the problem of combining heterogeneous modalities disappears, while the latter is useful for the detection of high-level concepts automatically and without the need for intervention by an expert. As a subsequent result, using the semantic analysis results, we can have a more detailed and improved documentation in order to provide more efficient access to the content.

As the world becomes increasingly dependent on digital resources, there is an important opportunity to develop a platform that enhances the transmission of traditional knowledge and skills by using current advances in the field of digital technologies. Platforms such as i-Treasures offer services for knowledge exchange between researchers and for the transmission of rare ICH know-how from LHTs to apprentices, acting as a means for stimulating creative and game industry and education as well as promoting local cultural tourism. A big challenge is to find the optimal technologies to capture, analyse, present and reuse ICH, which typically contains a huge wealth of multimodal information and corresponds to a rich knowledge domain. In the future, further advances in technologies for digitisation (i.e. audio, visual and motion capture), e-documentation (3D modelling enriched with multimedia metadata and ontologies), e-preservation (standards), visualisation (virtual/augmented reality and gamification technologies) and reuse (e.g. applications for research and education) of ICH are expected to exploit the full potential of ICH and offer multiple benefits to the different stakeholders involved. So technology is no longer a threat to the survival of customs and traditions but a tool for their sustained development in an increasingly global twenty-first century.

Acknowledgements The research leading to these results has received funding from the European Community's Seventh Framework Programme (FP7-ICT-2011-9) under grant agreement no FP7-ICT-600676 'i-Treasures: Intangible Treasures—Capturing the Intangible Cultural Heritage and Learning the Rare Know-How of Living Human Treasures'.

References

1. F. Cameron, S. Kenderdine, *Theorizing Digital Cultural Heritage: A Critical Discourse* (MIT Press, Cambridge, 2010)
2. M. Ioannides, D. Fellner, A. Georgopoulos, D. Hadjimitsis (ed.), Digital Heritage, in *3rd International Conference, Euromed 2010*, Lemnos, Cyprus, Proceedings (Springer, Berlin, 2010)
3. K. Dimitropoulos, S. Manitsaris, F. Tsalakanidou, S. Nikolopoulos, B. Denby, S. Al Kork, L. Crevier-Buchman, C. Pillot-Loiseau, S. Dupont, J. Tilmanne, M. Ott, M. Alivizatou, E. Yilmaz, L. Hadjileontiadis, V. Charisis, O. Deroo, A. Manitsaris, I. Kompatsiaris, N. Grammalidis, Capturing the intangible: an introduction to the i-treasures project, in *Proceedings of 9th International Conference on Computer Vision Theory and Applications (VISAPP2014)*, Lisbon, 5–8 Jan 2014
4. N. Aikawa, An historical overview of the preparation of the UNESCO international convention for the safeguarding of intangible heritage. Museum Int. **56**, 137–149 (2004)
5. V. Hafstein, Intangible heritage as list: from masterpieces to representation, in *Intangible heritage*, ed. by L. Smith, N. Akagawa (Routledge, Abingdon, 2009), pp. 93–111
6. P. Nas, Masterpieces of oral and intangible heritage: reflections on the UNESCO world heritage list. Curr. Anthropol. **43**(1), 139–143 (2002)
7. M. Alivizatou, The UNESCO programme for the proclamation of masterpieces of the oral and intangible heritage of humanity: a critical examination. J. Museum Ethnogr. **19**, 34–42 (2007)
8. L. Bolton, *Unfolding the Moon: Enacting Women's Kastom in Vanuatu* (University of Hawai'i Press, Honolulu, 2003)
9. K. Huffman, The fieldworkers of the Vanuatu cultural centre and their contribution to the audiovisual collections, in *Arts of Vanuatu*, ed. by J. Bonnemaison, K. Huffman, D. Tryon (University of Hawai'i Press, Honolulu, 1996), pp. 290–293
10. S. Zafeiriou, L. Yin, 3D facial behaviour analysis and understanding. Image Vis. Comput. **30**, 681–682 (2012)
11. P. Ekman, R. Levenson, W. Friesen, Emotions differ in autonomic nervous system activity. Science **221**, 1208–1210 (1983)
12. O. Engwall, Modeling of the vocal tract in three dimensions, in *Proceedings, Eu-rospeech99*, Hungary, 1999, pp. 113116
13. S.Fels, J.E. Lloyd, K. Van Den Doel, F. Vogt, I. Stavness, E. Vatikiotis-Bateson, Developing physically-based, dynamic vocal tract models using Artisynth, in *Proceedings of ISSP* 6, 1991, pp. 419–426
14. M. Stone, Toward a model of three-dimensional tongue movement. Phonetics **19**, 309320 (1991)
15. P. Badin, G. Bailly, L. Reveret, M. Baciu, C. Segebarth, C. Savariaux, Three-dimensional linear articulatory modeling of tongue, lips and face, based on MRI and video images. J. Phon. **30**(3), 533–553 (2002)
16. M. Stone, A three-dimensional model of tongue movement based on ultrasound and X-ray microbeam data. J. Acoust. Soc. Am. **87**, 2207 (1990)
17. O. Engwall, From real-time MRI to 3D tongue movements, in *Proceedings, 8th International Conference on Spoken Language Processing (ICSLP)*, Jeju Island, Vol. 2, 2004, pp. 1109–1112
18. M. Stone, A. Lundberg, Three-dimensional tongue surface shapes of English consonants and vowels. J. Acoust. Soc. Am. **99**(6), 37283737 (1996)
19. N. Henrich, B. Lortat-Jacob, M. Castellengo, L. Bailly, X Pelorson, Period-doubling occurences in singing: the "bassu" case in traditional Sardinian "A Tenore" singing, in *Proceedings of the International Conference on Voice Physiology and Biomechanics*, Tokyo, July 2006

20. N. Henrich, L. Bailly, X. Pelorson, B. Lortat-Jacob, Physiological and physical understanding of singing voice practices: the Sardinian Bassu case, AIRS Start-up meeting, Prince Edward Island, 2009
21. W. Cho, J. Hong, H. Park, Real-time ultrasonographic assessment of true vocal fold length in professional singers. J. Voice **26**(6), 1–6 (2012)
22. G. Troup, T. Griffiths, M. Schneider-Kolsky, T. Finlayson, Ultrasound observation of vowel tongue shapes in trained singers, in *Proceedings of the 30th Condensed Matter and Materials Meeting*, Wagga, 2006
23. T. Coduys, C. Henry, A. Cont, TOASTER and KROONDE: high-resolution and high-speed real-time sensor interfaces, in *Proceedings of the Conference on New Interfaces for Musical Expression*, Singapore, 2004, pp. 205–206
24. F. Bevilacqua, B. Zamborlin, A. Sypniewski, N. Schnell, F. Guedy, N. Rasamimanana, Gesture in embodied communication and human-computer interaction, in *8th International Gesture Workshop*, 2010, pp. 73–84
25. M. Caon, Context-aware 3D gesture interaction based on multiple kinects, in *Proceedings of the First International Conference on Ambient Computing, Applications, Services and Technologies*, Barcelona, 2011, pp. 7–12
26. M. Boucher, Virtual dance and motion-capture. Contemp. Aesthet. **9**, 10 (2011)
27. R. Aylward, J.A. Paradiso, Sensemble: a wireless, compact, multi-user sensor system for interactive dance, in *Proceedings of the International Conference on New Interfaces for Musical Expression (NIME06)*, Paris, Centre Pompidou, 2006, pp. 134–139
28. D. Drobny, M. Weiss, J. Borchers, Saltate!: a sensor-based system to support dance beginners, Extended abstracts on Human factors in Computing Systems, in *Proceedings of the CHI 09 International Conference* (ACM, 2009, New York), pp. 3943–3948
29. F. Bevilacqua, L. Naugle, C. Dobrian, Music control from 3D motion capture of dance. CHI 2001 for the NIME workshop (2001)
30. C. Dobrian, F. Bevilacqua, Gestural control of music: using the vicon 8 motion capture system, in *Proceedings of the Conference on New Interfaces for Musical Expression (NIME)*, National University of Singapore, 2003, pp. 161–163
31. M. Raptis, D. Kirovski, H. Hoppe, Real-time classification of dance gestures from skeleton animation, in *Proceedings of ACM SIGGRAPH/Eurographics Symposium on Computer Animation*, New York, 2011, pp. 147–156
32. D.S. Alexiadis, P. Kelly, P. Daras, N.E. O'Connor, T. Boubekeur, M.B. Moussa, Evaluating a dancer's performance using kinect-based skeleton tracking, in *Proceedings of the 19th ACM International Conference on Multimedia* (New York, ACM, 2011), pp. 659–662
33. S. Essid, D.S. Alexiadis, R. Tournemenne, M. Gowing, P. Kelly, D.S. Monaghan et al., An advanced virtual dance performance evaluator, in *Proceedings of the 37th International Conference on Acoustics, Speech, and Signal Processing (ICASSP)*, Kyoto, 2012, pp. 2269–2272
34. G. Alankus, A.A. Bayazit, O.B. Bayazit, Automated motion synthesis for dancing characters: motion capture and retrieval. Comput. Anim. Virtual Worlds **16**(3–4), 259–271 (2005)
35. M. Brand, A. Hertzmann, Style machines, in *Proceedings of the 27th Annual Conference on Computer Graphics and Interactive Techniques (SIGGRAPH 2000)* (ACM Press, 2000), pp. 183–192
36. D. Bouchard, N. Badler, Semantic segmentation of motion capture using laban movement analysis, in *Proceedings of the 7th International Conference on Intelligent Virtual Agents*, Springer, 2007. pp. 37–44
37. K. Kahol, P. Tripathi, S. Panchanathan, Automated gesture segmentation from dance sequences, in *Proceedings of the Sixth IEEE International Conference on Automatic Face and Gesture Recognition (FGR04)*, Seoul, 2004, pp. 883–888
38. J. James, T. Ingalls, G. Qian, L. Olsen, D. Whiteley, S. Wong et al., Movement-based interactive dance performance, in *Proceedings of the 14th annual ACM International Conference on Multimedia* (ACM, New York, 2006), pp. 470–480

39. A.-M. Burns, M.M. Wanderley, Visual methods for the retrieval of guitarist fingering, in *Proceedings of the Conference on New Interfaces for Musical Expression* (IRCAM-Centre, Pompidou, 2006), pp. 196–199
40. Vision par ordinateur pour la reconnaissance des gestes musicaux des doigts, Revue Francophone d'Informatique Musicale [Online] Available at: http://revues.mshparisnord.org/rfim/index.php?id=107. Accessed 13 July 2013
41. D. Grunberg, Gesture Recognition for Conducting Computer Music (n.d.) [On line] Available at: http://schubert.ece.drexel.edu/research/gestureRecognition. Accessed 10 Jan 2009
42. J. Verner, MIDI guitar synthesis yesterday, today and tomorrow, an overview of the whole fingerpicking thing. Record. Mag. **8**(9), 52–57 (1995)
43. C. Traube, An interdisciplinary study of the timbre of the classical guitar, PhD Thesis, McGill University, 2004
44. Y. Takegawa, T. Terada, S. Nishio, Design and implementation of a real-time fingering detection system for piano performances, in *Proceedings of the International Computer Music Conference*, New Orleans, 2006, pp. 67–74
45. J. MacRitchie, B. Buck, N. Bailey, Visualising musical structure through performance gesture, in *Proceedings of the International Society for Music Information Retrieval Conference*, Kobe, 2009, pp. 237–242
46. M. Malempre, Pour une poignee de danses, Dapo Hainaut (ed.) (2010)
47. T. Calvert, W. Wilke, R. Ryman, I. Fox, Applications of computers to dance. IEEE Comput. Graph. Appl. **25**(2), 6–12 (2005)
48. Y. Shen, X. Wu, C. Lua, H. Cheng, *National Dances Protection Based on Motion Capture Technology*, Chengdu, Sichuan, vol. 51 (IACSIT Press, Singapore, 2012), pp. 78–81
49. W.M. Brown, L. Cronk, K. Grochow, A. Jacobson, C.K. Liu, Z. Popovic et al., Dance reveals symmetry especially in young men. Nature **438**(7071), 1148–1150 (2005)
50. D. Tardieu, X. Siebert, B. Mazzarino, R. Chessini, J. Dubois, S. Dupont, G. Varni, A. Visentin, Browsing a dance video collection: dance analysis and interface design. J. Multimodal User Interf. **4**(1), 37–46 (2010)
51. J.C. Chan, H. Leung, J.K. Tang, T. Komura, A virtual reality dance training system using motion capture technology. IEEE Trans. Learn. Technol. **4**(2), 187–195 (2011)
52. I. Cohen, A. Garg, T. Huang, Emotion recognition from facial expression using multilevel HMM, in *Proceedings of the Neural Information Processing Systems Workshop on Affective Computing*, Breckenridge, 2000
53. F. Bourel, C. Chibelushi, A. Low, Robust facial expression recognition using a state-based model of spatially-localized facial dynamics, in *Proceedings of IEEE International Conference on Automatic Face and Gesture Recognition*, Washington, 2002
54. B. Schuller, S. Reiter, R. Mueller, A. Hames, G. Rigoll, Speaker independent speech emotion recognition by ensemble classification, in *Proceedings of the IEEE International Conference on Multimedia and Expo*, Amsterdam, 2005, pp. 864–867
55. C. Busso, Z. Deng, S. Yildirim, M. Bulut, C. Lee, A. Kazemzadeh, S. Lee, U. Neumann, S. Narayanan, Analysis of emotional recognition using facial expressions, speech and multimodal information, in *Proceedings of the International Conference on Multimodal Interfaces* (ACM, New York, 2004), pp. 205–211
56. R. Picard, E. Vyzas, J. Healey, Toward machine emotional intelligence: analysis of affective physiological state. IEEE Trans. Pattern Anal. Mach. Intell. **23**(10), 1175–1191 (2001)
57. F. Nasoz, C. Lisetti, K. Alvarez, N. Finkelstein, Emotion recognition from physiological signals for user modeling of affect, in *Proceedings of the International Conference on User Modeling*, Johnstown, 2003
58. C. Lisetti, F. Nasoz, Using non-invasive wearable computers to recognize human emotions from physiological signals. EURASIP J. Appl. Signal Process. **11**, 1672–1687 (2004)
59. D. McIntosh, A. Reichmann-Decker, P. Winkielman, J. Wilbarger, When the social mirror breaks: deficits in automatic, but not voluntary, mimicry of emotional facial expressions in autism. Dev. Sci. **9**, 295–302 (2006)

60. F. Esposito, D. Malerba, G. Semeraro, O. Altamura, S. Ferilli, T. Basile, M. Berard, M. Ceci, Machine learning methods for automatically processing historical documents: from paper acquisition to XML transformation, in *Proceedings of the First International Workshop on Document Image Analysis for Libraries (DIAL, 04)*, Palo Alto, 2004, pp. 328–335
61. A. Mallik, S. Chaudhuri, H. Ghosh, Nrityakosha: preserving the intangible heritage of Indian classical dance. ACM J. Comput. Cult. Herit. **4**(3), 11 (2011)
62. M. Makridis, P. Daras, Automatic classification of archaeological pottery sherds. J. Comput. Cult. Herit. **5**(4), 15 (2012)
63. A. Karasik, A complete, automatic procedure for pottery documentation and analysis, in *Proceedings of the IEEE Computer Vision and Pattern Recognition Workshops (CVPRW)*, San Francisco, 2010, pp. 29–34
64. S. Vrochidis, C. Doulaverakis, A. Gounaris, E. Nidelkou, L. Makris, I. Kompatsiaris, A hybrid ontology and visual-based retrieval model for cultural heritage multimedia collections. Int. J. Metadata Semant. Ontol. **3**(3), 167–182 (2008)
65. M. Liggins, D.L. Hall, J. Llina, *Handbook of Multisensor Data Fusion, Theory and Practice*, 2nd edn. (CRC Press, Boca Raton, 2008)
66. O. Punska, Bayesian approach to multisensor data fusion, PhD. Dissertation, Department of Engineering, University of Cambridge, 1999
67. S. Nikolopoulos, C. Lakka, I. Kompatsiaris, C. Varytimidis, K. Rapantzikos, Y. Avrithis, Compound document analysis by fusing evidence across media, in *Proceedings of the International Workshop on Content-Based Multimedia Indexing*, Chania, 2009, pp. 175–180
68. S. Chang, D. Ellis, W. Jiang, K. Lee, A. Yanagawa, A.C. Loui, J. Luo, Largescale multimodal semantic concept detection for consumer video, in *Proceedings of the International Workshop on Workshop on Multimedia Information Retrieval (MIR '07)*, September, 2007, pp. 255–264
69. R. Huber-Mörk, S. Zambanini, M. Zaharieva, M. Kampel, Identification of ancient coins based on fusion of shape and local features. Mach. Vision Appl. **22**(6), 983–994 (2011)
70. D. Datcu, L.J.M. Rothkrantz, *Semantic Audio-Visual Data Fusion for Automatic Emotion Recognition* (Euromedia, Porto, 2008)
71. M. Koolen, J. Kamps, Searching cultural heritage data: does structure help expert searchers?, in *Proceedings of RIAO '10 Adaptivity, Personalization and Fusion of Heterogeneous Information*, Paris, 2010, pp. 152–155
72. L. Bai, S. Lao, W. Zhang, G.J.F. Jones, A.F. Smeaton, Video semantic, content analysis framework based on ontology combined MPEG-7, in *Adaptive Multimedia Retrieval: Retrieval, User, and Semantics, Lecture Notes in Computer Science*, July, 2007, pp. 237–250
73. S. Dasiopoulou, V. Mezaris, I. Kompatsiaris, V.K. Papastathis, G.M. Strintzis, Knowledge-assisted semantic video object detection. IEEE Trans. Circuits Syst. Video Technol. **15**(10), 1210–1224 (2005) (Special Issue on Analysis and Understanding for Video Adaptation)
74. J. Lien, T. Kanade, J. Cohn, C. Li, Automated facial expression recognition based on facs action units, in *Proceedings of the 3rd IEEE Conference on Automatic Face and Gesture Recognition*, Nara, 1998, pp. 390–395
75. P. Mulholland, A. Wolff, T. Collins, Z. Zdrahal, An event-based approach to describing and understanding museum narratives, in *Proceedings: Detection, Representation, and Exploitation of Events in the Semantic Web Workshop in Conjunction with the International Semantic Web Conference*, Bonn, 2011
76. I. Kollia, V. Tzouvaras, N. Drosopoulos, G. Stamou, A systemic approach for effective semantic access to cultural content. Semant. Web – Interoperability, Usability Appl. **3**(1), 65–83 (2012)
77. A. Gaitatzes, D. Christopoulos, M. Roussou, Reviving the past: cultural heritage meets virtual reality, in *Proceedings of the 2001 Conference on Virtual Reality, Archeology, and Cultural Heritage*, ACM, 2001, November, pp. 103–110
78. M. Ott, F. Pozzi, Towards a new era for cultural heritage education: discussing the role of ICT. Comput. Hum. Behav. **27**(4), 1365–1371 (2011)
79. K.H. Veltman, Challenges for ICT/UCT applications in cultural heritage, in *ICT and Heritage*, ed. by C. Carreras (2005), online at http://www.uoc.edu/digithum/7/dt/eng/dossier.pdf

80. J.R. Savery, T.M. Duffy, Problem-based learning: an instructional model and its constructivist framework. Educ. Technol. **35**, 31–38 (1995)
81. M. Mortara, C.E. Catalano, F. Bellotti, G. Fiucci, M. Houry-Panchetti, P. Petridis, Learning cultural heritage by serious games. J. Cult. Herit. **15**(3), 318–325 (2014)
82. E.F. Anderson, L. McLoughlin, F. Liarokapis, C. Peters, P. Petridis, S. de Freitas, Serious games in cultural heritage, in *Proceedings of the 10th International Symposium on Virtual Reality, Archaeology and Cultural Heritage VAST*, ed. by M. Ashley, F. Liarokapis. State of the Art Reports (2009)
83. M. Ott, F. Pozzi, ICT and cultural heritage education: which added value? in *Emerging Technologies and Information Systems for the Knowledge Society*, ed. by Lytras et al. Lecture Notes in Computer Science, 5288 (Springer, Berlin, 2008), pp. 131–138
84. X. Rodet, Y. Potard, J.-B. Barriere, The CHANT project: from the synthesis of the singing voice to synthesis in general. Comput. Music J. **8**(3), 15–31 (1984)
85. G. Berndtsson, The KTH rule system for singing synthesis. Comput. Music J. **20**(1), 7691 (1996)
86. P. Cook, Physical models for music synthesis, and a meta-controller for real time performance, in *Proceedings of the International Computer Music Conference and Festival*, Delphi, 1992
87. P. Cook, Singing voice synthesis: history, current work, and future directions. Comput. Music J. **20**(3), 3846 (1996)
88. G. Bennett, X. Rodet, Synthesis of the singing voice, in *Current Directions in Computer Music Research*, ed. by M.V. Mathews, J.R. Pierce (MIT Press, Cambridge, 1989), pp. 19–44
89. H. Kenmochi, H. Ohshita, Vocaloid–commercial singing synthesizer based on sample concatenation. Presented at Interspeech 2007, Antwerp, 2007, pp. 4009–40010
90. A. Kitsikidis, K. Dimitropoulos, S. Douka, N. Grammalidis, Dance analysis using multiple kinect sensors, in *International Conference on Computer Vision Theory and Applications (VISAPP)*, IEEE, Vol. 2, 2014, January, pp. 789–795

Part III
Content Use and Re-use

Chapter 6
3D Digital Libraries and Their Contribution in the Documentation of the Past

Marinos Ioannides, Rob Davies, Pavlos Chatzigrigoriou, Eirini Papageorgiou, Georgios Leventis, Vasiliki Nikolakopoulou, and Vasilis Athanasiou

Abstract From the ancient library of Alexandria 2300 years ago, the objectives of the collection of information has a common fundamental base: to gather, preserve, and promote knowledge, thus helping in the intellectual and cognitive evolution of humanity. Today, the information revolution has given the ability to scientists, educators, researchers, and individuals not only to use a variety of digital libraries as an information source but also to contribute to these libraries by uploading data that they create, leading to a massive production of knowledge that we need to verify, manage, archive, preserve, and reuse. Cultural heritage data is a category in digital libraries that needs much attention, because of its crucial role in helping us to interact with the past and learn, promote, and preserve our cultural assets. Digital documentation of tangible and intangible heritage, data formats and standards, metadata and semantics, Linked Data, crowdsourcing and cloud, use and reuse of data, and copyright issues are the rising challenges that we try to address in this chapter, through literature review and best practice examples. At the end of this analysis, this chapter tries to predict the near future of digital heritage libraries, where 3D digital assets will be part of augmented, virtual, and mixed reality experiences.

Keywords Digital libraries • Digital documentation • 3D reconstruction • Semantic annotation • Ontology • 3D library • Crowdsourcing

M. Ioannides (✉)
Digital Heritage Research Lab, Cyprus University of Technology, 30 Archiepiskou Kyperianou, 3036 Limassol, Cyprus
e-mail: marinos.ioannides@cut.ac.cy

R. Davies • P. Chatzigrigoriou • E. Papageorgiou • G. Leventis • V. Nikolakopoulou • V. Athanasiou
Cyprus University of Technology, 30 Archbishop Kyprianou Str., 3036 Lemesos, Cyprus
e-mail: p.chatzigrigoriou@cut.ac.cy; e.papageorgiou@cut.ac.cy; georgios.leventis@cut.ac.cy; v.nikolakopoulou@cut.ac.cy; vasilis.athanasiou@cut.ac.cy

M. Ioannides et al. (eds.), *Mixed Reality and Gamification for Cultural Heritage*,
DOI 10.1007/978-3-319-49607-8_6

6.1 Digital Libraries

6.1.1 History

Knowledge is power is a common statement nowadays, but the wish of mankind to store and thus obtain access to knowledge and to the possibilities which unfold through and beyond it dates back to the ancient times of human history, when many famous libraries were founded across the whole known world, such as the Royal Library of Alexandria in Egypt and the Library of Pergamum in Anatolia, to store and safeguard knowledge in their premises. The story of physical libraries has evolved up to contemporary times, maintaining this initial goal: to provide access to knowledge.

Through their relation to the physical library, digital libraries (DLs) aim to collect, archive, catalogue, and classify items of digital content and make it accessible for detection, retrieval, and use by users. The digital aspect of physical libraries began in the 1970s with "library automation systems" [1], which catalogued data according to authority control rules and in relation to physical objects contained in a library. The task of these systems was mainly to manage and assist access to physical content. Their functions were limited and their role rather static. In the following decade (1980s), these automated catalogues became more advanced. Digital libraries (DLs) themselves started as content-centered or hierarchical databases [2] providing content collected and in service of special and limited user communities (librarians, researchers) and as institutions providing services for a social cause.

A DL is "fundamentally a resource that reconstructs the intellectual substance and services of a traditional library in digital form" [3]. Its advent was made possible in the early 1990s [4] with the introduction of networked, multitasking, and multiuser-oriented databases, on the one hand, through the inception of the World Wide Web (www), Hypertext Transfer Protocol (http), web browsers, and hyperlinks [5], which have vastly reduced the constraints of place, time, and content. As a result of the Internet boom, "info overload" [5] emerged alongside the need to efficiently store, detect, retrieve, and use the vast amount of digital information created. On the other hand, the above goals became achievable through the development of standard schemas which have a strict organizational structure and are sufficiently generic in order to allow the metadata incorporation of multiple and multifaceted data and, by these means, to facilitate the retrieval of the incorporated knowledge. Such metadata schemas are, for example, Dublin Core (DC) [6], which was introduced in 1995 to incorporate metadata from the domain of libraries, and the Lightweight Information Describing Objects (LIDO), which was introduced in 2009 in order to support the full range of descriptive information about museum objects.[1]

[1]http://network.icom.museum/cidoc/working-groups/lido/what-is-lido/

In 2010 IFLA/UNESCO defined digital libraries as follows [7]:

> A DL is an online collection of digital objects, of assured quality, that are created or collected and managed according to internationally accepted principles for collection development and made accessible in a coherent and sustainable manner, supported by services necessary to allow users to retrieve and exploit resources.

Electronic [8], hybrid, digital, three-dimensional, virtual, and cyber are some of the adjectives used in the last three decades, attempting to describe the library of the new era, as the concept evolved along with the terminology.

6.1.2 Evolution

From catalogues pointing to bookshelves and content-centered databases, DLs have evolved to become service providers for professional communities with special interest (researchers, scholars, etc.), wider public audiences, and other individual users. DLs include digitization actions which turn "physical into digital" [9] and "tangible into intangible" and manage data acquisition quality. Their evolution accords with the capability of the system to manage complex and diversified types of data. DLs aim not only to collect and archive their data (static function) but also to present their digital content to the user in a comprehensive, accessible way (management function) and in multimedia form. Huge amounts of digital files need to be organized in a structured way in order to facilitate the detection of this information by the user. DLs also seek to incorporate means to preserve existing digital data, taking into account constantly changing technologies, so that their digital collections are preserved and remain sustainable [2].

Starting from a reliable repository-centered approach, which has a rather static character, DLs have extended further to become central info storage hubs that can also keep track of different forms of data in the various stages of transformation [10]. Managing cultural heritage (CH) information and the opportunity to retrieve and browse a digital object have been added. During this process, the issue of "authenticity" in the digital world arose, leading to the London Charter (2009), by which the "intellectual transparency" of data was declared. The obligation to keep stored data as simple as possible, as well as to discern fact from interpretation, became crucial, along with the idea of a credibility audit (metadata and paradata) [11].

More recently, technology evolution has gradually enabled the shift from text-content repositories, where the text and 2D multimedia information (text, image, video) were described through metadata in a table form, toward geometry-based spaces, where surface data capture of 3D objects such as monuments allows both geometrical and structural information to be documented (geometric reconstruction). Apart from technological evolution, the capturing of 3D models of real-world objects became necessary to protect and preserve our CH objects, which are components of our cultural identity but frequently subject to natural and man-made disasters. The information has become three-dimensional (3D). 3D objects are described in 3D context and "3D semantics" [12], with digests of which DLs have become a knowledge hub to harvest 3D. Emphasis in 3D documentation of sites and built CH (architecture, archaeology, etc.) on the one hand and the rapid production of 3D models provided online to users on the other hand [13] are equally significant with regard to the issue of data interoperability.

From that point onward and due to the absence of metadata for 3D CH objects, 3D digitization and e-documentation has increasingly gained ground, while the "formation of 3D collections" [14] available to a wider audience with the use of 3D technology has turned into a major objective for DLs. The lack of ways to describe 3D objects initiated the creation of new data formats in order to support the "online existence of the 3D models" [15] inside 3D DLs, providing structured levels of detail. At the same time, issues have arisen in relation to further investigation of the metadata and the semantics of the 3D objects, the management of the "big data" created as well as the access to them (restrictions, copyrights, open data), and their dissemination to the public and the creative industries. Data sharing, use, and reuse of the vast amount of data involved in a 3D DL are in need of the development of enriched e-infrastructures that will facilitate these goals and are currently under further investigation and implementation in Europe.

Computer vision algorithms focusing on semantic image analysis by automated feature extraction from digital 3D representations[2] and image-based retrieval of information open a new path in the field of 3D DLs. More specifically, this is about scaled geometric representations of real 3D objects within a fully modeled 3D space. For this reason, the gathering of high-quality 3D data from large and distributed sites by automated means, the generation of new semantic meaning from solid models, and the interconnection between CH objects are of utmost importance, as characteristically indicated in the ongoing DigiArt project (2015–2018).

In any case, open archiving protocols, free open-source software for building and distributing DL collections, distributed repositories and interoperability, data harvesting, data preservation, and attention to sustainability indicate that DLs have evolved into a transdisciplinary sector, a multifaceted reality, and a new 3D world, which can be used in different areas of interest (such as creative industry, engineering, environment, education, etc.). Moreover, from being content and service providers, DLs have now shifted their emphasis in favor of a user-centric approach. The content they have is not only publicly accessed but furthermore enhanced and/or created by users. "User-friendly content" turns into "user-shaped content," which promotes creativity and upgrades the user into an "info configurator," promoting the personalization of the information's essence and providing new immersive experiences to users in a virtual or augmented environment.

Today, digital technology has dramatically eased the creation and dissemination of digital content. The amounts of digital information created and distributed inside

[2]http://digiart-project.eu/digiartpublications/fact-sheet/

the "information space" have led to an exponential growth of new digital information. According to UNESCO [7], "the digital universe is doubling in size every 2 years and will grow tenfold between 2013 and 2020." On the basis of the volume of the digital data as well as because of the fact that most of its content has an ephemeral nature, a compelling new issue is addressed, regarding the identification of significant digital heritage and early intervention through selection processes, in order to ensure the long-term preservation of (selected) digital objects.

6.1.3 From 2D GIS and 3D Models to BIM and HBIM

Especially in the field of monument conservation and management of built CH, there has been an ongoing process in recent years regarding the creation of an "information and knowledge hub" where all the data available for a monument will be gathered, compared, and shared. Such data can be those extracted from the on-site traditional documentation of the monument (measurements made with traditional instruments, remarks, croquis, etc.), those extracted with contemporary instruments (photogrammetry, laser scanners, drones, etc.) which provide 3D surface models, or the shape of the building extracted according to geometric laws of construction and compared with the type and the "charaxes" according to architectural pattern manuals. Documentation about the history of the monument, structural analysis, former interventions upon it, irregularities in its form, as well as distortions and the disposition of elements will also be included in this "information and knowledge hub."

The aforementioned task requires the organization of multilevel databases which vary in content and context but interrelate to each other, in a way that also secures the quantity and quality as well as the future access and reuse of the collected data.

One of the ways to collect, group, and manage various data in a systemic and unified way concerning regional, urban, building, or object scale (cities, sites, monuments, artifacts, etc.) is the two-dimensional geographic information system (2D GIS). The various data inserted in the database of a GIS system in the form of descriptive information interrelate with the 2D drawings, altering the provided representational knowledge according to the user's aim and desired level of detail on each occasion. The aim is to create significant broad content, aligned to widely recognized standards and also to act as a convenient tool for the facilitation of risk assessment, decision-making, and implementation activities such as conservation and restoration. Its use is extensively applicable and useful on an urban scale, while on the scale of individual buildings, the connection of vast descriptive information only to 2D products opens up possibilities for further development.

At the same time, the need arises for the definition of an international spatial data infrastructure for architectural heritage [16]. This need has its origin in the fact that there are various methodologies regarding heritage documentation and different "vocabularies and thesauri" are used in the field of conservation, while the "uniqueness" of each monument turns its categorization into a difficult endeavor. A spatial heritage information system in accordance with international standards needs to be defined to include the homogenization of structural information and the affiliation of different data typologies used in every country. Subsequently, not only spatial information needs to be standardized but also the related metadata.

On the other hand, the technology supports and develops three-dimensional reproduction applications which enable geometrical reconstruction. The 3D models, either produced on a scientific or on a photorealistic modeling basis [14], are supplemented by multiple interrelating libraries and algorithms. 3D models integrate large amounts of digital data, the reuse of which is of utmost importance. The retrieval and the reuse of these data is achievable through 3D semantics, by which meaningful context is given to the content of a 3D object, which is not explicit or not contained in the geometric data [17]. But the necessity for relating in a parametric way the geometrical information with the vast thematic information stored in a database remains an issue.

This gap in parametrical interconnection of the 3D representation model with its data has led to the development of a single management system, in which all the 2D and 3D information are interlinked, the building information modeling (BIM) system. BIM provides a virtual model of a built space in which structural elements, architectural elements, and elements of infrastructure are structured in a concise database which secures the logical correlations among them.

In the field of CH and monuments' conservation, this management system is called historic building information modeling (HBIM) system. HBIM allows the user to obtain a detailed 3D model in the form of a georeferenced spatial information structure [16], combined with all the related content information, which is collected and structurally inserted within the system's database. HBIM starts from a detailed survey of the building, taking into account the geometrical complexity and the multidiversity of historic constructions, while the parametric modeling of the elements and the interaction of the user with the model within the HBIM remain a challenge.

Worth mentioning is that BIM and HBIM provide a fertile platform for the collaboration of interdisciplinary team groups: BIM in the architecture, engineering, and construction (AEC) industry, and HBIM in the sector of cultural heritage and restoration. BIM focuses on new constructions, whose elements are predefined by the designers (architects, engineers), while HBIM focuses on old constructions such as monuments, whose elements rarely apply to linearities, regularities, simplifications, homogenosity, and isotropic behavior. Moreover, instead of "building" a (new) construction (BIM), in HBIM, after surface capturing, the (already constructed) 3D object is virtually "decomposed" into its structural elements in order for the assembly of construction, alongside the irregularities, to be revealed in the logic of "reverse engineering" (Fig. 6.1).

Fig. 6.1 Example of 2D GIS (*upper left*) for the Church of Panagia Asinou (UNESCO Monument) and proposal for 3D HBIM with textual and multimedia enrichment (Source of the photos: http://www.itn-dch.eu/, © 2016 FP7-PEOPLE Marie-Curie Project ITN-DCH, reprinted with permission)

6.2 Digital Libraries and Cultural Heritage: The State of Play

At the beginning of the twenty-first century, the technology had reached a point where the digitization and massive storage of data was economically efficient, and on the other hand, due to human threat and massive environmental destruction, there was a need for massive digitization. This fact has led to the formation of a high interest in turning the material into digitized content, for the information to be easily detected and retrieved and the knowledge to be widely and equally accessible. The concept of "digital libraries" has been established, while at the same time, a demand has developed for further evolution of the technology in order to facilitate the exponential growth of the created digital data (big data) and their preservation.

6.2.1 International Best Practices

Nowadays, the publicly accessed "space" of a library opens up much more widely within the DL "universe" to form the "information space" and "inhabited information spaces," which are effective social workspaces where digital information can be created, explored, manipulated, and exchanged [2]. DL systems and DL management systems are constantly evolving e-infrastructures, providing services to a number of DLs and their users. The ones developed within the EU DELOS Network of Excellence on Digital Libraries project are characteristic examples. Another example of them is The European Library (TEL), which is in fact both an aggregator of the digital collections and bibliographic data contained in partner libraries and institutions and a service provider. Its portal has free access, is addressed to researchers, and is multilingual, facilitating search and content detection through a subject-approach classification system and a powerful and enriched support informative system.

"Europeana" in Europe and "Digital Public Library of America" (DPLA) in the USA are two well-known international examples of DLs. Both of them share the same ambitious goal of bringing together the riches of the continent's libraries, archives, museums, CH repositories, and making them available to the general public for professional, educational, and recreational use[3] through a single portal.

Europeana was launched in 2008, and its vision is to unite Europe, a continent of different nations and multifaceted heritage, through culture. "Its fundamental belief is that culture is a catalyst for social and economic change, so that the world can be transformed with culture" [18]. It is based on "partnerships" with cultural and commercial stakeholders, leading to an extended network among organizations, institutions, and individuals that have safeguarded CH for years and becoming their "showcase" and "representative voice" to the world.

The role of Europeana is multiple and extends from harvesting metadata from numerous aggregators across Europe by using Open Archives Initiative Protocol for Metadata Harvesting (OAI-PMH) to central indexing and collocating items normally kept physically and institutionally separate [19], while the digital content remains on the host site and is accessed through a link. Furthermore, Europeana is working on the creation of interoperable standardized metadata in order to maximize the retrieval of the objects from the repositories, while an in-process consideration is the development of a new cloud-based infrastructure. Europeana's collaborations with several multidisciplinary professionals in CH offer it the leading advantage of providing access to authentic, credible, and quality material. Ten percent of the European culture, comprising artifacts, artworks, photographs, maps, books, newspapers, videos and film materials, sounds, etc., not only in 2D but also in 3D format,[4] is already digitally available, of which (10 %) 3 % is currently available online.

At the same time, the challenge is to promote and accelerate the digitization of the next 90 % of the European CH. Europeana supports the memory carriers and encourages them to open up their collections. Another challenge is to convert the digitized 10 % into something more usable by other sectors in real life, by making more of the content available online, preferably in open formats.

---

[3]http://strategy2020.europeana.eu/

[4]http://www.europeana.eu/portal/search?q=3D

Embracing technology and further development of standards, Linked Open Data (LOD) and metadata, multilingualism, changing copyright regulations, and more open licensing conditions will in the future ensure a greater level of accessibility and turn Europeana from a portal (for visiting only) into a more immersive platform (for creating). This transformation will facilitate user interaction and create value for distinct but interrelated groups of users. Through this platform, professionals and organizations that have heritage to share can interact, alongside people and entrepreneurs who want to use and reuse the content.

This freedom can promote user engagement, unlock peoples' creativity, and create new information to pass on to the future generations. Revealing Europe's CH to the eyes of its citizens can improve the condition of society, promote the understanding of ourselves and of each other among people and nations, and transform peoples' visions and lives [18]. In this all-embracing vision, Europe's vast cultural wealth will produce not only societal but also economic benefits. Unlocking business potential and combining it with cultural innovation will provide prosperous fields for the development of new business models, transforming lives in the process. However, tailoring user experiences according to the type of user (professionals, creative industry, and individual end users) remains a challenging field for Europeana.

Valuing the spirit of collaboration, DPLA furthermore encourages the public to share its content by using Smart App applications services and promoting the use and the reuse of data contained in the repository. Its extroversion expands beyond its own borders through collaboration with Europeana. Through the use of a customized search engine, it helps users to retrieve, link, combine, organize, and visualize data from both these sources.

It is worth mentioning that the evolution of DLs has been supplemented by many relevant funded research projects and initiatives[5] which have sought answers to knowledge-sharing, networking, and technology-development questions. The DL Initiative in the USA and the DELOS Initiative in Europe [1] played a key role in the DL sector for the research and development of effective services regarding the integration and retrieval of highly diversified information media. Moreover, IFLA has supported large-scale international DL initiatives: current examples are the World Digital Library[6] (WDL) project and the National Libraries Global (NLG) project [20].

WDL provides access to digital material according to place, period, topic, type of item, language, and contributing institution on a timeline with interactive maps. Not only the supplementary texts of the material but all of the metadata and descriptions are searchable through WDL in seven languages.

NLG aims to network the digital collections of national libraries in Asia and Oceania (AO) for wider access. The desired outcome of NLG is the creation of an access, discovery, and learning platform for participating library and educational

[5]https://ec.europa.eu/digital-single-market/en/node/77423

[6]https://www.wdl.org/en/about/

institutions to share digital content. This collaboration will be governed by a content-sharing policy framework formulated and implemented with the agreement of the participating institutions.

Last but not least, the initiatives of private organizations such as the Google Institute should be mentioned. At the beginning of the twenty-first century, Google set the goal of digitizing millions of books and making every sentence of them detectable. The project involved many top university libraries, turning Google into the single largest repository of digitized published material existing at that time. The goal was to facilitate or even provide access to library materials and information, which would have been hard or even impossible for users to find by using traditional means. Many questions have arisen from this, among them the danger of the extinction of traditional libraries and copyright issues. The Google Libraries project was renamed to Google Book Search Project, and the effort of creating a DL within which every book can be browsed via keyword search continues, pointing to a new digital era. Moreover, at the same time, we are facing the revolutionary growth of different social media products, especially Facebook and YouTube, which are at the moment the largest repositories of their kind in the world.

6.2.2 *Intersectoral Understanding: Overcoming Language Obstacles*

"If the digital heritage is the 'content', then the metadata provide the 'context'" [21]. This quote states very clearly how crucial is the issue of contextualization for the authentic preservation and recreation of the story of the past.

Up to the first decade of the twenty-first century, DLs were offering ways to organize the big data of digital information but were focused mainly on classification and based around text sources. The need for structured vocabularies has emerged. Classification and taxonomy systems have been created by many institutions (e.g., Getty, UNESCO, ICOM (International Council of Museums), ICOMOS (International Committee for Monuments and Sites), Council of Europe), by funded projects (e.g., RICHES), as well as by individual states (e.g., England, Italy, Canada, USA). INSCRIPTION, MIDAS, CERIF, HEREIN, NOMENCLATURE, MoRPHE, NMR, PARKS, CDWA, AAT, CONA, TGN, and ULAN are only some of the widespread structured vocabularies used by libraries worldwide.

The above vocabularies and classification systems provide an extensive list of object terms in different thematic areas and relate each object term to others within a hierarchical taxonomy. Due to the fact that the needs of each institution are diverse [22], some of these standardized vocabularies provide controlled flexibility by allowing the specialized user to add new terms within the vocabulary in order to express finer points of distinction among similar but subtly different objects.[7] It is

[7]http://community.aaslh.org/nomenclature-faqs/

clear that the vocabularies establish only a convention for object names, in order to facilitate data retrieval, and in any case do not substitute for fuller descriptions. Thesauri provide terminological tools for the identification of terms and concepts in various fields of science. For example, the HEREIN thesaurus (2014) provides the aforementioned service in the field of CH, TGN thesaurus does likewise in the field of geographic names, AAT in the field of art and architecture, etc.

Moreover, metadata schemes and ontologies have been designed to describe the object's contextual background, facilitating the retrieval of data and enhancing its value, such as DC, LIDO, and CIDOC Conceptual Reference Model (CIDOC-CRM) [6], all of which are also ISO standards.

The extended use of different classification systems and thesauri among institutions has led to the need for the development of a metadata schema able to map the existing original metadata into a common output schema in order to secure interoperability between the metadata preserved in each memory institution and to support the full range of descriptive information about all forms of CH. Projects such as CARARE [15] have focused on this direction for the documentation of 3D CH objects.

An important factor for structured vocabularies is the issue of multilinguality and the translation of terms. In addition, in many cultures, local words exist for the description of the same object. So the attempt to describe an object with terms understandable to every culture and the adoption of a common international "glossary" meet with a number of difficulties.

The EU-funded program Europeana v3.0[8] is moving toward providing multilingual access to digital CH content and overcoming language barriers. In this context, Europeana prepared a resource and best practices aggregator for realizing multilingual access to CH content in DLs. The newest version of the White Paper [23] summarizes the main state-of-the-art findings in the domain of access to digital CH and focuses on four pillars of multilingual CH information systems: (a) data, (b) access system, (c) user interactions, and (d) user interface (UI). Query translation process, multilingual enrichment of content metadata with semantic resources, and automatic detection of user's language are set into use in order to make sure that users can actually easily detect and retrieve data even in languages that they are not familiar with.

A quite new approach to the issue of communication is "image based" retrieval, where an image is analyzed, its features are automatically extracted, and through an enriched metadata context, the object of the picture becomes recognizable. DigiArt (2015–2018)[9] and ArchAIDE (2016–2019)[10] are characteristic examples of contemporary ongoing projects that will work on the domain of feature extraction, recognition, and automatic classification of 3D objects harvested in DL.

---

[8]http://pro.europeana.eu/blogpost/help-us-tear-down-language-barriers-together#sthash.Vd3Pxw3d.dpuf

[9]http://digiart-project.eu/project/about-us/

[10]https://www.unipi.it/index.php/english-news/item/7156

This new technological development which allows the image-based recognition of 3D objects overcomes the obstacles of interdisciplinarity, multilinguality, and multiculturalism all at once and creates a fertile ground for the actual "democratization of culture" [24], by using what is common to the sense of vision of humans. The perception of the (digital) world will turn from conceptual to multimodal and sensational.

6.3 Digital Library Content: Current Possibilities, Challenges, Risks, and Limitations

The evolution in the field of DLs and the democratization of the digitized knowledge rely actively upon the achievements of some pioneering international projects and the added value each one of them has developed. European Union initiatives for preservation of the European CH have resulted in a substantial number of research projects in the field. Their objectives, tools (vocabularies, metadata standards, semantics, ontologies), as well as the way to link information to its description may vary, yet the core goal remains the same: provide an enhanced user experience on the way to acquisition and individualization of knowledge.

6.3.1 Past and Current Developments

One of the initial EU CH projects was Epoch[11] (2004–2008). Epoch was a large network of European institutions focusing on research in areas including (a) field recording, (b) data organization, (c) reconstruction and visualization, (d) heritage education, and (e) planning for sustainability. The main objective of the project was to facilitate data retrieval and also to develop digital tools in the field of CH. Moreover, EPOCH's main goal was to stimulate the cooperation among researches on CH documentation, to enable information exchange instead of simply storage, and to set up one common information space [25].

Following Epoch, the EU project FOCUS K3D (2008–2010) recognized the necessity of 3D in CH repositories and the need for greater quality and quantity of 3D digitized content. FOCUS K3D was an encouragement for a new approach in techniques and ideas in the field of semantic 3D media. FOCUS K3D was addressed not only to the CH community but to every scientist, developer, and creator from academia or industry who had strong interest in 3D. Research in semantics was the main objective of this project, and the main outcome was a research road map in 3D shape semantics (FOCUS-K3D 2010).

[11] http://epoch-net.org/site/

Simultaneously 3D-COFORM[12] (2008–2012) concentrated its research interest and established a new attitude toward 3D documentation, the holistic approach. The three main directions emphasized in their research were (a) 3D capture/acquisition and processing; (b) integration of 3D digital objects, with metadata and related textual information; and (c) generative modeling and visualization. Deployment of tools, especially leading to assistance in 3D digitization and 3D documentation for the formation of 3D collections, as well as boosting industrial sectors such as eMuseum with the partnership of world-class museums (Victoria Albert Museums as full partner) and creative industry, was another significant factor of 3D-COFORM (3D-COFORM 2013).

The EU CARARE[13] (2010–2013) project was designed to involve and support Europe's digital heritage network in (a) making 3D digital content available to Europeana and (b) aggregating digital content and delivering services and enabling access to 3D and virtual reality (VR). CARARE's contribution was huge in the community as it ingested over two million items (10 % of all digital content), content metadata for 75 separate collections, a workflow for metadata harvesting from providers to Europeana, and the establishment of 3D as a content type in Europeana. CARARE developed map-based search (geographic information) and has enabled information to be captured about the provenance of 3D objects [26].

At present, EU H2020 DigiArt[14] (2015–2018) is looking into providing a new cost-efficient solution for the capture, processing, and display of cultural artifacts. With the expansion of technology such as drones/unmanned aerial vehicles, new techniques have arisen which offer alternative methods of 3D mass digitization and reconstruction. DigiArt objectives are (a) to develop methods for gathering 3D data, (b) provide an open-source 3D scanner, (c) develop software to handle point cloud data and 3D volumetric modeling and (d) methods for semantic meaning, (e) create immersive experiences, and (f) boost the CH and creative industry with 3D content and provide modern and efficient tools. DigiArt's breakthrough is to establish automation by using compliant robots for capture and processing of data [27].

As an overall result of the last decade of investment, DL content has evolved rapidly through these pioneer projects. Their contribution was significant as we have seen improvement in (a) enrichment of content in Europeana, (b) accessing content, (c) 3D models, (d) virtual reality–augumented reality technology, and (e) tools production.

6.3.2 Visualization of 3D Content and the Challenges of Virtual, Augmented, and Mixed Reality

Virtual, augmented, and mixed reality (VR, AR, and MR) have reached a point of evolution where they can offer realistic, interactive, and online 3D objects and 3D

[12]http://3d-coform.eu/

[13]http://carare.eu/eng

[14]http://digiart-project.eu/

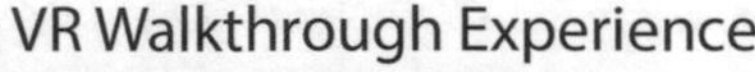

Fig. 6.2 Virtual reality walkthrough for the Church of Panagia Asinou, a UNESCO Monument in Cyprus, using smartphone and VR glasses

worlds on a wide variety of systems. Recent years have witnessed a revolution in VR systems from pioneer companies (Oculus Rift, HTC Vive, PlayStation VR, Samsung VR, Google Cardboard, etc.), where they can provide attractive and immersive experiences for educational, entertainment, and training purposes [28]. Augmented reality (AR) is a mixture of reality and virtual world where the virtual world engages based on computer-generated sensory input [29]. According to Ronald Azuma [30], in an augmented reality, 3D virtual objects are integrated into a real 3D environment. So by using AR technologies, the user is able to watch in real time the real world enhanced with virtual objects (Fig. 6.2). AR supplements reality and enhances user's perception of the real world by providing information which could not be directly accessed in real time in the 3D world. According to the AR system called "Augmenta," the view of the world which is offered to the user is enhanced because "the mind receives consciousness rather than creating it." Worth mentioning is also that besides adding objects to a real environment, AR can equally remove or hide them from the user's sight.

At the moment, this technology is being used in museum installations, tourist attractions, maps, magazines, flyers, etc. There is also impatience for "Magic Leap," which should be available in the coming years. Magic Leap is a truly convincing AR system that is working on a head-mounted virtual retinal display which superimposes 3D computer-generated imagery over real-world objects by projecting a digital light field into the user's eye. It has been characterized as the world's most secretive start-up and, to date, has raised 1.4 billion USD from a list of investors, including Google and Alibaba [31, 32]. These techniques, along with virtual (imaginary simulated world) and mixed reality (reality interacting with virtual world), are expected to dominate the digital world in the future [33]. The ability to integrate the public in understanding, use, and interaction with CH will provide a powerful tool for the preservation of CH assets. A user-friendly environment where the public will become educated and informed about CH requires planning, research, and evaluation before it is launched. A cautious and simple approach is needed, since the specific type of technology could easily be transformed into a nonfunctional and unusable experience. A booming area in manufacturing technology is currently 3D printing. This revolutionary technology is more accessible to laboratories and individuals, having evolved rapidly to result in cost reduction. In the CH field, 3D printing could open a new branch with endless possibilities, considering that there is access to millions of 3D models. Since image-based 3D modeling has become popular enough and easy to use with mobile phones, everyone now has the opportunity and tools to create a high-quality 3D model (Autodesk 123D Catch, VisualSFM, etc.) or the option to download a high-quality model from 3D DLs. One step further is offered by private companies to customers: the option to print their model for them and mail it to their chosen address.

6.3.3 Standards for 3D Web Retrieval and Discovery

As the World Wide Web was growing, the need to extend its boundaries became necessary. In 1994 David Raggett proposed at the first WWW conference to incorporate VR environments in the World Wide Web. Moreover, in 1995, VRLM was the first 3D web format, certified in 1997 by ISO [34]. VRML (Virtual Reality Modelling Language) is a text file format where vertices and edges can be specified, along with UV map texture (This process projects a texture map onto a 3D object. The letters "U" and "V" denote the axes of the 2D texture because "X", "Y" and "Z" are already used to denote the axes of the 3D object in model space). Besides, the progression of VRLM gave X3D (Xtensible 3D) to the community in 2001, along with prototypal features including (a) EXtensible Markup Language (XML) integration that assembled the format to be cross-platform, (b) accessible by smart devices, and (c) rendered in real time. Since then, 3D formats have changed along with the evolution of web browsers that support 3D content. The technical features (shaders, animation, user interactions, networking, security, etc.) have seen tremendous progression. What started in 1994 gave birth to a number of other 3D web formats (WebGL, Java 3D, Unity, etc.) [35]. These formats can be classified according to their characteristics, such as (a) simplicity, (b) compatibility, (c) quality, (d) interactivity, and (e) standardization.[15]

The EU CARARE project stated that even though 3D content is available in Europeana, there is still the need to reinforce its quality, quantity, and variety. It recommended 3D PDF open format as the most suitable for publishing 3D models to Europeana, since the absence of a format that could contain 3D model, images, and text, and, at the same time, be interactive was undeniable. In addition, the main advantages of using 3D PDF were that (a) it is an ISO standard and open format, (b) no plug-in is needed, and (c) it is secure [36].

3D web formats also include those that are not be viewable in a web browser but could be accessed through the Web and reused offline. This category of formats consists of two subcategories: private (due to copyrights) – which includes formats such as Autodesk 3ds Max (.max), Autodesk Maya (.ma), and Cinema 4D (.c4d) – and open format standards – which are accessible by everyone. DLs that are open to the public are the only suitable source for discovering 3D CH high-quality models. In commercial libraries where professionals or amateurs upload their 3D models, the cost for a quality 3D model is high (and the availability is limited). With the

[15]https://en.wikipedia.org/wiki/Web3D

ongoing increase in 3D DLs as analyzed so far, there is a continuing need for efficient retrieval of 3D models of CH assets from DLs. The vital factor in addressing this need is the metadata and the links between them.

6.4 Metadata and Interoperability

Metadata is the key in accessing, identifying, retrieving, and enriching information about a CH digitized asset. Metadata is data about data, and when it comes to a DL, "it" applies for any kind of resource description [37]. Metadata provide information about "how," "when," and "by whom" a particular set of data was collected and how data is formatted.[16] Therefore, the range of the description they provide varies between persons, for example, from the creator of the CH asset to technical information about the digital asset, such as the file format or the scanning techniques used for the digitization of the asset. This variety of descriptive components facilitates the organization of the resources, supports archiving, provides digital identification, enriches the asset's contextual background, and adds value to its original one.

Although the importance of metadata has been widely recognized and taken into account since the introduction of Web 3.0, or "the Semantic Web," their efficient implementation is still problematic due to the vastness of the produced raw data, in combination with the imprecise concepts used in the CH domain (such as the concept of the "monument"). In the networked era, where the new technological affordances are linking pieces of information that enable participatory editing and dissemination, the integration of digital content from libraries, archives, and museums is an ongoing challenge. The rapid growth in digital object repositories and the development of many different metadata schemas have contributed to their complex implementation [37, 38].

Usually, metadata are produced and corrected manually by experts in the subject domain. Creators of the digital asset and/or archivists or repository administrators register all of the descriptive, structural, technical, archival, and legislative information [37, 39, 40]. While human-expert intervention, in this case from the CH sector, benefits metadata quality and authentication [41], the possibility of automatically generated metadata still remains an open research question.

After their creation, metadata need to be converted into a machine readable form in order to store, transmit, and exchange information about their structure, content, or appearance. The most common of these encoding metadata schemas are Hypertext Markup Language (HTML), EXtensible Markup Language (XML), Resource Description Framework (RDF), MAchine-Readable Cataloguing (MARC), and Standard Generalized Markup Language (SGML) [37].

[16]http://www.webopedia.com/TERM/M/metadata.html

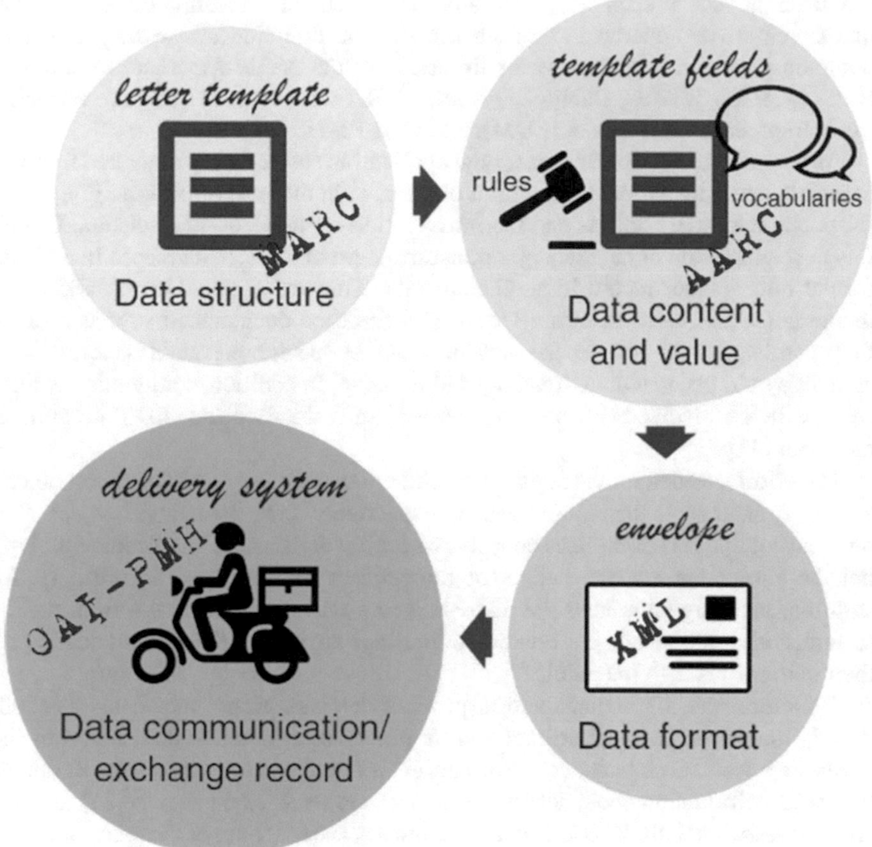

Fig. 6.3 The four different types of metadata schemas

Metadata schemas can be viewed as standardized structures describing the categories of information that should be recorded (Fig. 6.3) [42]. Categories of information is a group of metadata elements that define a purpose [39]. Those elements vary as the user interfaces vary from each other, depending on the user needs, as well as the affiliations that provide the information about heritage assets. This is the reason why there are various common metadata schemas and rules that need to be followed for an e-document description. The plethora of such local and international schemas, although they are being created in order to achieve better content description, has led to several common problems, such as multiple and, as a result, inaccurate definitions of terms and incomplete identification protocols, conventions, and new encoding schemes, leading to the question "why all libraries do not just use a single schema?" [38, 42].

The answer lies in the nature of the domain and the nonobjective definitions and interpretations of the digital objects by the libraries' diverse user groups as well as the different uses of such definitions and the objects' classification systems. Some of the initiatives undertaken through time in the direction of creating a single, common standardized structure for libraries are the Anglo-American Cataloging Rules (AACR), MARC, Dublin Core (DC), VRA Core (Visual Resource Association), Europeana Data Model (EDM), and OAI-PMH.

As user needs change over time, new applications use existing metadata formats to enable new interactions with digital objects, as in the case of the emerging need for documenting 3D objects and the introduction of the CARARE schema. Often, this new adaptation of data requires transformation of a metadata record in a given format into another record in another format. This act is called crosswalking or mapping [39]. If these metadata crosswalks could be documented so that institutions can learn from past experiences and domain-specific metadata issues, digital content would become more trustable and findable. In addition, community awareness will be evolved in creating easier and standardized EDM-compliant metadata [41].

The efforts needed for the digitization and documentation of a 2D cultural object are of a greater scale than those needed, respectively, for a 3D cultural object. Not only have numerous disciplines contributed for 3D digitization and documentation, but the equipment and the budget of the process are increased accordingly. In addition, such digital models are addressed to a wide range of users, from architecture, conservation, and preservation of heritage artifacts to the communication of their cultural value to the public.[17]

Therefore, the 3D documentation process demands richer metadata: detailed description of the physical artifact and its provenance; detailed description of its digital representation; technical information and quality assurance of the methods followed; information about access, licensing, and reuse of the created 3D models and any associated digital content; and moreover, the mapping of those metadata to unified aggregators such as EDM in order to achieve search, discovery, and reuse of the content created. What is more important for the description of a 3D digital object is defining its semantic 3D media, as an endeavor in encoding all the knowledge and the complexity that a shape divulges [17].

6.5 Semantics, Ontologies, and Linked Data

Metadata are strictly related to semantics, since they have been proposed as a mechanism for expressing the "semantics" of information as a means to facilitate information tracing, retrieval, understanding, and use [43]. According to Peirce and his broader view on language and logic, semantics are one of the three core branches of semiotics, the study of signs [44]. Semantics are the "logic proper"; they are the "carriers" of the meaning. But meaning can be considered as a "locally

[17]http://3dicons-project.eu/eng/Guidelines-Case-Studies

constructed" artifact [45], thus making the carrier of meaning fully subjective and multi-interpretable.

Accordingly, a digital cultural object's semantic signature can have multiple representations by the different disciplines and users involved in the CH domain. The necessity for some form of common language in order to share a common space of understanding emerges. Here fit metadata schemas, which have become enormous due to the difficulty in embracing all these different representations and meanings "created" from diverse affiliations among the domain in one single representation of knowledge.

Formal ontology has emerged as a "knowledge representation infrastructure for the provision of shared semantics to metadata, which essentially forms the basis of the vision of the Semantic Web" [46]. Considering the abundance of vocabularies and thesauri in CH and the fact that the domain is dominated by publicly accessible information, the Semantic Web technology could be widely applicable in such a knowledge-rich domain. Transdisciplinarity and multidisciplinarity are also present. The combination of carefully designed metadata following a domain's representative ontology, thesauri, and controlled vocabularies developed by many relevant institutions is a challenging endeavor for "semantic systems," which requires the coincidence of the effort of many scientific, engineering, and management disciplines to become a reality [43], including artificial intelligence, knowledge management in software engineering, database management, philosophy, and library and archival science, just to name a few.

Core ontologies of relationships are fundamental to schema integration, going beyond special terminologies. The main vision is not only to aggregate content with finding aids, as DLs are used to providing their users with, but also to become actively involved in practical knowledge management by integrating digital information into transdisciplinary networks of knowledge [47]. The most popular core ontology for CH is the CIDOC-CRM. CIDOC-CRM is an ISO standard ontology which constitutes a common language for the domain experts and a potentially extensible semantic framework that any memory institution can adopt and extend.

Transdisciplinary networks of knowledge (Fig. 6.4) could be the vestibule of the notion of Linked Data; networks that support access to, as well as use and reuse of, the integrated knowledge embedded in the data and metadata, that is, structured data that can be interlinked and become more useful through semantic queries.[18] The core concept of Linked Data is to turn the World Wide Web into a global multimodal database. Complying with four proposed steps, set by Tim Berners-Lee, initiator of the Linked Data project, developers can query links of data from multiple sources instantly and combine them using Semantic Web standards for data interchange (RDF) and data queries (SPARQL (Simple Protocol and RDF Query Language)).[19,20] The idea of the proposed steps is to (a) use URIs (Uniform

---

[18]https://en.wikipedia.org/wiki/Linked_data

[19]https://www.w3.org/TR/ld-glossary/#linked-data

[20]https://www.w3.org/TR/ld-bp/#CONVERT

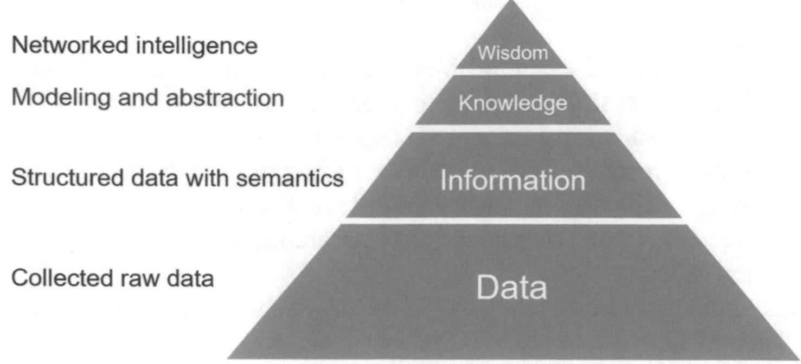

Fig. 6.4 "Knowledge management and modeling" [48] (© 2007 by SAGE Publications, reprinted with permission). *According to signatories to STM Permissions Guidelines (as of 23 August 2016), publisher is a member of STM, and the notification is not required ("automatic" process)* doi:10.1177/0165551506070706

Resource Identifier) in order to name the data records; (b) use HTTP URIs so that data records can be human and user-agent readable; (c) provide useful information by using the open web standards, such as RDF, SPARQL, or Web3D records;[21] and finally (d) include links to other related data records using their URIs when publishing on the Web (see footnote 17).

The Semantic Web and its applicability to the CH domain constitute the prevailing research agenda tendency. However, the current metadata approaches, their relation to semantics, and the reasons of their failure must be considered first. The huge number of metadata elements (fields) constituting a standardized schema has a direct bearing on metadata richness, which in turn directly affects semantics interoperability [38]. Interoperability is not actually a matter of metadata's nature but has its origins in semantics. Interoperability is, by definition, related to sharing and exchanging. Thus, semantic metadata interoperability is the sharing and exchanging of information meaning, and therefore, its goal is to "carry" information through negotiated meanings of the terms and expressions that are considered as standards. However, current metadata schemas, followed by different approaches intended to solve the interoperability issue, are deeply authoritative and hierarchical, and since they have been created by domain experts, they often fail to represent the user's view [38, 49, 50].

One could argue that, given the current schemas and the wide recognition of user involvement in metadata creation, first, DLs should look at which of the existing metadata standards are representing user's needs and expectations, and if so, how they have been devised. Second, further investigation must be focused on the efforts made by various affiliations, such as museums, to semantically enrich their collections with user feedback through social media and Web 2.0 technologies, such as social tagging and folksonomies [50, 51]. The risks here are mainly focused on

[21]http://www.web3d.org/

quality assurance: at which level and with what means the users can create, interfere, and change the CH semantic landscape.

Linked Data, on the other hand, can strengthen reusability and integration of metadata, acting as a large-scale aggregator. Although aggregation and data abstraction into a common format and schema ensure a level of consistency and interoperability, the process can impoverish metadata richness [52]. Thus, research needs to be conducted on techniques and methodologies that allow data to maintain its original abundance and remain enhanced with additional information by the users.

Lastly, it is argued[22] that the Semantic Web technologies, such as RDF and Web Ontology Language (OWL), can improve semantic extension and interoperability by identifying resources and metadata attributes (relations) via URIs and relating them to each other. This enables automated agents to access the Web more intelligently and perform more tasks in support of users.[23] Unfortunately, the efficient implementation of such technologies in metadata practices is still in its infancy.

Concluding, in spite of the existing pluralism in metadata schemas, they fail to address real problems and practical needs in the field. What still remains a challenge for DLs is to adapt their practices to a more user-centered approach. Semantic interoperability in the CH domain must provide access to multiple interpretations of a 3D digital object, beyond the main semantic problems related only to its physical characteristics and its geometry.

6.6 User Needs and Interfaces

User-centered approaches are an ongoing challenge for every institution that targets diverse user groups and, hence, diverse user needs. Deeper understanding of users' needs would create more focused and personalized experiences, revealing users' primary demands. A combination of users' needs and the content they want to access, manipulate, and/or create should form the minimum design requirements for user interfaces. However, most of the current DLs' interface approaches are creating a gap between expectations of users and practices followed by experts in archives and collections [53], when ideally, actual user interface (UI) and user experience (UX) design experts basing their work on user studies and gathering user requirements before creating the final interface should be leading these practices.

Due to the nature of 3D digital documentation, ranging from small objects, such as archaeological coins, to built heritage, such as monumental buildings, quality requirements become even more strict. Hence, it is of high priority for institutions to focus on quality and precision, forgetting the user's view. For instance, most DLs' interfaces apply this notion to their search results, where the user is expected

[22]https://www.w3.org/TR/webont-req

[23]https://en.wikipedia.org/wiki/Semantic_Web

to enter terminologies from thesauri, taxonomies, or classification systems that are not as familiar to them as to a librarian.

At the same time, major applications of the Web era, like Google, focus on attracting more users toward their services with interactions that reflect the reality of the ordinary users' world, where it is common to make typographical errors [38]. The example of Google is worth investigating as far as effective design interface principles are concerned. Simplicity positively affects usability and, by extension, ease of use [54]. Google keeps its interface simple, while its metadata are rich. In addition, keeping the interface simple provokes "addiction" in users, who tend to shift to simpler and more flexible interfaces, as they prefer to focus more on the content [55, 56].

The existing gap further affects the semantic annotations of the described objects. The semantic alignment between an interface and user's expectations denotes the correlation of objects and operations between user and system on a conceptual level [57]. Because of the semantically rich domain of CH, a user can have different or multiple intentions with a simple query. For instance, in a simple keyword search, a sufficient user interface could provide the user with information of what the collection is about, since the content is of user's prior concern. Hence presenting, from the input of the first letters, what the possible results of the search might be is akin to giving the idea of what this collection of objects is about through such simple interactions. Overall, what seems to be an emerging theme is that the search needs to become deeply user centered [19, 51].

However, the case of semantic content-based 3D retrieval has many limitations compared with 2D. This is because there is no canonical 3D representation from the point of view that there are many approaches to describe 3D shape representations, such as surface-, volume- and structural-based representations, which are not all equivalent but are expressed differently and, consequently, have different semantics [58]. How can these representations now be semantically grouped in a functional content-based organization in order to be meaningful to users and possible to reuse? Those are still open research questions affecting the organization and representation of the final user interface.

The importance of understanding the diverse user needs of an application to be developed is reflected in the ways that the interface is built. UX design is valuable in filtering those needs and presenting familiar and intuitive interfaces to the user. For instance, in order to reuse and create new DCH content for educational purposes (Fig. 6.5), the needs and perceptions of the educators and the students must be investigated first. For example, depending on the age of the students and their prior knowledge, the content presented should be different both in appearance and in length [59].

In conclusion, while the content is available through revolutionary, cost-effective technology (e.g., 3D models generated through sets of photographs), the importance should also be focused on the collection and accurate definition of the appropriate metadata. Since metadata provide the context, the statement that "the metadata is the interface" by Arnold Arcolio is fundamental [53]. Rich contextualization of content would create meaningful experiences, which, integrated with

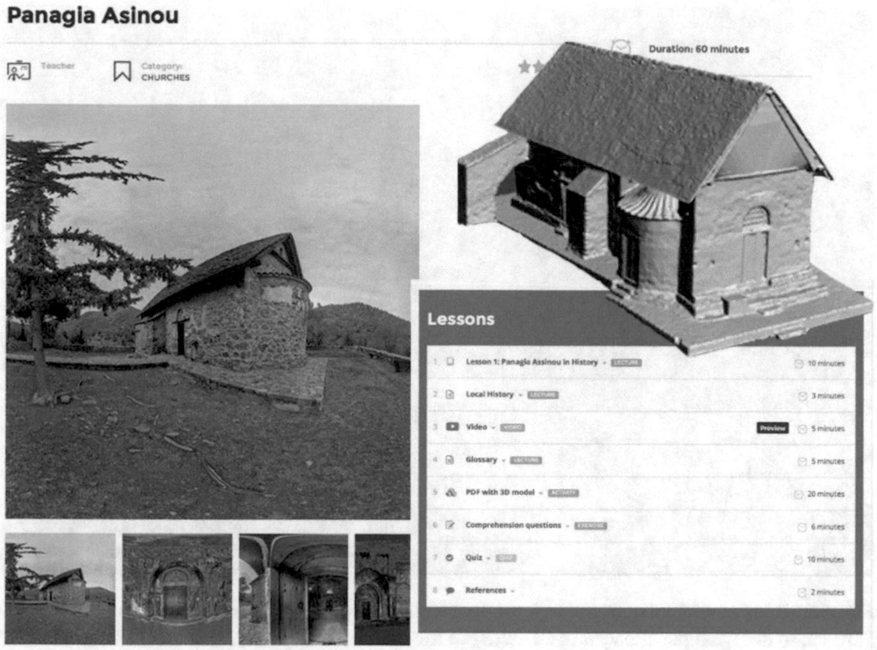

Fig. 6.5 Screenshots of the website of the Panagia Asinou online course. 2D content, 3D sections, and other surveying products were used for educational purposes (Source: http://wp.digitalheritagelab.eu/, © 2016 the Europeana Space project, reprinted with permission)

the emerging, immersive technologies of mixed reality, would change entirely the way users perceive the CH world.

6.7 Reuse, Copyright, and Licensing

Copyright laws are not the same in every country, although—thanks to international treaties and EU legislation—the majority of countries have similar rules on what it is protected by copyrights. There are three interested groups in copyrights of CH data: the author(s), the owner(s), and the user(s) of the work. These parties have different and often divergent interests [60]. In the DL space, some "users" have evolved into "creators" by reusing the CH data and developing what is known as "user-generated content." The balance between authors, owners, users, and creators is a—complicated—responsibility of policy makers, taking into consideration that many sectors depend on reusing CH data (Fig. 6.6).

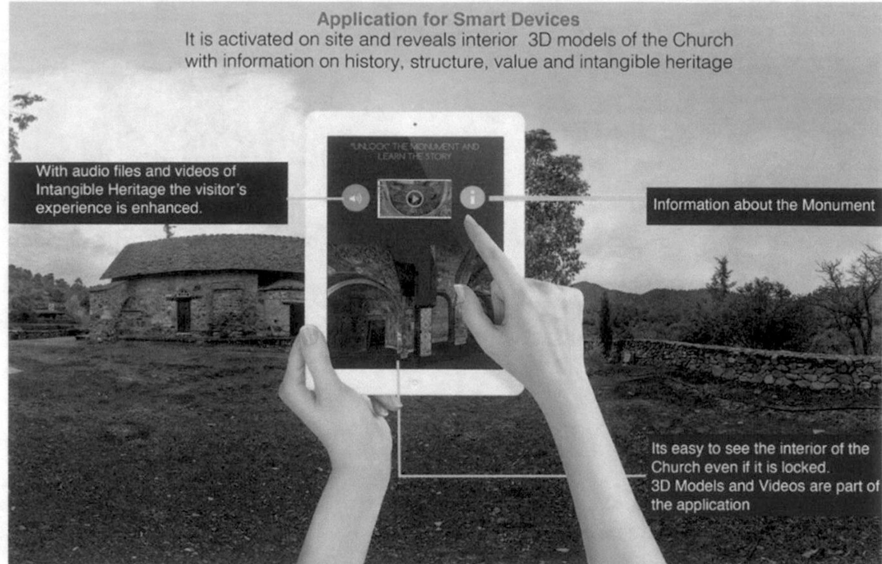

Fig. 6.6 Reusing CH data creates new content for applications on a variety of CH fields, such as tourism. In this example, the visit to a UNESCO Monument in Cyprus (Church of Panagia Asinou) is enhanced with information, and the interior is unlocked with the help of 3D models

6.7.1 The Open Data Agenda

It is obvious that copyrights are a challenging issue in the field of digital CH. More specifically, DLs are facing the same difficulties as museums, heritage organizations, and institutions when it comes to providing text, sound, and video digital collections openly to the world. Open access, as well as use and reuse of that content, is frequently prevented [60]. As digital technology facilitates new practices and techniques, we constantly observe a race between copyright laws around the world and the movement to share information. Copyright restrictions have trouble to keep pace since—in the new digital era—infringing copyright laws is easier than ever before [61]. At the same time, the Digital Agenda for Europe promotes the creation, production, and distribution of digital content and services for a creative, vibrant single market [62]. Reuse of digital CH content is taking place now in Europe, characterized by the Europeana projects (Europeana Creative, E-Space, Europeana Food and Drink, etc.), where experimental business models, innovative approaches, and services are developed using Europe's biggest—in digital items—library [63].

The reuse of digital CH content leads to copyright issues, which all the abovementioned projects are dealing with. Open access reuse of digital CH data is important in many ways because it (1) enhances creative entrepreneurship, opening new jobs and moving the economy in vital sectors such as galleries, libraries, museums, television, film, crafts, arts, music, etc.; (2) promotes research, especially in humanities and social sciences, encouraging information accessibility and dissemination, in ways that were not available before [64]; and (3) adds great value for education, where everyone can learn, copy, and share knowledge in and out of the classroom [60]. In 2011 Vice President for the Digital Agenda of the European Commission, Neelie Kroes, publicly appealed to cultural institutions to open up control of their data, asking them to exploit this wonderful opportunity to show how cultural material can contribute to innovation and how it can become a driver of new developments [65]. A number of NGOs in open data and CH have been pushing strongly policy makers (including the EU) toward this idea, with "Open Knowledge" and "OpenGLAM" being the most characteristic examples. Open Knowledge coordinates over 20 domain-specific working groups, focusing on activities around open knowledge and acting as a bridge between organizations and initiatives. OpenGLAM is a global network of people that work to open up cultural data and content, helping cultural institutions to take their first steps to this direction [60].

The terms "open data" and "open content" are used often in digital heritage but occasionally mixed or confused as concepts. Intellectual property (IP) laws distinguish "data" and "content." Both can be freely used and reused by anyone with the requirement to attribute (at most), but (1) "data" is mainly used for metadata about cultural works/artifacts, and (2) "content" is the result of the creative work/artifact (including images, videos, audio and text files, etc.). Legal documents that allow people to reuse digital heritage content under conditions are licenses, with public licenses most common for open content. Another frequent misinterpretation is between "public licenses" and "open licenses," with the latter allowing not only the free use, reuse, and redistribution but also the commercial and derivative work of the digital heritage data. There are two widely used types of open licenses: "Creative Commons licenses" (CC) have been developed for use with data and creative work, and "Open Data Commons License" has been designed for use with databases [60].

6.7.2 Creative Commons Licenses

Keeping in mind how essential the ability to use and reuse is for digital CH databases, there are two types of licenses that strongly promote the idea of sharing: The Open Data Commons Public Domain Dedication and License (PDDL) and the Creative Commons Zero Universal Public Domain Dedication (CC0). Both licenses allow reusing digital heritage data and content, for any purpose without restrictions. Similar to these licenses (PDDL and CC0) is the copyleft license, which allows open distribution, modification, and reuse but restricts any produced work to be distributed under the same terms [60]. Another common type of license is the "attribution license," which places a single condition on users of the licensed material: to attribute any public use of the data in a manner specified in the license. Attribution licenses are the Open Data Commons Attribution License (ODC-BY), the Creative Commons Attribution License (CC-BY), the Open Database License (ODbL), and the Creative Commons Attribution-ShareAlike License (CC-BY-SA). The abovementioned license types are preferable for digital heritage data and

Legal Code
Human Readable
Machine Readable
Creative Commons copyright licenses incorporate a unique and innovative "three-layer" design. Each license begins as a traditional legal tool, the Legal Code layer.
The Commons Deed (also known as the "human readable" version of the license) is a handy reference for licensors and licensees, summarizing and expressing some of the most important terms and conditions.
In order to make it easy for the Web to know when a work is available under a Creative Commons license, there is a "machine readable" version of the license written into a format that software systems, search engines, and other kinds of technology can understand.

Fig. 6.7 The three layers of Creative Commons licenses (Source: http://creativecommons.org/licenses/?lang=en, by Creative Commons is licensed under CC-BY 3.0/Partially edited from original)

content, because they allow creative reusing of CH data. The Creative Commons license (CC) is the best-known example in the attempt to open publicly the available digitized content. Their smart design of three layers ensures that the spectrum of rights is not just a legal text but a framework that creators and the Web itself can understand (Fig. 6.7).

Open data is not only the aim for CH digital data but also a process through which cultural institutions, stakeholders, and users are learning and evolving. In order the information to be truly accessible, it needs to be embedded in the users' daily network life [66]. However, to successfully involve users' daily web surfing with digital CH, the data should follow standards and procedures for aggregation, archiving, and sharing, which are important variables for preservation.

6.8 Aggregation, Standards, and Archiving

Due to various threats to CH assets, the need to digitize them massively has arisen rapidly in modern society, leading to a huge amount of data. Through the participation of the crowd by capturing multimedia representations of these CH assets, these data became even more chaotic, leading to a need to find ways of managing, archiving and preserving these big data to open repositories and "encyclopedias" such as Wikipedia. However, this digital content needs to be archived, along with its semantic information, by following specific metadata schemas such Dublin Core[24] can be facilitated, resulting in more descriptive asset information.

6.8.1 The Cloud

The present era is conditioned by the impact of technology in daily life. Cloud computing (aka "the Cloud") constitutes a part of this technological evolution. It is a type of computing relying on shared resources on both hardware (servers, processing power, etc.) and software (databases, virtual environment for applications, etc.). A study conducted by analysts at Gartner [67] showed the Cloud as the most crucial technology for use by both public and private sectors [68], pointing out that the constant evolution of cloud computing contributed significantly to events in the information technology field, as giant companies such as Google, Microsoft, etc. exploit this new technology in a beneficial way for their customers who seek robust platforms at a reasonable cost.

Like most information systems, the Cloud has advantages as well as disadvantages in practice. A few things that promote its broader use to both people and organizations are (1) access to theoretically unlimited storage capability and scalability, (2) comprehensive backup and recovery capabilities, (3) mobility enabling access from anywhere with a web connection, and (4) cost efficiency depending on the provided services. On the other hand, there are some weak points that must be overcome, which include (1) the security of the Cloud, mainly in the management of sensitive data; (2) compatibility issues among data formats; (3) limited control to the back-end infrastructure; and (4) in the case of migration from one system to another, issues caused due to vendor lock-in.

According to [69] and [70], the cloud environment is differentiated into three hosting deployment models based on the given control and access: (1) the private cloud, where the infrastructure is being exploited by a single company or organization and can be managed either by third parties or internally; (2) the public cloud, where its infrastructure is controlled by a company that offer its resources to the public under billing plans on a monthly or yearly basis; and (3) the hybrid cloud, which constitutes a combination of public cloud providers (such as Microsoft's Azure, Amazon's Web services, etc.) with the infrastructure of private cloud, where the provided environment differentiates allowing companies to store "sensitive" data on the private cloud while exploiting the hardware resources of the public cloud.

In conclusion, DLs should plan to use the services offered by the Cloud to their benefit. Since the maintenance of DLs can be really expensive, cloud systems can become a cost-efficient solution, because the nature of their services will allow DLs to pay only for those resources that they actually use. DLs can be constantly online

[24]http://network.icom.museum/cidoc/working-groups/lido/what-is-lido/

by exploiting the cloud infrastructure, which provides a backup scenario in case of hardware failure. Within the scope of cloud services, administrators have the ability to develop their own web-based applications in order to enrich user experience as well as the tools for their virtual interaction with the digital content.

6.8.2 Existing Online Repositories

DLs are organized gateways to digital resources as they are specially oriented toward users, to whom they provide information and access to the digital cultural assets hosted in various repositories. Repositories offer the availability of collections stored often adhering to open access principles, making information retrieval (using harvesting methods) by DLs an easy task to perform. However, data storage is a crucial question in information technology, requiring definition of how important our data (including the metadata) is, whether or not we should encrypt it partially or in whole, and where we want to store it. There is now a wide variety of storage methods (online repositories, servers, cloud systems) from which organizations or individuals can choose. More specifically, as far as the CH field is concerned, there are a huge number of assets that need to be digitized in order to be stored and eventually preserved.

Nowadays, advanced online repositories support a plethora of file formats, but their main disadvantage is that users have to pay a considerable amount of money for storing their precious assets. Accordingly, a lot of institutions have looked to creating their own repositories using an open-source package such as DSpace,[25] where not only can they create a place to store the digital content they may have, along with their metadata in relational databases, but they can also configure the access that corresponding users will have to these assets. In the wider context of CH assets, cultural landscapes represent combined works of humankind and nature,[26] which are strongly connected to the intangible values that people wanted to depict. As they constitute structures of great importance to the cultural community, their exported data through digital means (e.g., laser scanning techniques, photogrammetry, 3D models) needs to be stored online. To that end, a nonprofit organization was established named CyArk,[27] which is dedicated in storing the cultural data that comes from the use of laser scanning technologies and digital modeling techniques in archeological or historic landscapes to their online repository called 3D Heritage Archive, providing the opportunity to be open and freely accessible to all.

Furthermore, since these repositories are open and accessible to everyone, they exploit the most common, widespread, mostly open (not governed by copyrights or licenses) file formats in order to facilitate their use and reuse (see Sect. 6.7.2).

[25]http://www.dspace.org/

[26]http://whc.unesco.org/en/culturallandscape/

[27]http://www.cyark.org/

Depending on the use, there are different file formats for images, for videos, for audio, for 3D representations, and for texts. The most important ones are .gif, .png, .jpeg2000, .mkv, .vrml, .x3d, .pdf, .html, .fla, .aac, etc.

Unfortunately, many cultural assets are not available to the public since they are in private collections or remain stored for years in warehouses of OpenGLAM because of lack of space or even copyright restrictions. A query in Europeana for available digitized objects (in July 2016) indicated that images amount to 54.37 % of them, while the remaining 45.63 % are separated into texts (41.82 %), videos (2.08 %), audio (1.68 %), and 3D objects (0.05 %).

6.9 Digital Preservation

Digital assets stored in various repositories should be preserved in an innovative way by following certain strategies relative to their importance to cultural community. Taking into consideration [71, 72], we may define *digital preservation* in terms of CH as the procedure of maintaining a cultural asset unchanged, accessible, and exploitable through time.

These digital portrayals are characterized by a different complexity than their true-size representations, as they may contain various multimedia formats which are bilateral with users, like a video, an application, etc. [73]. Due to the fact that we live in a rapidly evolving technological era, these digital assets are more and more vulnerable to becoming technologically obsolete, which is why methods for their conservation need to be applied in conjunction with their life cycle (see Sect. 6.10) as well as with their semantic elements, metadata, and the relationships between components [74, 75]. Furthermore, the issue of obsolescence is not the only challenge faced during the preservation of digital content, as its complex and dynamic nature constitutes another crucial factor in its management and funding, affecting both its authenticity and integrity, since these digital representations often cannot be interpreted in a proper manner.[28]

A specific strategy aiming at long-term preservation has been established by a nonprofit membership cooperative, Online Computer Library Center (OCLC), which is dedicated to furthering access to information, as well as to reducing its costs. Additionally, OCLC's preservation strategy focuses on (1) the loss estimation of digital content among popular formats, (2) assessment of preservation actions that should be administered, (3) semantic relations as well as the metadata required for every digital asset, and (4) finally, the access criteria that should be given to users [76]. There are other strategies of digital preservation that should be mentioned, such as (1) the migration of data to new technologically advanced systems, along with their conversion to other formats so as to be broadly accessible; (2) the encapsulation of digital collections by enriching their semantic relations in order to

[28]https://en.wikipedia.org/wiki/Digital_preservation

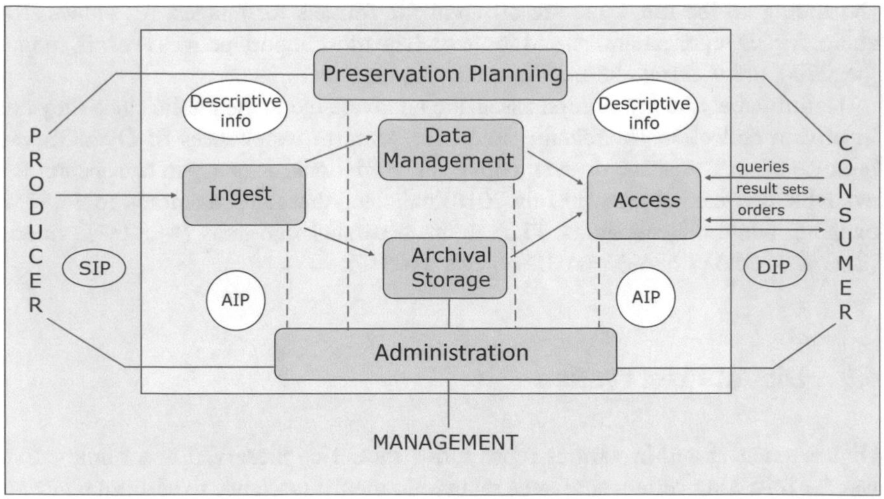

Fig. 6.8 OAIS functional entities (Source: https://commons.wikimedia.org/w/index.php?curid=9882077/ by Poppen is licensed under Public Domain/Revised Artwork of the original)

be interpreted properly; and (3) the emulation of an obsolete preservation environment by recreating the environmental conditions that existed during digital content creation [77].

For many years, it was believed that archiving digital cultural assets in hardware storage such as CDs, DVDs, hard disk drives (HDDs), and online repositories was the best route toward their long-term preservation. Hardware deterioration (cracks on disk surface, mistreatment, damage caused by falls, etc.) over time and the constant evolution of repositories in supporting newer file formats were not fully taken into account. But these factors do lead to a loss of our digital assets. In order to avoid this loss, some of the strategies described above need to be implemented. Furthermore, the sustainability and upgrade of technological equipment to be fully operational and compatible with newer digital formats in the future, together with their software development, need to be considered in order to emulate legacy and digital preservation environments [78]. The migration to newer virtual environments, implementing appropriate management policies, as well as proper preservation strategies, may lead to a potentially successful integrated preservation system that overcomes the obsolescence and interoperability issues affecting digital cultural assets [74].

A powerful reference model called "Open Archival Information System (OAIS)" (Fig. 6.8) has been developed by CCSDS (The Consultative Committee for Space Data Systems)[29] for the purpose of preserving digital content by using the encapsulation strategy. OAIS administers a theoretical perspective of transferring digital content between entities, limiting the possibility of components' loss [79]. In

[29]http://public.ccsds.org/default.aspx

addition to its theoretical perspective, OAIS is the key feature for architectural comparison of various data models, as well as being widely used for comparing preservation approaches in order to allow optimal selection.[30]

Digital preservation is an essential part of a digital asset's life cycle, as we need to ensure its future reuse by representing in a proper way the semantic relations as well as the required metadata, along with its digital content.

6.10 Crowdsourcing and User Contribution

Crowdsourcing is undoubtedly the most efficient new business organization and development process in the information society, since nowadays, a tremendous number of users connect to others by sharing information and being willing to help them in various ways. These users provide immense quantities of data (aka big data), which in most times are governed by complexity that makes the task of their management a difficult case. Crowdsourcing is a compound of the words *crowd* and *outsource*, which has been delineated as the practice of engaging a public group in order for certain goals or objectives to be achieved. The first attempt to define crowdsourcing was made by [80]. In addition to the aforementioned term, four main pedestals were given, which are distinguished in (1) the crowd, (2) the crowdsourcer, (3) the task, and (4) the platform that uses the crowdsourcing [81].

However, considering the millions of people willing to contribute in CH affairs, the target group should be first designated, as well as their motivation, since the work must be of high quality [82]. In an effort to label the possible crowdsourcers, research on their profiles [83] was necessary in order to find out who carries the most work in a crowdsourced CH project. This study showed that a specific group of people who are really interested in the domain of CH carry out the majority of work, and it is possible that they may work at home. Moreover, crowdsourcing can raise the importance of CH objects by captivating the interest of visitors in an interactive way, where they may contribute to the annotation and enrichment of these objects [84].

Crowdsourcing is a crucial part in the life cycle (Fig. 6.9) of a digitally constructed CH asset through all its steps. From an asset's creation to its distribution, crowdsourcing represents an important factor, since both individuals and organizations have the opportunity to digitally construct a cultural asset and share it directly with the general public through social media (Facebook, Twitter, etc.), their websites, and blogs. These assets need to be preserved in repositories either locally or in cloud systems by following certain strategies in order not to become technologically obsolete. Crowdsourcing may contribute further to their use and reuse after proper consideration of any copyright restrictions (see Sect. 6.7.1) that may occur.

[30]https://en.wikipedia.org/wiki/Open_Archival_Information_System

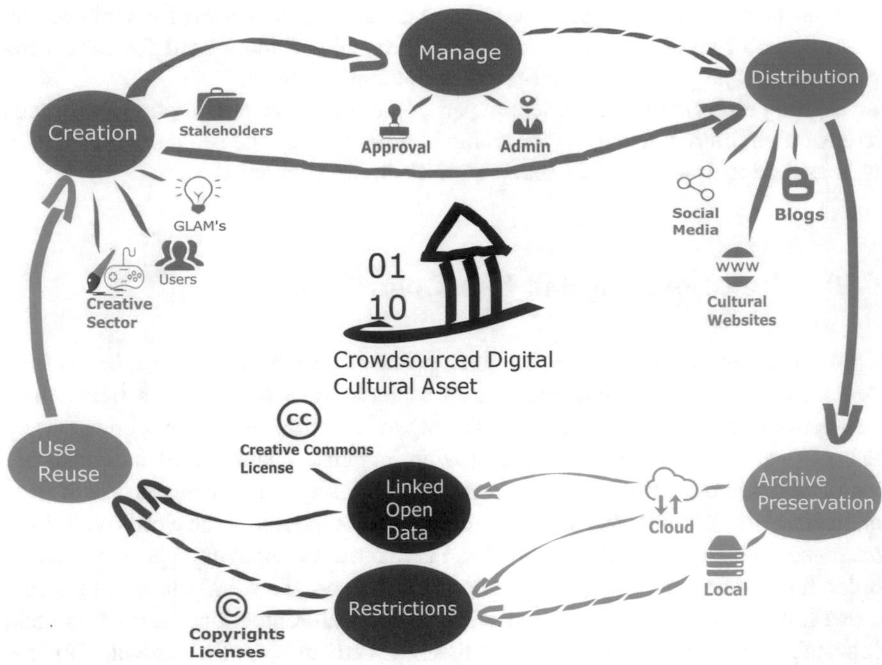

Fig. 6.9 Life cycle of a digital CH asset

Due to the free nature of crowdsourcing, a lot of questions may arise, as the number of users is—theoretically—infinite. These issues constitute a challenge in establishing the credibility of a digital crowdsourced cultural asset, since its quality is not ensured, for example, because a lot of users may create numerous digital creations of the same asset in low resolution. Moreover, as far as geolocation is concerned, users may have the ability to mark a CH landscape in a different location, resulting in confusion regarding its actual location. Another crucial issue is the liability of linked metadata, as editing by inexperienced users may cause digital CH assets not to be semantically enriched properly, leading to historic distortion. Over recent years, the number of crowdsourced photographs that are uploaded on a daily basis to media hosting platforms has been increased rapidly due to Instagram's[31] impact on people, as they started to discover a passion for digitizing and storing online the aspects of their daily routine. A typical example of this distributed material constitutes the cross-posting of filtered images from Instagram to Flickr,[32] as shown by a study [85] conducted in May 2015 by Flickr's researchers in a joint effort with a professor from the academia, which found that the application of filters to images for their enhancement makes them more popular among these online communities. Although this idea appears strong, it has a major

[31]https://www.instagram.com/?hl=en

[32]https://www.flickr.com/

disadvantage when the accuracy of shared information is concerned, as someone may take a photo of a monument, edit it by distorting its colors, and upload it using a caption irrelevant to its historic importance, succeeding in this way in creating an erroneous impression of that asset. Moreover, toward the same direction, another social platform called Pinterest[33] is under way as interested parties may search for media uploaded by others and "point it" to their account, making in such way a personal photo album of variable-quality photos of CH assets.

6.11 The Future

There has been significant technical progress in capturing, creating, archiving, preserving, and visualizing 3D digital items, and there are many demonstrations of 3D DLs, linking the technology areas and serving 3D DLs' data, using augmented, virtual, or mixed reality. The rapid growth of ICT (Information and Communication Technology) infrastructures and World Wide Web applications is having a huge impact on the policy makers of the "memory institutions," a term introduced by Lorcan Dempsey in an attempt to include libraries, archives, and museums [86]. Policy makers of the twenty-first century seem to have started dealing with the idea of an emerging convergence of these institutions due to their apparent similarities, especially in their online activities [87]. In all openness, emerging Web technologies, such as Linked Open Data, cloud computing, and crowdsourcing, are leading CH institutions to share and make available their content to anyone, everywhere, with the vision of an integrated, cross-cultural heritage web [87] that connects the history of nations and their CH assets to a unified presented knowledge of the past.

Sustainable DLs could support this vision, but there are many things to consider to achieve successful economic, social, and environmental sustainability which should support equitable access to all users, conform to specific design and usability guidelines, and support the personal, institutional, and sociocultural aspect of the users as well as the policy makers, according to the respective countries, regions, and affiliations [88]. According to the Digital Library Reference Model (DRLM) [89], three categories of actors are identified and are fundamental to the operation of a DLs service: end users (content creators and content consumers), managers (designers and DL system administrators), and DL software developers. The interaction of the aforementioned three major categories would provide DLs with the view of the activities needed to achieve efficient creation, management, use, and reuse of information.

DLs have been transforming from memory institutions [90] to become more user-centered and interactive systems, as they do not only carry memories of the

[33]https://www.pinterest.com/

past into the present but also convey cultural messages and create the "present in the future" through user filters and vast distribution channels. This transforms the core of DLs into a dynamic self-growing organism. However, repositories are platform dependent, as software vendors develop their own platforms, making the migration from one system to another a difficult technical accomplishment. Considering the future prosperity of digital repositories, they need to evolve over time toward an open repository environment while maintaining current preservation strategies as well as implementing new one. To this end, multilingual metadata and commonly agreed open standards need to be considered. Open standards can also help with copyright and intellectual property issues, promoting the use and reuse of the digitized or born-digital content. Copyright restrictions are a fundamental barrier for the future deployment of 3D DLs, since they inhibit sharing intentions on the part of creators and prevent the reuse opportunities. Interoperable and multilingual metadata, commonly agreed open standards and protocols, as well as preservation and sustainability of the content of 3D DLs will, on the one hand, facilitate communication among DLs and their extroversion and, on the other hand, promote the dissemination of the collected knowledge and equal access to it, in support of education, life-long learning, self-awareness, human values, and cultures beyond geographic and social boundaries.

In the sector of built CH, the creation of a repository where all the information regarding the building will be included (HBIM) is in need of the construction of a 3D DL as an online collection of digital materials and elements concerning the building. Even in this case, an open issue remains: the construction of a library of architectural elements, parametrically controlled, where every change of a parameter causes a change in the shape of the element [91]. There are three points for such open 3D HBIM DLs that should be taken into account: (1) these elements should not be oversimplified in shape, (2) they should be able to be transformed appropriately in order for their shape to be aligned to the irregularities of the shape of the actual historical object, and (3) the ways such a library can function interoperably between different BIM platforms.

In the future of 3D HBIM DLs, we expect further development of the accuracy of geometric visualization of the actual object on the one hand and, on the other, of the attachment (preferably automatically) of the descriptive thematic information to the 3D model in order for it to become "articulated" [16] and essentially useful for the professionals in the field of monument conservation. As far as semantic content-based 3D retrieval and its limitations are concerned, there have been suggestions for 3D retrieval systems based on similarity space (similarity type, addressed feature, and invariance properties) [58], as well as a combination of 3D media, with what already exists in the field of text, image, audio, and video retrieval [17]. HBIMs will be a standard part of the holistic digital documentation of documents, providing reverse engineering information to professionals and stakeholders and thus helping them to understand the past and design the future.

The future of DLs includes the full accessibility to all kinds of information, as an actual step toward the democratization of digitalized knowledge. At the same time, the reform of information based on the reconstruction of related pieces of information through personalized filters (user interests, needs, characteristics, general personality) will lead to new opportunities concerning the remodeling of knowledge as we now know it. Knowledge should exceed the level of "common" or "collective" and should harmonize with the level of each individual user, hence becoming extremely variable and multisided. Users could eventually be able to become the "info configurator" of their own information universe, taking at the same time full responsibility for both their own personal growth and societal integration and social development. The core meaning of democratization of knowledge will be actually implemented. In this direction, management of 3D DL data (metadata, meta-metadata, semantics, storage, formats, preservations, and copyrights) will play the most important role.

In the near future, having the opportunity to virtually travel in space, between different 3D CH sites, and in time, between different periods, users will be able to form their own virtual environment with the help of smart software serving custom information. New technology will help us process the huge amounts of CH digital data, identifying interpretations and extracting new answers to the questions about our rich CH history. We are expecting powerful experiences where different 3D digital artifacts will be collected in the same virtual space, creating an evolution of André Malraux's "Imaginary Museum" [92], using automatic contextualization and semantic similarities of different CH DLs according to users' preferences. In this direction, holistic documentation is essential, since it will give the necessary added value to the digital CH assets.

References

1. M. Agosti, Digital libraries, in *Information Retrieval* (2011), p. 307
2. L. Candela, G. Athanasopoulos, D. Castelli, K. El Raheb, P. Innocenti, Y. Ioannidis, A. Katifori, A.Nika, G.Vullo, S. Ross, *Digital Library Manifesto* (2011)
3. M. Scadle, E. Greifeneder, Defining a digital library. Libr. Hi Tech. **25**, 169–173 (2007)
4. L.C. Borgman, What are digital libraries?: competing visions. Inf. Process. Manage. **35**, 227–243 (1999)
5. P. Linde, Introduction to digital libraries – Memex of the future, in *Conference on Electronic Publishing* (Blekinge Institute of Technology, 2006), pp. 15–32
6. K. Sotirova, J. Peneva, S. Ivanov, R. Doneva, M. Dobreva, in *Digitization of Cultural Heritage – Standards, Institutions, Initiatives* (1972)
7. IFLA/UNESCO, IFLA/UNESCO Manifesto for Digital Libraries (2010)
8. D.J. Crane, creating services for the digital library. Online Inf. 96. Proc. Twent. Int. Online Inf. Meet. London, 3–5 Dec 1996 (1996), pp. 397–401
9. V. Bachi, A. Fresa, C. Pierotti, C. Prandoni, The Digitization Age: Mass Culture is Quality Culture. Challenges for cultural heritage and society. http://resources.riches-project.eu/digitization-age-mass-culture-is-quality-culture/ (2016)

10. EPOCH/IST, Excellence in Processing Open Cultural Heritage D.1.12 – Publishable Final Activity Report (2008)
11. H. Denard, London Charter (2009)
12. FOCUS-K3D, Public Annual Report 2010 Summary of Activities (2010)
13. 3D ICONS, Guidelines and Case Studies (2014)
14. 3D-COFORM, D.1.5 – (3D COFORM) Project Final Report (2013)
15. Europeana/CARARE Project, D1.8 – Final Report (2013)
16. D. Oreni, From 3D content models to HBIM for conservation and management of built heritage. Lectures Notes Computer Science (including Subser. Lect. Notes Artif. Intell. Lect. Notes Bioinformatics). 7974 LNCS, pp. 344–357 (2013)
17. C.E. Catalano, M. Mortara, M. Spagnuolo, B. Falcidieno, Semantics and 3D media: current issues and perspectives. Comput. Graph. **35**, 869–877 (2011)
18. EUROPEANA, We transform the world with culture (2015)
19. T. Hill, D. Haskiya, A. Isaac, H. Manguinhas, V. Charles, *Europeana Search Strategy* (2016)
20. N.L. Choh, National Libraries Global (NLG) : A Proposal (2014)
21. UNESCO/PERSIST Content Task Force, The UNESCO/PERSIST Guidelines for the selection of digital heritage for long- term preservation (2016)
22. P. Ronzino, K. Fernie, C. Papatheodorou, A. Rc, H. Wright, J. Richards, D3.2: Report on project standards Authors (2013)
23. Europeana, White Paper on Best Practices for Multilingual Access to Digital Libraries (2016)
24. R. Anttonen, K.H. Victoria Ateca-Amestoy, T. Johansson, A.K. Annukka Jyrämä, K.K.-B. Kaari-Kiitsak Prikk, M. Luonila, J.-M. Kõlar, K.P. Beatriz Plaza, T. Pusa, M.S. Anna Ranczakowska-Ljutjuk, A.Ä. Ira Stiller, Managing Art Projects with Societal Impact, Helsinki (2016)
25. D. Arnold, Excellence in Processing Open Cultural Heritage D.1.12 – Publishable Final Activity Report (2008)
26. K. Fernie, M.D.R. Partners, D1.8 – Final Report (2013)
27. DigiArt: Fact Sheet, http://digiart-project.eu/digiartpublications/fact-sheet/
28. Papagiannakis et al., Mobile AR/VR rendering and animation in gamified heritage sites (2016)
29. M. Graham, M. Zook, A. Boulton, Augmented reality in urban places: contested content and the duplicity of code. Trans. Inst. Br. Geogr. **38**, 464–479 (2013)
30. R. Azuma, A survey of augmented reality. Presence Teleoperators Virtual Environ. **6**, 355–385 (1997)
31. I. Lapowsky, Magic Leap CEO Teases "Golden Tickets" for Its Augmented-Reality Device, http://www.wired.com/2015/02/magic-leap-reddit/
32. E. Huet, Magic Leap CEO_Augmented Reality Could Replace Smartphones – Forbes, http://www.forbes.com/sites/ellenhuet/2015/02/24/magic-leap-ceo-augmented-reality-could-replace-smartphones/?utm_campaign=AR&utm_content=12737607&utm_medium=social&utm_source=twitter#3be5b7ce55da
33. V. McKalin, Virtual Reality vs. Augmented Reality, http://www.augment.com/blog/virtual-reality-vs-augmented-reality/
34. D. Raggett, Platform Independent, https://www.w3.org/People/Raggett/vrml/vrml.html
35. Web3D Consortium, What is X3D?|Web3D Consortium, http://www.web3d.org/realtime-3d/x3d/what-x3d
36. M.E. Masci, A.De Santis, K. Fernie, D. Pletinckx, 3D in the CARARE project: providing Europeana with 3D content for the archaeological and architectural heritage: The Pompeii case study, in *Proceedings of 18th International Conference on Virtual System Multimedia, VSMM 2012 Virtual System Information Society* (2012), pp. 227–234
37. K. Ivanova, M. Dobreva, P. Stanchev, G. Totkov, Access to Digital Cultural Heritage: Innovative Applications of Automated Metadata Generation. Plovdiv University Publishing House, Paisii Hilendarski (2012)

38. G. Alemu, B. Stevens, P. Ross, G. Alemu, B. Stevens, P. Ross, Towards a conceptual framework for user-driven semantic metadata interoperability in digital libraries: a social constructivist approach. New Libr. World. **113**, 38–54 (2012)
39. M. Foulonneau, J. Riley, *Metadata for Digital Resources: Implementation* (Systems Design and Interoperability, Elsevier, New York, 2014)
40. B. Glushko, Metadata and Metadata Standards. Lecture presentation at Berkley School of Information, USA 2006 (2008)
41. Europeana Metadata Quality Task Force, Report and Recommendations from the Task Force on Metadata Quality, p. 54 (2015)
42. M.W. Elings, G. Waibel, Metadata for all: descriptive standards and metadata sharing across libraries, archives and museums (2007)
43. M.-A. Sicilia, Metadata, semantics, and ontology: providing meaning to information resources. Int. J. Metadata Semant. Ontol. **1**, 83–86 (2006)
44. C.S. Peirce, Collected Papers of CS Peirce, ed. by C. Hartshorne, P. Weiss, A. Burks, 8 vols (1931)
45. T. Brasethvik, A semantic modeling approach to metadata. Internet Res. **8**, 377–386 (1998)
46. M.-A. Sicilia, M.D. Lytras, *Metadata and Semantics* (Springer Science & Business Media, London, 2008)
47. M. Doerr, S. Stead, Harmonized models for the Digital World CIDOC CRM, FRBROO, CRMDig and Europeana EDM, in *Tutorial 15th International Conference on Theory and Practice of Digital Libraries*, TPDL, Berlin (2011)
48. J.E. Rowley, The wisdom hierarchy: representations of the DIKW hierarchy. J. Inf. Sci. **33**(2), 163–180 (2007)
49. K.H. Veltman, Syntactic and semantic interoperability: new approaches to knowledge and the semantic web. New Rev. Inf. Netw. **7**, 159–183 (2001)
50. J. Trant, B. Wyman, Investigating social tagging and folksonomy in art museums with steve museum, in *Collaborative Web Tagging Workshop at WWW*, Edinburgh (2006)
51. G. Schreiber, A. Amin, L. Aroyo, M. van Assem, V. de Boer, L. Hardman, M. Hildebrand, B. Omelayenko, J. van Osenbruggen, A. Tordai, J. Wielemaker, B. Wielinga, Semantic annotation and search of cultural-heritage collections: the multimediaN E-culture demonstrator. Web Semant. **6**, 243–249 (2008)
52. V. De Boer, J. Wielemaker, J. Van Gent, M. Hildebrand, A. Isaac, J. Van Ossenbruggen, G. Schreiber, Supporting linked data production for cultural heritage institutes: The Amsterdam museum case study. Lecture Notes Computer Science (including Subser. Lect. Notes Artif. Intell. Lect. Notes Bioinformatics). 7295 LNCS (2012), pp. 733–747
53. J. Schaffner, The Metadata is the Interface: Better Description for Better Discovery of Archives and Special Collections. Synthesized from User Studies (2009)
54. J. Lee, D. Lee, J. Moon, M.-C. Park, Factors affecting the perceived usability of the mobile web portal services: comparing simplicity with consistency. Inf. Technol. Manage. **14**, 43–57 (2013)
55. J. Nielsen, *Designing web usability: the practice of simplicity New Riders Publishing* (Indianapolis, Indiana, 2000)
56. L. Tischler, The Beauty of Simplicity, http://tc.eserver.org/37581.html (2005)
57. H. Obendorf, *Minimalism, Simplicity and Rules of Design* (Springer, London, 2009), pp. 97–121
58. B. Bustos, D.W. Fellner, S. Havemann, D.A. Keim, D. Saupe, T. Schreck, Foundations of 3D Digital Libraries: Current Approaches and Urgent Research Challenges. Bibliothek der Universität Konstanz (2007)
59. M. Ioannides, P. Chatzigrigoriou, V. Bokolas, V. Nikolakopoulou, V. Athanasiou, Educational use of 3D models and photogrammetry content: the Europeana space project for Cypriot UNESCO monuments, in *Proceedings of 4th International Conference on Remote Sensing and Geoinformation of Environment*, ed. by K. Themistocleous, D.G. Hadjimitsis, S. Michaelides, G. Papadavid, SPIE Digital Library, Cyprus, April (2016)

60. S. Whatley, Europeana Space: Final Report on the Content Space and Legal Aspects (2016)
61. C. Morrison, J. Secker, Copyright literacy in the UK: a survey of librarians and other cultural heritage sector professionals. Libr. Inf. Res. **39**, 75–97 (2015)
62. EU, ICT PSP Work Programme 2012. 78 (2012)
63. D.R. Tobergte, S. Curtis, Europeana creative: where cultural heritage and creative industries meet to re-use Europe's digital memories. J. Chem. Inf. Model. **53**, 1689–1699 (2013)
64. M. Terras, Opening access to collections: the making and using of open digitised cultural content. Online Inf. Rev. **39**, 733–752 (2015)
65. N. Kroes, Foreword: culture and open data: how can museums get the best from their digital assets? Uncommon Cult. **2**, 5–7 (2011)
66. G.G. Waibel, R. Erway, Think global, act local – library, archive and museum collaboration. Museum **24**, 323–335 (2009)
67. Gartner Inc., Gartner Identifies the Top 10 Strategic Technologies for 2011, http://www.gartner.com/it/page.jsp?id=1454221 (2011)
68. Q. Zhang, L. Cheng, R. Boutaba, Cloud computing: state-of-the-art and research challenges. J. Internet Serv. Appl. **1**, 7–18 (2010)
69. Venkatesh, Cloud computing security issues and challenges. Int. J. Comput. Sci. Inf. Technol. Res. **2**, 122–128 (2014)
70. S. Stead, Cloud Computing and Cultural Heritage IT (2012)
71. M. Hedstrom, 1998-Digital preservation: a time bomb for digital libraries. Comput. Hum. **31**, 189–202 (1997)
72. N. Beagrie, N. Semple, P. Williams, R. Wright, Digital Preservation Policies. Part 1: Final Report. Strategies 60 (2008)
73. D. Lavoie, Thirteen Ways of Looking at… Digital Preservation. D-Lib Mag. 10 (2004)
74. R. Moore, Towards a theory of digital preservation. Int. J. Digit. Curation. **3**, 63–75 (2008)
75. G. Chowdhury, From digital libraries to digital preservation research: the importance of users and context. J. Doc. **66**, 207–223 (2010)
76. K. Sotirova, J. Peneva, S. Ivanov, R. Doneva, M. Dobreva, Digitization of Cultural Heritage–Standards, Institutions, Initiatives (2015)
77. M. Ferreira, A. Baptista, J. Ramalho, An intelligent decision support system for digital preservation. Int. J. Digit. Libr. **6**, 295–304 (2007)
78. K. Lee, O. Slattery, R. Lu, X. Tang, V. Mccrary, The state of the art and practice in digital preservation. J. Res. Natl. Inst. Stand. Technol. **107**, 93–106 (2002)
79. J. Spence, Preserving the cultural heritage. Aslib Proc. **58**, 513–524 (2006)
80. J. Howe, The rise of crowdsourcing. Wired Mag. **14**, 1–5 (2006)
81. N. Colasanti, R. Frondizi, M. Memeguzzo, The "Crowd" revolution in the public sector: from crowdsourcing to crowdstorming. IFKAD Proceedings (2016)
82. R. Spindler, An evaluation of crowdsourcing and participatory archives projects for archival description and transcription. Arizona State Univ. Libr. 26 (2014)
83. R. Holley, Crowdsourcing: how and why should libraries do it? D-Lib Mag. 16 (2010)
84. D. McKinley, Crowdsourcing cultural heritage 101, http://nonprofitcrowd.org/crowdsourcing-cultural-heritage-101/ (2015)
85. S. Bakhshi, D.A. Shamma, L. Kennedy, E. Gilbert, Why we filter photos and how it impacts engagement. Assoc. Adv. Artif. Intell. (2015)
86. L. Dempsey, Scientific, Industrial, and Cultural Heritage. A Shared Approach: A Research Framework for Digital Libraries, Museums and Archives, http://www.ariadne.ac.uk/issue22/dempsey (2000)
87. J. Trant, Emerging convergence? Thoughts on museums, archives, libraries, and professional training. Museum Manage. Curatorsh. **24**, 369–387 (2009)
88. G. Chowdhury, Sustainability of digital libraries: a conceptual model and a research framework. Int. J. Digit. Libr. **14**, 181–195 (2014)
89. The Digital Library Reference Model: The Digital Library Reference Model (2010)

90. RICHES, Digital Libraries, Collections, Exhibitions and Users. Exploring the status of digital heritage mediated by memory institutions (2015)
91. S. Boeykens, Using 3D Design Software, BIM and Game Engines for Architectural Historical Reconstruction, in *Proceedings of 14th International Conference on Computer Aided Architecture Design Futures*, pp. 493–509 (2011)
92. A. Malraux, *Museum Without Walls* (Secker & Warburg, London, 1967)

Chapter 7
Enriching and Publishing Cultural Heritage as Linked Open Data

Nikolaos Simou, Alexandros Chortaras, Giorgos Stamou, and Stefanos Kollias

Abstract In the last decade, a lot of effort has been put by the cultural community around the world into digitization and aggregation activities. The main outcome of these was the development of portals like Europeana, DPLA, DigitalNZ, and National Library of Australia, which are collecting and providing access to the public digitized cultural assets from Europe, America, New Zealand, and Australia, respectively. Their main objective, however, is not only to bring the public closer to culture but also to efficiently represent information about cultural objects that will make them useful to various target groups like teachers, students, and developers by also permitting their creative reuse. The best practice for fulfilling this requirement is the publication of such information according to the Linked Open Data (LOD) principles. In this chapter, we present the tools developed and the methodology adopted through the participation of our group in aggregation activities for enriching and publishing cultural heritage as Linked Open Data.

Keywords Linked Open Data • Semantic alignment • Enrichment • Metadata interoperability • Europeana • Aggregation

7.1 Introduction

Massive digitization and aggregation activities all over Europe and the world have shaped the forefront of digital evolution in the cultural heritage domain during the past few years. Following the increasing support at the European level, as well as the emerging involvement of major IT companies, there has been a variety of converging actions toward multimodal and multimedia cultural content generation from all possible sources (i.e., galleries, libraries, archives, museums, audiovisual archives, etc.). The creation and evolution of Europeana,[1] as a unique point of

[1]http://www.europeana.eu

N. Simou (✉) • A. Chortaras • G. Stamou • S. Kollias
School of Electrical and Computer Engineering, National Technical University of Athens, Iroon Polytechneiou 9, Zografou 15780, Greece
e-mail: nsimou@image.ntua.gr; achort@cs.ntua.gr; gstam@cs.ntua.gr; stefanos@cs.ntua.gr

M. Ioannides et al. (eds.), *Mixed Reality and Gamification for Cultural Heritage*, DOI 10.1007/978-3-319-49607-8_7

access to European cultural heritage, has been one of the major achievements of these efforts. At the moment, more than 50 million objects, expressing the European cultural richness, are accessible through the Europeana portal. Similar initiatives have led to the creation of the Digital Public Library of America[2] (DPLA), which brings together the riches of America's libraries, archives, and museums and makes them freely available to the world. The main aim of DPLA is to expand this crucial realm of openly available materials and to make those riches more easily discovered and more widely usable and used. DigitalNZ[3] and National Library of Australia[4] share the same objectives with Europeana and DPLA, but they use content collected from New Zealand and Australia, respectively.

The creation of these cultural portals, together with the rapid growth of Internet resources and digital collections, has been accompanied by a proliferation of metadata schemas, each of which has been designed according to the requirements of particular user communities, intended users, types of materials, subject domains, project needs, etc. Several national bodies and cultural institutions that deal with cataloguing and documentation of cultural heritage have developed different forms and standards.

Metadata standards, in general, are requirements that are intended to establish a common understanding of the meaning or semantics of the data to ensure correct and proper use and interpretation of the data by its owners and users. To achieve this common understanding, a number of characteristics or attributes of the data have to be defined, also known as metadata. Many institutions have been working toward the development of standards to make documentation uniform in order to systematically document, keep, and consult objects and archive records, not only for the physical preservation of the cultural heritage asset but also for the preservation of its related information for future reference [1, 2].

These institutions have defined guidelines and indications that help in gathering information about an asset, such as adopting thesauruses and controlled vocabularies for the standardization of the terms. Some of these data standards have been defined within a national framework, such as the ICCD (Central Institute for Catalogue and Documentation) schema (Italy) and the MIDAS (Moving Image Database for Access and Re-use of European Film Collections) standard (England); others aim at guaranteeing data interoperability, such as LIDO (Lightweight Information Describing Objects) and the EuScreen schema, which are CIDOC-CRM (CIDOC Conceptual Reference Model) [3] and EBUCore [4, 5] compliant, respectively.

The most prominent metadata schema at the moment is the Europeana Data Model (EDM) [6, 7]. EDM is aimed at being an integration medium for collecting, connecting, and enriching the descriptions provided by Europeana content providers. It is a major improvement on the Europeana Semantic Elements (ESE), the basic data model that Europeana began its life with. Each of the different heritage sectors represented in Europeana uses different data standards, and ESE reduced these to the lowest common denominator. EDM reverses this reductive approach and is an attempt to transcend the

[2]https://dp.la/

[3]http://www.digitalnz.org/

[4]https://www.nla.gov.au/

respective information perspectives of the sectors that are represented in Europeana—the museums, archives, audiovisual Europeana Data Model Primer collections, and libraries. EDM is not built on any particular community standard but rather adopts an open, cross-domain Semantic Web-based framework that can accommodate the range and richness of particular community standards such as LIDO for museums, EAD (Encoded Archival Description) for archives, or METS (Metadata Encoding and Transmission Standard) for digital libraries.

One of the main advantages of EDM compared with other cultural metadata standards and also the main reason Europeana made the shift from ESE to it is its native Resource Description Framework (RDF) and Linked Open Data (LOD) support. Linked Open Data is the best practice for easily sharing and reusing web sources, which is the main objective of the aforementioned cultural portals that have emerged in the last decade. In this chapter, we present the workflows and respective tools that can be used in a typical aggregation scenario for the ingestion and manipulation of cultural metadata as well as the methodology that can be adopted for their publication as Linked Data.

The rest of the chapter is organized as follows: Section 7.2 presents the necessary background for the reader in order to fully understand the Linked Open Data principles as well as the tools and methods presented in this chapter for enriching cultural sources. Section 7.3 presents the overall workflow employed, while Sect. 7.4 describes the MINT platform and its main functionalities that have been used for establishing semantic interoperability. Section 7.5 describes the techniques used for enriching cultural metadata and also presents the application of these techniques for enriching metadata of the Europeana Fashion project. Finally, the established results are presented, together with the more expressive retrieval capabilities that can be offered by taking advantage of the publication of metadata as Linked Data.

7.2 Background

7.2.1 RDF and Linked Open Data

During the last few years, the Web has evolved from a global information space of linked documents to one where both documents and data are linked. This evolution has resulted in a set of best practices for publishing and connecting structured data on the Web, known as Linked Data. In few words, Linked Data is simply about establishing typed relations between web data from a variety of sources. These may be as diverse as databases maintained by two organizations in different geographical locations or simply heterogeneous systems within one organization that, historically, have not easily interoperated at the data level. Technically, Linked Data refers to data published on the Web in such a way that it is machine readable, its meaning is explicitly defined, it is linked to other external datasets, and it can in turn be linked to from external datasets [8].

The main difference between the hypertext Web and Linked Data is that the former is based on Hypertext Markup Language (HTML) documents connected by untyped hyperlinks, while Linked Data relies on documents containing data in Resource Description Framework (RDF) format [9]. However, rather than simply connecting these documents, Linked Data uses RDF to make typed statements that link arbitrary things in the world.

As it is implied by its name, RDF is a standard for describing resources, and a resource can be considered as anything we can identify. The following examples present the way things work with RDF, taking into account the cultural heritage domain, the fact that the main thing usually described is a cultural object, as well as the Europeana Data Model.

The resource, CHOExample (CHO stands for cultural heritage object), is shown as a rectangle and is identified by a Uniform Resource Identifier (URI), in this case "http://.../CHOexample." On top of the URI and within the same rectangle, the type of this resource is shown—that is, *edm:ProvidedCHO*, a class used in EDM for characterizing cultural resources. It is also a URI, but as URIs are rather long and cumbersome, the diagram shows it in XML qname form. The part before the ":" is called a namespace prefix and represents a namespace. The part after the ":" is called a local name and represents a name in that namespace. Resources also have properties. Figure 7.1 shows only one property, that is, the title of the resource. A property is represented by an arc, labeled with the name of the property. Strictly, however, properties are also identified by a URI. Each property has a value. In this case, the value is a literal, that is, a string of characters (Mona Lisa), but the value of a property can be another resource, as shown in Fig. 7.2.

In detail, what is depicted in Fig. 7.2 is the relationship between a resource that is of type *edm:ProvidedCHO* and a resource that is of type *ore:Aggregation*, which is mandatory for all the ProvidedCHOs in EDM. The former is described by properties such as *dc:title* and *dc:description* (not shown in this example for simplicity) that actually describe the cultural heritage object. The *ore:Aggregation* resource is described by properties that provide information about the aggregation process itself such as the owner of the CHO (*edm:provider*, *edm:dataProvider*), the rights (*edm:rights*) that are applied to it, and the links that can be used from someone for either viewing the CHO and its metadata at the provider's site (*edm:isShownAt*) or viewing directly the digitized version of the CHO (*edm:isShownBy*). By having this

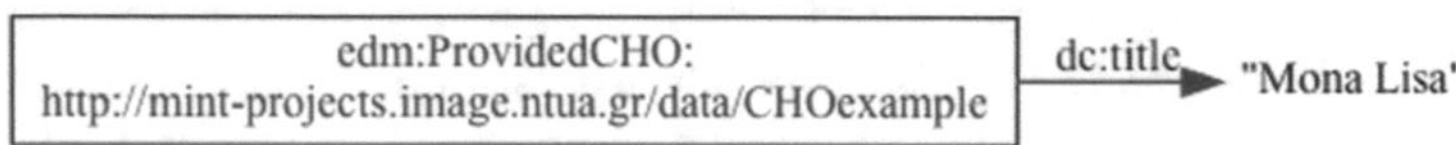

Fig. 7.1 A graphical representation of an RDF triple—literal value

Fig. 7.2 A graphical representation of an RDF triple—resource value

relationship as mandatory, Europeana verifies the connection of the CHO with the aggregation information.

The examples described above are actually RDF statements. Each statement asserts a fact about a resource. A statement has three parts:

- The subject is the resource from which the arc leaves.
- The predicate is the property that labels the arc.
- The object is the resource or literal pointed to by the arc.

A statement is sometimes called a triple, because of its three parts. The RDF statements are saved on a special type of database, called triplestore, supporting the SPARQL protocol (SPARQL Protocol and RDF Query Language). SPARQL is a W3C (World Wide Web Consortium) recommendation [10], and it is the semantic query language for retrieving and manipulating RDF statements.

Using RDF, the Web of Data may more accurately be described as a Web of Things in the world, described by data on the Web. Berners-Lee [11] outlined a set of "rules" for publishing data on the Web in a way that all published data becomes part of a single global data space:

1. Use URIs as names for things.
2. Use HTTP URIs so that people can look up those names.
3. When someone looks up a URI, provide useful information using the standards (RDF, SPARQL).
4. Include links to other URIs so that people can discover more things.

These have become known as the "Linked Data principles" and provide a basic recipe for publishing and connecting data using the infrastructure of the Web while adhering to its architecture and standards.

7.2.2 Semantic Enrichment

Semantic enrichment is a very broad term used to describe the process of adding additional statements to those already existing so that machines can understand some aspects of the data and gain knowledge about the relations that exist among the several data items. Traditional semantic enrichment can take the form of tagging, annotating, categorizing, or classifying the data items [12]. Thus, a metadata scheme, apart from the standard free-text fields (such as title, description, creator, etc.), contains also additional, specialized fields for the description of certain aspects of the data items with controlled vocabulary values (e.g., subject, keyword, category, etc.) and, if appropriately populated, can provide an increased level of semantic characterization of the dataset.

In the context of the Semantic Web and the Linked Open Data technologies, semantic enrichment takes up a different dimension. It is not sufficient anymore to devise or agree to a closed list of words and use it as a vocabulary in order to semantically characterize a data collection, since this limits the possibilities that the local content can be understood and reused by other machines and used for establishing relationships with other similar data sources. In contrast, it is desirable to use established, machine-understandable vocabularies to describe the data. Typically, such vocabularies form part of the LOD cloud, and their use transforms a local dataset to a dataset understandable in the same way by any other machine of the Web. In this case, the metadata values are not anymore simple keywords but URI resources of the respective vocabulary scheme.

The use of URI resources for metadata descriptions permits also the use of richer knowledge representation and organization systems. The URI resources that describe a certain domain and establish the domain vocabulary can be structured as taxonomies, thesauruses, or even ontologies. A taxonomy is a hierarchically structured vocabulary, and a thesaurus can contain also simple types of relations between the resources (such as similar, related, etc., resource), while an ontology is a formal description of a domain that permits the definition of complex relationships between resources through the provision of axioms and hence the inference of new knowledge. In the Semantic Web, the formal way to define a thesaurus is using the Simple Knowledge Organization System (SKOS) [13], while an ontology can be defined using Web Ontology Language (OWL) [14].

The major difficulty in performing semantic enrichment lies in the way to do it. Manual tagging can be performed by domain experts and has very high precision, but it cannot be applied to large volumes of already existing content. The alternative is the use of automatic semantic enrichment, in which the generation of the metadata values is performed automatically by a software system. Such systems traditionally rely on natural language processing (NLP), word disambiguation, information retrieval, machine learning, and named-entity extraction techniques [15–17]. They are scalable, but depending on the domain and the form and quality of the data, they can have a relatively low level of accuracy. The compromise is the use of semiautomatic semantic enrichment, in which the software systems generate some enrichments and then the domain experts review them in order to validate or reject them.

7.3 Overall Architecture

The overall workflow consists of three main steps, the metadata ingestion, their transformation to a common reference schema, and finally their publication as Linked Data (see Fig. 7.3).

Cultural portals such as Europeana, DPLA, and others are built from cultural content provided by various organizations and smaller providers. This fact implies different content and metadata management systems and, in turn, different types of metadata, which creates the need for semantic interoperability. In order to achieve semantic interoperability with external web applications, first the ingestion of provider's metadata is required. The main requirement for this step is the support of different delivery protocols such as HTTP upload, FTP, or OAI-PMH (Open Archives Initiative Protocol for Metadata Harvesting) and also the support of different formats in which metadata can be delivered such as CSV, XML, and JSON. Furthermore, this process needs to be agnostic to the metadata standard used

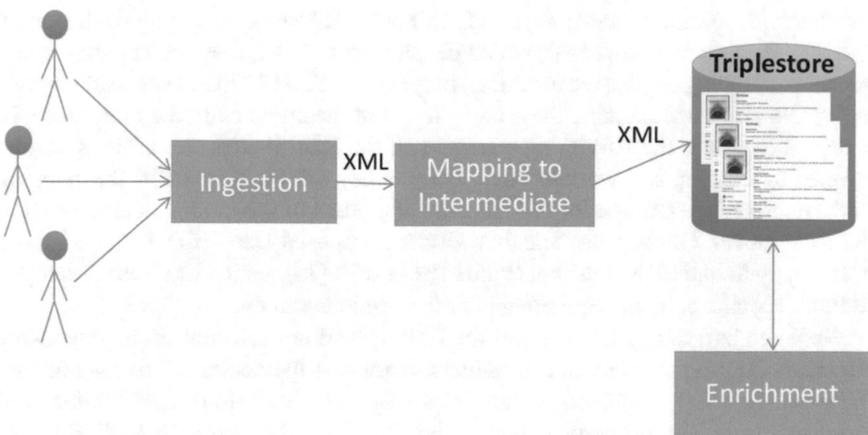

Fig. 7.3 Overall workflow

by the various content providers, since each one of them may deliver well-structured metadata of an established metadata standard or proprietary metadata used by their in-house management system. During this step, all the metadata are collected and are homogenized to XML. The reasons why this is done are the following:

- XML is a well-established representation for metadata.
- XSLT, which is a language for transforming XML documents into other XML documents, can be employed for easily transforming the metadata to the common reference schema (see the next step of the workflow).
- RDF offers a serialization in XML, meaning that all the RDF statements described in the previous section can be represented in XML.

The next step is the selection of a harvesting schema and the creation of semantic alignments (or semantic mapping) of all the properties providers use in their original metadata to properties and classes of this schema. This schema needs to have well-defined semantics—using established standards such as Dublin Core—while it also needs to be expressive enough for adequately describing the cultural objects. Additionally, in order to fulfill the Linked Open Data requirements, this schema needs to provide an RDF serialization for the creation of RDF triples.

In the case of Europeana, EDM plays the role of both the aggregation schema and the RDF data model that can be used for the Linked Open Data publication. This, however, is not always the case; sometimes, a different intermediate schema and RDF model are employed, although this increases the overall complexity. The main reason this often happens is the familiarity of the content providers with a specific intermediate schema and their lack of RDF knowledge. In particular, aggregation of large amount of metadata requires the involvement of the content providers in the actual process, because they are the ones who know the in-house metadata schemas best, and they are the only capable persons for mapping them to an intermediate schema. Hence, specific cultural content communities happen to be familiar with specific schemas such as LIDO or CARARE (Connecting Archaeology and Architecture in Europeana), which despite the fact that they are expressive and capable of holding expressive metadata, they are not Linked Open Data ready. In this chapter, we will not examine these cases to avoid the complexity they introduce. In short, cases where the harvesting schema and the RDF model are different can be covered by the proposed workflow simply by adding one more step after the mapping to the intermediate schema for the semantic alignment of the intermediate schema to the RDF model. Our approach deals with the Europeana Data Model [6] and, more precisely, with the EDM-Fashion Profile (EDM-FP) [18], which has been developed to fulfill specific content requirements of the fashion domain.

Once the harvesting schema and the RDF model are selected, RDF statements are created during the semantic alignment process of metadata. Let us assume that the example CHO discussed earlier originally had the "Mona Lisa" value in a provider's in-house property called "label." During the mapping to EDM, this property is aligned to the *dc:title* property of the ProvidedCHO, resulting in the triple depicted in Fig. 7.1. A good selection of the URIs is really important at this step for the publication according to the Linked Data principles. The interested reader is referred to [19] and [20], which provide guidelines and strategies for selecting and maintaining cool URIs for the Semantic Web. Finally, the resulting triples are transferred to the triplestore, from where they are accessed using SPARQL endpoint for enrichment and consumption in general.

7.4 Semantic Interoperability Using MINT

In this section, we present the MINT services that are used for the metadata aggregation and transformation. We mainly focus on MINT's aggregation workflow—which has been successfully adopted by many Europeana feeder projects such as AthenaPlus,[5] EuropeanaFashion,[6] CARARE,[7] EUScreen [21], and other—and its mapping editor, which facilitates the mapping of providers' data to any XML schema.

7.4.1 The MINT Platform

MINT[8] is an open source, Web-based platform for the ingestion, mapping, and transformation of metadata records. Semantic interoperability is achieved through the use of well-defined metadata models and the alignment of the providers'

[5]http://www.athenaplus.eu/

[6]http://www.europeanafashion.eu/

[7]http://www.carare.eu/

[8]http://mint-wordpress.image.ntua.gr/mint-end-user-documentation/

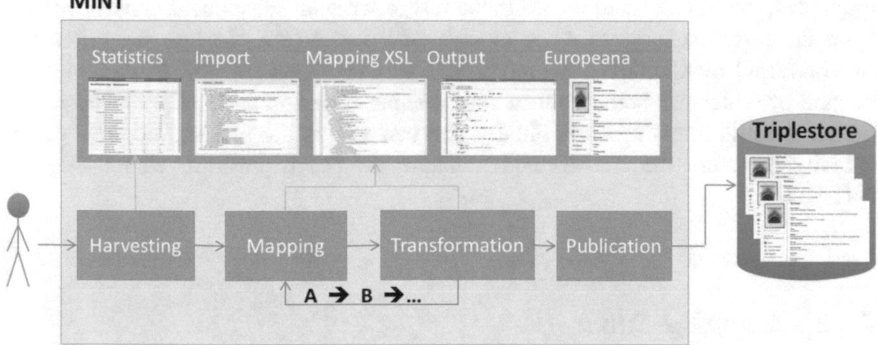

Fig. 7.4 The MINT workflow

metadata to them, thus conforming to their requirements. The metadata ingestion workflow, as illustrated in Fig. 7.4, consists of four main procedures:

- The harvesting of provider's metadata
- The mapping or semantic alignment to the intermediate schema
- The transformation of the input metadata, resulting in a set of metadata in the intermediate schema format
- The publication of the metadata as Linked Open Data through their transfer to a triplestore

More specifically, the platform offers a user and organization management system that allows the deployment and operation of different aggregation schemes with corresponding user roles and access rights. Registered users can start by uploading their metadata records in XML or CSV serialization, using the HTTP, FTP, and OAI-PMH protocols. Users can also directly upload and validate records in a range of supported metadata standards (XSD). XML records are stored and indexed for statistics, previews, access from the mapping tool, and subsequent services. Handling of metadata records includes indexing, retrieval, update, and transformation of XML files and records. XML processors are used for validation and transformation tasks as well as for the visualization of XML and XSLT.

The next step is the mapping procedure, for which MINT uses a visual mapping editor for the XSL language. Mapping is performed through drag-and-drop and input operations, which are translated to the corresponding code. The editor visualizes the input and target XSDs, providing access to and navigation of the structure and data of the input schema, and the structure, documentation, and restrictions of the target one. Mappings can be applied to ingested records, edited, downloaded, and shared as templates.

During the third step, users can transform their selected collections using complete and validated mappings in order to publish them in available target schemas for the required aggregation and remediation steps. Preview interfaces present the steps of the aggregation such as the current input XML record, the XSLT code of mappings, the transformed record in the target schema, subsequent transformations from the target schema to other models of interest (e.g., Europeana's metadata schema), and available HTML renderings of each XML record. In this way, the content provider has better control over his/her metadata and the produced results during the alignment process. Finally, the last step is the publication process that actually transfers the transformed metadata to the triplestore, where they are enriched.

7.4.2 Mapping Editor

Metadata mapping is the crucial step of the ingestion procedure. It formalizes the notion of a metadata crosswalk, hiding the technical details and permitting semantic equivalences to emerge as the centerpiece. It involves a user-friendly graphical environment (Fig. 7.5 shows an example mapping opened in the editor) where interoperability is achieved by guiding users in the creation of mappings between input and target elements. User imports are not required to include the respective schema declaration, while the records can be uploaded as XML or CSV files. User's mapping actions are expressed through XSLT stylesheets, that is, a well-formed XML document conforming to the namespaces in XML recommendation. XSLT stylesheets are stored and can be applied to any user data, exported and published as a well-defined, machine-understandable crosswalk, and shared with other users to act as template for their mapping needs.

The structure that corresponds to a user's specific import is visualized in the mapping interface as an interactive tree that appears on the left-hand side of the editor. The tree represents the snapshot of the XML schema that is used as input for

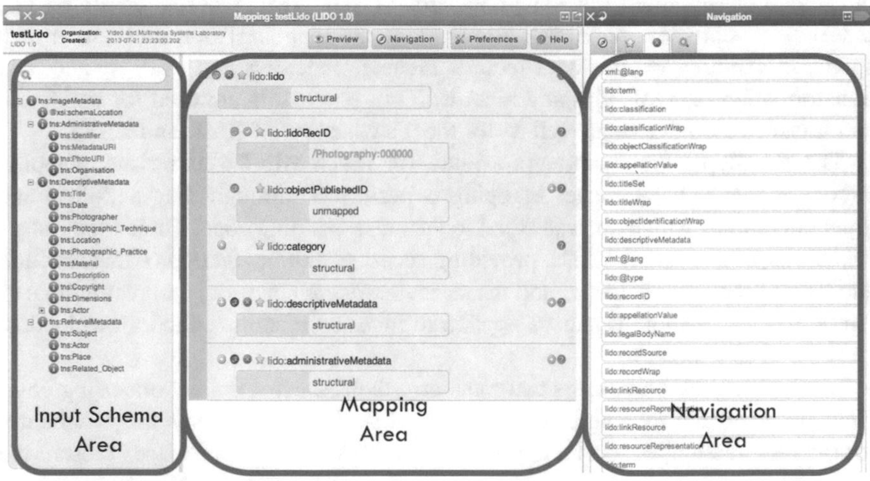

Fig. 7.5 The MINT mapping editor (screenshot of MINT)

the mapping process. The user is able to navigate and access element statistics for the specific import, while the set of elements that have to be mapped can be limited to those that are actually populated. The aim is to accelerate the actual work, especially for the nonexpert user, and to help overcome expected inconsistencies between schema declaration and actual usage.

On the right-hand side, buttons correspond to high-level elements of the target schema and are used to access their corresponding subelements. These are visualized on the middle part of the screen as a tree structure of embedded boxes, representing the internal structure of the complex element. The user is able to interact with this structure by clicking to collapse and expand every embedded box that represents an element, along with all relevant information (attributes, annotations) defined in the XML schema document. To perform an actual (one-to-one) mapping between the input and the target schema, a user has to simply drag a source element from the left and drop it on the respective target in the middle.

The user interface of the mapping editor is schema aware regarding the target data model and enables or restricts certain operations accordingly, based on constraints for elements in the target XSD. For example, when an element can be repeated, then an appropriate button appears to indicate and implement its duplication. Several advanced mapping features of the language are accessible to the user through actions on the interface, including:

- *String manipulation functions for input elements*: During the mapping process, the original values can be modified using a variety of string processing functions.
- *m-1 mappings, with the option between concatenation and element repetition*
- *Constant or controlled value assignment*
- *Conditional mappings that allow the user to set different mappings according to the values used in the metadata and the composition of conditions using AND and OR operators*
- *Value mappings editor (for input and target element value lists)*

7.5 The Europeana Fashion Use Case

Fashion is an important part of the European cultural heritage. It permeates different spheres of daily life, economy, society, and culture. It is not only a consumer good but also a form of art, creativity, and craftsmanship that should be preserved and known by a broader audience. Fashion is showing increasing interdisciplinary links with other fields of knowledge such as arts, culture, and sociology, and not only communication, mass production, and consumption. Today, fashion is acknowledged as an important cultural system with a consolidated historical dimension.

Since the beginning of the twentieth century, some of the most important cultural institutions and museums of applied arts in Europe have begun collecting and preserving garments, accessories, catalogues, fashion magazines, and other documents and materials related to fashion. This has resulted in a growing number of impressive and unique collections. Especially since the 1980s, these collections have increased considerably also thanks to many donations by private institutions and famous designers.

The Internet has become the principal source of information for the fashion world and industry through a wide range of websites, portals, blogs, social networks, etc. The virtual dimension has become a fundamental territory for the creation, diffusion, consumption, and study of fashion, requiring a global recognition. The difficulty of collecting and studying the enormous amount of knowledge produced within the Web has become an urgency of the contemporary study of fashion. However, there is an evident lack of structured, easy searchable, and reliable contents. At present, searching these digital materials is difficult and is likely to become even more complicated as digital content on fashion continues to grow in a scattered way.

To tackle the abovementioned issues, in 2012 a project called Europeana Fashion has been started. Europeana Fashion is an initiative whose aim is to bring together and engage fashion institutions (galleries, libraries, archives, museums, and creative industries) in the valorization and exploitation of fashion heritage online. One of its main objectives is to establish, keep alive, and enrich a fashion database and portal through which more than 800,000 fashion objects can be accessed, shared, and promoted online, and which brings together more than 35 public and private archives and museums, coming from 13 European countries, in order to collect and give public access to high-quality digital fashion content, ranging from historical dresses to accessories, catwalk photographs, drawings, sketches, videos, and fashion catalogues.

Europeana Fashion is part of the Europeana network, whose overall purpose is to provide open access to different types of content from different types of European cultural heritage institutions.

7.5.1 The Europeana Fashion Profile

As an integration medium for collecting, connecting, and enriching the descriptions provided by the Europeana content providers, the Europeana Data Model (EDM) has been developed [6]. As such, it includes an extensive set of elements (classes and properties) found in the content provider's descriptions. Given that taking into account all possible elements would be rather impossible, EDM identifies an extensive essential set of elements, expected to cover most provider needs. The elements contained are both elements reused from other namespaces and new elements introduced by EDM. It is important to mention at this point that EDM was not designed to exhaustively cover all possible needs of the providers that would join the Europeana information space; it has been designed as an open set, that is, as a set that can be extended as new providers join the Europeana information space.

One such extension is EDM-FP [18], which builds on EDM and other existing standards to support the documentation of fashion-related content, as submitted to

Table 7.1 The EDM-FP properties used to extend EDM

Name	Description
gr:color	Color
edmfp:localType	Original object name
edmfp:technique	Method, technique, or tool
mrel:aut	Author
mrel:clb	Collaborator
mrel:cur	Curator of an exhibition
mrel:drt	Director
mrel:ill	Illustrator
mrel:ivr	Interviewer
mrel:pht	Photographer
edmfp:stylist	Stylist
mrel:dsr	Designer
mrel:edt	Editor
mrel:ive	Interviewee
mrel:pro	Producer
mrel:sds	Sound designer
mrel:spn	Sponsor
mrel:std	Set designer
edmfp:model	Model (employed to display or promote the object)
edmfp:hairstylist	Hairstylist
edmfp:makeupArtist	Makeup artist

the Europeana Fashion project. EDM-FP provides a rich expressivity for describing fashion items. It inherits from EDM typical general metadata properties found in most metadata description schemes and provides also special fashion-related properties, as well as properties relating fashion items to the agents that have participated in their life cycle. A list of the properties that EDM-FP adds to EDM is presented in Table 7.1.

Examples of the core properties of EDM inherited by EDM-FP that will be used in the sequel are *dc:title*, *dc:description*, *dc:type*, *dcterms:created*, *dcterms:spatial*, and *dcterms:medium*, which provide the title, the description, the type of item (e.g., whether it is a fashion show, a photograph, a dress, a fashion accessory, etc.), the creation date, the materials used for the construction of the item, and the information about the locations associated with the item, respectively.

In the following (Fig. 7.6), the metadata as provided by the Victoria and Albert Museum are presented (in-house proprietary format), together with the outcome of the mapping process that results into an EDM-FP data record (Fig 7.7).

As can be observed, in-house properties such as *Object_name_1*, *Physical_description*, *Object_production_place*, and *Materials_techniques_note* are aligned to the EDM-FP properties *dc:title* and *edmfp:localType*, *dc:description*, *dcterms:medium*, and *dcterms:spatial*, respectively.

```
<item>

  <Object_name_1>Parasol</Object_name_1>

  <Physical_description>A parasol with handle of composition ivory carved
with a lily-of-the-valley design, the canopy of Brussels bobbin lace ap-
plied to machine-made net, over black silk taffeta. Lined with white silk
taffeta and trimmed with black satin ribbon raced with white satin. Great
Britain, 1870-1880. Linen, silk, composition ivory, machine
made.</Physical_description>

  <Object_production_place>Great Britain</Object_production_place>

  <Dimensions>Length 69.0cm (unspecified); Width 7.5cm, Depth 7.5cm
(closed)</Dimensions>

  <Acquisition_source_funder_credit_line>Given by Mrs Emma
Kent</Acquisition_source_funder_credit_line>

  <Materials_techniques_note>artificial ivory</Materials_techniques_note>

  <Materials_techniques_note>Brussels lace</Materials_techniques_note>

  <Materials_techniques_note>silk taffeta</Materials_techniques_note>

  <Object_production_date>1870/1880</Object_production_date>

</item>
```


Fig. 7.6 Metadata as originally provided by the Victoria and Albert Museum

7.5.2 Fashion Thesaurus

Since EDM-FP is an RDF vocabulary, it specifies the types of values that each property is allowed to take, which in general may be either literals or URIs. In order to assign values to properties, such as *dc:type*, *gr:color*, and *dcterms:medium*, that are expected to associate fashion objects to concrete resources rather than to textual descriptions, in the context of LOD, a vocabulary of fashion-related values is required. The need for such a vocabulary in Europeana Fashion that should be used in combination with EDM-FP and allow the publication of the data according to the LOD publication principles was addressed by the definition of the Fashion Thesaurus.

The Fashion Thesaurus assembles all concepts used in the fashion domain in a controlled, structured hierarchy. The Fashion Thesaurus is based on the Arts and Art & Architecture Thesaurus (AAT). It is structured as an SKOS hierarchy of concepts (URI resources) that covers four main categories: *fashion object*, *fashion event*, *material*, and *technique* (including *color*), used in the production of fashion objects. The thesaurus is multilingual and supports 11 languages, and for each concept, a preferred label and any alternative labels for each language are provided. It contains about 1100 concepts that range from broad concepts such as *costume*,

```
<rdf:RDF>

        <edm:ProvidedCHO

                rdf:about="http://mint-pr.image.ntua.gr/europeana-
            fashion/VA_T.127-1933">

        <dcterms:extent>

            Length 69.0cm (unspecified); Width 7.5cm, Depth 7.5cm
        (closed)

        </dcterms:extent>

        <dcterms:medium>artificial ivory</dcterms:medium>

        <dcterms:medium>silk taffeta</dcterms:medium>

        <dcterms:medium>Brussels lace</dcterms:medium>

        <dcterms:provenance>Given by Mrs Emma Kent</dcterms:provenance>

        <dcterms:spatial>

            <edm:Place><skos:prefLabel>Great Brit-
    ain</skos:prefLabel></edm:Place>

    </dcterms:spatial>

        <dc:date>1870/1880</dc:date>

        <dc:description xml:lang="en">

A parasol with handle of composition ivory carved with a lily-of-the-
valley design, the canopy of Brussels bobbin lace applied to machine-made
net, over black silk taffeta. Lined with white silk taffeta and trimmed
with black satin ribbon raced with white satin. Great Britain, 1870-1880.
Linen, silk, composition ivory, machine made.

        </dc:description>

        <dc:title>Parasol</dc:title>

        <dc:type re-
    source:about="http://thesaurus.europeanafashion.eu/thesaurus/10145"/>

        <edmfp:localType>Parasol</edmfp:localType>

    </edm:ProvidedCHO>

</rdf:RDF>
```

Fig. 7.7 Extract of the Victoria and Albert metadata in EDM-FP

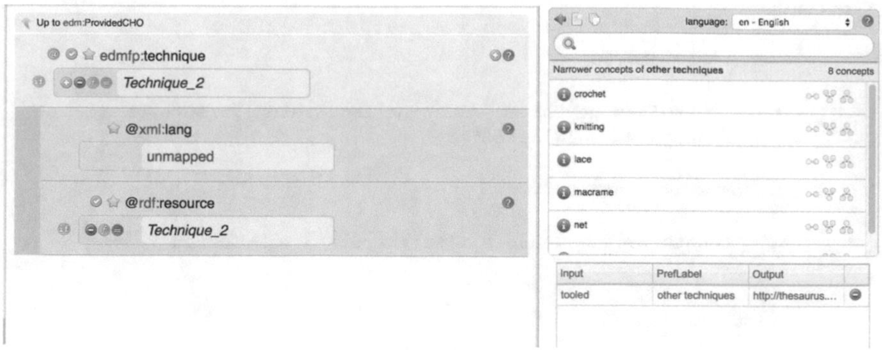

Fig. 7.8 SKOS vocabulary mapping using MINT (screenshot of MINT)

costume accessory, *non-digital medium* (*subconcepts* of *fashion object*), *exhibition* (subconcept of *fashion event*), *natural fiber*, *animal origin* material (subconcepts of *material*), *weaving technique*, and *mechanical transformation* (subconcepts of *technique*) to low-level concepts such as *banyan* (a *costume*), *marriage crown* (a *costume accessory*), *engraving* (a *nondigital medium*), *fashion exhibition* (an *exhibition*), *merino wool* (a *natural fiber*), *marabou feather* (an *animal origin material*), *brocatelle* (a *weaving technique*), and *carding* (a *mechanical transformation*).

The use of vocabularies in metadata empowers them since they allow their discovery in multiple languages and also provide a homogenized curation that makes searchability of records more effective. It is worth mentioning at this point that MINT offers functionality for the providers to characterize their records using vocabularies even if they do not hold in-house vocabulary URIs. This can be done in two ways. A content provider can either characterize a set of records with the same vocabulary URI or align in-house values to one of the Europeana Fashion vocabulary URIs. In detail, as shown in Fig. 7.8, the provider can first map the in-house values to an EDM-FP property—in this case, technique is mapped to *edmfp:technique*—controlled by a vocabulary and then map the internal values (tooled) to vocabulary URI value (other techniques) by navigating to the vocabulary.

7.5.3 Thesaurus-Based Enrichment

The intended use of the Fashion Thesaurus was to provide URI resources as values for the four most important fashion-related EDM-FP properties mentioned above that can accept controlled vocabulary values, namely, *dc:type*, *dcterms:medium*, *edmfp:technique*, and *gr:color*. Nevertheless, its use was optional, and it was left to the discretion of each content provider to use the Fashion Thesaurus resources to model the contributed content. This allows for cases where the thesaurus may be missing extraordinary terms and gives the providers the option to keep the values in their original proprietary format when submitting their datasets to the Europeana Fashion aggregator.

This resulted in a notable heterogeneity among the metadata contributed by the several providers, not only with respect to the metadata properties that were actually used but also with respect to the property values that were used.

In order to alleviate this effect and enhance the semantic characterization of the Europeana Fashion datasets by aligning them with the Fashion Thesaurus, we performed a thesaurus-based semantic enrichment process with a twofold aim: first, to identify literal values with the corresponding Fashion Thesaurus terms in the cases where the providers chose to use textual descriptions instead of the respective Fashion Thesaurus concepts and, second, to detect the occurrence of additional Fashion Thesaurus concepts in the detailed, textual descriptions of the items that were not included in the relevant metadata properties. For example, in the metadata extract presented above, the values for the properties *dcterms:medium* and *edmfp:technique* are clearly amenable to enrichment by identifying the textual values with the respective Fashion Thesaurus resources. Moreover, by analyzing the detailed item description, new information can be discovered (e.g., linen as *dcterms:medium* and black as *gr:color.*) that is not present in the properties originally submitted by the provider.

The thesaurus-based enrichment process was performed in the following steps:

First, as a preprocessing step, we associated each Fashion Thesaurus concept to the EDM-FP property that can have it as a potential value (e.g., *dress*, *bag* to *dc:type*, *red*, *blue* to *gr:color*, *silk*, *linen* to *dcterms:material,* etc.). Thus, by exploiting the hierarchy of Fashion Thesaurus, we associated all subconcepts of the *fashion object* and *fashion event* concepts to the *dc:type* EDM-FP property; all subconcepts of the *material* concept to the *dcterms:medium* property; all subconcepts of the *technique* concept, excluding the subconcepts of *color*, to the *edmfp:technique* property; and all subconcepts of the *color* concept to the *gr:color* property.

Next, for each Fashion Thesaurus concept, and for each one of the 11 supported languages, we generated a list of regular expressions capturing the textual variations in which the concept may appear in the textual descriptions of the items. The regular expressions were constructed using the preferred and alternative labels of each concept provided in the Fashion Thesaurus (e.g., for the concept *red*, the regular expression *\bred\b* was created for English, *\brot(e|es|er|en|em)?\b* for german, *\bross[oiea]\b* for italian, *vermelh[oa]s? || encarnad[oa]s?* for portuguese, etc.).

The main processing step consisted in checking for occurrences of the above-constructed regular expressions within the values of the *dc:type*, *dcterms:medium*, *edmfp:technique*, and *gr:color* properties of the items that contained a literal value. Note that the detection of occurrence of concepts within textual descriptions can also be done using more advanced techniques that rely on NLP. However, given the limited scope of the Fashion Thesaurus vocabulary and the use of a standardized language in the textual descriptions, the use of regular expression matching provided reasonable-quality results. So, we considered each regular expression match as a potential enrichment and represented it by generating a new RDF triple having as subject the identifier of the item, as predicate the EDM-property associated to the Fashion Thesaurus concept for which the matched regular expression was constructed, and as object the associated Fashion Thesaurus resource.

The above process covers the first part of the twofold enrichment process specified above, namely, the identification of literal values used in the specialized metadata EDM-FP properties with the Fashion Thesaurus concepts. In order to cover the second part as well, that is, the detection of the extra occurrences of Fashion Thesaurus concepts in the general textual descriptions of the items, we applied the same processing on the *dc:title* and *dc:description* values of all items.

7.5.4 DBpedia-Based Enrichment

With the above-described thesaurus-based enrichment process, we enhanced the semantic richness of the content provided to the Europeana Fashion aggregator by increasing its interlinking with the Fashion Thesaurus vocabulary. However, an additional level of metadata enrichment is still possible: Several EDM-FP properties, in particular the properties that relate items with agents and places, usually contain textual values that correspond to named entities for which external URI resources, identifiable in the LOD cloud, exist. In particular, properties such as *dcterms:spatial*, *mrel:pht*, *mrel:dsr*, *edmfp:stylist*, and *edmfp:model* normally have as values names of well-known places and persons, for most of which an LOD resource exists (e.g., "Great Britain" may be mapped to the DBpedia resource http://dbpedia.org/resource/Great_Britain).

In order to cover this enrichment opportunity, we recurred to the use of DBpedia, which is one of the richest general-purpose LOD resources and applied a DBpedia-based enrichment process on the entire Europeana Fashion dataset. To achieve this, first, we created an index-based DBpedia lookup service. In particular, we indexed all strings that are used as labels of DBpedia resources for the languages used in the Europeana Fashion project. To account for occasional misspellings and nonstandard name uses, the index supported also fuzzy retrieval. Then, for each fashion item, we looked up in the index all agent and place names included in its *dcterms:spatial*, *mrel:pht*, *mrel:dsr*, *edmfp:stylist*, *edmfp:model*, etc., properties. To improve the accuracy of the results, we filtered the results using DBpedia ontology, which assigns specific types to each concrete DBpedia resource. Thus, when enriching the *dcterms:spatial* values, we searched for DBpedia resources that are instances of *dbpedia:Place*; when enriching the *mrel:dsr* values, we searched for DBpedia resources that are instances of *dbpedia:FashionDesigner* or *dbpedia:Company*, etc. From the results of the lookups, we constructed additional RDF enrichment triples. Note that since the index we built supported fuzzy retrieval, the matches returned by the lookup service were accompanied by a confidence score. To build the final enrichment set, only the matches with high confidence scores were kept.

As an example, the enriched metadata elements of the examples presented before are shown in Fig 7.9.

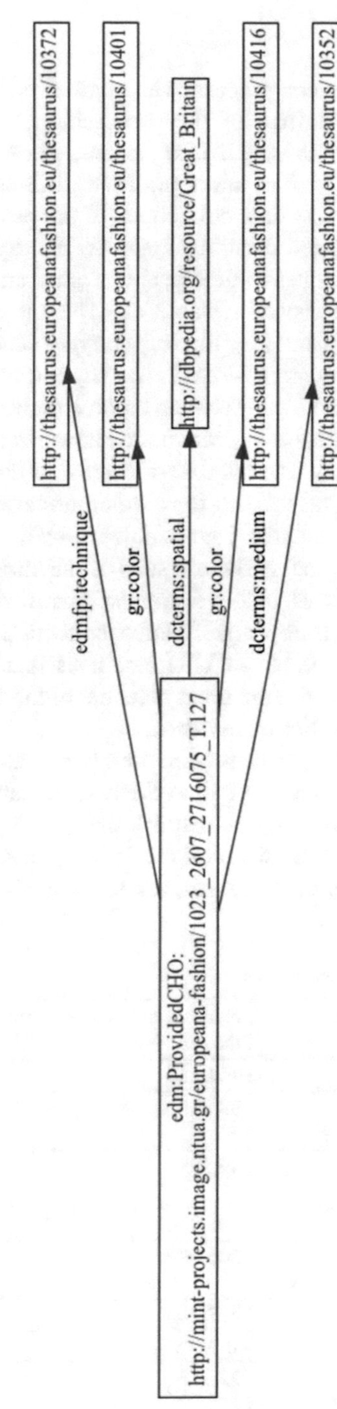

Fig. 7.9 Results of enrichment on a record

7.6 Results

The above-described enrichment process was applied on the entire Europeana Fashion dataset, which at the time of the processing contained 682,488 items from 29 providers. The data was very heterogeneous, since it came from different providers, who kept different information and used different conventions for the description of their datasets. The data collections of the providers differed also in the type of content, which ranged from fashion show photographs, fashion journal pages, and fashion design sketches to medieval costumes and fashion accessories.

The enrichment results are shown in Table 7.2. The outcome of the enrichment process were values (URI resources) for the *dc:type*, *dcterms:medium*, *edmfp:technique*, *gr:color*, *dcterms:spatial*, *mrel:dsr*, *mrel:pht* (the remaining mrel properties were not used in the provided metadata so no enrichments were computed), and *edmfp:model* metadata properties, which are shown in the first column of the table. The second column shows the number of values for the respective properties that existed in the original dataset, the third column shows the number of new values that were produced, and the fourth column shows the total number of metadata values, both the original and the results of the enrichment.

As can be seen, the process that we applied contributed to the significant semantic enrichment of the Europeana Fashion collection metadata, leading to almost a duplication of the number of URI resources that are used as metadata property values. This demonstrates the great potential of the enrichment process for the generation of LOD publication-ready data.

It should be noted, however, that the enrichment process that we applied was fully automatic and was not subjected to a systematic human validation in order to detect and reject false positives. In this respect, the quality of the results was not formally evaluated in terms of the standard recall and precision metrics. However, the limited scope of the Fashion Thesaurus, the fact that all items belonged to the

Table 7.2 Results of the enrichment process

EDM property	Number of instances before enrichment	Number of instances created by the enrichment	Total number of instances
dc:type	1,573,623	444,824	2,018,447
dcterms:medium	116,006	88,590	204,596
edmfp:technique	11,698	40,551	52,249
gr:color	44,950	106,914	151,864
dcterms:spatial	0	506,099	506,099
mrel:dsr	0	227,203	227,203
mrel:pht	0	139	139
edmfp:model	0	22,854	22,854
TOTAL	1,746,277	1,437,174	3,183,451

same narrow domain, and the fact that textual values that were enriched were written in a standardized domain-specific language all resulted in a reasonable, expected quality for the enrichments.

7.7 Conclusion

In this chapter, we presented the workflows and respective tools used for the ingestion and manipulation of cultural metadata as well as the methodology adopted for enriching them and publishing them as Linked Open Data. Cultural content is of great significance and interest. Portals such as Europeana and DPLA deliver to students, teachers, scholars, and the public incredible resources while also enabling new and transformative uses of our digitized cultural heritage. By the publication of cultural content as Linked Data, it can be easily consumed, making, in that way, the implementation of various applications that use it much simpler.

Moreover, cultural content can be enriched by its linking to external data, as presented through the Europeana Fashion use case, allowing in this way for more expressive search and retrieval. For example, a consumer can query to pick Europeana Fashion records of a specific material, type, or color, or he/she can even combine these characteristics to get very specific results. The enrichment process that results in the use of vocabularies' terms in the metadata also permits a hierarchical, faceted view of cultural records, as shown in Fig. 7.10. The hierarchy of the vocabulary is shown on the left and the user can filter out the results by picking the desired term.[9] It should be noted, however, that enrichment results have not undergone a validation process to eliminate false positives. The validation needs human interaction, and the setting up of an interface to perform it by the museum curators is included in our ongoing work.

The outcome of this work, together with the tools developed, also sets a strong basis for the creation of appealing games. In detail, the better the quality of the metadata and content on a cultural heritage object is—meaning that it is described sufficiently so that someone can easily identify it, discover it, and reuse it—the more complex application scenarios can be supported. A game scenario for fashion experts that can be implemented by exploiting the results of enrichments can be one where the user would be asked to answer questions regarding the material and technique employed for the creation of a dress. As presented, the material and technique values that describe the fashion records come from a multilingual vocabulary; thus, not only an enumerated list for them is available, allowing the selection of the correct material and technique, along with some negatives for giving choices to the user, but also the selection of multiple languages. This game scenario could be further enhanced by using elements such as the country the fashion object comes from or the designer. These elements are also part of the metadata that

[9]Available at http://ipa.image.ntua.gr:9040/assets/index.html#collectionview/5704c53b75fe242d7baf5034/

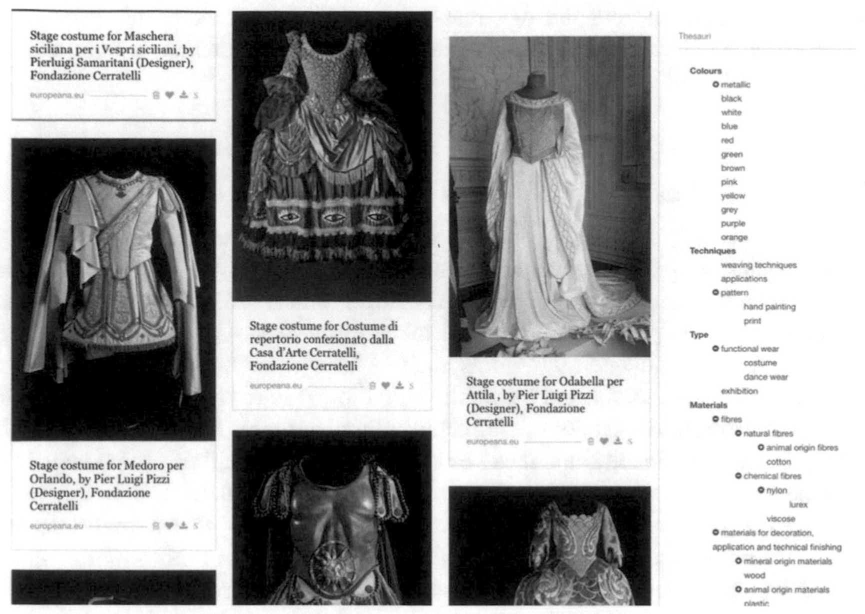

Fig. 7.10 Faceted search on Europeana Fashion content using vocabularies (screenshot of WITH; source of the photos: www.europeanafashion.eu)

describe the fashion objects, and their values can be easily linked to existing Linked Open Data sources such as Geonames and DBpedia to obtain additional information, such as coordinates and description in multiple languages in the case of countries and biographical information and related works in the case of designer.

Current work includes further improvement in the MINT services by extending them to offer more advanced normalization and refine functionalities, permitting in this way better results in resource discovery from literals. In addition, we intend to continue our work on semantic enrichment of established vocabularies such as AAT (Art & Architecture Thesaurus), ULAN (Union List of Artist Names), and TGN (Thesaurus of Geographic Names) by the implementation of services that content providers could use to get the possible terms back. Apart from this, WITH,[10] which is a new tool we are working on, has been recently released. WITH is rather simple to use and familiarize with, and its user can create collections using records either collected from various existing cultural portals (e.g., Europeana, DPLA, DigitalNZ, Rijksmuseum, The British Library, or other sources that may be supported) or transformed through MINT or even directly uploaded to WITH. In its current form, WITH provides also an Application Programming Interface (API) from third-party developers for reusing content from collections into applications. WITH focuses on media and content convergence and also on the promotion and creative reuse of cultural content, which are among the hot topics for future EU policy and the H2020 Digital Agenda.

[10] http://withculture.eu/

Acknowledgements This research was partially supported by the Europeana Fashion (CIP-ICT-PSP.2011.2.1) and the Europeana Space (CIP-ICT-PSP-2013-7) projects.

References

1. R. Letellier, R. Eppich (eds.), *Recording, Documentation and Information Management for the Conservation of Heritage Places* (Routledge, 2015)
2. P.Patias, in *Cultural Heritage Documentation*. International Summer School Digital Recording and 3D Model, 2006
3. D. Martin, The CIDOC conceptual reference module: an ontological approach to semantic interoperability of metadata. AI Mag. **24**(3), 75 (2003)
4. T. Buerger, J.-P. Evain, P.-A. Champin, *W3C Media Annotation Working Group RDF Ontology (ma-ont)*, http://www.w3.org/TR/2011/PR-mediaont-10-20111129/ (2011)
5. J.P. Evain, *EBU Core Metadata Set EBU*, http://archive.ert.gr/wp-content/uploads/2016/02/EBU%20Core%20(tech3293v1_3).pdf (2009)
6. M. Doerr, S. Gradmann, S. Hennicke, A. Isaac, C. Meghini, H. van de Sompel, in *The Europeana Data Model (EDM)*. World Library and Information Congress: 76th IFLA General Conference and Assembly, pp. 10–15, August 2010
7. A. Isaac, R. Clayphan, *Europeana Data Model Primer*, http://pro.europeana.eu/files/Europeana_Professional/Share_your_data/Technical_requirements/EDM_Documentation/EDM_Primer_130714.pdf (2010)
8. C. Bizer, T. Heath, T. Berners-Lee, Linked data—the story so far, in *Semantic Services, Interoperability and Web Applications: Emerging Concepts* (2009), pp. 205–227
9. G. Klyne, J. Carroll, *Resource Description Framework (RDF): Concepts and Abstract Syntax* (2006)
10. E. Prud'hommeaux, A. Seaborne, *SPARQL Query Language for RDF*, https://www.w3.org/TR/rdf-sparql-query/ (W3C Recommendation, 2008)
11. T. Berners-Lee, *Linked Data—Design Issues*, https://www.w3.org/DesignIssues/LinkedData.html (2006)
12. M. Clarke, P. Harley, How smart is your content? Using semantic enrichment to improve your user experience and your bottom line. Science Editor 37:2 (2014)
13. A. Miles, S. Bechhofer, *Skos Simple Knowledge Organization System*, https://www.w3.org/TR/skos-reference/ (W3C Recommendation, 2009)
14. D.L. McGuinness, F.V. Harmelen, OWL web ontology language, in *Encyclopedia of Database Systems* (Springer US, 2009)
15. D. Nadeau, S. Sekine, A survey of named entity recognition and classification. Lingvisticae Investig. **30**(1), 3–26 (2007)
16. J. Daiber, M. Jakob, Ch. Hokamp, P.N. Mendes, *Improving Efficiency and Accuracy in Multilingual Entity Extraction*. Proceedings of the 9th International Conference on Semantic Systems (I-Semantics), 2013
17. J.R. Finkel, T. Grenager, Ch. Manning, in *Incorporating Non-Local Information into Information Extraction Systems by Gibbs Sampling*. Proceedings of the 43nd Annual Meeting of the Association for Computational Linguistics (ACL 2005), pp. 363–370, 2005
18. Europeana Data Model Fashion Profile (EDM-FP), http://pro.europeana.eu/files/Europeana_Professional/EuropeanaTech/EuropeanaTech_taskforces/Mapping_Refinement_Extension/Case_studies/EuropeanaFashion/EDM-FP%20specification.docx (2012)
19. T. Berners-Lee, *Cool URIs Don't Change*, https://www.w3.org/Provider/Style/URI.html (1998)
20. L. Sauermann, R. Cyganiak, *Cool Uris for the Semantic Web*, https://www.w3.org/TR/cooluris/ (2010)
21. L. Kaye, *Content Selection and Metadata Handbook*, http://blog.euscreen.eu/wp-content/uploads/2010/10/Content-Selection-and-Metadata-Handbook_public.pdf (2011)

Chapter 8
Digital Memory and Integrated Data Capturing: Innovations for an Inclusive Cultural Heritage in Europe Through 3D Semantic Modelling

Federica Maietti, Roberto Di Giulio, Marcello Balzani, Emanuele Piaia, Marco Medici, and Federico Ferrari

Abstract Starting from different applications in 3D integrated laser scanner survey of heritage buildings and sites, this chapter will illustrate advanced procedures in 3D surveying and modelling of complex buildings, focusing on the ongoing European project "INCEPTION—Inclusive Cultural Heritage in Europe through 3D semantic modelling", funded by the EC within the Programme Horizon 2020. The project methodology proposes the enhancement of efficiency in 3D data capturing methodologies, procedures and devices beyond current standards, especially as regards their suitability and aptitude for tangible cultural assets, characterized by nonconventional features, locations and geometries. Within the overall documentation process, the semantic enrichment of 3D models will enable an inclusive approach for accessing and understanding European cultural heritage through digital documentation.

Keywords Integrated data capturing • Digital documentation • Semantic modelling • 3D laser scanner survey • Cultural heritage

8.1 Introduction

Innovative ICT applications and advanced "storytelling" attitudes of 3D reconstructions, including augmented and virtual reality, are becoming more and more widespread in communicating and enhancing tangible and intangible cultural heritage.

Information and communication technologies are constantly evolving, and new digital media are increasingly used for accessing, understanding and preserving

F. Maietti (✉) • R. Di Giulio • M. Balzani • E. Piaia • M. Medici • F. Ferrari
Department of Architecture, University of Ferrara, via Quartieri 8, 44121 Ferrara, Italy
e-mail: federica.maietti@unife.it; roberto.digiulio@unife.it; marcello.balzani@unife.it; emanuele.piaia@unife.it; marco.medici@unife.it; federico.ferrari@unife.it

M. Ioannides et al. (eds.), *Mixed Reality and Gamification for Cultural Heritage*,
DOI 10.1007/978-3-319-49607-8_8

cultural heritage; ICTs allow new experiences and enjoyment of cultural sites giving the opportunity to approach more easily something that very often is perceived as distant and unattractive. Multimedia interactive guides realized in 3D for museums, exhibitions and archaeological sites, smart phone applications, touchscreens, multimedia books with dynamic images and virtual reality are just some examples of new possibilities to learn, understand and access cultural heritage. Enriching semantically the 3D models and improving the applications of virtual and augmented reality, the understanding of the European cultural heritage will be more accurate and will go beyond the virtual tours; these tools will allow everyone to add a rich diversity of contexts and interpretations to the 3D models through interactive, storytelling and wiki-oriented approaches using mobile devices [1].

Documentation processes are becoming more and more relevant, and the nearly 10 years of research and experimentation have been characterized by an attempt to focus efforts and contribute to the enrichment of representational knowledge of existing elements. Heritage documentation is basic for understanding our legacy and our cultural identity.

The newly developed technologies for the automatic acquisition of geometric data are innovative elements that allow us to create databases of high-definition, three-dimensional morphometric data [2].

These archives of architectural and archaeological data allow to collect dimensional data and integrate them with information related to structures and materials, state of conservation, diagnostic analysis and historical data, making the data capturing an overall integrated process in supporting sustainable decision strategies for conservation, restoration and enhancement of cultural heritage.

The development of criteria for multilevel organization of databases is mainly oriented to preservation and restoration work but also contributes to the enhancement, promotion, management and enjoyment of cultural heritage sites. The database contains 3D models obtained by the use of laser scanner and all the topographic, photographic, diagnostic and structural data associated with them. Databases allow users to consult and update all data, providing an important foundation for the management, preservation, maintenance and enhancement of heritage sites [3].

In this framework, digital technologies are very relevant because they are able to survey very rapidly heritage buildings and sites by collecting millions of spatial coordinates. These 3D acquired data can be used not only for documentation and monitoring purposes but also for digital application (such as virtual tours, virtual tourism, digital reconstructions, etc.) and to create integrated 3D database for preservation, diagnostics, restoration and management procedures (Fig. 8.1).

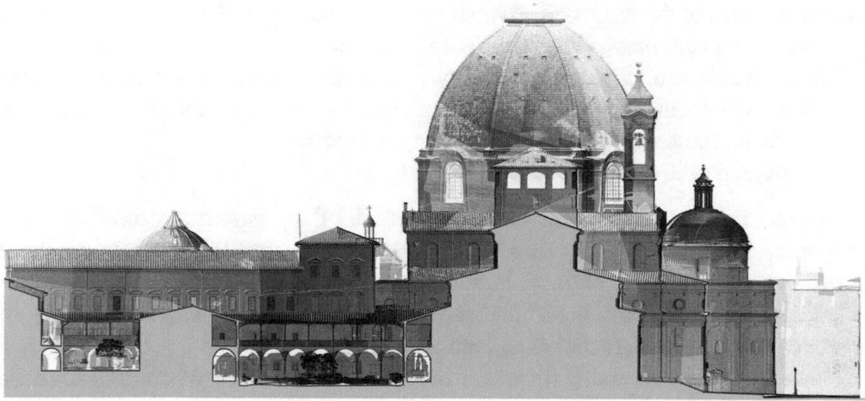

Fig. 8.1 Florence, environmental section cutting the cloister of San Lorenzo; in the background the Medici Chapels and the Laurenziana Library (© 2003 DIAPReM centre, reprinted with permission)

8.2 Digital Memory and Integrated Data Capturing

8.2.1 INCEPTION Objectives and Strategies

The European Project "INCEPTION—Inclusive Cultural Heritage in Europe through 3D semantic modelling", funded by the EC within the Programme Horizon 2020, aims to solve the shortcomings of state-of-the-art 3D reconstruction by significantly enhancing the functionalities, capabilities and cost-effectiveness of instruments and deployment procedures for 3D laser survey, data acquisition and processing.

The INCEPTION[1] main aim is focused on innovation in 3D modelling of cultural heritage through an inclusive approach for time-dynamic 3D reconstruction of heritage sites and on the possibility to create an inclusive understanding of

[1]The project, started in June 2015, will be developed by a consortium of 14 partners from 10 European countries led by the Department of Architecture of the University of Ferrara (scientific coordinator Prof. Roberto Di Giulio) which makes use of the facilities and researchers of the Laboratory TekneHub, Ferrara Technopole, belonging to the Construction Platform of the Emilia-Romagna High Technology Network. Academic partners of the consortium, in addition to the Department of Architecture of the University of Ferrara, include the University of Ljubljana (Slovenia), the National Technical University of Athens (Greece), the Cyprus University of Technology (Cyprus), the University of Zagreb (Croatia), the research centres Consorzio Futuro in Ricerca (Italy) and Cartif (Spain). The clustering of small- and medium-sized enterprises includes DEMO Consultants BV (the Netherlands), 3 L Architects (Germany), Nemoris (Italy), RDF (Bulgaria), 13BIS Consulting (France), Z + F (Germany) and Vision and Business Consultants (Greece).

The project has been applied for the Work Programme Europe in a changing world—inclusive, innovative and reflective societies (Call—Reflective Societies: Cultural Heritage and European Identities, Reflective-7-2014, advanced 3D modelling for accessing and understanding European cultural assets).

European cultural identity and diversity by stimulating and facilitating collaborations across disciplines, technologies and sectors.

Within this overall framework, the project is developing cost-effective procedures and enhancements for on-site 3D survey and reconstruction of cultural heritage artefacts, buildings, sites and social environments.

This objective is achieved by:

- Enhancing the efficiency of three-dimensional data capturing procedures and devices, especially their suitability and aptitude for the physical cultural resources and assets: cultural heritage sites, historical architectures, archaeological sites and artefacts that are characterized by smart handling of nonconventional characteristics, locations and geometries.
- Developing new methods for condition assessment survey of cultural heritage which are based on predictive analysis (diagnostic, conservative, morphometric) and non-destructive procedures and supported by economically sustainable technologies and devices.
- Optimization of hardware and software instruments for easy scan system, rapid capture of main features/geometric data and automated data output in an H-BIM environment.
- The integrated data capturing methodology will be accomplished by the implementation of a common protocol for data capturing and related enhancement of functionalities, capabilities and cost-effectiveness of data capturing technologies and documentation instruments. The protocol considers quality indicators, time consumption, cost-effectiveness, results' accuracy and reliability and useful data to be recorded for heritage applications.

The INCEPTION project faces the changing role of 3D digital models in heritage representation and their collaborative use across disciplines increasing knowledge, enhancement and dissemination through digital models in order to promote the inclusiveness and accessibility of European cultural heritage.

Breaking down the barriers caused by the sector segmentation, a "common framework" for the interpretation of European cultural identity and diversity through 3D documentation of cultural heritage [4] sites and buildings will be established (Fig. 8.2).

8.2.2 Integrated 3D Laser Scanner Survey for Cultural Heritage

Methods and processes for data collection are continuously developing and today are characterized by an effective interdisciplinary. Skills on 3D laser scanner survey, diagnostic procedures and historical researches, as well as about environmental condition assessment or management of metric and dimensional data,

Fig. 8.2 Florence, visualization of the point cloud of the dome of the *Sagrestia Nuova* by Michelangelo coloured by intensity values (© 2003 DIAPReM centre, reprinted with permission)

support the vision of integrated digital documentation [5] for cultural heritage assessment.

The INCEPTION's approach to the improvement of the understanding of European cultural identity and diversity is focused on the 3D data capturing and modelling of heritage buildings and sites, through digital representation of the shape, appearance and conservation condition,[2] in addition to a set of semantic information able to enrich research and deployment applications.

3D laser scanner technologies allow creating high-definition databases based on even more detailed three-dimensional morphometric data. These "digital archives" are an extremely valuable research tool in cultural heritage field: the so-called geometric memory is essential for knowledge, understanding, protection and sustainable conservation of cultural heritage.

The concept of geometric memory is related to documentation and data filing by means of 3D data acquisition technologies characterized by high-speed procedures and the creation of high-density and accurate data.

Starting from "geometric memory", it is possible to extract not only geometric aspects but also many different data for the enhancement of documentation and information for conservation, diagnostics, monitoring and restoration project and for heritage promotion, valorization and enhancement [6].

The three-dimensional model produced by a 3D survey, referred to a specific degree of accuracy and precision depending on the performance specifications of the instruments and the complexity of the data acquisition process, is represented by

[2]See Chap. 10, "Data collection for estimation of resilience of cultural heritage assets".

a set of X, Y, Z coordinates that can be retrieved and examined by anyone at any time, as will be deeply explained in the next sections of the document.

The 3D survey follows an organization able to highlight the steps of its achievement and to retrace the registration process and data fusion. The obtained 3D model, certificate with a certain degree of accuracy and precision related to the performance specifications of the instrument and the complexity of acquisition, can be queried by everyone even after the measurement phase.

The degree of flexibility offered by this system allows researchers to transfer organizational and interpretive work into the laboratory or off-site, decoupling the data acquisition process from the exclusive purpose of producing a measurement and making the collection of measurement data exportable, updatable and implementable. Geometric configuration is the basis of knowledge of heritage spatial and architectural outlines and the support for layering many different information such as shapes and textures, highly descriptive quality in terms of material characteristics and state of conservation, etc. The geometric memory is an essential cognitive support to organize the 3D database, which can include also other types of survey data (infrared, spectrophotometric, structural). This allows an investigation approach that exploits the effectiveness of morphological navigation [7]. The 3D database presents itself as a whole entity, where it is possible, for example, to decide to:

- Cut off parts (to better display others)
- Filter data (taking, time to time, the density and stratification consistent with the purpose of the survey)
- Place the observer in a free condition with respect to the planimetric position of the acquisition itself
- Navigate into the three-dimensional model and browse and query through different informative levels (Fig. 8.3)

Operating within a context of hundreds of millions of organized three-dimensional coordinates allows, for example, to read through volumetric correspondences of architectures and sites.

This procedure can be extremely powerful in helping the historical analyses, checking and monitoring the heritage architectures and sites [8] and setting up interactive metric databases able to provide at any time information about the surveyed object.

In particular, the precision, the acquisition speed of metric data and the opportunity to use these data to build 3D geometric models and to carry out conservative and structural analyses are very advantageous features. The results obtained until now have shown that it is possible to organize databases of a great variety and nevertheless complementary to each other, to allow a global view of heritage knowledge, preservation, conservative and managing issues (Fig. 8.4).

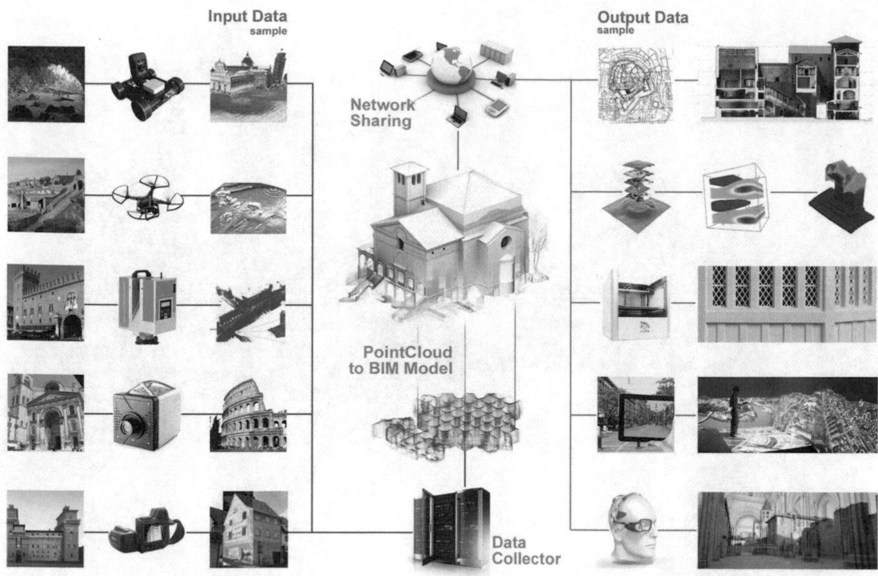

Fig. 8.3 Scheme of the integrated documentation procedure of the INCEPTION project (© 2014 DIAPReM centre, reprinted with permission)

8.2.3 Cultural Heritage Through Time and Space Dimension

INCEPTION project is focused on innovation in 3D data capturing and modelling of heritage buildings and sites. The overall approach to the survey of heritage "spaces" and geometric dimensions (different from the survey of objects and artefacts) is the opportunity to explore and improve the multilayered conceptual dimension of European heritage. At the same time, one of the main challenges of the INCEPTION project is to realize innovation in 3D modelling of cultural heritage through an inclusive approach for time-dynamic 3D reconstruction of built and social environments. This feature will allow the creation, visualization and analysis of 3D H-BIM models of cultural heritage over time, with emphasis on how the modelled cultural heritage evolves over time in association with its built and social environments.

The architectural space becomes the foundations, the common core and the "connection" for the creation of a protocol for optimizing the 3D documentation of cultural heritage. The methodology sets as a priority the unconventional features/geometries, unique and complex within heritage, avoiding the "segmentation" of data acquired and facilitating data access and use through an inclusive approach.

State-of-the-art and interdisciplinary references analysed and checked during the first research stages, together with wide on-site tests and experiences, include the most recent contributions in the field of survey, representation, modelling and database management for cultural heritage.

Fig. 8.4 Piazza dei Miracoli, Pisa. Visualization of data extraction generated from the 3D database for a perspective view (© 2006 DIAPReM centre, reprinted with permission)

The main used methodologies face the problem of the complexity of current tools and the processing of results obtained by using new technologies in representation over the 2D and 3D conventions. These outcomes are very often surprising but sometimes impoverished in the expressive vocabulary of the representation of a proper reference model, which allows investigating the tangible material as well as the intangible intentions.

Architectural space geometry is an essential tool to handle the spatial expression of a drawing useful to accomplish knowledge and conservative process; survey and representation of heritage architectural spaces are an effective tool for exploring the form from the two-dimensionality to the three-dimensionality of reality and vice versa.

An international comparison and interdisciplinary analysis of several indicators (within documentation, data acquisition and processing) aimed at the knowledge of the heritage through the 3D modelling and database querying and data extraction has been accomplished; the future steps will develop advanced 3D modelling in a BIM environment to enhance the understanding of cultural heritage.

Innovation is related to the focus on the heritage spaces (at an architectural and urban scale), one of the most important "containers" of cultural expressions identified in the evolution of the concept of European identity.

The project develops an integrated approach able to investigate the potential of spaces in order to create new cultural connections and awareness; the architecture is an outstanding example of the multilayered conceptual dimension of European heritage.

The 3D survey of heritage architectural space needs a common protocol for data capturing and related enhancement of functionalities, capabilities and cost-effectiveness of technologies and documentation instruments. The protocol considers the uniqueness of each site, quality indicators, time consumption, cost-effectiveness, data accuracy and reliability, additional data and semantic proprieties to be recorded for heritage applications and adaptability to different sites with different historical phases (Fig. 8.5).

The combination of innovative methodologies and protocols, processes, methods and devices will enhance the understanding of European cultural heritage by means of 3D models bringing new knowledge, collaboration across disciplines and time and cost saving in develop and use of 3D digital models. The innovative procedures and applications will enable remote communication and collaboration across professionals, experts, architects, etc. and will increase the operation fields in cultural heritage.

The integration of digital data and the possibilities of reuse digital resources are an important challenge for the protection and conservation of the historical buildings as well as for an efficient management in the long term. The need of a future reuse of such a broad and descriptive source of measurement data demands new applications to facilitate information accessing collected in three-dimensional databases without compromising the quality and amount of information captured in the survey.

The 3D survey of heritage "spaces" means:

- To understand how the space (defined by its geometric morphometric characteristics) can be the interface/connection with time dimension; the space/time relation can be an easy (and affordable) and understandable (and therefore inclusive) metaphor of memory (collective and European).
- To understand how space (architectural, urban and environmental) has its own dynamic characteristic that not only gives the chance of an understandable navigation and discovery but also identifies the option of choosing which is the basis of the definition of culture: what to choose and to store in a certain time and why.

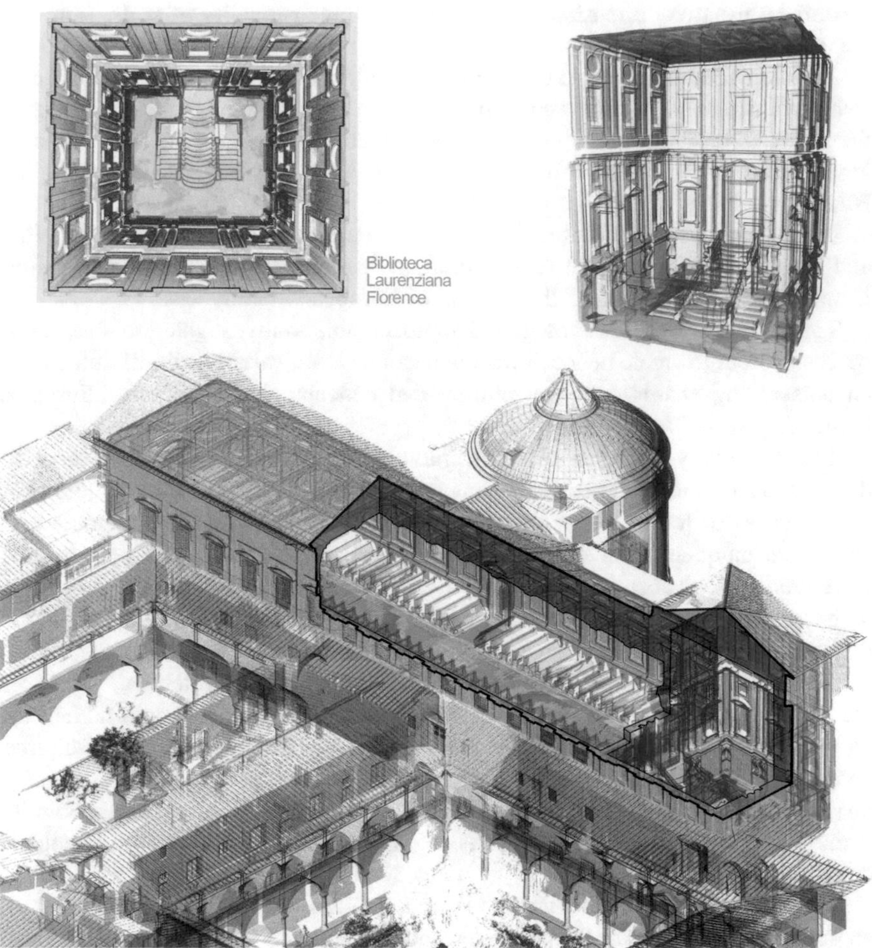

Fig. 8.5 Laurenziana Library, Florence, by Michelangelo, an example of complex architectural "space" to be detected; view of the data extraction generated from the 3D database of the interior spaces and the 3D point cloud model in *silhouette*, mixing grey scale and intensity values (© 2003 DIAPReM centre, reprinted with permission)

- To understand that only through space (and its complexity) it is possible to collect a high level of multifunction knowledge strongly linked to the multiscale representation process.

The identification of the multifunction and multiscale role of the model allows the exploitation of uneasy and complex resources (obtained by the collection of geometric shape and not just of the architectural and urban context) at different levels over time and by different actors. Here it is the value of accessibility/affordability of the process that until now has been barely allowed to spatial scale but through a mere visual navigation often uninterpreted, an approach very far from the knowledge, understanding and conservative needs.

Working at heritage architecture and site scale will allow the identification of the cultural heritage buildings semantic ontology and data structure for information catalogue. During the second year, activities will be addressed to a modelling approach within the 3D semantic Heritage-BIM: the integration of semantic attributes with hierarchically and mutually aggregated 3D geometric models is indispensable for the management of heritage information. 3D parametric and semantic modelling will lead to the development of semantic 3D reconstructions of heritage buildings and sites, integrated with additional documents (i.e. pictures, maps, literature) and intangible information.

The 3D data integration is consistent with the trend of open linked data and big data, which are recommended procedures for displaying and sharing the semantic web context. INCEPTION would fit perfectly into the ongoing research projects in order to identify the right and useful technologies in order to support the future of web of data. It will try to give a response to the data use in relation to the possible correlations (tourist development, accessibility, historical reconstructions, real-time identification of the state of conservation, etc.).

INCEPTION main scopes and objectives include the generation of data sets and the creations of synergies with digital libraries,[3] and the INCEPTION 3D standard will be integrated into the Europeana EDM format (Fig. 8.6).

8.3 Semantic Enrichment and Inclusive Approach

8.3.1 3D Semantic Models to Manage the Time Dimension

Within INCEPTION, the time-dynamic 3D reconstruction will become part of the modelling and of model deployment. The time dimension is part of the most significant steps of the project, starting from the 3D survey and documentation. The so-called INCEPTION "time machine" will be developed as an open-standard semantic web platform.

Looking at that objective, the heritage documentation and the optimized data acquisition protocol are related to the "time dimension" since survey, integrated digital documentation, representation and semantic enrichment are parts of the time-dynamic 3D reconstruction process [9].

Historical data and documentation are part of the knowledge management and holistic documentation aimed at the hierarchical organization of information about heritage buildings and sites based on semantic approach; heritage documentation process includes historical documents and historical drawings (when available) or

[3]See Chap. 5, "3D Digital Libraries in Cultural Heritage and their contribution in the documentation of the past".

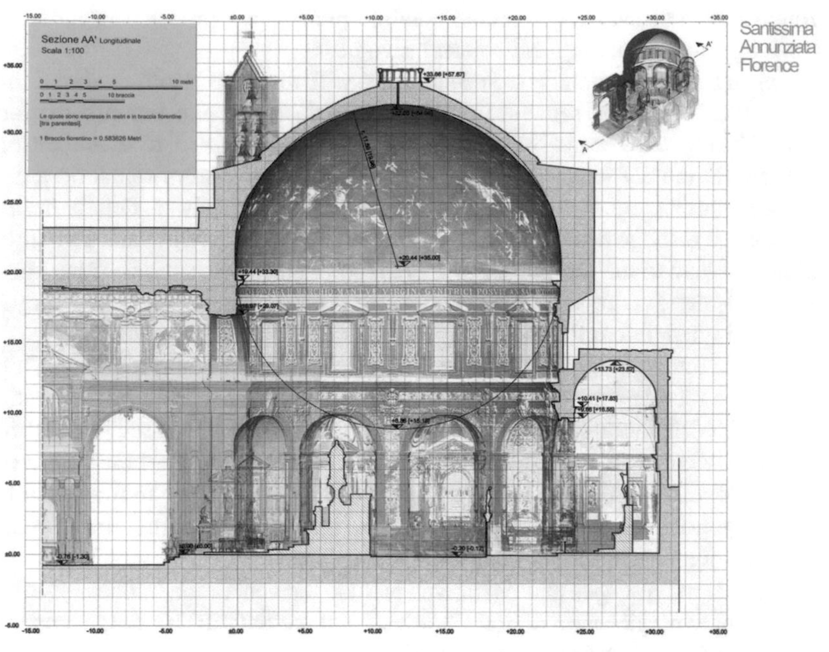

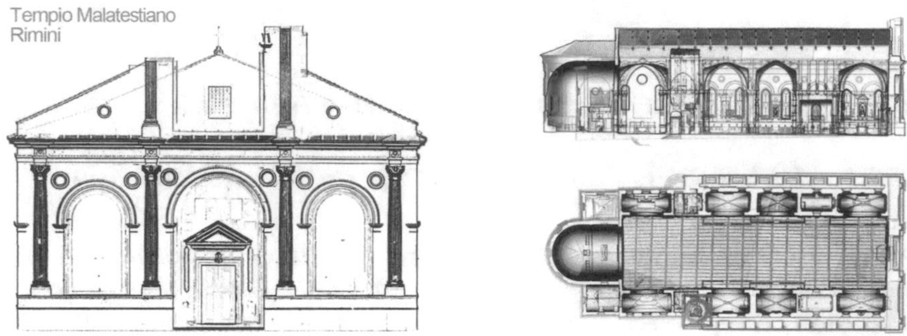

Fig. 8.6 Leon Battista Alberti, Santissima Annunziata in Florence and Tempio Malatestiano in Rimini, comparison of 3D databases for querying and extracting horizontal and vertical section and geometric analysis (© 2004 DIAPReM centre, reprinted with permission)

iconographies, pictures, etc., as well as documentation about previous interventions of restoration.

The 3D survey is able to "work over time", by layering different information (including comparison with previous surveys acquired by different technologies) and relating the metric-morphological data to the historical documentation and additional information within the semantic approach; acquired data can be integrated over time with additional survey.

3D data capturing and documentation at different times of geometries, shapes and constructive and formal conditions allow to generate a four-dimensional database, comparing different 3D models. Time frames are one of the informative layers included in the development of methods for semantic organization and glossary definition for cultural heritage buildings; including time dimension in the 3D modelling development, it is possible to describe building evolution and different phases or previous interventions.

In case of ruins or partially lost architectures, it is possible to virtually reconstruct the building shape in a specific time lag with the help of historical documentations. Reconstructions and simulations related to specific historical periods, moving across time and space, are possible within the semantic web platform.

Heritage maintenance and real-time asset management and monitoring and periodic condition assessment allow verifying the state of conservation over time. Semantically enriched 3D models allow to transmit the heritage building through time and space in an accessible way and through interoperable formats to a wide range of users, experts and non-experts.

Applications for analysis and understanding of cultural heritage through time and space involve on-site augmented reality based on INCEPTION H-BIM [10] (same place and same time), off-site virtual reality by INCEPTION mobile apps (different place, same time), INCEPTION semantic web collaboration platform (same place, different time) and INCEPTION "time machine" for analysis of culture and identity (different place, different time) [11].

Since time definition is also used by documentations related to the building, in the time machine tool properties linked to the model should be available for a specific period of time. Another issue is that in cultural heritage domain, time is not always known or perfectly indicated on specific events or could be defined in relation with other events.

The implementation of the dynamic structure of the INCEPTION platform through models and reconstructions/simulations related to specific historical periods allows to "move across time and space" enabling features like time machines, and it is connected also with time planning of interventions. Users will be provided with a dashboard for accessing survey data, i.e. cloud of points, and building 3D historical simulations.

A possible data model to manage the "time dimension" in cultural heritage 3D models is through ontologies. Semantic data models have been applied and exploited in several ways in virtual museums and cultural heritage artefacts, but time representations have always been a critical point. Time, as a measure, is a mathematical entity, but it is also descriptive of events closely interlaced with intangible properties (like architectural styles, environmental description, authors and usage, which often have not a strictly defined time span). Time definition is also applied by related documentations about the building, so in the time machine tool properties linked to the model should be available for a specific period.

Different references mean different meanings and applications, so defining a time span for a physical entity could imply an evolution, transforming it in another entity or its replacement. Physical properties related to the style description should deal with their relation with model changings through time; some not precise phrasal indication (e.g. in the mid of the seventeenth century) in related documentation has to be taken into account, and granularity of time measure could affect performance and usability.

8.3.2 Advancement in 3D Data Capturing: Towards an Enriched Semantic Modelling

Differently from other research field, where the quantitative data are mainly collected to prove or explore a hypothesis, for what may concern survey procedures, the quantitative data could become the starting point.

Quantitative data are anything that can be expressed as a number: indeed, the collection of 3D data generates arrays of numerical data that should define geometries. Generally, different technologies and methodologies of 3D data capturing could acquire different types of quantitative raw data (point clouds, reflectivity, colourimetric value, etc.) that need to be interpreted to become significant. Conversely, qualitative data cannot be generally expressed as a number but defines the key to understand the digital description provided from the 3D captured data. The quantitative data represent the whole surveyed object that need to be qualitatively interpreted to understand single elements that define the building as well as its materials, additions, ratios, etc.

According to this, the main challenge in 3D digital data management towards H-BIM could be defined in the capability of H-BIM models to merge quantitative and qualitative data into a semantic integrated 3D model [12].

As well as three-dimensional scanners are a technology now widely used in the field of cultural heritage survey and the field of restoration and conservation, the Building Information Modelling systems, starting from the development of CAD, are becoming tools more and more used for the documentation of cultural heritage, as well as semantic web technologies [13, 14] (Fig. 8.7).

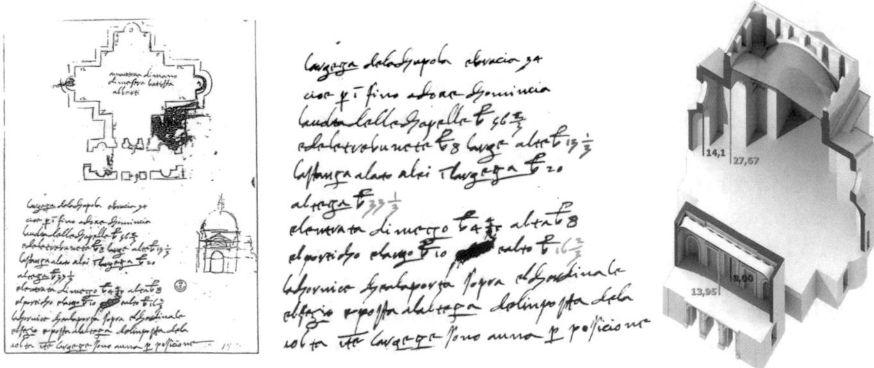

Fig. 8.7 Leon Battista Alberti, San Sebastiano, Mantua. The BIM model obtained from the point cloud is used as graphical verification of measures starting from the drawing by Antonio Labacco, beginning of the sixteenth century (© 2015 DIAPReM centre, reprinted with permission)

The integration between BIM environments and three-dimensional acquisition technologies is one of the challenges to be faced in order to guarantee a truly collaborative process in the heritage preservation sector.

Starting from the implementation of the 3D data capturing protocol for heritage applications and the identification of the cultural heritage buildings semantic ontology and data structure for information catalogue, the project will develop guidelines for 3D parametric and semantic modelling in a Heritage-BIM environment, based on open BIM standard, improving a "BIM approach" for cultural heritage.

3D models generated through INCEPTION methods and tools will be accessible for many different users. Semantic enrichment will generate 3D models for multiple purposes depending on the needs and level of knowledge of the end users. The semantic enrichment will link geometric information for 3D visualization, historical information and geotechnical data as well as structural information for material conservation, maintenance and refurbishment.

An open-standard format and semantic ontology to generate high-quality, reliable and interoperable models of H-BIM will be used in order to manage point clouds in the overall process to generate 3D models without compromising the high quality and accuracy of surveyed data [15].

Semantic H-BIM allows users not only to access but also to interact with the models, allowing spatial and multi-criteria queries in a virtual 3D environment. The end users will be able to access information utilizing a standard browser, and they will be able to query the database using keywords and an easy search method.

INCEPTION semantic modelling approach will resolve the existing barriers between data collection and documentation, as well as between model creation and analysis/interpretation (Fig. 8.8).

8.4 Future Developments and Innovations: VR and AR in Heritage Applications

INCEPTION will allow model utilization and deployment: queries, visits, uploads and downloads, and access through apps will allow a completely new kind of analysis about needs, behaviours, expectations of CH customers and operators.

The models will be delivered through INCEPTION platform in already existing apps for a myriad of purposes. With this feature, the models will be applied for research, tourism, building maintenance, specific studies, etc. It will be tested also using virtual and augmented reality applications on tablets and smart phones.

Moreover, the digital model generated will be readily exported to VRML, X3D or equivalent formats which are appropriate for VR/AR applications, multimedia edition, conceptualization in a computer scenario and historical recreations (Fig. 8.9).

Fig. 8.8 San Sebastiano, Mantua. Hybrid visualization of point cloud and meshed model towards the H-BIM (© 2015 DIAPReM centre, reprinted with permission)

Thanks to virtual reality, it is possible to rebuild past worlds, monuments and ancient cities: because of the possibility of comparing different historical periods and their physical transformation, architecture and archaeology need to deeply explore this technology to enhance the understanding of cultural heritage.

Moreover, AR can be used to aid archaeological and architectural research, by augmenting features onto the modern landscape, enabling researcher to formulate conclusions about site placement and configuration or to more general users to understand what they are looking at. Computer-generated models can be superimposed into a real life to rebuild ruins, buildings, landscapes or even ancient characters as they formerly existed. This technology can be useful only on the field because it needs real-world environment or objects to be augmented.

To better understand the difference from VR and AR, it could be useful to refer to the definition of mixed reality (MR). It is the merging of real and virtual worlds to

Fig. 8.9 Example of augmented reality by using applications on smart phones (© 2016 DIAPReM centre, reprinted with permission)

produce new environments and visualizations where physical and digital objects coexist and interact in real time. Mixed reality takes place not only in the physical world or the virtual world but is a mix of reality and virtual reality, encompassing both augmented reality and augmented virtuality. In 1994, Paul Milgram and Fumio Kishino defined a mixed reality as "...anywhere between the extrema of the virtuality continuum" (VC), where the virtuality continuum extends from the completely real through to the completely virtual environment with augmented reality and augmented virtuality ranging between (Fig. 8.10).

8.5 Conclusion

The need of a future reuse of such a broad and descriptive source of measurement data demands new applications to facilitate information accessing collected in three-dimensional database without compromising the quality and amount of information captured in the survey.

Looking at the future development of the INCEPTION platform, the integration of qualitative and quantitative data, beginning from the data capturing phase, will allow the possibility to make qualitative query on quantitative data within a database of multiple CH buildings and, therefore, to better understand the cultural European complexity from its tangible heritage.

Fig. 8.10 Example of augmented reality by using applications on tablet devices within the archaeological site of Pompeii (© 2015 DIAPReM centre, reprinted with permission)

Databases allow users to understand how each survey phase was carried out (scans, topographic support, image acquisition, etc.) and thus to obtain the maximum possible amount of morphological information; this procedure means to work with complex interfaces that are based on the programming languages of the software used to complete the survey itself.

Furthermore, VR and AR applications are becoming increasingly important in the preservation, protection and collection of our cultural and natural history; making easier the access to monuments, artefacts, building and culture, these technologies are actually enhancing the learning process, motivating and understanding of certain events and historical elements for the use of students and researchers [16].

Currently, efforts in developing the user interface are concentrated on providing direct or partially controlled access to the large three-dimensional scale models, also by means of immersive navigation. The creation of large digital spaces properly set up in terms of both form and dimensions will make possible to navigate, enter and extract its qualities and specifications (measurements, colours, materials, historical documentations, conservation records) in real time.

However, the user's needs and desire for knowledge might be somewhat stymied by such complicated interfaces that could be hard to understand.

Current efforts are focused on creating immersive and easy-to-use 3D visualizations that can be accessed from a wide range of users.

The field of experimentation underlying the integrated, interdisciplinary research effort shares many aspects (dimension and complexity of the data) with heritage surveys, and the results obtained so far give us reason to hope that these optimization processes can be exported.

New simplified navigation interfaces are also being developed for users with lower levels of expertise to facilitate access to and navigation of the three-dimensional models.

It is thus clear that new visualization and communication modes for the geometric and measurement information have to be conceived and developed in step with the development and application of three-dimensional surveys.

Acknowledgements The research project "INCEPTION—Inclusive Cultural Heritage in Europe through 3D semantic modelling" has received funding from the European Union's H2020 Framework Programme for research and innovation under grant agreement no. 665220.

References

1. R. Di Giulio, in *Towards Sustainable Access, Enjoyment and Understanding of Cultural Heritage and Historic Settings*, ed. by R.P. Borg, P. Gauci, C.S. Staines. Proceedings of the International Conference SBE Malta 2016. Europe and the Mediterranean: Towards a Sustainable Built Environment, Valletta, Malta, 16–18 March 2016 (Gutenberg Press, Malta, 2016), pp. 269–277
2. F. Maietti, M. Balzani, N. Santopuoli, in *Innovative Technologies for Restoration in Pompeii. The 3D Morphometric Survey in via dell'Abbondanza*, ed. by R. Amoeda, S. Lira, C. Pinheiro, F. Pinheiro, J. Pinheiro. Proceedings of the "International Conference Heritage 2008—World Heritage and Sustainable Development", vol. II, Vila Nova de Foz Coa, Portugal, 7–9 May 2008 (Green Lines Institute for Sustainable Development, Barcelos, 2008), pp. 549–559
3. F. Maietti, F. Ferrari, M. Medici, M. Balzani, in *3D Integrated Laser Scanner Survey and Modelling for Accessing and Understanding European Cultural Assets*, ed. by R.P. Borg, P. Gauci, C.S. Staines. Proceedings of the International Conference SBE Malta 2016. Europe and the Mediterranean: Towards a Sustainable Built Environment, Valletta, Malta, 16–18 March 2016 (Gutenberg Press, Malta, 2016), pp. 317–324
4. D.M. Jones (ed.), *3D Laser Scanning for Heritage. Advice and Guidance to Users on Laser Scanning in Archaeology and Architecture* (English Heritage Publishing, Swindon, 2011)
5. N. Yastikli, Documentation of cultural heritage using digital photogrammetry and laser scanning. J. Cult. Herit. **8**, 423–427 (2007)
6. M. Ioannides, N. Magnenat-Thalmann, E. Fink, R. Zarnic, A.-Y. Yen, E. Quak (eds.), in *Digital Heritage. Progress in Cultural Heritage. Documentation, Preservation, and Protection.* 5th International Conference, EuroMed 2014, Limassol, Cyprus, 3–8 November 2014, Proceedings (Springer International Publishing, 2014)
7. P. Martín Lerones, J. Llamas Fernández, A. Melero Gil, J. Gómez García-Bermejo, E. Zalama Casanova, A practical approach to making accurate 3D layouts of interesting cultural heritage sites through digital models. J. Cult. Herit. **11**(1), 1–9 (2009)
8. F. Maietti, M. Balzani, F. Ferrari, in The integrated survey aimed at the regeneration of the urban scene in the historical urban fabric, *Drawing & City. Culture Art Science Information*, ed. by A. Marotta, G. Novello. Proceedings of the XXXVII Convegno Internazionale dei Docenti della Rappresentazione—XII Congresso Unione Italiana Disegno—Torino, 17–19 Settembre 2015 (Gangemi Editore, 2015), pp. 657–662

9. L. Taffurelli, L. Fregonese, in *Transmission of Cultural Heritage Through Time and Space by Digital 3D Models*. Proceedings of XXIII CIPA Symposium—Prague, Czech Republic, 12–16 September 2011
10. P. Bonsma, I. Bonsma, R. Sebastian, A.E. Ziri, S. Parenti, F. Maietti, P. Martín Lerones, J. Llamas, B. Turillazzi, E. Iadanza, in *Roadmap for IT Research on a Heritage-BIM Interoperable Platform Within INCEPTION*, ed. by R.P. Borg, P. Gauci, C.S. Staines. Proceedings of the International Conference SBE Malta 2016. Europe and the Mediterranean: Towards a Sustainable Built Environment, Valletta, Malta, 16–18 March 2016 (Gutenberg Press, Malta, 2016), pp. 283–290
11. C. Dore, M. Murphy, in *Integration of Historic Building Information Modeling (HBIM) and 3D GIS for Recording and Managing Cultural Heritage Sites*. In Virtual Systems and Multimedia (VSMM), 18th International Conference (IEEE, 2012), pp. 369–376
12. N. Hichri, C. Stefani, L. De Luca, P. Veron, G. Hamon, From point cloud to BIM: a survey of existing approaches. Int. Arch. Photogramm. Remote Sens. Spat. Inf. Sci. **XL-5/W2**, 2 (2013)
13. P. Pauwels, R. Bod, D. Di Mascio, R. De Meyer, in *Integrating Building Information Modelling and Semantic Web Technologies for the Management of Built Heritage Information*. Digital Heritage International Congress (DigitalHeritage), vol. 1 (IEEE, 2013), pp. 481–488
14. S. Logothetis, A. Delinasiou, E. Stylianidis, in *Building Information Modelling for Cultural Heritage: A Review*. ISPRS Annals of the Photogrammetry, Remote Sensing and Spatial Information Sciences, vol. II-5/W3, 2015. 25th International CIPA Symposium 2015, Taipei, Taiwan, 31 August–04 September 2015
15. I. Toschi, P. Rodríguez-Gonzálvez, F. Remondino, S. Minto, S. Orlandini, A. Fuller, Accuracy evaluation of a mobile mapping system with advanced statistical methods. ISPRS Int. Arch. Photogramm. Remote Sens. Spat. Inf. Sci. **XL-5/W4**, 245–253 (2015)
16. Z. Noh, M.S. Sunar, Z. Pan, in *A Review on Augmented Reality for Virtual Heritage System. Learning by Playing. Game-Based Education System Design and Development*. 4th International Conference on E-Learning and Games, Edutainment 2009, Banff, Canada, 9–11 August 2009. Proceedings (Springer, Berlin Heidelberg, 2009), pp. 50–61

Part IV
Geospatial

Chapter 9
Five-Dimensional (5D) Modelling of the Holy Aedicule of the Church of the Holy Sepulchre Through an Innovative and Interdisciplinary Approach

Antonia Moropoulou, Andreas Georgopoulos, Manolis Korres, Asterios Bakolas, Kyriakos Labropoulos, Panagiotis Agrafiotis, Ekaterini T. Delegou, Petros Moundoulas, Maria Apostolopoulou, Evangelia Lambrou, George Pantazis, Lydia Kotoula, Alexandra Papadaki, and Emmanouil Alexakis

Abstract The Church of the Holy Sepulchre (Church of the Resurrection) is one of the most important historical sites of Christianity. The current Aedicule structure is the result of various construction phases, damages and destructions, reconstructions, and protection interventions, and as such, it serves as an emblematic case study for five-dimensional (5D) modelling. The innovative and interdisciplinary approach adopted for the modelling of the Holy Aedicule of the Church of the Holy Sepulchre utilizes data from the following: (a) architectural documentation: Description of the current form and structure, as well as its evolution through the ages, based on historic documentation; (b) analysis of construction phases: The construction phases were revealed by a ground-penetrating radar (GPR) survey that was implemented within an integrated methodology, which enabled the technique to identify the various interfaces; (c) geometric documentation: Generation of a 3D

Petros Moundoulas was deceased at the time of publication.

A. Moropoulou (✉) • A. Bakolas • K. Labropoulos • E.T. Delegou • M. Apostolopoulou • E. Alexakis
Laboratory of Materials Science and Engineering, School of Chemical Engineering, National Technical University of Athens, Zografou, Greece
e-mail: amoropul@central.ntua.gr; abakolas@mail.ntua.gr; klabrop@central.ntua.gr; edelegou@central.ntua.gr; mairi_apostol@hotmail.com; alexman@central.ntua.gr

A. Georgopoulos • P. Agrafiotis • E. Lambrou • G. Pantazis • L. Kotoula • A. Papadaki
Laboratory of Photogrammetry, School of Rural and Surveying Engineering, National Technical University of Athens, Zografou, Greece
e-mail: drag@central.ntua.gr; pagraf@central.ntua.gr; litsal@survey.ntua.gr; gpanta@survey.ntua.gr; lydiakotoula@outlook.com; al.i.papadaki@gmail.com

M. Korres
School of Architecture, National Technical University of Athens, Zografou, Greece
e-mail: mankor@otenet.gr

M. Ioannides et al. (eds.), *Mixed Reality and Gamification for Cultural Heritage*, DOI 10.1007/978-3-319-49607-8_9

high-resolution model, through an automated image-based method and through using terrestrial laser scanning; (d) materials documentation: A wide range of analytical and nondestructive techniques have been used in order to characterize the building materials and extract data for fusion in 5D modelling; and (e) 5D modelling: visualization of the historic construction phases of the Holy Aedicule of the Church of the Holy Sepulchre. The integrated modelling which, after the above analysis, includes enhanced information covering all aspects of the Aedicule structure, geometry, and materials and forms the basis for the creation of an innovative tool that induces mixed reality (MR) with the focus on the Aedicule's structural evolution (time factor—4D) and on its materials (5D).

Keywords Architectural • Geometric and materials documentation • 5D modelling and visualization

9.1 Introduction

The Church of the Holy Sepulchre (Church of the Resurrection) is one of the most important historical sites of Christianity. Within this Church, the Holy Aedicule is built, which contains the tomb of Jesus Christ. The current Aedicule structure is the result of various construction phases (Fig. 9.1), damages and destructions, reconstructions, and protection interventions [1–4].

The Church dates back to 325 AD, when Emperor Constantine I ordered the construction of a basilica incorporating the tomb of Jesus Christ, within the Holy Aedicule (Fig. 9.1a, by Theo Mitropoulos). The Holy Tomb was carved outside, possibly in a polygonal form, with an entrance on its eastern side (Fig. 9.1a, by Theo Mitropoulos), whereas the interior had a rectangular form and on its northern side the arcosolium. At the start of the seventh century, the exterior surfaces of the polygonal monolithic Aedicule were covered by marble plates, columns, and metal fences to protect it from visiting pilgrims.

The Church of the Holy Sepulchre was damaged by fire in 614 when the Persians invaded and destroyed Jerusalem. The Aedicule's exterior and interior surfaces and decorations were destroyed, including partial destruction of the burial chamber, along its east–west axis (Fig. 9.1b, by Theo Mitropoulos). In 622, Christians were allowed to rebuild churches and monasteries. Modestus, the abbot of the Monastery of St. Theodosius, rebuilt the Church of the Holy Sepulchre and destroyed parts along the east–west axis of the Aedicule which were restored with masonry (Fig. 9.1c, by Theo Mitropoulos). In 1009, the Caliph of Egypt Al-Hakim ordered the complete destruction of the church; the Holy Aedicule is destroyed down to ground level. During the reign of Constantine Monomachus, Patriarch Nikiforos persuaded the Emperor to offer money for the reconstruction of the Holy Sepulchre (1027–1048). Parts destroyed by Al-Hakim were restored with masonry, the Aedicule regaining its former Constantinean plan form, and its exterior surfaces covered with stone plates, enveloped by 12 columns (Fig. 9.1d, by Theo Mitropoulos).

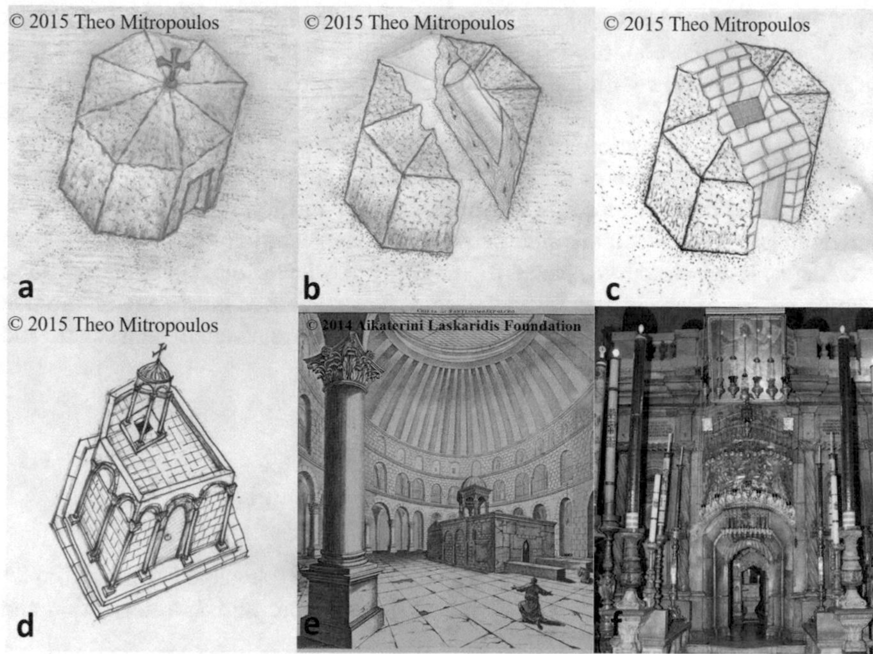

Fig. 9.1 The construction phases of the Holy Aedicule of the Church of the Holy Sepulchre throughout history (© 2014 Aikaterini Laskaridis Foundation, reprinted with permission—© 2015 Theo Mitropoulos, reprinted with permission)

After the arrival of the Crusaders (1099), the Church of the Holy Sepulchre was renovated in a Romanesque style and added a bell tower. A vestibule (Chapel of the Angel) was added at the eastern side of the Aedicule in 1119 (Fig. 9.1e, by Cornelis de Bruyn, 1714). Following various conquerors, Jerusalem fell in 1517 to the Ottoman Turks, who remained in control until 1917.

In 1808, an accidental fire became uncontrolled, which caused the dome of the Rotunda to collapse over the Aedicule, inflicting severe damage to it. According to historic sources [5], the Holy Tomb remained intact, but the Aedicule structure was heavily damaged and buried under the Rotunda dome ruins. After permission, the official architect Nikolaos Komnenos rebuilt the Aedicule in the contemporary Ottoman Baroque style, effectively embedding the remaining core of the burial chamber within the new, larger, Aedicule structure. The restored Church was inaugurated on 13 September 1810 and came into its present form (Fig. 9.1f, May 2015).

Since the 1810 reconstruction, in all external faces except the west end, the marble shell presents a strong buckling. By 1947, the deformation of the external construction of the Aedicule was already as intense as today, forcing the British authorities to take immediate measures in the form of an iron "frame" along the flanks, which through strong wooden wedges prevented any further outward movement of the stones already affected by the buckling mechanism. More recently, the

National Technical University of Athens, after invitation from His All Holiness, Beatitude Patriarch of Jerusalem and All Palestine, Theophilos III, signed a programmatic agreement with the Jerusalem Patriarchate and implemented an innovative research titled "Integrated Diagnostic Research and Strategic Planning for Materials, and Conservation Interventions, Reinforcement and Rehabilitation of the Holy Aedicule in Church of the Holy Sepulchre in Jerusalem". Within this framework, an array of nondestructive techniques, in conjunction with materials characterization, and architectural and geometric documentation were performed to elucidate the construction phases of the Holy Aedicule, the materials they are composed of, to assess the preservation state of the Aedicule, and to provide basic layering information for the assessment of its current state against static and seismic loads.

9.2 Interdisciplinary Approach: Study Overview

The innovative and interdisciplinary approach adopted to enable 5D modelling of the Holy Aedicule of the Church of the Holy Sepulchre utilizes information and data from the following:

- *Architectural documentation*: Description of the current form and structure, as well as its evolution throughout the ages, based on historic documentation.
- *Analysis of construction phases*: The construction phases were revealed by a ground-penetrating radar in situ survey, implemented within an integrated methodology, which enabled the technique to identify the various interfaces.
- *Geometric documentation*: Generation of a 3D high-resolution model, through an automated image-based method and through using terrestrial laser scanning. The 3D representation of the results of the prospection with GPR for the internal structure of the Holy Aedicule was considered highly useful as it actually enables the 5D representation of the historic construction phases.
- *Materials documentation*: A wide range of nondestructive and laboratory (Analytical) techniques were used for the assessment of the condition and the characterization of the various building materials of the holy monument.
- *5D modelling*: To enable the potential for a 4D modelling, the time factor has to be accounted for, suggesting the historic construction phases of the holy monument. The aforementioned architectural documentation could provide such data validated by the analysis of the construction phases and the geometric documentation. Data fusion from material documentation and characterization will eventually enable 5D modelling.

The typical 3D model is, thus, enriched by the fusion of information from various disciplines, i.e., architecture, civil, surveying, and chemical engineering.

Within this framework, the gamification approach could be adopted transforming the above 5D model into an emblematic case study for smart educational and heritage applications.

9.3 Architectural Form and Structure of the Holy Aedicule

The present form of the Holy Sepulchre, which exists without alterations since 1810, is a result of repair and restoration of the earlier building after the catastrophic fire of 1808. The exact form of the earlier building, also a result of a restoration of an even earlier form, which is closer to the initial form surrounding the Holy Grave Rock, appears in 1609 drawings together with a brief description, a citation on the dimensions and notes [6].

For a better understanding of the structural connection of the new construction with the previous one, Prof. M. Korres, based on newer drawings (made by the National Technical University of Athens), on the ones of 1609, and on his own measurements and observations, composed Fig. 9.2 depicting the present form, the earlier latent construction enveloped by the present building's exterior masonry, and the area of possible existence of the Holy Grave Rock inside the latter.

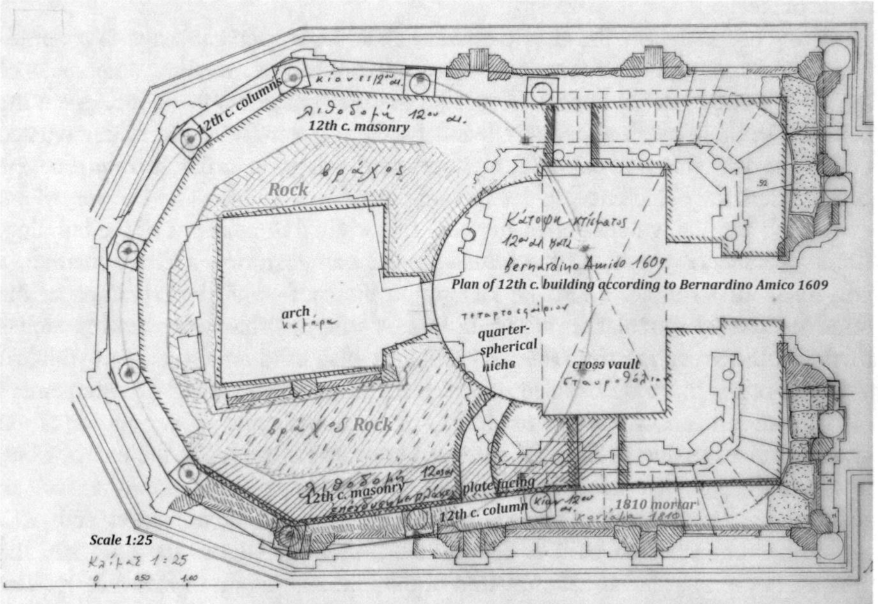

Fig. 9.2 Holy Aedicule, depicting: (a) the present form (*black color*), (b) the earlier latent construction (*red color*) enveloped by the present building's exterior masonry, (c) the potential extent of the Holy Rock (*green color*) inside the Aedicule structure [5]

In the earlier building, the western part, which was polygonal as it is on the present building, instead of being exactly semicircular, was shaped like a horseshoe, and, therefore, it was wider than the other part toward the east. Nevertheless, the sides of the polygon corresponded to 30° arcs, and the columns that existed before them stepped on a circular arc's spokes, on 15°, 45°, and 75° positions north and south of the western semi-axis of the building. To put it in another way, if the aforementioned shape was not interrupted by the east projecting part, it would be a normal dodecagon. In any case, the horseshoe-like form of the building must have been perceived as a result of a merger of a dodecagon and a parallelogram with a west front markedly narrower than the diameter of the dodecagon. So it is most likely that this form was really a product of the attachment of a vestibule in a first regular dodecagon building with columns standing before each of its corners.

Obviously, such a dodecagon cannot be other than the primary dodecagon around the Holy Grave according to the historical tradition. In that initial state, the solid mass behind the 12 columns must have been the carved rock and not surrounding masonry. The lining of the rock with masonry has given the whole, at least externally, the appearance of a building made entirely of hewn stones.

During the drastic overhaul of the building, that is, its extension toward the east, with the result that only the western part remained from the original full dodecagon, a canopy (initially dodeka style) was erected on its roof, almost above the site of the burial chamber, obviously in symbolic accordance to the original form and, in any case, to protect the Holy Sepulchre from the rain falling through the open-air oculus of the dome.

During the 1808 fire, the Holy Sepulchre must have been subjected to a combination of damages, not only because of the violent fall of massive components of the giant wooden dome but also from the thermal attack on the stone, given the combustion of so much material. Obviously, the recovery of the form that existed before the fire was not possible, nor desirable, since, in order to reinforce the construction, very thick new masonry would need to be added almost everywhere externally, and that would drastically alter the original dimensions of the building. Kalfas Komnenos preserved the initial general composition—a dimer internal, a polygonal western end, a circular canopy on the roof—and the repetition of the original external modulation with pilasters or columns that were bearing arches rhythmically projecting from the wall studs. He also used architectural rhythmical elements of his time. He decided to enrich the interior with a drastic enlargement of the vestibule, an increase in the height of the domes, and proper conformation of the surfaces, using rhythmical elements coherent to those on the exterior but, in any case, finer. He apparently pursued some metric proportions to ensure an academic–numerological perfection of the architectural composition and of a certain symbolism: The bulk of the building, that is, without the base and the parapet, has a length of 8.325 m, width of 5.55 m, and height of also 5.55 m. The simple arithmetic connection 2:2:3 of these dimensions is an essential part of the whole architectural concept.

The enlargement of the Aedicule regarding its exterior dimensions, the enlargement of the Chapel of the Angel regarding its interior dimensions, and the reorientation and enlargement of the burial chamber were accomplished by adding new masonry to the exterior of the surviving Crusader building phase one. This would necessitate removal of any surviving lining stones from the previous construction period and carving of the surviving masonry wherever required. Obviously, at elevated heights the masonry would be entirely new, since the previous Aedicule was lower than the newer one and had sustained significant damage due to the fire. In addition, he performed carving of the surviving old masonry, wherever its thickness justified such a laborious approach, to enlarge the interior space. The coexistence of old and new masonries at the interior and exterior of the Aedicule is verified by the ground-penetrating radar prospection of the structure.

9.4 Analysis of the Construction Phases

Ground-penetrating radar (GPR) is an established nondestructive electromagnetic technique that can locate objects or interfaces within a structure. GPR was utilized in order to reveal information about the interior structure of the Aedicule, i.e., the interior layers of its masonries, as well as the assessment of their preservation state and cohesion, in conjunction with macroscopic deformations.

The GPR survey was implemented within an integrated methodology, which was based on the preceding three steps (architectural documentation, geometric documentation, materials characterization) of the overall innovative and interdisciplinary approach, and followed a carefully designed survey matrix, to ensure that the main aims of the GPR survey were achieved without the need for excessively extensive measurements that would distract the religious functions of the Aedicule.

The ground-penetrating radar system used in this survey was a MALÅ Geoscience ProEx system with 1.6 and 2.3 GHz antennae. The MALÅ Geoscience GroundVision 2 software was used for data acquisition. The GPR scans were processed with the MALÅ Geoscience RadExplorer v.1.41 software after application of the following filters: DC removal, time-zero adjustment, amplitude correction, and band-pass filtering. The application of filters enhanced weak peaks and layers that were not readily identifiable in a nonprocessed radargram. The scan after its processing with the aforementioned filters still remains a distance–time graph. The horizontal axis corresponds to the displacement of the antenna over the surveyed surface, whereas the vertical axis of the graph corresponds to the time elapsed between the moment the electromagnetic pulse is emitted from the antenna on the surface, its diffusion within the masonry, its encounter with an interface of materials of different electrical properties, its partial reflection toward the exterior surface, and its detection by the receiver antenna. For the conversion of the scan into a two-dimensional section distance and depth (X axis versus Depth $-Z$ axis), the calculation of the pulse velocities throughout all observed layers is required. Stone blocks of the parapet at the roof and a stone block from the seat outside the entrance to the Aedicule were used as standards to calibrate the pulse velocities for the GPR analysis. Thus, the velocities and dielectric constants were calculated and used in the velocity models of the remaining areas, representing the exterior stone panels and the Holy Rock, as they have a similar synthesis. Based on this calibration, a velocity of $v = 11.58$ cm/ns ($\sigma = 1.02$ cm/ns) was calculated, which corresponds well with that of similar materials of the bell tower of the Church of the Holy Sepulchre [7].

The pulse velocity of the Komnenos construction phase was calculated by adjusting the velocity model in the southern masonry of the Chapel of the Angel, so that the thickness of the masonry measured by a georadar coincides with the actual one. The pulse velocity of the Crusader building phase was calculated by comparing scans from the exterior and the interior and optimizing the velocity model so that common targets coincide spatially. Figure 9.3 presents in a descriptive approach the various layers within the Aedicule structure, as analyzed by GPR. Figure 9.3 is based on Fig. 9.2 and retains the plan of the current structure and the exterior boundary of the eleventh/twelfth-century building (red outlines). The BN3 plane and the longitudinal axis conceptually define the four quadrants A1–A4.

Starting from the southwest quadrant of the Aedicule, and analyzing with the aforementioned methodology, the following internal interfaces were revealed: (a) exterior panel, (b) Kalfas Komnenos construction phase, (c) Crusader construction phase, (d) the Holy Rock, (e) masonry between the Holy Rock and interior

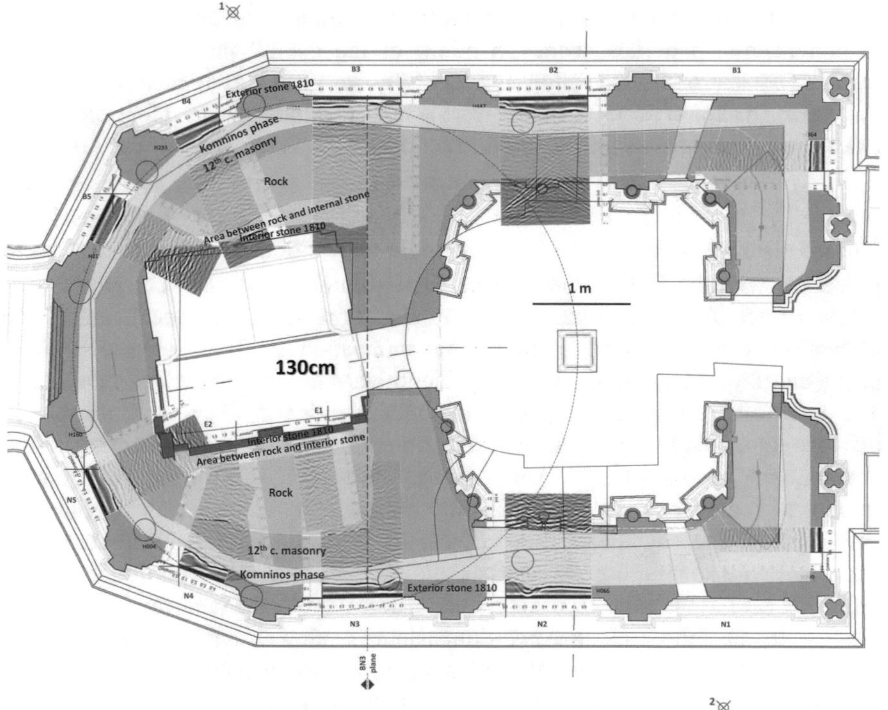

Fig. 9.3 Layering within the Holy Aedicule (cross section at height level 130 cm) as identified by the GPR analysis [5]

panel, and (f) interior panel. The exterior panel has a varying thickness of 10–15 cm. Moving toward the interior, an interface is observed at a depth of 30–40 cm. The layer between the exterior panel and this interface corresponds to the Kalfas Komnenos construction phase and is indicated in Fig. 9.3 as a yellow-colored zone. Moving further toward the interior, the GPR scans reveal the presence of a second interface, at a depth of approximately 50–60 cm. The layer between the red dashed curve—internal boundary of the Komnenos construction phase—and this second interface corresponds to the twelfth-century masonry, i.e., the Crusader construction phase.

The combined analysis of the horizontal and vertical GPR scans at the southern quadrant, both from the exterior (areas N3, N4, and N5) and from the interior (areas E1 and E2), allowed the per-height identification of the boundary of a third internal interface. The volume within this interface is theorized to correspond to the Holy Rock, after its consecutive carvings of its original volume. In Fig. 9.3, the Holy Rock is depicted as an orange-colored area. The GPR analysis shows that the Holy Rock possibly extends to a height of approximately 2 m. Above this height, the GPR scans indicate masonry, possibly constructed after the 1808 fire, although parts of the twelfth-century constructions could not be excluded from being present. Scanning of the interior of the Holy Tomb, it is estimated that the interior panels at areas E1 and E2 have a thickness of 5–6 cm. The area between the Holy Rock and the E1 and E2 panels appears to be masonry with an average stone size of approximately 10 cm.

A systematic differentiation of the horizontal scans in area B3 is observed on a vertical plane BN3 (indicated with a blue dashed line in Fig. 9.3, which is perpendicular to the longitudinal axis of the Aedicule intersecting areas B3 and N3 at their mid-axis. To the west side of this BN3 plane, the construction layers are those described above. To the east side of this plane, the revealed layering is interrupted in respect to its western continuity, regarding the layer corresponding to the twelfth-century masonry, since reflections from the parts of the scans that belong to quadrants of the Chapel of the Angel are present in different depths. The analysis leads to the theorization that to the east side of plane BN3, the structure consists only of masonry, without any rock volume being present in this area. Possibly the interior of the semicircular niche is the result of deep carving and supplementation with a new masonry, so that the area around the entrance to the Holy Tomb obtained its new geometry.

At the Chapel of the Angel, GPR indicates parts of the northern side and the eastern side of the Crusaders' masonry were retained (Fig. 9.3). Deep carving was performed to their interior to facilitate the northward expansion of the Chapel. The old wall was retained—on the north part of the Chapel of the Angel—probably to the full length of the Chapel, up to the façade area [5]. The retained height is probably approximately up to 1.5 m above the interior floor level, corresponding to the height of the entrance of the northern staircase and its first three steps. Above that height, the masonry is most probably entirely new, constructed during the 1810 restoration works. Correspondingly, at the southern part of the Chapel of the Angel, the GPR analysis indicates that retaining of the Crusaders' masonry phase occurs only at the southeastern corner (Fig. 9.3), up to a height similar to the one on the northeastern corner.

9.5 Geometric Documentation

The geometric documentation carried out produced a 3D high-resolution model, through the combination of automated image-based method and using terrestrial laser scanning. Using the final model, it was possible (i) to extract the eventually necessary conventional two-dimensional products, such as, e.g., horizontal and vertical sections, and facades; (ii) to produce suitable visualizations for the support and design of the restoration interventions; and (iii) to virtually visualize the internal structure of the Holy Aedicule in three dimensions.

9.5.1 Data Acquisition

All current measurements and works were based on the important past efforts for the geometric documentation of the Church of the Holy Sepulchre and the Holy Aedicule [8–14].

This present geometric documentation aims at the production of the necessary base material on which the structural and material prospection studies will be based. For the needs of this documentation, it was decided to produce a high-resolution three-dimensional model and to perform specialized highly accurate geodetic measurements for the production of conventional 2D base material on the one hand and for the documentation of the deformations and deviations of the construction today on the other. Due to the peculiarities of the object of interest, and the crowds of pilgrims always present inside and around the Aedicule, most of the works for the data acquisition took place after the closure of the Church. The methodology implemented for the production of the above-described products applied the most contemporary geomatic techniques and specialized instrumentation. Briefly, an automated 3D-imaging methodology based on high-resolution digital images, terrestrial laser scanning, and high accuracy geodetic measurements were implemented.

For the image-based approach, digital image sequences from varying distances were collected using a calibrated professional Canon EOS-1Ds Mark III full-frame CMOS digital camera with 21MP resolution (5616 × 3744 pixels) and 6.4 μm pixel size, aiming to reconstruct the 3D scene of the Holy Aedicule through structure from motion (SfM) and dense image matching (DIM) techniques. These techniques are the state of the art in reconstructing 3D scenes and offer high reliability and high accuracy as a cost- and time-effective alternative to the use of scanners. For this purpose, different lenses with a varying focal length (16, 50, 135, and 300 mm) were used. The image acquisition took place under low natural lighting conditions and during the night, exploiting the existing artificial lighting. No additional light sources were used (flash, studio flash, etc.). Therefore, the use of a photographic tripod was necessary since in some cases, the exposure time was up to 30 s. A total of 3,757 images were captured requiring up to 59.3 GB of hard drive space. However, a selection process was applied in order to ensure a highly accurate result according to the requirements of the study and the significance of the object. Finally, distances were accurately measured on the Holy Aedicule in order to scale the final 3D model. Problems in the acquisition processes such as lighting conditions and camera-to-object relative positioning as well as difficulties in the alignment step and mesh optimization are also encountered without reducing the accuracy of the final results. These problems included, among others, the large distances between the object and the camera, the poor or inadequate lighting, the continuous population of the area by pilgrims, and the smoke from the candles, which create faded areas on the images or unpredictable optical deformations due to the refraction effect caused by the temperature difference in the air.

In addition, laser scanning was also employed, in order to cover the areas where image acquisition was impossible, e.g., the dark and smoked interiors of the two domes of the Holy Aedicule and the two staircases leading to the construction's roof. The two techniques act complementarily to each other. For this procedure the terrestrial laser scanner FARO 3D X 330 was chosen as it is a lightweight third-generation scanner, which uses the phase-shift method for measuring distance. It has the ability of collecting 1 million points per second with an accuracy of 2–3 mm in its space position. It can record points 360° around the vertical axis and 300° around the horizontal axis. For the complete coverage of the Holy Aedicule, special scanning strategy was designed, in order to avoid gaps in the point clouds on one hand and to record all necessary details on the other. For that purpose, it was necessary to acquire overlapping scans from different scan positions. In total, 58 scans were needed, of which 13 were around the Holy Aedicule, 8 on top of its roof, 8 in the two staircases, 10 from the Rotunda gallery, and 19 on the inside. The total number of points collected was 65 million for the outside and 42 million for the inside.

The density of the scans was selected to 1 point every 5 mm, in order to record all fine details, even those necessary at a later stage. The time required for each scan varied depending on the distance of the scanner to the object, a fact which differentiates the total number of points necessary. In any case, the time for each scan was not more than a few minutes.

9.5.2 Data Processing and Results

The creation of the final accurate three-dimensional model from the digital images is a complicated procedure requiring large computation cost and human effort. It includes the already mentioned collection of geometric data in limited space and time, the selection of the images, the 3D point cloud extraction, the creation of the surface, the noise filtering, and the merging of individual surfaces. It is important to note that in such cases, the detail of the surface is very important; thus the noise filtering must be a carefully implemented procedure. The initial data were processed using various software packages in order to produce the final accurate 3D model of the Holy Aedicule. After careful selection of the necessary images and the creation of thematic folders, the radiometric correction of the imagery took place aiming at their quality improvement by minimizing the effects of the shadows and dark areas. Then, the images are imported into the software that implements SfM and DIM techniques. Subsequently, the dense point cloud is exported and imported into another software package in order to be subjected to a time-consuming process for removing outliers. Finally, the processed point clouds are merged and exported again in order to be scaled. The SfM technique for the orientation of the images and the 3D point cloud extraction procedure were realized through the use of Agisoft's PhotoScan® software, which has been extensively evaluated for increased accuracy in prior research internationally and also of the Laboratory of Photogrammetry [12].

For the full coverage of the Holy Aedicule and the creation of a complete 3D model, images were captured from many different locations. It is important to note that for every part of the 3D model, the sparse point clouds consist of 10,000–60,000 points. After an inspection of the alignment results, the generation of the dense point cloud model took place. At this stage, the Agisoft PhotoScan® algorithms, based on the estimated camera positions, calculate depth information for each camera to be combined into a single dense point cloud. It is noted that the dense point cloud of each part of the 3D model of the Holy Aedicule consists of about 35,000,000 points and the entire model of about 280,000,000 points. At this stage the color is attributed to each point based on the images where it appears. In Fig. 9.4, upper left, the outside colored point cloud of the Holy Aedicule is presented.

The processing of the Holy Aedicule point cloud was realized within the Geomagic Studio®, MeshLab®, and CloudCompare® software. To sort out the outliers, several filtering algorithms were applied using various software packages [Geomagic Studio, MeshLab, and Cloud Compare (CC)]. In addition, algorithms were applied in order to make the point cloud uniform in terms of point spacing and to reduce its density. Finally, the processed dense point clouds are wrapped into meshes. Figure 9.4 upper right illustrates the part of the 3D model of the dome, which is one of the more complex parts of the Holy Aedicule. Through the created 3D model, it is possible to identify vulnerable and destroyed areas of the Holy Aedicule with no physical access to them.

The laser scanner data were thoroughly examined for their completeness in situ, i.e., before the departure of the team from Jerusalem. For that purpose, test registrations of the point clouds were performed in order to establish this possibility on one hand and their completeness on the other. After these tests, additional scans were required sometimes from very unconventional scan positions.

The final point cloud registration was performed in the Laboratory of Photogrammetry of NTUA. As the volume of data was huge, it was decided to perform

Fig. 9.4 *Upper left* The colored point cloud of the Holy Aedicule. *Upper right* The 3D model of the dome textured. *Lower* Part of the registered point clouds inside the Holy Aedicule [5]

the registration separately for the inside and outside parts of the Holy Aedicule. For the point cloud registration, at least three points are required. This role was undertaken by the special targets, whose coordinates in the common reference system were carefully determined. Hence after registration the point clouds were also referenced to the common system. The accuracy achieved for the registrations was of the order of 2–3 mm. In Fig. 9.4 *lower*, a sample of the registered point clouds is shown.

For registering and georeferencing the three-dimensional models of the Holy Aedicule which were produced with the methods described to the common reference system, specially targeted points were put in suitable positions on the inside and outside of the Holy Aedicule and also in the surrounding area. In total 38 control points were used.

9.5.3 Inserting GPR in 3D

The 3D representation of the results of the nondestructive prospection with GPR for the internal structure of the Holy Aedicule was considered highly useful as it actually enables the 5D representation of the historic construction phases. For the creation of this innovative 3D model of the internal structure of the Holy Aedicule, as this was interpreted from the GPR data, an interdisciplinary scientific methodology was developed. The methodology applied was specially designed and adapted for this specific application, as it has not been implemented in this way in the past. Finally, the 3D surface model created was incorporated into the existing high-resolution 3D model of the interior of the Holy Aedicule, where its position in relation to the reference system and also to the various details was established. This initial innovative step toward the relation of the GPR data and high-resolution 3D models definitely enables the study of the Holy Aedicule and offers additional data to the experts. In addition, this related model verifies the precision and accuracy of the measurements and observations by the members of the interdisciplinary team.

The contribution of this 3D visualization and relation of the interpreted GPR measurements are very important for this study, as it represents the internal structure of the Holy Aedicule, which is not directly visible. The main aim is to enable the advanced interpretation of the initial GPR observations from the experts and the feeding of the structural study with this invaluable information. For the creation of this innovative 3D model of the internal structure of the Holy Aedicule, as this was interpreted from the GPR data, an interdisciplinary scientific methodology was developed. The boundary lines of the various materials detected were available in 2D sections at 23 known elevations in the form of JPG images. They covered the Holy Aedicule from a height of 0.3 m up to 2.9 m from the internal floor. It was foreseen that these sections had at least two points of reference, which were determined in the common reference system. In this way their georeference was enabled and also they were directly related to the 3D model.

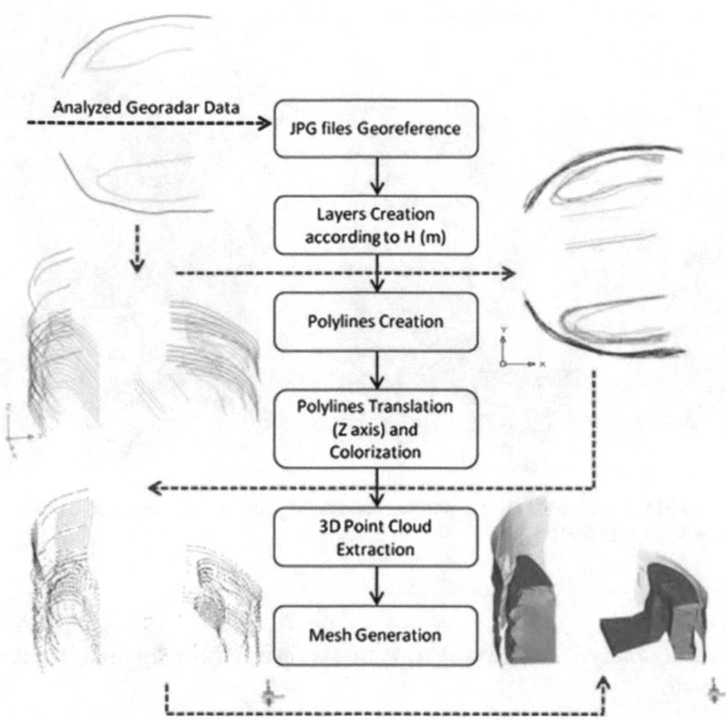

Fig. 9.5 Flowchart of the methodology developed for the creation of the 3D model of the internal structure of the Holy Aedicule

The methodology applied was specially designed and adapted for this specific application, as it has not been implemented in this way in the past (Fig. 9.5). Initially the 23 images of the 2D sections of GPR were georeferenced. Subsequently they were placed in various layers according to their height attribute. They would contain the digitized border lines/2D sections.

Afterward, each of these lines was transferred to its own height. In this way the 2D information was converted to 3D. Then points were extracted from the drawn polylines in a .txt file. This file was imported into a point cloud and surface processing software, where the desired surface is created and is subject to the final processing for its integration and completion with the help of careful interpolation (Fig. 9.6 left).

Finally, the 3D surface model created was incorporated to the existing high-resolution 3D model (Fig. 9.6 right) of the interior of the Holy Aedicule, where its position in relation to the reference system and also to the various details was established. This initial innovative step toward the relation of the GPR data and high-resolution 3D models definitely enables the study of the Holy Aedicule and offers additional data to the experts. In addition, this related model verifies the precision and accuracy of the measurements and observations by the members of

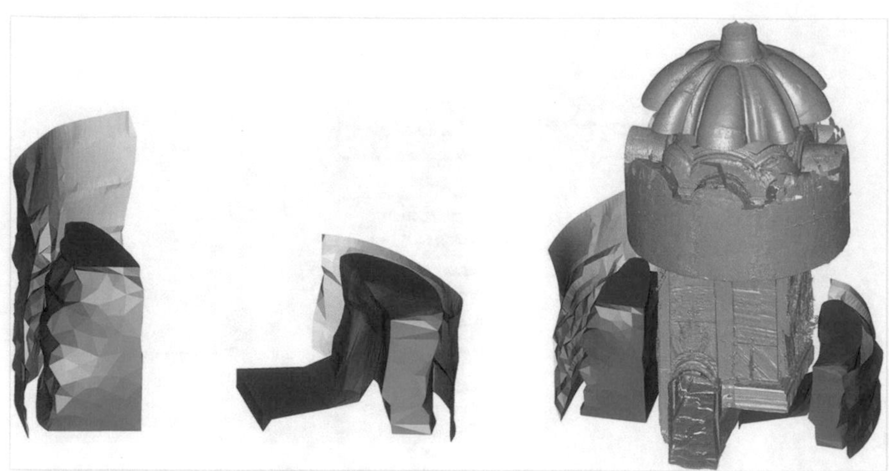

Fig. 9.6 *Left* 3D visualization of the prospection findings. *Right* The scanned 3D model (*gray*) integrated with the 3D GPR data

the interdisciplinary team. However, it needs further investigation, research, and development.

9.5.4 Visualizations from the 3D Model

From the three-dimensional model, it is possible to visualize the Holy Aedicule with simple procedures in order to better understand its structure and for the proposals for its restoration to be based on solid ground. In addition, the eventual restoration works can be better designed and programmed.

Initially a vertical section was implemented to the 3D model. This section appears in Fig. 9.7 left with texture. It should be noted that this texture is originating from the high-resolution images. Corresponding sections can be applied in any position and at any angle. Finally, in Fig. 9.7 *right* a horizontal section at a very low height is presented, in order to highlight the marvelous marble inlays of the Holy Aedicule floor set by the architect Komnenos.

9.6 Materials Characterization

Members of the Laboratory of Material Science and Engineering, School of Chemical Engineering NTUA, conducted an in situ diagnostic study for assessing the extent of material decay and the conservation state of the Holy Aedicule of the

Fig. 9.7 *Left* Visualization of a vertical section from the 3D model with texture. *Right* horizontal section of the 3D model where the floor is shown

Church of the Holy Sepulchre. The present section is part of the study under the title "*Materials & Conservation, Reinforcement and Rehabilitation Interventions in the Holy Edicule of the Holy Sepulchre*" [5].

A macroscopic observation survey over the Sacred Monument reveals the extent of certain deformation of the external facades of the Monument (Fig. 9.8), suggesting detachment of the façade building material from the internal substrate due to that buckling. These deformations could have a great impact on the Sacred Monument's static and dynamic correspondence to loads contributing in a negative way to its longevity. This is the reason why the cause of the effect has to be determined and reversed. To do so, first a nondestructive testing assessment of the materials' compatibility and condition took place making use of the infrared thermography and the fiber-optical microscopy.

In order to determine the materials' decay and the origination of this decay (causes), the need to study the building materials with laboratory techniques arises. Characterization of historic materials is subjected to sampling limitations imposed by the sensitive nature of built cultural heritage—in which the nondestructive techniques present a clear advantage over destructive analytical testing—and refers

Fig. 9.8 External facades deformations

to a range of analyses. In the present study, material characterization measurements will be utilized not only as data for the integrated 5D modelling but also for visualization purposes such as texturing and rendering of visual objects. In particular, optical microscopy measurements are processed and then used for texturing the mesh (UV Mapping) of the historic construction phases' 3D models (4D modelling). Additionally, nondestructive testing and material characterization measurements (infrared thermography, X-ray diffraction, mercury intrusion porosimetry) enable data fusion from heterogeneous datasets.

9.6.1 Sampling

In order to identify the causes behind the external marble masonry deformations, the building materials' preservation state has to be examined with laboratory techniques and make an evaluation of their decay, physical, chemical, and mechanical properties. The extracted samples (building materials: building stones, mortars, plasters) were collected from crucial parts around the Monument. Core samples were also extracted (Fig. 9.9), in order to ensure that building materials coming from all the historic construction phases of the Holy Monument would be included in the study.

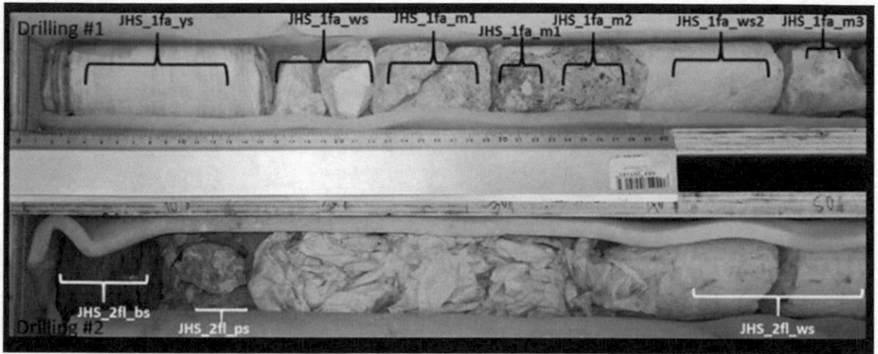

Fig. 9.9 *Upper* Façade core sample: Three building stones and three mortar samples. *Lower* Floor core sample: Three building stone samples

9.6.2 Nondestructive Testing

Infrared Thermography

Infrared thermography measurements were performed for the nondestructive inspection of the architectural surfaces of the Holy Aedicule of the Church of the Holy Sepulchre in order to collect data indicative to: the decay of the building materials, the physicochemical compatibility among each other by identifying defective areas, the presence of nonvisible components inside a wall, and the presence of moisture and the study of its transportation mechanisms. The particular method-technique records the infrared radiation emitted from the testing materials providing their thermal radiation map, which is associated with the microstructure and their surface morphology. The thermal variations of the testing material are recorded and rendered where the different colors correspond to different temperatures.

From the examination of the south façade of the Holy Aedicule, it is verified that the long intervals of the pilgrims burning candles cause strong thermal stresses to the building stone of the façade, apart from the obvious esthetic degradation, due to accumulation of soot and oil deposits. This can be deduced from the higher temperature by 1.5 °C of the building stones neighboring the flame of the candle (Fig. 9.10). The anisotropic heat distribution over the surface of the building stone and subsequently in the deeper layers of the wall via the mechanism of heat induction and the maintenance of that temperature difference at least by 0.5 °C 3 h after burning the candles out proves the topical thermal heterogeneity. The aforementioned action taking place on a daily basis causes corresponding changes in the thermo-hygrometric behavior of the building materials in the masonry, accelerating their deterioration.

Fiber-Optical Microscopy

Fiber optic microscope (FOM) is a nondestructive microscope that can be utilized in situ to acquire magnified, visible-spectrum images. FOM is a microscope system

Fig. 9.10 IR-thermal inspection of the south façade of the Holy Aedicule of the Church of the Holy Sepulchre

integrating advanced optics, fiber optics, and digital components. Whereas in traditional optical microscopy a sample is required to be placed at the microscope, with FOM, no sampling is required, and the image can be acquired in situ. In the field of cultural heritage protection, FOM is employed to identify differences in the texture and composition of surfaces, for materials classification (e.g., classifications of mortars) and for the study of the decay phenomena (alveolation, hard carbonate crust, etc.); to investigate the materials' surface morphology; to identify defects in historic building materials, for material characterization; to classify decay typologies for porous stones; to evaluate cleaning interventions, consolidation interventions, and incompatible interventions; and to study the preservation state of mosaics.

A part of the Holy Rock of Golgotha coming from the core sample illustrated in Fig. 9.9, is examined through Optical Microscopy, as illustrated in Fig. 9.11. Macroscopically, has off-white color with visible craters all over its range. The examination with the polarizing microscope (Fig. 9.11 *lower left*) reveals opaque metallic minerals which probably are ferric (Fe) oxides and hydroxides as suggested by the off-orange color revealed from the fiber optical microscope measurements in the same figure.

9.6.3 Laboratory Techniques: Petrographic and Mineralogical Characterization

In order to determine the origin, the micro-texture, and structure of the rocks, the optical mineralogy analysis in thin section is equipped. From the XRD examination (Fig. 9.12, left) of the same sample, it is slightly bituminous and mainly consists of micrite calcite at approximately 98 %. Opaque metallic minerals are also found, as shown from the polarized microscope measurement in Fig. 9.11, which are iron oxides

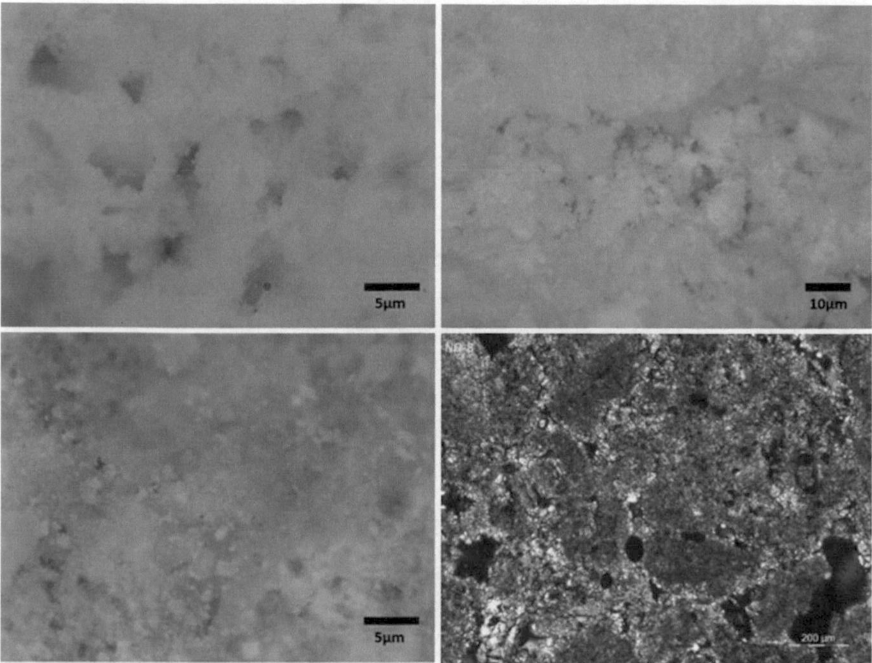

Fig. 9.11 *Upper* and *lower left* Microscope fiber optic measurements using lens 50× (scale 10 µm) and lens 120× (scale 5 µm). *Lower right* Polarizing microscope measurement

at <2 %. This sample is characterized as a micritic limestone. The pore size distribution, as determined from the microstructural analysis with mercury intrusion porosimetry, is presented in Fig. 9.12, right. From the microstructural analysis for the same sample, the measured characteristics were: Specific surface area is 0.256 m^2/g, total porosity 22.37 %, average pore radius 0.005 µm, and bulk density 3.08 g/cm^3.

9.7 Five-Dimensional (5D) Modelling of the Historic Construction Phases

Based upon the sketches of Fig. 9.1 coming from the historic documentation of the Holy Aedicule provided by the Architect of the Technical Service of the Jerusalem Patriarchate, Dr. T. Mitropoulos [2], the visualization of the first two construction phases of the Holy Aedicule has been realized with the open-source computer graphics software Blender. According to the historic documentation, the Holy Tomb was carved outside, possibly in a polygonal form, with an entrance on its eastern side (Fig. 9.1a). In order to represent the real texture of the Holy Tomb, FOM measurements from the Holy Rock of Golgotha sample (Fig. 9.7) were processed and used to create a new “virtual material” within Blender. The mesh

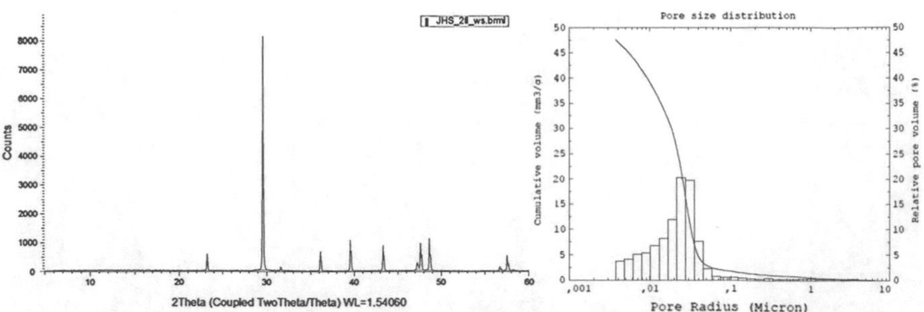

Fig. 9.12 *Left* XRD pattern. *Right* Pore size distribution

Fig. 9.13 The Holy Aedicule—two construction phases (*left* and *right* models) and the demolished state in the *middle*

of the 3D model was unwrapped and the UV mapping of the mesh polygons based upon the "virtual material" previously constructed. The rendered result of the first construction-phase textured 3D model is illustrated in the left part of Fig. 9.13. In order to texture the demolished (by the Persians Fig. 9.1b) part of the Holy Tomb, another processed FOM measurement from a cracked section of the sample used to create one more "virtual material" for texturing the specific area of the rendered 3D model as illustrated in the middle part of Fig. 9.13. Due to the fact that there are no documented information for the masonry building materials (stones and mortars) from the Modestus reconstruction phase (Fig. 9.1a), a random masonry material has been used for texturing the reconstructed masonry as presented (rendered) in the right part of Fig. 9.13. In conclussion, 3D visualization of the first and the second construction phases of the Holy Tomb has enabled the 4D modelling, whereas material data fusion (i.e. texture), realize the 5D modelling.

The 3D models representing the historic phases have been fitted upon the dimensions of the real Holy Rock of Golgotha as they are illustrated in Fig. 9.14. Based on the analysis presented at the end of the previous chapter, the interpolation of the

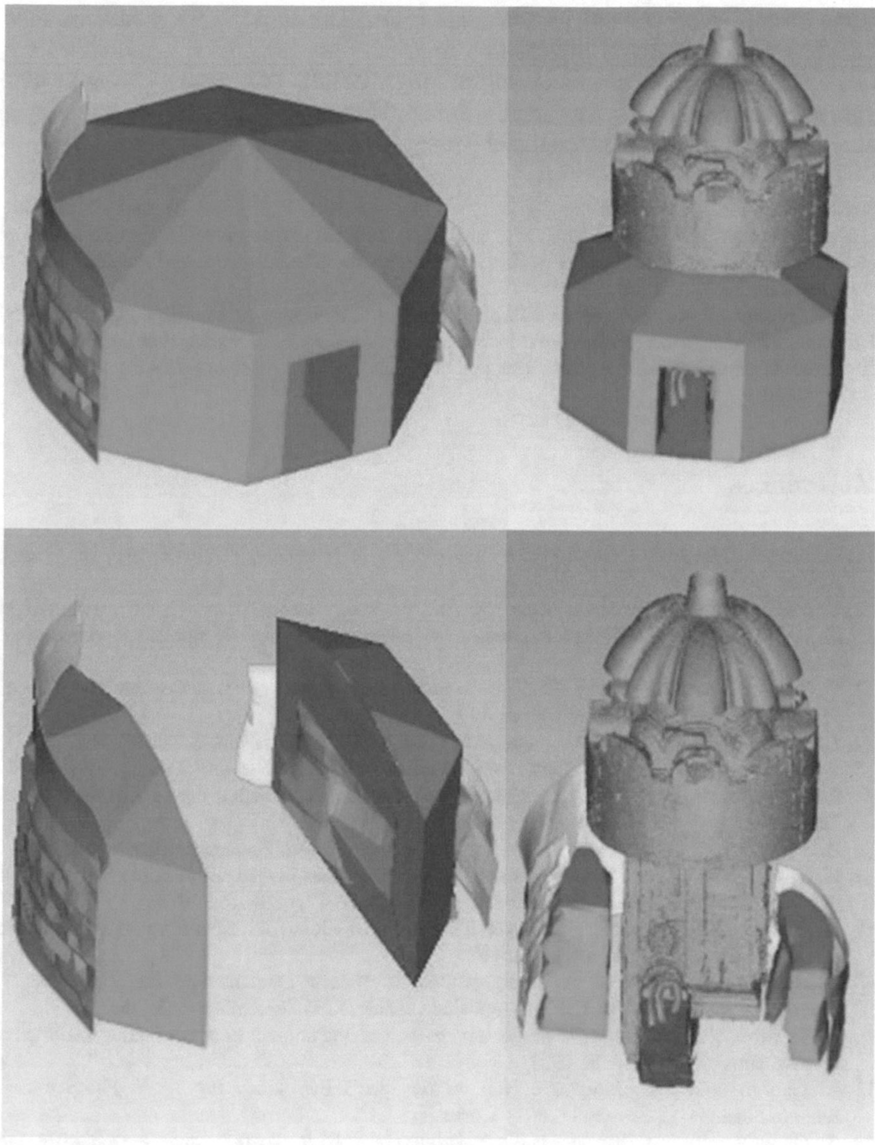

Fig. 9.14 Fitting the 3D models in the real dimensions as estimated by the GPR measurements

GPR measurements in different heights gave an estimation of the real dimensions of the Holy Rock of Golgotha volume over which the historic construction-phase 3D models were adjusted.

The work presented so far contains enhanced information covering all aspects of the Aedicule structure and forms the basis for the creation of an innovative tool that induces mixed reality (MR) with the focus on the Aedicule's structural evolution (time factor—4D) and on its materials (5D). The typical 3D model is, thus, enriched by the fusion of information from various disciplines, i.e., architecture, civil, surveying, and chemical engineering. Within this context, gamification approach can be adopted that can transform the above 5D model into an emblematic case study for smart educational and heritage applications.

Acknowledgments His Beatitude the Patriarch of Jerusalem, Theophilos III, that took the initiative to perform the program agreement by NTUA with title "*Integrated Diagnostic Research Project and Strategic Planning for Materials, Interventions Conservation and Rehabilitation of the Holy Aedicule of the Church of the Holy Sepulchre in Jerusalem*".

His Paternity the Franciscan Custos of the Holy Land, Rev. f. Pierbattista Pizzaballa, and His Beatitude the Armenian Patriarch in Jerusalem, Nourhan Manougian, that authorized His Beatitude the Patriarch of Jerusalem, Theophilus III, and NTUA to perform this research.

References

1. G. Lavvas, *The Holy Church of the Resurrection in Jerusalem* (The Academy of Athens, Athens, 2009)
2. T. Mitropoulos, *Ο Πανίερος Ναός της Αναστάσεως Ιεροσολύμων—Το έργο του Κάλφα Κομνηνού* (Ευρωπαϊκό Κέντρο Βυζαντινών και Μεταβυζαντινών Μνημείων, Θεσσαλονίκη, 2009)
3. D. Pringle, *The Churches of the Crusader Kingdom of Jerusalem. A Corpus*. The City of Jerusalem, vol III (Cambridge University Press, Cambridge, 2010)
4. S.S. Montefiore, *The Biography Paperback* (Weidenfeld & Nicolson, Great Britain, 2011)
5. A. Moropoulou, *Materials & Conservation, Reinforcement and Rehabilitation Interventions in the Holy Edicule of the Holy Sepulchre* (National Technical University of Athens, Athens, 2016)
6. B. Amico, *Trattato delle piante et imagini dei sacri edificii di Terrasanta* (Roma, 1609)
7. K. Labropoulos, A. Moropoulou, Ground penetrating radar investigation of the bell tower of the church of the Holy Sepulchre. Constr. Build. Mater. **47**, 689–700 (2013)
8. M. Biddle, M.A.R. Cooper, S. Robson, The Tomb of Christ, Jerusalem: a photogrammetric survey. Photogramm. Rec. **14**(79), 25–43 (1992)
9. D. Balodimos, G. Lavvas, A. Georgopoulos, in *Wholly Documenting Holy Monuments*. Paper Presented at the XIX CIPA Symposium, Antalya, 30 September–4 October 2003
10. V.C. Corbo, *Il Santo Sepolchro di Gerusalemme*, vol 3 (Publication of the Studium Biblicum Franciscanum 29, Jerusalem, 1981)
11. A. Georgopoulos, M. Modatsos, Non metric bird's eye view. Int. Arch. Photogramm. Remote Sens. **34**(5), 359–362 (2002). Corfu
12. A. Georgopoulos, in *Photogrammetric Automation: Is It Worth?* Paper Presented at the Virtual Archaeology Museums & Cultural Tourism, Delphi, 23–26 September 2015
13. G. Lavvas, *The Church of the Holy Sepulchre in Jerusalem* (Academy of Athens, Athens, 2009)
14. G. Tucci, V. Bonora, in *Geomatic Techniques and 3D Modeling for the Survey of the Church of the Holy Sepulchre in Jerusalem*. Paper Presented at the XXIII CIPA Symposium, Prague, 12–16 September 2011

Chapter 10
Historic BIM for Mobile VR/AR Applications

Luigi Barazzetti and Fabrizio Banfi

Abstract This chapter presents the latest advances in historic building information modeling (HBIM) that have been transformed into models for mobile apps based on augmented and virtual reality. The chapter aims to demonstrate that a complex model based on HBIM can be used in portable devices to extract useful information not only for specialists in architecture, engineering, and construction industry and cultural heritage documentation and preservation but also for a wide user community interested in cultural tourism.

Keywords 3D modeling • BIM • Built environment • Mixed reality

10.1 BIM for Cultural Heritage Documentation and Preservation

Since its early days, building information modeling (BIM) has provided new digital instruments for integrated and collaborative projects in the architecture, engineering, and construction (AEC) industry [1]. In recent years, economic challenges have caused a surge in interest in smart technologies for the whole building life cycle: design, construction, operation, maintenance, renovation, and demolition [2, 3]. Here, BIM plays a fundamental role.

The main advantage of an approach based on BIM is that it provides a virtual model of a facility, in which architectural and structural elements (e.g., walls, doors, windows, pillars) and mechanical, electrical, and plumbing services are structured in a database. Elements have relationships (e.g., a door fits into a wall), parametric geometry (i.e., elements are defined by specific parameters such as width or height), and attributes (e.g., energy data, material properties).

BIM technology is not limited to buildings. BIM can be used for many projects related to the built environment, such as civil infrastructures [4], for example, highways, bridges, tunnels, and dams. In addition, BIM can also be applied to

L. Barazzetti (✉) • F. Banfi
Politecnico di Milano, via Ponzio 31, 20133 Milan, Italy
e-mail: luigi.barazzetti@polimi.it; fabrizio.banfi@polimi.it

M. Ioannides et al. (eds.), *Mixed Reality and Gamification for Cultural Heritage*,
DOI 10.1007/978-3-319-49607-8_10

restore, adapt, and reuse existing valuable constructions, including historic structures [5].

Historic BIM (HBIM) [6] is intended as the application of BIM technology to historic buildings, which are digitally surveyed with images and laser scans [7–17]. Here, the complexity of historic constructions, with their irregular geometry, inhomogeneous materials, variable morphology, alterations, damages, and various construction stages, makes the creation of an accurate and detailed model using HBIM a challenging task.

The aim of this chapter is to investigate the possibility of using an accurate model based on HBIM in mobile devices, starting from a detailed survey of a building. Different specialists interested in preservation policies and sustainable management, cultural heritage documentation, disaster prevention, improved risk management, conservation, cost-effective maintenance, and restoration techniques (e.g., architects, archaeologists, restorers, historians, conservators, and engineers) can exploit the benefits of improved team collaboration using HBIM.

On the other hand, the practical applications of HBIM are not limited to professionals. Particular attention is also paid to a wider user community and applications in various fields, including built environment education, interactive learning, cultural tourism, and gamification, among others (Fig. 10.1).

Currently, wider use of HBIM is expected thanks to its close relationship with the latest developments in the technology industry. Cloud computing allows optimized collaboration with multiple devices, including advanced tools for modeling and simulation [18, 19]. Game engines can be exploited for real-time rendering to generate immersive and interactive BIM environments based on virtual reality (VR) and augmented reality (AR).

Mobile devices play an essential role in stimulating interactions between people (including specialists and so-called casual users) and digital cultural heritage. This is useful in the creation of knowledge and preservation of cultural heritage. Handheld mobile devices (mainly smartphones and tablets) can be used for productive work or for personal and recreational purposes (Fig. 10.2). Today, mobile devices are used in various scientific disciplines (e.g., medicine, education, simulated training) because of their highly flexible nature and the real-time access to information they provide: it is normal to digitize notes, send and receive invoices, scan barcodes, or make payments. At the same time, they allow for simple exploitation of digital models coupled with additional information (the "I" in HBIM).

The use of advanced visualization techniques for three-dimensional (3D) models transferred to mobile devices is not new in the AEC industry. For instance, efficient techniques for photorealistic visualization are required to present projects to clients. This is usually carried out in 3D rendered environments or 360° panoramic images, which allow users to navigate virtual scenes with varying levels of immersion and interactivity.

Because HBIM is available in 3D, there is a direct connection between digital models and advanced visualization techniques based on AR and VR. Starting from laser scanning and photogrammetric point clouds, the manual generation of

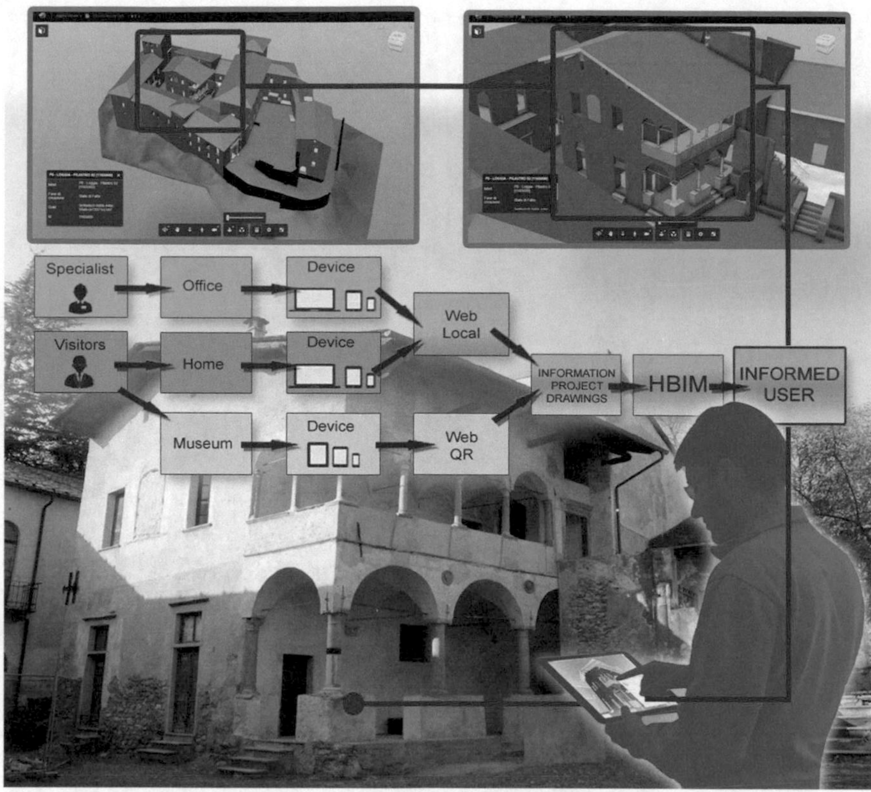

Fig. 10.1 Possible flowcharts for different operators interested in products generated from a model based on HBIM

two-dimensional (2D) project boards can be avoided (or at least reduced) using BIM.

Advanced modeling techniques allow for the generation of parametric 3D models, from which traditional project boards (plans, sections, elevations) can be automatically generated [20]. On the other hand, the level of detail that is achievable with laser scanning and photogrammetric point clouds could provide reconstructions with a huge number of polygons [21], too many to be simultaneously visualized on mobile devices. Scalable procedures able to display only specific parts of a model become mandatory. Integration with realistic visualization techniques able to provide a high level of visual fidelity is another important issue in which visibility and occlusion problems, lighting conditions, visual effects, and photorealistic textures play essential roles.

The graphic quality of a 3D model has great importance for the transmission of visual information. Several parameters determine the quality of the final visualization, which is strictly dependent on project requirements. The main aspects relate to, for example, the features of mobile devices, the resolution and image format

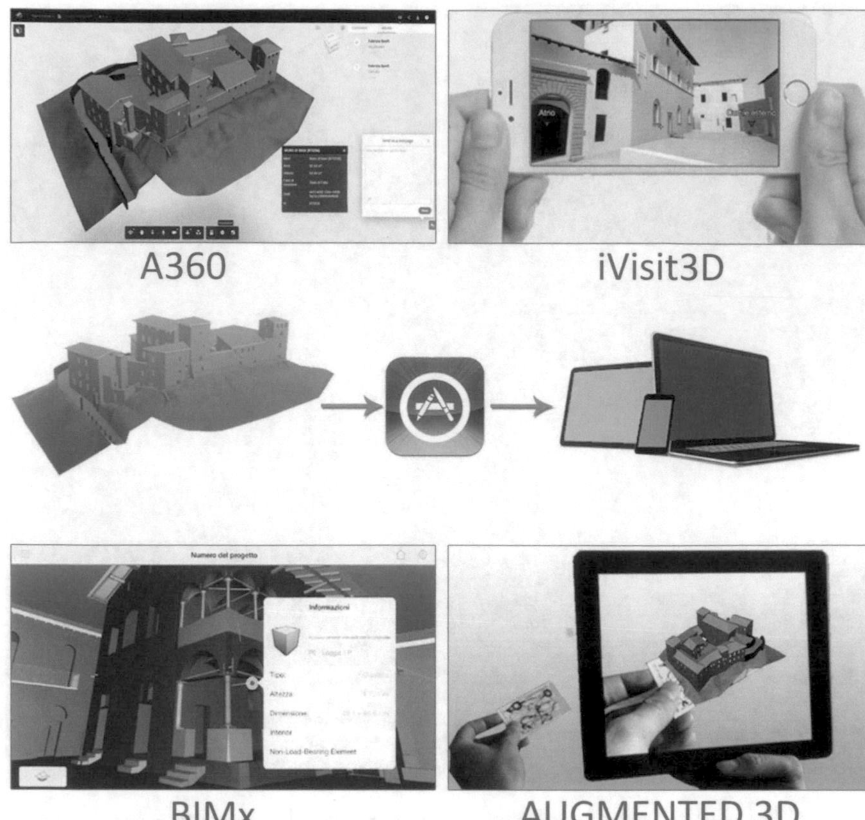

Fig. 10.2 Apps allow the use of HBIM in mobile devices

associated with geometry (e.g., size and number of pixels, radiometric and geometric resolution, depth, texture), rendering engines, and the limits of the mapping system in which the 3D model will be displayed.

BIM technology is based on software for parametric modeling, which replaces the traditional production of "pure geometry" models (direct modeling) with sets of predefined libraries, including building fabric systems and mechanical and electrical objects [22]. Architectural, structural, and mechanical, electrical, and plumbing (MEP) elements chosen from existing databases also contain information for material characterization. Materials for visual mapping can therefore be chosen from native object databases (such as local databases of BIM software and online repositories) or generated as new elements to customize the different visual properties.

This work describes some VR and AR applications designed to run on mobile devices. An accurate and detailed model based on HBIM was turned into several application-specific formats for smartphones and tablets. Results are illustrated and discussed using the case study of Castel Masegra, a castle located in the city of

Sondrio (Lombardy region, Italy). A detailed and accurate HBIM model (500 MB in Autodesk Revit file format) was generated from laser scanning and photogrammetry, which provided a huge point cloud comprised of 7.5 billion points. The various structural elements of the castle were modeled following their logic of construction (how the construction was assembled) as well as chronological, material, and stratigraphic aspects. The model was then simplified and exported into different file formats to try out different mobile applications for both professional workers and casual users interested in digital tourism.

10.2 Conversion of a Survey into Parametric Geometry: Beyond Direct Modeling

HBIM requires a detailed digital reconstruction from point clouds acquired by laser scanning and photogrammetric techniques. The modeling can be carried out by manual, semiautomated, or automated procedures [23–25]. Because dense point clouds reveal the geometric complexity and diversity of historic constructions, parametric modeling is not a trivial task (Fig. 10.3).

Most commercial BIM software packages available on the commercial market were developed for modern and regular buildings. Objects have prefixed shapes, parameters, and attributes that do not reflect the real characteristics of historic constructions along with their anomalies (e.g., tilted walls, variable thickness, and unique decorative and structural elements). Although some BIM software packages have specific tools (family editors) for the generation of ad hoc objects, predefined functions for parametric 3D modeling are not always sufficient for detailed projects, especially if the virtual model must be an accurate digital representation for documentation, conservation, and restoration (not just a visual model).

Most 3D documentation projects from dense point clouds are carried out with direct modeling techniques, in which static 3D models are generated without advanced parametric representation. This is not sufficient in BIM projects where parametric objects allow the user to modify shapes by setting specific parameters stored in a database [26]. The parametric 3D model is intended as an advanced computer technology able to manage information for the automatic generation of drawings (e.g., sections, plans), reports, design analysis, schedule simulation, thermal and structural analysis, facilities management, and much more. Semantics cannot be neglected in BIM. Objects know where they belong, how they relate to other objects, and what they consist of [27].

A synthesis of the basic requirements for parametric objects is provided in [28]. More specifically, parametric objects:

- Contain geometric information and associated data and rules
- Have nonredundant geometry, which allows for no inconsistencies

Fig. 10.3 Point clouds (*right*) are converted into a detailed HBIM model (*left*)

- Have parametric rules that automatically modify associated geometries when inserted into a building model or when changes are made to associated objects
- Can be defined at different levels of aggregation
- Have the ability to link to or receive, broadcast, or export sets of attributes, for example, structural materials, acoustic data, energy data, or cost, to other applications and models

The choice of structural elements that require parameterization and the kind of parameterization required represent a new paradigm for HBIM. As mentioned earlier, historic buildings are often characterized by geometric anomalies, including walls with variable thicknesses, tilted columns, and voids and floor deflections, for example. Here, predefined structural elements with a consistent logic of construction and unique shape are not available in existing data repositories.

The creation of new object libraries (for each specific case study) might be a solution. However, producing a new library is a very time-consuming work. Some authors have developed new methods for capturing the geometric complexity in a

Fig. 10.4 Example of irregular vault with additional parameterization of the thickness following survey of intrados with point clouds

parametric way [29], facilitating the use of BIM technology in cultural heritage documentation.

An example of a historic object with additional parameterization is shown in Fig. 10.4. The umbrella vault of Castel Masegra was surveyed with laser scanning point clouds and photogrammetry to create an accurate digital model. Point clouds can capture only the external surface of the vault (intrados), whereas BIM requires a parametric representation with solid objects and their internal structure (layers). Because information about the thickness of the vault was not available, the parameterization of the extrados was generated through a dynamic thickness. The method uses an interactive offset [30, 31] of the different parts of the vault. Obviously, semantics must be added to create an effective vault object consistent with the floor upstairs and the lateral walls.

10.3 The Importance of the "I" in HBIM

Building information modeling is more than a 3D model. It is a rich database of the facility, in which the 3D model provides interactive access to a variety of information, including, for example, materials, thermal properties, and layers. The word

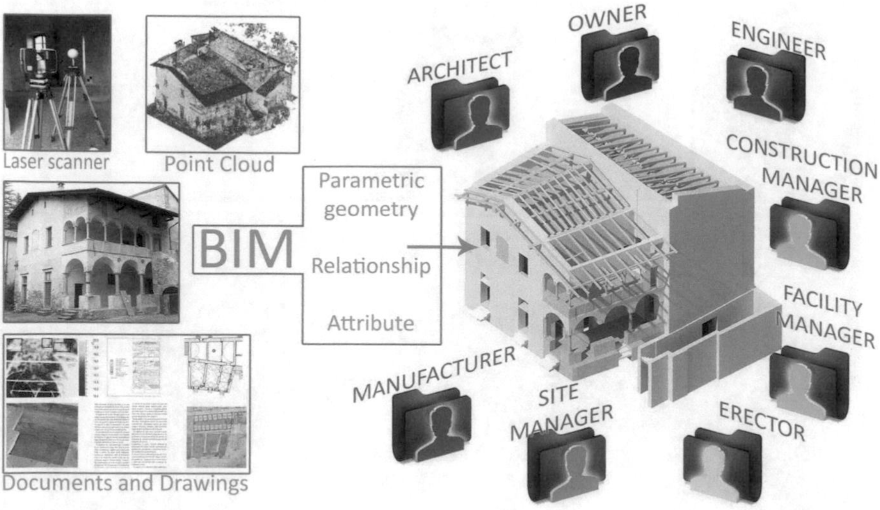

Fig. 10.5 Information from multiple data sources can be integrated into HBIM, which is becoming a common platform for the different professional workers involved in the project

information in the acronym BIM plays a fundamental role. A database that includes semantics and object properties is mandatory to create and manage meaningful information about the building. BIM software packages (e.g., Revit, ArchiCAD, AECOsim Building Designer, Teckla) allow users to electronically collaborate at different levels, from basic configurations based on isolated (independent) processing on different platforms (desktop and mobile) to an integrated data access via cloud services [32], which is fundamental to ensure a consistent exchange of information.

The availability of multiuser information makes BIM a shared platform for all professional operators involved in a project (Fig. 10.5). BIM is designed as a 3D information model of the construction industry, with expected improvements in the overall project workflow for the opportunity to share information and facilitate decision making.

As mentioned earlier, the 3D model is not only a graphic representation of the construction; it is an advanced computer technology that can be used to manage information for the automatic generation of drawings (e.g., sections, plans), reports, design analyses, schedule simulations, thermal and structural analyses, facilities management, and much more. BIM is a so-called seven-dimensional solution able to share information throughout the building life cycle, thereby eliminating data redundancy, data reentry, data loss, miscommunication, and translation errors. If the first three dimensions refer to geometry, 4D simulation adds time (e.g., the sequential phases of a project before the construction phase or the transition from the design phase to the construction phase), 5D provides a direct link to costs (e.g., cost management), 6D relates to building life cycle management, and 7D concerns facility and asset management.

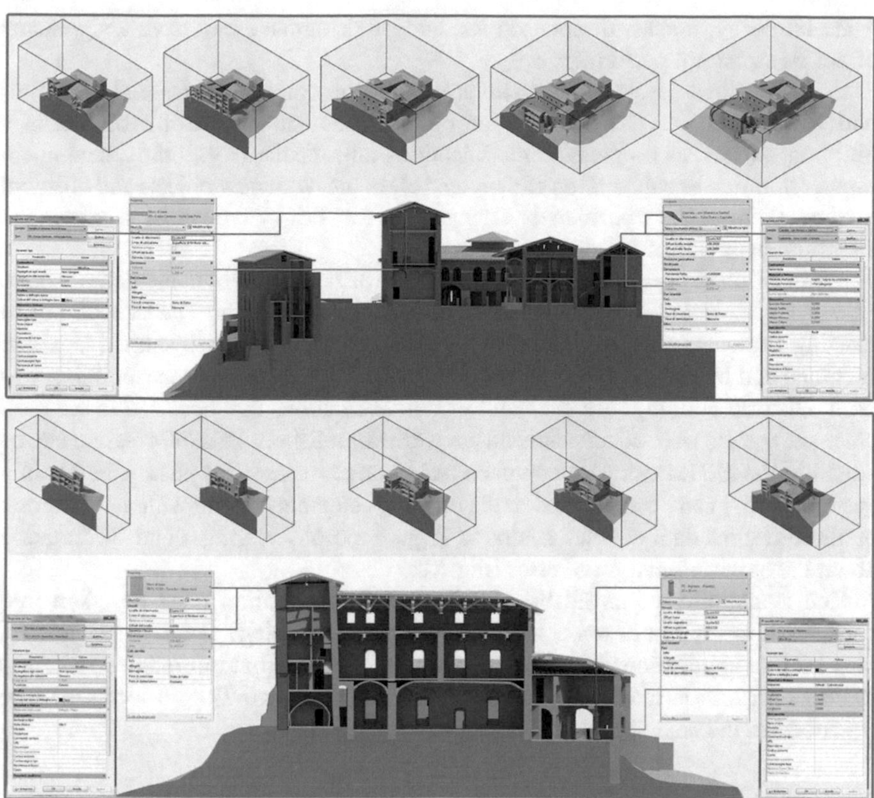

Fig. 10.6 Information incorporated into the database of the building (for the different structural elements) comprises a fundamental part of a complete BIM project

The case of historic buildings surveyed with photogrammetry and laser scanning poses new challenges not only in terms of the complexity of geometry but also the basic information that is usually required to enrich an HBIM database (Fig. 10.6).

The survey cannot be limited to the acquisition of geometric data. The survey is intended as an exhaustive analysis of the building, including a historical analysis, because the different construction stages reflect the modifications to the building, the identification of materials, technological aspects, stratigraphic analysis, and information from other inspections such as destructive and nondestructive tests, and infrared thermography. Information from additional analysis with nondestructive (e.g., thermography, sonic tests, geo-radar), minor destructive (e.g., flat jack, coring), or destructive (sampling) tests may be available in conservation and restoration projects. The mechanical characterization of the materials used in historic buildings, along with their internal composition, represents another significant challenge. Buildings are made up of heterogeneous materials (e.g., bricks in combination with mortar, stones), and construction elements have variable morphologies, with alterations, repairs, demolitions, or additions occurring over time.

Material decay, cracks, disconnections, and other damage can have a significant effect on structural performance.

A diagnostic analysis can be extremely useful in combining material properties and geometric data. The deterioration of materials and historical evolution of a building, as well as progressive modifications and repairs (e.g., infills, new openings, restoration or substitution of damaged elements with new objects and different materials), must be considered. Changes in the original conditions affect the structural behavior of buildings.

As mentioned previously, the identification of the different construction stages cannot be neglected in the analysis of historic constructions. The availability of existing drawings (not only modern project boards but also historic plans and sections) can be extremely useful for understanding how a particular building was built. Historic buildings are the result of transformations that occurred in the past, where new parts were added while others were demolished. This information can be stored in the HBIM using an approach based on chronological phases, in which a specific period can be associated to the different elements, along with a description of the different data sources available (e.g., reports, drawings) and information about the expected margin of error (Fig. 10.7).

The availability of an HBIM enriched with information must be taken into consideration for future reuse in mobile devices. As things stand at the present, only mobile applications based on BIM can preserve digital information, whereas information loss is inevitable for most AR and VR apps. These aspects will be described in the next section.

10.4 HBIM in Mobile Devices Through Augmented and Virtual Reality

The use of BIM on mobile devices is becoming increasingly important for collaborative projects involving many different specialists. The ability to work with mobile apps connected to a centralized cloud service allows specialists to pursue a strategy of simultaneous exploitation and exploration of BIM, sharing rich digital information at different levels.

Examples of mobile applications integrating BIM technology were proposed in [33], where a virtual panoramic environment was developed to show the construction progress. A mixed reality tool to support professionals in the AEC industry was developed in [34], whereas AR and BIM were integrated in [35] to detect construction defects.

Recent years have witnessed the realization of mobile BIM applications for training, education, and simulation. Projects aimed at developing learning tools for energy issues (such as heating, ventilation, and air-conditioning) were proposed in [36, 37]. A simulation of evacuation was proposed in [38], including Web-based

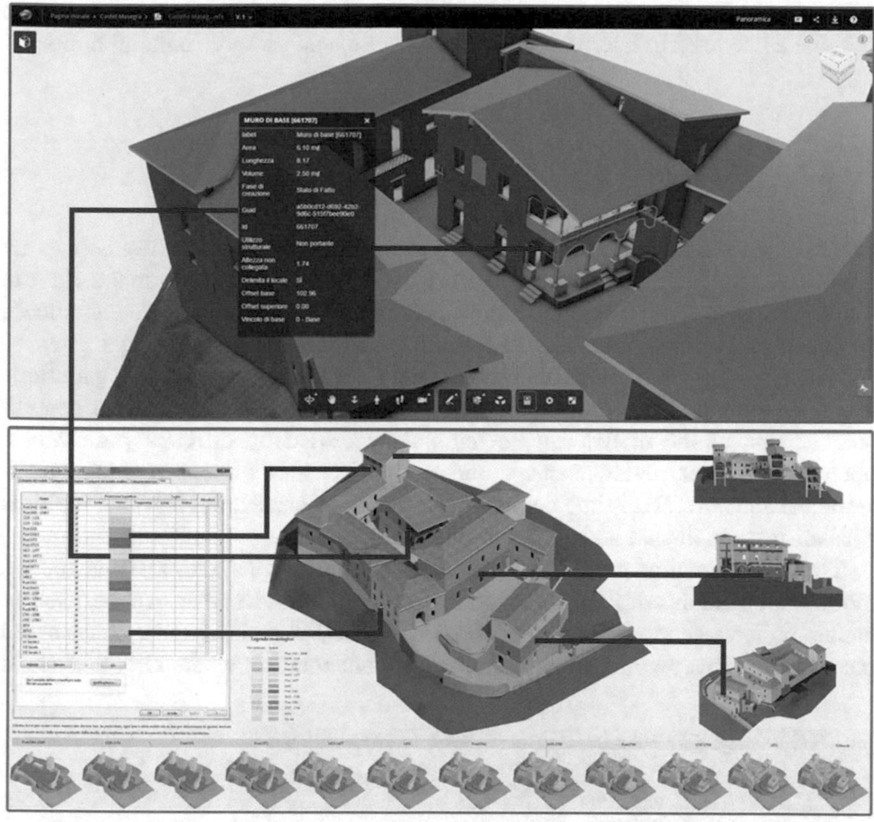

Fig. 10.7 Information on chronological phases can be integrated in different objects

visualization tools and serious games. Approaches to the sustainable management of buildings were proposed in [39] by means of a serious game.

Nowadays, several applications for so-called mobile BIM are available on the Internet. Most BIM applications can be downloaded from the Apple Store or Google Play. Examples include Autodesk 36, Buzzsaw Mobile, Tekla BIMsight Mobile, Graphisoft BIMx, SketchUp Viewer, BIManywhere, Structural Synchronizer, McNeel iRhino, LCi Sightspace3D, BIM 360 Glue, Navigator Pano Review, Revizto Viewer, InfraWorks 360, and others.

The aim of this chapter is to demonstrate that HBIM technology can be used on mobile devices not only by specialists in AEC industry fields and cultural heritage preservation but also by a wider user community interested in digital reconstructions and virtual tourism. The use of HBIM with mobile applications for VR and AR could represent a new opportunity for modeling and understanding cultural heritage. Mobile AR and VR deliver advanced multimedia contents with high levels of entertainment. The combination of geometry and digital information encapsulated in a model based on HBIM with AR and VR has the potential to become a new way to interpret, understand, reuse, and preserve cultural heritage.

10.4.1 HBIM in Mobile Apps for Specialists

Different mobile applications able to handle models based on BIM technology are available on the Internet. The main idea is to move the use of BIM from the office to the construction site, providing a new collaborative environment for architects, engineers, customers, producers, and builders, among others. Nowadays, growing attention is being paid to apps integrating cloud technology for connecting multiple users, avoiding multiple project versions with possible inconsistencies. A centralized version of the model can be remotely accessed by different professional operators, who can review, inspect, and edit project files without expensive hardware and software. Real-time communication can be carried out between multiple specialists through chat and e-mail notifications.

The first application presented in this work is Autodesk 360 (A360) (Fig. 10.8), a mobile application with an associated cloud-based service that can be used to handle projects generated in Autodesk Revit. A360 is defined as “a cloud-based platform that gives you access to storage, a collaboration workspace, and cloud

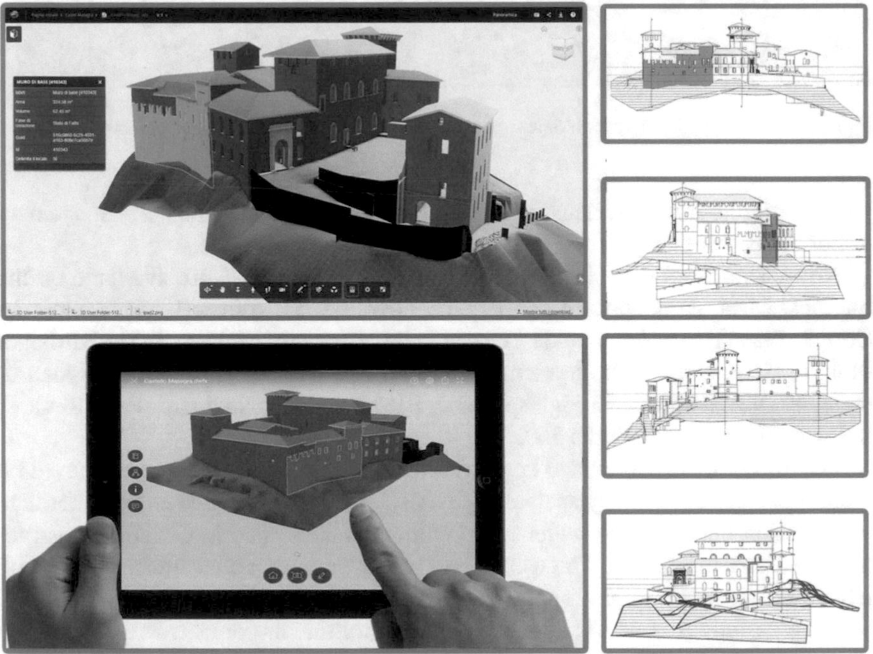

Fig. 10.8 BIM of Castel Masegra in A360

services to help you dramatically improve the way you design, visualize, simulate, and share your work with others anytime, anywhere."

The system provides 3 GB of free storage space; a monthly, quarterly, or annual subscription includes 25 GB and the access to cloud computing services for rendering, optimization, energy analysis, and structural analysis. Files cannot exceed 2 GB in size. A360 provides real-time visualization of 2D and 3D models with different predefined views (e.g., 3D views or planar visualization for plans and sections) to facilitate access to different parts of the model. Object properties can be reviewed, and reports of the different activities in progress can be visualized and modified.

The Web browsers that are supported include Google Chrome, Mozilla Firefox, and Microsoft Internet Explorer for 2D visualization (e.g., plans, sections, elevations), whereas 3D visualization is only supported by Google Chrome and Mozilla Firefox. A mobile application is also available to fill the gap between office and construction site. The mobile app supports more than 100 file formats used in the AEC industry, including 2D and 3D formats (e.g., .dwg, .dwf, .ipt, .iam, .idw, .rvt, . sldprt, .sldasm, .asm, .nwd, .nwc, .catpart, .catproduct, .f3d), and can be used to access e-mail attachments and files from Dropbox, Box, Google Drive, OneDrive, iCloud, or Buzzsaw, for example.

Specific functions are available for reviewing and navigating models through intuitive touch-based functions (zoom, pan, rotate); tools for annotation, markup, and comment are available as well.

The HBIM project of Castel Masegra (Autodesk Revit file format) was saved in the .dwf file format to preserve object information. Object properties (e.g., level, type, category) can be exported during the creation of the mobile version, so that the HBIM database remains available in smartphones and tablets.

Graphisoft BIMx (Fig. 10.9) is another application that can be used to handle BIM files converted into a new format for portable devices. BIMx provides cloud-based data access with free (mainly for clients) and low-cost versions (mainly for specialists). Hyperlinks between specific objects of the model can be generated to connect Web browsers, an Facilities Management (FM) database, or a product catalog application.

BIMx cannot directly use BIM files generated with Autodesk Revit. A preliminary conversion using the interoperable Industry Foundation Class (IFC) format was needed to import the model in ArchiCAD. Although IFC files should be in interoperable file formats for an efficient exchange of information between different BIM packages (from Revit to ArchiCAD in this case), the conversion may cause errors, especially in connection with complex shapes, object textures, and material properties. This results in a loss of information for some parts of the model.

The visualization of the model of the castle imported into BIMx was very fluid, with the opportunity to create dynamic sections with a slider and smooth transitions between two and three dimensions. Indeed, BIMx has powerful visualization functions to walk or fly around naturally on mobile devices and 3D glasses for an immersive environment. The advanced interaction level is surely attractive for the direct use of HBIM outside the office.

Fig. 10.9 Mobile version of Castel Masegra in BIMx

10.4.2 Panoramic Virtual Tour from HBIM

Panoramic virtual tours are based on rendered photospheres at an angle of 360°. Single panoramic images or complete tours can be generated from 3D digital models. A static (panoramic) image is usually generated by projecting the world (e.g., a scene visible from a specific point) on a sphere, which is then mapped using specific cartographic projections (e.g., equirectangular, spherical). For this reason, the visualization offered by panoramic images is not carried out in a pure 3D environment, even though the visual effect is remarkable.

The final visualization is based on a predefined set of images placed at different locations, which correspond to different rooms of the original building. Virtual navigation is also quite fluid on mobile devices with limited performances because the output is not a complete 3D model, only a combination of static images.

The tour is created using a set of linked panoramic images, so that users can visit the different rooms available, including indoor and outdoor spaces. Images derived from a 3D model can also be coupled with panoramic images acquired using a rotating camera and stitched with automated software for panoramic photography (e.g., PTGui, Autopano, 360 Panorama, Photosynth, AutoStitch Panorama, DMD Panorama, Sphera, Pano). This combines digital models and real photographs.

The application used for the tour of the castle is iVisit 3D, which is based on the rendering engine Artlantis (Fig. 10.10). Thanks to Artlantis, users can produce

Fig. 10.10 Graphic interface of Artlantis, used to handle model exported from Revit

professional renderings with advanced visual effects available in a large library of shaders, textures, and 3D objects. Each element has several customizable parameters (properties such as adjustable reflection, transparency, representation scale, and brightness, for example), which can be adjusted directly from the graphical interface of the software. A simple so-called drag-and-drop tool allows users to associate a wide range of materials or textures to different objects, enriching the 3D model with synthetic images, photographs, rectified images, and orthophotos generated with photogrammetric or computer vision techniques.

Graphic performance depends on the level of detail of textures associated to the surfaces of models based on HBIM. File formats like .3ds and .obj can be imported in the software without losing the morphological complexity of complex elements. This is a very important aspect, which requires the translation of the HBIM into a format that can be imported in Artlantis. This conversion comes at a cost: the creation of a pure geometry model (in this case the .3ds file format was chosen), which results in an information loss.

The creation of the virtual tour is a simple procedure that includes mapping textures and setting lighting conditions. It is sufficient to set different points of view, which can also be directly linked in an immersive visualization (direct movement from a panoramic image to another) or connected through an overall keyplan visible during navigation.

The final result is delivered as a small .pno file that can be visualized on mobile devices as well as additional files generated from Artlantis for visualization through Web browsers. The use of such panoramic visualization is very simple, attractive, and fluid, so that the method has great potential for presentation and dissemination activities.

10.4.3 HBIM and Augmented Reality

The opportunity to combine BIM and AR (which overlays digital information on the real world) holds remarkable promise for several applications in the AEC industry [40–42]. The main idea is to move the use of 3D models from the office (more generally, from known spaces with predefined conditions) to the construction site, which is intended as a dynamic place where continuous modifications are in progress. This kind of applications must still reach full technological maturity in terms of technical issues related to automated localization, tracking, and alignment in the case of complex scenes that change over time.

Typical applications based on AR are related to the visualization of a 3D model starting from printed drawings (e.g., plans, elevations, and sections). Project boards can be used as markers to exploit different visualizations of objects, such as architectural and structural models with MEP services. Starting from a reference object (e.g., the map of a specific floor), multiple 3D contents can be easily inspected and reviewed. This represents not just a different way to visualize predefined 3D models; AR can be envisioned as a new approach to understanding projects.

It is clear that BIM holds great promise for use on mobile devices and applications based on AR. The extraction of 3D information directly from a BIM model and the use of mobile AR can improve the collaboration between contractors and different specialists involved in the project. Although AR applications are mainly carried out in the office (or in so-called controlled conditions), the opportunity to work with automated geolocalization tools at a construction site is attractive not only because it allows one to evaluate construction progress but because it can also reveal hidden objects such as subsurface utilities, clash detection, and assisted work and facilitate operator training and the simulation of future scenarios.

AR is also very attractive for dissemination activities that stimulate better interactions between people (e.g., expert operators, tourists) and a built heritage. A model based on HBIM can be the starting point for specialists who are mainly interested in the preservation and restoration of cultural heritage or a wider user community interested in visual products derived from HBIM.

The example in Fig. 10.11 shows that the model of the castle can be turned into an informative product for tourists. The tested application is AR-media, which consists of different plug-ins for 3D modeling software, such as Autodesk 3ds Max, Sketch Up, Cinema 4D, Vectorworks, Nemetschek Scia Engineer, and Autodesk Maya. The final visualization is carried out with AR-media Player, which is

Fig. 10.11 Model of caste coupled with AR. The 3D model in AR-media was generated from the HBIM in Revit

available for Windows and OS X (desktop), including the mobile app downloadable from Google Play and Apple Store. In addition, AR-media Player supports several head-mounted displays, such as eMagin and i-glasses.

AR-media allows for correlations between 3D models and multiple markers (a brochure on the castle in this case), so that its elements can be visualized from different points of view. Objects can be structured in multiple layers and visualized independently, including a visualization with synchronized slides for a sort of presentation with specific functions for advanced animations and transitions, such as rigging and morphing.

In the Revit model, the castle was converted from thc original BIM format to .fbx format, which was then imported in Autodesk 3ds Max. This led to an information loss regarding object properties. After importing the 3D model in 3ds Max, it is possible to link the model with specific markers. The procedure is very simple and intuitive. The model can be saved in the .armedia format, resulting in a model of limited size that can be transferred to mobile devices. After running the mobile application, the model will be automatically displayed when the camera captures the marker.

10.5 Conclusion

Mobile devices play a fundamental role in promoting interactions between people and digital cultural heritage in different ways: connecting people and heritage, creating knowledge, and preserving cultural heritage.

Historic building information modeling holds great promise for use on mobile applications based on AR and VR, leading to new opportunities and alternative approaches to data representation, organization, and interaction for the operators in the field of cultural heritage documentation and preservation. On the other hand, practical applications are not only limited to specialists in digital documentation, restoration, and conservation or experts in the AEC industry. New applications can be developed for a wider user community interested in cultural tourism. Here, AR and VR, coupled with HBIM, can promote interactions between users and cultural heritage.

Particular attention must be paid to interoperability requirements, standards, and protocols for the efficient use of digital reconstructions in both BIM packages and VR/AR applications. Standardized procedures and formats are needed for the reliable exchange of digital information, starting at the first phases of work (data acquisition) to the delivery of outputs in various formats, which can be used with multiple devices through cloud-based services.

This chapter started with a simple consideration: the use of BIM technology is becoming increasingly important in the field of construction. This means that the availability of 3D models in mobile devices, along with functions and tools for authoring, editing, documenting, sharing, searching, and navigating, is expected to eventually serve as a bridge between office and construction site. As things presently stand, only personal computer systems with large enough monitors can be used for concrete work (say, productive work) in which the model and its associated database are handled. On the other hand, new mobile applications will play a primary role in onsite (productive) work, where project documentation is currently carried out with printed project boards. Advances in algorithm development, along with the availability of new portable devices for VR and AR (such as the Samsung Gear VR, Microsoft HoloLens, and emerging technologies such as Magic Leap), will hold great promise when it comes to the complete integration of HBIM on mobile devices.

References

1. S. Azhar, M. Khalfan, T. Maqsood, Building information modeling (BIM): now and beyond. Aust. J. Constr. Econ. Buil. **12**(4), 15–28 (2012)
2. D. Bryde, M. Broquetas, J.M. Volm, The project benefits of building information modelling (BIM). Int. J. Proj. Manag. **31**(7), 971–980 (2013)
3. K. Kensek, D. Noble, *Building Information Modeling: BIM in Current and Future Practice* (Wiley, Hoboken, NJ, 2014), p. 432

4. H. Son, F. Bosché, C. Kim, As-built data acquisition and its use in production monitoring and automated layout of civil infrastructure: a survey. Adv. Eng. Inf. **29**(2), 172–183 (2015)
5. Y. Arayici, Towards building information modelling for existing structures. Struct. Surv. **26**, 210–222 (2008)
6. M. Murphy, E. Mccgovern, S. Pavia, Historic building information modelling—adding intelligence to laser and image based surveys of European classical architecture. ISPRS J. Photogramm. Remote Sens. **76**, 89–102 (2013)
7. A. Baik, A. Alitany, J. Boehm, S. Robson, Jeddah historical building information modelling "JHBIM"—object library. ISPRS Ann. Photogramm. Remote Sens. Spat. Inf. Sci. **2**(5), 41–47 (2014)
8. R. Brumana, D. Oreni, A. Raimondi, A. Georgopoulos, A. Breggiani, in *From Survey to HBIM for Documentation, Dissemination and Management of Built Heritage: The Case Study of St. Maria in Scaria d'Intelvi*. Digital Heritage International Congress, Marseille, France, pp. 497–504, 2013
9. S. Fai, K. Graham, T. Duckworth, N. Wood, R. Attar, in *Building Information Modeling and Heritage Documentation*. 23rd International CIPA Symposium, p. 8, 2011
10. S. Fai, M. Filippi, S. Paliaga, Parametric modelling (BIM) for the documentation of vernacular construction methods: a BIM model for the Commissariat Building, Ottawa, Canada. ISPRS Ann. Photogramm. Remote Sens. Spat. Inf. Sci. **2**(5/W1), 115–120 (2013)
11. S. Fai, J. Rafeiro, Establishing an appropriate level of detail (LoD) for a building information model (BIM)—West Block, Parliament Hill, Ottawa, Canada. ISPRS Ann. Photogramm. Remote Sens. Spat. Inf. Sci. **2**(5), 123–130 (2014)
12. N. Hichri, C. Stefani, L. De Luca, P. Veron, Review of the "as-built BIM" approaches. Int. Arch. Photogramm. Remote Sens. Spat. Inf. Sci. **40**(5/W1), 6 (2013)
13. M. Murphy, E. Mccgovern, S. Pavia, Historic building information modelling (HBIM). Struct. Surv. **27**(4), 311–327 (2009)
14. D. Oreni, R. Brumana, B. Cuca, in *Towards a Methodology for 3D Content Models. The Reconstruction of Ancient Vaults for Maintenance and Structural Behaviour in the Logic of BIM Management*. 18th International Conference on Virtual Systems and Multimedia—Virtual Systems in the Information Society, Milan, Italy, pp. 475–482, 2012
15. R. Quattrini, E.S. Malinverni, P. Clini, R. Nespeca, E. Orlietti, From TLS to HBIM: high quality semantically-aware 3D modeling of complex architecture. Int. Arch. Photogramm. Remote Sens. Spat. Inf. Sci. **40**(5/W4), 367–374 (2015)
16. A. Scianna, S. Gristina, S. Paliaga, in Experimental BIM applications in archaeology: a workflow. *Digital Heritage, Progress in Cultural Heritage: Documentation, Preservation, and Protection*. Lecture notes in computer science, vol 8740, pp. 490–498, 2014
17. R. Volk, J. Stengel, F. Schultmann, Building information modeling (BIM) for existing buildings—literature review and future needs. Autom. Constr. **38**, 109–127 (2014)
18. L. Barazzetti, F. Banfi, R. Brumana, G. Gusmeroli, D. Oreni, M. Previtali, F. Roncoroni, G. Schiantarelli, BIM from laser clouds and finite element analysis: combining structural analysis and geometric complexity. Int. Arch. Photogramm. Remote Sens. Spat. Inf. Sci. **40** (5/W4), 345–350 (2015)
19. C. Dore, M. Murphy, S. Mccarthy, F. Brechin, C. Casidy, E. Dirix, Structural simulations and structural analysis—historic building information model (HBIM). Int. Arch. Photogramm. Remote Sens. Spat. Inf. Sci. **40**(5/W4), 351–357 (2015)
20. V. Patraucean, I. Armeni, M. Nahangi, J. Yeung, I. Brilakis, C. Haas, State of research in automatic as-built modelling. Adv. Eng. Inform. **29**(2), 162–171 (2015)
21. F. Fassi, C. Achille, L. Fregonese, Surveying and modelling the main spire of Milan Cathedral using multiple data sources. Photogramm. Rec. **26**(136), 462–487 (2011)
22. D. Oreni, R. Brumana, F. Banfi, L. Bertola, L. Barazzetti, B. Cuca, M. Previtali, F. Roncoroni, Beyond crude 3D models: from point clouds to historical building information modeling via NURBS. Lect. Notes Comput. Sci. **8740**, 166–175 (2014)

23. I. Brilakis, M. Lourakis, R. Sacks, S. Savarese, S. Christodoulou, J. Teizer, A. Makhmalbaf, Toward automated generation of parametric BIMs based on hybrid video and laser scanning data. Adv. Eng. Inform. **24**(4), 456–465 (2010)
24. P. Tang, D. Huber, B. Akinci, R. Lipman, A. Lytle, Automatic reconstruction of as-built building information models from laser-scanned point clouds: a review of related techniques. Autom. Constr. **19**, 829–843 (2010)
25. C. Thomson, J. Boehm, Automatic geometry generation from point clouds for BIM. Remote Sens. (Basel) **7**(9), 11753–11775 (2015)
26. L. Barazzetti, Parametric as-built model generation of complex shapes from point clouds. Adv. Eng. Inform. **30**, 298–311 (2016)
27. The Foundation of Wall and Ceiling Industry, *Building Information Modeling: Understanding and Operating in a New Paradigm* (Foundation of the Wall and Ceiling Industry 513 West Broad Street, Suite 210, Falls Church, VA, 2009), p. 32
28. C. Eastman, P. Teicholz, R. Sacks, K. Liston, *BIM Handbook: A Guide to Building Information Modeling for Owners, Managers, Designers, Engineers and Contractors*, 2nd edn. (Wiley, Hoboken, NJ, 2011), p. 626
29. L. Barazzetti, F. Banfi, R. Brumana, M. Previtali, Creation of parametric BIM objects from point clouds using NURBS. Photogramm. Rec. **30**(152), 339–362 (2015)
30. L. Piegl, W. Tiller, *The NURBS Book*. Monographs in Visual Communication (Springer, Berlin, 1995), p. 646. ISBN 978-3-642-97385-7
31. L. Piegl, W. Tiller, Computing offsets of NURBS curves and surfaces. Comput. Aided Des. **31**, 147–156 (1999)
32. A. Redmond, A. Hore, A. Alshawi, R. West, Exploring how information exchanges can be enhanced through cloud BIM. Autom. Constr. **24**, 175–183 (2012)
33. L.M. Waugh, B. Rausch, T. Engram, F. Aziz, in *Inuvik Super School VR Documentation: Mid-Project Status*. 15th International Conference on Cold Regions Engineering, Quebec, Canada, p. 10, 19–22 August 2012
34. P.S. Dunston, X. Wang, An iterative methodology for mapping mixed reality technologies to AEC operations. J. Inf. Technol. Constr. **16**, 509–528 (2011)
35. C. Park, D. Lee, O. Kwon, X. Wang, Framework for proactive construction defect management using BIM, augmented reality and ontology-based data collection template. Autom. Constr. **33**, 61–71 (2013)
36. Z. Shen, L. Jiang, K. Grosskopf, C. Berryman, in *Creating 3D Web-Based Game Environment Using BIM Models for Virtual On-Site Visiting of Building HVAC Systems*. Construction Research Congress 2012 © ASCE 2012, pp. 1212–1221, 2012
37. L. Yang, *BIM Game: A "Serious Game" to Educate Non-Experts About Energy Related Design and Living*, Doctoral dissertation, Massachusetts Institute of Technology, MA, p. 100, 2009
38. U. Rüppel, K. Schatz, Designing a BIM-based serious game for fire safety evacuation simulations. Adv. Eng. Inform. **25**(4), 600–611 (2011)
39. H. Dib, N. Adamo-Villani, Serious sustainability challenge game to promote teaching and learning of building sustainability. J. Comput. Civil Eng. **28**, 11 (2014)
40. S. Dong, V.R. Kamat, SMART: scalable and modular augmented reality template for rapid development of engineering visualization applications. Vis. Eng. **1**(1), 17 (2013)
41. X. Wang, M. Truijens, L. Hou, Y. Wang, Application of collaborative mobile system in AR-based visualization, data storage and manipulation: a case study of LNG project. Lect. Notes Comput. Sci. Springer **8091**, 221–226 (2013)
42. X. Wang, M. Truijens, L. Hou, Y. Wang, M. Lavender, Y. Zhou, Integrating augmented reality with building information modelling: onsite information sharing and communication for liquefied natural gas industry. Autom. Constr. **40**, 96–105 (2014)

Chapter 11
Data Collection for Estimation of Resilience of Cultural Heritage Assets

Roko Zarnic, Vlatka Rajcic, and Barbara Vodopivec

Abstract Cultural heritage assets, the bearers of historic evidence, are under continuous pressure from change, deterioration, and destruction. Therefore, there is a need to identify and monitor the related risks and to develop appropriate measures for increasing the resilience of cultural heritage. The activities for establishing a European system for data collection and its application in the field of preventive conservation are an ongoing process, where the issue of risks and resilience is well addressed. Recently, there has been an interest in developing a model of built heritage resilience related to mitigation and reaction on sudden environmental impacts, following the resilience models of contemporary buildings. However, these models cannot be simply extended to heritage buildings because of their specific character. In this chapter, a contribution to an acceptable resilience model of heritage buildings is presented.

Keywords Cultural heritage asset • Significance • Data • Cultural heritage services • Resilience model

11.1 Introduction

Since the beginning of this century, the interest in resilience rather than in vulnerability of objects exposed to disaster came in to focus in research and mitigation activities of societies worldwide. The number of publications, documents related to

R. Zarnic (✉)
Faculty of Civil and Geodetic Engineering, University of Ljubljana, Jamova 2, 1000 Ljubljana, Slovenia
e-mail: roko.zarnic@fgg.uni-lj.si

V. Rajcic
Faculty of Civil Engineering, University of Zagreb, Kacica-Miosica 26, 10000 Zagreb, Croatia
e-mail: vrajcic@grad.hr

B. Vodopivec
Research Centre of the Slovenian Academy of Science and Arts, Novi trg 2, 1000 Ljubljana, Slovenia
e-mail: barbara.vodopivec@zrc-sazu.si

M. Ioannides et al. (eds.), *Mixed Reality and Gamification for Cultural Heritage*,
DOI 10.1007/978-3-319-49607-8_11

preparedness of communities, international events, and investments in research and application of research results is increasing. This is reflected also in the field of cultural heritage safeguarding, where recently the increased interest of the EU Commission can be seen in the promotion of the research through calls in Horizon 2020. However, resilience is still a new term for those with a traditional approach to cultural heritage protection, although it is closely related to the well-established term of "preventive conservation." Experts in the domain of risk reduction and disaster recovery are familiar with the meaning of resilience and the implementation of its idea, but a wider society of experts and stakeholders involved in heritage preservation and use still need to be better informed about it. Clear definitions contribute to a better understanding, as it has been demonstrated by an overview of definitions of resilience in [1]. However, in continuation, the recent definition of IPCC [2] will be followed: "resilience is the ability of a system and its component parts to anticipate, absorb, accommodate, or recover from the effects of a hazardous event in a timely and efficient manner, including through ensuring the preservation, restoration, or improvement of its essential basic structures and functions." Resilience applies to both people and the built and natural environment and is shaped by both physical and social factors.

A comprehensive review and discussion on heritage and resilience is presented in [3], where the role of cultural heritage in disaster risk reduction is examined. The authors quote the outcome document of the UN Conference on Sustainable Development (Rio + 20) [4]: "many people especially the poor, depend directly on ecosystems for their livelihoods, their economic, social and physical well-being, and their cultural heritage," in order to stress the importance of heritage safeguarding not only because of its memory value but also because of its role in the economies of many countries worldwide. Cultural heritage is a powerful asset for inclusive economic development, but it is important that societies recognize its potential. The well-established term "ecosystem services" can be well applied to the cultural heritage domain by introducing the analog term "cultural heritage services," as it will be discussed in continuation of this chapter. Introducing this term, clear links between the economic potential of ecosystems and cultural heritage can be established in order to understand the economic potential of heritage assets in particular geographic location. Identification of the economic potential of a cultural heritage asset in a certain society brings forward the awareness of its value and the need for its protection. Consequently, the attention is focused on risks and safeguarding, and the currently popular issue of resilience can serve as an inclusive framework for a new understanding of heritage in the era of climate and societal changes. In this sense, resilience is understood in a wider sense than only in technical terms of disaster risk reduction as it will be explained further in this chapter. The Thimphu Document 1 [5] points to the wider aspects of heritage protection: "the protection of cultural heritage should be promoted, not only because of its intrinsic historic or artistic value, but also because of the fundamental spiritual and psycho-social support and the sense of belonging it provides to communities during the disaster recovery phase, as well as the contribution it makes towards building resilience to the increasing frequency and intensity of disasters and adaptation to climate change". Following the idea of holistic approach to cultural heritage understanding, preservation, and usage, resilience should be understood also as the ability of cultural heritage to recover from unfavorable impacts in its total dimension, ranging from spiritual to material contents and significances.

Studies of cultural heritage engage an extremely large area of professions and activities, where a profound understanding of heritage and its significances is of primary importance. There are many definitions of cultural heritage significance based on internationally well-established doctrines developed within universities, institutions, and international organizations such as UNESCO. In this chapter, the attempt to summarize and group various significances of cultural heritage is presented in order to encompass the entire area of heritage aspects that should be considered when resilience is studied. However, the significances can be identified and studied only if appropriate and reliable data are collected, preserved, and presented in a way that can be used for various purposes, and one of them is the issue of resilience. In today's era of rapid development of IT-based techniques and tools, data collection, storage, and usage seem relatively easy tasks, but such an opinion is misleading. The large amount of available data demands systematic data management and the supporting of an entire set of activities related to cultural heritage preservation, where the increasing of resilience is an important one.

11.2 Significances of Built Heritage

11.2.1 Background of the Definition of Cultural Heritage Significances

In general, the heritage can be grouped into two categories: cultural property, including tangible and intangible objects, and natural heritage. Each of them can be further divided into subgroups, where built heritage can be one of them within the cultural property. Built heritage interacts with the surrounding natural heritage and is an environment for intangible heritage through activities performed in and around the built heritage.

Significances of heritage buildings with architectural and artistic character combine tangible and intangible aspects of cultural heritage. Interdisciplinary research resulted in the definition of significances as described in [6].

Significances were defined on the following contextual bases:

- Detailed knowledge of the research object
- Detailed knowledge of the history and the theory of conservation
- Detailed knowledge of each specific space and context

Those substantive bases determine significances such as:

- Multidisciplinary
- Descriptive (nonmaterial) and measurable (material) properties

Fig. 11.1 The overview of built heritage significances

- Globally and locally defined according to the context and location
- Universal and specific according to the type of heritage

Definition of significances was carried out in five consecutive steps:

1. Identification
2. Comparative analysis
3. Semantic aggregation
4. Definition of significance
5. Significance tree modeling

Although significances were defined for the built heritage in particular (Fig. 11.1), their broad contextual basis allows them to be used also for other types of heritage. In such a case, the significance structure needs to be reconsidered and reassessed prior to its use. Since the significance scheme simplifies aspects of individual scientific disciplines that need to be addressed, an assessment of heritage significance should still be derived primarily from the evaluation process based on each discipline's methodology.

11.2.2 Definition of Cultural Heritage Significances

Geospatial/Geometric Significances

Geospatial and geometric significances are related to geographic position, cultural landscape characteristics, and geometry of asset. A geographic information system

(GIS) is a system designed to capture, store, manipulate, analyze, manage, and present all types of spatial or geographical data. A cultural landscape, as defined by the World Heritage Committee, is the cultural property that represents the combined works of nature and of man. It is a landscape designed and created intentionally by man, an organically evolved landscape that may be a relict (or fossil) landscape or a continuing landscape. Geometry of cultural heritage asset is defined by the shape of the building and includes presentation of plan, cross sections, facades, architectural details, etc.

State of Preservation
State of preservation is a condition in which cultural heritage asset has been kept by means of regular maintenance and periodic interventions. It is defined by the current condition of materials and structure. The condition of materials is defined by the current characteristics of the materials and the level of decay and damage assessed by the identification of hazards that caused the damages. Condition of structure is defined by structural assessment taking into account the level of material decay and damages of structural elements and components. Maintenance and previous interventions are defined by the assessment of the effects of regular maintenance and previous interventions (preintervention works, conservation, restoration works) on the state of preservation.

Environmental Significances
Environmental significance is related to the sustainability aspects, in particular to the environmental value in terms of protection of environment (restoration and conservation of land, reduction in pollution, and construction waste), as well as in terms of the relationship between heritage and environment/space (embedment of heritage in the space, interaction of natural and cultural heritage, restoration of heritage as a part of spatial planning). Energy efficiency defines the heritage asset in terms of sustainable use of resources in the case of its renewal (reuse of materials, the use of compatible materials), increasing the occupancy comfort by energy-efficient renovation, and the rational use of energy during the use of heritage asset. Landscape significance defines the heritage value emerging from an interaction between the cultural heritage and cultural landscape. A typical example is an environment in which palaces surrounded by gardens compose a unique space of high cultural value. Spatial significance defines spatial heritage value derived from its placement in the local environment, cityscapes, dominant urban silhouettes, etc. It defines contextual integration of a heritage asset in the area as a basis for development opportunities.

Hazards and Risks
Hazards and risks define measurable potential of harmful impacts to heritage assets. They may be natural (long term and sudden) or human induced (intentional and unintentional). They are quantifiable and can be measured or indirectly determined by their consequences. Hazards and risks can be estimated by probabilistic risk assessment, and consequently reduction measures can be undertaken. Human induced defines one or more unintended (improper decision-making, economic

activities, accidents) or intended (vandalism and terrorism, riots, war) impacts induced by human activity. Long-term natural hazards are one or more environment-caused impacts, such as biodegradation, climate change, wind, water (groundwater, atmospheric water), solar radiation, particle pollution, aerosols, long-term load, and geological conditions (including local peculiarities). Short-term (sudden) natural hazards are one or more environment-induced impacts through an unexpected occurrence, such as a storm, fire, flood (flash flood, surface flooding), earthquake, landslide, avalanche, tsunami, volcano, etc.

Esthetic Significances

Esthetic significance defines the artistic features such as concept, form, color, etc., often referred to as the artistic value. It includes also the visual characteristics attributed to heritage by values assessment and interpretation, such as beauty, sublimity, esthetics of archaeological remains, etc. In the broadest sense, esthetic importance derives from the intense experience of heritage in terms of all the senses employed (smell, hearing, and touch). Architectural significance relates to the authorship [extraordinary, typical, the most valuable achievement of a certain author(s)], typology (remarkable, typical example of a certain period), and technological value or achievement (a typical example of a particular workmanship, form and style, advance in the design approach, material and structural characteristics). Integrity defines integrity, i.e., high level of preservation of those heritage values that define significance and protection regime of the asset. It is understood as the absence of adverse effects of subsequent interventions, additives, neglect, improper use, and degradation processes. Rarity defines the rareness, the exceptionality of a heritage asset. It can also be measurable, when a particular heritage asset is rare because it is a unique example of a certain historic period, culture, and author or has any other rare significance.

Cultural-Symbolic Significances

Cultural-symbolic significance defines values associated with the concept of "here" and "now": these are the ideas, habits, actions, attitudes, and in a broader sense, cultural- and civilizational-related values. Cultural significance is sometimes associated with the term civilization and as such defines how certain features of heritage are seen and understood according to each specific context. The symbolic meaning is defined on the basis of the symbols associated with the heritage unit (legends, myths, literature, etc.). In a very broad interpretation, the cultural-symbolic significance may be associated with the feelings of attachment to the heritage site (genius loci). Spiritual-religious significance defines the value derived from religious or other sacred heritage importance. It may be linked to the practices, beliefs, and learning of a particular religion. Novelty defines stylistic unity and ideal condition of the asset (including removal of all later additions). According to novelty, the importance of heritage results from the subsequent recovery, reconstruction, and other interventions that lead to new stylistic unity or return to the previous "ideal state," which may even never have existed. The appearance of "novelty" has priority over the appearance of "patina" in this concept. Novelty is rejected in contemporary conservation theory, but in practice the approach may still be found.

Secular significance derives from the irreligious feelings of awe, wonder, and from the respect of certain heritage asset or values associated with it. It is closely associated with the type of so-called intentional monuments.

Social Significances

Social significance defines characteristics of heritage, which create the so-called social capital: promotion and facilitation of social networking, creation of social cohesion, and sense of community (identity). It is also associated with the potential of heritage to foster development of society. Educational significance defines the potential of heritage for formal and vocational education as well as, in a wider sense, learning from the past. Management significance covers the management structure and plan of the heritage asset, as well as the protection regime including legal protection (e.g., listed asset), ownership, and accessibility. It refers to the development policy based on the heritage exploitation, including definition of its function and usage. Scientific significance defines the value and potential of heritage for the development of science. Heritage conservation can contribute to the development of new materials, techniques, tools, approaches, and research findings. Preservation process contributes to scientific advances in several disciplines; therefore, it has the potential for multi- and interdisciplinary development of science.

Historic Significances

Historic significance encompasses characteristics that bear witness to the past and illustrate a specific development of historical significance. It can be derived from the link of the asset with certain persons and/or events and for its documentary and archival value. Definition of the criteria is always a result of scientific study and consequent understanding of the heritage. Archaeological significance defines the value of the heritage, based on archaeological findings and on a definition of the archaeological importance of these findings as witnesses of a certain development. It also embraces a definition of a site's archaeological potential (defined on the previous research, confirming not yet excavated archaeological site). Authenticity defines the degree of authenticity and originality of the asset as a whole and of its elements. It is assessed on the basis of preservation level of the original shape and design, materials, purpose and use, traditions, location, as well as of resources related to heritage and defining its value. Authenticity embraces the concept of "age value" which defines evident link of the asset with the past, identifiable as a result of the natural aging cycle without apparent restoration procedures and the effects of premature aging (e.g., Patina). Technological significance defines the value of a heritage as a bearer of information about the stage of technology development. It includes craft skills and craft value associated with methods of material production and construction processes, as well as industrial and technological development (industrial, technical heritage).

Economic Significances

Economic significance defines economic value of heritage, which can be measured either with financial (expressed in money/price) or other methods (contingency methods). Indirect development effects of heritage preservation are related to social significance. Nonuse value defines the value that cannot be offered and sold on the market and therefore cannot be expressed in financial terms. It is related to general awareness about the existence of the asset, to its availability for general public access and to conservation necessity for its preservation in order to be available to subsequent generations. The use value defines economic importance determined on the basis of the concept of utility, which can be expressed in financial terms. The market value of heritage stems from goods and services that can be offered and sold on the market (fees, wages) and are reflected in the price. Measurements can be performed with economic methods. Investment potential defines effects of investments in cultural heritage asset (reconstruction, restoration, etc.). The bases for assessment are conservation plans and feasibility studies, which include financial and economic analysis (indirect economic and developmental effects among others).

11.2.3 Cultural Heritage Services

Natural and cultural heritage are linked because the natural environment enabled development of cultures that created heritage assets. But, nature and its ecosystems also enabled survival of societies and development of their economic activities. Humans benefit from ecosystems in various ways, and these benefits are nowadays expressed by the term ecosystem services. In [7] authors explain how the new initiatives started at the end of the last century in economics to evaluate the services that nature provides. The value of these services can be broken down roughly as shown in Fig. 11.2. The authors suggest to use the same approach to evaluate the economic potential of cultural heritage by introducing the term of cultural heritage services. The idea of cultural heritage services has been introduced and discussed during the Interreg IVC project HISTCAPE—historic assets and related landscapes (http://www.histcape.eu), which outcomes are presented in publication [8]. Ecosystem services and cultural heritage services are linked through comparable values and uses that are offered both by natural environment and by human-built environment. Both environments are equally exposed to long-term environmental impacts due to climatic changes and sudden events (natural disasters). But even more dangerous are human-induced influences, among which wrong decisions are, besides war destructions, the most dangerous.

The idea of interaction of ecosystem services and cultural heritage services is put forward as an opportunity for creation of jobs and for the increase in the well-being of societies in protected areas as Natura 2000. It is closely related to important issues of sustainable reuse, assessment, and renovation of historic buildings and monuments in rural areas. For example, vernacular architecture solutions could be implemented, using local traditional materials and techniques. This, on the one hand, could be an example of nature-based solution and, on the other hand, could contextualize constructions and preserve the cultural heritage as illustrated in [9].

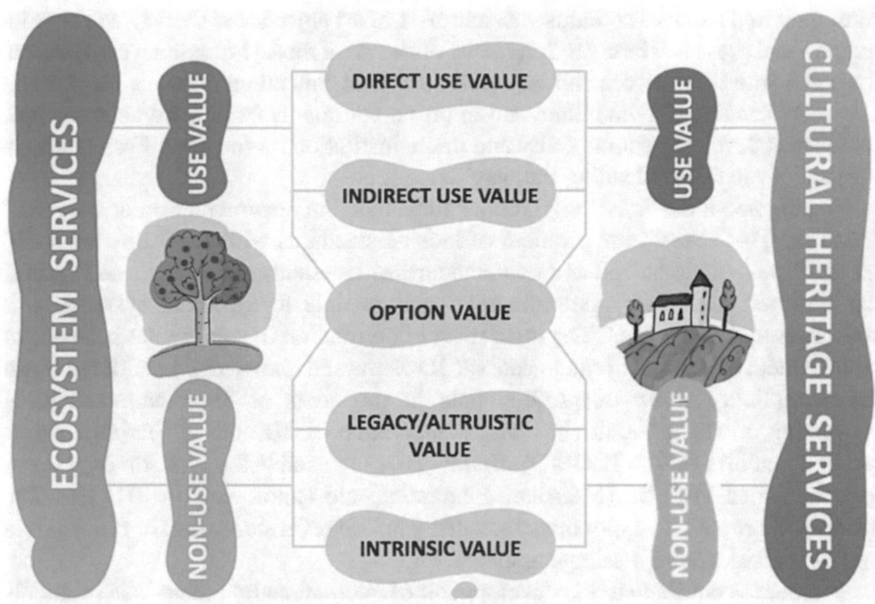

Fig. 11.2 Interconnections between ecosystem and cultural heritage services

11.3 Built Heritage Database Systems

11.3.1 Overview of Current Systems

In many countries, there are well-established systems and tools used to inventory and document cultural heritage. They reflect the tradition of cultural heritage protection, and the local approaches and understandings condition their content structure. In some countries, there are several systems for data collection, which are not connected together. Therefore, a straight comparison of data on heritage assets is not possible. The overview of currently used approaches in seven countries (Croatia, Czech Republic, Greece, Israel, Italy, Poland, and Slovenia) was presented during the 1st EU-CHIC Workshop held in Vienna in 2010 (www.eu-chic.eu) [10]. The Ad Hoc Group for Inventory and Documentation within the Technical Co-operation and Consultancy Programme related to the Integrated Conservation of the Cultural Heritage contributed the most complete effort in harmonization of approaches on at least a basic level by developing three standards related to historic buildings, monuments, archaeological sites, and heritage objects [11]. Earlier, the importance of international documenting standards for protection of cultural heritage has been recognized within the Getty art history information program [12]. The importance of establishing a systematic approach to data collection and usage in the Internet era has been clearly stated in [13]: “The great collective repository of our cultural heritage scattered around the world in libraries, museums, and archives contains vast numbers of art objects and literary works from the past and present. These are fragments of the great mosaic of human civilization. To make sure these pieces can be accessed across collections in ways that benefit our understanding of humankind and improve our quality of life, we need to work together in developing community and multi-institutional Web sites. Fortunately, a handful of models are leading the way".

Writing about the "missing grammar for the digital documentation of the past," Ioannides [14] stresses the problem of lack of standards with the following statement: "Due to unorganized and non-standardized methods of use of these IT tools, the achieved results are predominantly incompatible for different systems, presentations and future use." The most recent contribution to solving the problem of management of cultural heritage data on 3D assets and knowledge is initiated by an interdisciplinary group of professionals in the areas of 3D data acquisition, processing, modeling, archiving, and preservation of 3D cultural heritage assets led by Ioannides [15] to ICOMOS Board (2016) to establish a task force group of experts named MeSeOn (Metadata, Semantics, and Ontologies for 3D CH). The group will propose the guidelines for setting up MeSeOn standards for the tangible and intangible cultural heritage assets.

In order to contribute to the development of internationally recognized protocols for data collection, experts from fourteen European countries, Israel, and Egypt pooled their efforts in the development of the model for the so-called Cultural Heritage Identity Card. It has been developed within the EU-financed Coordinated Action EU-CHIC (FP7-ENV-2008-1 no. 226995, 2009/12). The idea of Identity Card originates from the COST Action C5: "Urban Heritage-Building Maintenance," 1996–2000 [16]. The general conclusion stressed in the final report was that there is a serious lack of reliable data on European urban heritage and a pressing need to collect it, in order to support the ongoing process of refurbishment of existing buildings. COST C5 Action concluded that there are great variations in the systems of establishing and evaluating data from buildings in the European countries. The responsibility for collecting data depends on the administrative structure in each country. Planning of broad activities, such as preventive strengthening or even post-earthquake measures in European earthquake-prone areas or energy preservation measures, can be better based on mutually developed methodology. The basic rules and approach can be developed from the existing European standards and codes. However, no generally accepted approach existed that would lead to European methodology.

The creation of a Pan-European protocol for data collection is just the first step in the ambitious process. The essential part of the data in this protocol is related to the identification of risks to which heritage assets are exposed. It is well known that the vulnerability of assets is one of the main criteria for intervention in asset management in order to increase its resilience. The final aim of the process is to develop a general approach to resilience assessment of heritage assets based on the identification of risks that can be generalized by the introduction of risk indicators.

11.3.2 European Cultural Heritage Identity Card

The main objective of the EU-CHIC Project was to develop and test guidelines that are required for the efficient compilation and storage of data pertinent to each asset under observation. Data can be collected and well maintained only if the appropriate protocols are developed and applied. The documentation protocol can be understood as an envelope with a set of rules, which establish and define the categories of data needed for achievement of a targeted goal. If the protocol for cultural heritage is defined, it can be applied to built heritage, archaeological sites, cultural landscape, heritage objects, and to collections of artifacts. A protocol can be composed of several layers regarding the type of data, their amount, and nature. During their lifetime, the heritage assets have been constantly exposed to external natural influences that increased the material and structure decay processes and to alterations of use and interventions in their structure. The necessary data for evaluation of consequences of events in the assets' lifetime can be collected from different sources and documents, but an on-site inspection is the only way to assess the current state of an asset. From the assessment of an asset under observation and knowledge gained from studying similar cases, a prediction of future behavior can be estimated. The important data for estimation, besides the ones collected by inspection, are risks resulting from events that may happen in the future life of an asset. Sufficient amount of reliable data is necessary for a basis in decision-making that determines and thus influences the future life of an asset. Those who are responsible for an asset should always be ready to answer the simple question: "What will be the consequences of my decisions?"

The collecting of detailed data on cultural heritage assets engages a significant amount of effort by professionals and researchers, which means also the engagement of a significant amount of funds. Therefore, the owners or the responsible organization of authority have property rights and can exploit the data according to their needs. However, a certain amount of data should be given to the interested public for general use (research, education, tourism, etc.). On the other hand, sensitive data that are under the owners' control are needed for management and all other decisions related to ownership of asset. As an answer to these dilemmas, a new structure of data has been developed. It was visualized in the form of an iceberg and named "EU-CHIC Iceberg" or, in short, "CHICBERG" (Fig. 11.3).

Data, which in their total volume create the Identity Card, are divided into two groups (Table 11.1). The "upper" group of data is open to general public use. The "lower" two groups of data are the sensitive ones and of high value to the owner of the asset. Therefore, these can be used only with their permission. Following this scheme, the Cultural Heritage Identity Card is not a single document of the asset but a set of documents that contains comprehensive information and is created and updated during the entire lifetime of an asset. The updating follows the changes to the asset after the initial creating of files. Therefore, the system of three levels is established as presented in Table 11.1. The first level of the Card contains data collected mainly from publicly available sources with additional information about

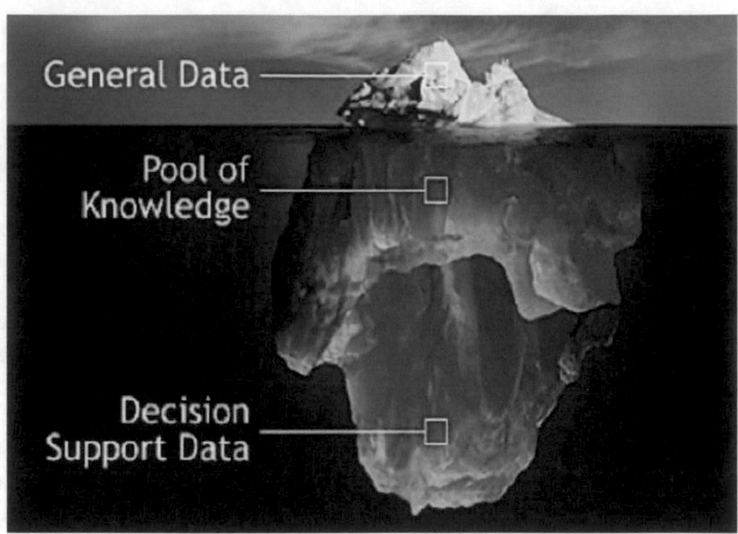

Fig. 11.3 The scheme of CHICBERG

the current physical condition and the major risks to which the asset may be exposed. The original intention of the Card was to establish a system that would enable comparison between assets of the same type across Europe and the Mediterranean countries. The first level of the Card is designed to meet this goal.

The existing standards [11] form an important, well-established system, and the intention of the EU-CHIC is not to compete or replace it but to integrate them to a wider and more ambitious system. The first level of the Card is meant as an introduction to lower, more important levels because the basic information about an asset given in the first level is elaborated in detail in the second level named Pool of Knowledge. The structured knowledge, as presented in Table 11.1, is a basis for the most important aim of the system: support for decision-making that is of crucial importance for the conservation of a cultural heritage asset. One of the most important issues is the prevention of a heritage asset from risks. Risks can be identified not only from past events in the area of heritage asset location but also from the scientific prediction of potentially harmful events. The variety of risks and concurrency of events can be managed by the introduction of risk indicators that enable good prediction of influences even when the amount of reliable data is in sufficient.

Major risks may be divided into two categories regarding their source: environmental and human induced (Table 11.2). The environmental risks are the consequences of either long-term impacts or sudden events. Long-term impacts are expressed in terms of environmental factors that affect the asset, and the results appeared over a long period of time. Sudden environmental impacts are expressed in terms of events that affect the asset in a relatively short time interval (measured in minutes or at most in hours) and its occurrence could not be foreseen in advance. The human-induced impacts might be the consequence of regular economic

Table 11.1 The content of the Cultural Heritage Identity Card

Public data General data obtained by identification	
Name, location, legal status, type, dating, function, major risks, materials, structure, state of conservation	
Owner-controlled data Detailed information on the cultural heritage asset	
Nonphysical aspects	Physical aspects
History Art history Museology Sociology Ethnology Cultural landscape Legal issues Economic issues Previous interventions Conservation Valuation methods	Geospatial aspects Geometry of asset Risks Archaeology Architecture Materials Structure Movable objects Current condition Energy efficiency Surveying techniques
Decision support Knowledge implementation procedures	
Intervention decision-making Decision impact analysis Site management	

activities, of other unintended sources of harmful influence to heritage asset, or the consequence of intended harmful influences. Among the most dangerous and relatively frequent unintended influences are improper decisions made due to the lack of knowledge or data. These are serious reasons for wrong reactions from responsible persons.

Therefore, the key target of EU-CHIC Protocol is its support to decision-making procedures. The third part of the "CHICBERG" is intended to exploit the knowledge collected and is the core of the Identity Card. Available data collected in the second section should be organized in a way that makes them suitable for various purposes of management, such as intervention decision-making, decision impact analysis, and site management. A good example is the usage of data for regular monitoring and inspection of historic buildings and monuments, as developed and applied by the "Monumentenwacht" organization in the Netherlands and in the Flanders region of Belgium.

Decision-making can be made easier if experiences gained from successful cases are exchanged and compared. The EU-CHIC aims to contribute to the simplification of comparison of general data on heritage assets and to the international exchange of knowledge and experience gained from heritage conservation. It may also be a basis for the development of a Pan-European system for regular monitoring, inspection, and maintenance of historic buildings, monuments, and sites.

Conservation of cultural heritage is related to high costs, and required interventions generally exceed available funding. It is, therefore, necessary to prioritize

Table 11.2 List of hazards to which the heritage assets are exposed

Environmental hazards	
A: Long-term influences	B: Sudden events
A1: Bio-attack	B1: Wind storm
A2: Climate condition fluctuations	B2: Fire
A3: Aeolic impact	B3: Flood
A4: Water (atmospheric, ground)	B4: Earthquake
A5: Solar radiation	B5: Landslide
A6: Particle matter and aerosols	B6: Avalanche
A7: Long-term loading	B7: Tsunami
A8: Geological and geotechnical conditions	B8: Volcano
Human-induced hazards	
C: Unintended influences	D: Intended events
C1: Economic activities	D1: Vandalisms
C2: Accidental events	D2: Riots
C3: Improper decisions	D3: Wars

renovation interventions. Multicriteria assessment can lead to scientifically sound and informed decisions about interventions. The research carried out with the purpose of establishing a multicriteria method for the assessment of architectural heritage is under progress in Slovenia. In [6] the methodology used to develop the multicriteria method is explained. Its main elements are critical content analysis of relevant literature, comparative analysis between the Slovenian and international space, and the identification of relevant criteria and sub-criteria for the decision method. The course and results of empirical research, based on interviews with selected experts, are presented together with the results of the criteria importance ranking based on the Analytic Hierarchy Process (AHP) method. The research presented in the paper is interdisciplinary and brings together the tangible and intangible aspects of cultural heritage. The obtained results confirm that rational determination of relative importance of individual criteria for the assessment of architectural heritage can help decision-makers to identify buildings with higher refurbishment priority.

11.3.3 Environmental Impact on Historic Structures

Long-term environmental factors affect both the state of preservation and structural condition of historic buildings and monuments, provoking serious decays to them. In this chapter, the impact of environmental agents to the structure of historic buildings and monuments will be presented. The examined building materials are timber, masonry, and iron cast, which are the most common in historic buildings and monuments.

Many historic structures include timber as structural elements like timber beams, roofs, pillars, or timber frames. Timber elements are usually in combination with other building materials, mostly masonry, due to their ability to enhance the stability of the structure [17]. On the other hand, masonry (limestone, marble, granite, etc.) is the most common building material in cultural heritage. From ancient times, people used masonry for the construction of monumental buildings. Even though masonry is the most durable material through time, it shows significant susceptibility to environmental factors. Cast iron became a very popular building material during the nineteenth century. Cast iron's ability to carry more loads led to its mass production and use in big structures such as columns and ornamental parts of buildings [18].

In Table 11.3, an attempt to judge the impact of long-term environmental factors to the structural properties of historic structures is presented. The judgment is provisional and illustrative and is based on the understanding of authors as generated from their professional experiences. It should be understood as a suggestion for future assessments of impact of long-term processes to resistance of structures to natural disastrous actions.

Timber is the most vulnerable among building materials. Environmental factors like the presence of insects and humidity can penetrate timber structures causing severe interior damage or aggravate already existing decays. Insolation causes brittleness, while geological conditions and loads threaten the building's stability. Regarding masonry, it shows great susceptibility to environmental impact, but the decays are mainly on the surface of the buildings or in depth of millimeters (or maximum some centimeters). Therefore, their impact leads to detachments and material loss, but these do not cause great damage to the structure. Nevertheless, the combination of long-term loads and the geological conditions with sudden events (earthquake, fire) as well as human impact (vandalism, war) could threaten the masonry structures. As far as iron cast is concerned, the environmental factors that affect it the most are its exposure to water (seawater and acid rainwater) and particle matters. Because of water's impact, phenomena like rusting (oxidation) and graphitization occur. Depending on the material's properties, components, and the grade of its exposure to these factors, rust can cause severe decay and even total loss of the materials' components. Moreover, the conversion of iron to soluble iron oxide thus causes the historic structure to be weakened.

11.3.4 Influence of Improper Decisions

The environmental impact cannot be human controlled, and the only way to mitigate it is in increasing the resilience of heritage assets. In contrast, the human-induced impacts can be controlled and limited by establishing adequate safety measures. One of the most successful and important strategies is in spreading awareness and knowledge, especially among the institutions and persons responsible for decision-making. An illustrative example of decision-making is reported in [19]. The author reports about the examination of the extent to which disaster risk reduction is considered within the management systems of various World Heritage

Table 11.3 Influence of long-term impacts on structural properties of building

Impact	High	Medium	Low
Timber			
A1	XX	X	
A2	XX		
A3		X	X
A4	XX	X	
A5	X	XX	
A6			X
A7	XX		
A8	XX		
Masonry			
A1			X
A2	X	X	X
A3			X
A4	X	XX	X
A5			X
A6			XX
A7	XX	X	
A8	XX	X	
Cast iron			
A1		X	X
A2	X	X	
A3		X	
A4	X	X	
A5		X	
A6	X		
A7	XX	X	
A8	XX	X	

X, less frequent occurrences; XX, more frequent occurrences

properties. He focused particularly on those that appear to be most exposed to disaster risks. The study surveyed 60 World Heritage properties and identified 41 properties in 18 countries as being most at risk from natural and human-induced hazards according to the World Risk Index (http://whc.unesco.org/en/soc). The source of information were UNESCO archives on the management systems established for the World Heritage properties. The aim of the research was to determine the extent to which the relevant disaster risks are identified and addressed. The research discovered the following facts:

- The risks were not identified within the management plans in 37 % of cases.
- The risks were identified, but no concrete plans or reference to mitigating them were established in management plans in 30 % of cases.
- The risks were identified, but mitigation included in management plans considered mainly visitor safety in 3 % of cases.

- The risks were identified, and plans to mitigate them were considered in management plans, but to an insufficient extent, or where there is a concern regarding their effective implementation in 20 % of cases.
- The risks and mitigation of these were presented in an effective and extensive Risk Preparedness Plan in 10 % of cases.

The results of research clearly show that in the management of World Heritage properties, risk reduction is not among the highest of priorities in spite of the vulnerability of heritage assets to hazards. Surprisingly, only in 6 out of 60 properties the risk and mitigation contingency was presented in an effective and extensive Risk Preparedness Plan. It would be interesting to study case by case and learn about the reasons for the lack of attention paid to risks. As mentioned before, human technology even nowadays cannot yet influence the occurrence of natural hazardous events, but at least decision-makers can do much more to mitigate them. In this context, the importance of reliable information supported by adequately managed data collections is of primary importance.

11.4 Resilience Model for Built Heritage

11.4.1 Resilience Model of Contemporary Buildings

The concept of resilience is developed in the domain of earthquake engineering, but earthquake is only one of the sudden environmental impacts that endanger heritage buildings. However, the knowledge developed in this area can be transferred and enlarged to all other risks to which heritage assets are exposed. As part of the conceptualization of a framework to enhance the seismic resilience of communities in the USA [20], in 2003 seismic resilience has been defined as the ability of a system to reduce the chances of a shock, to absorb such a shock if it occurs (abrupt reduction of performance), and to recover quickly after a shock (reestablish normal performance).

More specifically, a resilient system is one that shows:

- Reduced failure probabilities
- Reduced consequences from failures, in terms of lives lost, damage, and negative economic and social consequences
- Reduced time for recovery (restoration of a specific system or set of systems to their "normal" level of functional performance)

A broad measure of resilience that captures these key features can be mathematically expressed and thus calculated. Resilience depends on the quality of the asset. Specifically, performance can range from 0 to 100 %, where 100 % means no degradation in quality and 0 % means total loss. An earthquake or any other disastrous event that occurs within a short time period could cause sufficient damage to the asset such that the quality measure is immediately reduced (from

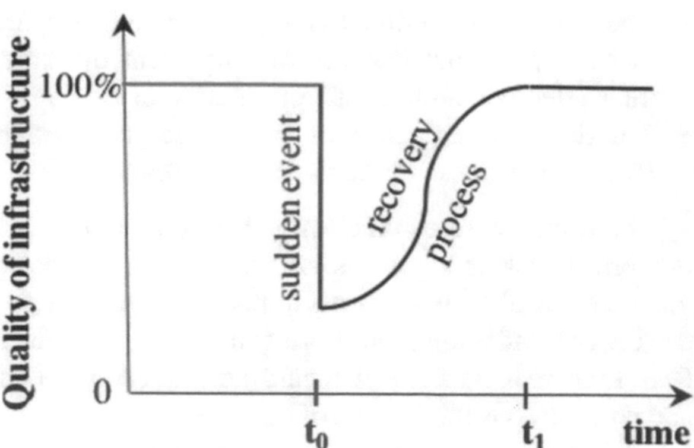

Fig. 11.4 Resilience model following [20]

100 to 50 %, or in the worst case of a collapse to 0 %). Restoration of the asset is expected to occur over a period of time to be completely repaired and become functional once again (indicated by a quality of 100 %).

When the resilience of existing, contemporary infrastructure endangered by earthquakes is observed (Fig. 11.4), the basic assumption is that the infrastructure is 100 % resilient at the time of occurrence (t_0) of earthquake and that the same resilience can be restored by appropriate intervention in a certain time period (t_1). In the case of built heritage, the situation is more complex because the resilience of heritage asset depends on the state of its preservation, including the conditions of materials, structure, maintenance, and previous interventions.

11.4.2 Proposal of Resilience Model for Built Heritage

The assumption of resilience model proposed here for cultural heritage assets (Fig. 11.5) differs from the model for contemporary structure because of the specific nature of the cultural heritage asset. It was 100 % ($R_0 = 1$) resilient at the time of its creation. Various long-term and sudden impacts occurred during its lifetime, measured in centuries or even millennia (Fig. 11.5a). In the present time (t_1), the resilience of the asset is much lower than the initial one ($R_1 < R_0$). Practically it cannot be completely restored to its original state but only to the best achievable ones ($R_1 < R_2 < R_0$). Theoretically, it would be possible to reach the initial resilience (R_0) only in cases when the complete documentation of the initial state is available and reconstruction in its parts would be allowed. Documentation is complete only if it contains both, data on tangible characteristics and intangible values of asset. The solution of the problem becomes even more demanding if in observed, present time (t_1) in (Fig. 11.5b) the additional sudden drop (R_e) of resilience occurs due to natural or human-induced impact.

Extended research is needed to quantify resilience, particularly for some types of critical assets. For critical assets for which the deliverable is not a simple engineering unit, such as for the case of a heritage endangered by human-induced hazards,

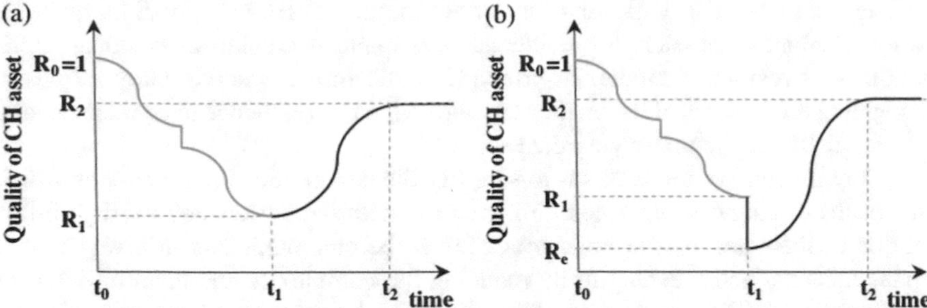

Fig. 11.5 Resilience model of cultural heritage asset in the case of long-term (**a**) and in the case of sudden (**b**) environmental or/and human-induced impacts

the quantification is almost impossible. However, it is worthwhile to start research in this area, which is completely new, though the future progress and outcomes are not very predictable.

Resilience for both physical and social systems can be further defined as consisting of the following properties [20]:

- Robustness: strength or the ability of elements, systems, and other measures of analysis to withstand a given level of stress or demand without suffering degradation or loss of function.
- Redundancy: the extent to which elements, systems, or other measures of analysis exist that are substitutable, i.e., capable of satisfying functional requirements in the event of disruption, degradation, or loss of functionality.
- Resourcefulness: the capacity to identify problems, establish priorities, and mobilize resources when conditions exist that threaten to disrupt some element, system, or other measures of analysis. Resourcefulness can be further conceptualized as consisting of the ability to apply material (i.e., monetary, physical, technological, and informational) and human resources in the process of recovery to meet established priorities and achieve goals.
- Rapidity: the capacity to meet priorities and achieve goals in a timely manner in order to contain losses, recover functionality, and avoid future disruption.
- In the specific cases of heritage assets, additional properties should be identified.

The basic idea of further research in the cultural heritage domain is to apply the theory of resilience for the development of efficient measures for preservation of cultural heritage assets. It is obvious that for each type of environmental or human-induced impact, mathematical models of resilience should be developed, but all may emerge from the above explained idea (Fig. 11.5). The main problem is not in the mathematical formulation of a model but in reliable and realistic input data for calculation of resilience. In the case of a heritage asset being exposed to several different categories of impacts, the total resilience is a combination of partial resiliencies associated with every relevant impact. And as mentioned above, an earthquake is only one of them.

The use of the risk indicators for definition and, where it is possible, quantification of input parameters for resilience assessment is crucial for practical application on a resilience model. In principle, indicators can serve many purposes, depending on the level at which they are applied, on the audience to be reached, and on the quality of the underlying data sets.

A key function of indicators is to simplify the communication process by which the results of analysis and accounting are provided to the users and to adapt information to their needs. The indicators need to be communicated in a way that is understandable and meaningful by reducing the complexity and level of detail of the original data. Due to this simplification and adaptation, the indicators may not always meet strict scientific demands to demonstrate causal chains. They rather represent trade-offs between their relevance for users and policies, their statistical quality, and their analytical soundness and scientific coherence. Indicators therefore need to be embedded in larger information systems—such as databases, accounts, monitoring systems, and models.

11.5 Conclusions

In the current era of rapid ICT development, their application in heritage conservation domain is not yet sufficient. Although the main actors in the heritage conservation discipline are still considered as one that follow the conservative principles, the use of ICT tools is well-accepted among majority of them. A very positive move in this direction has been achieved during the International Conferences on Cultural Heritage and Digital Libraries EUROMED 10, 12, and 14, where the large area of possibilities and already developed technologies and applications in the cultural heritage domain were presented. The architecture of the presented European Cultural Heritage Card (EU-CHIC) is open to further upgrading that gives the opportunity for the rising of its quality by a wide application of ICT. But the main role of ICT will be in providing data and models for resilience assessment using the risk indicators. As stressed earlier, the quality and quantity of reliable documentation is crucial for the restoring of resilience of heritage assets. The important part of documentation is the visualization of the asset as a whole and in parts, including details that may be of crucial importance in restoring monuments and historic buildings. The long-term preservation of data is another crucial issue that still needs to be addressed in a proper way. The current storage media may not be sufficiently durable and resistant to various influences. Therefore, new media should be developed and be made available in order to assure long-term preservation of stored data.

Acknowledgments The ongoing research work that is the basis of this chapter is supported by the European Commission (EC). The research through the Initial Training Networks for Digital Cultural Heritage: Projecting our Past to the Future (ITN-DCH, FP7-PEOPLE-2013-ITN-Marie-Curie Action: "Initial Training Networks" Project reference 608013 funded under FP7-PEOPLE from 2013-10-01 to 2017-09) engage early-stage researchers from different countries. The research is partially based on results of EC-financed Coordinated Action EU-CHIC (FP7-ENV-2008-1 no. 226995, 2009/12). The future results of the recently started Horizon 2020 project INCEPTION—Inclusive Cultural Heritage in Europe through 3D semantic modelling (H2020-REFLECTIVE-7-2014 no: 665220, 20152019)—will contribute to intended further development of the resilience model. The authors acknowledge the support of the European Commission to their research.

References

1. S.B. Manyena, The concept of resilience revisited. Disasters **30**(4), 434–450 (2006)
2. C.B. Field et al. (eds.), *Managing the Risks of Extreme Events and Disasters to Advance Climate Change Adaptation: Special Report of the Intergovernmental Panel on Climate Change* (Cambridge University Press, Cambridge, 2012)
3. R. Jigyasu et al., *Heritage and Resilience: Issues and Opportunities for Reducing Disaster Risks* (UNESCO Worrld Heritage Centre, Geneva, 2013), p. 52
4. Assembly, UN General, The future we want. Resolution **66**, 288 (2012)
5. Thimphu Document 1, Outcome of the International Conference on Disaster Management and Cultural Heritage, Thimphu, Bhutan, 2010
6. B. Vodopivec et al., Renovation priority ranking by multi-criteria assessment of architectural heritage: the case of castles. Int. J. Strateg. Prop. Manag. **18**(1), 88–100 (2014)
7. I.J. Bateman, R.K. Turner, Valuation of the environment, methods and techniques: the contingent valuation method, in *Sustainable Environmental Economics and Management: Principles and Practice* (Belhaven Press, London, 1993), pp. 120–191
8. R. Eppich (ed.), *Cultural Heritage, Landscape & Rural Development: Good Practice, Methodology, Policy Recommendations and Guidelines for Rural Communities: HISTCAPE: Historic Assets and Related Landscapes* (2014), http://histcape.eu
9. V. Rajčić, Croatian traditional vernacular wooden architecture, in *HISTCAPE and Beyond*, ed. by B. Vodopivec et al. (2014), pp. 9–14
10. R. Žarnić et al., *Heritage Protection. From Documentation to Interventions* (2012), http://www.eu-chic.eu
11. Council of Europe, *Guidance on Inventory and Documentation of the Cultural Heritage, Prepared by Ad Hoc Group for Inventory and Documentation Within the Technical Co-operation and Consultancy Programme* (Council of Europe Publishing, Strasbourg, 2009), http://archives.icom.museum/object-id/heritage/core.html
12. R. Thornes, E. Fink, *Protecting Cultural Objects Through International Documentation Standards: A Preliminary Survey* (Getty Art History Information Program, Santa Monica, CA, 1995)
13. E.E. Fink, in *Sharing Cultural Entitlements in the Digital Age: Are We Building a Garden of Eden or a Patch of Weeds?* Museums and the Web Conference, pp. 5–8, 1997
14. M. Ioannides et al., in *Standards in Cultural Heritage: The Missing Grammar for the Digital Documentation of the Past*. XX CIPA Symposium, 2005
15. M. Ioannides, R. Žarnić, V. Rajčić, R. Davies, G. Papagiannakis, M. Hagedorn-Saupe, in *How to Manage (Model, Archive, Retrieve, Preserve and Exchange) Cultural Heritage Data on 3D Assets and Knowledge?* Communication to ICOMOS Board, pp. 1–3, 2016
16. F. Hofmann et al. (ed.), *COST Action C5: Urban Heritage—Building Maintenance: Final Report* (EUR 20447, EC Directorate-General for Research, Brussels, 2002), http://bookshop.europa.eu/en/cost-action-c5-pbKINA20447/?CatalogCategoryID=ANIKABstUgUAAAEjCJEY4e5L
17. M.B. Bagbancı, Examination of the failures and determination of intervention methods for historical Ottoman traditional timber houses in the Cumalıkızık Village, Bursa–Turkey. Eng. Fail. Anal. **35**, 470–479 (2013)

18. A. Davey, *Maintenance and Repair Techniques for Traditional Cast Iron-Short Guide* (Historic Scotland, 2013), pp. 2–4, 6, http://conservation.historic-scotland.gov.uk/publication-detail.htm?pubid=9908
19. P. Antoniou, in *Concern for Disaster Risk Reduction in the Management of World Heritage Properties*. A research through the archives of the World Heritage Centre, UNESCO, 2012
20. M. Bruneau et al., A framework to quantitatively assess and enhance the seismic resilience of communities. Earthq. Spectra **19**(4), 733–752 (2003)

Chapter 12
Virtual Reconstruction of Historical Architecture as Media for Knowledge Representation

Sander Münster, Cindy Kröber, Heide Weller, and Nikolas Prechtel

Abstract 3D reconstructions have always been an important medium for teaching, illustrating and researching historical facts and items, especially architecture. While 3D reconstructions in academic contexts aim at an accurate virtual representation of a historic original, various knowledge communication effects influence a creation and understanding of virtual representations. From a temporal point of view, architecture usually lasts beyond a human lifespan, and concepts, ideas and messages of deceased builders are available only via sources—either through the architectural object itself or by descriptions or depictions of it. While a creational process of virtual representation is often performed by cross-disciplinary workgroups, an exchange of knowledge between involved individuals is characterised by the need for a synchronisation of personal mental models and organisational and cooperational learning. Moreover, architectural representations address a wide and heterogeneous audience. All described processes are highly supported by visual media, such as images, virtual models or the architectural object itself. To explore knowledge-related phenomena, the authors performed four stages of investigation using qualitative and quantitative research methods. While a first research stage focuses on the scope and overall relevance of virtual architecture within the field of digital heritage, a second stage investigates phenomena due to a creation of virtual architectural representations. A third stage examines how skills and competencies for creating virtual architectural representations evolve during a project and if teaching facilitates the development. Finally, a fourth stage evaluates design approaches for virtual building representations to make them comprehensible for an audience.

S. Münster (✉) • C. Kröber • H. Weller
Media Center, Dresden University of Technology, 01062 Dresden, Germany
e-mail: sander.muenster@tu-dresden.de; cindy.kroeber@tu-dresden.de; heide.weller@tu-dresden.de

N. Prechtel
Institute for Cartography, Dresden University of Technology, 01062 Dresden, Germany
e-mail: nikolas.prechtel@tu-dresden.de

M. Ioannides et al. (eds.), *Mixed Reality and Gamification for Cultural Heritage*,
DOI 10.1007/978-3-319-49607-8_12

Keywords Historic architecture • Digital 3D reconstruction • Cultural heritage • Visual communication • Knowledge representation • Information sciences

12.1 Introduction

While historical picture sources usually provide elusive and fragmentary impressions, digital three-dimensional reconstructions of historical architecture and their depictions offer the chance to convey holistic and more easily accessible ideas and knowledge. Until 2000, virtual 3D modelling technologies and computer-generated images of cultural heritage objects were used merely as a digital substitute for physical models [1, 2]. Nowadays, 3D models are widely used in presenting historic items and monuments to the general public [3] as well as in research [4] and education [5]. Recent case studies of 3D applications aim at presenting 3D models in a multipurpose way, due to the great effort involved in their creation. Moreover, virtual reconstructions in academic contexts intend a close representation of a historical original or intention of the historical builder. While a reconstruction of still extant architecture is challenging from mostly technical aspects, such as complete and accurate data acquisition and handling or an efficient and comprehensive algorithmic model creation, technical workflows for a modelling of no longer extant or never-realised architecture are widely established, similar to other 3D modelling tasks in engineering and architectural design. Specific challenges for such interpretative reconstructions are their need for coping with historic sources or interdisciplinary workflows.

12.1.1 Research Objectives

While a key interest of a scientific community as well as funding institutions in this particular field is on the development of technical solutions like platforms and libraries, an investigation of user requirements and usage scenarios is rarely in focus. Against this background, an overarching interest of our current research activities is to investigate how digital methods correspond with visual cultural heritage research and education, in particular in the context of virtual 3D reconstruction of architectural heritage. Regarding this overarching research interest, further questions arose from this investigation. As one major finding, strategies and workflows within 3D reconstruction projects evolved over time and have adapted on demand. While these strategies and workflows resulted from "trial and error", it seems interesting to investigate an effect of the teaching of project participants that could enhance a project quality in terms of workflows and cooperation quality. Moreover, our previous investigations focussed on the production process of visual media but did not investigate its reception by an audience. This leads to the question of how virtual architectural representations should be designed in order to support the perception of inherited knowledge of an object. Against this background, our main research questions are:

- What scenarios, phenomena and strategies are related to the use of virtual 3D reconstruction methods within visual cultural heritage research and education?
- What implications can be deduced for an appropriate design of media and workflows?

12.2 Theoretical Concepts

12.2.1 Knowledge

Out of plenty of possible research interests on a virtual representation of architecture, this article focuses on aspects of knowledge representation. This is closely related to concepts of intrapersonal knowledge such as reasoning or memorisation as well as for groups of persons and their communication and joint mental modelling [6] (Table 12.1).

Besides a perspective on knowledge holders, concepts like "visual reasoning" or "embodied knowledge" [8, 9] focus on an object which contains and represents knowledge and which may be, for example, architecture. A well-established and hierarchical classification of information and knowledge is the distinction between *signs, data, information* and *knowledge* (c.f. Table 12.1). According to this definition, knowledge does not only include a perception and cognition of signs but also aspects of their relevance and mental connection ability for a recipient [7]. Regarding a typology of knowledge, a main distinction is between declarative and procedural knowledge or—widely similarly used—"knowing how" and "knowing what" [10]. Declarative knowledge stands for factual knowledge, while procedural knowledge refers to "a knowledge of the flow and transformation processes" [11]. Closely related is the distinction between explicit and tacit knowledge [12]. While explicit knowledge can be articulated and is transferable, tacit knowledge denotes a dimension of knowledge which builds on the experience of the individual and includes, for example, "insights, intuitions, and hunches" [13, p. 8] and cannot be articulated or transferred by default.

Table 12.1 Classification scheme [c.f. 7]

Sign	
Data	Perceptible signs
Information	Data which are useable for an individual
Knowledge	Information which are relevant and mentally connectable for an individual

12.2.2 Representation

The aspect of representation addresses the replacement of a represented knowledge object by a, e.g. lingual, pictorial or architectural knowledge representing an object. Aspects of representation are closely related to semiotics and model theory. From the point of semiotics, an object can be represented by a sign which a recipient could identify as symbolisation for that object [14]. Such symbols can represent linguistic and iconic characters but also, for example, gestures. Character meaning or application contexts are dependent on the conventions and the epistemic culture of the application area and the culture of the user [15]. On this basis, Bertin developed a specific graphic semiology [16] which subsumes and analyses the various degrees of freedom of a graphic design. Based on the laws of the Gestalt theory [c.f. 17], a generalised assumption is that only differences and similarities can be perceived between visual signs [18]. While semiotics focus on the function and shape of signs, model theory focuses on the relation between an original and a model as its abstraction [19]. According to the established explanation scheme, a model is a simplified or abridged image of an original, while a "pragmatism" of said component means a subjective purpose orientation [20]. Closely related is the Common Grounds approach as one of the most common explanation models for a joint understanding of knowledge. It originates in cognitive psychology and explains factors and recommendations for successful communication [21]. For a successful knowledge transfer between two individuals, their knowledge, beliefs and assumptions must be synchronised [22]. Especially for a communication between individuals with different cultural as well as disciplinary backgrounds or levels of expertise, aspects such as varying meanings of the same terms or, in an opposite manner, a usage of different terms for the same content is relevant [23]. Closely related to such effects is the fact that the differences are not known in advance, but usually appear only in the course of a more intensive communication.

12.2.3 Roles of Architecture

Related to communication and representation, architecture addresses several functions. On the one hand, architecture represents concepts, ideas and messages of the builders and manifests and transfers these to the public. In that function architecture can work as common ground to symbolise attributes like power via building height, or wealth via ornamentation and overwhelming craftsmanship, or for more sophisticated concepts like an arrangement of parts of medieval cathedrals which represent the Corpus Christi [24]. On the other hand, architecture is the object of discussion and is represented by various media and embedded in various contexts. Even if a perception of architecture and its virtual representation contain multisensual components, the most dominant way is to conceive architecture visually. Related to knowledge processing, a virtual representation of architecture includes knowledge

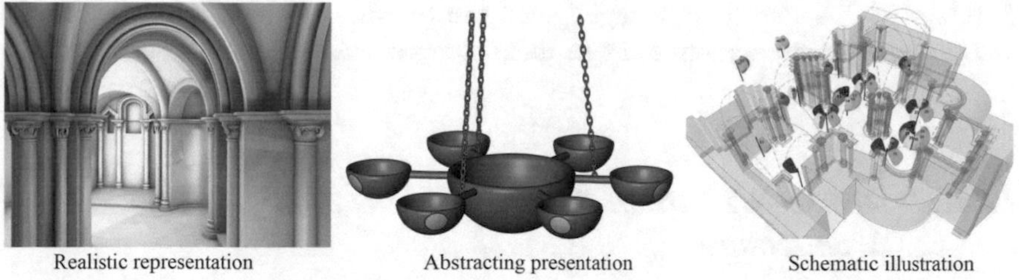

Realistic representation | Abstracting presentation | Schematic illustration

Fig. 12.1 Qualities of architectural representation

transfers between a historic builder, individuals involved in a creation process and an addressed audience. Moreover, knowledge exchange between these stakeholders is affected by various and primarily visual media. From a temporal point of view, architecture usually lasts beyond a human lifespan. Concepts, ideas and messages of deceased builders are available only via sources—either by the architectural object itself or by descriptions or depictions of it. While a creational process of virtual representation is often performed by cross-disciplinary workgroups, an exchange of knowledge between involved individuals is characterised by the need for a synchronisation of understanding beliefs and several processes of organisational and cooperational learning, which are highly supported by visual media, too. Moreover, a reception of an architectural representation by an audience primarily takes place through visual media as well and depends on the qualities of the architectural representation (c.f. Fig. 12.1).

12.3 Research Design and Results

From a disciplinary point of view, especially information sciences [25] as well as visual humanities provide approaches and methods to investigate knowledge-related phenomena associated with visual, virtual representations of historical architecture. Regarding these different epistemic approaches and our research interest, we combined various theory-driven and empirical methodical approaches for research and performed various stages of analysis and explorative assessment. Moreover, a leading paradigm was to identify and explore phenomena and generate hypotheses using qualitative and quantitative research methods. At a glance, a first research stage focuses on a scope and an overall relevance of virtual architecture within the field of digital heritage. A second stage investigates phenomena due to the creation of virtual architectural representations and especially focuses on the role of visual media. While former stages analysed projects in progress or finished ones, in a third stage we performed a practice project to examine how cross-disciplinary development of skills and competencies for creating virtual architectural representations evolves during a project and if teaching facilitates the development. A fourth stage highlighted the question of how to design virtual architectural representations to make them comprehensible to an audience.

12.3.1 Discussing Virtual Representations of Historical Architecture

Research Design
A first-stage research interest was to identify a scope and an overall relevance of virtual architecture within a discussion in the scientific field. It included the content analysis of publications in the field of digital heritage in order to examine current use scenarios and field of research. Prior to the task, three experts were asked to examine the most respected conferences and publications. As another prerequisite all the publications included had to be written in English and be available online. In an initial sample, 452 journal articles and conference proceedings were included [26]. An extended sample contained in total 2584 publications (Table 12.2). An investigation took place via qualitative and quantitative content analysis with the development of a categorisation and its quantification [27] (Table 12.2).

Findings and discussion
Focussing on a role of architecture within cultural heritage projects, objects reconstructed through 3D modelling are often architectural structures, mostly religious buildings like churches or temples (Fig. 12.2). Moreover, architecture is a prominent topic in academic discourse too. With regard to keywords listed in articles, "architecture" and related variants rank third among the top article keywords and are the most-named type of object (c.f. Fig. 12.3).

Related to research aspects regarding virtual historical architecture, the users fall into a multitude of disciplines: the discourse-leading disciplines of cultural heritage

Table 12.2 Sample (publications)

	Publication	Volume	No.
Sample 1	3DArch Conf.	2005–2009	112
	CAA Conf.	2007, 2009	130
	VAST Conf.	2003–2007, 2010	105
	J. Digital Heritage	From 2000	52
	Various Publication	1999–2011	79
Sample 2	3DArch Conf.	2005–2013	237
	CAA Conf.	1990–1992, 1994–2001, 2004–2009, 2011	963
	VAST Conf.	2003–2006, 2008–2012	202
	Euromed Conf.	2006–2012	456
	CIPA Conf.	1999–2001, 2005–2013	935
	J. Cultural Heritage	From 2000	52
	J. Heritage in the Digital Era	1/2013	7

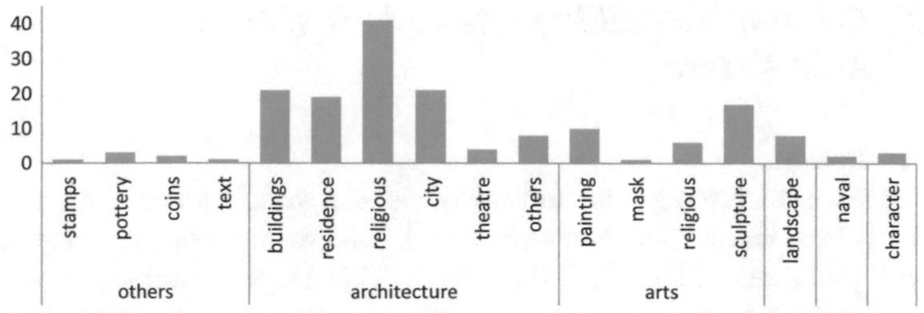

Fig. 12.2 Types of objects ($n = 175$ projects described in 452 publications)

Fig. 12.3 Tag cloud of TOP 50 keywords ($n = 10{,}504$ keywords out of 2063 publications)

studies and archaeology are accompanied by, e.g., architectural and cultural history studies, art history or museology. They all provide specific use cases beyond reconstruction and visualisation: an evaluation of historic sources and their correspondence [4, 28], the detection of geometric principles in historic creational processes as well as the classification and systematisation of historic architecture in respect to dependencies, similarities or singularities [28]. Even suppositious objects, such as idealistic buildings designed from architectural principles like the traditional Chinese or Vitruvian system [29], are created using 3D construction technologies. Regarding a reception of resultant virtual representations of architecture, apart from main purposes of virtual 3D reconstructions such as education and research, general modes of information retrieval include browsing, i.e. a self-determined search within data repositories; location or context-related information presentations, e.g. within exhibitions; or location-based augmented reality applications [30, 31]. These possibilities are connected to individual interests and presuppositions of a user. Alternatively, in the next research stage, the influence of the creators within the creation process of virtual representations of historical architecture will be investigated.

12.3.2 Creating Virtual Representations of Historical Architecture

Research Design

A second stage analysed production scenarios and workflows to examine knowledge transfer and related phenomena and workflows within project workgroups and creational processes [32] (c.f. Table 12.3). This stage contained a survey of 26 project reports to examine current production scenarios of virtual 3D reconstructions for never-built or no longer extant architecture. An investigation took place via inductive and deductive qualitative content analysis to identify and classify project constellations and related phenomena. While an investigation of publications provides only a retrospective view on communication and exchange during the creation process, four case studies were included to examine knowledge-related aspects and their evolution during a creation process of digital heritage objects. The leading paradigm for an evaluation of this stage was a mixed methods approach, including heuristic frameworks and grounded theory [33]. As data in all four cases, a total of nine interviews with key role team members took place; in addition, six direct and participating observations of team meetings were carried out. Also a significant number of documents, including log files, communication data, protocols, sources and model renderings, were included in the investigation (Table 12.3).

Findings and Discussion

As pointed out in former articles, a creation of virtual historical architecture is mostly performed by cross-disciplinary teams within projects [34]. Moreover, a reconstruction is highly correlated with the use of visual media. In all observed projects, especially for architecture that is no longer extant or has never been built, historic plans and panoramas have widely been the most important sources for creating a virtual reconstruction. These historical sources usually do not contain all information required for a virtual reconstruction but show various errors, smoothness or inexactness of depiction or lack coherence between different sources. To bridge such uncertain or contradictive information, an interpretation would include logical implications such as analogies to similar objects and requirements of

Table 12.3 Sample (projects)

	Project	Material
Reports	26 project reports describing interpretative 3D reconstruction projects	Published reports, 1999–2011
Cases	Roman City (*no longer extant*)	Interviews, Documents
	Palace Gardens (*never realised*)	Interviews, Direct observation, Documents
	Church Interior (*never realised*)	Interviews, Participating Observation, Communication Data, Documents
	Necropolis (*no longer extant*)	Published project report, Interviews

systems such as the Vitruvian architectural system or would simply rely on inner-model logic as with common boundaries of modelled parts [35]. Regarding a creational workflow, a main element of all 3D reconstruction projects is the creation of a virtual 3D model. To make these models visually perceptible, it is necessary to transfer them into rendered images or physical objects again, i.e. as visualisations, animations, interactive content or manufactured prototypes. Regardless of whether an object is extant or does not physically exist, there are two major modes of reconstruction available during the production process. A *digitisation mode* assumes well-researched attributes which are available as data or images for modelling and can be used for model creation without further historical research. Such stages usually progress quite quickly, while a second mode requires an interpretation or interpolation and progresses at a much slower pace. This could occur if no directly accessible information is available, sources do not agree with one another, or different scientific hypotheses are available and research is required to gain information prior to reconstruction. While "digitisation" stages of easy to transfer parts mostly occur at the beginning of reconstruction projects, especially beginning project teams would set a benchmark for qualities to achieve through such fast progression. In later stages, "interpretation" work gains more importance and causes a slower progress of projects. As pointed out in a former publication [36], several factors influence a reconstruction process and lead to certain strategies for communication, cooperation and quality management within these projects. Especially when working groups with different disciplinary backgrounds are involved, visual media would be intensively used to foster communication and quality negotiations. For example, common strategies for quality negotiation in such projects are based on a comparison between source images and images of the created virtual reconstruction of architecture. While widely established symbols like arrows are used in all projects, some projects created their own graphical codices or metaphors for communication. Moreover, several projects successfully adopted highly standardised conventions from architectural drawings for interdisciplinary exchange.

12.3.3 Learning Virtual Representations of Historical Architecture

Research Design

Research in Stages 1 and 2 analysed ongoing or terminated projects in mostly professional contexts. Moreover, a third stage focussed on an investigation of personal and organisational learning processes during a complete project lifecycle and explored possibilities to facilitate these processes via education. Supported by the *Saxon Centre for Teaching and Learning in Higher Education*, an educational project was performed aiming at the creation of an audio-visual guide for smartphones which describes certain places of interest and no longer extant construction stages for the cathedral in Freiberg in eastern Germany [37]. The project dated from April to October 2014 and involved 30 student participants belonging to the fields of art history, linguistics and geoscience. For the project-based work, ten student teams were formed involving students of the humanities focussing on a research and textual description of certain historical aspects and students of geosciences to perform virtual reconstructions and animations to emphasise the results. Regarding the implications from cognitive apprenticeship [38], the first project phase spanned 6 weeks and included a teaching of project-relevant competencies within weekly courses and two additional study trips to the cathedral. Courses were offered for students of each discipline to build knowledge in their field of expertise. Joint sessions were performed to teach object-related knowledge about the historical cathedral and to equip student teams with knowledge and best practice for project management and communication based on implications gathered in research stage 2. A second phase of the educational project lasted for another 12 weeks and included a production of visual and textual assets by student work groups and was supported by coaching offered for each discipline. During the educational project, several types of evaluation took place to monitor the progress of work and effects of education. Two joint group discussions—mid-second phase and at the end of the project—were expected to identify problems and to estimate the success of didactic guidance and the students' adaptation of practices and strategies. In addition, students were asked via questionnaires at the beginning of the educational project, at the end of phase one, and at the end of phase two ($n = 15$; $n = 11$; $n = 7$) to query their satisfaction and individual needs. An analysis of all evaluations took place via inductive and deductive qualitative content analysis [27].

Findings and Discussion

As a general finding, most of the students involved in the educational project were highly trained in dealing with methods of their certain disciplines but had no former experience in performing interdisciplinary teamwork. The most appropriate interest for students to participate had been to learn about methods from other disciplines. According to findings of the second stage, a cross-disciplinary sharing of knowledge, ideas and research methods evolved over time. As highlighted in [39], a mental processing and problem-solving workflow differs highly for textual and visual media. Moreover, epistemic cultures [40] of art history and language studies as humanities disciplines are closer to each other than of geosciences. As a consequence, especially a synchronisation between text- and image-related disciplines was challenging and time consuming. Similar to findings from research stage 2, strategies for information sharing and communication evolved over time and in view of a practical cooperation within the student teams. Facilitating factors were an intense communication and mutual empathy of teammates, a commitment to objectives and a personal involvement [c.f. 41–43]. Moreover, interest and ability in discovering and understanding of foreign methods were fostered. In opposition, especially a high level of professional competency and ambition as well as a low level of personal involvement hindered a successful cooperation within teams. A teaching of knowledge and visual techniques in phase one was estimated as too theoretical and overwhelming by many of the students. However, the supervision and coaching of teams by lecturers and research assistants in phase two were estimated as helpful. The phenomenon of the slow evolvement of task-related competencies over time for complex problems and without having (much) prior experience is widely researched and explained by theories. According to a problem-solving process, solution quality and progress highly depend on prior real or imagined experiences of individuals for a certain situation [44] and the availability of extant patterns for a solution [45]. Moreover, according to cognitive load theory [38, 46], especially during the early stages of the education, a high cognitive workload was affected by a high number of simultaneous tasks like team building and organising, task structuring and an improvement of required professional competencies [47, 48]. Related to the role of architecture within the educational project, several phenomena can be drawn. The availability of the cathedral in Freiberg facilitated a cross-disciplinary discussion by making design and spatial relations of architecture directly feasible for all team members. Moreover, abstract, non-nomothetic information like multiple reconstruction alternatives or relational information could be properly transferred via media such as text or speech. Even if architecture and architectural representation lack the ability to transfer these types of information, they provide a boundary object [49] for communication and knowledge sharing. A majority of the project participants estimated that a discussion and exchange of more abstract concepts, as, for example, a genesis of certain parts of the cathedral, became more transparent in situ. Moreover, textual and visual media are highly complementary to each other. Regarding the resulting application and the ambition to illustrate complex phenomena, a mutual description and depiction enhanced the quality and clarity of information presentation [50]. The targeted application relied on various media; therefore, competencies for selecting, processing and combining of media are needed to be developed. The process calls for a role switching where student workgroups work as designers of learning media dedicated to information and entertainment of others. The anticipation of user needs for usability, user experience and instructional design need to be considered [c.f. 51].

12.3.4 Recognising Virtual Representations of Historical Architecture

Research Design

A fourth stage investigated practical implications and user testing for a design of virtual architecture. While investigations by game studies focus on final products [52] and their relation to an original, our interest was to explore how various levels of detail would affect the recognition of buildings and city structures. Based on implications from research literature, six varying designs for a no longer extant building block were developed, which was formerly located in the city of Dresden in Germany and originally built in the late nineteenth century. An evaluation included two studies to (a) compare design alternatives for buildings and (b) prove a visual usability of the former preferred design alternative. From a methodical point of view, both studies employed a “thinking aloud” method from usability testing [53, 54], by which test users perform several given tasks within an application and comment on their doings and thoughts. In the first case, six users (age: 23–52, 2 male and 4 female) compared and negotiated six design alternatives [55]. A second test involved 15 people with various levels of expertise with virtual architectural representation (5 experts, 4 novices, 6 no answer) which performed tasks including the identification of certain buildings within a virtual city model and the description of their unique features, i.e. a building type and certain attributes.

Results and Discussion

A well-established approach to categorising qualities of architectural representation is provided by the level of detail (LOD) scheme. LOD distinguishes between five different levels; while LOD 1 means a block model as an extruded footprint of a building, LOD 2 includes a building block, its height and a certain roof design, and LOD 3 adds a photo texture of a facade. Moreover, LOD 4 stands for a highly detailed modelling of a building hull, including all unique features, and LOD 5 declares a highly detailed modelling of inner and outer building features [56]. While the LOD scheme provides just a rough classification scheme, it may help to identify which of certain features are most essential to identify a single building within a building block and to identify a building as unique in comparison to others. By research literature, the following features are suggested as potentially influencing:

- Basic shape, including a simplified footprint of a building
- Height of a building
- Roof shape
- Façade photo texture (e.g. windows, storeys, etc.)
- Building details (e.g. chimneys, balconies, etc.)

Expanding on this classification, six design alternatives were created with varying features (Fig. 12.4). All tests were performed within a modified Google Earth environment, including several freedom degrees for a user to change the viewpoint. More generally, it highly depends on a (virtual) context and any given information to identify a building and estimate its scale in a virtual environment [57]. Especially block models (LOD 1) need additional clues. This additional information can be provided either by a higher level of detail in case of a single building (e.g. by adding roof structures), by providing auxiliary visual clues (e.g. via a map overlay as a ground plan for a building) or by combining various buildings with differing heights into building blocks. Regarding the interest to identify a single building from a group of buildings, especially its basic shape, a unique height and an individual roof colour which is different from surrounding buildings foster recognition, while an individual façade photo texture is perceptible

Fig. 12.4 Design alternative example

only in close views. Regarding opportunities to identify a certain building as unique, especially its basic geometry and hcight and an individual roof shape provide important visual clues. Moreover, a façade and additional building details did influence a distinction of a certain building in a lesser way. To sum up, little visual information is actually needed to identify a single building and to distinguish buildings from each other—(relatively) independent from novice or expert users. While these findings in general are widely supported, e.g. by cognition psychology [58], and provide some rough implications for designing virtual, interactive architectural models, a more sophisticated investigation and detailed implications for an appropriate LOD of architectural representation would have to include other presentation forms, such as animation or visualisations, various building types from different cultural and temporal backgrounds. Moreover, it would be highly interesting to investigate in detail how a level of expertise and a professional background would affect recognition of architecture. While, for example, visual reasoning [59] is one main key to a mental engagement with virtual models, various levels of abstraction impose different demands varying with a particular discipline and the *professional vision* capabilities [60]: Novices typically perceive holistic impressions, while experts mentally employ visual *pattern recognition* [61] strategies, e.g. comparing rendered 3D models with pictorial sources or mental models. Archaeologists are trained to judge on rather "realistic" visual impressions [59], while more abstract representations are more familiar among architects.

12.4 Conclusion

A major challenge for an expression and explication of knowledge is to build a common ground of understanding. While more sophisticated code patterns like language require a synchronisation of individual interpretation and understanding, architectural structures as natural, in the sense of "everyday experienced", visual media are highly suitable to build a common ground for interdisciplinary and expert-novice communication.

What scenarios, phenomena and strategies are visible by our research? Even if an intensive use of images, especially as sources for 3D reconstruction of no longer extant objects and for a depiction of results, is widely known, the range of functions and the crucial importance of images during a creation of virtual representations of architecture seem surprising. Especially for communication and for negotiation, visual media are widely used within a creation workflow. While there are many efforts to make knowledge embodied in a reconstruction visible in its outcomes, there are only a few possibilities and practically used approaches to make cross-disciplinary decision and creation processes transparent [62]. That seems especially important, since multiple authors, implicit professional vision processes and visual reasoning are relevant within such processes. A development of procedures and strategies for cooperation within projects for creating virtual representations of architecture evolves slowly, mostly due to emerging problems and urgent demands. Related competencies are highly based on implicit knowledge and experience. As a consequence, teaching of implications and best practices prior to a project work is less effective than coaching during the project work. While project work, cross-disciplinary cooperation, and complex problem solving processes are an essential part of modern professional work, academic learning mostly focuses on explicit and theoretical knowledge as well as disciplinary ambition and less on its practical application in complex scenarios. More attention to project-based learning and related competencies in academic education in general would probably enhance cooperation quality and project progress. Regarding a level of detail which is necessary to recognise architectural buildings, relatively little visual information is needed to allow viewers to distinguish buildings from each other or to identify a single building and to gain information about its spatial relation and shape. Due to this issue, architectural and landscape models provide an appropriate approach to structure and access further space-related information, for example, historical sources, background information and relations, in a visual way [63].

What implications can be deduced for an appropriate design of media and workflows deduced? As an overarching finding for all particular studies, daily contact with the forms and structures of architecture and built space in everyday life create a strong familiarity with their characters, symbols and representations. Though architecture is adequate for transporting knowledge about a shape and spatial setting of objects, it also facilitates a communication and knowledge exchange for more abstract and sophisticated concepts. It functions as a shared metaphor. Especially historical architecture is rarely comprehensively described by historical sources. A major issue is to bridge uncertainties within a creational process as well as to show vagueness and blurriness of sources for generated visualisations. A common approach to visualize the vagueness of a reconstruction within images is to use abstracted, non-photorealistic visualisation [64]. As shown in our research, even high levels of visual abstraction and schematic appearance are suitable to make architecture recognisable for an observer. This allows to make different source qualities and levels of certainty visible, e.g. by schematic visualisation [65–67]. Architecture and built structures are the most relevant objects of 3D modelling in cultural heritage and most prominent in related academic discourses. As shown in our research, virtual models rely on individual contributions from different authors. Moreover, a multiplicity of intuitive decisions is included in such media. Against the background of an inclusion of virtual models into an academic discourse, both an academic culture and mechanisms to make digital models and generated visualisations scientifically linkable and able to discuss have to be established. Especially in the humanities, affinity and competence of scholars regarding digital research methods are only little developed [68]. Against this background, a method-related development of competencies of scholars and users related to the production, evaluation and usage of digital reconstructions is still an ongoing main challenge.

What are the limitations of this study? This study performs an explorative research using methods from social sciences. In consequence, various concepts and phenomena can be sketched, but from the available data only limited, more general implications and negotiations are possible. A next research stage will be to operationalise the knowledge transfer and transformation process with special regards to its academic context and to investigate these issues using quantitative testing approaches. As an initial step on this way, we are currently developing a classification scheme for academic reconstruction projects [69] to determine types and factors of knowledge-related functions.

Acknowledgements Research on usability aspects took place within a reconstruction project dealing with historic Dresden and Terezin in the context of the Holocaust. A test for visual usability was conducted by Josefine Brödner, Katharina Hammel and Cindy Kröber. The authors want to acknowledge the support of Dr. Lars Schlenker (Dresden University of Technology) who provided information on architecture-based learning.

References

1. B.J. Novitski, *Rendering Real and Imagined Buildings. The Art of Computer Modeling from the Palace of Kublai Khan to Le Corbusier's Villas* (Rockport Pub, Gloucester, 1998)
2. D.H. Sanders, More than pretty pictures of the past. An American perspective on virtual heritage, in *Paradata and Transparency in Virtual Heritage*, ed. by A. Bentkowska-Kafel, H. Denard, D. Baker (Ashgate, Burlington, 2012), pp. 37–56
3. M. Greengrass, L.M. Hughes, *The Virtual Representation of the Past. Digital Research in the Arts and Humanities* (Ashgate, Aldershot, 2008)
4. D. Favro, In the eyes of the beholder. Virtual reality re-creations and academia, in *Imaging Ancient Rome: Documentation, Visualization, Imagination*, ed. by L. Haselberger, J. Humphrey, D. Abernathy. Proceedings of the 3rd Williams Symposium on Classical Architecture, Rome, 20–23 May 2004. J. Roman Archaeol. (Portsmouth, 2006), pp. 321–334
5. R. El Darwich, Modelle, in *Handbuch Medien im Geschichtsunterricht*, ed. by H.-J. Pandel, U.A.J. Becher, 3rd edn. (Wochenschau-Verlag, Schwalbach, 2005), pp. 580–591
6. J.A. Cannon-Bowers, E. Salas, S.A. Converse, Shared mental models in expert team decision making, in *Individual and Group Decision Making: Current Issues*, ed. by N.J. Castellan Jr. (Lawrence Erlbaum Associates, Inc., Hillsdale, 1993), pp. 221–246
7. U. Hasler Roumois, *Studienbuch Wissensmanagement. Grundlagen der Wissensarbeit in Wirtschafts-, Non-Profit- und Public-Organisationen*, vol 2954, 2nd edn. (Orell Füssli, Zürich, 2010)
8. R. Arnheim, *Visual Thinking* (Rütten & Loening, München, 1969)

9. D.C. Gooding, Cognition, construction and culture. Visual theories in the sciences. J. Cogn. Cult. **4**, 551–593 (2004)
10. G. Ryle, *The Concept of Mind* (University of Chicago Press, Chicago, 1949)
11. P. Baumgartner, *Der Hintergrund des Wissens. Vorarbeiten zu einer Kritik der programmierbaren Vernunft* (Kärntner Druck- und Verlagsgesellschaft, Klagenfurt, 1993)
12. M. Polanyi, *The Tacit Dimension*, 18th edn. (University of Chicago Press, Chicago, 1966)
13. I. Nonaka, H. Takeuchi, *The Knowledge-Creating Company. How Japanese Companies Create the Dynamics of Innovation* (Oxford Press, New York, NY, 1995)
14. M.G. Müller, S. Geise, *Grundlagen der Visuellen Kommunikation* (UVK, Konstanz, 2015)
15. H. Schumann, W. Müller, *Visualisierung. Grundlagen und Allgemeine Methoden* (Springer, Berlin, 2000)
16. J. Bertin, G. Jensch, *Graphische Semiologie* (Diagramme, Netze, Karten. de Gruyter, Berlin, 1974)
17. R.J. Gerrig, P.G. Zimbardo, *Psychology and Life*, 19th edn. (Allyn & Bacon, Boston, MA, 2010)
18. J. Bollmann, W.G. Koch, *Lexikon der Kartographie und Geomatik* (Spektrum Akademischer Verlag, Heidelberg, 2001)
19. B. Mahr, *Das Wissen im Modell* (Technische Universität, Fakultät IV, Berlin, 2004)
20. H. Stachowiak, *Allgemeine Modelltheorie* (Springer, Wien, 1973)
21. A. Repko, Integrating interdisciplinarity. How the theories of common ground and cognitive interdisciplinarity are informing the debate on interdisciplinary integration. Issues Integr. Stud. **25**, 1–31 (2007)
22. H.H. Clark, *Using Language* (Cambridge University Press, Cambridge, 1996)
23. R. Bromme, Beyond one's own perspective. The psychology of cognitive interdisciplinarity, in *Practising Interdisciplinarity*, ed. by P. Weingart, N. Stehr (University of Toronto Press, Toronto, ON, 2000), pp. 115–133
24. R. Horst, *Die Sakraltopographie der Romanischen Jakobus-Kathedrale* (Studien zur Kunstgeschichte des Mittelalters und der Frühen Neuzeit, Korb, 2012)
25. W.G. Stock, M. Stock, *Handbook of Information Science* (de Gruyter, Berlin, 2013)
26. S. Münster, T. Köhler, S. Hoppe, 3D modeling technologies as tools for the reconstruction and visualization of historic items in humanities. A literature-based survey, in *Across Space and Time*, ed. by A. Traviglia. Selected Papers from the 41st Computer Applications and Quantitative Methods in Archaeology Conference, Perth, 25–28 March 2013 (Amsterdam University Press, Amsterdam, 2015)
27. P. Mayring, Qualitative content analysis. Forum Qual. Sozialforschung **1**(2), Art. 20 (2000)
28. S. Bürger, Unregelmässigkeit als Anreiz zur Ordnung oder Impuls zum Chaos. Die virtuose Steinmetzkunst der Pirnaer Marienkirche. Z. Kunstgesch. **74**(1), 123–132 (2011)
29. S. Zhang, R. Lu, C. Liu C, ACAML—a markup language for ancient Chinese architecture, in *Revive the Past. Computer Applications and Quantitative Methods in Archaeology (CAA)*, ed. by M. Zhou, I. Romanowska I, Z. Wu, P. Xu, P. Verhagen. Proceedings of the 39th International Conference (Pallas Publications, Amsterdam, 2011), pp. 285–295
30. K. Walczak, W. Cellary, A. Prinke, Interactive presentation of archaeological objects using virtual and augmented reality, in *On the Road to Reconstructing the Past. Computer Applications and Quantitative Methods in Archaeology (CAA)*, ed. by E. Jerem, F. Redő, V. Szeverényi. Proceedings of the 36th International Conference (Archaeolingua, Budapest, 2011)
31. M. Zöllner, M. Becker, J. Keil, Snapshot augmented reality–augmented photography, in *11th International Symposium on Virtual Reality, Archaeology and Cultural Heritage (VAST 2010)*, ed. by A. Artusi, M. Joly-Parvex, G. Lucet, A. Ribes, D. Pitzalis (Eurographics Association, Paris, 2010), pp. 53–56
32. S. Münster, in *The Role of Images for a Virtual 3D Reconstruction of Historic Artifacts*. International Communication Association (ICA) Annual Meeting, London, 17–21 June 2013
33. A. Bryant, K. Charmaz, *The SAGE Handbook of Grounded Theory* (Sage, Thousand Oaks, CA, 2010)

34. S. Münster, L. Schlenker, T. Köhler, Common grounds and representations in cross-disciplinary processes, in *Knowledge and Management Models for Sustainable Growth*, ed. by D. Carlucci, G. Schiuma, J. Spender (Institute of Knowledge Asset Management, Basilicata, 2014), pp. 579–589
35. S. Münster, P.-H. Jahn, M. Wacker, in *Bildlichkeit im Zeitalter der Modellierung. Operative Artefakte in Entwurfsprozessen der Architektur und des Ingenieurwesens. eikones*, ed. by S. Ammon, I. Hinterwaldner. Von Plan- und Bildquellen zum virtuellen Gebäudemodell. Zur Bedeutung der Bildlichkeit für die digitale 3D-Rekonstruktion historischer Architektur (Wilhelm Fink Verlag, Munich, 2017), pp. 255–286
36. S. Münster, Workflows and the role of images for a virtual 3D reconstruction of no longer extant historic objects. Ann. Photogramm. Remote Sens. Spat. Inf. Sci. **II-5/W1**(XXIV International CIPA Symposium), 197–202 (2013)
37. C. Kröber, S. Münster, An app for the Cathedral in Freiberg—an interdisciplinary project seminar, in *Competencies, Challenges, and Changes in Teaching, Learning and Educational Leadership in the Digital Age. Papers from the CELDA 2014*, ed. by D.G. Sampson, J.M. Spector, D. Ifenthaler, P. Isaias (Springer, Berlin, 2016), pp. 303–318
38. A. Collins, J.S. Brown, S.E. Newman, *Cognitive Apprenticeship: Teaching the Craft of Reading, Writing and Mathematics*, Technical Report No. 403, University of Illinois, Cambridge, 1987
39. H. Mintzberg, F. Westley, Decision making: it's not what you think, in *Handbook of Decision Making*, ed. by P.C. Nutt, D. Wilson (Wiley-Blackwell, Oxford, 2010), pp. 73–82
40. K. Knorr-Cetina, *Epistemic Cultures. How the Sciences Make Knowledge* (Harvard University Press, Cambridge, 1999)
41. V. Bartsch, M. Ebers, I. Maurer, Learning in project-based organizations: the role of project teams' social capital for overcoming barriers to learning. Int. J. Proj. Manag. **31**(2), 239–251 (2013)
42. C. Pilbeam, Coordinating temporary organizations in international development through social and temporal embeddedness. Int. J. Proj. Manag. **31**(2), 190–199 (2013)
43. L.O. Oyedele, Analysis of architects' demotivating factors in design firms. Int. J. Proj. Manag. **31**(3), 342–354 (2013)
44. H. Tsoukas, *Complex Knowledge* (Oxford University Press, Oxford, 2006)
45. H.A. Simon, Theories of bounded rationality, in *Decision and Organization*, ed. by C.B. McGuire, R. Radner (North-Holland Publishing Company, Amsterdam, 1972), pp. 161–176
46. T. Hatcher, B. Hinton, J. Swartz, Graduate student's perceptions of university team-teaching. Coll. Stud. J. **30**(3), 367–376 (1996)
47. D.M. Wegner, Transactive memory. A contemporary analysis of the group mind, in *Theories of Group Behavior*, ed. by B. Mullen, G.R. Goethals (Springer, New York, NY, 1986), pp. 185–208
48. C. Argyris, D.A. Schön, *Organizational Learning. A Theory of Action Perspective* (Addison-Wesley, Reading, MA, 1978)
49. S.L. Star, J.R. Griesemer, Institutional Ecology, "Translations" and Boundary Objects. Amateurs and Professionals in Berkeley's Museum of Vertebrate Zoology 1907–1939. Soc. Stud. Sci. **19**(4), 387–420 (1989)
50. Paivio A, Dual coding theory and education (draft), in *Pathways to Literacy Achievement for High Poverty Children* (The University of Michigan School of Education, 29 September–1 October 2006)
51. J. Nielsen, *Usability Engineering* (Academic, Salt Lake City, 1993)
52. J.L. Torn, *The Virtual Cityscapes of Rock Star Games*. International Communication Association (ICA) Annual Meeting, London, 17–21 June 2013
53. S. Krug, *Don't make me think!: a common sense approach to web usability*, 2nd edn. (New Riders Pub, Berkeley, CA, 2006)

54. J. Rubin, D. Chisnell, *Handbook of Usability Testing. How to Plan, Design, and Conduct*, 2nd edn. (Wiley Publishing, Inc., Indianapolis, IN, 2008)
55. H. Weller, *Generalisierte 3D-Gebäuderepräsentation im Spannungsfeld von Primärinformation, Modellierungsaufwand und Wiedererkennbarkeit am Beispiel eines 3D-Stadtmodells von Dresdens um 1940*, Diploma thesis, TU Dresden, Dresden, 2013
56. G. Pomaska, *Web-Visualisierung mit Open Source. Vom CAD-Modell zur Real-Time-Animation* (Herbert Wichmann Verlag, Heidelberg, 2007)
57. A. Yaneva, Scaling up and down. Extraction trials in architectural design. Soc. Stud. Sci. **35**(6), 867–894 (2005)
58. G.D. Rey, T. Wehr (eds.), *Kognitive Psychologie. Ausgewählte Grundlagen- und Anwendungsbeispiele* (Berlin, 2008)
59. B. Tversky, Spatial schemas in depictions, in *Spatial Schemas and Abstract Thought*, ed. by M. Gattis (MIT Press, Cambridge, 2002), pp. 79–112
60. C. Goodwin, Professional vision. Am. Anthropol. **96**(3), 606–633 (1994)
61. H.A. Simon, Invariants of human behavior. Annu. Rev. Psychol. **41**, 1–19 (1990)
62. S. Münster, N. Prechtel, Beyond software. Design implications for virtual libraries and platforms for cultural heritage from practical findings, in *Digital Heritage. Progress in Cultural Heritage: Documentation, Preservation, and Protection*, ed. by M. Ioannides, N. Magnenat-Thalmann, E. Fink, R. Žarnić, A.-Y. Yen, E. Quak, vol LNCS 8740 (Springer, Cham, 2014), pp. 131–145
63. N. Prechtel, S. Münster, in *3D Research Challenges in Cultural Heritage II*, ed. by S. Münster, M. Pfarr-Harfst, P. Kuroczyński, M. Ioannides. Cultural heritage in a spatial context – towards an integrative, interoperable, and participatory data and information management (Springer, Cham, 2016), pp. 272–288
64. J.E. Packer, Digitizing Roman imperial architecture in the early 21st century. Purposes, data, failures, and prospects, in *Imaging Ancient Rome: Documentation, Visualization, Imagination*, ed. by L. Haselberger, J. Humphrey, D. Abernathy. Proceedings of the 3rd Williams Symposium on Classical Architecture, Rome, 20–23 May 2004. J. Roman Archaeol. (Portsmouth, 2006), pp. 309–320
65. M. Danielová, *Visual Reconstruction of Archaeological Data of the Sanctuary of Diana at Nemi, Italy*, Master thesis, Munich, 2014
66. D. Lengyel, C. Toulouse, Darstellung von unscharfem Wissen in der Rekonstruktion historischer Bauten, in *Von Handaufmaß bis High Tech III. 3D in der historischen Bauforschung*, ed. by K. Heine, K. Rheidt, F. Henze, A. Riedel (Verlag Philipp von Zabern, Darmstadt, 2011), pp. 182–186
67. F.I. Apollonio, M. Gaiani, Z. Sun, in *3D Modeling and Data Enrichment in Digital Reconstruction of Architectural Heritage*. International Archives of the Photogrammetry, Remote Sensing and Spatial Information Sciences XL-5/W2, XXIV International CIPA Symposium, Strasbourg, 2–6 September 2013, pp. 43–48
68. S. Albrecht, in *Scholars' Adoption of E-Science Practices: (Preliminary) Results from a Qualitative Study of Network and Other Influencing Factors*. XXXIII. Sunbelt Social Networks Conference of the International Network for Social Network Analysis (INSNA), Hamburg, 21–26 May 2013
69. S. Münster, C. Kröber, H. Weller, N. Prechtel, in *3D Research Challenges in Cultural Heritage II*, ed. by S. Münster, M. Pfarr-Harfst, P. Kuroczyński, M. Ioannides. Researching knowledge issues on virtual historical architecture (Springer, Cham, 2016), pp. 362–374

Part V
Presence

Chapter 13
Gamified AR/VR Character Rendering and Animation-Enabling Technologies

Margarita Papaefthymiou, Steve Kateros, Stylianos Georgiou, Nikos Lydatakis, Paul Zikas, Vasileios Bachlitzanakis, and George Papagiannakis

Abstract In recent years, the popularity of mixed reality (MR) environments has increased as they provide attractive and immersive experiences for educational, entertainment, and training purposes. The increasing advances of Augmented Reality (AR) and Virtual Reality (VR) hardware and software technologies also constitute an interesting area of research. In this work, we present the main pipeline followed for creating virtual character-based AR experiences, specifically in cultural heritage environments. Our main goal in this chapter is to compare different software methodologies for creating VR environments and present a complete novel methodology for authoring life-sized AR virtual characters and life-sized AR crowd simulation using only modern mobile devices. One important aspect of these environments that we focus on is creating realistic and interactive virtual characters via procedurally generated body and facial animations which are illuminated with real environment light. Virtual characters' transformations are handled efficiently using a single mathematical framework, the 3D Euclidean geometric algebra (GA), and the conformal geometric algebra (CGA) which is able to handle translations, rotations, and dilations. Using such a single algebraic framework, we avoid conversions between different mathematical representations; as a result, we achieve more efficient performance. We also compare the efficiency of different GA code generators—(a) the Gaigen library, (b) libvsr, and (c) Gaalop—so that a future user of GA can choose the most appropriate, currently available s/w library that will provide the most optimal and efficient results. Our main research involves the following questions: (a) Are novel, low-cost, modern HMDs suitable as VR platforms? (b) Which are the most appropriate s/w platforms needed to realize such VR digital heritage gamified experiences? (c) Can we

M. Papaefthymiou (✉) • S. Kateros • S. Georgiou • N. Lydatakis • P. Zikas • V. Bachlitzanakis • G. Papagiannakis
Institute of Computer Science, Foundation for Research and Technology—Hellas, 100 N. Plastira Str., 70013 Heraklion, Greece

Department of Computer Science, University of Crete, Voutes Campus, 70013 Heraklion, Greece
e-mail: mpapae@ics.forth.gr; kateros@csd.uoc.gr; georgiou@csd.uoc.gr; lydatakis@csd.uoc.gr; zikas@csd.uoc.gr; csd3058@csd.uoc.gr; papagian@ics.forth.gr

M. Ioannides et al. (eds.), *Mixed Reality and Gamification for Cultural Heritage*, DOI 10.1007/978-3-319-49607-8_13

achieve more efficient AR scene authoring? (d) Can we achieve more efficient AR animation interpolation and skinning using a single mathematical framework employing GA?

Keywords Augmented reality • Rendering • Animation • Geometric algebra • Illumination • Mobile precomputed radiance transfer • Procedural character animation systems • Conformal geometric algebra • Virtual reality • Animation blending • Skinning • GPU-based skinning • Virtual character simulation • AR crowd simulation • Virtual characters • Crowd simulation

13.1 Introduction

In this chapter, we aim to compare different software methodologies for real-time VR in digital heritage sites of both intangible and tangible cultural heritage and the generation of interactive, immersive MR environments. The software technologies that we compare are the OpenGL Geometric Application framework (glGA) [1] and the Unity game engine. Moreover, we propose a complete methodology for robust authoring of life-sized AR virtual characters [2] and life-sized AR crowd simulation using only mobile devices. We author and fully augment life-sized animated virtual characters in any open scene in less than a minute, and we are able to load that augmentation in the same scene within a few seconds. Our characters are illuminated using real environment light with HDR environment maps and are powered by SmartBody [3], a character animation platform that supports many character animation capabilities like locomotion, object manipulation, gazing, speech synthesis, and lip syncing.

To handle rotations of the AR characters, we use Euclidean GA, a mathematical framework that provides a single, convenient all-inclusive algebra for representing orientations and rotations of objects in three or higher dimensions, a compact and geometrically intuitive formulation of transformation algorithms, and an easy and immediate computation of rotors (subsuming quaternions and complex numbers). GA rotors are simpler to manipulate than Euler angles, more numerically stable, and more efficient than rotation matrices for the composition of transformations, avoiding the problem of gimbal lock. CGA extends the usefulness of the 3D GA by expanding the class of rotors to include translations and dilations (uniform scaling). Using the conformal model of GA that combines translation, rotation, and dilation, we generate an all-inclusive algorithm for real-time animation interpolation and GPU-based geometric skinning of animated, deformable virtual characters. Using this model, we represent transformations in a single representation, and we avoid converting from one mathematical representation to another. We also compare the efficiency of different GA code generators—(a) the Gaigen library, (b) libvsr, and (c) Gaalop—so that a future user of GA libraries can choose the most appropriate one that will give the most optimal and efficient results.

The results of this work will allow us to (a) provide a methodology for populating life-sized realistic and interactive virtual characters and crowd simulation in AR using only mobile devices; (b) unify and improve the performance of previously separated linear and quaternion algebra transformations; (c) fully replace quaternions for rotation interpolation with faster GA rotors; (d) generate an efficient animation blending and GPU-based skinning algorithm using CGA, a single geometric algebraic framework that supports rotation, translation, and dilation; and (e) compare software methodologies for creating VR environments.

Figure 13.1 shows the pipeline for creating AR/VR applications. At the beginning, is needed to capture and process the illumination and geometry data. Next, the virtual characters are created, and some of their movements are captured through a motion capture system. The next is to construct the static 3D models needed for the AR/VR applications and capture the HDR light probes that describe the environment light. In AR, an appropriate application is needed to extract the 3D feature points for performing markerless SLAM-based camera tracking that allows the augmentation of the virtual characters and the 3D static models in the environment. The libraries used for the development of such an application are the glGA framework, the SmartBody animation platform, the RVO library, and the Metaio SDK. glGA is responsible for loading, rendering, and illuminating the virtual characters using HDR light probes. The SmartBody animation platform is responsible for advanced, behavioral body and face animations. RVO is responsible for controlling the behavior of a crowd simulation, such as locomotion and collision avoidance. The Metaio SDK is used for performing markerless SLAM-based camera tracking. Historical information is used for creating different scenarios in order to present intangible data of the cultural heritage site.

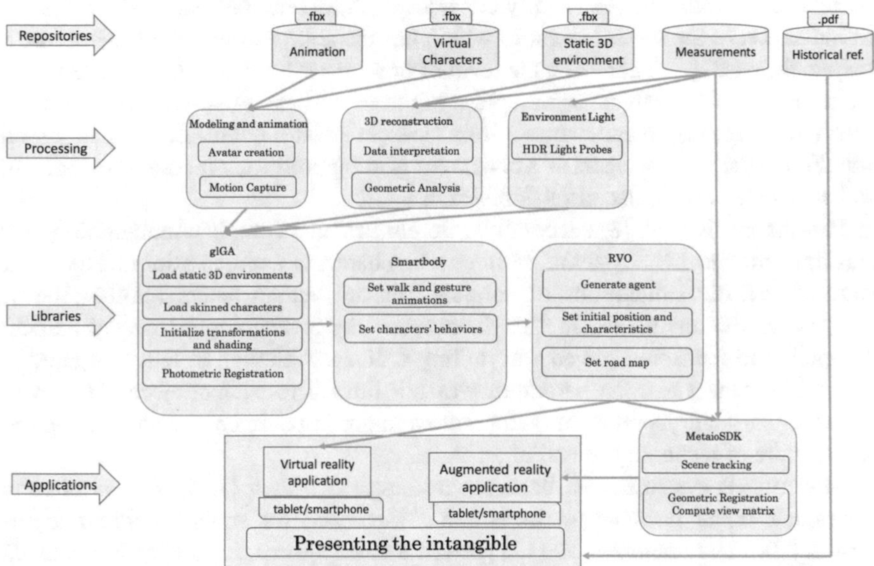

Fig. 13.1 The pipeline for creating AR/VR applications

Here is an overview of the content of each section:

- In Sect. 13.2, we provide previous work on the creation of MR environments and related work in handling transformations using GA.
- In Sect. 13.3, we present our novel results obtained from our comparison of the Unity 3D game engine and the glGA framework.
- In Sect. 13.4, we give an overview of 3D Euclidean GA and CGA mathematical frameworks used for handling transformation of our virtual characters.
- In Sect. 13.5, we describe the methodologies and the pipeline followed for populating interactive and realistic virtual characters and crowd simulation in AR.
- In Sect. 13.6, we propose an efficient algorithm for AR scene authoring using GA rotors and an efficient single mathematical framework for animation interpolation and GPU-based skinning using CGA.
- In Sect. 13.7, we provide our visual results, the comparison of our animation interpolation and GPU-based skinning algorithm with quaternions and dual quaternions, and a comparison of the efficiency of different GA code generators.
- In Sect. 13.8, we conclude and we present potential future work.

13.2 Previous Work

MR games [4] elude one's cognitive system and produce a sense of being physically present in the real as well as the virtual gaming world. This "sense of being there" is also known as presence [5, 6]. Presence is considered a paramount factor when using MR environments, especially considering digital heritage sites, since it gives an indication of the virtual scenario which has the ability to pull the subject into a "trip to the past" [7]. Therefore, the level of presence is fundamental to understanding the extent of the subject's perception of the scenario as a real-world experience, even though the origin and nature of this variable are still not clear. MR has gained attention in the last few years as a consumer gaming product, a medium for training and education, which also attracts research interest.

Papagiannakis et al. [8] successfully demonstrated a complete methodology for real-time mobile MR systems with virtual character augmentations. The work featured realistic simulations of animated virtual human actors (clothes, body, skin, face) who augmented real environments (the archaeological site of ancient Pompeii) and reenacted staged storytelling dramas. Although initially targeted at cultural heritage sites, the paradigm was not limited to such subjects. However, portability, usability, and form factor were a major impediment for wider adoption of that suite of technologies and algorithms.

Modern AR systems have been progressing since then [1, 5, 9], and already component-based frameworks have been researched for mobile outdoor applications [10, 11]. Langlotz et al. [12] present a novel system that allows in-place 3D content creation for mobile augmented reality in unprepared environments. The work described two different tracking techniques in order to create a feature database of the environment while the user runs the AR application. One tracking technique is for large working environments and the other for small workspaces. If the feature database exists, the user can retrieve it from the server with a query.

The SmartBody [3] animation framework that we use in this work, which is described in [13], provides a pipeline for incorporating high-quality humanoid assets into a virtual character and quickly infuse that character with a broad set of behaviors that are common to many games and simulations, including lip syncing and nonverbal behaviors. In this work, we provide a novel integration of the framework for mobile AR scenes, featuring life-size, interactive virtual characters and a markerless SLAM-based camera tracking system that allows the augmentation of any indoor or outdoor scene in less than a minute [2].

GA and CGA mathematical tools used in our work for handling transformations of the virtual characters attract research interest in many areas of computer science and engineering and particularly in computer graphics as it is shown that they can produce more efficient and smooth results than other algebras. Dorst et al. [14] present applications of GA and CGA in the field of computer graphics and provide useful examples written in C++ using the Gaigen library and code generator. Some of these applications are interpolating rotations, recursive ray tracing for illumination, constructing binary space partition (BSP) trees, handling rotations with rotors, and handling intersections for collision detection and shadows. Papagiannakis et al. [11, 15] propose two alternative methodologies for implementing real-time animation interpolation for skinned characters using geometric algebra rotors. They compare their methodology with alternative animation blending techniques, such as quaternion linear blending and dual-quaternion SLERP interpolation, and show that they achieve shorter computation time, lower memory usage, and higher visual quality results compared to other methods. Moreover, Wareham et al. [16] propose a method for pose and position interpolation using CGA that can also be extended to higher dimension spaces. Wareham and Lasenby [17] propose a method for interpolating smoothly between two or more displacements that include rotation and translation using CGA. Also, Kavan et al. [18] present an interpolation method of rotation and translation for skinning using dual quaternions with fast performance. Magnenat-Thalmann et al. [19] introduce matrix operation approach for skin deformation which overcomes the problem of vertex collapsing. Magnenat-Thalmann et al. [20] propose joint-dependent local deformation (JLD) operators for moving hands and grasping an object, which also provides hand deformation while moving.

In our work, we use GA for handling rotations of the virtual characters and implementing animation interpolation and skinning. We compare our method with standard quaternions, linear algebra matrices, and dual-quaternions blending and skinning algorithms and illustrate how our CGA-GPU-inclusive skinning algorithm can provide results as smooth as and more efficient than state-of-the-art methods mentioned previously.

13.3 Comparison of Unity 3D Game Engine and glGA Framework

We created VR games for the Knossos Heritage site (Fig. 13.2) using the novel Oculus Rift DK1 HMD in order to compare the Unity 3D game engine and the glGA framework. From this comparison [21], the following novel results were obtained:

- Oculus Rift DK1 by itself is not yet a minimum VR platform. Head and hand tracking (rotations including translations) should be coupled to the underlying s/w framework as also found in [22] in order to avoid "breaks in presence." Recent RGB-D-based algorithms and open frameworks from FORTH provide such ready-to-be-integrated solutions [23, 24], and we are currently in the process of integrating them. Instrumental to this approach is having complete source code support and usage of C++11; thus our own glGA framework has a clear advantage in this process, rather than other commercial frameworks.
- Unity provided an easy-to-use, rapid prototyping environment with high-visual 3D realism (shadow-mapped point lights as well as HDR area lights and sky-boxes). However, our current VR games have so far indicated (we have not yet finalized a formal user study) that a coherent, low-realism 3D world can lead to higher presence by the participants: if you are targeting a visually realistic environment, it is more likely to generate breaks in presence [25]. This is because the human brain will expect many things that we are not yet able to achieve technically: perfect physics, sound, and force feedback so that your hand does not penetrate an object, objects breaking into pieces, etc. Having a lower realistic environment lowers user expectations, resulting in a more consistent presence feeling.
- Oculomotor (avoiding eye strain) and bodily comfort (e.g., asking the user to sit to prevent feelings of disorientation and nausea) are key factors to provide a positive user VR experience. In order to maintain as much VR immersion as possible from game start to finish, multiple s/w and h/w parameters have to be constantly reevaluated and adjusted, which is a challenging task. As a good starting point, we found that the Oculus best practice guidelines [22, 25, 26] as well as other similar guidelines from other researchers [27] allow adjustment and intensification of the VR experience.

Fig. 13.2 Roman Agora suite of VR minigame shells in our Unity-based VR game

13.4 Review of Geometric Algebra Framework Used for Handling Transformations of Virtual Characters

GA [14, 28, 29] is a mathematical framework that provides a convenient mathematical notation for representing orientations and rotations of objects in three dimensions, a compact and geometrically intuitive formulation of algorithms, and an easy and immediate computation of rotors.

13.4.1 3D Euclidean Geometric Algebra

The basis vectors for the three-dimensional Euclidean geometric algebra space are the orthonormal bases e_1, e_2, and e_3, which are the basic elements for generating the GA. The products of GA are the outer product, the inner product, and the geometric product. The outer product, often called wedge product, is denoted by ^ and is computed with the following equation:

$$\begin{aligned} a{\wedge}b &= (a_1e_1 + a_2e_2 + a_3e_3) + (b_1e_1 + b_2e_2 + b_3e_3) \\ &= (a_1b_2 - a_2b_1)e_1{\wedge}e_2 + (a_2b_3 - a_3b_2)e_2{\wedge}e_3 \\ &\quad + (a_3b_1 - a_1b_3)e_3{\wedge}e_1 \end{aligned} \tag{13.1}$$

where a and b are GA vectors. A higher level dimensionality oriented subspace can be constructed by defining the outer product between GA vectors. Such a subspace is called blade, and a k-blade denotes a k-dimensional subspace. For example, a vector is 1-blade, the outer product of 2 vectors is 2-blade, called a bivector; the outer product of 3 vectors is 3-blade, called a trivector, etc. A bivector represents a plane, and a trivector represents a 3D volume. The bivectors of the 3D Euclidean GA are $e_1{\wedge}e_2$, $e_2{\wedge}e_3$, and $e_3{\wedge}e_1$, and the trivector is $e_1{\wedge}e_2{\wedge}e_3$. The highest blade element is called pseudoscalar and is denoted by I. For example, the pseudoscalar in 3D Euclidean space is I_3. The inner product, often called dot product, is denoted by $\cdot$ and it is used to compute distance and angles. The inner product is computed using the equation below:

$$a \cdot b = |a||b|cos\varphi \tag{13.2}$$

where φ is the angle formed by the vectors a and b. The geometric product is a mixed grade product: it consists of a scalar (0-blade) and a bivector (2-blade) and is called multivector. The geometric product is computed using the equation below:

$$ab = a \cdot b + a{\wedge}b = |a||b|(cos\varphi + Isin\varphi) = |a||b|e^{I\varphi}. \tag{13.3}$$

The duality of a GA element is denoted by * and gives a blade that represents the orthogonal complement of that subspace. For example, the duality of a bivector equals to a vector that is perpendicular to this bivector and vice versa. The duality is defined with the equation below:

$$A^* = \mathrm{A}/\mathrm{I} = -AI. \tag{13.4}$$

The basic element used to handle rotations of any multivector in GA is a rotor and is usually denoted as R and is computed using the exponential formula below:

$$R = e^{I_3 u \frac{\varphi}{2}} \tag{13.5}$$

where φ is the angle of rotation, and u is the axis of rotation. The interpolated rotation between two rotors R_1 and R_2 in N steps is given by:

$$R_N = e^{log\left(R_2 R_1^{-1}\right)*N}. \tag{13.6}$$

To rotate a multivector A, we sandwich it between the rotor R and its inverse rotor R^{-1} as shown below:

$$RAR^{-1}. \tag{13.7}$$

13.4.2 Conformal Geometric Algebra

CGA is a 5D space algebra which is able to handle 3D transformations (conformal transformations) like translations, rotations, and dilations by expanding the 3D Euclidean geometric algebra with two additional basis vectors. These additional basis vectors are e_- and e_+, with opposite signatures, which are defined such that:

$$e_+^2 = 1, \qquad e_-^2 = -1, \qquad e_+ \cdot e_- = 0. \tag{13.8}$$

Using the basis vector e_- and e_+, two additional basis vectors are defined: e_0 the 3D point at the origin and e_∞ the infinity point, both of which are null:

$$e_0^2 = 0, \qquad e_\infty^2 = 0 \tag{13.9}$$

and are constructed as follows:

$$e_\infty = e_- + e_+, \qquad e_0 = \frac{1}{2}(e_- - e_+). \tag{13.10}$$

Table 13.1 Representation of entities with CGA (x is the 3D point in the 3D Euclidean GA model) (© 2016 Springer)

Entity	Inner product null space	Outer product null space
Point	$P = x + \frac{1}{2}x^2 e_\infty + e_0$	–
Sphere	$S = P - \frac{1}{2}r^2 e_\infty$	$S^* = P_1 \wedge P_2 \wedge P_3 \wedge P_4$
Plane	$\pi = n + de_\infty$	$\pi^* = P_1 \wedge P_2 \wedge P_3 \wedge e_\infty$
Circle	$Z = S_1 \wedge S_2$	$Z^* = P_1 \wedge P_2 \wedge P_3$
Line	$L = \pi_1 \wedge \pi_2$	$L^* = P_1 \wedge P_2 \wedge e_\infty$
Point pair	$P = S_1 \wedge S_2 \wedge S_3$	$P^* = P_1 \wedge P_2$

13.4.2.1 Representing Entities in CGA

Conformal geometric algebra (CGA) is able to represent basic 3D primitives using inner and outer products which are (a) point, (b) sphere, (c) plane, (d) circle, (e) line, and (f) point pair. Table 13.1 shows how these entities are represented with CGA.

13.4.2.2 Transformations in CGA

Translators In the conformal space we can translate a vector x with a translator rotor with the formula below:

$$T = e^{-\frac{1}{2}te_\infty} = 1 - \frac{1}{2}te_\infty \tag{13.11}$$

where t is the vector that represents translation $t = t_1e_1 + t_2e_2 + t_3e_3$.

Rotors Rotor operator in CGA space is constructed using the exponential equation:

$$R = e^{-b\frac{\varphi}{2}} = e^{I_3u\frac{\varphi}{2}} = cos\left(\frac{\varphi}{2}\right) - uI_3sin\left(\frac{\varphi}{2}\right) \tag{13.12}$$

where φ is the angle of rotation, b is the plane of rotation, and u is the axis of rotation.

Dilators The dilation operator gives the scaling of factor d about the origin e_0 using the formula below:

$$D = 1 + \frac{1-d}{1+d}e_\infty \wedge e_0. \tag{13.13}$$

Motors In CGA, a transformation that includes rotation and translation, called displacement versor or motor, is given by:

$$M = RT \tag{13.14}$$

where R is the rotor and T is the translator. The following formula is used to linearly interpolate between two motors M_1 and M_2 in N steps:

$$\mathrm{M_N} = \mathrm{M_1}*(1 - \mathrm{N}) + \mathrm{M_2}*\mathrm{N}. \tag{13.15}$$

The following equation is used to apply the motion to a rigid body A, where M^{-1} is the inverse of the motor M:

$$MAM^{-1}. \tag{13.16}$$

13.4.3 Representing Quaternions and Dual Quaternions with Geometric Algebra

Quaternions of the form $Q = 1 + (xi + yj + zk)$ are represented in CGA based on four blades: the scalar and three 2-blades. Dual quaternions of the form:

$$\begin{aligned} Q &= Q_1 + \in Q_2 \\ &= 1 + (x_1 i + y_1 j + z_1 k) + \in(1 + (x_2 i + y_2 j + z_2 k)) \\ &= 1 + (x_1 i + y_1 j + z_1 k) + (\in + x_2 i \in + y_2 j \in + z_2 k \in) \end{aligned} \tag{13.17}$$

where Q_1 and Q_2 are quaternions are represented in CGA based on eight blades: a scalar, six 2-blades, and one 4-blade. Table 13.2 shows the correspondence of quaternions and dual quaternions with CGA blades.

13.5 Creating Interactive and Realistic Virtual Characters

Table 13.2 Representing quaternions and dual quaternions in CGA (© 2016 Springer)

Quaternion	Dual quaternion	CGA
1	*1*	e
i	i	e_1^e_2
j	j	e_3^e_1
k	k	e_2^e_3
–	$k\epsilon$	e_∞^e_1
–	$j\epsilon$	e_∞^e_2
–	$i\epsilon$	e_∞^e_3
–	ϵ	e_1^e_2^e_3^e_∞

Our glGA framework enables creating realistic and interactive virtual characters by providing a wide range of capabilities. Specifically, it allows real-time global illumination using HDR environment maps and provides procedurally generated body and facial animation to the characters using the SmartBody animation platform (Fig. 13.1).

13.5.1 Rendering Virtual Characters for AR and VR

glGA is a lightweight, shader-based C++ computer graphics (CG) framework which is developed for educational as well as research purposes. glGA is a cross-platform application development framework and supports many mobile and desktop platforms. glGA contains many operations like compiling and loading shaders, textures, sounds, animations, and loading 3D static meshes as well as rig meshes.

glGA supports from simple 3D models to animated, skinned characters. In order to help students visualize the externally rigged virtual characters (e.g., Collada or MD5 models), glGA provides the functionality required to parse the bone tree in real time and retrieve the transformation matrix from each one of the joints. These matrices are then passed as uniform and vertex attribute parameters to the vertex shader.

13.5.1.1 Markerless AR Tracking for AR

For performing markerless SLAM-based 3D camera tracking for AR applications, we have integrated in our glGA framework the Metaio SDK [1], as illustrated in Fig. 13.1. The user can utilize the capabilities of the Metaio SDK in two ways. The user must create a 3D map using the Toolbox mobile application and then pass this file to the application bundle using a Desktop File Transfer application. Alternatively, he can create a 3D map at runtime. However, creating the 3D map using the second way has a limitation: you cannot extend the 3D map. In our work, we propose a way to load the 3D map created by Toolbox directly from the device: the user must create the 3D map using the Toolbox mobile application, send it via e-mail, open the e-mail, select the file, and open it with our application. We achieve this by modifying the property list in the .plist file. The user must define the file extension types that the application will support (Uniform Type Identifier (UTI)) by setting to the "public.filename-extension" the name "3dmap". Also, we add the identifier for the custom UTI. When the user opens the .3dmap with the application, the function: -(BOOL) application:(UIApplication *) application openURL:(NSURL *) urlsource Application:(NSString *) source Application annotation:(id)annotation in AppDelegate is called automatically. By using the variable URL, we extract the full path of the 3D map and set it as the Metaio SDK configuration file.

13.5.2 Real-Time Global Illumination Using PRT Methods

To achieve real-time global illumination, we use precomputed radiance transfer (PRT) techniques. Our work so far includes diffuse unshadowed and shadowed PRT for static objects, supported also by mobile devices.

When using glGA framework to create AR environments, the user has the ability to adjust the exposure in order to change the intensity of the light of the objects based on the light in the real world. We give this functionality to the user because base on the time that it is tracking, the light may have different intensity in comparison to the intensity captured in the environment map.

13.5.2.1 Shadowed-Transfer and Unshadowed-Transfer PRT Implementation

The first step is to generate random samples using the Monte Carlo integration. We divide the sphere's surface in *RxR* cells where $R = \sqrt[2]{s}$ and s is the number of samples. To generate the samples, we generate a random point in every cell. Then, we convert the points to vector coordinates and we compute the Spherical Harmonics (SH) coefficients for each sample using the Boost library. The second step (precomputed) is to compute the coefficients that represent the incident radiance coming from the environment map for each vertex. We sum up for each sample, for each SH coefficient, the multiplication of dot product of the vertex normal and the direction of the sample and the spherical harmonic value. The dot product gives a positive value if the ray is inside the upper hemisphere. Then, we divide the result with the number of samples. For the shadowed-transfer PRT, we multiply the dot product with the visibility term (1 if the vertex is visible, otherwise 0). Equation 13.18 is used for shadowed-transfer PRT, where ρ_x is the albedo at vertex x, $L_i(x, \omega_i)$ is the incoming light to vertex x from direction ω_i, $V(\omega_i)$ is the visibility term from direction ω_i, and $N_x \cdot \omega_i$ is the dot product between vertex normal and direction ω_i:

$$L(x) = \int_{\Omega} L_i(x, \omega_i) V(\omega_i) \max(N_x \cdot \omega_i, 0) d\omega_i. \tag{13.18}$$

We implement shadows by constructing binary space partitioning (BSP) tree and specifically *k-d* tree. Since we construct it, we are able to define if a vertex is illuminated or not from a certain direction by ray casting.

At runtime, we compute the light coefficients based on the input HDR environment map. Firstly, we compute the light coming from the environment map for every generated sample by converting the Cartesian coordinates of the sphere to image coordinates. Each light coefficient equals to the summation of the product of the light coming from the sample direction and the SH coefficient. We multiply the

Fig. 13.3 VR character illuminated with shadowed-diffuse PRT with different exposures

result with the probability 4**PI* and divide it with the number of samples. The final color of each vertex equals to the summation of the product of the light coefficients with the vertex coefficients. Figure 13.3 shows a VR character illuminated with shadowed-diffuse PRT with different exposures.

13.5.3 Interactive Characters with Procedural Animation

glGA virtual characters are powered from SmartBody platform, a versatile character animation framework. SmartBody animation system is infused with a wide range of capabilities, such as locomotion, object manipulation, gazing, speech synthesis, and lip syncing. In the next section, we describe all the necessary steps for any computer graphics framework to easily integrated with SmartBody, in order to harness its advanced character behavioral capabilities. Figure 13.4 shows an augmented life-sized virtual character on a mobile device, performing gestures created with the SmartBody library at the Kourion Archaeological Site.

13.5.3.1 Integration of SmartBody into Any Modern Shader-Based CG Framework

We integrated SmartBody with glGA in order to be able to have a wide range of behaviors for our characters and be able to use an animation designed for a certain character in another one (retargeting).

The main idea is to create a character in SmartBody with a deformable mesh instance, assign him/her an animation, take the transformation matrix on the current frame of each bone of the character, and pass it to the corresponding skeleton data structure in glGA. In this way, SmartBody can be integrated into any computer graphics framework in order to utilize their character animation generators.

We used the following suggested SmartBody integration method [3, 13]:

1. In your engine/simulation, create a character. Simultaneously, create a SmartBody character in the SmartBody context with the same name.

Fig. 13.4 Augmented life-sized virtual character on a mobile device, performing gestures created with the SmartBody framework at Kourion Archaeological Site

2. Implement the SBSceneListener interface which handles character creation/deletion and modification of SmartBody characters and perform the equivalent actions in your engine/simulation.
3. Send SmartBody commands to control the character and change the scene every frame as needed.
4. Query SmartBody every frame to obtain the character state and change the engine/simulation character's state to match it.

Character behaviors such as speaking, gesturing, or other animated performance can be controlled by sending explicit commands using the behavioral markup language (BML).

13.5.4 AR Crowd Simulation Behavior

We have implemented life-sized AR crowd simulation [30] using the glGA framework (Fig. 13.5).

13.5.4.1 Collision Avoidance and Path Generation

For the simulation of crowd movement, the RVO2 [31] collision avoidance library was used. The initialization of the agents is done offline by specifying the characteristics of each agent such as the maximum speed and radius. After this step it starts to simulate the crowd, and each agent moves toward the goal position that we have set while avoiding collisions with other agents. For the animation management, we used SmartBody to alternate between walking and idle animations. The path followed by the agent is most of the times a straight line. If any obstacles appear in front them, they will try to overpass it as much as possible. The ORCA algorithm

Fig. 13.5 Life-sized AR crowd simulation on a mobile device (*left*) and on Fibrum HMD (*right*) (© by ACM 2016, reprinted with permission)

[32] used by RVO aims for the shortest path possible which is always a straight line, but this is not always preferable, especially when controlling a crowd.

To make the agents walk on a certain path, we need to define their goal positions and create a road map. A road map is like a graph, so it needs multiple points to represent a walking path. These points are stored in a unique vector for each agent as goal points. The agent has to reach all the goals of the road map to complete the path and come back to an idle state. Once a goal is reached, another will take its place in the vector and so on. Until every goal is reached, the agent continues to calculate the next velocity vector based on the goal points provided.

On each frame, RVO computes the velocity vectors for each agent. These vectors are used to determine the direction of the agent, but we also use them to find their actual rotation. The agent's body should always point in the direction of walking, and to do that we need to know in what direction he is planning to go. Velocity vectors are two-dimensional vectors, so by calculating the angle of each one with a common coordinate system, we can define the angle of the agent. This result is converted to a quaternion representation to generate the character's rotation matrix.

13.6 Handling Virtual Characters Transformations with Geometric Algebra

We use GA as the main framework that handles transformations of virtual characters [33]. We aim to enhance the conformal model of geometric algebra (CGA) [14, 28] as the mathematical background for character animation control [11] and specifically for animation blending and GPU-based geometric skinning (character deformation). We also use the Euclidean model of GA for robust authoring (rotation) of the augmented reality scene. The elements of CGA that handle transformations (CGA motors) can support translation, rotation, and dilation (uniform scaling) of joints under a single, GPU-supported mathematical framework and avoid conversion between different mathematical representations in contrast to quaternions and dual quaternions that support only rotation and rotation and translation, respectively. Hence our main novelty is the replacement of different types of algebras and the conversions between CPU and GPU, such as linear algebra matrices, quaternions, dual quaternions, and Euler angles for animation interpolation and skinning, with a single mathematical representation and CGA motors which can optimally handle the composition of translation, rotation, and scaling joint transformations and interpolations. The next section gives a detailed review of a geometric algebra mathematical framework. We implemented the following algorithm using the GA Gaigen library.

13.6.1 AR Scene Authoring with Geometric Algebra

We handle rotations of the AR scene objects with the use of GA by replacing Euler angles with Euclidean GA rotors. With the use of GA, we produce more efficient results in terms of visual quality. GA rotors are easier to manipulate than Euler angles, more numerically stable and more efficient than rotation matrices. Moreover, GA rotors do not produce discontinuities to the rotation by avoiding the problem of gimbal lock.

Our main novelty lies in the replacement of Euler angles with fast and robust GA rotors while the user rotates the objects of the AR scene.

As a first step, we set the initial rotation of the scene on each axis, and we compute the current GA rotor. We convert Euler angles to quaternion representation, and we compute the angle and the axis of the quaternion in order to compute the current GA rotor. To compute the rotor, we use the following exponential equation:

$$R = e^{-I_3 u \frac{\varphi}{2}}$$

where I_3 is the pseudoscalar, φ is the angle of rotation, and u is the axis of rotation. Our implementation gives the use the ability to rotate the scene on the global axis or on the object's local axis.

When we rotate on a local axis, we rotate the GA basis vectors with the current GA rotor (R_{cur}) in order to define the new local coordinate system. We rotate the coordinate system by sandwiching the 3D Euclidean GA basis vectors (e_1, e_2, e_3) between the current GA rotor and its inverse rotor. For example, to rotate the basis vector e_1, we use the formula $rot\_e_1 = R_{cur} e_1 R_{cur}^{-1}$ as deduced from Eq. (13.7). In this way, we compute the new rotated basis vectors rot_e$_1$, rot_e$_2$, and rot_e$_3$ which are used to define the new planes of rotation (bivectors) by constructing the outer product between the new rotated basis vectors, which are rot_e$_1$^rot_e$_2$, rot_e$_2$^rot_e$_3$, and rot_e$_3$^rot_e$_1$ on x, y, and z axis, respectively. When we change the axis of rotation, we need to define the new local coordinate system. When rotating on the same axis, we need to change the angle of rotation, recompute the current rotor, and multiply it with the previous rotor. We compute the current rotor using the following equation as deducted from Eq. (13.5):

$$R = e^{v\frac{\varphi}{2}}$$

where v is the plane of rotation, and φ is the angle of rotation. In contrast, when we rotate in a global coordinate system, the planes of rotation are defined by constructing the outer product between the GA basis vectors (e_1, e_2, e_3), i.e., e_1^e_2, e_2^e_3, and e_3^e_1.

13.6.2 Animation Interpolation and GPU-Based Skinning

Our main novelty, is the employment of conformal GA motors as fast, drop-in replacements for quaternion algebra and dual quaternion algebra during animation blending for skinned characters. In the following approach, we represent rotation combined with translation and dilation with CGA motors, and we use linear interpolation to interpolate the motors between the two keyframes of the character animation. We implemented the following algorithm [34] with CLUCalc scripting language and generate C++ optimized code using Gaalop Precompiler.

Rotation, translation, and scaling of the two keyframes of the animation are represented as CGA motors representation. The ASSIMP library provides the rotation of the animation in quaternion representation. In order to avoid converting quaternion to CGA rotor on each frame, we add an additional field to the structure of the bone (CGA rotor field) of the ASSIMP library, and we precompute the quaternion as CGA rotor representation. The following steps show how we convert rotation and translation to motor representation using the CLUCalc scripting language:

1. Convert translation vector to 3D Euclidean geometric algebra vector with the help of the basis vectors e$_1$, e$_2$, and e$_3$, where transX, transY, transZ are the Euclidean translation vectors:
   translationGA=transX*e1+transY*e2+transZ*e3.
2. Convert 3D GA vector (translationGA) to CGA translator rotor using the Eq. 13.11, where einf is the infinity point:
   translationCGA=1 – 0.5*translationGA*einf.
3. Compute the angle and the axis of the quaternion using GLM mathematical library functions:
   float angle=angle(quaternion),
   vec3 axis=axis(quaternion).

4. Similar to Step 1, we convert the axis (axis.x, axis.y, axis.z) of the quaternion to a 3D GA point:
   vector=VecN3(axis.x, axis.y, axis.z).
5. Construct a line that represents the axis of the quaternion using the line equation in Table 13.1:
   axis = vector^VecN3(0,0,0)^einf.
6. Compute the duality of the line, e.g., the plane of rotation (bivector) (Eq. 13.4):
   plane=*axis.
7. Construct rotor representation: $R = \exp(-0.5$*angle*plane).
8. Motor is computed as the geometric product of the translator and rotor (Eq. 13.14):
   motor=translationCGA*R.

After expressing the source and destination rotation and translation to CGA motors, we interpolate them based on a factor number that defines the animation interpolation step. We compute the motor from source (M_{src}) to destination (M_{dst}) motor in N steps using the linear Eq. (13.15), which is written in CLUCalc script as follows:

```
Interpolated=Msrc*(1−alpha)+Mdst*alpha.
```

To construct the dilator of a key frame, we use Eq. (13.13), which is written in CLUCalc script as follows:

```
Dilator=1+(1−d1)/(1+d1)*einf^e0
```

where d1 is the scaling of the keyframe. To interpolate between two dilators, we use the following CLUCalc script formula:

```
finalD=Dilator+(Dilator2-Dilator)*alpha
```

where Dilator is the source dilator, Dilator2 is the destination dilator, and alpha the factor of interpolation. Final transformation is computed by the geometric product of motor and dilator as follows:

```
final=interpolated*finalD.
```

13.6.3 GPU-Based Skinning Algorithm Description

In our method, we handle geometric skinning using CGA motors in the vertex shader. To apply transformation on the vertices, we sandwich the position of the vertex between the motor and its inverse motor. We generate a code that transforms a point using motor that comprises rotation, translation, and dilation using CLUCalc scripting language as follows:

```
motor=translation*rotation*dilation,
newPoint=motor*VecN3(x,y,z)*~motor.
```

Gaalop precompiler generates motor as a 12-element vector which we convert it to a matrix representation of type mat3x4 (build-in type of GLSL) in order to be able to use it in the vertex shader. In the vertex shader, we declare a uniform array which comprises the bones' transformations of type mat3x4.

Each vertex of the skinned character may be influenced by four bones, each one with a different weight. We transform the vertex with each bone separately using the code generated from the Gaalop precompiler:

```
vec4 pos1=transformP(BonesVersors[BoneIDs[0]],pos.x,pos.y,pos.z),
vec4 pos2=transformP(BonesVersors[BoneIDs[1]] pos.x,pos.y,pos.z),
vec4 pos3=transformP(BonesVersors[BoneIDs[2]],pos.x,pos.y,pos.z),
vec4 pos4=transformP(BonesVersors[BoneIDs[3]],pos.x,pos.y,pos.z),
```

and we compute their weighted average based on the weight of each bone:

```
vec4 finalpos=pos1*Weights[0]+pos2*Weights[1]+pos3*Weights[2] +
pos4*Weights[3].
```

13.7 Results

In this section, we present our visual results of AR applications in indoor as well as outdoor environments.

Figure 13.6 shows a life-sized AR character on a mobile device at Asinou Church, and Fig. 13.7 shows life-sized AR crowd simulation on a mobile device. For authoring the geometric and photometric AR scene in 1 minute, firstly, we create a 3D map of the scene using Toolbox and then we send it via e-mail and open it using our application. Next, we manage the size, position, and rotation of the character to achieve a life-sized augmentation and then we manage the shading of the object by adjusting the exposure in order to be consistent with the scene. Finally, we save the transformations in order to have the same transformation when relaunching the app.

Next, we compare our animation blending and GPU-based skinning approach with quaternions and dual quaternions. We obtained the following results using the

Fig. 13.6 Life-sized AR character on mobile device at Asinou Church

Fig. 13.7 Life-sized AR crowd simulation on a mobile device

platform described in Table 13.3. The characters used to obtain the results are of . dae format, loaded with Assimp Library, and consist of 42–54 joints and 3,851–1,4985 triangles.

Table 13.3 Platform characteristics used to run our experiments (© 2016 Springer)

Platform	OS X 10.11.3
Processor	2.5 GHz Intel Core i7
Graphics Card	NVIDIA GeForce GT 750 M 2048 MB
Compiler	LLVM 7.0

Table 13.4 Comparison of animation blending of time in msecs of quaternions, dual quaternions, and CGA-GPU-inclusive algorithm (© 2016 Springer)

	Character 1		Character 2		Character 3	
Method	Time (ms)	Fps	Time (ms)	Fps	Time (ms)	Fps
Quaternions (rotations only)	0.0004	59.6	0.0017	59.6	0.0012	59.6
Dual quaternions (rotations and translation)	0.0003	59.6	0.0016	59.6	0.0009	59.6
CGA-GPU-inclusive algorithm (rotations, translations)	0.0003	59.6	0.0017	59.6	0.0012	59.6
CGA-GPU-inclusive algorithm [rotations, translations, and dilations (scaling)]	0.0005	59.6	0.0022	59.6	0.0015	59.6

Table 13.4 shows the time in msecs for each animation blending method and the average frame rate (fps) for animation blending and skinning for three different characters. The characters used have the following characteristics:

- Character 1: polygon count: 2,548; number of bones: 52
- Character 2: polygon count: 135,976; number of bones: 54
- Character 3: polygon count: 14,985; number of bones: 43

The first method is quaternions that support rotation combined with translation matrices, the second one is dual quaternions which combine translation and rotation, and the third one is our method, "CGA-GPU inclusive algorithm," which combines rotation, translation, and scaling. In Table 13.4, we also present a CGA-GPU-inclusive algorithm with only rotation and translation in order to be comparable with quaternions and dual quaternions. In the case of Character 1, we have nonidentity dilation; for that reason, this character is slower than in the method without dilation. Our results show that our algorithm is equally efficient with quaternions and dual quaternions in terms of performance and frame rate but is superior in terms of single mathematical algebraic representation in CPU and GPU. We did not notice any significant errors in our algorithm during the necessary conversions between different mathematical representations. Table 13.5 summarizes the contribution of our CGA-GPU-inclusive algorithm compared to Euler-angles, transformation matrices, quaternions, and dual quaternions.

We also focused on comparing the efficiency of three different GA code generators—(a) the Gaigen library, (b) libvsr, and (c) Gaalop—using our animation blending methodology so that a future user of GA libraries can choose the most appropriate one that will give the most optimal and efficient results. Table 13.6

Table 13.5 General comparison of Euler angles/transformation matrices, quaternions and dual quaternions with our method, CGA-GPU-inclusive algorithm (© 2016 Springer)

Methodology	Rotation	Translation	Dilation	Performance	Single representation
Euler-angle/ transformation matrices	√	Matrices only	Matrices only	• Gimbal lock • Transformation matrices may produce numerical errors, not efficient	Transformation matrices only
Quaternions	√	–	–	• Interpolated only at the origin • Need conversion to transformation matrix to transform point	No translation No dilation
Dual quaternions	√	√	–	• Interpolated only at the origin, need conversion to transformation matrix to transform point	No dilation
Our method: CGA-GPU-inclusive algorithm	√	√	√	• Efficient performance • Interpolate around any axis • Can transform any entity	√

Table 13.6 Average time (msecs) for each animation blending method for the three characters (© 2016 Springer)

Method	Character 1	Character 2	Character 2
GA Gaigen	0.0013	0.0025	0.0015
GA Gaalop	0.0015	0.0027	0.0020
CGA Gaalop	0.0003	0.0017	0.0012
GA Versor	0.0075	0.0019	0.0016
CGA Versor	0.0082	0.0020	0.0015

shows the average time in msecs for the animation blending implemented with GA and CGA using the three different code generators for the three characters.

13.8 Conclusions and Future Work

In this work, we compared different software methodologies for creating VR environments, and we proposed a method for robust authoring of geometric and photometric AR scenes in less than a minute with life-sized VR characters and life-sized crowd simulations. We handled rotations of the AR objects using GA rotors, and we achieved higher-quality results by avoiding the problem of gimbal lock. Moreover, we implemented a global illumination algorithm for unshadowed as well as shadowed diffuse static objects using PRT methods, which we have integrated in the glGA framework. Furthermore, we have integrated a character animation platform, SmartBody, with the glGA framework. Such integration allows complex interactions with virtual characters through AR.

We also presented an efficient algorithm for authoring the AR scene using 3D Euclidean GA animation-blending method and a GPU-based skinning algorithm using CGA motors that combine to a unique mathematical representation translation, rotation, and scaling. Our results show that our method achieves high performance and smooth results as well as quaternions and dual quaternions. However, our method allows handling blending and skinning without the need to use any other algebraic framework in contrast to quaternions and dual quaternions, which can handle only rotations and rotations and translations, respectively. Using our animation-blending method, we compared the efficiency of three different GA code generators—(a) the Gaigen library, (b) libvsr, and (c) Gaalop—so that a future user of GA libraries can choose the most appropriate one that will give the most optimal and faster results.

Our main focus is to expand and improve the robust, easy, and fast AR authoring of 3D scenes involving both static as well as animated virtual characters, lit with natural scene HDR image-based light. Moreover, we aim to give the user the ability to interact with the virtual characters in order to better connect the real world with the virtual world. We also aim to achieve interpolation using logarithms of motors for rotation, translation, and scaling in the vertex shader. Lastly, we intend to extend our CGA framework by applying GA for global illumination and, specifically, for rotating spherical harmonics for PRT for real-time rendering.

When visiting an archaeological site, especially when it is not well preserved, there is a lot of information that is hard to assimilate. Facts about the daily habits of the residents, how the buildings looked when they were populated, and even details considering missing artifacts need a visual representation to aid the visitors' perception. Reflecting on this need for visualization, AR and VR applications act as a medium for simulating these details and presenting the intangible part of the cultural heritage site. The mixed reality simulations will give an opportunity for education by providing the users a series of different games (game-based learning) and scenarios for learning about the everyday life of the residents. The virtual characters will be able to perform a wide range of different human-like activities in order to simulate different scenarios that present ceremonies and events that take place at the specific cultural heritage site. One important aspect of virtual characters is illumination consistency. Virtual characters will be lit with the natural scene light in order to look more realistic and immersive, which provide cues that the virtual characters are a real part of the environment. Other important aspects are efficiency, performance, and having smooth deformations of the characters. With the CGA animation blending and skinning algorithms, we can achieve a high frame rate and smooth deformations without artifacts.

Acknowledgments The research leading to these results has received funding from the European Union People Programme (FP7-PEOPLE-2013-ITN) under grant agreement nr. 608013.

References

1. G. Papagiannakis, P. Papanikolaou, E. Greasidou, P. Trahanias, glGA: an opengl geometric application framework for a modern, shader-based computer graphics curriculum. Eurographics **2014**, 1–8 (2014)
2. M. Papaefthymiou, A. Feng, A. Shapiro, G. Papagiannakis, in *A Fast and Robust Pipeline for Populating Mobile AR Scenes with Gamified Virtual Characters*. SIGGRAPH Asia 2015 Mobile Graphics and Interactive Applications, SA '15 (ACM, New York, NY, 2015), pp. 22:1–22:8
3. A. Shapiro, *Building a Character Animation System* (Springer, Berlin, 2011)
4. B.H. Thomas, A survey of visual, mixed, and augmented reality gaming. Comput. Entertain. **10**(1), 3:1–3:33 (2012)
5. A. Egges, G. Papagiannakis, N. Magnenat-Thalmann, Presence and interaction in mixed reality environments. Vis. Comput. **23**(5), 317–333 (2007)
6. M. Ponder, B. Herbelin, T. Molet, S. Scherteneib, B. Ulicny, G. Papagiannakis, N. Magnenat-Thalmann, D. Thalmann, in *Interactive Scenario Immersion: Health Emergency Decision Training in Just Project*. Proceedings from the 1st International Workshop on Virtual Reality Rehabilitation (VRMHR2002), pp. 87–101, 2002
7. A. Lewis Brooks, S. Brahnam, L.C. Jain, Technologies of inclusive well-being at the intersection of serious games, alternative realities, and play therapy, in *Technologies of Inclusive Well-Being—Serious Games, Alternative Realities, and Play Therapy* (2014), pp. 1–10
8. G. Papagiannakis, S. Schertenleib, M. Ponder, M. Arevalo, N. Magnenat-Thalmann, D. Thalmann, *Real-Time Virtual Humans in AR Sites*. 1st European Conference on Visual Media Production CVMP, pp. 273–276, 2004
9. L. Gun, M. Billinghurst, in *A Component Based Framework for Mobile Outdoor AR Applications*. SIGGRAPH Asia 2013 Symposium on Mobile Graphics and Interactive Applications (SA '13), pp. 173–179, 2013
10. Z.P. Huang, P. Hui, C. Peylo, D. Chatzopoulos, Mobile Augmented Reality Survey: A Bottom-Up Approach. Technical report, HKUST Technical report, 2013
11. G. Papagiannakis, E. Greasidou, P. Trahanias, M. Tsioumas, Mixed-reality geometric algebra animation methods for gamified intangible heritage. Int. J. Herit. Digit. **3**, 683–699 (2015)
12. T. Langlotz, S. Mooslechner, S. Zollmann, C. Degendorfer, G. Reitmayr, D. Schmalstieg, Sketching up the world: in situ authoring for mobile augmented reality. Pers. Ubiquit. Comput. **16**(6), 623–630 (2012)
13. A. Feng, Y. Huang, Y. Xu, A. Shapiro, Fast, automatic character animation pipelines. Comput. Anim. Virt. Worlds **25**(1), 3–16 (2014)
14. L. Dorst, D. Fontijne, S. Mann, *Geometric Algebra for Computer Science* (Morgan Kaufmann, San Francisco, CA, 2007)
15. G. Papagiannakis, in *Geometric Algebra Rotors for Skinned Character Animation Blending*. SIGGRAPH Asia 2013 Technical Briefs, SA '13 (ACM, New York, NY, 2013), pp. 11:1–11:6
16. R. Wareham, J. Cameron, J. Lasenby, in *Applications of Conformal Geometric Algebra in Computer Vision and Graphics*, ed. by H. Li, P.J. Olver, G. Sommer. IWMM/GIAE, Lecture Notes in Computer Science, vol 3519 (Springer, Berlin, 2004), pp. 329–349
17. R. Wareham, J. Lasenby, in *Mesh Vertex Pose and Position Interpolation Using Geometric Algebra*. Articulated Motion and Deformable Objects, 5th International Conference, AMDO 2008, Port d'Andratx, Mallorca, Spain, 9–11 July 2008, Proceedings, pp. 122–131, 2008
18. L. Kavan, S. Collins, J. Žára, C. O'Sullivan, Geometric skinning with approximate dual quaternion blending. ACM Trans. Graph. **27**(4), 105:1–105:23 (2008)

19. N. Magnenat-Thalmann, F. Cordier, H. Seo, G. Papagianakis, in *Modeling of Bodies and Clothes for Virtual Environments*. Cyberworlds, 2004 International Conference on, pp. 201–208, November 2004
20. N. Magnenat-Thalmann, R. Laperrière, D. Thalmann, in *Joint-Dependent Local Deformations for Hand Animation and Object Grasping*. Proceedings on Graphics Interface '88 (Canadian Information Processing Society, Toronto, ON, 1988), pp. 26–33
21. S. Kateros, S. Georgiou, M. Papaefthymiou, G. Papagiannakis, M. Tsioumas, A comparison of gamified, immersive VR curation methods for enhanced presence and human–computer interaction in digital humanities. Int. J. Herit. Digit. Era **4**(2), 2015 (2016) (also presented in "The 1st International Workshop on ICT for the Preservation and Transmission of Intangible Cultural Heritage", EUROMED2014)
22. S. Kuntz, *Sébastien Cb Kuntz, Creating VR Games—The Fundamentals* (2014), pp. 1–10. http://cb.nowan.net/blog/2014/01/27/creating-vr-games-the-fundamentals/#more-1642
23. I. Oikonomidis, N. Kyriazis, A. Argyros, in *Tracking the Articulated Motion of Two Strongly Interacting Hands* (2012)
24. M. Pateraki, H. Baltzakis, P. Trahanias, Visual estimation of pointed targets for robot guidance via fusion of face pose and hand orientation. Comput. Vis. Image Underst. **120**, 1–13 (2014)
25. S. Kuntz, *Gamasutra: Sebastien Kuntz's Blog—Lessons from the VR Field* (2014), pp. 1–9. http://www.gamasutra.com/blogs/SebastienKuntz/20140112/208452/Lessons_from_the_VR_field.php
26. Oculus VR Best Practices Guide, *Oculus VR Best Practices Guide* (2014), pp. 1–53. http://static.oculusvr.com/sdk-downloads/documents/OculusBestPractices.pdf
27. Giving Oculus Rift demos: Best practice|RenderingPipeline, *Giving Oculus Rift Demos: Best Practice*|RenderingPipeline (2014), pp. 1–6. http://renderingpipeline.com/2014/09/giving-oculus-rift-demos-best-practice/
28. D. Hestens, G. Sobczyk, *Clifford Algebra to Geometric Calculus: A Unified Language for Mathematics and Physics (Fundamental Theories of Physics)* (Springer, Dordrecht, 1984)
29. K. Kanatani, *Understanding Geometric Algebra: Hamilton, Grassmann, and Clifford for Computer Vision and Graphics* (A K Peters/CRC Press, Boca Raton, FL, 2015)
30. P. Zikas, M. Papaefthymiou, V. Mpaxlitzanakis, G. Papagiannakis, in *Life-Sized Group and Crowd Simulation in Mobile AR*. Proceedings of the 29th International Conference on Computer Animation and Social Agents (CASA '16) (ACM, New York, NY, 2016), pp. 79–82
31. J. van den Berg, S. Patil, J. Sewall, D. Manocha, M. Lin, in *Interactive Navigation of Multiple Agents in Crowded Environments*. Proceedings of the 2008 Symposium on Interactive 3D Graphics and Games, I3D '08 (ACM, New York, NY, 2008), pp. 139–147
32. J. van den Berg, M.C. Lin, D. Manocha, in *Reciprocal Velocity Obstacles for Real-Time Multi-Agent Navigation*. IEEE International Conference on Robotics and Automation (IEEE, 2008), pp. 1928–1935
33. M. Papaefthymiou, D. Hildenbrand, G. Papagiannakis, A conformal geometric algebra code generator comparison for virtual character simulation in mixed reality. Adv. Appl. Clifford Algebr., 1–16 (2016) (also presented in GACSE workshop, CGI 2016, Heraklion, Greece, June 2016)
34. M. Papaefthymiou, D. Hildenbrand, G. Papagiannakis, An inclusive conformal geometric algebra GPU animation interpolation and deformation algorithm. Vis. Comput., 1–9 (2016) (also presented in CGI 2016, Heraklion, Greece)

Chapter 14
Experiencing the Multisensory Past

Alan Chalmers

Abstract The world is multisensory. All five major senses, visuals, audio, smell, feel and taste, are important to how we, humans, perceive the world around us. Furthermore, the interaction of the senses—cross-modal effects—can significantly affect our understanding of an environment, with one sensory stimuli even being ignored in the presence of other more dominant stimuli. This is as true now as it was in the past. So if we are to attempt, through computer simulation, to understand how a past environment may have been experienced, it is essential that these virtual reconstructions are multisensory, otherwise we run the very real risk of misrepresenting the past.

Keywords Virtual experiences • Multisensory • Kalabsha • Medieval pottery • Real Virtuality

14.1 Introduction

Modern computer technology enables computer reconstructions of ancient sites to be done in a straightforward manner. However, the vast majority of these are based on artistic interpretation rather than physical accuracy [1, 2]. Although techniques for capturing the geometry of a site, such as laser scanning and structure from motion (SfM), can provide millimetre accuracy, this only applies to existing remains. Any parts of the site that are missing still have to be "filled in".

How a site may have been experienced in the past is, of course, dependent on far more than just its geometry. We humans perceive the world with all our senses (visuals, audio, smell, feel and taste). If we are to try and gain an understanding of the past, then we need to experience the reconstruction of the ancient site using all our senses. Furthermore, the senses need to be authentically simulated. For example, as Fig. 14.1 shows, a Roman site which is illuminated with simulated modern lighting (left) appears very different to the one in which the lighting is authentically simulated with olive oil lamps that the Romans would have used [3, 4].

A. Chalmers (✉)
WMG, University of Warwick, Coventry, UK
e-mail: alan.chalmers@warwick.ac.uk

M. Ioannides et al. (eds.), *Mixed Reality and Gamification for Cultural Heritage*,
DOI 10.1007/978-3-319-49607-8_14

Fig. 14.1 Roman site lit by simulated (*left*) modern lighting (*right*) olive oil lamps [3] (© Devlin and Chalmers 2001, reprinted with permission)

Furthermore, humans perceive the world in real time, and thus any simulated multisensory experience of the past needs to be interactive, enabling the user to respond naturally to the experience. To provide this interactivity, the multiple sensory stimuli need to be computed and delivered in real time. Despite many advances in hardware and software over the decades, the physically accurate simulation of, for example, just the light within an environment can still take many seconds to compute.

Fortunately a human is not a "physics engine". Our brains are simply unable to process all the sensory input we receive at any given moment. Rather, based on who we are, including any previous experience, we initially attend to those stimuli in a scene that is most salient or important for the task being undertaken [5, 6]. Human perception also possesses the ability to "fill in" details in a scene which may not actually be physically present. Key factors that may influence the perceptual importance of different aspects of a real scene are a person's experience (including skill fade [7]), knowledge and ability and the activity that he/she is undertaking. Furthermore, a high level of familiarity with the environment (or habituation) may make the user perceive less [8]. Deliberate preconditioning on the other hand, or the intensity and nature of the task being performed, can force the user to attend to stimuli that they would otherwise ignore [9, 10], while cross-modal effects, that is, the interaction of the senses, can be so significant that some sensory information may even be ignored [9].

This chapter will present the latest advances for achieving high-fidelity multi-sensory (visuals, audio, smell, feel and taste) reconstructions of past heritage environments in real time. Termed Real Virtuality [11], such approaches exploit knowledge of human perception to capitalize on the interplay between stimulus saliency, the sensory capabilities of the user and the scenario task goals in order to maximise stimulus fidelity where it is most needed and downplay those aspects which are likely to go unnoticed. This ensures those multisensory parts of a scene which are being attended to, are computed at the high–highest fidelity, while unattended parts of a scene can be computed and delivered in a much lower quality, and *the user will not be aware of this quality difference*.

14.2 Multisensory Perception

Sensory perception research to date has primarily focussed on the functional properties of one and sometimes two senses. However, in the real world, the human brain processes the separate sensory inputs and concurrently tries to couple them to a common event [12]. How multisensory integration may occur and when this might be the strongest was suggested by Stein and Meredith [13] as:

- *Spatial rule*: when the contributing unisensory stimuli originated from approximately the same location
- *Temporal rule*: when the contributing unisensory stimuli originate at approximately the same time
- *Inverse effect*: when the contributing unisensory stimuli are relatively weak when considered one at a time

In the real world, there is an intimate linkage between the dominant and minor senses [12]. The key to an authentic model of perception is the combination and integration of multiple sources of sensory information.

Everyone responds to multisensory stimuli differently. Not only is the quality of our sensory organs different, but we can also be affected by motivation and personality [14], linguistic experience [15], gender [16], attention [17] and the ageing process [18].

When confronted with multiple stimuli, one modality can dominate. Furthermore, different integration strategies can occur at different points of time and due to prior knowledge [19]. Although much research has been done in cognitive neuroscience [20], none of this has considered multisensory integration in virtual environments.

Fortunately, to deliver a perceptually equivalent "real-world experience" to the user via a computer simulation, it is only necessary to deliver the "appropriate" level of sensory stimulation to the user for each sense. It is not necessary to integrate these senses in any way during delivery, as the brain will do this naturally.

If it would be possible to accurately compute all the physics associated with presenting the stimuli, then, as in the real world, the user would simply process those parts of the stimuli which are necessary for the perception of the environment at that time. Even if we fully understood all the physics, such physical accuracy in real time is beyond computing capabilities for many years to come. A key feature to increase our ability to achieve Real Virtuality on current computers is to understand the limitations of the human brain, which is simply not able to process all the sensory input we receive every moment of the day. Rather we selectively process these sensory inputs to build up a useful, but not necessarily accurate, perception of our environment.

14.2.1 The Perception Equation

The perception of an environment, *P*, may be described in its simplest form as a function over time of task (*t*) and preconditioning (*ρ*) [CF08]:

$$P(t,\rho)=\omega_v V+\omega_a A+\omega_s S+\omega_t T+\omega_f F+\omega_\delta \Delta$$

where V = Visuals, A = Audio, S = Smell, T = Taste and F = Feel. Δ is a "distraction factor" indicating how focussed the user is on the environment. The ω_i are threshold weighting values below which difference between the real environment and its virtual representation would be noticeable. For simplicity $\Sigma\omega_i \leq 1$.

In a virtual simulation, therefore, as long as the precision of each of the sensory stimuli is computed to be above the ω_i threshold, the resultant virtual experience will be "perceptually equivalent" to the real experience [21].

14.3 Real Virtuality

Interactivity is a key feature of virtual reality (VR) systems. While it is possible to simulate fully the physics of how sensory stimuli propagate in an environment, even with modern computer hardware, a single time step can take several seconds, well beyond the 25 frames per second required for interactivity. VR systems thus typically reduce the level of realism in order to achieve the required frame rate [21]. While many applications do not in fact require a high level of physical accuracy [22], there are others for which such realism is essential if the simulated real experience is not to be compromised in the virtual world.

14.3.1 Visuals

A real-world scene can contain a wide range of light from areas in bright sunshine to those in a dark shadow. The ration between the maximum and minimum light intensity in a scene is known as the dynamic range [23]. In fact, a candle in a dark room has a much higher dynamic range than a scene which is evenly lit with sun light. At any level of adaption, with no noticeable adaption, the human eye is able to see a contrast ratio of approximately 20 stops, that is, 10^{20} (1,048,5761): 1.

Fig. 14.2 HDR image of the temple of Kalabsha: (*left*) tone-mapped image (*right*) different 8 stop "exposure slices" of the original HDR image

Traditional imaging technology, on the other hand, is only able to capture and display eight stops. Emerging high-dynamic-range (HDR) methods however are able to capture and deliver digitally up to 20 stops, the full range that the human eye can see [23].

Where the dynamic range of the display matches that of the captured lighting, the images can be displayed in a straightforward manner [24]. For example, the current HDR display from SIM2 is capable of displaying $\leq$14 stops (Sim2 [25]). If the captured scene contains 14 stops, then this can be displayed directly onto this HDR display. If the scene contains more than 14 stops, or the display is a LDR display capable of only displaying 8 stops, then an 8-stop "exposure slice" can be displayed, Fig. 14.2 (right), or the images can be mapped to the lower dynamic range, known as tone mapping, to ensure an enhanced viewing experience that preserves the perceptual appearance of the real scene on the available display, Fig. 14.2 (left) [23].

14.3.2 Audio

In the real world, sound is directional and is heard outside the head (unlike when listening to, for example, an iPod when the sound appears to be inside the head). 3D audio may be captured using a four-microphone-capsule tetrahedral array which is set up with the four capsules very close together and protected with a full windshield. The audio is then converted into a binaural output for rendering over headphones or via a B-format to Ambisonic conversion to any loudspeaker system of known configuration. To simulate 3D sound virtually on the other hand, it is necessary to have a geometric model of the environment, the sound source and location from where it is emanating and the listener's position. An impulse response function for the virtual environment encodes the delays and attenuations from the sound source. This impulse response function can then be convolved with the source signal to determine the virtual 3D audio. A number of methods have been developed to accurately model the propagation of sound within a 3D environment, see [26] for an overview.

Having modelled the sound propagation, it is also necessary to accurately simulate the acoustic effects of the listener's head and shoulders (their head-related transfer function), as these directly influence how we each individually hear sound [27]. Furthermore, head tracking needs to be undertaken to ensure that when the listener moves his/her head, the sounds moves as well [28].

14.3.3 Feel

A human's skin is our largest sensory organ. When touched, sensors in the dermis layer of the skin convey the details of the touch to the brain. A human is able to determine approximately 20 different types of "feel" sensation, including heat, cold, pain, pressure, etc. The sensors are not distributed uniformly within the skin; some parts of the body contain more than others, such as our hands, lips, face, neck, fingertips and feet. Furthermore, our tongue contains more nerve endings for pain than for heat, so it is relatively easy to burn our mouths if we eat something too hot, and it really hurts if we bite our tongue.

Known as haptics, simulating feel in virtual environments has been investigated for many years. A key challenge is that even the most modern haptic device has a limited number of sensors, typically of the order of tens, while, for example, the human hand consists of millions of specialised tactile sensors all working in parallel [29].

Simulating feel in a passive virtual experience is significantly easier than in an experience which involves user interaction. In a passive experience where the user, for example, undergoes the experience while standing is a single position; the only sensations that may need to be simulated could be temperature, humidity and perhaps the feel of any wind. This can be achieved by means of a personal air conditioner system. Thus, in a recreation of prehistoric cave art, feel simulation would include the constant 12 °C of a cave interior [30], while for a recreation of a Byzantine church on Cyprus, the impact on the sudden change in temperature from the hot exterior to the cool interior of the church should be considered [31]. If the user is sitting, positioning him/her in an actual reconstruction of the ancient seat should in this mixed reality situation satisfy the skin as to the authenticity of the seating experience [11]. Real motion, such as the movement of a ship, can be captured on a real ship through accelerometers and recreated via a simple "motion platform".

14.3.4 Smell

Smell is an important sense for humans that can affect mood, memory, emotion and even the choice of a mate. Despite the importance of smell in an experience, it is seldom used when recreating the past. An exception is the Jorvik Viking Museum in York which uses smell to enhance the visitor experience. Built on the site of the Viking-age city of Jorvik, visitors ride through a reconstruction of the village complete with all its tenth-century smells. In addition, smell boxes have been introduced next to the display of objects, including the smell of iron, leather, beef and wood [32]. Research has shown that inclusion of smell at the Jorvik Viking Museum helps visitors to remember what they have seen [33].

Humans detect smell through molecules. This is a biochemical reaction and thus cannot be simulated digitally. Furthermore, any aroma which we detect may comprise of only a few or perhaps many thousand different smell molecules. For example, the smell of coffee comprises hundreds of different smell molecules, but, to the non-expert, this is simply detected as "coffee". A smell can be captured by sucking the air across an automated thermal desorption tube. The odour molecules stick to the fine granular material in the tube. The chemical composition of the smell can be determined in a laboratory by passing the trapped molecules through a gas–liquid chromatography instrument to separate the mixture of odorants into consistent molecules and then passing this through a mass spectrometer. The result is a histogram of the molecules present. A trained molecular scientist often assists in identifying the odour molecules, as current mass spectrometers are not precise and can miss some molecules.

Smell in a virtual environment can be achieved by releasing a small amount of the required smell directly to the user's nose. Although it may not be possible to create the full complexity of any smell, this is in fact not necessary, as the human nose (for non-experts) is quite poor at determining the exact smell composition or concentrations. Close approximations of the required smell can often be created from key odorant markers, and the human nose will be unaware of the difference between this and the original smell, particularly in the presence of other sensory stimuli.

14.3.5 Taste

The molecules of food are chemicals detected by taste receptors in the mouth and the olfactory receptors in the nose. There are five primary tastes: salty, sour, bitter, sweet and umami (from the Japanese for "tasty"—which corresponds roughly to the taste of glutamate) [34]. How we perceive food is also influenced by its texture, its temperature, what it looks like and environmental factors, such as where we are eating and with whom, etc. [35–37]. Despite the fact that research on the perception of taste started as long ago as the late 1500s (by the French physician and philosopher Jean Fernel), very little work has been done on virtual flavour. In 2003, Iwata et al. [38] presented their food simulator: a haptic interface to mimic the taste, sound and feeling of chewing real food. A device in the mouth simulated the force of the type of food and a bone vibration microphone provided the sound of biting, while the chemical simulation of taste was achieved via a micro injector. More recently, work from Ranasinghe et al. [39] has shown that it is possible to simulate the sensation of some of the primary tastes by direct electrical and thermal stimulation of the tongue. Narumi et al. [40] demonstrated how cross-sensory perception could influence a user's enjoyment of food by superimposing virtual colour onto a real drink, while the MetaCookie + project [41] changed the perceived taste of a cookie using visual and auditory stimuli. This previous work has shown the potential for using multisensory stimuli to manipulate flavour perception in virtual environments, but much more needs to be done.

Taste has recently been included in the Jorvik Viking Museum in York [32]. Seafood was a key part of the diet of Viking Jorvik, with archaeological evidence of many types of fish being eaten, including carp, pike, salmon, eel, herring bones and oysters. To deliver taste at the Jorvik Viking Museum, visitors will be given samples of unsalted, dried cod and mead, a beverage made of fermented honey [32].

14.4 Case Studies

14.4.1 Kalabsha

Build at Kalabsha (Talmis) in 30 BC during the reign of the Roman Emperor Octavius Augustus, the temple of Kalabsha was dedicated to the Nubian fertility and solar deity god Mandulis. With the building of the Aswan High Dam in 1959, it was necessary to dismantle and move the temple to a new site before it disappeared under the rising waters of the river Nile. With the support of the West German government and under careful archaeological supervision, the German civil engineering firm Hochtief fully recorded the site and began dismantling it in November 1961 [42]. Over 13,000 blocks and 20,000 t of stone were taken and stored ready to be reassembled at the new site. By November 1963, the temple had been rebuilt at a site 750 m south of the Aswan High Dam, Table 14.1.

The position and orientation of Egyptian temples were accurately determined using astronomy. In particular, the axis of the building to the inner sanctuary was aligned so sunlight would only enter the sanctuary at sunset on the summer solstice. This helped in determining the length of the year [43]. Real Virtuality allows the

Table 14.1 A new location and orientation for the temple of Kalabsha

	Original location	New location
Latitude (DMS)	23 33′ 0 N	24 4′ 60 N
Longitude (DMS)	32 52′ 0E	32 52′ 60E
Altitude	172 m	141 m

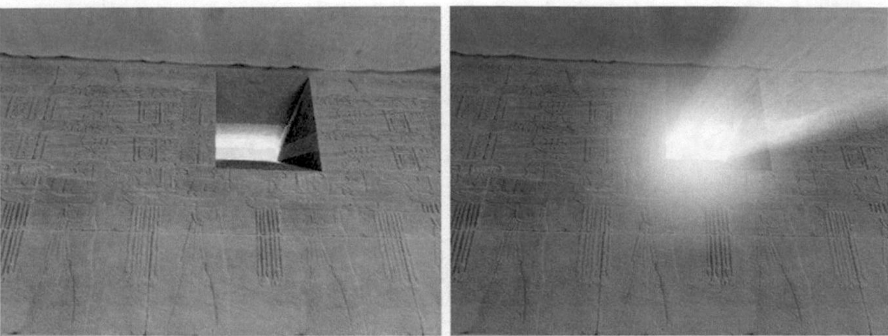

Fig. 14.3 Computer reconstruction of Kalabsha (*left*) without and (*right*) with dust [45] © Eurographics Association 2005

temple of Kalabsha to be experienced as it might have been in 30 BC, with the original orientation and location recreated virtually.

The multisensory perception of Kalabsha in the past would have been dominated by the heat of the Egyptian sun contrasting with the cool interior of the inner sanctuary and included the quiet prevalent in the interior and the smell produced by the sesame oil lamps. A key feature of any authentic reconstruction of this site, and others in Egypt, is the need to include the ever-present Egyptian dust [44], Fig. 14.3.

14.5 Medieval Pottery

14.5.1 Medieval Pottery

Medieval pottery is brightly coloured. The question that intrigues archaeologists [BCM97] is:

> *Were they brightly colored because they had to be to be seen, or could they be seen fine and the people just wanted some color in their otherwise monotonous lives?*

Furthermore, only the top half of some jugs are glazed and decorated (glazing was expensive at the time [46]). Is this perhaps indicative of how they were illuminated in use, perhaps by daylight through windows or from torches hung on walls? Glazing on the top, when lit from above, should result in the pots appearing more colourful. As discussed in Sect. 14.3.1, the appearance of colour can change depending on the types of light source present. An accurate reconstruction of not only the lighting but also the other sensory stimuli within the medieval environment is thus a vital step in comprehending attitudes to colour, shape and decoration, including any symbolic meaning in the use of colour on pottery.

Figure 14.4 shows the medieval environment lit by modern lighting and the animal tallow candles of the period. Investigation of the simulated environment clearly showed that the pots had to be brightly coloured in order to be seen in the

Fig. 14.4 Medieval environment lit by (*left*) modern light (*right*) animal tallow candles

"murky" medieval interiors. Glazing the top of the pots was shown to be important when lit from above. The simulations also "shed some light" on perhaps why there was no blue pottery in England before the sixteenth century. There was blue pottery in Syria at the time and established trade links between Syria and England. As there is very little blue in animal tallow candlelight, the blue pottery would have been difficult to see within medieval English buildings. The sixteenth century saw the introduction of chimneys and bigger windows, allowing a lot more natural light into the buildings [46].

14.6 Discussion

The authentic multisensory simulation of past environments using Real Virtuality is potentially the most far-reaching and flexible way of exploring human perceptions in the past. Human perception has not changed significantly in the last 40,000 years. We experience environment with all our five senses, exactly as our ancestors would have done. Although our perceptions are undoubtedly influenced by "twenty-first century baggage", using Real Virtuality, we can investigate past environments in a safe, repeatable and controlled manner. Although we will never know exactly how a past environment may have appeared, to quote Sherlock Holmes, "... when you have eliminated the impossible, whatever remains, however improbable, must be the truth".

References

1. P. Martinez, *Digital Realities and Archaeology: A Difficult Relationship or a Fruitful Marriage?* Proceedings of the 1st International Symposium on Virtual Reality, Archaeology, and Cultural Heritage VAST 2001, 9–16, 2001
2. P. Miller, J. Richards, The good, the bad and the downright misleading: archaeological adoption of computer visualization. Comput. Appl. Quant. Methods Archaeol. 19–22 (1994)
3. K. Devlin, A.G. Chalmers, in *Realistic Visualisation of the Pompeii Frescoes*. AFRIGRAPH 2001 (ACM SIGGRAPH Publications, 2001), pp. 43–48
4. A. Gonçalves, L. Magalhães, J. Moura, A. Chalmers, *Accurate Modelling of Roman Lamps in Conimbriga Using High Dynamic Range*. VAST'08: Proceedings of the Symposium on Virtual Reality, Archaeology and Cultural Heritage, 2008
5. L. Itti, C. Koch, A saliency-based search mechanism for overt and covert shifts of visual attention. Vision Res. 40(10–12), 1489–1506 (2000)
6. A.L. Yarbus, Eye movements during perception of complex objects, Chapter VII, in *Eye Movements and Vision*, ed. by L.A. Riggs (Plenum Press, New York, NY, 1967), pp. 171–196
7. B. Leonard, L. Martin, in *Literature Review on Skill Fade*. Human Factors Integration Defence Technology Centre/2/WP10.3/2, Version No. 1/25, May 2007
8. S. Marsland, U. Nehmzow, J. Shapiro, *Novelty Detection on a Mobile Robot Using Habituation*. From Animals to Animats: The 6th International Conference on Simulation of Adaptive Behaviour, 2000
9. A. Mack, I. Rock, in *Inattentional Blindness*. Proceedings of Symposium on Interactive 3D Graphics, Massachusetts Institute of Technology Press, 1998
10. D. Nunez, E.H. Blake, in *Conceptual Priming as a Determinant of Presence in Virtual Environments*. Afrigraph 2003, ACM SIGGRAPH, pp. 101–108, 2003
11. A.G. Chalmers, D. Howard, C. Moir, in *Real Virtuality: A Step Change from Virtual Reality*. SCCG'09 (ACM Press, 2009)
12. G. Calvert, C. Spence, B. Stein, *The Multisensory Handbook* (MIT Press, Cambridge, MA, 2004)
13. B. Stein, M. Meredith, *The Merging of the Senses* (MIT Press, Cambridge, MA, 1993)
14. T.G. Giolas, E.C. Butterfield, S.J. Weaver, Some motivational correlates of lipreading. J. Speech Hear. Res. **17**, 18–24 (1974)
15. K. Sekiyama, Y.J. Tohkura, McGurk effect in non-English listeners: few visual effects for Japanese subjects hearing Japanese syllables of high auditory intelligibility. Acoust. Soc. Am. **90**, 1797–1805 (1991)
16. J. Irwin, D. Whalen, A sex difference in visual influence on heard speech. Percept. Psychophys. **68**(4), 582–592 (2006)
17. A. Alsius, J. Navarra, R. Campbell, S. Soto-Faraco, Audiovisual integration of speech falters under high attention demands. Curr. Biol. **15**(839–843) (2005)
18. J. Townsend, M. Adamo, F. Haist, Changing channels: an fMRI study of aging and cross-modal attention shifts. NeuroImage **31**(4), 1682–1692 (2006)
19. M.O. Ernst, H.H. Bülthoff, Merging the senses into a robust percept. Trends Cogn. Sci. **8**, 162–169 (2004)
20. T.S. Andersen, K. Tiipanna, M. Sams, Factors influencing audiovisual fission and fusion illusions. Cogn. Brain Res. **21**, 301–308 (2004)
21. A.G. Chalmers, A. Ferko, in *Levels of Realism: from Virtual Reality to Real Virtuality*. In SCCG'08: Spring Conference on Computer Graphics, ACM SIGGRAPH Press, pp. 27–33, 2008
22. J. Ferwerda, in *Three Varieties of Realism in Computer Graphics*. Proceedings SPIE Human Vision and Electronic Imaging, pp. 290–297, 2003
23. F. Banterle, A. Artusi, K. Debattista, A.G Chalmers, *Advanced High Dynamic Range Imaging*. (CRC Press, Boca Raton, 2011). ISBN: 978-156881-719-4

24. H. Seetzen, W. Heidrich, W. Stuerzlinger, G. Ward, L. Whitehead, M. Trentacoste, A. Ghosh, A. Vorozcovs, High dynamic range display systems. ACM Trans. Graphics **23**(3) (2004)
25. SIM2 HDR 47 Engineering display series, http://hdr.sim2.it/. Feb 2017
26. V. Hulusic, C. Harvey, K. Debattista, N. Tsingos, S. Walker, D. Howard, A.G. Chalmers, Acoustic rendering and auditory-visual cross-modal perception and interaction. Comput. Graphics Forum **31**(1), 102–131 (2012)
27. N. Tsingos, E. Gallo, G. Drettakis, in *Perceptual Audio Rendering of Complex Virtual Environments*. SIGGRAPH 2004 (ACM Press, 2004), pp. 249–258
28. V. Hulusíc, C. Harvey, K. Debattista, N. Tsingos, S. Walker, D. Howard, A.G. Chalmers, Acoustic rendering and auditory-visual cross-modal perception and interaction. Comput. Graphics Forum 31(1), 102–131 (2012)
29. A. Saddik, The potential of haptic technologies. IEEE Instrum. Meas. Mag. **10**(31), 10–17 (2007)
30. K.A. Robson Brown, A.G. Chalmers, T. Saigol, C. Green, F. d'Errico, An automated laser scan survey of the Upper Palaeolithic rock shelter of Cap Blanc. J. Archaeol. Sci. **28**, 283–289 (2001)
31. E. Zányi, Y. Chrysanthou, J. Happa, V. Hulusic, A.G. Chalmers, in *The High-Fidelity Computer Reconstruction of Byzantine Art*. Cyprus IV International Congress of Cypriot Studies, April 2008
32. Jorvik Viking Centre, http://jorvik-viking-centre.co.uk/contact-us/press/forget-3d-discover-vikings-in-4d-this-summer/. Jul 2015
33. J. Aggleton, L. Waskett, The ability of odours to serve as state-dependent cues for real-world memories: can Viking smells aid the recall of Viking experiences? Br. J. Psychol. **90**, 1–7 (1999)
34. H. Abdi, What can cognitive psychology and sensory evaluation learn from each other? Food Qual. Prefer. **13**, 445–451 (2002)
35. C.M. Delahunty, J.R. Piggott, Current methods to evaluate contribution and interactions of components to flavour of solid foods using hard cheese as an example. Int. J. Food Sci. Technol. **30**, 555–570 (1995)
36. E.T. Rolls, Taste, olfactory, and food reward value processing in the brain. Prog. Neurobiol. **127–128**, 64–90 (2015). doi:10.1016/j.pneurobio.2015.03.002
37. J. Verhagen, L. Engelen, The neurocognitive bases of human multimodal food perception: sensory integration. Neurosci. Biobehav. Rev. **30**, 613–650 (2006)
38. H. Iwata, H. Yano, T. Uemura, T. Moriya, *Food Simulator*. ICAT'03: Proceedings of the 13th International Conference on Artificial Reality and Telexistence (IEEE Press, 2003)
39. N. Ranasinghe, A. Cheok, R. Nakatsu, E. Yi-Luen Do, in *Simulating the Sensation of Taste for Immersive Experiences*. ImmersiveMe '13 (ACM Multimedia, 2013)
40. T. Narumi, M. Sato, T. Tanikawa, M. Hirose, in *Evaluating Cross-Sensory Perception of Superimposing Virtual Color onto Real Drink: Toward Realization of Pseudo-gustatory Displays*. 1st Augmented Human Interaction Conference (ACM, 2010)
41. T. Narumi, S. Nishizaka, T. Kajinami, T. Tanikawa, M. Hirose, in *MetaCookie+*. Virtual Reality Conference (IEEE, 2011)
42. G. Wright, *Kalabsha: The Preserving of the Temple* (Gebr. Mann Verlag, Berlin, 1972)
43. S. Quirke, *The Cult of RA: Sun Worship in Ancient Egypt* (Thames and Hudson Distributors LTD, New York, NY, 2001)
44. F. Kahnert, Reproducing the optical properties of fine desert dust aerosols using ensembles of simple model particles. J. Quant. Spectrosc. Radiat. Transfer **85**, 231–249 (2003)
45. V. Sundstedt, D. Gutierrez, F. Gomez, A. Chalmers, in *Participating Media for High-Fidelity Cultural Heritage*. Proceedings of the Conference on Virtual Reality, Archaeology and Cultural Heritage. Eurographics (VAST'05), 2005
46. D.H. Brown, A.G. Chalmers, A. McNamara, in *Light and the Culture of Colour in Medieval Pottery*. The International Conference of Medieval and Later Archaeology, Brugge, October 1997

Chapter 15
Multimodal Serious Games Technologies for Cultural Heritage

Fotis Liarokapis, Panagiotis Petridis, Daniel Andrews, and Sara de Freitas

Abstract This chapter describes how multimodal serious games can create an immersive experience to enhance the visitor's experience. The creation of more engaging digital heritage exhibitions by seamlessly integrating technologies to provide a multimodal virtual and augmented reality experience is presented. In engaging exhibitions, participants can switch between different modes of exploring the physical artefacts at the museum and can explore these artefacts further through serious games, user interfaces, virtual reality and augmented reality. Different types of interaction paradigms are also illustrated. Moreover, a framework for multimodal cultural heritage is proposed based on the above technologies. Finally, future research directions for creating new opportunities for scientific research are presented.

Keywords Multimodal interfaces • Augmented reality • Virtual reality • Human–computer interaction • Serious games • Cultural heritage

15.1 Introduction

Learning institutions such as archives, libraries and museums play a central role in the preservation and distribution of cultural knowledge in our society. These institutions need to ensure the preservation of our cultural heritage whilst simultaneously allowing it to be accessed. However, traditional physical storage systems for documents and artefacts lack scalability and long-term sustainability. Learning institutions are thus recognizing the need to embrace new technologies for digital

---

F. Liarokapis (✉)
Faculty of Informatics, Masaryk University, Brno, Czech Republic
e-mail: liarokap@fi.muni.cz

P. Petridis • D. Andrews
Business School, Aston University, Birmingham, UK
e-mail: p.petridis@aston.ac.uk; d.andrews@aston.ac.uk

S. de Freitas
Murdoch University, Murdoch, WA, Australia
e-mail: S.deFreitas@murdoch.edu.au

M. Ioannides et al. (eds.), *Mixed Reality and Gamification for Cultural Heritage*,
DOI 10.1007/978-3-319-49607-8_15

acquisition, content management (including cataloguing) and subsequent public exhibition. Learning history is fundamentally dependent upon intangible narratives, often accompanied by illustrations and historical facts [1]. To promote better absorption of knowledge, the greatest possible degree of involvement from learners in the learning process is desirable. Experiential learning [2] advocates learning through experience and learning by doing. However, digitization of the learning environment often implies experiences that become abstract subsets of their real-world counterparts, and therefore cracks can emerge in the exploratory learning model between action, (virtual) experience and reflection [3]. These often manifest themselves as a negative transfer due to inadequate fidelity or through reports of cognitive overload as learners struggle to address the additional demands required to reflect on virtual experiences in the context of real-world events [4, 5]. Hence, it is necessary to narrow the gap between virtual and real spaces, enabling experiential learning techniques to be more readily and effectively applied.

In recent years, multimodal serious games technologies, such as virtual reality (VR) and augmented reality (AR), have emerged as areas of particular interest as methods for visualizing a museum's digital artefacts in differing contexts. The technologies associated with these new visualization techniques have been typically limited by high initial costs, restricting its use. However, the advent of low-cost computing devices, GPUs and 4/5 K displays, coupled with increasing Internet broadband speeds, has made the implementation of virtual museums increasingly cost-efficient. Some characteristic examples of visualization technologies that augment traditional multimedia and which learning institutions can now cost-effectively employ to engage and immerse their visitors in websites or exhibitions include: Web3D, VR, AR and XML. Such technologies can be employed using a simple repository-driven architecture, whereby visitors can access virtual museums embedded with rich multimedia content, navigate through those virtual environments (VEs), interact with objects in virtual reality browsers (i.e. VRML/X3D clients that embed on a web browser) and use AR interfaces that captivate the visitor. Authoring tools, such as modern games engines, allow the creation of an interactive VE to set the context for historical artefacts, which supports platforms, such as the web and mobile (android and IOS).

The rest of the chapter is structured as follows: Firstly, the concept of serious games and gamification is explained. Next, the most significant technologies for immersive heritage applications are presented including both visualization and interaction. Moreover, a generic multimodal environment for cultural heritage is proposed. Finally, conclusions and future work are presented. It is worth mentioning that the results of this book chapter are directly connected to digital libraries in cultural heritage. In particular, the content existing in digital libraries can be used to create novel multimodal serious games experiences. This may include any type of multimedia content including 3D information, audio, metadata, images and videos.

15.2 Serious Games

The increasing use of games in non-entertainment contexts is transforming everyday lives and most importantly injecting more fun in everyday contexts [6]. The power of games to immerse, engage and motivate [7] and the capabilities of games to foster and facilitate cognitive gain, awareness and behavioural change have encouraged more games of this nature to be deployed in real-life settings. Most of these games are however bespoke and do not support reusability. There are initiatives, where game making is part of a pedagogy that will allow learners to learn while creating and developing games in line with the current perceptions of considering learners as designers and creators of content and processes. The need to add fun and competition in everyday activities has seen gamification, defined as the use of game mechanics in non-game context, being applied as a strategy to not only engage but also sustain participation (see next section). One of the best examples of 'gamification'—or how games are pervading our lives—is the example of serious games, educational gaming as well as games, and virtual worlds that are specifically developed for educational purposes reveal the potential of these technologies to engage and motivate beyond leisure time activities [8]. Hamari [9] summarized existing initiatives that have impacted teaching and training. These approaches were based loosely on player types, and they demonstrated that personalization is key to motivation.

When it comes to the state of the art in serious game development, the easy answer is that it is identical to the state of the art in entertainment game development. Both types of games share the same infrastructure, i.e. technology base, or as Zyda [10] notes, 'applying games and simulations technology to non-entertainment domains results in serious games'. Over the past decade, there have been tremendous advances in entertainment computing technology, i.e. 'today's games are exponentially more powerful and sophisticated than those of just 3 or 4 years ago' [11], which in turn is leading to very high consumer expectations. Modern real-time computer graphics can achieve near photorealism, and virtual game worlds are usually populated with massive amounts of high-quality content, creating a rich user experience. The programmable rendering pipeline of modern consumer graphics hardware allows the use of new lighting and shading models that produce highly convincing visuals. The games' rendering systems are usually implemented to be scalable to the underlying hardware, ensuring that the best possible visuals are presented on every computer that they run on. Virtual game worlds also make extensive use of recent AI developments for the creation of realistic non-player characters (NPCs), i.e. virtual actors that can have meaningful interactions with human players. Examples for this would be bestselling games, such as the recent Fallout3 or the immensely successful massively multiplayer online game (MMOG) World of Warcraft (WoW), which both create persistent virtual worlds.

It should be noted, however, that the state of the industry—as opposed to the state of the art—in serious games lags behind the state of the industry in entertainment games. The main reason for this difference between serious games and entertainment games can be found in the games' production values, i.e. whereas modern entertainment games frequently have production budgets of tens of millions of US dollars with development teams that can number several hundreds of developers who can target high-end entertainment systems, serious games are usually created by small teams with moderate budgets who develop for low-to-medium spec computer systems. This gap can be overcome with recent developments in procedural methods that can be used to automatically generate much of the game content, including the actual game world (terrain, vegetation, buildings, etc.) and the virtual entities that populate it (character/creature animations, NPC behaviour). This greatly reduces development time and allows much more extensive and detailed virtual worlds to be created on small development budgets.

15.3 Gamification

The power of games to immerse and motivate [12] and the capabilities of games to change perceptions and views [13] have created a more positive approach to games and new game genres. More use of games in non-entertainment contexts, such as training [14], are transforming everyday lives, and multiplayer and social games communities are changing social interactions, leading to greater capabilities for social learning and interactions and importantly more fun in everyday contexts [15]. Efficacy can be further achieved by better understanding the target audience and pedagogic perspectives to make learning experiences more immersive, relevant and engaging. Gamification is the deliberate implementation of features of games in contexts not normally associated with games. Organizations incorporate gamification in order to encourage participants to feel a certain way, exhibit a certain behaviour and/or perform a certain action, which may not occur otherwise. Gamification has attracted widespread attention from academia within a short period of time. This has resulted in disparate approaches to, and applications of, research into gamification.

Deterding et al. [16] defined gamification as the application of game elements and digital game design techniques to non-game problems, such as business and social impact challenges. Gamification is discussed in relation to a broader movement exploring the evolution of digital games technologies in the context of human–computer interaction. It is argued that gamification is one of the more recent applications of games design principles that have been studied since the prominence of video games in the 1980s. Due to the popularity of video games, researchers were interested in identifying aspects that made them appealing and whether these could be transferred to other software related to productivity [17, 18]. To motivate the users to work towards these goals, gamification implements an accomplishment-based reward system. Points, stars and badges are often 'given' to users for completing important tasks; gamification is a quite recent concept, but it has a great potential, and it was added to the Gartner Hype Cycle

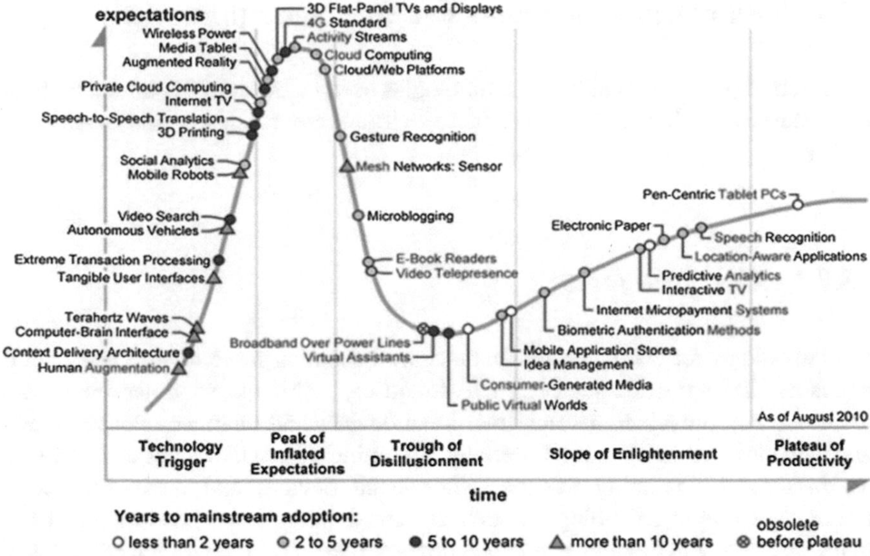

Fig. 15.1 Gartner Hype Cycle for emerging technologies (copyright [19])

for 2011 (Fig. 15.1). Gartner group predicts that gamification will be adopted by every CIO, IT planner and enterprise architect as it closely relates to their business [19].

The result of this growing interest is that applications of gamification are extensive. Since the term 'gamification' was adopted by research communities in 2011, a rapid proliferation of varied studies has been produced within a short period of time. Methods for business applications of gamification were originally championed in books and blog articles by authors such as [20, 21]. In a recent review, [22] explain how such methods were challenged or expanded by scholars from various other fields, distancing the research from business contexts. Although attempts have been made to direct gamification research following these developments, these have been from the perspective of human–computer interaction (HCI) [22]. While such studies may offer valuable insight into the design and evaluation of interactive systems, a coherent research agenda for gamification in business contexts has yet to emerge from these enquiries.

Gamification was recently applied successfully in websites in order to increase customer engagement, create loyalty and brand awareness. There are several successful gamification examples like Zero Emission from Nissan used for its ecological model Nissan Leaf. Another successful gamification application is Kobo Reading Life that tries to gamify reading; NIKEiD is an e-commerce gamified application allowing users to design their own shoes, and the most popular designs gather points. Various applications of gamification can be found in the industry of health and wellness: Keas, FitBit and Lose It. Motivation and learning also offer examples like Stick.com, MindSnacks and EnglishAttack.

15.4 Technologies for Immersive Heritage Applications

This section presents a number of technologies used in multimodal cultural heritage environments including user interfaces, virtual environments and augmented reality.

15.4.1 User Interfaces

User interfaces for computer applications are becoming more diverse and readily available. 2D interaction devices, such as mouses, keyboards, windows, menus and icons, are still prevalent, but non-traditional devices and interfaces can be created and embedded into museum exhibitions. These include spatial input devices, such as trackers, 3D pointing devices, whole-hand devices and three-dimensional multisensor output technologies, such as semi-immersive or head-mounted displays, spatial audio systems and haptic devices [23–25]. In the design and deployment of these technologies, new challenges have arisen; humans often find it difficult to understand the concept of pseudo or virtual 3D spaces and how to perform actions within them [26]. Although we live in a 3D world, the real world contains visual cues which help us to understand the environment we live in and interact with, which can be absent from a computer simulation [25]. Therefore, the design of the interface and interaction technique is an important consideration when seeking to create effective and engaging experiences. It is clear that simply adapting windows, icon, menu and pointing device (WIMP) interaction styles to 3D does not provide a complete solution to this problem [25].

To establish specific user interface requirements, the designer must first identify the tasks occurring relevant to each application scenario [27]. According to Wuthrich [28], tasks in 3D virtual space can be broken down into three elementary actions: selection/grabbing, positioning with N degrees of freedom (DOF) and deformation. Research carried out by Subramanian [29] has shown that an increase in the number of available DOF in an interaction device can improve performance; however, instead of increasing the DOF of an input device, we must exploit specific tasks in order to decrease dimensionality, making the interactivity intuitive and easy to grasp for a wider audience. For example, if the user needs only to rotate the object, it makes no sense to allow simultaneous translation [30, 31]. Hence, when a task requires 1 or 2 DOF of freedom, a 2D input device can be more effective than a 3D input device [29, 30]. A combination of 3D input devices with a 2D input device is called a hybrid interface [25]. In certain contexts, hybrid interfaces have been shown to improve performance over solely 2D or 3D interfaces [29].

15.4.2 Virtual Environments

Virtual museums take advantage of innovative digital technologies in order to display, preserve, reconstruct and store collections. They can provide a valuable resource for the end user, enabling efficient and remote learning of their local heritage in diverse, multimodal fashion. A relevant study examined similarities and differences among the sites in relation to visitors' expectations, perceptions of learning opportunities, engagement in motivated learning behaviours and perceptions of the learning experience [32]. The primary source of the educational value of the virtual museums is considered as the ability of users to take, manipulate, redistribute and redescribe digital objects [33]. Moreover, a conceptual model has been used as a guideline in designing and evaluating virtual museum in terms of efficiency, ease of use and satisfaction [34].

An example of such a museum is the Virtual Egyptian Antiquity Museum [35]. VEs have already been employed within the domain of cultural heritage. Applications, such as Virtual Ancient Egypt [36], present users with digital recreation of ancient artefacts. Events, such as a battle in a computer-generated scene, can also be recreated to allow users to move around and watch from any angle or location. First-hand experience is, however, not commonly advocated by these environments. A more ubiquitous approach has included the use of portable devices during a visit to a historical site. Santangelo et al. [37] proposed the use of a personal digital assistant (PDA) with ad hoc built-in information retrieval functionalities to assist visitors of a historical site in a natural manner instead of traditional audio/visual pre-recorded guides. An information retrieval service is included and is easily accessible through spoken language interaction. The system uses the advantages of chatbot and speech recognition technologies, allowing for natural interaction with the user.

The 3DMURALE project [38] developed 3D multimedia tools to record, reconstruct, encode and visualize archaeological ruins such as the ancient city of Sagalassos in Turkey using virtual reality. These tools were applied to buildings, building parts, statues, stratigraphy, pottery, terrain geometry, textures and texture materials. The Ename 974 project developed a non-intrusive interpretation system to convert archaeological sites into open-air museums, called TimeScope-1 [39]. The architecture is based on 3D computer technology originally developed by IBM, called TimeFrame. Visitors enter a specifically designed on-site kiosk, wherein real-time video images and other architectural reconstructions are superimposed onto monitor screens.

The Foundation of the Hellenic World (FHW) has produced a number of VR applications for representing the Olympic Games in ancient Greece [40]. A characteristic example is 'Walk through Ancient Olympia' (Fig. 15.2), where the user, apart from visiting the historical site, learns about the ancient games themselves by interacting with non-player characters (NPC), such as athletes in the ancient game of pentathlon.

Fig. 15.2 Ancient Olympia walk through (copyright [42])

15.4.3 Augmented Reality Environments

Augmented reality (AR) is a collection of interactive technologies that merge real and virtual content and provide accurate registration in three dimensions [41]. In the past years, AR has been applied experimentally for a number of cultural heritage applications including both indoor environments such as museums and outdoor environments, like tourist guides. ARCHEOGUIDE [42] provided an interactive AR guide for the visualization of archaeological sites. The system was based on mobile computing, networking and 3D visualization providing users with a multimodal interaction user interface. A similar project is LIFEPLUS [43], which explored the potential of AR aiming to allow users to experience a high degree of realistic interactive immersion. The broader scope of this system allows the rendering of realistic 3D simulations of virtual humans, animals and plants in real time. The ARCO system (Fig. 15.3) developed tangible interfaces that allow museum visitors to visualize museum artefacts in an interactive table-top AR environment [44]. Furthermore, AR has been experimentally applied to make it possible to visualize incomplete or broken real objects as they were in their original state by superimposition of the missing parts [45].

Another approach to AR in context of historical heritage showed how drawings and paintings can be superimposed to the live camera view and how to filter the scene images to keep the same presentation style as the included objects [46]. Time

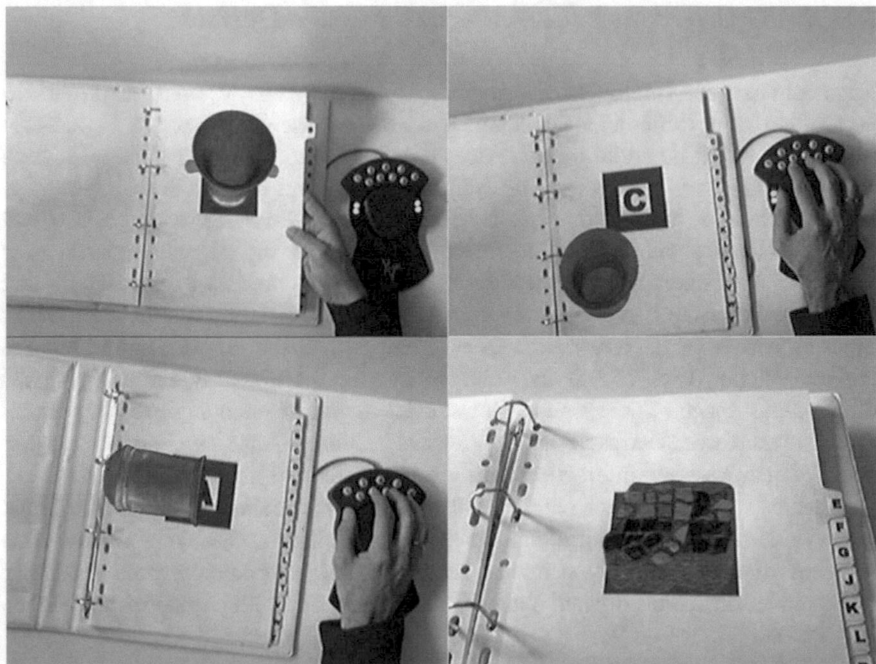

Fig. 15.3 The ARCO project learning book interaction examples

Warp was an outdoor AR mobile game placed in the city of Cologne (Germany), which combined artificial static and animated objects with sound [47]. The Dublin AR project [48] investigated 26 international and domestic tourists' requirements for the development of a mobile AR tourism application in urban heritage. The CorfuAR project [49] supported personalized recommendations in a mobile AR environment. Finally, a mobile AR tourist guide for examining user experiences in urban environments was recently proposed [50]. The main features of the AR touristic application were evaluated with 30 healthy volunteers, and results showed that users found the sensor approach easy to use and intuitive. The majority reported fast adaptation to the AR application.

15.5 Interactions for Cultural Heritage

This section presents an overview of the characteristic approaches in human–computer interaction for cultural heritage systems.

15.5.1 Interactions with Active and Passive Devices

The use of game technologies, with the integration of games, VR and AR provides a compelling set of technologies with which to build a museum interactive. Figure 15.4 illustrates several potential input devices useful for interacting with the museum's digital heritage collections ranging from standard input devices such as the keyboard and mouse, joystick through to bespoke replicas complete with tracking and sensor electronics and through the use of natural processing language interfaces or brain computer interfaces (see next section). Physically touching a virtual artefact may narrow the gap between what we perceive as a virtual and real object [51]. In order to enrich users' experience in a virtual world, the authors have used the Novint Falcon (Fig. 15.4a) in order to support virtual navigation in three-dimensional space. The system allows users to experience high-fidelity three-dimensional force feedback that represents texture, shape, weight, dimension or/and dynamics upon interaction with virtual artefacts (Fig. 15.4b) [51].

Another way to interact with virtual museum, particularly for museum kiosk displays, is through a multimodal interface providing access to a replica of a museum artefact. Multimodal input systems process two or more combined user input modes in a coordinated manner with the multimedia system output (see Fig. 15.5).

15.5.2 Interactions with Sound Interfaces

Sound can sometimes be the Cinderella aspect of virtual environments and interfaces, with much attention lavished on the visual fidelity of a given scene and the sound being very much a secondary or even tertiary concern. However, in the cultural heritage sphere, much application of sound has been used to give a better

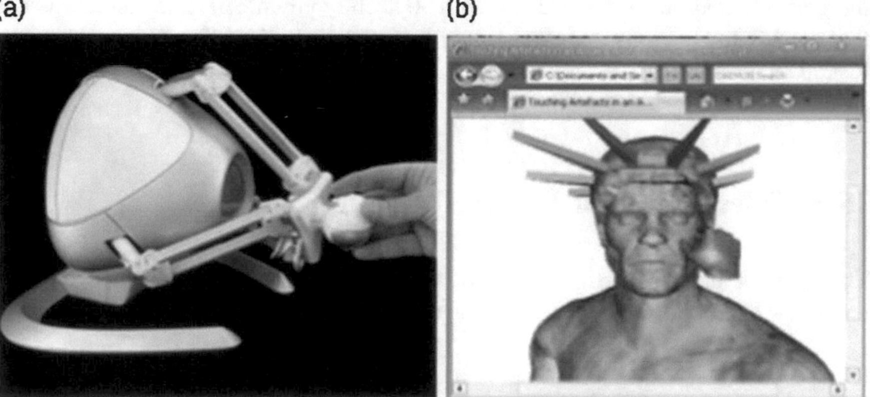

Fig. 15.4 Falcon interaction

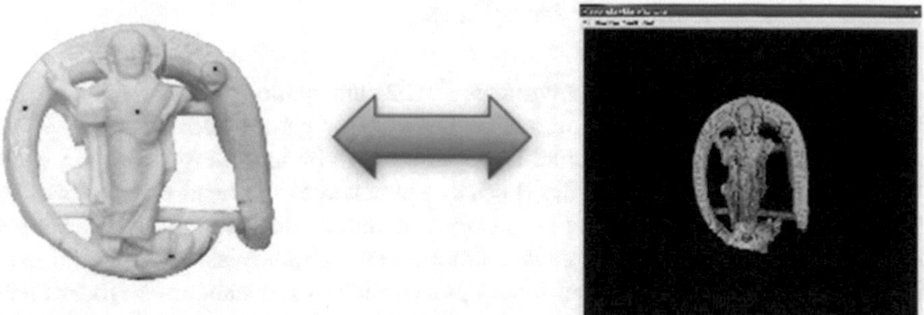

Fig. 15.5 Replica for museum kiosks

sense of place and immersion for certain displays. This is usual in the form of a son et lumière non-interactive experience, e.g. the Blitz experience at the Coventry Transport Museum, or even audio guides giving a commentary as you are directed around a location. Although, what could perhaps be considered an audio, only AR can be constructed by allowing the commentary to be location sensitive and permitting the user to choose their own route around the site of interest, e.g. the audio tour of the National Gallery in London. One primary problem with the use of audio content is its actual generation, especially in the area of speech. This can be seen as on a sliding scale from auto-generated text-to-speech conversion software, providing a cheap but low-quality robotic voice, to recording of live vocal talent, resulting in expensive but high-quality voice, with solutions like that of Phonetic Arts [www.phonetc-arts.com] providing hybrids between the two extremes, using a real voice as the basis of a phonetic text-to-speech conversion system.

Going beyond audio purely as output, we should not ignore the potentially useful implementation of audio input for multimodal interfaces, especially with the use of natural speech interaction. The primary benefit of such input is that it, in principle, does not require the user to learn how to use a seemingly complex interface or device, they just talk. Further, it also allows visually impaired users a means of using the system, especially in concert with broader audio output. Over in the interactive entertainment sphere, there are a number of instructive audio-based examples. The Pit [www.studiohunty.com/itp] is a purely audio game for the Xbox 360 where the player is put in the role of a hungry monster at the bottom of a pit and must navigate to their prey using purely stereo audio, a work by Ian Parberry [52] to convert the classic text-based game Colossal Cave Adventure into an audio-only experience, which used off-the-shelf, text-to-speech and speech-to-text systems. Finally, it should also be noted that the primary reason for speech recognition being added to the recently released kinetic peripheral for the XBox 360 is that it is in the spirit of the device in expanding the potential user base to those not accustomed to using the standard games controllers.

15.5.3 Brain–Computer Interfaces

Non-invasive brain–computer interfaces (BCIs) are getting a lot of attention as alternative human–computer interaction devices for games and virtual environments. Non-invasive BCIs operate by recording the brain activity from the scalp with electroencephalography (EEG) sensors attached to the head on an electrode cap or headset without it being surgically implanted. However, they still have a number of problems, and they cannot function as accurately as other natural user interfaces (NUIs) and traditional input devices such as the standard keyboard and mouse. The raw EEG is usually described in terms of frequency ranges: gamma (γ) >30 Hz, beta (β) 13–30 Hz, alpha (α) 8–12 Hz, theta (θ) 4–8 Hz and delta (δ) <4 Hz [53]. Delta (δ) waves with the lowest frequencies of all the brainwaves are most apparent in deep sleep states, where conscious brain activity is minimal. Theta (θ) waves appear in a relaxed state and during light sleep and meditation. Alpha (α) waves are typically associated with meditation and relaxation, more so than any other waves. Beta (β) waves are connected to alertness and focus. Gamma (γ) waves can be stimulated by meditating while focusing on a specific object.

BCIs can be used under a range of interaction paradigms to either enhance or replace existing methods for interaction. Their use as a control input alone is limited as a consequence of the difficulty in achieving precision with such a device, though EEG control approaches have been demonstrated to allow users to control a mouse pointer or perform other tasks by thought alone [54]. More interesting in this context is the ability to use them to supplement other modes of interaction: allowing one variable controlled by EEG has the potential to allow an additional DOF to be implemented without complicating other interaction methods. Furthermore, the ability of biofeedback devices to monitor user states such as alpha and beta wave activity, muscle activity or galvanic skin response can allow a designer insight into the state of the user and allow architectures to be developed that respond accordingly [55]. The notion of an ‘intelligent conversational agent’ driven by biofeedback has been explored in previous research [56], and the use of such AI in cultural heritage as a guide, educator and curator is of increasing interest. Furthermore, the inclusion of biofeedback devices within the architecture allows increased support for disabled users, allowing users incapable of physical interaction with the system an alternative medium for interaction.

In terms of controlling cultural heritage serious games, an interactive serious cultural heritage game was developed based on commercial BCI headsets (Fig. 15.6) controlling virtual agents in the ancient city of Rome [57]. Initial results indicate that brain–computer technologies can be very useful for the creation of interactive serious games.

In another study, two different EEG-based BCI devices were used to fully control the same serious game [58]. The first device (NeuroSky MindSet) uses only a single dry electrode and requires no calibration. The second device (Emotiv EPOC) uses 14 wet sensors requiring additional training of a classifier. User testing was performed on both devices with 62 participants measuring the player

Fig. 15.6 Ability to control events using the Emotiv device (*left*) and NeuroSky (*right*) (copyright [60])

experience as well as key aspects of serious games, primarily learnability, satisfaction, performance and effort. Recorded feedback indicated that the current state of BCIs can be used in the future as alternative game interfaces after familiarization and in some cases calibration. Comparative analysis showed significant differences between the two devices. The first device provides more satisfaction to the players, whereas the second device is more effective in terms of adaptation and interaction with the serious game.

15.6 A Generic Multimodal Environment for Cultural Heritage

According to Oviatt, multimodal interfaces offer the 'potential to greatly expand the accessibility of computing to diverse and non-specialist users, and to promote new forms of computing not previously available' [59]. The flexibility of multimodal interfaces allows for better alternation of input modalities, preventing overuse and physical damage arising from a repeated action during extended periods of use. Moreover, multimodal interfaces can be exploited to provide customizable digital heritage applications and scenarios [60]. The main benefit for the users is that they can switch between different types of mixed reality environments and perform different tasks. Typical examples include web-based virtual and augmented reality interfaces and immersive virtual reality and augmented reality systems [60]. Several different interface techniques can be employed to make exploration of the user experience much more interesting.

15.6.1 System Architecture

A diagram that illustrates interaction and visualization technologies employed in the proposed multimodal mixed reality system is presented in Fig. 15.7. The system supports various interaction modes that can be grouped in three categories: brain–computer interface (BCI) interaction, natural speech interaction and interaction with haptic devices. The interactive experience can be enhanced with the use of haptic devices, such as the Novint Falcon, where tactile feedback can be incorporated into the interaction with artefacts. Haptic interfaces are designed to communicate through the subtle and sensitive channels of tactile senses associated with the tactile definition of a virtual object. Additionally the system supports interactions with several standard input devices and interaction sensors such as the Spacemouse, the Spacepilot, Isense Inertia cube, etc. The system supports interaction with BCIs such as the NeuroSky mindwave and the EPOC Emotiv headsets. The NeuroSky contains a dry sensor and it can be used without prior training. In the case of the Emotiv, this device uses 14 wet sensors and allows the user to 'train' their EEG (brainwave) and EMG (facial muscle activity) response to manipulate linear variables. Hence, an object can be moved by self-induction of an EEG state or facial expression, allowing for a breadth of new interaction paradigms for manipulating objects and interacting with virtual characters. Furthermore, evidence linking the attentive state of learners to EEG activity can be capitalized upon to create interaction modalities that respond to attention [56], facilitating increased learning transfer as well as interaction [58].

3D visualization and haptic interaction can also be realized through this architecture on a web browser, a virtual gallery environment, a person using a physical replica of an artefact or a haptic device to control and explore the virtual artefact and through several AR examples. The proposed system provides an extendable, device-independent interface, which allows the user to set up various I/O devices across different virtual environments or gaming engines. Such a multimodal mixed reality interface allows users to select the best visualization mode for a particular application scenario. Although not all of the functionality implemented in these systems was transferred to our MR interface, the main capability is the multimodal switching between a VR and an AR visualization domain in real time. The basic idea behind this is based on the concept explored in a previously implemented interface [60].

In this work, we focus on the details of the multimodal interface. The VR interface provides assistance and other relevant information to the heritage users. The challenge is to provide a high level of immersion to the users through specialized displays and interaction devices. The interface operates on different types of processing devices such as dedicated workstations and ultra-mobile personal computers (UMPCs). On dedicated workstations, since they are much more powerful, a VR engine is capable of delivering high-end immersion in real-time performance. The AR interface makes use of the real environment to superimpose audio-visual and other relevant information to users. The accurate registration of

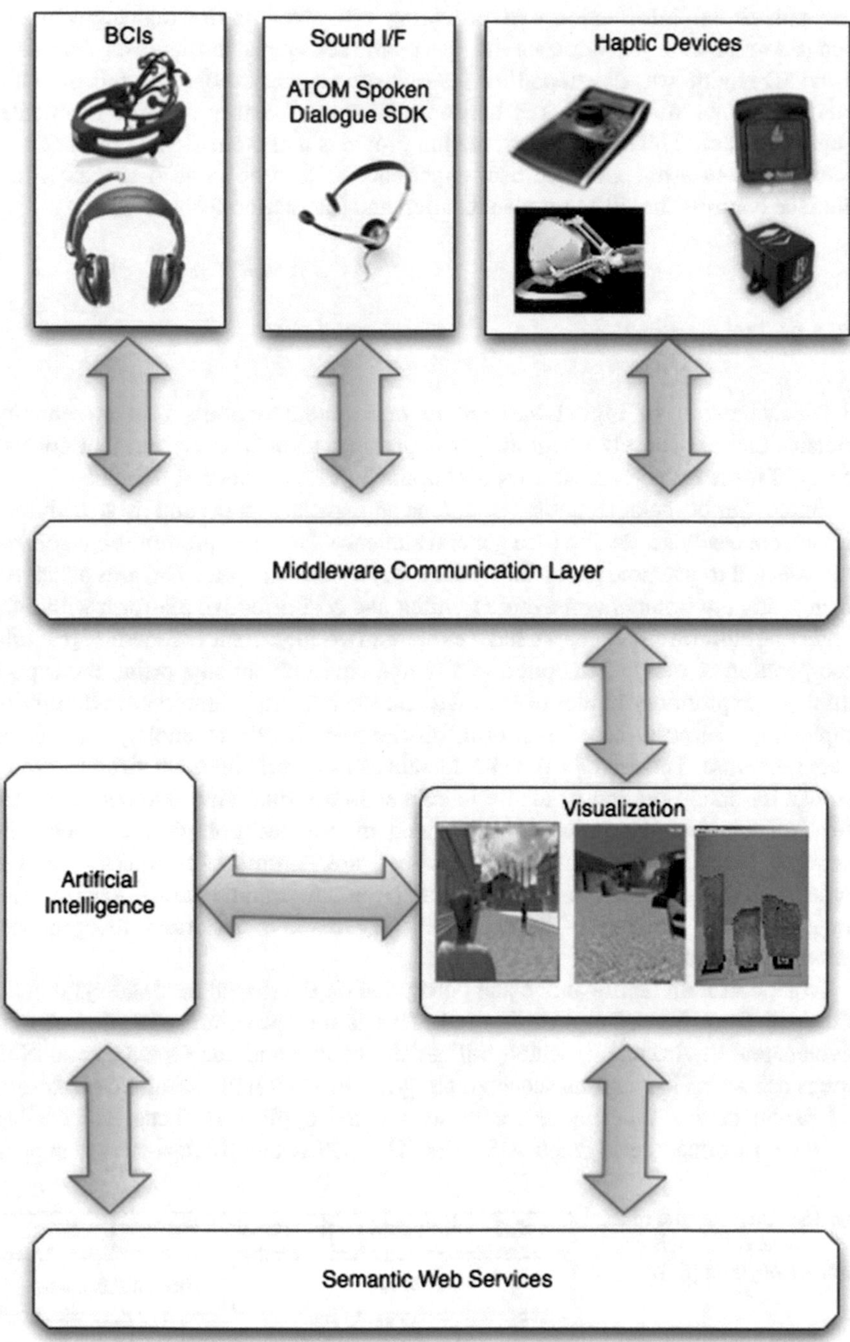

Fig. 15.7 Multimodal reality interface

real and virtual information and providing effective multimedia augmentation alongside real-time performance are the main challenges in this task. An audio-visual 3D engine was developed for the realistic augmentation. The mixed reality interface allows users to switch between the virtual reality and the augmented reality interface. This type of presentation provides a combined view of the above technologies offering a unique user experience. The user-focused graphical user interface controls the different visualization and interaction technologies.

15.6.2 Visualization

The visualization of digital heritage in our system exploits two presentation domains that are loosely integrated. It is possible to build a system that consists of any of these two domains: a Web3D domain (VR) and an AR domain.

Employing bespoke technologies can be an expensive task, and these technologies are not easily accessible for a general audience. Hence to promote engagement, it is essential to promote accessibility for a wider demographic. Towards achieving an engaging environment on a more familiar and cost-effective platform within the context of cultural heritage, we have explored two important parameters [61]: the incorporation of tactile perception in a virtual environment supporting the experiential and exploratory model of learning and the need to promote accessibility by employing a browser-based platform, off-the-shelf haptic technology and open-source software. The use of a Web3D domain can support hands-on virtual learning through the incorporation of tactile interfaces in a virtual environment. We capitalize on the fact that Internet access and mobile technologies, coupled with graphical user interfaces and web browsers, are common in education and at home [62]. An abstraction layer provided through middleware allows a wide range of haptic devices to be supported. Figure 15.8 illustrates the proposed software architecture.

To support both tactile and visual perception on the digital heritage system, the H3D API from SenseGraphics is used. This is an open-source haptic software development environment, which utilizes the open standards OpenGL and X3D alongside haptics in a unified scene graph. With the H3D API, being cross-platform and haptic device independent, a browser-based application becomes feasible. Unlike most other scene-graph APIs, the H3D API is chiefly designed to support

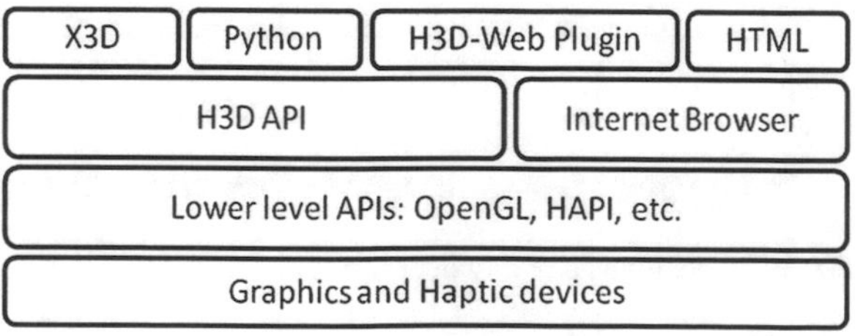

Fig. 15.8 Architecture of a browser-based VE with haptics (copyright [63])

a rapid development process. An off-the-shelf haptic device (Novint Falcon) has been employed due to its usability and stability within the domain of haptic-based games. It is also supported by H3D and does not require prior technical skills and experience.

15.6.3 Web-Based Virtual Environment

The web-based virtual environment consists of two main components: artefact development and web deployment. The artefact development component incorporates the 3D visual and the relevant haptics definition. The 3D Visual rendering of the object is based on an X3D (the extensible 3D file format), an ISO open standard scene-graph design that is easily extended to offer new functionality in a modular way and is based on XML, which is the standard mark-up language used in a wide variety of applications and is especially popular on the web. In tandem with XML for web semantics, models from the Rome Reborn [63], mainly in a 3D Studio Max format, were repurposed and translated into X3D to provide the visual scene graph, which was then extended with haptic functionality.

For the haptic definition, H3D provides a full XML parser for loading scene-graph definitions of X3D extended with haptic functionality. With the haptic extensions to X3D via H3D API, tactile definition was incorporated into the scene graph. Furthermore, Python scripting enables more behaviour to be included in the scene, such as the deformable behaviour of a soft texture upon interaction. Figure 15.9 demonstrates real-time interaction with virtual artefacts, where tactile and visual feedback respective of the texture, shape and material of the artefacts upon interaction could enrich users' experience through exploratory engagement.

For the web deployment, HTML encapsulates the scene-graph definitions developed using the H3D API, which can be displayed on the web browser via the H3D-Web plug-in. Figure 15.10 illustrates a haptic-enabled browser, where users

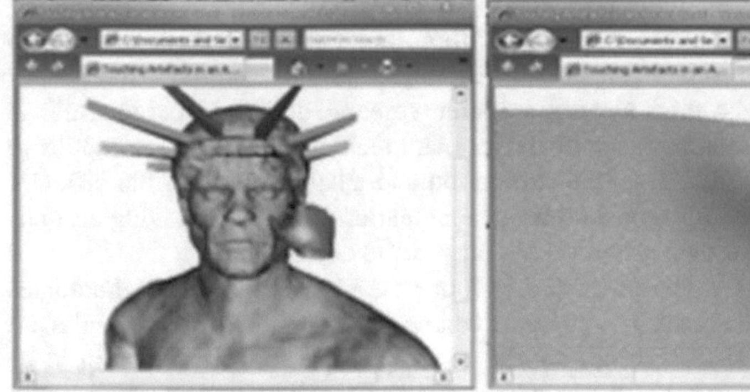

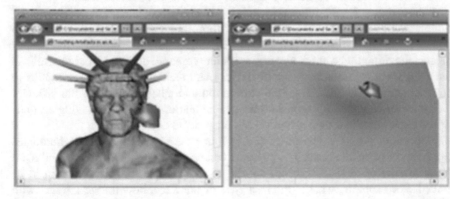

Fig. 15.9 Haptic interaction (hand cursor) with a rigid artefact and a soft surface (copyright [53])

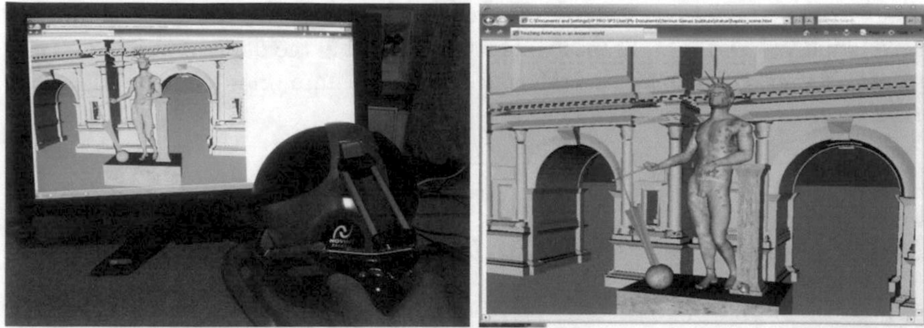

Fig. 15.10 Ancient Rome on a haptic-enabled web browser with a Novint Falcon device

can experience tactile feedback from real-time interactions with the artefacts over the web using a Novint Falcon device. The system is based on client–server architecture. The client side is responsible for the runtime processing, such as rendering. The web content including the haptic-enabled visualization resides at the server side [51].

15.7 Conclusions and Future Challenges

Learning institutions, such as museums and art galleries, play a significant role in heritage preservation and have only recently started to metamorphose into hybrid institutions that can accommodate both physical and digital resources. This chapter has outlined the emerging technologies for multimodal serious games and virtual environments in cultural heritage. Moreover, a novel multimodal interaction interface suitable for adoption by learning institutions, allowing them to create interactive content through a combination of AR, VR and web visualization, was proposed. The system allows these learning institutions to utilize several haptic devices to create more interactive and immersive experiences for users.

Future research will ultimately entail using various technologies to support multimodality in a cultural heritage institution or art gallery setting in order to enhance experience and engagement. Although several examples have been presented within this context already, sufficient research does not exist to establish the effectiveness and acceptance of devices and technologies, such as haptics to complement physical artefacts, the correlation and amalgamation of the different technologies to create a balanced sensory stimulation towards achieving an optimized experience and the feasibility of a large-scale deployment.

Depending on the environment (i.e. indoor or outdoor), different technologies can be used. In an ideal scenario, the same technologies should be operational in all types of environments. There are a number of open questions that remain to be solved. For example, what is the best type of interface, how do we interact with different types of content and what is the required level of immersion and realism.

We are in the beginning of a new era of visualization and interaction hardware devices and software systems in the near future, and the predictions are strongly suggesting that we are going to encounter a completely different user experience. However, the impact of multimodal serious games technologies influences a number of sectors such as creative and game industry, museums, EU policy towards CH digitalization, growth and education.

Acknowledgements The authors would like to thank Human–Computer Interaction Laboratory members for their support and inspiration.

References

1. S. Arnab, P. Petridis, I. Dunwell, S. de Freitas, in *Touching Artefacts in an Ancient World on a Browser-Based Platform*, ed. by Y. Xiao, T. Amon, R. Muffoletto. Proceedings of the IADIS International Conference on Computer Graphics, Visualization, Computer Vision and Image Processing. International Association for Development of the Information Society (IADIS), 2010.
2. D. Kolb, *Experiential Learning: Experience as the Source of Learning and Development* (Prentice Hall, Inc., New Jersey, 1984)
3. S. de Freitas, T. Neumann, The use of 'exploratory learning' for supporting immersive learning in virtual environments. Comput. Educ. **52**(2), 343–352 (2009)
4. S. Warburton, in *Defining a Framework for Teaching Practices Inside Virtual Immersive Environments: The Tension Between Control and Pedagogical Approach*. Proceedings of RELive '08 Conference, 2008
5. B. Parker, F. Myrick, A critical examination of high-fidelity human patient simulation within the context of nursing pedagogy. Nurse Educ. Today **29**(3), 322–329 (2009)
6. J. McGonigal, *Reality Is Broken: Why Games Make us Better and How They Can Change the World* (Jonathan Cape, London, 2008)
7. R. Garris, R. Ahlers, J.E. Driskell, Games, motivation, and learning: a research and practice model. Simul. Gaming **33**, 441–467 (2002)
8. E.F. Anderson, L. McLoughlin et al., in *Serious Games in Cultural Heritage*. Proceedings of the 10th VAST International Symposium on Virtual Reality, Archaeology and Cultural Heritage—STARs Session, Eurographics, Malta, pp. 29–48, 2009
9. J. Hamari, J. Koivisto, H. Sarsa, in *Does Gamification Work?—A Literature Review of Empirical Studies on Gamification*. Proceedings of the 47th Hawaii International Conference on System Sciences, Hawaii, USA, 2014
10. M. Zyda, From visual simulation to virtual reality to games. IEEE Comput. **38**(9), 25–32 (2005)
11. B. Sawyer, in *Serious Games: Improving Public Policy Through Game-Based Learning and Simulation*. Whitepaper for the Woodrow Wilson International Center for Scholars, 2002
12. D. Panzoli, A. Qureshi et al., Levels of interaction (LoI): a model for scaffolding learner engagement in an immersive environment. Intelligent tutoring systems. Lect. Notes Comput. Sci. **6095**, 393–395 (2010)
13. S. de Freitas, Game for change. Nature **470**(7334), 330–331 (2011)
14. P.D. Mautone, V.A. Spiker, M.R. Karp, in *Using Serious Game Technology to Improve Aircrew Training*. Proceedings of the Interservice/Industry Training, Simulation and Education Conference (IITSEC) December 2008, Orlando, Florida, 2008
15. J. McGonigal, *Reality Is Broken: Why Games Make us Better and How They Can Change the World* (Jonathan Cape, London, 2011)

16. S. Deterding, R. Khaled et al., *Gamification: Towards a Definition*. CHI 2011 Gamification Workshop Proceedings, Vancouver, BC, Canada, 2011
17. S. Deterding, The lens of intrinsic skill atoms: a method for gameful design. Human Comput. Interact. **30**, 294–335 (2015)
18. O. Korn, *Industrial Playgrounds: How Gamification Helps to Enrich Work for Elderly or Impaired Persons in Production*. Proceedings of the 4th ACM SIGCHI Symposium on Engineering Interactive Computing Systems, pp. 313–316, 2012
19. Gartner Group, *Press Release. Gartner Says by 2015, More Than 50 Percent of Organizations that Manage Innovation Processes Will Gamify Those Processes* (2011), Available from http://www.gartner.com/newsroom/id/1629214
20. G. Zichermann, C. Cunningham, *Gamification by Design: Implementing Game Mechanics in Web and Mobile Apps*, 1st edn. (O'Reilly Media, Sebastopol, CA, 2011)
21. K. Werbach, D. Hunter, *For the Win: How Game Thinking Can Revolutionize Your Business"* (Wharton Digital Press, Philadelphia, PA, 2012)
22. K. Seaborn, D.I. Fels, Gamification in theory and action: a survey. Int. J. Human Comput. Stud. **74**, 14–31 (2015)
23. D. Bowman, E. Kruijff, J. LaViola, I. Poupyrev, 3D user interface output hardware, in *3D User Interfaces: Theory and Practice* (Addison Wesley, Boston, MA, 2004), pp. 29–86
24. D. Bowman, E. Kruijff, J. LaViola, I. Poupyrev, 3D user interface input hardware, in *3D User Interfaces: Theory and Practice* (Addison Wesley, Boston, MA, 2004), pp. 87–134
25. D. Bowman, E. Kruijff, J. LaViola, I. Poupyrev, An introduction to 3D user interface design. Presence Teleop. Virt. Environ. **10**(1), 96–108 (2001)
26. K. Herndon, A. Van Dam, M. Gleicher, The challenges of 3D interaction. Siggraph Bull. **26**(4), 36–43 (1994)
27. D. Aliakseyeu, J.B. Martens, S. Subramanian, M. Rauterberg, in *Interaction Techniques for Navigation through and Manipulation of 2D and 3D Data*. Proceedings of Eight Eurographics Conference on Virtual Environments, 2002
28. C.A. Wuthrich, in *An Analysis and a Model of 3D Interaction Methods and Devices for Virtual Reality*. Proceedings of the Eurographics Workshop, 1999
29. S. Subramanian, D. Aliakseyeu, J.B. Martens, in *Empirical Evaluation of Performance in Hybrid 3D and 2D Interfaces*. Proceedings of Human Computer Interaction—Interact'03, pp. 916–919, 2003
30. P. Petridis, K. Mania, D. Pletinckx, M. White, in *Usability Evaluation of the EPOCH Multimodal User Interface: Designing 3D Tangible Interactions*. Proceedings of the Interactive Technologies and Sociotechnical Systems: Lecture Notes in Computer Science, 2006
31. P. Petridis, M. White et al., in *Exploring and Interacting with Virtual Museums*. CAA 2005: The World in Your Eyes, Tomar, Portugal, 2005
32. J. Packer, R. Ballantyne, Motivational factors and the visitor experience: a comparison of three sites. Curator Mus. J. **45**(3), 183–198 (2002)
33. S. Bayne, J. Ross, Z. Williamson, Objects, subjects, bits and bytes: learning from the digital collections of the National Museums. Mus. Soc. J. **7**(2), 110–124 (2009)
34. N. Rahim, T.S.M.T. Wook, A.M. Zin, in *Developing Conceptual Model of Virtual Museum Environment Based on User Interaction Issues*, ed. by H.B. Zaman, P. Robinson, M. Petrou, P. Olivier, T.K. Shih. Proceedings of the Second International Conference on Visual Informatics: Sustaining Research And Innovations—Volume Part II (IVIC'11) (Springer, Berlin, Heidelberg, 2011), pp. 253–260
35. The Virtual Egyptian Antiquity Museum, (1 December 2007). Available from http://www.touregypt.net/museum/
36. J. Jacobson, in *The Virtual Egyptian Temple*. ED-MEDIA: Proceedings of the World Conference on Educational Media, Hypermedia and Telecommunications, 2005
37. A. Santangelo, A. Augello et al., in *A Chat-Bot Based Multimodal Virtual Guide for Cultural Heritage Tours*. Proceedings of the 2006 World Congress in Computer Science Computer Engineering and Applied Computing, Las Vegas, Nevada, 2006

38. J. Cosmas, T. Itegaki et al., in *3D MURALE: A Multimedia System for Archaeology*. Proceedings of the ACM-SIGGRAPH Conference on Virtual Reality, Archaeology and Cultural Heritage, Athens, Greece, pp. 297–306, 2001
39. D. Pletinckx, D. Callebaut et al., Virtual-reality heritage presentation at Ename. IEEE Multimedia **7**(2), 45–48 (2000)
40. A. Gaitatzes, D. Christopoulos, G. Papaioannou, in *The Ancient Olympic Games: Being Part of the Experience*. Proceedings of the 5th International Symposium on Virtual Reality, Archaeology and Cultural Heritage, pp. 19–28, 2004
41. R.T. Azuma, A survey of augmented reality. Presence Teleop. Virt. Environ. **6**(4), 355–385 (1997)
42. D. Stricker, P. Daehne et al., in *Design and Development Issues for ARCHEOGUIDE: An Augmented Reality Based Cultural Heritage On-Site Guide*. Proceedings of the International Conference on Augmented, Virtual Environments and Three-Dimensional Imaging, IEEE Computer Society, 2001
43. G. Papagiannakis, M. Ponder et al., in *LIFEPLUS: Revival of Life in Ancient Pompeii*. Proceedings of Virtual Systems and Multimedia (VSMM 2002), 2002
44. M. White, N. Mourkoussis et al., in *ARCO—An Architecture for Digitization, Management and Presentation of Virtual Exhibitions*. Proceedings of the CGI'2004 Conference, Hersonissos, Crete, June 2004 (IEEE Computer Society, Los Alamitos, CA, 2004), pp. 622–625
45. F. Liarokapis, M. White, Augmented reality techniques for museum environments. Mediterr. J. Comput. Netw. **1**(2), 90–96 (2005)
46. M. Zoellner, A. Pagani et al., in *Reality Filtering: A Visual Time Machine in Augmented Reality*. Proceedings of the 9th International Symposium on Virtual Reality, Archaeology and Cultural Heritage, Eurographics, Braga, Portugal, 2–5 December, pp. 71–77, 2008
47. I. Herbst, A.K. Braun, R. McCall, W. Broll, *TimeWarp: Interactive Time Travel with a Mobile Mixed Reality Game*. Proceedings of the 10th International Conference on Human Computer Interaction with Mobile Devices and Services (MobileHCI 2008), ACM Press, pp. 235–244, 2008
48. D.I. Han, T. Jung, A. Gibson, Dublin AR: implementing augmented reality in tourism, in *Information and Communication Technologies in Tourism 2014* (Springer, Cham, 2014), pp. 511–523
49. P. Kourouthanassis, C. Boletsis, C. Bardaki, D. Chasanidou, Tourists responses to mobile augmented reality travel guides: the role of emotions on adoption behavior. Pervasive Mob. Comput. Elsevier **18**, 71–87 (2015)
50. D. Střelák, F. Škola, F. Liarokapis, in *Examining User Experiences in a Mobile Augmented Reality Tourist Guide*. Proceedings of the 9th International Conference on PErvasive Technologies Related to Assistive Environments (Petra 2016), ACM Press, Corfu Island, Greece, 29 June–1 July, 2016
51. S. Arnab, P. Petridis, I. Dunwell, S. de Freitas, Enhancing learning in distributed virtual worlds through touch: a browser-based architecture for haptic interaction, in *Serious Games and Edutainment Applications*, ed. by M. Ma, A. Oikonomou, L.C. Jain (Springer, London, 2011), pp. 149–167
52. T.E. Roden, I. Parberry, D. Ducrest, Toward mobile entertainment: a paradigm for narrative-based audio only games. Science of computer programming. Spec. Issue Aspects Game Program. Elsevier **67**(1), 76–90 (2007)
53. S. Sanei, J.A. Chambers, *EEG Signal Processing* (Wiley, Hoboken, NJ, 2013)
54. J. Knezik, M. Drahansky, Simple EEG driven mouse cursor movement. Comput. Recognit. Syst. 2 **45**, 526–531 (2007)
55. M. Ninaus, S.E. Kober et al., Neurophysiological methods for monitoring brain activity in serious games and virtual environments: a review. Int. J. Technol. Enhanc. Learn. **6**(1), 78–103 (2014)

56. G. Rebodello-Mendez, I. Dunwell et al., in *Assessing Neurosky's Usability to Detect Attention Levels in an Assessment Exercise*. Proceedings of the 13th International Conference on Human-Computer Interaction, Springer, Berlin, Heidelberg. Lecture Notes in Computer Science, vol 5610/2009, San Diego, CA, USA, 19–24 July, pp. 149–158, 2009
57. A. Vourvopoulos, F. Liarokapis, P. Petridis, in *Brain-Controlled Serious Games for Cultural Heritage*. Proceedings of the 18th International Conference on Virtual Systems and Multimedia, Virtual Systems in the Information Society, IEEE Computer Society, Milan, Italy, 2–-5 September, pp. 291–298, 2012
58. F. Liarokapis, K. Debattista, A. Vourvopoulos, P. Petridis, A. Ene, Comparing interaction techniques for serious games through brain-computer interfaces: a user perception evaluation study. Entertain. Comput. Elsevier **5**(4), 391–399 (2014)
59. S. Oviatt, Multimodal interfaces, in *Handbook of Human-Computer Interaction* (Lawrence Erlbaum, New Jersey, 2002)
60. M. White, P. Petridis, F. Liarokapis, D. Plecinckx, Multimodal mixed reality interfaces for visualizing digital heritage. Int. J. Archit. Comput. (IJAC) Special Iss. Cult Herit Multi-Sci 5 (2), 322–337 (2008)
61. S.A. Brewster, Impact of haptic 'touching' technology on cultural applications, in *Digital Applications for Cultural Heritage Institutions*, ed. by J. Hemsley, V. Cappellini, G. Stanke (Ashgate, Burlington, VT, 2005), pp. 273–284
62. A. Frisoli, *The Museum of Pure Form* (2007), Available from http://www.pureform.org/
63. B. Frischer, *The Rome Reborn Project. How Technology Is Helping us to Study History*, OpEd (University of Virginia, 2008)

Part VI
Intangible Heritage

Chapter 16
Modelling Life Through Time: Cultural Heritage Case Studies

Simon Sénécal, Nedjma Cadi, Marlène Arévalo, and Nadia Magnenat-Thalmann

Abstract This chapter describes how to create, animate and interact with virtual humans in the context of cultural heritage. Our case studies are previous European projects that our lab participated in, such as ERATO, LIFEPLUS, EPOCH and CALVIN. Our contribution to these projects was to show the state of the art of virtual humans and interactive applications. First we talk about modelling and how to generate avatar components (head, body and clothes) based on physic, spatial and external information: picture, 3D scans and measurements. Then we move on to the intangible part, where we explain how to capture and use motion to animate the avatar in various situations and semantic contexts, via different forms of gesture, expression and lip synchronization. Finally, we focus on the interaction loop between the detection of visitors and the reactions/expressions of the avatar, the dynamics and the integration of metadata such as pictures, storytelling and information that enrich user experience through an exhibition presented at the world's biggest museum of computer science: Lady Ada.

Keywords Cultural heritage • Digital documentation • 3D reconstruction • Semantic annotation • Virtual humans • Animation • Clothes

16.1 Introduction

Virtual restitution of highly complex heritage sites requires accurate choices for each phase of the modelling, texturing or lighting processes, and special attention must be paid when preparing models for real-time simulations with virtual historical characters. Furthermore, precise and reliable source data is critical for a scientifically correct and accurate restitution. Interpretative and comparative issues are also necessary when the restitution is targeting intangible heritage.

S. Sénécal (✉) • N. Cadi • M. Arévalo • N. Magnenat-Thalmann
MIRALab CUI, University of Geneva, Geneva, Switzerland
e-mail: senecal@miralab.ch; cadi@miralab.ch; arevalo@miralab.ch; thalmann@miralab.ch

M. Ioannides et al. (eds.), *Mixed Reality and Gamification for Cultural Heritage*,
DOI 10.1007/978-3-319-49607-8_16

16.2 Tangible Heritage

The definition of UNESCO cultural heritage is:

> The legacy of physical artefacts and intangible attributes of a group or society that are inherited from past generations, maintained in the present and bestowed for the benefit of future generations. Tangible heritage includes buildings and historic places, monuments, artefacts, etc., which are considered worthy of preservation for the future. These include objects significant to the archaeology, architecture, science or technology of a specific culture [1].

16.2.1 3D Modelling

For the restitution of tangible heritage, we have to model the various elements constituting scenes. To give life to these scenes, we create clothed virtual humans.

16.2.1.1 Body and Head Modelling

Body Modelling

With virtual humans, we consider mainly two issues. The first one is that a virtual body should correspond to real human body shapes. The second one is that virtual figures should have an appropriate 3D representation for the purpose of cloth simulation and animation.

Body modelling approaches available today allow the interactive design of human bodies either from scratch or by modifying existing models (e.g. commercial libraries such as Fuse [2], Poser [3], Daz 3D [4], etc.). However, they require user intervention and thus suffer from slow production time and lack of efficient control.

An automatic body creation methods, such as 3D body scanner (e.g. 3dMD [5], Size Stream [6], Human Solutions [7], Vitronic [8], etc.), gives accurate and realistic results as it captures the body shape of a person in three dimensions. The result is a 3D model that can be used as it is or modified.

Since every human body is different, the advantage of the body scanner technique is to obtain a 3D realistically textured human body model (Fig. 16.1). Due to its precision (millimetre based), it's possible to reconstruct any features of the body shape.

Also, we can generate a controllable diversity of appearance in body models using interpolation methods that start with range scan data and use data interpolation. Thus, the automatic modelling approach introduced by Seo and Magnenat-Thalmann [9] is aimed at realistic human models whose sizes are defined and controlled by numerous anthropometric parameters (Fig. 16.2).

In the context of reproducing historical figures, this method permits to modify and vary shapes easily to meet new needs (e.g. height, leg length, waist girth, etc.).

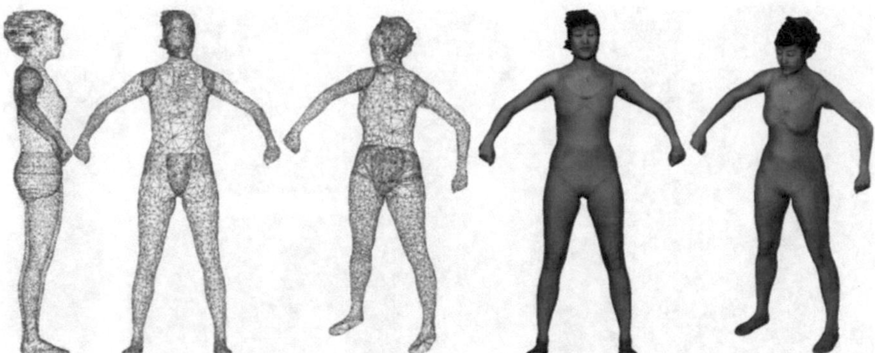

Fig. 16.1 3D Scanner results—acquisition, 3D mesh processing, texture mapping (MIRALab) (© 2006 Uni. Geneva/MIRALab, reprinted with permission)

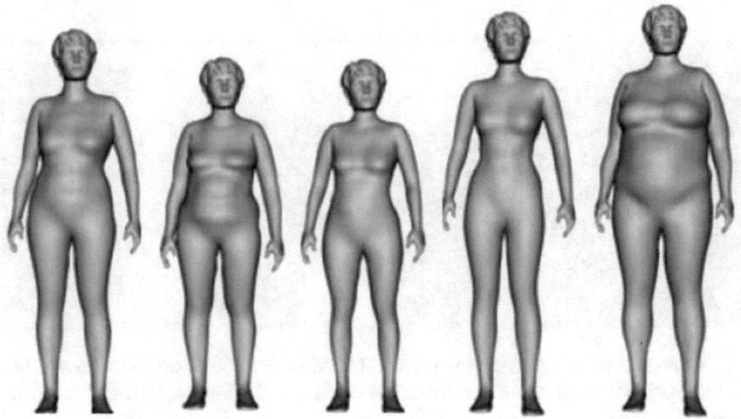

Fig. 16.2 Body models generated by controlling anthropometric parameters (MIRALab) (© 2004 Uni. Geneva/MIRALab, reprinted with permission)

Head Modelling

It's not just the body shape that provides an identification to a historical figure, but it is mainly the head and the face that give personality to the character.

To illustrate the process of head creation, we will take the example of the John Calvin project: The main difficulty is to obtain a 3D representation that accurately reflects and respects the character built upon the collective memory.

The 3D modelling of the reformer (the face, head and body) was based on an interpretation approach made from the iconographic data (Fig. 16.4). Somehow, we have produced animated 3D prints transcoded and adapted to today's world. Our John Calvin is not from the sixth century, it is a virtual artistic creation. Nevertheless, it is a representation of him. We sought to identify the lines of force and the inherent features of the model that produce the legendary John Calvin: emaciated profile of John Calvin, his long thin nose and his pointed beard (Fig. 16.3).

Fig. 16.3 3D reconstitution of John Calvin (International Museum of the Reformation and MIRALab) (© 2008 International Museum of the Reformation and Uni. Geneva/MIRALab, reprinted with permission)

Fig. 16.4 3D head modelling process (International Museum of the Reformation and MIRALab) (© 2008 International Museum of the Reformation and Uni. Geneva/MIRALab, reprinted with permission)

The process of creating an average human face is well established; however, to achieve a realistic, animated, engraving style, we have to make the best out of every step we do: from collecting references (iconographies, text description), planning before modelling, topology, texturing and rendering.

After having prepared our reference images (e.g. colour, distortion, etc.) in an image processing application, we imported them into our 3D application software to use them as a template for modelling. The techniques used were a mix between a polygonal and sculpting approach. Polygonal modelling was chosen to create the base mesh and generate a good topology, which was very significant for the head model to be able to deform well into our facial animation software.

The basic 3D model was then imported into a digital sculpting and painting commercial software (Zbrush), to be refined and detailed. To finalize the model, a texture painting process was applied to the 3D mesh by using the reference images of the reformer (Fig. 16.4).

16.2.1.2 Cloth Modelling

Clothing and accessories are essential tools for studying cultural and social history. These artefacts help to tell the story of status differences and class aspirations through the materials used and the cut of the garment.

Non-verbal communication is often assumed only to rely on the body language such as having the arms crossed or pupils dilated or even having clenched hands or fake smiles. However, the types of clothes we wear are a form of corporal communication. We could easily determine the age, gender, political opinions and social class of a person by their clothing style.

Modelling the clothes is a significant part. For that purpose, we use a platform for 3D virtual prototyping of garments called Fashionizer, which was developed in MIRALab, University of Geneva [10–13]. It integrates the design of 2D pattern, simulation of fabrics, virtual human animation, comfortability evaluation, real-time animation and visualization.

The Fashionizer platform is based on general mechanical and collision-detection schemes and allows for the simulation of multiple interacting garments and bodies. Combined with animation, Fashionizer is a powerful system allowing to compute the correct behaviour of cloth. To illustrate the process of creating and simulating the garments, we will take the example of the EPOCH project: The Abbey at the archaeological site of Ename in Belgium has been chosen for the 3D simulation of the daily life inside the Abbey during the twelfth century.

Design of the Patterns

The workflow of Fashionizer takes an analogy to what truly happens during the creation of "real clothing". A garment is composed of several 2D patterns, made of 2D polygons, connected by seam lines. The patterns describe the surface of a fabric. The dimension of these patterns corresponds to the size of the body to be dressed.

Therefore, careful research on the clothing culture of the monks' period is carried out, and the collected data, such as patterns of different garments, images and historical descriptions, are used as a base for the restitution of several types of clothes and their simulation around the bodies.

The clothes of the monks, the prior and subprior are the same. The monks wear a black *roccus* over a white tunic. Both are made of wool (raw, not smooth). A tunic is a long dress that reaches the feet. A *roccus* is a long coat with wide sleeves and a pointed cap (Fig. 16.5).

Placement of the Patterns Around the 3D Body

The patterns obtained in the previous part are placed around the virtual body, and the seaming process is executed. The seams force the patterns to approach each other and pull the matching pattern borders together during simulation (Fig. 16.6).

Garment Parameters

The garment properties, and particularly the physical parameters (e.g. cotton, linen, silk, etc.), are then adjusted to obtain a realistic behaviour. We have two categories

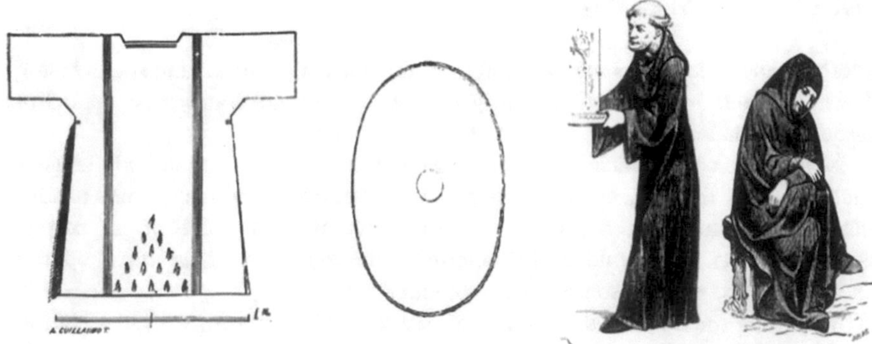

Fig. 16.5 Historical references of the monks' clothes (EU project EPOCH - MIRALab) (© 2004 FP6 Project EPOCH and Uni. Geneva/MIRALab, reprinted with permission)

Fig. 16.6 2D patterns in the 2D viewer, placement on the body in the 3D viewer (MIRALab) (© 2004 Uni. Geneva/MIRALab, reprinted with permission)

of parameters: environment (global parameters) and object (local parameters). Among the global simulation parameters, the major ones are gravity, collision distance and collision detection modes. Local parameters include elasticity, surface density, bending rigidity, friction values, Poisson coefficient and viscosity and non-linear elasticity values, which are the mechanical properties of the garment.

Fitting of the Garment

Once the texturing and garment property setting is done, we can start the "fitting" process, by applying mechanical simulation, which forces the surfaces to approach along the seam lines. The surface deforms according to the shape of the body. The

Fig. 16.7 Example of a clothed monk (MIRALab) (© 2004 Uni. Geneva/MIRALab, reprinted with permission)

simulation runs until the fabric has dynamically stabilized. The resulting position is a suitable starting point for garment simulation on the animated body.

Animation of Clothing
The realistic clothing animation is simulated according to the movement of the virtual human. This process is realized through collision detection and friction with the surface of the body. The mechanical parameters are regulated at this stage and are adapted to the visual information. The adjustments to the simulation parameters can be different from those used during the fitting process. The mechanical simulation gives realism to the animation of clothing on the virtual character by reproducing the exact behaviour of fabric (Fig. 16.7).

16.3 Intangible Heritage

16.3.1 The Use of Animated Virtual Humans in Historical Sites

Adding historically consistent virtual humans into virtual reconstruction allows adding the social aspect which is one of the relevant dimensions that we may consider while attempting a consistent restitution. It permits the creation of more realistic simulations with the inclusion of specific ambiences, atmospheres or dramatic elements. In the cases of a virtual simulation of an ancient site, the choice to stage a virtual re-enactment of a daily life scenario is made to enhance the virtual simulations with the inclusion of such dimensions.

In this section, we present different case studies where virtual humans re-enacted situations and activities typically performed during ancient times. These case studies are sort into two “categories” where animated virtual humans are used for either of the following:

- Inhabited virtual restitution of historical site where the virtual humans will perform specific actions and thereby attempt to bring a comprehensive simulation of the site (LIFEPLUS, ERATO)
- Virtual simulation of a historical figure where the principal objective is to help foster a better understanding of his life and actions. The key elements of the restitution will be then mainly based on the “image” that the virtual figure will drive based on behavioural aspects such as posture, head and clothes, body movements and gestures (Calvin).

16.3.2 Animating Virtual Humans

16.3.2.1 Body Animation and Skinning

Different approaches are possible for animating virtual characters. To obtain more realistic motion and expressions, we chose an optical motion capture system (VICON) for recording body and facial animation (Fig. 16.8).

Several video references were employed as a support for the motion capturing sessions: In all the case studies digitally recorded video sequences featuring real actors playing the scenario (to be virtually reproduced) are prepared with the assistance of the historical advisors. Then, a projector is used to screen the real actor’s performances in order to provide the motion-captured subject with an

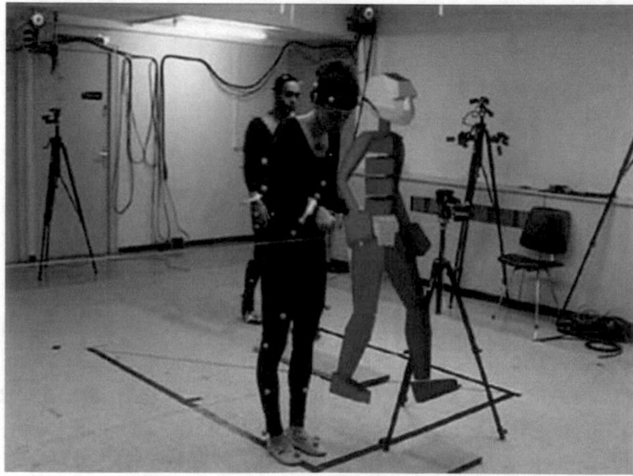

Fig. 16.8 Optical motion capture session—LIFEPLUS project (MIRALab) (© 2003 FP5 Project LIFEPLUS and Uni. Geneva/MIRALab, reprinted with permission)

appropriate reference to time, allowing the synchronization of his actions with the recorded sounds and dialogues.

The 3D body model is attached to the skeleton to perform the recorded animations. A proper skin attachment is essential for skeletal deformation. The attachment assigns for each vertex of the mesh, the affecting bones and corresponding weights. Once the 3D model is properly attached to the skeleton, transformation of the bone automatically drives transformation of the skin mesh (Fig. 16.9).

After the completion of the skinning process, the captured movements corresponding to the various parts of the scenario are converted to separate key-framed animations ready to be applied to our skeleton hierarchy that will drive the virtual characters.

For finger animation we opted for manual key framing; indeed the subtle motions of the fingers, nevertheless, are complex to capture. Due to their small scale, the high degrees of freedom of hands and frequent occlusions, optical motion capture of fingers requires a larger number of cameras to cover the same space and laborious manual post-processing (Fig. 16.10).

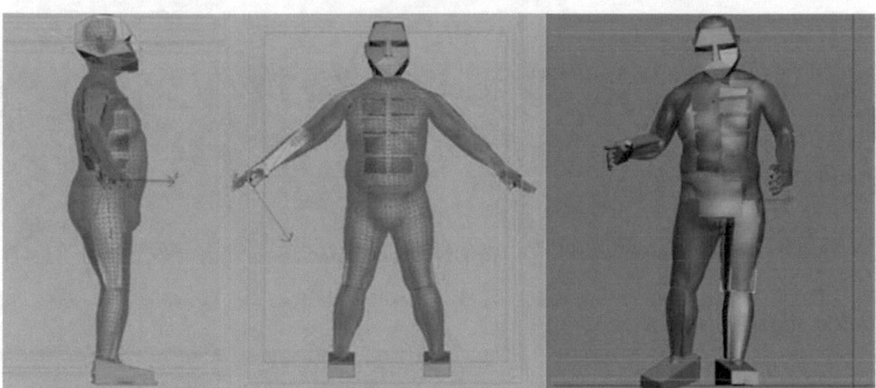

Fig. 16.9 Skinning process (MIRALab) (© 2002 Uni. Geneva/MIRALab, reprinted with permission)

Fig. 16.10 From motion capture to body animation—Calvin animation (MIRALab) (© 2008 Uni. Geneva/MIRALab, reprinted with permission)

Since the final animation resulting from the application of motion-captured data exhibits realistic motion behaviour but a limited flexibility, the different recorded tracks are connected to each other to produce smooth sequences featuring no interruption during their execution.

16.3.2.2 Facial Animation

There are various ways to animate the facial mesh, depending upon the application, the available tools and the desired performance.

In our case, the facial animation of our virtual character is built upon a mixed process between commercial software for capturing motion (VICON) and house-made software using MPEG-4 parameter system for facial animation (Fig. 16.11) [14]. The algorithm is based on general-purpose feature point-based mesh deformation, which is extended for a facial mesh using MPEG-4 facial feature points (Figs. 16.12 and 16.13).

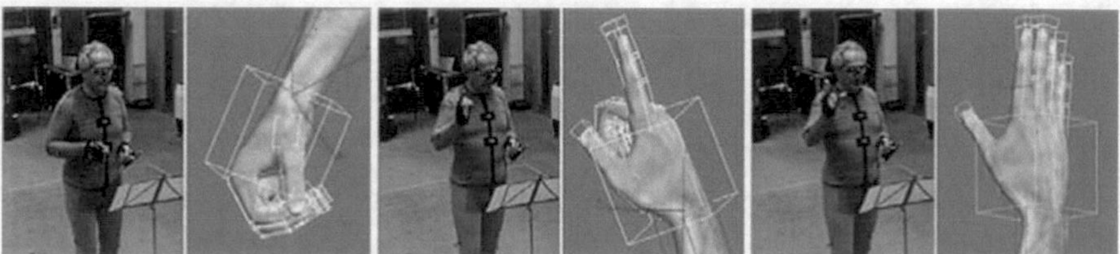

Fig. 16.11 Fingers manual animation—Calvin gesture (MIRALab) (© 2008 Uni. Geneva/MIRALab, reprinted with permission)

Fig. 16.12 Motion-captured data loaded on top of a virtual actor re-enacting a Greek drama—ERATO project (MIRALab) (© 2005 FP5 Project ERATO and Uni. Geneva/MIRALab, reprinted with permission)

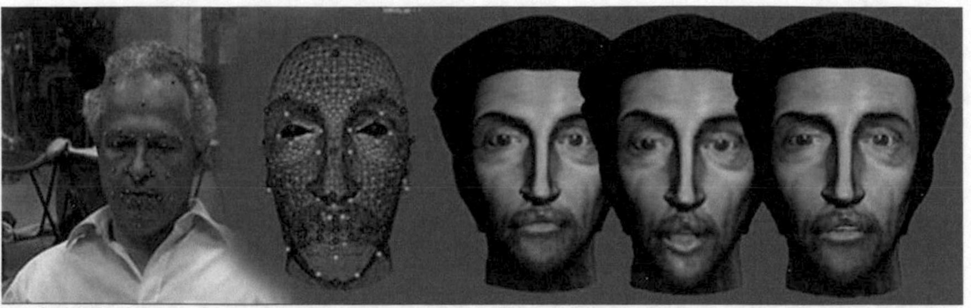

Fig. 16.13 From motion capture to 3D facial animation—Calvin facial animation (MIRALab) (© 2008 Uni. Geneva/MIRALab, reprinted with permission)

16.3.3 Virtual Humans Re-enacting Activities in Historical Sites

16.3.3.1 Inhabited Virtual Heritage Case Studies

In the following case studies, we present a real-time virtual re-enactment of a Roman play in a virtual Aspendos theatre [15] and a daily-life scenario at the augmented thermopolium in Pompeii [16]. In both cases, the role of virtual humans is to relate a story about social places and to convey information elements related to the way of life of that society.

After having gathered all the cultural and historical information and sources, the preparation of the 3D virtual humans, with their garments, props, musical instruments and masks, is done according to the specific restrictions inherent to real-time simulation. The different phases that were necessary to complete the modelling and animation of virtual human models are described in the section above.

Setting Up the Scenario

The preparation of the scenario was assigned to professional teams of screenwriters assisted by archaeologists and specialists whose role was to supervise and guide the process, thus ensuring the historical validity of the final results.

Five different scenario-based simulations were prepared for the two case studies:

Two scenarios describing daily life situations in Pompeii, taking place, respectively, in the thermopolium of Vetutius Placidus and in a garden of a villa located nearby, and three excerpts from Greek dramas to be re-enacted in the virtually restituted theatre of Aspendos, including the *Agamemnon* of Aeschylus, the *Antigone* of Sophocles and a choral song from the *Iliad* (Fig. 16.14).

The scenario involves several interactions between the virtual actors at the same time. In order to assist such complexity, a scripting language was implemented to control and drive such interactions.

Fig. 16.14 The selected sites: thermopolium Pompeii and theatre of Aspendos (MIRALab) (© 2005 Uni. Geneva/MIRALab, reprinted with permission)

Fig. 16.15 Excerpt from the on-site filmed live action reference footage (MIRALab) (© 2004 Uni. Geneva/MIRALab, reprinted with permission)

The case study of thermopolium of Vetutius (LIFEPLUS project)

Taverns were popular and characteristic social gathering places in ancient Pompeii. They were public establishments where hot food and drinks were served and where many people used to meet to eat, drink, play or simply talk.

The thermopolium of Vetutius Placidus was chosen for an AR real-time simulation. The structure of the considered building is simple and typical of the Roman period and is one of the best preserved at the archaeological site since most of its original furniture was found during the site's excavation (Fig. 16.15).

The implemented scenario is taking place inside the tavern's main entrance room. In order to achieve the transposition of the scripted scenario into the virtual simulation and to assist character modelling and animation phases, several references to real-world examples were employed. To support the creation of the virtual dresses, for instance, and to provide tangible physical references for their

Fig. 16.16 On-site historical data (EU project LIFEPLUS–MIRALab) (© 2003 FP5 Project LIFEPLUS and Uni. Geneva/MIRALab, reprinted with permission)

Fig. 16.17 Results: the integrated scenario staging the virtual characters inside the thermopolium (MIRALab) (© 2004 Uni. Geneva/MIRALab, reprinted with permission)

simulation, real prototype counterparts were designed, tested and commissioned to a tailor using the available historical data (Fig. 16.16).

The virtual characters performing the simulation were defined as acting as they normally would have in a real tavern and as exhibiting historically consistent outfits in order to mimic and virtually recreate specific scenes that can still be observed on the frescos on site and reproduce dialogues taken from inscriptions found there (Fig. 16.17).

The case study of Aspendos (ERATO project)

In this case, a Roman play simulation is staged in the virtual theatre of Aspendos, thus giving a better representation of the use of this space. Different stages were necessary to plan this scenario: the preparation of the simulated echoic 3D sound speeches and the recording of the motion-captured movements to be applied to the virtual actors, in order to re-enact the selected Roman play. The process for the implementation of the scenario and all the necessary operations needed to prepare the virtual actors for the real-time simulation are similar to the ones presented in the previous section (Figs. 16.18 and 16.19).

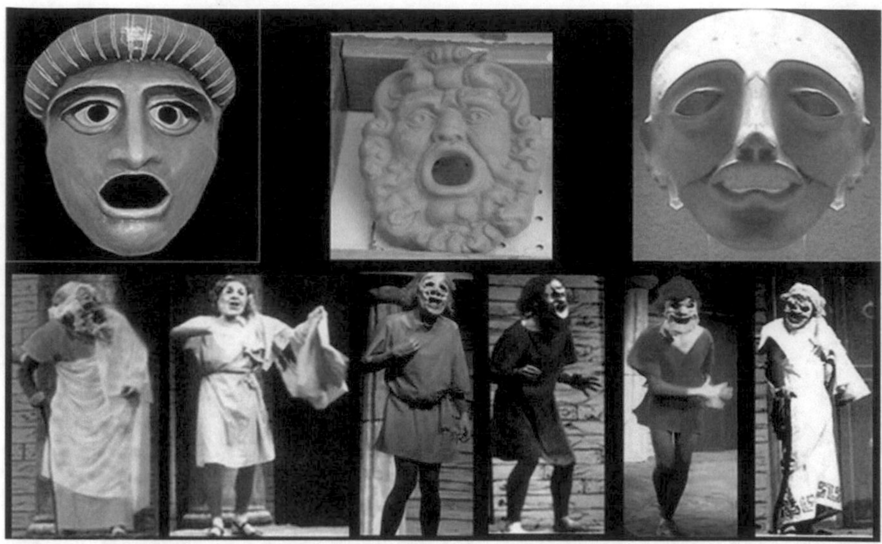

Fig. 16.18 Examples of Roman theatre masks (top) and actor's outfits (EU project ERATO–MIRALab) (© 2005 FP5 Project ERATO and Uni. Geneva/MIRALab, reprinted with permission)

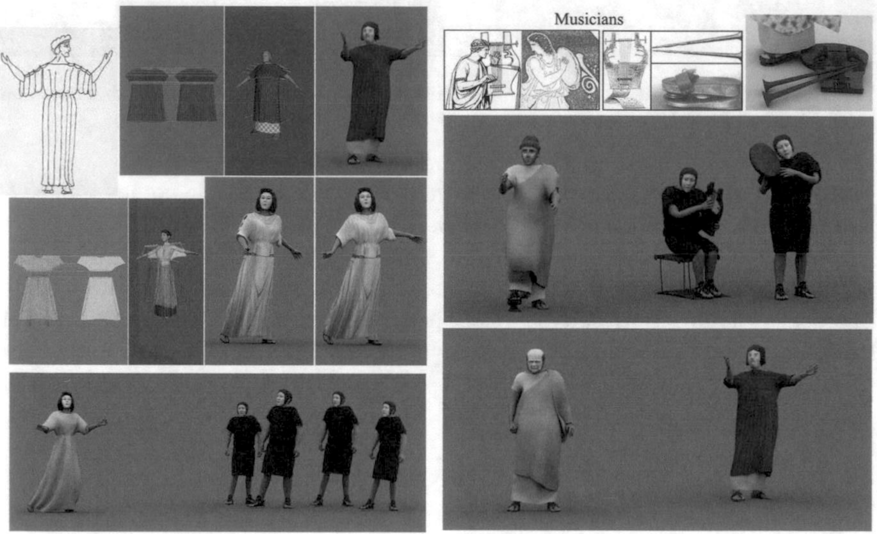

Fig. 16.19 Results: motion capture applied to virtual actors with masks and instruments (EU project ERATO–MIRALab) (© 2005 FP5 Project ERATO and Uni. Geneva/MIRALab, reprinted with permission)

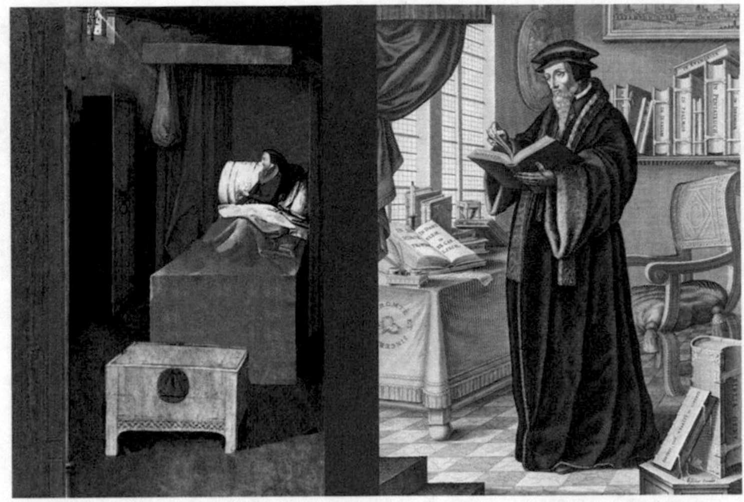

Fig. 16.20 Historical references (International Museum of the Reformation and MIRALab) (© 2008 International Museum of the Reformation and Uni. Geneva/MIRALab, reprinted with permission)

16.3.3.2 Virtual Simulation of a Historical Figure

Case Study: Simulation of John Calvin the Reformer

The principal objective of this simulation is to help foster a better understanding of a historical figure that belongs to the collective memory, John Calvin the Reformer (Ref article de Calvin). The Reformer has been simulated in 3D in his familiar surroundings and activities, featuring virtual representations of the reformation-era world and John Calvin's main occupations.

The 3D simulation of this mythic figure is based on the convergence of various historical data such as texts, stories and work of specialists of the Roman church reform (Fig. 16.20).

As a result, we provide 3D scenes depicting key moments in a day in the life of John Calvin [17]. We see him praying and preaching, arguing and advising, teaching, etc. The animation of the 3D Calvin was performed according to a scenario defined by historians and specialists of the reformation, who extracted from the historical texts explicit description of key moments in the life of the reformer which will constitute the intangible data that has to be transposed to the virtual word. A skilled theatre actor was hired for playing John Calvin's role. He was reading texts and tales while adapting the body language (movements of the head, the upper body, arms and finger gestures), thus strengthening his verbal expression while giving rhythm, action and artistic power to the scene (Fig. 16.21).

Fig. 16.21 Results: real-time scene with scripted scenario applied to virtual actors (MIRALab) (© 2009 Uni. Geneva/MIRALab, reprinted with permission)

16.4 Interactive Behaviour

16.4.1 Introduction

The restitution of an intangible scene is basically composed of two different tasks: reconstructing the tangible heritage of the cultural site and proposing a restitution of the intangible cultural heritage. See Arévalo et al. [18] and Foni [19] for a survey of the possible way to present a general classification of the different approaches that might be employed to constitute a visual representation of cultural heritage. A lot of work has already been done in the domain of virtual tangible heritage reconstruction (see [20–22]). The critical aspects in this specific area are the digitization and processing of the environment, the preparation of the lighting model and the modelling of the textures. In order to achieve an immersive cultural VR or AR application, including intangible content, the critical aspects are the modelling and animation of the virtual character. Indeed, the restitution of scenes involves virtual characters [23, 24].

In the last two decades, a lot of work has been done in the domain of virtual museum. Tangible and intangible restitution in virtual museums has to be historically precise, pedagogic and well designed. The additional difficulty is to provide an efficient application that satisfies the user's expectations. In this chapter, we present the different methods used to simulate interactive behaviour for virtual humans. We illustrate techniques based on our work for the special Lady Ada Byron's exhibition at the Nixdorf Museum in Germany (see Fig. 16.22 and [25]). A virtually modelled Lady Ada was projected onto a big wall screen inside a tunnel. She could react to the presence of people and talk to them, explaining historical clues related to her story.

We first look at tracking development, which allows the virtual character to sense the visitor, and then explain how this information is integrated to a global behaviour system that gives constituency to the virtual human and embed all necessary components.

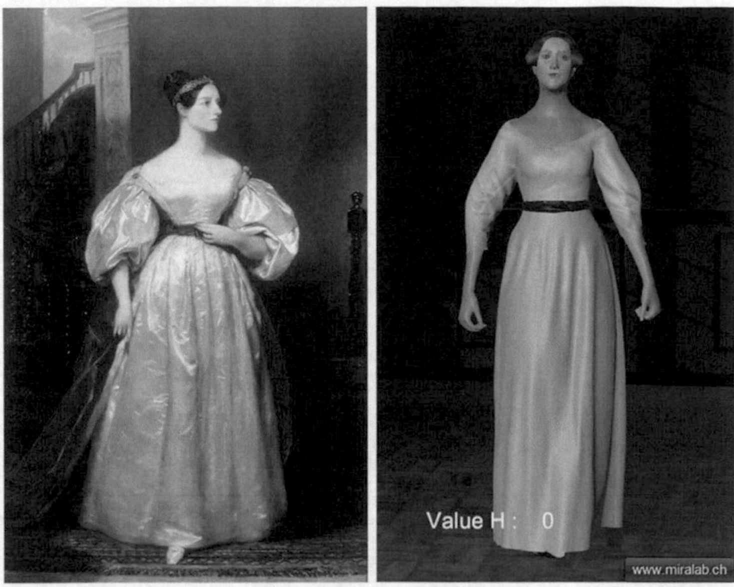

Fig. 16.22 Seventeenth-century painting and 3D reconstruction of Lady Ada Byron (MIRALab) (© 2015 Wikimedia Commons and Uni. Geneva/MIRALab, reprinted with permission)

Fig. 16.23 Tracked hand. The position of the centre of the hand is determined in real time by a Microsoft Kinect v1 that provides depth information (MIRALab) (© 2015 Microsoft and Uni. Geneva/MIRALab, reprinted with permission)

16.4.2 Tracking

To give senses to our VH, we need to get a stream of information about the behaviour of the passing people. Usually this means the use of sensors that can extract various information from the visitors, along the time and with sufficient accuracy. In our case study, we needed the position of the people at least 15 fps. This was made possible by the use of multiple sensors and tracking technology. The device Kinect v1 [26] (Microsoft Xbox 360), which was originally developed for home entertainment purposes, has also gained popularity in the scientific community [27, 28]. The Kinect is an infrared depth scanner and HD camera (720p), composed of an infrared (IR) projector, an infrared camera and an RGB camera (Fig. 16.23).

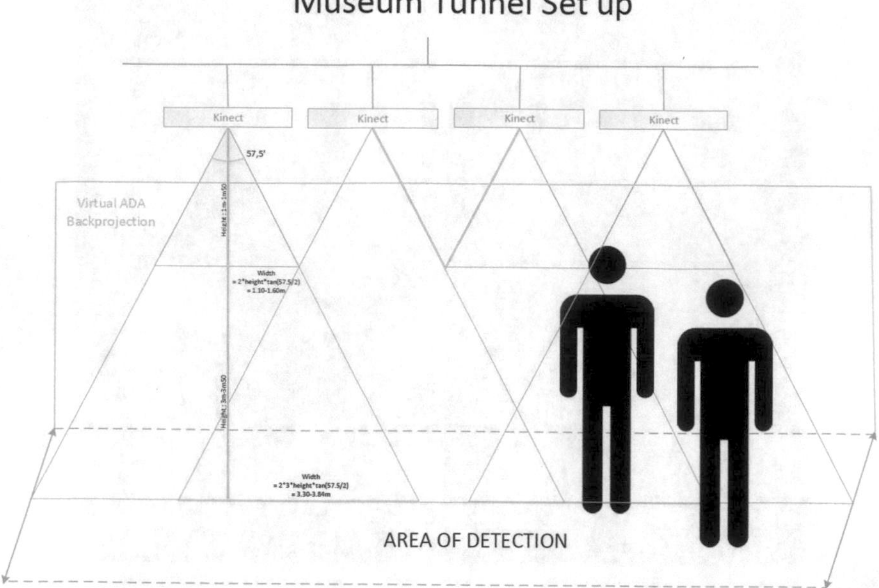

Fig. 16.24 Schematics of the sensor setup. On top are the four Kinects that detect people in a contiguous circular area (MIRALab) (© 2015 Uni. Geneva/MIRALab, reprinted with permission)

16.4.2.1 Acquisition

We set up 4 Kinect for Windows v1 side by side, such that the area covered by each Kinect is along the other one. All connected to a computer that will process the information and output on a video projector (Fig. 16.24).

16.4.2.2 Processing

The incoming data acquired is four images of depth at variable rates. We then have a buffer that waits to receive four images to then merge them into one to avoid missing the images. We extract blobs based on the depth information. We use a depth corresponding to a range of 40 cm, between 1.50 and 1.90 m above the ground, to be able to detect the most number of people. An additional function gives us the position of the centre of this detected blob over time. Another memory function ensures we know the position of the same person over time without misleading the person. The output is an array of the person's position over time, and so their trajectory.

16.4.3 Analysis

From the position of the user at a certain rate, we process these information to extract high-level information. Using Markov chains and statistical analysis, we define a spatial behaviour of people corresponding to their intentions based on a sequence of positions (around 40 positions). Therefore we know if the people are approaching the virtual human, going away or staying at their place. Two different information are outputted to the behaviour system:

- The spatial region where the people are at any time (near the screen, on the right, etc.)
- The intentions of the people that come from an analysis of the sequence of motion

These two pieces information are produced at different frequencies and will be integrated into the virtual human behaviour by replacing behaviour parameters when these information are changing. Therefore the behaviour loop is time independent of the tracking unit.

16.4.4 Behaviour Integration

The locomotion, gestures, speech and reaction of the avatar are driven by a behaviour management unit that guarantees the constituency and synchronization of the virtual human's visual behaviour. In the case of human–machine interaction for entertainment purposes, users expect a fast and reliable feedback from the interaction device, which is in this case the virtual human, as suggested in [29–31].

16.4.4.1 Behaviour Management System

The synchronization between the different possible actions of the virtual human and a huge reliability is essential for his credibility. Such objectives can be achieved using behaviour trees. Behaviour tree is a programming technique that allows management of errors and is well suited for real-time application (Fig. 16.25).

It is made of hierarchical states that can be an action, animation or modification of a variable. The behaviour in our case is oriented interaction: The VH passes from an idle state or static action to interaction mode where he is approaching the screen as people are coming and waves at them before talking.

16.4.4.2 Gaze

Having the virtual human looking at you even if you are moving is a common feature that is very important for credibility. We use position tracking and projected

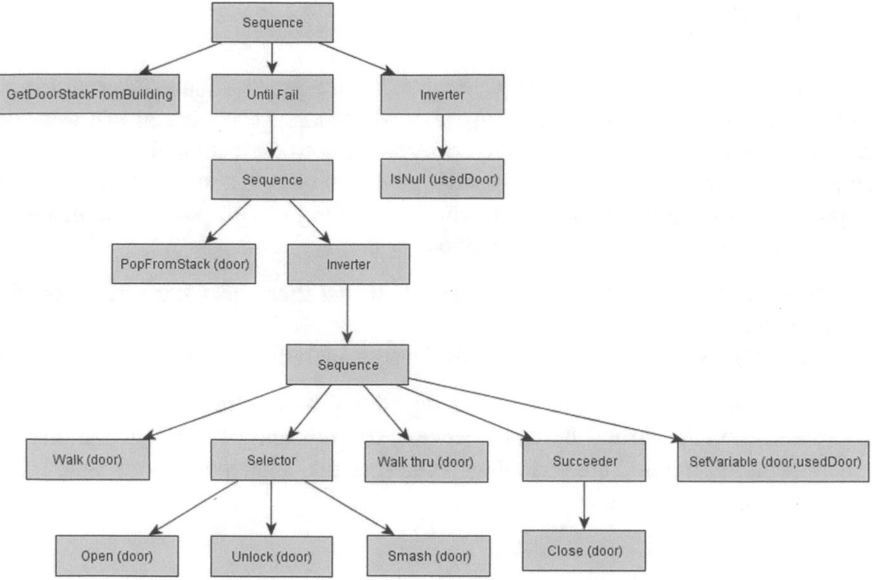

Fig. 16.25 Example of a behaviour tree illustrating how to open a door (Chris Simpson) (© 2014 Chris Simpson, reprinted with permission)

Fig. 16.26 Virtual Ada face close-up. The eyes follow the spectator motion (MIRALab) (© 2015 Uni. Geneva/MIRALab, reprinted with permission)

that into a plane so that every person in front of virtual Ada will feel that she is looking towards them (Fig. 16.26). An adjustment in depth is also necessary to avoid looking above people or in the case of children.

16.4.4.3 Locomotion

The motion of the virtual Ada should be related to the people's behaviour. Indeed, having the VH walking towards you when you approach him makes sense and is part of the believability. However, it is not necessary that virtual Ada gets close to the people. She can also walk away from them or exhibit other behaviours, as long as we feel the VH is somehow aware of the visitors. We use navigation system with pathfinding and root motion. Different techniques can be used for moving in space:

- Using the spatial motion embedded in the animation, if it is a long clip. It means we don't have precise control every second but roughly every 10 s.
- Using pathfinding and walk animation. This means the VH is already capable of walk animations. Then we can choose dynamically a place to go and the VH will move accordingly. Here again, we can follow either of the two following methods:
  - First move the virtual human in translation and/or rotation in the same time as the animation is playing. These two have to be synchronized to avoid a sliding effect.
  - Using so-called root motion. This allows the translation to be determined by the animation, which makes more sense and is much more easy to use, because no tuning is required. However, in that case the driving of the animation using pathfinding should be well thoughtout.

For virtual Ada, we defined six main spots that she is moving towards. The locomotion behaviour consists then in moving to a front spot when people are present and going to a back spot when nobody is there (Fig. 16.27). The gaze motion takes control of the joints around the head and overlays other animations such as lip syncing for talks, allowing constituent multiple animation at a time (e.g. talking and moving the head towards someone).

16.4.5 Emotion Recognition

Using the studies from [29, 32], we integrate an emotion recognition system based on body movement analysis. This allows the avatar to be aware of the emotion expressed by the people trying to interact with him. It will be then used during the avatar's talk to better communicate with the user (Fig. 16.28).

The emotion recognition system is based on an emotion model on one hand and a motion model on the other hand. A complete motion analysis is made in real time, then processed using statistical analysis. The recognition system output is an estimation of each people's emotion regarding the Russel classification. The motion of the virtual Ada will be influenced by the recognized emotion.

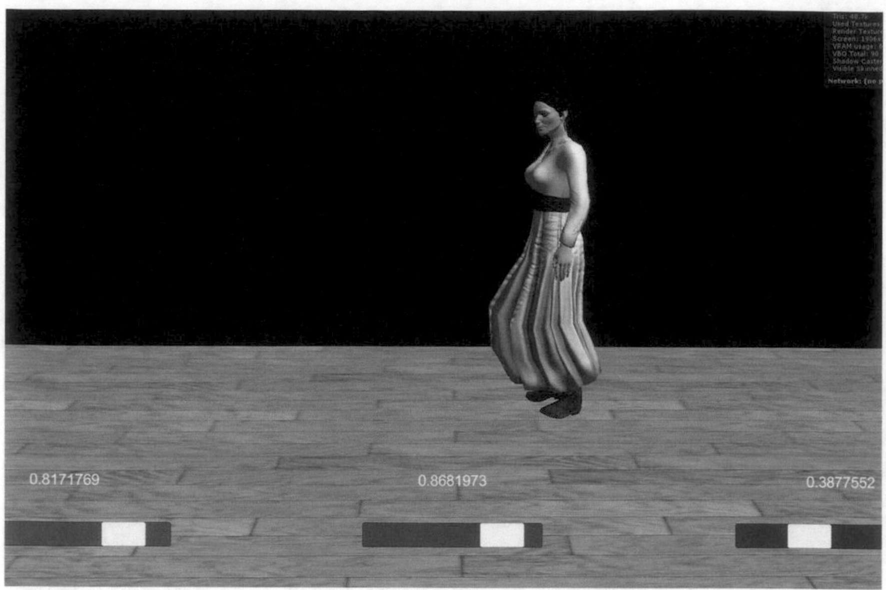

Fig. 16.27 Virtual Ada walking in a determined direction driven by the pathfinding algorithm (MIRALab) (© 2015 Uni. Geneva/MIRALab, reprinted with permission)

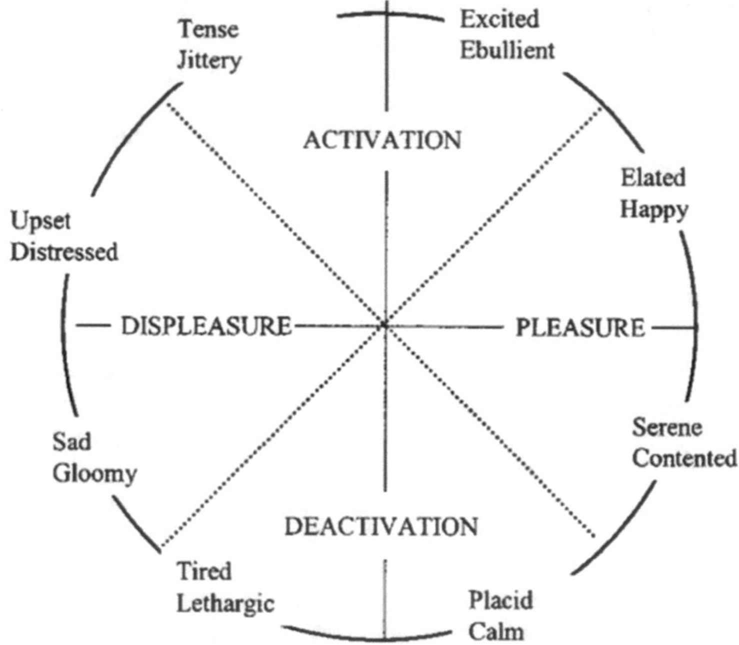

Fig. 16.28 Russel's continuous model of emotion. Each emotion is defined by a two-dimension coordinates, Pleasure and Arousal (American Psychological Association) (© *2003* American Psychological Association, reprinted with permission)

Fig. 16.29 Virtual character interaction with passing people in a tunnel. Sensors are located above the people and allow the interaction. Virtual Ada thanks the people for their visit to the exhibition and wishes them a good way back (MIRALab) (© *2015 Uni. Geneva/MIRALab*, reprinted with permission)

16.4.6 User Feedback and Application

A lot of adjustment has to be done on site as the timing of the virtual human behaviour needs to be tuned with the behaviour of multiple people in the real world. The real-time analysis and synthesis can be tricky and could result in bugs or blocked states. This is why the programme has to be bug resistant and running even if some parts of it are stuck. The result of the Ada exhibition (Fig. 16.29) is an interactive virtual human that reacts in accordance to visitor motion in a specific area. Position tracking, emotion recognition and behaviour analysis have been used to determine a precise state of the people.

16.5 Conclusion

Bringing a cultural context to life means to take into account a lot of information and constraints. Modelling a full human with his accessories and his clothes is already a challenge. We need then to model the environment and integrate the human inside the environment. Then the motion correlated with gesture and interaction has to be brought. Many decisions have to be made at different levels that will have consequences. The choice depends on what is the objective: what we want to show and what is the material at disposition. Depending on the way we want to interact (Kinect, position sensor, gesture sensor, distance, speech recognition), we can organize a different virtual human behaviour.

We showed through our examples corresponding to multiple European and side projects that each case study drove the development of the final application or research. For cultural heritage, the different resources to digitize can be complex and need careful attention. Furthermore, the interaction method should follow the educational requirements as for a specific use [33]. Current new techniques and devices allow for more virtual and augmented reality tours that can enhance the user's experience.

Acknowledgements This project has received funding from the European Union's Seventh Framework Programme for research, technological development and demonstration under grant agreement no 608013.

References

1. http://www.unesco.org/new/en/cairo/culture/tangible-cultural-heritage/
2. https://www.mixamo.com/fuse
3. http://my.smithmicro.com/poser-3d-animation-software.html
4. http://www.daz3d.com/
5. http://www.3dmd.com/
6. http://www.sizestream.com/
7. http://www.human-solutions.com
8. https://www.vitronic.com
9. N. Magnenat-Thalmann, H. Seo, F. Cordier, Automatic modeling of virtual humans and body clothing. J. Comput. Sci. Technol. **19**(5), 575–584 (2004)
10. P. Volino, N. Magnenat-Thalmann, Implementing fast cloth simulation with collision response, in *Computer Graphics International Proceedings, IEEE Computer Society* (2000), pp. 257–266
11. P. Volino, N. Magnenat-Thalmann, Accurate collision response on polygonal meshes, in *Computer Animation 2000 Proceedings, IEEE Computer Society* (2000)
12. P. Volino, N. Magnenat-Thalmann, Comparing efficiency of integration methods for cloth simulation, in *Computer Graphics International Proceedings* (2001)
13. N. Magnenat-Thalmann, P. Volino, F. Cordier, Avenues of research in dynamic clothing, in *Computer Animation 2000 Proceedings, IEEE Computer Society* (2002), pp. 193–202
14. T. Di Giacomo, C. Joslin, S. Garchery, H. Kim, N. Magnenat Thalmann, Adaptation of virtual human animation and representation for MPEG. Comput. Graph. **28**(4), 65–74 (2004)
15. A. Egges, S. Kshirsagar, N. Magnenat Thalmann, A model for personality and emotion simulation, in *Knowledge-Based Intelligent Information and Engineering Systems (KES2003)*, (2003), pp. 453–461
16. N. Magnenat-Thalmann, A. Foni, N. Cadi-Yazli, Real-time animation of ancient Roman sites, in GRAPHITE 2006

17. N. Magnenat-Thalmann, G. Papagiannakis, A. Foni, M. Arevalo-Poizat, N. Cadi-Yazli, Simulating life in ancient sites using mixed reality technology, in Spanish Computer Graphics Conference, invited paper, Seville (CEIG04) (2004)
18. M. Arévalo, N. Cadi-Yazli, N. Magnenat Thalmann, in *Proceedings of Progress in Cultural Heritage. Documentation, Preservation, and Protection 5th International Conference*, EuroMed 2014, Limassol, 3–8 Nov 2014
19. A.E. Foni, N.M.-T. George Papagiannakis, A taxonomy of visualization strategies for cultural heritage applications. J. Comput. Cult. Herit. **3**(1), 1–21 (2010)
20. A.E. Foni, G. Papagiannakis, N. Cadi-Yazli, N. Magnenat-Thalmann, Time-dependent illumination and animation of virtual Hagia-Sophia. Int. J. Archit. Comput. **5**(2), 283–301 (2007)
21. N. Magnenat-Thalmann, A.E. Foni, G. Papagiannakis, N. Cadi-Yazli, Real time animation and illumination in ancient Roman sites. IJVR **6**(1), 11–24 (2007)
22. G. Papagiannakis, N. Magnenat-Thalmann, Mobile augmented heritage: enabling human life in ancient pompeii. Int. J. Archit. Comput. **5**(2), 396–415 (2007)
23. A. Egges, G. Papagiannakis, N. Magnenat-Thalmann, Presence and interaction in mixed reality environments. Vis. Comput. **23**(5), 317–333 (2007)
24. K.C. Apostolakis, D.S. Alexiadis, P. Daras, D. Monaghan, N.E. O'Connor, B. Prestele, M.B. Moussa, Blending real with virtual in 3DLife, in *2013 14th International Workshop on Image Analysis for Multimedia Interactive Services (WIAMIS)*, IEEE (2013, July), pp. 1–4
25. http://www.hnf.de/en/sonderaustellungen/preview-ada-lovelace.html
26. https://developer.microsoft.com/en-us/windows/kinect/develop
27. A. Kitsikidis, K. Dimitropoulos, S. Douka, N. Grammalidis, Dance Analysis using Multiple Kinect Sensors. VISAPP2014, Lisbon, 2014, pp. 789–795
28. Q.-R. Mao, X.-Y. Pan, Y.-Z. Zhan, X.-J. Shen, Using Kinect for real-time emotion recognition via facial expressions. Front Inform. Technol. Electron. Eng. **16**(4), 272–282 (2015)
29. M.B. Moussa, N. Magnenat-Thalmann, Toward socially responsible agents: integrating attachment and learning in emotional decision-making. Comput. Anim. Virtual Worlds **24**(3–4), 327–334 (2013)
30. M. Gutiérrez, A. García-Rojas, D. Thalmann, F. Vexo, L. Moccozet, N. Magnenat-Thalmann, M. Spagnuolo, An ontology of virtual humans. Vis. Comput. **23**(3), 207–218 (2007)
31. Z. Kasap, N. Magnenat-Thalmann, Intelligent virtual humans with autonomy and personality: state-of-the-art. Int. Decis. Technol **1**(1, 2), 3–15 (2007)
32. S. Simon, L. Cuel, A. Aristidou, N. Magnenat-Thalmann, Continuous body emotion recognition system during theater performances, in *Conference of Animation and Social Agents*, CASA (2016)
33. N.E. O'Connor, Y. Tisserand, A. Chatzitofis, F. Destelle, J. Goenetxea, L. Unzueta, N.M. Thalmann, Interactive games for preservation and promotion of sporting movements, in *2014 22nd European Signal Processing Conference (EUSIPCO)*, IEEE, 2014, September, pp. 351–355

Chapter 17
Preservation and Gamification of Traditional Sports

Yvain Tisserand, Nadia Magnenat-Thalmann, Luis Unzueta, Maria T. Linaza, Amin Ahmadi, Noel E. O'Connor, Nikolaos Zioulis, Dimitrios Zarpalas, and Petros Daras

Abstract This chapter reviews an example of preservation and gamification scenario applied to traditional sports. In the first section, we describe a preservation technique to capture intangible content. It includes character modelling, motion recording, and animation processing. The second section is focused on the gamification aspect. It describes an interactive scenario integrated in a platform that includes a multimodal capturing system, a motion comparison and analysis, and a semantic-based feedback system.

Keywords Cultural heritage • Gamification • Sport preservation • Character modelling • Motion recording • Motion comparison

17.1 Introduction

Traditional Sports and Games (TSG) are a strong part of the identity of a society and a strong mechanism for the promotion of cultural diversity. This chapter aims to explain research done in order preserve and promote these TSG. The rich intangible cultural heritage expressed through TSG is inherently gamified. The preservation

Y. Tisserand (✉) • N. Magnenat-Thalmann
MIRALab CUI, University of Geneva, Geneva, Switzerland
e-mail: yvain.tisserand@miralab.ch; thalmann@miralab.ch

L. Unzueta • M.T. Linaza
Vicomtech IK4, San Sebastian, Spain
e-mail: lunzueta@vicomtech.org; mtlinaza@vicomtech.org

A. Ahmadi • N.E. O'Connor
INSIGHT, Dublin City University, Dublin, Ireland
e-mail: amin.ahmadi@dcu.ie; noel.oconnor@dcu.ie

N. Zioulis • D. Zarpalas • P. Daras
Centre for Research and Technology Hellas, Information Technologies Institute, Thessaloniki, Greece
e-mail: nzioulis@iti.gr; zarpalas@iti.gr; daras@iti.gr

M. Ioannides et al. (eds.), *Mixed Reality and Gamification for Cultural Heritage*,
DOI 10.1007/978-3-319-49607-8_17

and promotion of the cultural diversity through TSG is a challenging task due to trends in spectator and participative sports. Mainstream and commercial sports are generating more interest due to their access to high technology and mass media outreach. By developing a technological platform around the interpretation of digital content for TSG through a popular modern medium like gaming, their reach to wider audiences and their access to the general public will be increased. This work has been achieved within the framework of the EU RePlay project.

This work can be divided into two main steps. First of all, in order to preserve the TSG, the original game has to be captured. We propose to capture, model, and animate targeted TSG in 3D. The second step is to promote TSG; a gamification scenario will be described as well as its components. It includes an interaction system, a real-time multimodal 3D capturing system, a motion comparison module and a semantic-based feedback system.

17.2 Gamification for Traditional Sports and Games

17.2.1 Platform Overview

We present a multimodal 3D capturing platform coupled to a motion comparison system, in the context of a PLAY&LEARN scenario, which is based on the definition of storylines which highlight its main features and are used to extrapolate from the present into the future of TSG. The TSG considered in this work are the Gaelic sports from Ireland and Basque sports from France and Spain.

Next, we show a couple of examples of this kind of storylines and how the platform can be designed and built accordingly:

> John is a 10-year-old boy who plays Hurling at school. For his birthday, he got a Microsoft Kinect sensor with a new game called "Play against your Heroes". As stated in the box, the game allows John to play against several players. However, John is only interested in Hero1, who is one of his favourite Hurling players. The game should be played along and also includes a gadget that looks much like a Hurley. When the game starts, John has first to choose among the existing players. Of course, he chooses Hero1. He knows Hero1 is an expert in movement1, so he will try to mimic that movement1. The screen is divided into two parts. On the left part, John can see the movement1 played by Hero1. On the right part, he sees himself with the Hurley trying to mimic the movement. The Kinect captures his movement and presents it on a "puppet-like" avatar of himself. As he can see, there are several differences between his shot and movement1 from Hero1. Thus, he tries again to improve his performance.
>
> Sarah is a 12-year-old Pala player who wants to see how much she is improving her game. She has a Kinect at home, and she decides to buy the "Basque Ball game". On the screen, she can see herself and the national hero or heroine she has already chosen to compare her performance to the one of the national heroine and see how far hers is from that of her heroine. She tries to improve the movement, and she can check on the screen the trials she is doing and see if she is improving or not. She can play against any player too.

Thus, the PLAY&LEARN scenario focuses on children and teenagers having access to a low-cost motion capture set up (e.g., one Kinect sensor or a set of Kinect and wearable inertial measurement unit (WIMU) sensors) at home or school for them to learn and mimic the skills of a national/local hero. The user can optionally have a copy of an instrument related to the selected TSG (e.g., a hurley, a cesta, or a pala). The main goal of this scenario is to promote the TSG to children and thus encourage their participation. Users can learn, compare, and compete in the performance of sporting gestures and compare themselves to real athletes. Regarding the application, the player can initially configure his/her preferences (i.e., language, modality, the number of trials, and the hand to play). Then, the user must follow several steps (gain control of the Microsoft Kinect and watch the instructions and the 3D representation of the skill) before performing the skill. The user gets visual (two avatars side by side), semantic, textual, and score feedbacks.

A final issue is the estimation of the trajectory of the ball associated with the movement. As this is a home scenario, it does not seem to be feasible to have a real ball. However, the capturing platform can also estimate the ball trajectory to provide feedback to the player if WIMU sensors are included in the set up. This feedback does not show the real place where the ball should be, but positive/negative feedback based on the estimated trajectory of the ball and the accuracy of the performance of the skill. This is important for a positive reinforcement in an engaging strategy.

17.2.2 Description of the Infrastructure

In this scenario, different hardware configurations may be used. The simplest one consists of considering only one Microsoft Kinect sensor, while the most complex one considers a set of Kinects placed around the capture space and WIMU sensors placed on the user's body and the instrument related to the selected TSG. These different configurations depend on the space available for the set-up and the desired level of precision for the capture. Figure 17.1 shows a set up where one Kinect sensor is used and the user wears a set of WIMU sensors.

In this specific set-up, one Kinect sensor is used to capture the side-frontal view of the user. It is connected via USB to a PC running corresponding software for capturing and storing the streams. It should be placed no further than 4 m from the user. Regarding the WIMU sensors, they need to be placed at different segments of a subject. The WIMU data can be transferred to the PC via Bluetooth connection.

Correct sensor placement will provide the best body tracking performance for the Microsoft Kinect device. The sensor needs to be placed in a location so that it can see the entire body of the performer.

The sensor should be positioned between 0.6 and 1.8 m from the ground, ideally at least 15 cm above digital screens and also away from any speakers (at least 0.3 m). Additionally, the sensor needs to be placed near the edges of flat surfaces; otherwise, its bottom view will be clipped. Another important issue is the lighting conditions in which the sensor operates. The surrounding space needs to have enough bright light

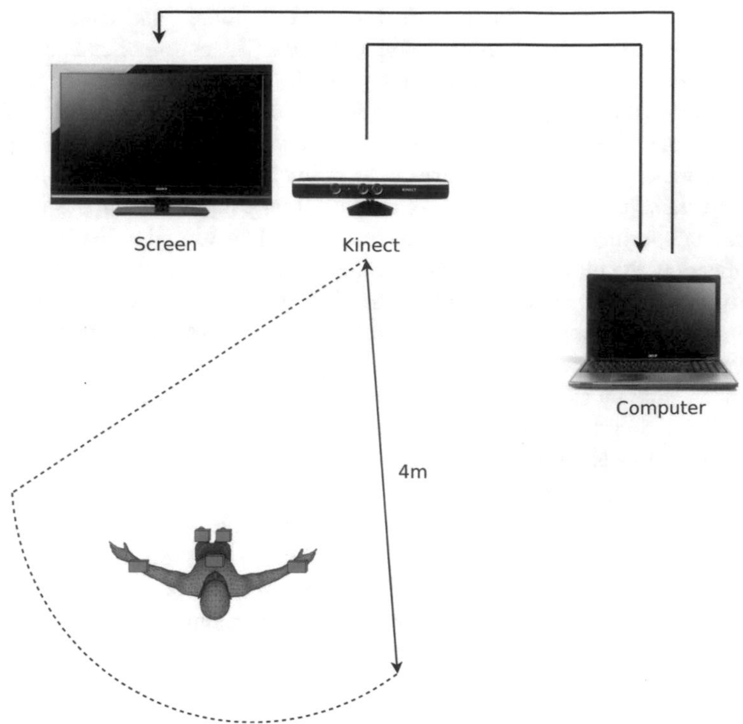

Fig. 17.1 Layout of the platform for the PLAY&LEARN scenario (Vicomtech) (© 2016 FP7 Project RePlay and Vicomtech-IK4, reprinted with permission)

and be equally lit. In any case, direct sunlight has to be avoided; thus, it needs to be placed away from windows, or they should be shaded during daylight usage.

Finally, in cases of reflective floors, it is recommended to place the sensor 1.1–1.2 m above the ground parallel to the floor. Otherwise, it should be placed lower (0.8 m above the floor) and rotated so that the depth camera only captures the user without the ground (Fig. 17.2). Such rules are not restrictive as long as the sensor can see the entire body of the user and the user can freely move around without having obstacles limiting the view of the sensor.

Besides the correct placement, extra attention has to be paid while using the Microsoft Kinect device. Despite being a state-of-the-art markerless motion tracking sensor, it suffers from some limitations regarding self-occlusion that need to be taken into account during its usage. First, users should try to keep most of their body parts directly visible to the sensor. Secondly, as the sensor was designed for frontal usage mainly with some rotational tolerance, it is recommended to keep the angle between the coronal plane of the user and the viewing direction of the sensor less than 45° (Fig. 17.3).

The platform including the Kinect and WIMU sensors should be portable and easy to handle in a plug-and-play mode. However, if the full configuration is used, a calibration phase must be considered, which should be done by a person with a

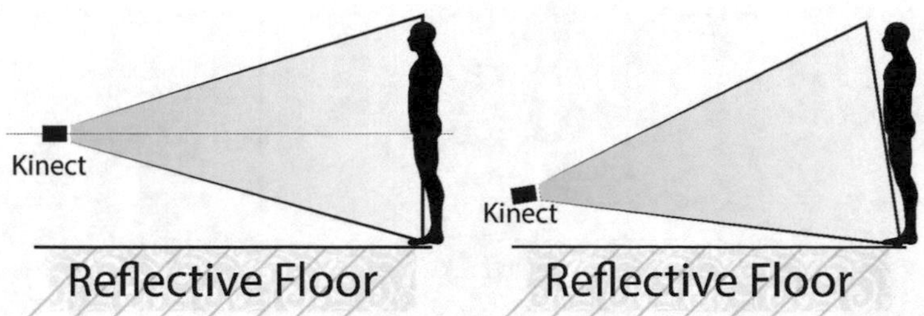

Fig. 17.2 Placement of the Microsoft Kinect in case of reflective floors (CERTH) (© 2016 FP7 Project RePlay and Centre for Research and Technology Hellas/CERTH, reprinted with permission)

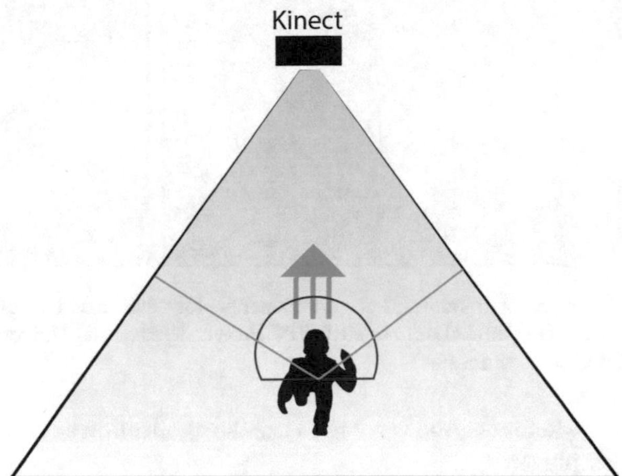

Fig. 17.3 Placement of the Microsoft Kinect for correct use (*top view*) (CERTH) (© 2016 FP7 Project RePlay and Centre for Research and Technology Hellas/CERTH, reprinted with permission)

basic technical knowledge about the system. Besides, the platform works on the basis of the "Quick Post" concept. This means that important feedback will be given as soon as possible, while other statistics should be provided later. In this way, the platform should give direct feedback.

17.2.3 Interaction Experience of the User

Figure 17.4 displays a diagram showing the relationship between the modules and components of the capturing platform.

The user opens the application at the "Preferences" screen (Fig. 17.5) to select the language in which the application will run, the modality (Gaelic sports or Basque pelota), the skills to be played, the number of trials, the hand normally

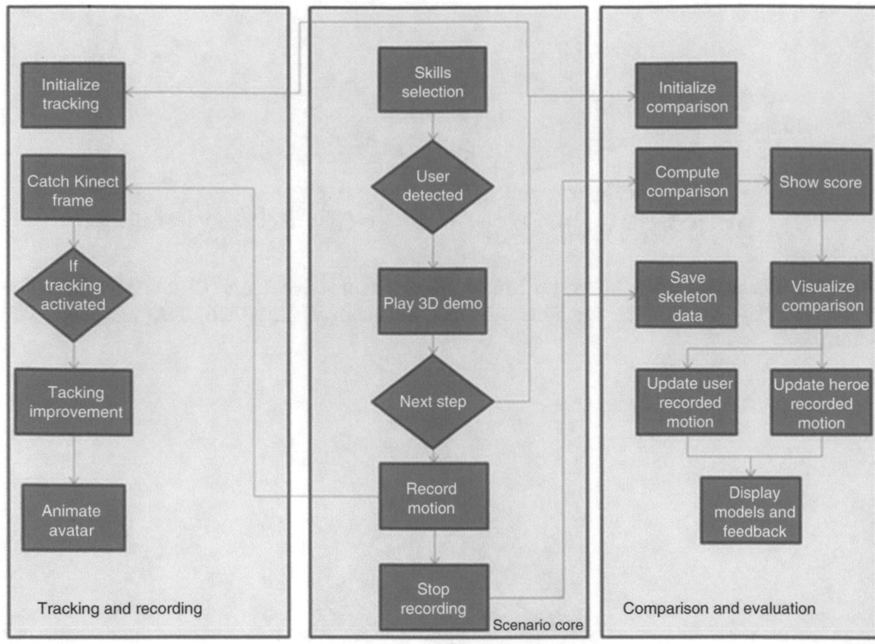

Fig. 17.4 Combination of modules and components for the coach application of the PLAY&LEARN scenario (MIRALab) (© 2016 FP7 Project RePlay and University of Geneva/ MIRALab, reprinted with permission)

used to play, and whether he/she is going to use the application as an experienced or non-experienced player.

Figure 17.6 displays the workflow of the capturing platform. To start the trial, the user must wave his/her right hand to be recognized by the Kinect sensor and to gain control of the movements of the avatar. Then, the user can watch the instructions to perform the current skill. Afterwards, the user can watch a 3D representation of the skill performed by a national hero. Finally, the user can perform the skill after the countdown, when the "Go" alert appears. In order to compare the skill, two avatars are presented side by side, one representing the performance of the national hero and the other one representing that of the player (Fig. 17.7).

17.3 Traditional Sport and Game Capture, Modeling, and Animation

To capture TSG skills in 3D, three main steps are required. First of all, we need to create the shape of the 3D avatar that represents the athlete; then we need to capture its movement; and, finally, we need to animate the 3D avatar according to the captured animations.

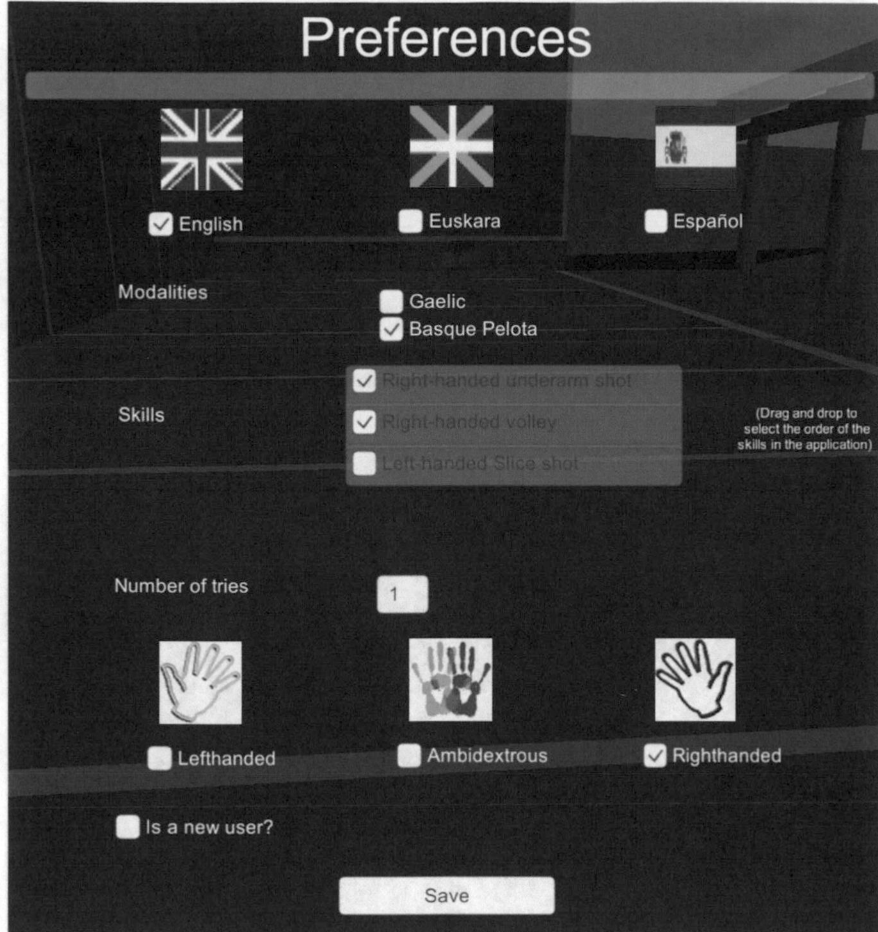

Fig. 17.5 Selection of the preferences in the PLAY&LEARN scenario (Vicomtech) (© 2016 FP7 Project RePlay and Vicomtech-IK4, reprinted with permission)

17.3.1 Avatar Creation

The time-consuming manual process of avatar creation has been replaced over time by several techniques. Different methodologies have been proposed and can be classified into three main categories: creative [1], reconstructive [2], and interpolation methods [3]. We propose a reconstruction-based technique that uses an image-based 3D scanner to capture the user in a fast and accurate manner. The post-processing time and the cost of the installation can be significantly decreased, compared to the previous generation of body scanners, such as the laser-based body scanner.

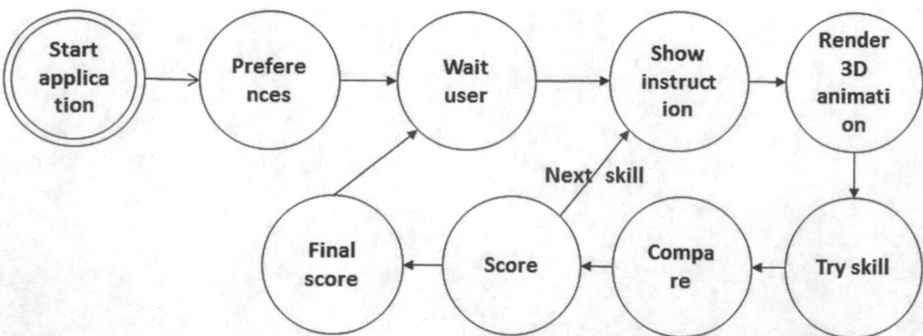

Fig. 17.6 Global flow of the PLAY&LEARN application (MIRALab) (© 2016 FP7 Project RePlay and University of Geneva/MIRALab, reprinted with permission)

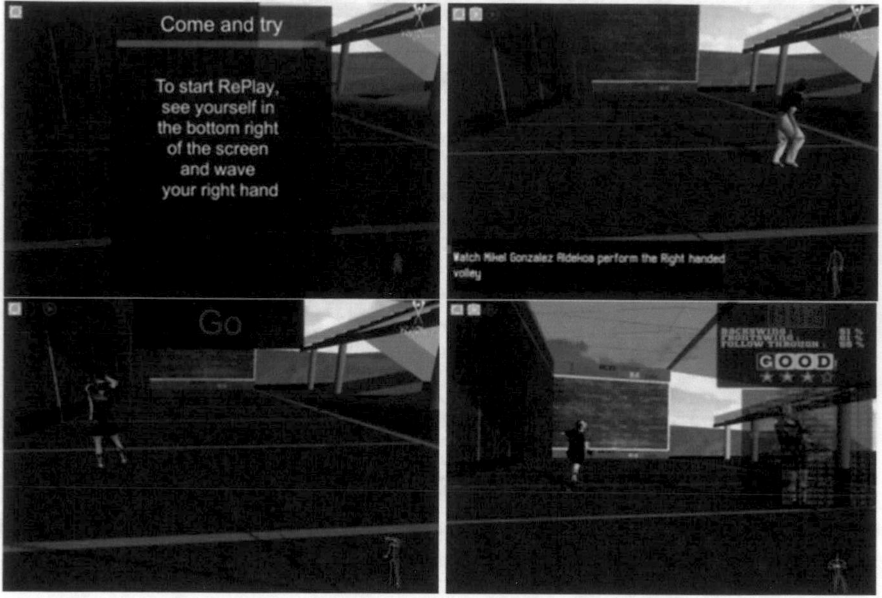

Fig. 17.7 Several screenshots of the capturing platform for the PLAY&LEARN scenario (MIRALab) (© 2016 FP7 Project RePlay and University of Geneva/MIRALab, reprinted with permission)

The system is based on photogrammetry technologies. It is composed of a large number of compact cameras that are synchronized and controlled by a computer. Within less than a second, pictures of the subject are taken by the camera cluster from different angles. This very short delay during the capture minimizes user movements, which drastically reduces the noise in the generated model. The images can then be used for 3D reconstruction. Finally, a virtual skeleton is inserted into the model to be able to animate it (Fig. 17.8).

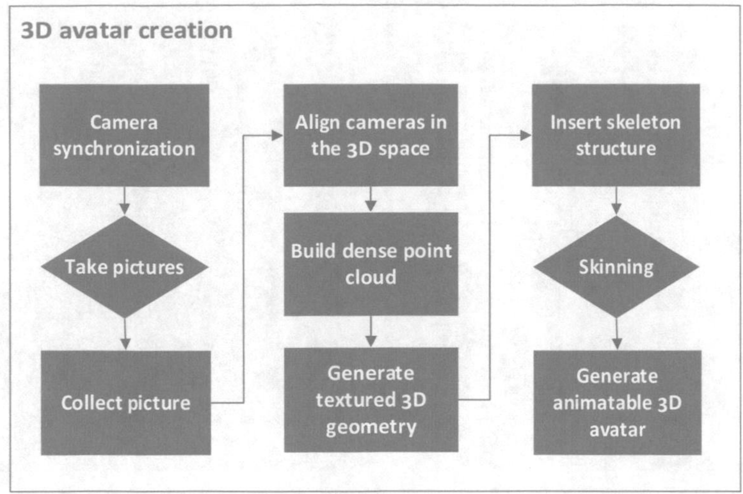

Fig. 17.8 3D avatar pipeline (MIRALab) (© 2016 FP7 Project RePlay and University of Geneva/ MIRALab, reprinted with permission)

Our system is composed of a cluster of 80 compact cameras. They have been placed onto a hexagonal structure. Our acquisition volume covers an adult human, and the number of cameras and their positions has been chosen accordingly. A made-to-measure green fabric has been placed over the support structure to control the light conditions and to facilitate the post-processing of the acquired data. To get diffuse light inside the scanner, flexible led ribbons have been attached to the support structure (Fig. 17.9).

All cameras are connected to a single computer. A dedicated library has been used to control, to synchronize and to take pictures with the camera remotely (CHDK). Custom scripts have been written to remotely control and synchronize the individual cameras, to adjust the zoom, to take shots, and to copy back recorded pictures to the controller computer. After a short synchronization step, we can remotely take a synchronized shot.

The user simply has to stand inside the structure and to hold the position for a second. Once the pictures are taken, they are automatically copied to the hard drive of the controller computer for reconstruction.

We use an image-based 3D reconstruction software (Agisoft PhotoScan) to generate the 3D avatar mesh. As input, it requires a set of images. An optional mask can be used for accelerated 3D reconstruction. The process can be divided into four steps: camera alignment, point cloud creation, mesh reconstruction, and texturing (see Fig. 17.10).

The camera alignment consists of two sub-steps. First, features are detected in all images. In the second step, the software tries to match the features pairwise in the set of images. Therefore, a sufficient overlap of the images is needed. It can be

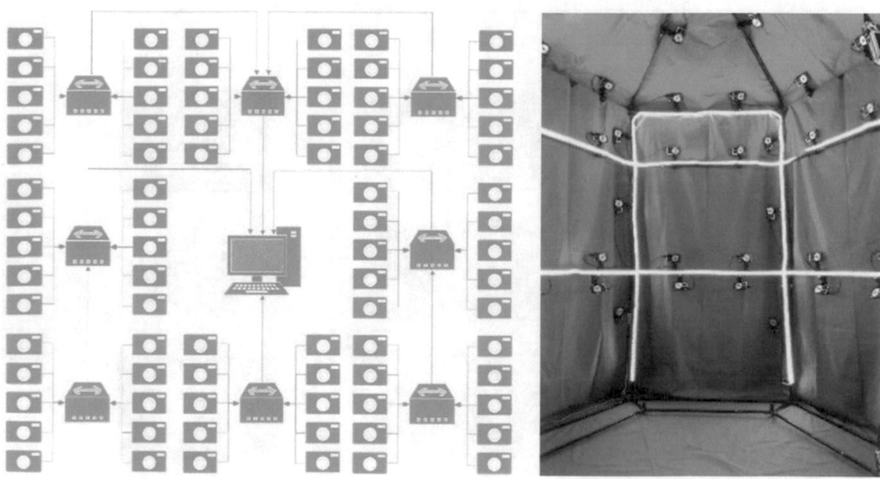

Fig. 17.9 Overview of the image-based 3D scanner (MIRALab) (© 2016 FP7 Project RePlay and University of Geneva/MIRALab, reprinted with permission)

Import dataset

Calculate camera position

Generate point cloud

Generate mesh

Generate texture

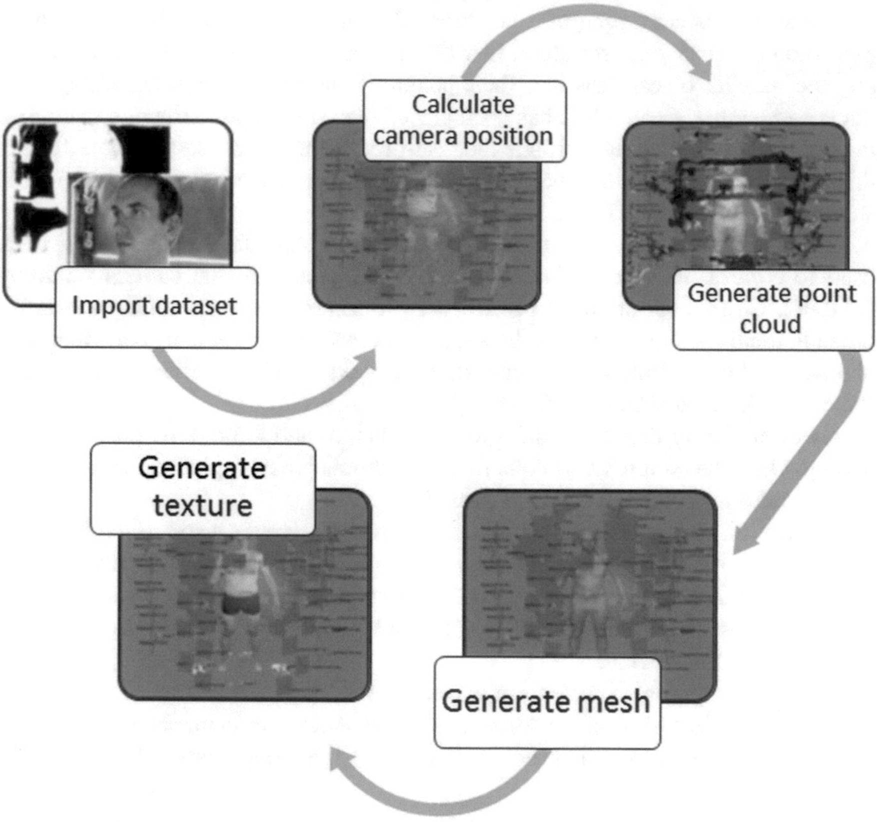

Fig. 17.10 3D reconstruction pipeline using the image-based method (MIRALab) (© 2016 FP7 Project RePlay and University of Geneva/MIRALab, reprinted with permission)

achieved by carefully controlling the position and zoom level of the cameras. Several tests have been conducted to develop our current set up.

We obtain a fully reconstructed and textured 3D. However, small corrections are needed to remove mesh artefacts in the obtained 3D model (Fig. 17.11). First, we apply Laplacian smoothing to reduce the noise and to smooth the mesh. Then, to reduce the number of polygons and to get a regular grid on the 3D mesh, we apply a Quadric Edge Collapse Decimation algorithm. As a result, we obtain a static mesh that represents the athlete.

A final step is then required in order to have a fully animatable 3D avatar. A virtual skeleton has to be added as well as virtual garments (Fig. 17.12). The result is a fully functional dressed 3D avatar that can be used and animated in any 3D platform.

17.3.2 Motion Capture

To capture sport skills with a high level of precision, we have chosen an optical motion capture system provided and controlled by Vicon. Due to sport constraints such as the skill's speed, field dimension or the specificity of accessories, a particular set up has been defined. A motion capture studio has been used with a large tracking space volume.

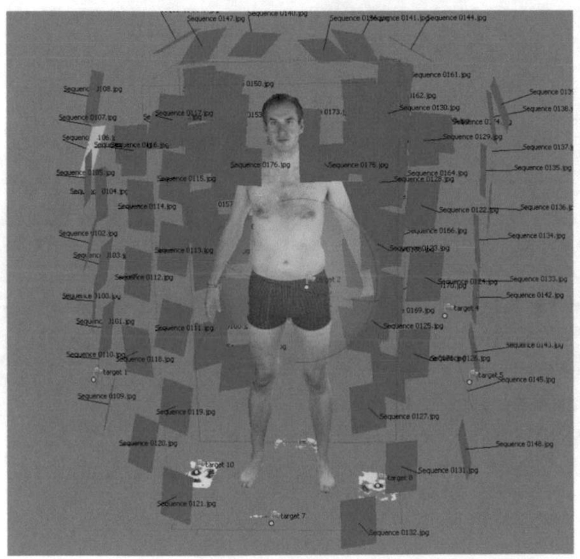

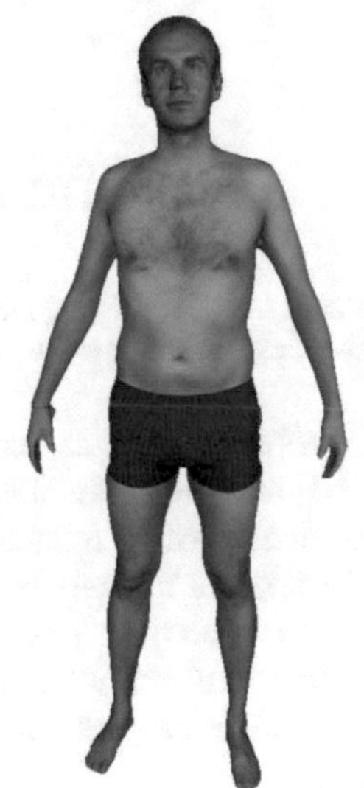

b. Cleaned model

Fig. 17.11 Example of 3D reconstructed avatar. (**a**) Textured model. (**b**) Cleaned model (MIRALab) (© 2016 FP7 Project RePlay and University of Geneva/MIRALab, reprinted with permission)

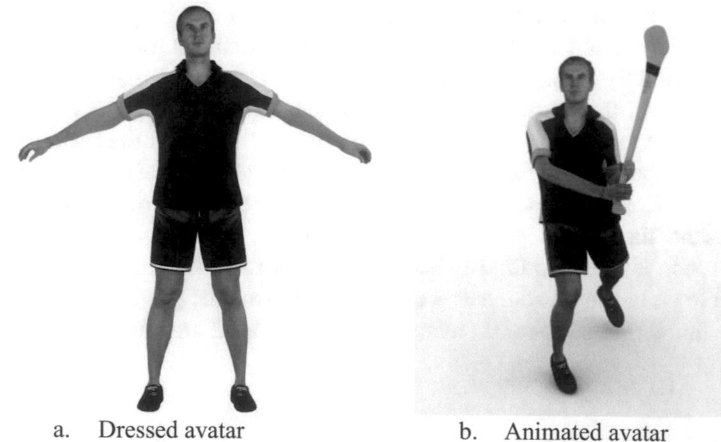

Fig. 17.12 Rigging, clothing, and animation of the 3D avatar. (**a**) Dressed avatar. (**b**) Animated avatar (MIRALab) (© 2016 FP7 Project RePlay and University of Geneva/MIRALab, reprinted with permission)

Fig. 17.13 Tracking camera set-up (Vicon) (© 2016 FP7 Project RePlay and Vicon Motion Systems Ltd, reprinted with permission)

More than 50 cameras have been used to track the athletes' movements with a high accuracy (Fig. 17.13). The "Plug In Gait" marker set up has been used. It is composed of 45 reflective markers used to track the full human body (Fig. 17.14). Some extra markers have also been used to track sport accessories.

As results, we obtained 180 records from eight athletes of different TSG. The output is an animation file that can be combined with a virtual avatar or that can be applied to a stick figure.

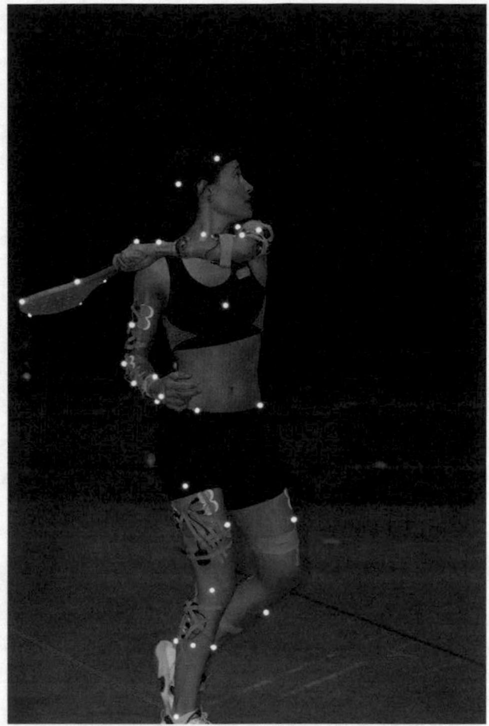

Fig. 17.14 Athlete being captured (MIRALab) (© 2016 FP7 Project RePlay and University of Geneva/MIRALab, reprinted with permission)

17.3.3 Avatar Animation

To animate the 3D avatar, a skeleton structure has to be added to the static mesh made using the image-based 3D scanner. The avatar is then animated by mixing the 3D avatar obtained using the 3D scanner and kinematic data. The output is a high-quality animation that includes a high frame rate (200 fps) and high level of precision. It is possible to render the animation with all recent graphical engines, including Unity3D and Unreal Engine. To increase the immersion, we designed some 3D environment to reproduce the TSG fields.

The animated avatar is then placed in a virtual context and can be shown to promote and preserve TSG in a gamification context (Fig. 17.15).

Fig. 17.15 3D avatar animated and placed in the 3D environment (MIRALab) (© 2016 FP7 Project RePlay and University of Geneva/MIRALab, reprinted with permission)

17.4 Real-Time Tracking

We chose wearable inertial sensors and the Microsoft Kinect since they are low-cost and are each gaining popularity in the area of human movement monitoring and gesture recognition due to their accuracy and potential for real-time applications. In the following section, we introduce these two sensor modalities as well as describe the advantages and disadvantages of each sensor with respect to motion capture.

Kinect: Since very recently, computer game users can enjoy a novel gaming experience with the Xbox, thanks to the introduction of the Microsoft Kinect sensor, where your body is the controller. Like the Nintendo Wii sensor bar, the Kinect device is placed either above or below the video screen. However, the Kinect adds the capabilities of a depth sensor to those of an RGB camera, recording the distance from all objects that lie in front of it. The depth information is then processed by a software engine that extracts, in real time, the human body features of players, thus enabling the interaction between the physical world and the virtual one. However, there are some disadvantages associated with Kinect including low frame rate, limited volume of capture, inaccurate joint orientation estimation, and lighting and occlusion problems.

WIMU: In general, a wireless/wearable inertial measurement unit, or WIMU, is an electronic device consisting of a microprocessor board, on-board accelerometers, gyroscopes and magnetometers, and a wireless connection to transfer the captured data to a receiving client. WIMUs are capable of measuring linear acceleration, angular velocity, and gravitational forces and are often used in MoCap systems. MEMS inertial sensors are being widely used in MoCap research due to the following reasons:

- They are miniaturized and lightweight so they can be placed on any part or segment of a human body without hindering performance.
- The cost of such sensors is falling dramatically as they start to persuade mass market consumer devices.
- They can be utilized to capture human movement/actions in real unconstrained environments (e.g., outdoor environments with variable lighting conditions) to obtain accurate results.
- They can be used to provide real-time or near-real-time feedback.

A possible solution to the limitations of the Kinect system is to combine the Kinect-based data with data from wireless inertial motion units (WIMUs) which can provide greater accuracy in the measurement of body segment angles and angular velocities and also have much higher sampling frequencies (e.g., up to 1024 Hz) at consistent rates. WIMUs can incorporate triaxial accelerometers and gyroscopes to determine angular measures and facilitate an accurate identification of key events which involve impact (e.g., ground contact when jumping and striking a ball in tennis). The use of WIMUs alone, however, is limited because of significant challenges in determining accurate joint center position necessary in the provision of visual feedback on the body's motion. This provides the motivation for fusing information from Microsoft Kinect and multiple WIMUs.

Different capturing modalities used within the RePlay platform provided different types of skeletons. Using the Microsoft Kinect can generate a relatively simple skeleton with 16 bones and 15 nodes as shown in Fig. 17.16a. It also provides 3D segment angles linked to each bone. Using the Kinect and different numbers of WIMUs can result in generating a fused skeleton which is more robust, reliable, and accurate than the skeleton generated by Kinect (Fig. 17.16b). The fused skeleton is the primary method to capture athletes' performance to be compared against that of a national hero within the RePlay platform. The main challenge to implement the fused skeleton is to obtain accurate 3D orientation using the WIMUs. In the following section, 3D orientation estimation using WIMUs is briefly discussed.

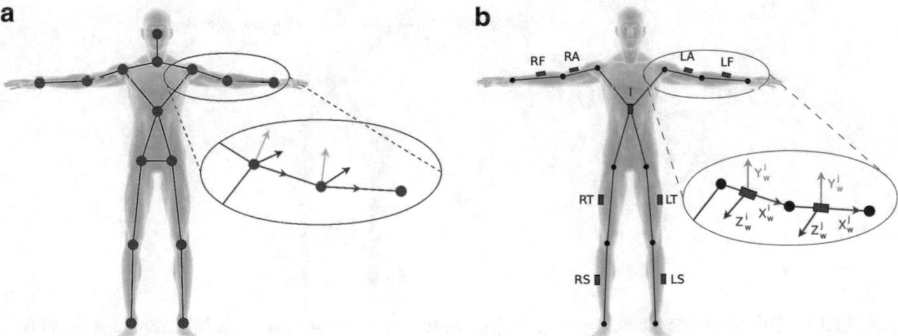

Fig. 17.16 (**a**) The 3D skeleton captured using the Microsoft Kinect sensor; (**b**) The 3D skeleton generated using Microsoft Kinect and 9 WIMUs are shown (INSIGHT) (© 2016 FP7 Project RePlay and Dublin City University/INSIGHT, reprinted with permission)

17.4.1 Orientation Estimation Using Inertial Sensors

Measuring accurate orientation plays an important role in sport activity applications as it enables coaches, biomechanists, and sport scientists to monitor and investigate athletes' movement technique in indoor and outdoor environments. Although there are different technologies to monitor athletes' technique and measure their body orientation, wearable inertial sensors have the advantage of being self-contained in a way that measurement is independent of motion, environment, and location. It is feasible to measure accurate orientation in 3D space by utilizing triaxial accelerometers, gyroscopes, and a proper filter. We employed a filter that utilizes a quaternion representation, allowing accelerometer data to be used in an analytically derived and optimized gradient descent algorithm to compute the direction of the gyroscope measurement error as a quaternion derivative [4, 5]. The filter has been shown to provide effective performance at low computational expense. Using such a technique, it is feasible to have a lightweight, inexpensive system capable of functioning over an extended period of time [4, 5].

17.4.2 Sensor Placement

Each inertial sensor device (WIMU) has to be placed on one segment of a subject in a predefined orientation. The location of the sensor on each body segment was chosen to avoid large muscles, as soft tissue deformations due to muscle contractions and foot-ground impacts may negatively affect the accuracy of joint orientation estimates. As it is shown in Fig. 17.17, the sensors and the x-axis and y-axis of each sensor are well aligned with the longitudinal axis of the corresponding bone for the upper body and lower body segments, respectively. It should be noted that

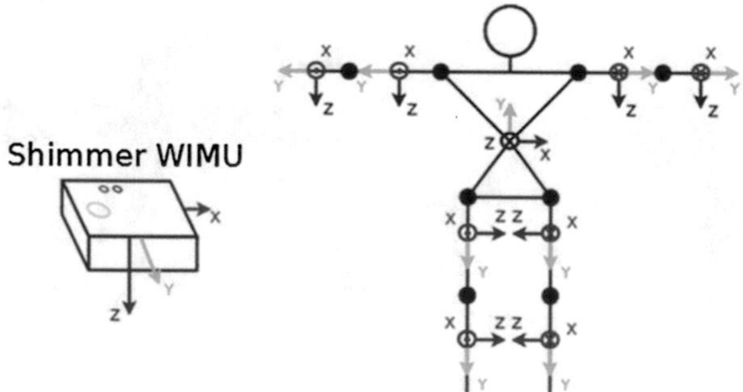

Fig. 17.17 Shimmer sensor orientation (*left*) and the sensor placement on different segments of a subject is illustrated (*right*). *Nine inertial sensors* are fixed to the subject's forearms, arms, thighs, shanks, and chest. These correspond respectively to the fused skeleton joints R/LF, R/LA, R/LT, R/LT and T (INSIGHT) (© 2016 FP7 Project RePlay and Dublin City University/INSIGHT, reprinted with permission)

the number of sensors used to be fused with the MS Kinect sensor is selectable (between one and nine).

17.4.3 Methodology

We designed and implemented the fused Kinect/WIMU skeleton using three separate information sources given by each modality [6]. The Kinect sensor provides the initial joint positions of our skeleton, as well as the global position of the subject's body over time. The WIMUs provide the orientation information, which we need to animate each bone of our fused skeleton over time.

First, we consider a reference skeleton provided by the Kinect sensor and the associated skeleton extraction algorithm. This reference skeleton is the starting point of our fused skeleton synthesis method and is built from a reference frame captured by the Kinect. We need this reference skeleton to be as accurate as possible to produce a stable result. In order to do this, the subject is asked to stand still in a T-pose with his/her palms facing the ground in front of the Microsoft Kinect sensor for 5 s to successfully obtain the reference skeleton. This is shown in following Fig. 17.18.

Secondly, for each subsequent frame captured by the two sensory modalities, we consider one specific joint captured by the Kinect algorithm and the rotational data provided by the WIMUs. The aim of this specific Kinect skeleton joint is to track the global displacement of the subject's body over time, as the WIMUs cannot provide this information easily. For stability and simplicity purposes, we choose to consider the *chest/torso* joint of the Kinect skeleton. As a result, the location of the

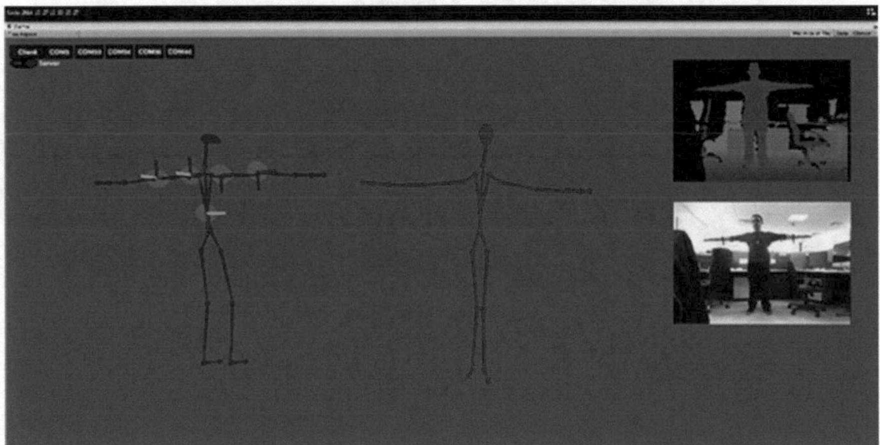

Fig. 17.18 T-Pose required by the RePlay platform to calibrate the fusion of a Kinect sensor and the WIMUs (INSIGHT) (© 2016 FP7 Project RePlay and Dublin City University/INSIGHT, reprinted with permission)

central joint of our fused skeleton is updated with respect to the displacement of this Kinect joint.

Finally, our fused skeleton is built from the reference skeleton. For each dataset captured by the WIMUs, each bone of our fused skeleton is rotated according to this rotational information in a hierarchical manner. This first process defines a new position for the starting and the ending points of our fused skeleton. For instance, the wrist position of the subject is affected by the orientation of the elbow, shoulder and torso, respectively. As such, once the orientation of the chest is obtained (as the root of the animated skeleton), then the remaining joint positions and orientations can be estimated. In other words, the rotated shoulder joints can be used to calculate the new position of the elbow joints. The hip joints, in turn, can be used to calculate the new position of the knee joints.

Two examples of the accuracy of the fused skeleton (in blue) and the Kinect skeleton (in red) are shown in Fig. 17.19. The point clouds captured by the Kinect are superimposed. It can be seen that the skeletons captured using the Kinect are not as stable, reliable, and accurate as those generated using the fused skeleton. For instance, it is evident in Fig. 17.19 (left) that due to the occlusion issue, the left knee is not detected correctly by the Kinect. Also in Fig. 17.19 (right), the right elbow, shoulder, and knee joints were not detected correctly by Kinect since the subject was performing fast movements inside the capturing volume.

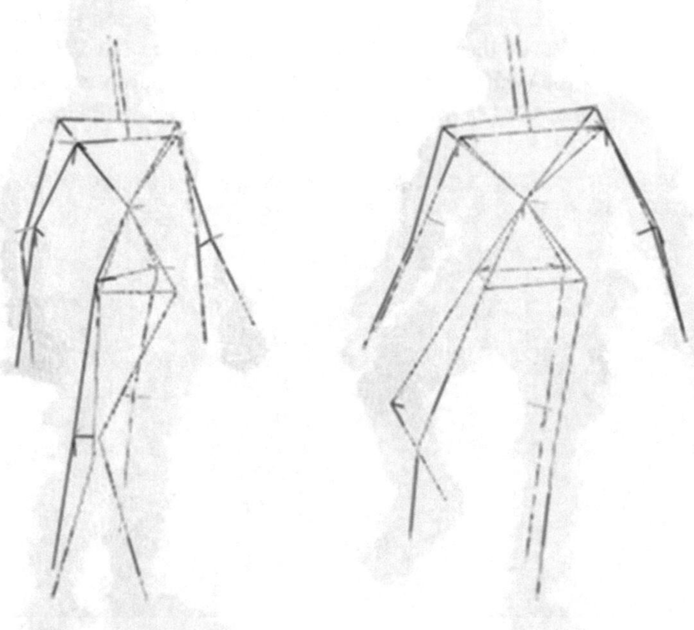

Fig. 17.19 Two examples of the accuracy of the fused skeleton (in *blue*) versus the Kinect skeleton (in *red*) (INSIGHT)

Table 17.1 Numerical analysis of the Microsoft Kinect and the fused skeleton results compared to the results from the Vicon system during the right knee flexion gesture with five trials (INSIGHT)

Joint angle	Left knee flexion RMSE	Left knee flexion NCC	Right knee flexion RMSE	Right knee flexion NCC
Kinect L-Elbow	16.73	0.13	9.93	0.61
Fusion L-Elbow	14.19	0.70	3.81	0.85
Kinect R-Elbow	12.06	0.41	10.34	0.56
Fusion R-Elbow	6.97	0.89	5.12	0.84
Kinect R-Knee	29.51	−0.63	26.94	−0.02
Fusion R-Knee	6.79	0.73	8.98	0.50
Kinect R-Knee	9.82	0.82	12.96	0.80
Fusion R-Knee	4.10	0.99	5.86	0.99

Table 17.1 shows a comparison of the performance of the Microsoft Kinect and the fused skeleton compared to the Vicon system. These results were measured during the performance of knee flexion, where the subjects were asked to raise their right knees up to about 90° before flexing/extending their knees. The subjects were also asked to be in a predefined pose (T-pose) and then flex and extend their right and left elbows.

The root-mean-square errors (RMSE) and the normalized cross-correlation coefficients (NCC) were measured during the whole trial [6]. It can be seen that the results obtained from the fused skeleton are always closer to those measured using the Vicon system. Five subjects participated in this experiment.

17.5 Comparison and Feedback

Even though TSG are games by definition, adherence to the gamification approach in the context of a computer game aims to familiarize users with TSG in engaging and educative ways. Thus, two gamification elements were implemented: (1) introducing digital-game-intrinsic principles like scoring that allow for competition among multiple players and (2) combining it with an educational aspect to engage the users and facilitate their continuous skill improvement. The followed gamification approach relies on guiding the player's performance to match that of their favourite hero's.

17.5.1 Compare and Score

Comparing a sport skill performance against a reference one and producing a representing score pose a big challenge, not only due to the complexity of the human motion but also because of the following issues:

- Non-uniform representations: Different modalities are used to capture the performance of a professional hero and those of the players. Excluding the purpose of preserving national hero performances, they also need to be captured in very high quality and detail, to serve as the "reference" motions in our evaluation method and to drive the comparison results. To ensure this, the "gold standard" professional motion capturing system of Vicon was used, while for the player skill performance motion capturing, the solution described in Sect. 17.3.2 was used.
- Noisy measurements: Using low-cost sensors for the performance capture of the players can introduce varying levels of noise.
- Varying execution speed.
- Coordination differences: Actual player performance deviates from that of the professional athlete due to inexperience and the skill level gap.
- Analysis of the motion: Each sport skill needs to be analyzed to identify its important characteristics and how its performance level can be assessed.
- Meaningful scoring and feedback: The outcome of the sport skill evaluation methodology should guide the player's improvement in performing it.

To overcome the above, the proposed solution's overview is illustrated in the logical pipeline of Fig. 17.20.

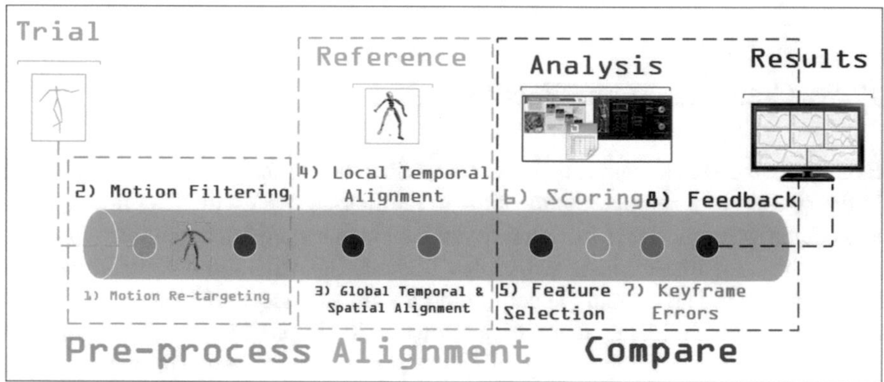

Fig. 17.20 The motion evaluation pipeline (CERTH) (© 2016 FP7 Project RePlay and Centre for Research and Technology Hellas/CERTH, reprinted with permission)

17.5.1.1 Preprocessing

The user's ("trial") captured motion has different signal characteristics than the captured hero performances ("reference"). As a result the first step of our preprocessing pipeline was motion retargeting, where, given a motion signal in a specific body structure format, it is transformed to another body structure format. Motion retargeting is achieved by extending the methodology described by Ahmadi et al. [7] only for the leg or to the whole body, so that the raw trial motion data captured by the low-cost motion capturing system are parameterized and retargeted to the reference motion's body structure. This step effectively offers the two motion sequences under comparison in a unified body format. Next, motion filtering is employed as the trial motion captured data contain noisy measurements that need to be filtered in order to correct erroneous pose estimations. Due to the nature of athletic action motion signals, characterized by sharp joint movements, an amplitude preserving filtering solution was opted for. More specifically, the least squares polynomial fitting Savitzky-Golay [8] filters were selected, whose properties rather than being defined in the frequency domain and then translated to the time domain are derived directly from a particular formulation in the time domain aiming to preserve higher moments, while smoothing and supporting inflexion at the same time. Another advantage of this choice is that due to its polynomial form, the filter itself can be differentiated, and thus, the derivatives can be seamlessly calculated, providing the velocity and acceleration feature estimations.

17.5.1.2 Alignment

Having the trial and reference motions expressed uniformly in the same body structure enables the alignment phase. However, in order to be compared, they need to be (1) spatially and (2) temporally aligned. The two-step temporal alignment procedure initially estimates the global temporal offset and the spatial relative pose transformation between the two sequences and then estimates local temporal alignment correspondences. In particular, quaternionic signal processing techniques are used by embedding the joint positions in pure quaternions and then first estimating their relative shift in time (global temporal alignment) through the maximum of the quaternionic cross covariance similar to Alexiadis and Daras [9]. Secondly, local temporal warping through the dynamic time warping (DTW) technique is employed using the same quaternionic representation of the joint positions with respect to the pelvis joint, for the resulting globally aligned motions. The distance used for calculating the DTW path when using pure quaternion is the three-dimensional Euclidean distance. As a result the rotational invariance achieved through the global rotation between the two motions (encoded in the phase of their cross covariance for time equal to zero) is instrumental to the local alignment step. This two-pronged temporal alignment strategy accounts for all the temporal inconsistencies either global (different start and end times as well as durations) or local (varying durations of each phase). In conclusion, it should be noted that in the work of Alexiadis and Daras [9], all the joints participated into the alignment calculations, but for the developed game, due to inexperienced users and in order to maintain high user experience levels while playing, the selection for the local alignment step was limited to one joint, the most informative one based on the weights defined in the following subsection. A visual example of the alignment methodology is shown in Fig. 17.21, with the "reference" motion in yellow and the "trial" in orange.

17.5.1.3 Compare

As aforementioned, the implemented evaluation scheme is a blend of achievement- and incentive-driven gamification principles with educative and learning elements. The learning element is based on offering teaching points, tailored to each specific skill, to guide players on how to correct their performance. These teaching points were mapped to motion features, and a weighted scheme is utilized based on a selected subset of these features, corresponding to the teaching points, and their weighted relative importance to drive a hybrid comparison method.

More specifically, each sport skill was initially analyzed after taking into account its teaching instructions into a set of phases and features with respect to each phase. These phases are the (a) backswing, (b) front swing, and (c) follow

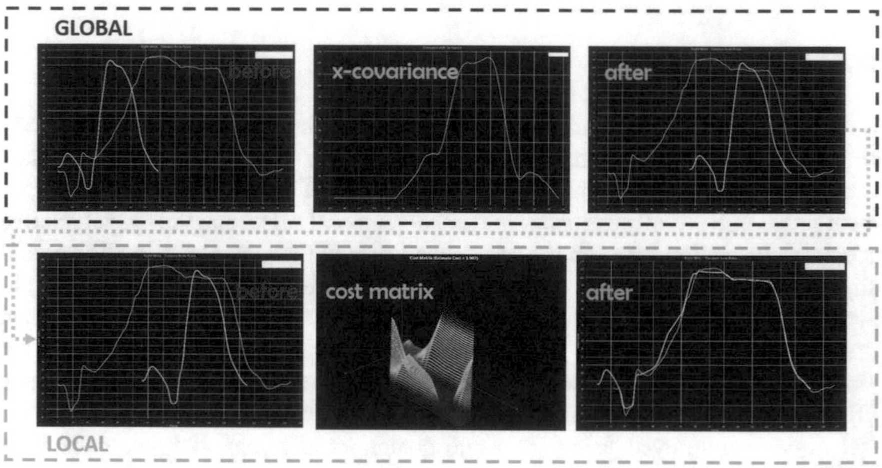

Fig. 17.21 The motion alignment methodology. *Top left:* Right-wrist relative position to the pelvis—initial reference and trial motion features. *Top middle*: The cross covariance of the reference and trial features. *Top right*: Trial and reference motion features after removing their global time shift. *Bottom left*: The now temporally and spatially aligned motion features are fed to the local alignment algorithm. *Bottom middle*: The 3D heat-map plot of the DTW cost matrix. *Bottom right*: The final temporally aligned reference and trial motion features (CERTH) (© 2016 FP7 Project RePlay and Centre for Research and Technology Hellas/CERTH, reprinted with permission)

through and are delimited by a set of key frames: (1) start of backswing, (2) start of front swing, (3) ball impact, and (4) end of follow through. The feature pool includes features like joint's velocity, acceleration and anthropometric angles (flexion, extension, abduction, adduction, etc.)

Given two aligned motion sequences, each phase's features are extracted and compared using the Structural Similarity Index metric (SSIM) in order to offer a feature-specific score. The SSIM proposed by Wang et al. [10] in the context of image quality analysis is utilized after adapting it for use with one-dimensional time-series data instead of images, and it is comprised of:

1. An amplitude term, scoring the average value of a set of measurements
2. A measurement distribution term, scoring the variance of a set of measurements
3. A structural term, scoring the temporal interdependencies of a set of measurements

A weighted combination of these three terms is calculated for each feature's time instant around a local neighbourhood (in time) and then averaged for that feature's phase duration, calculating its score. Then, the overall score is computed by averaging all the features dictated by the motion analysis schema created for that skill.

An example is presented in the Fig. 17.22, where the performance of a *handball—right-handed volley* skill—is being assessed. The flexion of the user's right

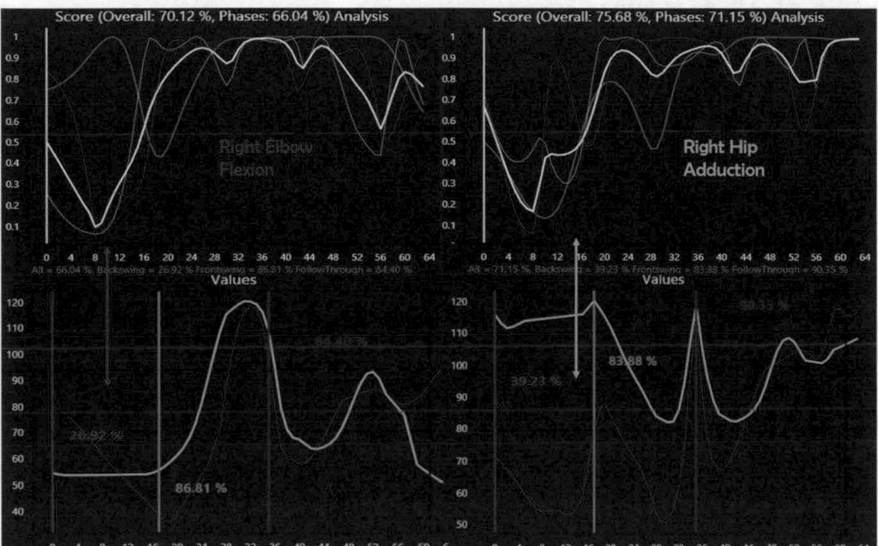

Fig. 17.22 Per feature scoring analysis example. *The trial* (*green*) and reference (*red*) motion features at the *bottom row* and the SSIM and its respective terms at the *top* one (amplitude term in *dark green*, distribution term in *orange*, structural term in *purple* and overall SSIM score in *light brown*). The *vertical lines* represent the motion's key frames (*red* for start of the backswing, *green* for start of the front swing, *blue* for the impact point and *black* for the end of the follow through. The coloured percentages denote each phase's score for that feature (*red* for the backswing, *green* for the front swing and *blue* for the follow through) (CERTH) (© 2016 FP7 Project RePlay and Centre for Research and Technology Hellas/CERTH, reprinted with permission)

elbow and the right hip's adduction were defined as two of the important motion features for this skill.

17.5.2 Feedback and Visualization

This analysis and interpretation of the performed skill with respect to the defined teaching points are ultimately driving the educational aspect of the game, the offered feedback that players receive. This returned feedback decomposes the scoring overview and identifies specific sources of error and areas of improvement with respect to the important key frames of the motion. The motion analysis schema associates specific features at specific key frames of the motion with the required teaching points and semantic instructions around them. Then an error metric is calculated for each of these key-frame features that is then used to decide which instruction is to be triggered. Consequently, the hybrid comparison method uses both temporal technique scoring and key-frame posture error estimations to provide feedback in numerous ways:

- Score percentage
- Semantic text feedback
- Visual animation feedback

First, the score is presented to the user with, optionally, detailed per feature scores and plots. Then two avatars are animated side by side using the alignment information to visually highlight corresponding postures during the performed action (Fig. 17.23). In parallel, this visual animation playback slows down when reaching erroneous key frames; pauses and annotates, by colour highlighting, the

Fig. 17.23 Visually annotated semantic feedback (CERTH) (© 2016 FP7 Project RePlay and Centre for Research and Technology Hellas/CERTH, reprinted with permission)

body segments involved with the error; and then displays the semantic feedback instructions to guide the player's improvement.

17.6 Conclusion and Results

The proposed platform has been implemented and tested together with TSG federation. A demonstrator has been set up for several events around Europe to promote TSG as well as the technology, where the participants filled a questionnaire about it. Thanks to the provided feedback, it has been concluded that one important parameter related to the ease of use is the understanding of the skill the participant had to mimic. In this case, the skill was completely understood by half of the participants, and the remaining understood the skill quite well. Another important parameter related to the ease of use is the understanding of the comparison between the user and the national hero to evaluate the visual feedback provided. The results of the questionnaires demonstrate that two-thirds of the participants understood quite well the comparison, while the percentage is similar in the case of "A bit" and "Nothing." Regarding the expected results, half of the participants agreed that the score was quite approximate to what they would have expected. Regarding the understanding of the numbers in the score (general score and percentages for each of the phases), two-thirds of the participants agreed on having understood the numbers very well. One important feature of the feedback is the semantic feedback, providing text-based instructions at the bottom of the screen with suggestions to improve the score. Half of the participants read most of the instructions and one third read all the instructions. Related to this question, participants were asked if they have followed the recommendations provided by the platform. The distribution of the responses clearly demonstrates that the feedback was taken into account mostly by half of the participants and completely by one third of them.

The biggest issue regarding the demonstrator is the accuracy of the Microsoft Kinect sensor in capturing challenging sport actions. The discrepancy between the capture quality of the Gaelic field trials and the Basque ones resides in the increased difficulty of the Microsoft Kinect sensor to appropriately track a kicking action. While the capture quality of the fist pass skills is at the same level of capturing quality as similar hand action skills, the capturing quality of the Punt Kick skill is less than half of that. Finally, due to either lighting conditions or sensor problems, the captured frame rates sometimes varied as seen in the frame rate distribution per trial. This issue can be improved in the future with the development of more robust techniques for human body pose estimation techniques from depth-sensing cameras, specifically designed for capturing motions of the targeted sports and games.

Acknowledgements This project has received funding from the European Union's Seventh Framework Programme for research, technological development and demonstration under grant agreement *FP7-601170 RePlay*.

References

1. P. Ratner, *3-D Human Modeling and Animation* (Wiley, New York, 2012)
2. B. Allen, B. Curless, Z. Popović, The space of human body shapes: reconstruction and parameterization from range scans, in *ACM Transactions on Graphics (TOG)*, ACM, Vol. 22, No. 3, 2003, July, pp. 587–594
3. M. Bastioni, Ideas and methods for modeling 3D human figures The principal algorithms used by MakeHuman and their implementation in a new approach to parametric modeling, pp. 1–6
4. S.O. Madgwick, A.J. Harrison, R. Vaidyanathan, Estimation of imu and marg orientation using a gradient descent algorithm, in *Rehabilitation Robotics (ICORR), 2011 I.E. International Conference, on* IEEE, 2011, pp. 1–7
5. A. Ahmadi, E. Mitchell, C. Richter, F. Destelle, M. Gowing, N.E. O'Connor, K. Moran, Toward automatic activity classification and movement assessment during a sports training session. IEEE Internet Things J. **2**(1), 23–32 (2015)
6. F. Destelle, A. Ahmadi, N.E. O'Connor, K. Moran, A. Chatzitofis, D. Zarpalas, P. Daras, Low-cost accurate skeleton tracking based on fusion of Kinect and wearable inertial sensors, in *Signal Processing Conference (EUSIPCO), 2014 Proceedings of the 22nd European*, IEEE, 2014, September, pp. 371–375
7. A. Ahmadi, F. Destelle, D. Monaghan, K. Moran, N.E. O'Connor, L. Unzueta, M.T. Linaza, Human gait monitoring using body-worn inertial sensors and kinematic modelling, in *SENSORS*, 2015 IEEE, pp. 1–4
8. A. Savitzky, M.J. Golay, Smoothing and differentiation of data by simplified least squares procedures. Anal. Chem. **36**(8), 1627–1639 (1964)
9. D.S. Alexiadis, P. Daras, Quaternionic signal processing techniques for automatic evaluation of dance performances from MoCap data. IEEE Trans. Multimedia **16**(5), 1391–1406 (2014)
10. Z. Wang, A.C. Bovik, H.R. Sheikh, E.P. Simoncelli, Image quality assessment: from error visibility to structural similarity. IEEE Trans. Image Process. **13**(4), 600–612 (2004)

Part VII
Ambient Intelligence and Storytelling

Chapter 18
Deployment of Robotic Guides in Museum Contexts

Maria Pateraki and Panos Trahanias

Abstract Recent advances in technology have provided new ways to present information and interact with visitors in public spaces. Relevant implementations range from the simple utilization of standard PCs that present minimal multimedia content to large theater halls that immerse visitors in virtual worlds or display fancy 3-D representations of exhibited items. Mobile robots provide an attractive alternative to the above, and, as technology becomes progressively available, the number of paradigms of robots in museums is steadily increasing. For this class of robots, human-like interactivity is an essential part of their functionality, aiming at correctly perceiving and understanding natural human behavior and also acting in ways that are familiar to humans using a variety of modalities. Motivated by the latest advances in mobile robots as museum tour guides, this chapter provides insight in how to develop robotic avatars with advanced navigation capabilities, vision-based tracking technologies for human–robot interaction, and personalized, choice-driven access to information in heritage sites.

Keywords Multimodal interaction • Augmented environments • Robotic guides • Environment mapping • Object tracking • Interfaces

18.1 Introduction

Access to cultural heritage and exhibits is a central issue in museums and exhibition galleries that is recently approached under a new, technological perspective. Although the cultural industries' practices in the case of museums and cultural

M. Pateraki (✉)
Institute of Computer Science, Foundation for Research and Technology—Hellas, Crete, Greece
e-mail: pateraki@ics.forth.gr

P. Trahanias
Institute of Computer Science, Foundation for Research and Technology—Hellas, Crete, Greece

Department of Computer Science, University of Crete, Crete, Greece
e-mail: trahania@ics.forth.gr

M. Ioannides et al. (eds.), *Mixed Reality and Gamification for Cultural Heritage*,
DOI 10.1007/978-3-319-49607-8_18

exhibits have remained practically unchanged for long, in recent years we have been witnessing a gradual adoption of novel technologies toward providing media-rich presentations of cultural exhibits and consequently offering innovative services to museum visitors to actively and energetically seek a broader audience.

The design and development of mobile robots capable of operating and providing services in populated environments is an area that has attracted the interest of the scientific community throughout the last couple of decades. Paradigms of such robots are deployed in hospitals, museums, trade fairs, office buildings, and department stores. In these environments, the mobile robots provide various services, including tasks like delivering, educating, informing, entertaining, and assisting people. In museum contexts, the central task of a robotic tour guide may be seen as to provide interactive tours to museum visitors. This concerns two types of visitors, those enjoying physical presence in the exhibition premises and remote visitors establishing a "virtual presence." Facilitating an immersive telepresence may enable people all around the world to visit the museum, using a Web interface through which they could watch the robot operate and send it to specific exhibit locations. In the case of professionals who need to critically study realistic views of exhibits as part of their work, immersive telepresence via robots offers a viable alternative to the current model that requires on-site visits, operating on a 24-h basis, 7 days a week, permitting thus more people to exploit its services at their convenience.

A very important factor for the acceptance of a robotic tour guide by the broader public is the degree to which the system smoothly interacts with both on-site and Web visitors. Therefore, most efforts in the development of such systems are concentrated in porting elements of human-to-human communication in human–robot interaction (HRI) to render robots more user friendly. The design and overall esthetics, the autonomous navigation in populated dynamic environments, the verbal and nonverbal cues for multimodal interaction, and the employed interfaces are discussed here to provide insight to the readers on the scientific challenges and requirements imposed by the specific application area. Research results in this area have potential applications in a range of other scenarios where artificial agents must interact with humans in natural settings, requiring essentially the same basic cognitive components. These concern a wide range of service robots exhibiting advanced levels of flexibility and efficiency, for example, in the context of domestic or health care applications or robots operating in public spaces such as trade shows or shopping malls.

18.2 Robot Design

The design of the robot and relevant characteristics should take into consideration the requirements of the specific application. The robot should have the ability to move autonomously in the museum area and to interact naturally with visitors of different characteristics and age groups. Due to the foreseen operation of the mobile robot in a public space, essential capabilities are required for autonomous navigation, such as the perception of its environment and the capability of navigating in a safe way, which also includes the avoidance of static and/or moving obstacles. Solutions to the autonomous navigation problem are discussed in Sect. 18.3. The usual sensory devices that are employed to facilitate robotic navigation are laser range scanners; the latter should be safety approved and placed in appropriate positions on the mobile robot, usually at a height of 20–30 cm. To guarantee maximum safety, the mobile robot must additionally be equipped with emergency stop buttons that set off the safety brakes of the motors in unexpected situations. Optionally, the platform may also integrate supplementary safety devices, such as radio-controlled emergency stop systems, that can be triggered via software running onboard or on a remote control computer.

The appearance and the overall robot esthetics are also important aspects in platform design. In interactions, the first impression is critical, and this applies in both human–human and human–robot contexts. The robot's exterior look can strongly influence a human's perception of the robot and its acceptability, that is, an aggressive appearance may instill fear while a friendly appearance may be an invitation to interact. Moreover, tour guide robots, being instances of social robots, need to have anthropomorphic features in order to be capable of meaningful social interactions. These include whole-body motion, proxemics (i.e., interpersonal distance), gestures, facial expressions, gaze behavior, head orientation, and linguistic or emotive vocalization. In this respect the design of the robot's head is of foremost importance; any kind of robotic head when directed at humans may result to bizarre reactions if the effects of its exterior look and feel and motion are not adequately considered. Whereas many anthropomorphic robot heads have a cartoonish or an exaggerated emotive caricature appearance, others feature a very human-like appearance with skin, teeth, and hair [1] (Fig. 18.1).

Indicative robot cases regard (a) Kodomoroid [6], developed by Hiroshi Ishiguro and coworkers, that is currently acting as a guide at the Miraikan museum in Tokyo and (b) the INDIGO robot that has been developed in the course of a European-funded project [7]. INDIGO guided visitors in the exhibition premises of the Foundation of the Hellenic World in Athens, Greece, and featured an anthropomorphic head, designed by HANSON Robotics.

A design challenge regards avoiding the so-called *uncanny valley* where the appearance and movement of the robot resemble more of an animate zombie than a living human. Designs that fall within the *uncanny valley* elicit a strong negative reaction from people. Mori [8] in 1970 originally formulated the theory to describe people's reactions to robots, though it can be applied to anything possessing human-like qualities including digital animation (e.g., [9]) and voices (e.g., [10]). As the human likeness of a stimulus increases, an individual's emotional response to the stimulus becomes more positive, but when human likeness nears perfection, the individual's emotional response sharply declines and becomes strongly negative. The region immediately following this decline is the *uncanny valley*. As an example, the physical appearance of the INDIGO robot's head laid in the area of the graph marked with the red circle (Fig. 18.2), the synthetic

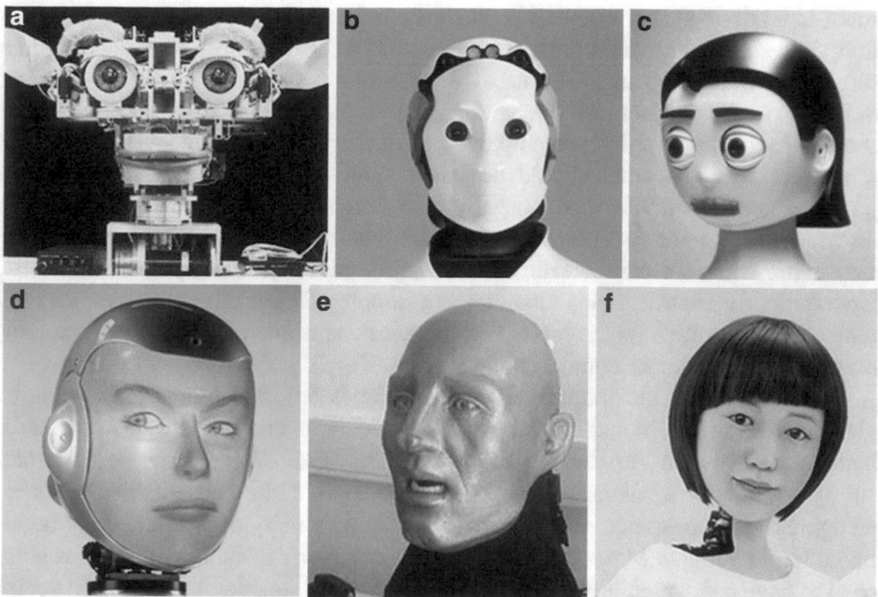

Fig. 18.1 Examples of anthropomorphic robot heads. (**a**) Kismet (reproduced from [2], © 2003 Elsevier, reprinted with permission), (**b**) Reem [3] (© PAL Robotics, Spain 2016, reprinted with permission), (**c**) Flobi (reproduced from [4], © 2012 Springer, reprinted with permission), (**d**) SociBot [5] (© Engineered Arts Limited 2016, reprinted with permission), (**e**) INDIGO, (**f**) Kodomoroid [6] (© Miraikan Museum 2014, reprinted with permission)

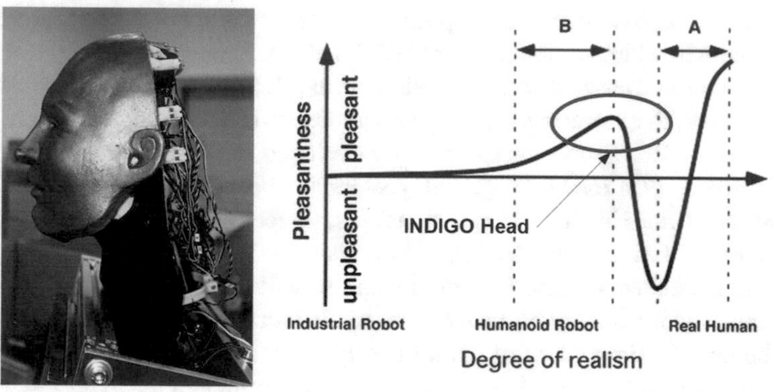

Fig. 18.2 The *uncanny valley* theory graph (*right*) and the selected area (marked with *red*) for the INDIGO anthropomorphic head (*left*)

skin was created using Frubber™, a patented silicone elastomer, and was painted with nonnaturalistic coloring to prevent it from looking like a human. Furthermore, it featured 31° of freedom, able to emulate 62 facial and neck muscular movements.

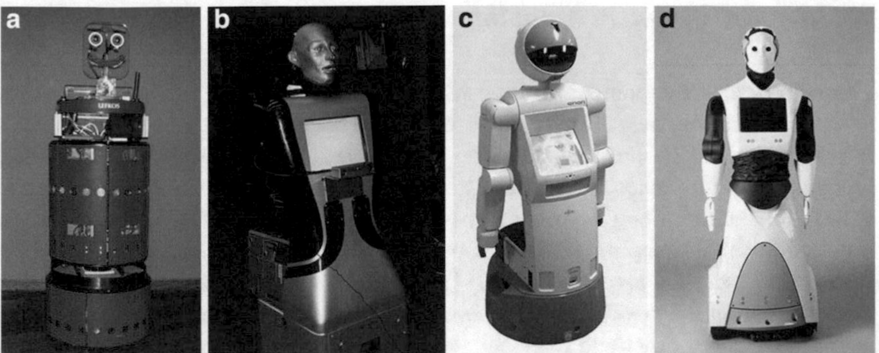

Fig. 18.3 Examples of mobile robotic guides. (**a**) TOURBOT, (**b**) INDIGO, (**c**) Enon (reproduced from [12], © 2011 Springer, reprinted with permission), (**d**) Reem-H2 [3] (© PAL Robotics, Spain 2016, reprinted with permission)

As the robot should have advanced mobility capabilities, the choice of a wheel-based robot versus a bipedal one is favored. The foremost reason is that wheel-based robots are extremely easy to design and build, whereas leg-based robots require complex mechanics and computation to maintain balance, orientation, efficiency, and speed. Moreover, legged robots require the system to generate an appropriate gait to move instead of just rolling with wheels. The fact remains that the stability, agility, and versatility of any existing bipedal machine does not even come close to that of the human biped [11]. Thus, paradigms aimed for robotic guides in public spaces used wheel-based platforms as shown in Fig. 18.3, such as the TOURBOT [13], Minerva [14], Rhino [15], Jinny [16], INDIGO [7], Enon by Fujitsu [12], and Reem by PAL robotics [3].

18.3 Autonomous Navigation in Dynamic Environments

The autonomous navigation of robots in open and dynamic environments, that is, environments containing moving objects (potential obstacles) whose future behavior is unknown, is an important challenge, requiring developers to solve several difficult research problems at the cutting edge of the state of the art. Accordingly, tasks that need to be addressed regard (a) simultaneous localization and mapping (SLAM) in dynamic environments; (b) detection, tracking, and filtering of dynamic objects; and (c) online motion planning and safe navigation.

18.3.1 Environment Mapping

The map of the environment that constitutes the robot's workspace is essential for autonomous robot navigation. If the pose (we use the term pose to refer to a robot's x–y location and its heading direction θ) of the robot is always known during mapping, building maps is relatively straightforward. On the other hand, if a map is available, determining the robot's poses can be done efficiently. In the literature, the mobile robot mapping problem is often referred to as the *simultaneous localization and mapping problem (SLAM)* [17–23]. This is because mapping includes both estimating the position of the robot relative to the map and generating a map using the sensory input and the estimates about the robot's pose. Most of today's mapping systems utilize motion and laser range measurements and are able to deal with noise in the sensor data; however, they usually assume that the environment is static during mapping. If a person walks through the sensor range of the robot during mapping, the resulting map will contain evidence about an object at the corresponding location. Moreover, if the robot scans the same area a second time and registers the two scans, the resulting pose estimates will be less accurate if the person has moved in between. Thus, dynamic objects can lead to spurious objects in the resulting maps and at the same time can make localization harder. In Sect. 18.3.2, different ways are discussed that deal with the dynamic objects in the environment.

In terms of mapping, two different techniques in 2-D are presented below, the first following a grid-based approach whereas the second a feature-based one, offering very promising alternatives, each one with its own merits.

Grid-Based Mapping

Grid-based methods are based on the concept of occupancy grids to map the environment, firstly introduced by the pioneering work of Moravec and Elfes [24] back in 1985 and extended further by others [25, 26]. In these approaches, the robot's environment is discretized into cells of fixed size. An occupancy value is assigned to each cell representing the probability that an obstacle exists in the physical location corresponding to this cell (Fig. 18.4). For localization, instantaneous sensory information acquired by the robot is matched with the occupancy

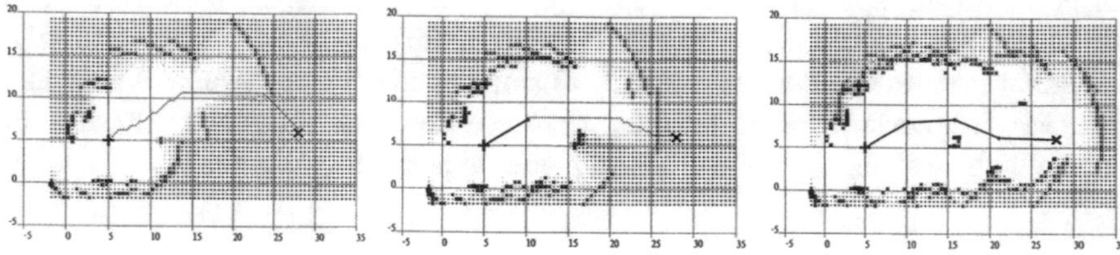

Fig. 18.4 Overhead view of incremental map building as an occupancy grid. Sonar measurements are employed in this process, whereas each point on the dark trajectory is a stop that allowed the sensor to collect new reading. The scale marks are in feet (© H.P. Moravec 1984, reprinted with permission)

grid map, and the location of the robot is calculated by considering areas of the map with high correlation.

The discussed mapping technique of [27] uses occupancy grid maps and realizes an incremental mapping scheme that has been previously employed with great success [26] to deal with environments of arbitrary shape. Mathematically, we calculate a sequence of robot poses $\widehat{l}_1, \widehat{l}_2, \ldots$ and corresponding maps by maximizing the marginal likelihood of the t-pose and map relative to the $(t-1)$-th pose and map:

$$\hat{l}_t = \underset{\hat{l}_t}{\operatorname{argmax}} \left\{ p\left(s_t \middle| l_t, \hat{m}\left(\hat{l}^{t-1}, s^{t-1}\right)\right) \cdot p\left(l_t \middle| u_{t-1}, \hat{l}_{t-1}\right) \right\} \quad (18.1)$$

In Eq. (18.1) the term $p\left(s_t \middle| l_t, \hat{m}\left(\hat{l}^{t-1}, s^{t-1}\right)\right)$ is the probability of the most recent measurement s_t given the pose l_t and the map $\hat{m}\left(\hat{l}^{t-1}, s^{t-1}\right)$ constructed so far. The term $p\left(l_t \middle| u_{t-1}, \hat{l}_{t-1}\right)$ represents the probability that the robot is at state l_t, provided that the robot was previously at state $\widehat{l}_{t-1}$ and has carried out (or measured) the motion u_{t-1}. The resulting pose $\widehat{l}_t$ is then used to generate a new map $\widehat{m}$ via the standard incremental map-updating function presented in Moravec and Elfes [24]:

$$\hat{m}\left(\hat{l}^t, s^t\right) = \underset{m}{\operatorname{argmax}}\, p\left(m \middle| \hat{l}^t, s^t\right) \quad (18.2)$$

The overall approach can be summarized as follows. At any point in time $t-1$, the robot is given an estimate of its pose $\widehat{l}_{t-1}$ and a map $\hat{m}\left(\hat{l}^{t-1}, s^{t-1}\right)$. After the robot moved further on and after taking a new measurement s_t, the robot determines the most likely new pose $\widehat{l}_t$. It does this by trading off the consistency of the measurement with the map [first term on the right-hand side in (18.1)] and the consistency of the new pose with the control action and the previous pose [second term on the right-hand side in (18.1)]. The map is then extended by the new measurement s_t, using the pose $\widehat{l}_t$ as the pose at which this measurement was taken. To maximize (18.1) a 2-D scan matching approach is utilized, which is an extension of the one presented in [28]. To align a scan relative to the map constructed so far, an occupancy grid map $\hat{m}\left(\hat{l}^{t-1}, s^{t-1}\right)$ [24, 28] is computed out of the sensor scans obtained so far. Additionally to previous approaches, small Gaussian errors are integrated in the robot pose when computing the maps. This avoids that many cells remain unknown especially if t is small. Additionally, it increases the smoothness of the map and corresponding likelihood function to be optimized and thus facilitates the range registration. To maximize the likelihood of a scan with respect to this map, a hill-climbing strategy is applied.

Feature-Based Mapping

In feature-based approaches, maps are composed of specific, easily identifiable features of the environment, such as planes, corner points, and line segments

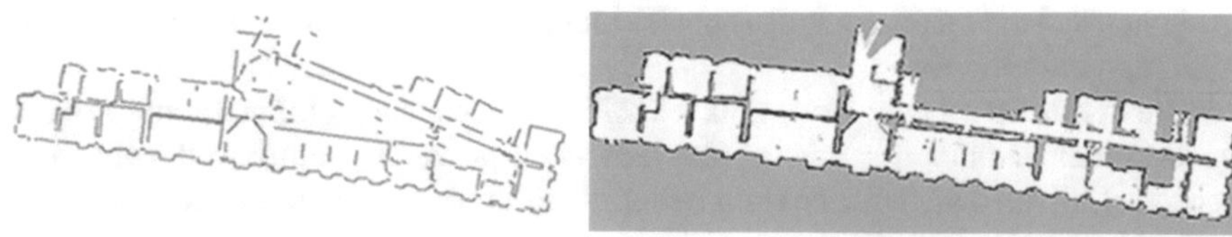

Fig. 18.5 Line feature map (*left*) and occupancy grid map (*right*) of an exhibition site generated by a mobile robot (reproduced from [35], © 2003 Springer, reprinted with permission)

[29]. Similarly to grid-based approaches, feature-based approaches tend to view the localization problem as a matching problem between sensor observations and model features of the a priori metrically correct feature map. The most successful feature-based approaches rely on filtering methods, such as Kalman filters, in order to track the robot position [30, 31].

The technique presented in Baltzakis [32] and Baltzakis and Trahanias [29] relies on line features and corner points extracted out of laser range measurements. It uses a combination of a discrete (hidden Markov) model and a continuous (Kalman-filter) model [33] and applies the expectation–maximization (EM) algorithm [28, 34] to learn globally consistent maps. The proposed EM algorithm iterates a Kalman smoother-localization step (E-step) and a map recalculation step (M-step) until the overall process has converged or until a certain number of iterations have been carried out. To detect and close loops during mapping, the algorithm relies on the global localization capabilities of a hybrid method based on a switching state-space model [33]. This approach applies multiple Kalman trackers assigned to multiple hypotheses about the robot's state. Hypotheses are dynamically generated by matching corner points extracted from measurements with corner points contained in the map. Hypotheses that cannot be verified by observations or sequences of observations become less likely and usually disappear quickly, and the resulting map always corresponds to the most likely hypothesis. Figure 18.5 shows a typical map of an exhibition site resulting from this process.

Summarizing on the above, the grid-based method is more adequate in environments with no clearly defined structure (walls, corridors, corners, etc.) at the price of slightly decreased loop-closing capabilities. When the environment structure becomes evident, feature-based methods can be employed to render more robust loop closing.

18.3.2 Detection, Tracking, and Filtering of Dynamic Objects

Whereas most contemporary mapping methods are able to deal with noise in the odometry and the sensor data, these methods assume that the environment is static during mapping. However, in public spaces such as museums or trade fairs, the environment cannot be regarded as static during a mapping session. There exist several approaches to mapping in dynamic environments [36]. One popular way to achieve this is to use features corresponding to dynamic objects and to track such objects while the robot moves in its environment [27, 37]. Accordingly, prior to updating the map, measurements that correspond to dynamic objects can be filtered out. In the work of Hähnel et al. [27], persons are tracked in range scans, and corresponding data are removed during the registration and mapping process. Other notable works on updating maps or improving localization in populated environments are the work of Burgard et al. [15], Montemerlo et al. [38], and Fox et al. [25]. These methods require a given and fixed map which is used for localization and for the extraction of the features corresponding to the people.

Figure 18.6 shows results from two different environments, namely, a map of the Byzantine and Christian Museum in Athens and a populated corridor environment of the University of Bonn. In both sites the people tracker of Hähnel et al. [27] was incorporated into the mapping process. As can be observed, the robot was able to detect moving people so that the resulting map provides a better representation of the true state of the static environment.

Further to the above, a common problem with respect to object detection is that various objects, such as chairs, tables, and shelves, are not correctly represented in the two-dimensional (2-D) laser range scans used for navigation. To overcome this problem and prevent possible collisions, existing systems additionally use visual information. According to the method developed in [39], the 2-D structure acquired with the laser range scanner is used to compute a 2.5-D representation of the environment by assuming vertical planar walls for all obstacles in the 2-D map. Camera information is then exploited to (a) validate the correctness of the constructed model and (b) qualitatively and quantitatively characterize inconsistencies between laser and visual data wherever such inconsistencies are detected. Figure 18.7 illustrates a typical application example in a corridor environment at the Institute of Computer Science (ICS) of the Foundation for Research and Technology—Hellas (FORTH), in Heraklion, Greece. In this case, the robot travels along a

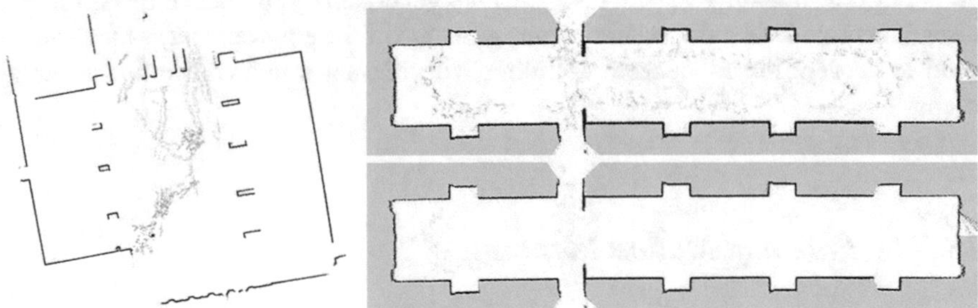

Fig. 18.6 Map of the populated exhibition hall of the Byzantine and Christian Museum in Athens with measurements labeled as belonging to dynamic objects shown in *orange* (*left*). Maps created for the populated corridor environment of the University of Bonn without and with people filtering (*right*) (reproduced from [27], © 2003 by Taylor & Francis, reprinted with permission)

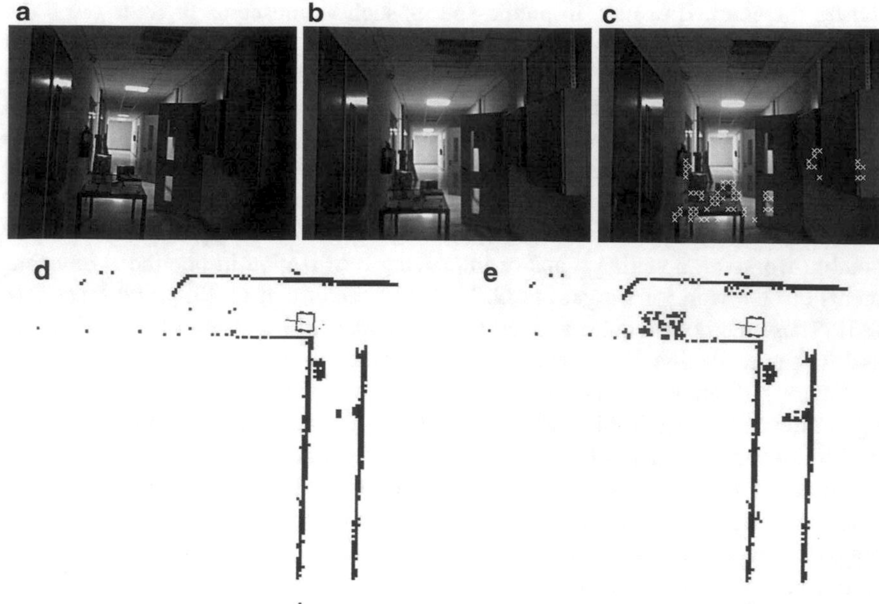

Fig. 18.7 (**a**, **b**) Images acquired at successive points in time, (**c**) results of obstacle detection superimposed on the image shown in (**b**). (**d**) Occupancy grid map computed with laser data only. (**e**) Occupancy grid maps computed based on the fusion of vision and laser data (reproduced from [35] © 2003 Springer, reprinted with permission)

corridor with several objects that are invisible to the laser scanner, such as the table, the fire extinguisher, and the wall cabinet. Figure 18.7a, b show the images grabbed by the robot at two consecutive moments in time. Figure 18.7c shows the results of obstacle detection. Regions with inconsistencies are marked with crosses. As can be verified, objects that cannot be detected with the range finder are successfully detected with the proposed technique. Finally, Fig. 18.7d, e shows the occupancy grid maps obtained without considering visual information and after fusing vision and laser information, respectively. The map generated by the fusion of vision and laser data provides a more accurate representation of the environment, which can be used to prevent the robot from colliding with obstacles not visible in the range scans.

18.3.3 Path and Motion Planning

The mobile robot path-planning task is formulated as that of finding a collision-free route, through an environment containing obstacles, from a specified start location to a desired goal destination using a representation of the environment and certain optimization criteria. Moreover, the robot must be able to follow the generated path while detecting and avoiding unexpected obstacles that block its way. The first task, known as the path-planning task (or off-line planning), assumes perfectly known and stable environment, while the second task, known as the motion planning and obstacle avoidance task (or online planning), focuses on dealing with uncertainties when the robot traverses the environment. The path planning particularly addresses the following question: *what is the best way to go there?* Several strategies exist [40, 41]; however, most systems often use a global path planner, as in [32, 41], which finds optimal paths to the desired target taking into account the topology of the map. Produced paths are guaranteed to be optimal according to an a priori defined cost function (e.g., shortest path). Paths are then split into an ordered set of subgoals which are given sequentially to the motion planner module. The motion planner module takes into account the robot dynamics and produces motion commands in order to reach them avoiding at the same time collisions with unexpected obstacles that may occur.

Global Path Planner

The value iteration algorithm [42] is a standard algorithm used for global path planning. The algorithm is based on dynamic programming that iteratively propagates values through the map according to (a) obstacles defined in the map, (b) the position of the target, and (c) an a priori defined cost function. The solution is a two-dimensional histogram of potentials with maximum values at places of obstacles and only a single minimum at the position of the target. By following the gradient of the histogram, the robot is guaranteed to traverse a minimum cost path (e.g., shortest path) to the target.

The value iteration algorithm initializes by setting the values of all histogram cells to infinity, except for the value of the cell corresponding to the target point which is set to zero. That is, each cell value $H_{x,y}$ is initialized as:

$$H_{x,y} = \begin{cases} 0, & \text{if cell } (x,y) \text{ corresponds to the target point} \\ \infty, & \text{otherwise} \end{cases} \tag{18.3}$$

Cell values are updated iteratively, until convergence is achieved, according to the following rule:

$$H_{x,y} \leftarrow \min_{\substack{k=-1,0,1 \\ l=-1,0,1}} \{H_{x+k,y+l} + Prob(occ(x,y)) + \sqrt{k^2+l^2} \tag{18.4}$$

where $Prob(occ(x, y))$ is the probability that the position corresponding to cell (x, y) is occupied by an obstacle and is given by the occupancy grid map. $\sqrt{k^2+l^2}$ is the distance that the robot has to transverse in order to move from cell $H_{x+k,y+l}$ to cell $H_{x,y}$. Both those terms constitute the cost function.

What makes the proposed global path planning algorithm suitable for the given application scenario is that the produced histograms depend only on the map and the target point location. Once the histogram is computed for a target, the robot can

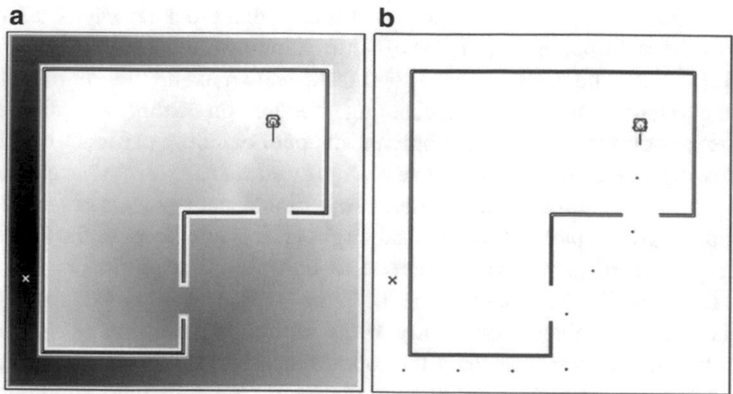

Fig. 18.8 Operation of the global path planner. (**a**) Results of the value iteration algorithm. (**b**) Intermediate points constituting the resulting global path (reproduced from [32], © 2004 H. Baltzakis, reprinted with permission)

easily find the optimal path to the target by simply following the gradient of the histogram, regardless of its position within the map. In other words, the histogram is computed once, according to the desired target, and remains the same either until the goal is reached or until another goal is defined. Even if the robot's belief about its state changes dramatically, the histogram does not have to be recomputed. Figure 18.8 displays the computed histogram for an artificial map. Darker areas indicate lower histogram values while lighter areas indicate higher histogram values. The global minimum of the resulting histogram is at the position of the specified target point (indicated by an "*x*"). The optimal path is easily computed by following the gradient of the histogram, and subgoals are defined along this path, marked by dots "·" in Fig. 18.8b. These subgoals are then passed to the motion planner module, described in the next section.

Motion Planner

Online motion-planning methods utilize recently collected range data in order to steer the robot toward a desired target, avoiding at the same time collision with obstacles that may block its way. Popular methods based on vector field histogram (VFH) [43], potential fields [44], or dynamic windows [45] treat the problem locally, directing the robot into executing globally suboptimal paths to its destination point, that is, the robot sticks on the initial planned path obtained by the global path-planning module. Furthermore, they do not consider a *predictive navigation* framework, that is, do not utilize future motion prediction of humans and/or other objects to decide on what is the "*best*" approach the robot should employ. Namely, the robot can decide at any time step to either change completely its path to its goal position in order to follow an unblocked path or perform a detour. The detour will be executed well before the robot gets too close to the obstacles, and in addition the robot may have foreseen that after performing this detour it will be able to complete its path to the goal position without any other obstructions. Furthermore, the robot

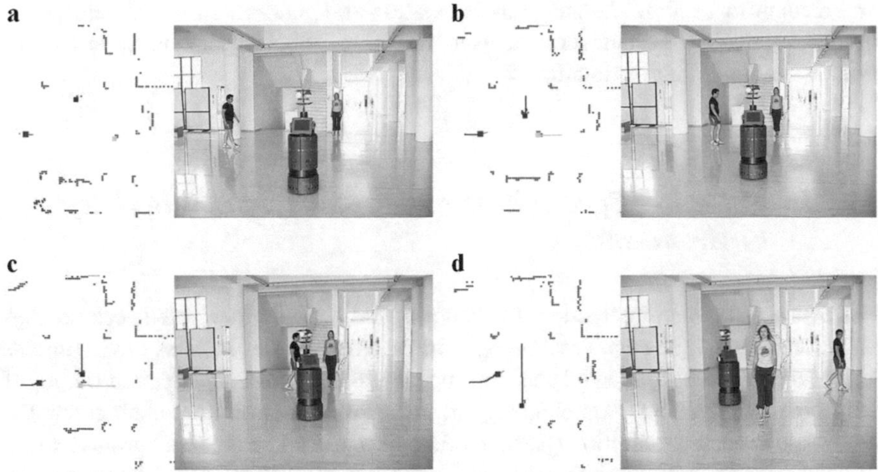

Fig. 18.9 Avoiding two moving objects with a detour [47]. (**a–d**) The robot detects early in its movement that its path to the goal point, the stairs, will be completely blocked by the two persons moving. Hence, it starts making a detour well before it faces any of the two persons (reproduced from [47], © 2010 Springer, reprinted with permission)

can also decide to change its speed of movement to a lower one to allow an obstacle to move away from its motion path or bypass the obstacle by increasing its speed.

Along these lines, Foka and Trahanias [46, 47] treat the navigation problem in a probabilistic manner based on a partially observed Markov decision process (POMDP). Probabilistic planning is performed under the predictive navigation framework where future motion prediction is employed for effective obstacle avoidance. Motion prediction refers to the estimation of the final destination of a human's or another object's motion trajectory. This kind of prediction provides information that is utilized for effective obstacle avoidance since the robot is able to plan in awareness of predicted changes in the environment (see results in Fig. 18.9).

18.4 Human–Robot Interaction

Early museum tour-guide projects [28, 48, 49] mainly focused on the autonomy of the mobile robots with less emphasis on the interaction part. Over the last few years, much research has been carried out in the area of multimodal interaction; however, relevant systems, such as REA [50] and Steve [51] developed by MIT Lab and the University of Southern California, respectively, all considered multimodal interaction and intelligent communication with embodied agents, but they were not directly relevant to natural interaction with mobile autonomous robots. More recently, projects like INDIGO [7] further advanced human–robot interaction (HRI) by exploiting additional relevant technologies, such as speech synthesis and recognition, natural language interpretation and generation, visual perception, human–robot dialog management, user modeling, robotic personality and emotional state, and facial animation.

18.4.1 Automatic Speech Recognition and Synthesis in Noisy Environments

For natural language interaction, the robotic guide should integrate speech recognition technology, be capable of recognizing spoken phrases in noisy environments and of advanced speech synthesis, and be capable of producing spoken output of very high quality. The main challenge in museums and exhibition centers that the automatic speech recognition (ASR) module needs to address is background noise, namely, coping with far-talk ASR problems but also with real external noises. Noise robustness in ASR is a vast topic, spanning research literature over 30 years, and interested readers are referred to the review of Li et al. [52]. A natural way to deal with noise in the acoustic environment is to use multistyle training [53], which trains the acoustic model with all available noisy speech data. The hope is that one of the noise types in the training set will appear in the deployment scenario. However, it is hard to enumerate during training all noise types and SNRs encountered in test environments. Recently, noise suppression techniques based on input from multiple microphones have shown impressive results in noisy conditions [54]. Similar approach was followed in the INDIGO HRI system by performing training on noise-contaminated data and incorporating acoustic modeling. Speech recognition rates were also substantially improved by using predictions from the dialog manager to dynamically restrict the lexical and phrasal expectations at each dialog turn.

Furthermore, the speech synthesis module of the INDIGO system [55] is based on unit selection technology, generally recognized as producing more natural output compared to previous technologies such as diphone concatenation or formant synthesis. The main innovation that is demonstrated is support for emotion, a key aspect of increasing the naturalness of synthetic speech. This is achieved by combining emotional unit recordings with run-time transformations. With respect to the former, a complete "voice" comprises three subvoices (neutral, happy, and sad), based on recordings of the same speaker. In addition to the statically defined subvoices, the speech synthesis module implements dynamic transformations (e.g., emphasis), pauses, and variable speech speed. The system combines all these capabilities in order to dynamically modulate the synthesized speech to convey the impression of emotionally modulated speech.

18.4.2 Visual Detection and Tracking of Humans

In addition to laser-based tracking aiming at motion planning (see Sect. 18.3.3), the robot should also be able to recognize and track faces and hands of the people around it using information from available cameras. This serves the extraction of user IDs and provision of further input for the analysis of communicative signals conveyed by the head, body, and hands, as well as other actions involving hands and objects in the scene. Two main issues need to be addressed. The first concerns tracking objects and maintaining their unique IDs during the whole sequence, which calls for sophisticated modeling of the objects' trajectories and/or a complex model to describe/track each object's shape and the associated dynamics (i.e., how the shape changes over time). The second regards the effective operation of the visual perception system under difficult conditions regarding occlusions, variable illumination, moving cameras, and varying background (see Fig. 18.10).

Different approaches to human detection and tracking have been proposed, utilizing motion cues [56], color [57, 58], depth [59], and feedback from tracking [60]. Skin color provides an effective means for hand and face localization so as to support gesture and action recognition. The idea behind this category of approaches is to build appropriate color models of human skin and then classify image pixels based on how well they fit to these color models. On top of that, various segmentation techniques can be used to cluster skin-colored pixels together into solid blobs that correspond to human hands and/or human faces.

In this respect, the work of Baltzakis et al. [61, 62] that have also been part of the INDIGO [7], as well as of the JAMES [63] systems, can potentially solve difficult tracking problems without any explicit assumptions about the trajectory of the tracked objects or their shape. According to this work, foreground, skin-colored pixels are identified according to their color and grouped together into skin-colored blobs. Information about the location and shape of each tracked blob is maintained by means of a set of pixel hypotheses which are initially sampled from the observed blobs and are propagated from frame to frame according to linear object dynamics computed by a Kalman filter. The distribution of the propagated pixel hypotheses provides a representation for the uncertainty in both the position and the shape of the tracked object.

At the final stage, an incremental classifier [62] is used to maintain and continuously update a belief about whether a tracked hypothesis corresponds to a facial

Fig. 18.10 Images captured by the cameras of the robot at the premises of an exhibition site—Foundation of the Hellenic World—FHW, Athens, Greece

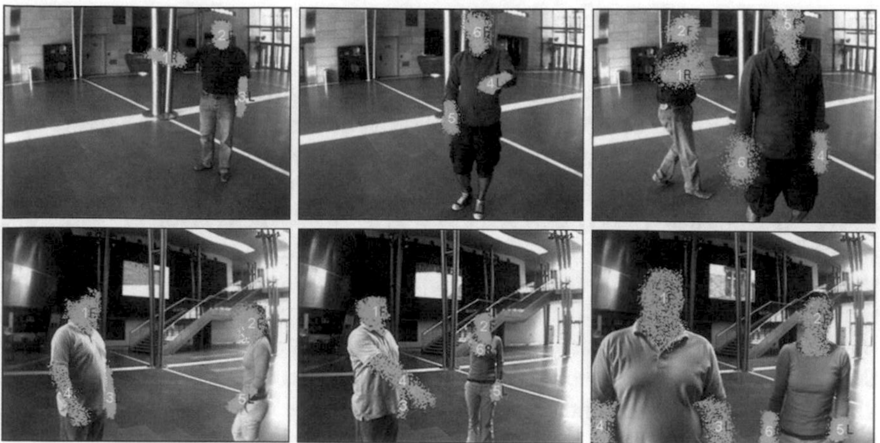

Fig. 18.11 Indicative tracking results from two different sequences acquired in the foyer of the Hellenic Cosmos Center of the Foundation of the Hellenic World (INDIGO's application environment). In all cases the algorithm succeeds in correctly tracking all hypotheses (*numbers*) that correspond to the hands and faces of each person (with *red*)

region, a left hand, or a right hand. For this purpose, a simple yet robust feature set is used, which conveys information about the shape of each tracked blob, its motion characteristics, and its relative location with respect to other blobs. The class of each track is determined by incrementally improving a belief state based on the previous belief state and the likelihood of the currently observed feature set.

Figure 18.11 shows indicative results obtained in two video sequences captured in the foyer of the Hellenic Cosmos Center of the Foundation of the Hellenic World in Athens, Greece, the application environment of INDIGO. As can be easily observed, the algorithm succeeds in keeping track of all the three hypotheses despite the occlusions introduced at various parts of each sequence and in classifying each hypothesis as face (F), left hand (L), or right hand (R).

18.4.3 Visual Attentive Cues for Intention Estimation

Apart from recognizing that a visitor is approaching the robot (based on information from human detection and tracking) and treating it as a signal of a dialog opening, also of particular interest is the focus of attention of a person before or during an interaction with a robot. A body of literature suggests that gaze, head pose, and body (i.e., torso) orientation play an important role during social interaction and, in particular, are used and perceived as a signal of attention, establishing them as important nonverbal communiques.

As with detection and tracking (see Sect. 18.4.2), solutions for visual pose estimation are challenged with respect to invariance in lighting variability, human

Fig. 18.12 Qualitative results of torso and head pose estimation (reproduced from [67], © 2015 Springer, reprinted with permission)

appearance, and visual characteristics. The emergence of low-cost real-time depth cameras, such as the Kinect™ sensor [64], led to numerous important approaches to the pose extraction and tracking problems for the body (e.g., [59]) and face (e.g., [65]), significantly pushing forward the state of the art. Despite the fact that most of the contemporary approaches perform well in usual cases, when dealing with complex, realistic interaction scenarios involving multiple users, limiting factors appear due to explicit or implicit requirements for an initialization phase and occlusions. Additionally, the anthropometric and kinematic inconsistencies encountered in many of the non-model-based approaches usually result to erroneous pose extraction and, thus, may severely deteriorate performance. The majority of methods focus on either the head or the torso due to their difference in appearance and the different types of features that can be extracted. In [66, 67] a model-based framework is adopted, able to overcome key limitations in free-form interaction scenarios and issues of partial occlusions. The method is competent at treating different body parts, including the torso and head, in a unified manner by formulating the *top view re-projection (TVR)* concept. Figure 18.12 illustrates results from experiments involving single and multiple persons, acting and interacting arbitrarily in the scene.

18.4.4 Gesture Interpretation

Further to verbal modes of communication, for example, the ability to accept requests in spoken form, nonverbal modes like gestures complement human-like interactivity of a robotic tour guide. Example gestures may include the *"pointing"* gesture (the user points to an exhibit and asks the robot for information or points down and asks the robot to "come here"), the *"stop"* gesture (the user blocks the way of the robot and opens his/her hands), the *"thumbs up"* gesture (the user performs a *"thumbs up"* sign to approve or answer *"yes"* to a question by the robot), the *"thumbs down"* gesture (the user expresses disapproval or answers *"no"* to a question by doing the thumbs down gesture), or the *"I want your attention gesture"* [the user waves his/her hand(s)]. For the recognition of static gestures,

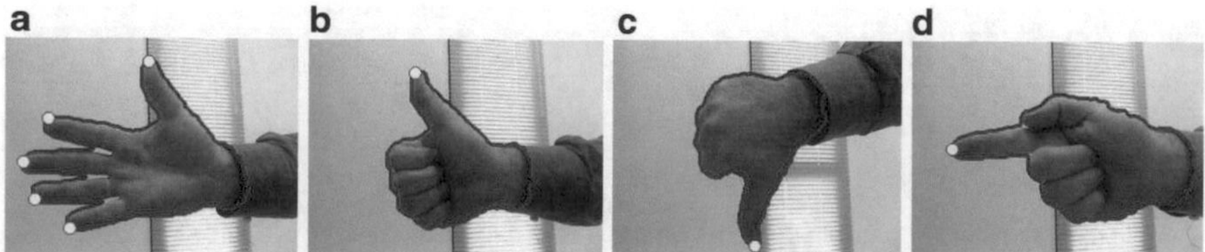

Fig. 18.13 (**a**) The "stop" gesture, (**b**) the "thumbs up" gesture, (**c**) the "thumbs down" gesture, (**d**) the "point" gesture. Detected hand contours and fingertips are also shown (reproduced from [68], © 2009 Zabulis and Baltzakis, reprinted with permission)

Fig. 18.14 Recognition of pointing (*left*) and waving (*right*) gestures, based on the classification of arm trajectories (© 2010 Sigalas, reprinted with permission)

that is, gestures in which the information to be communicated lies in the hand and finger posture at a certain moment in time, a rule-based technique may be followed, simply by detecting the number of fingertips and their relative location with respect to the hand centroid [68] (see Fig. 18.13). Especially for the case of pointing gestures, information from a head pose can be combined [69], assuming the most common type of deictic gesture, that is, the one that involves the index finger pointing at the object of interest and the user's gaze directed at the same target. For gestures like *waving*, which involve arm movement, algorithms based on the classification of arm trajectories to gestures can be used [70] (see Fig. 18.14).

18.5 Interfaces

The employment of intuitive human–robot interfaces is of paramount importance to the acceptance and success of the overall system. The interfaces should be tailored to the type of user; clearly there are similarities as well as important differences between distant and on-site users.

Web Interfaces

A variety of Web-based tele-operation interfaces for robots have been developed in the context of relevant projects, including the Mercury Project [71] and the "Telerobot on the Web" [72]. The mobile robotic platforms Xavier Rhino and Minerva [14, 15] could also be operated over the Web. Their interfaces relied on

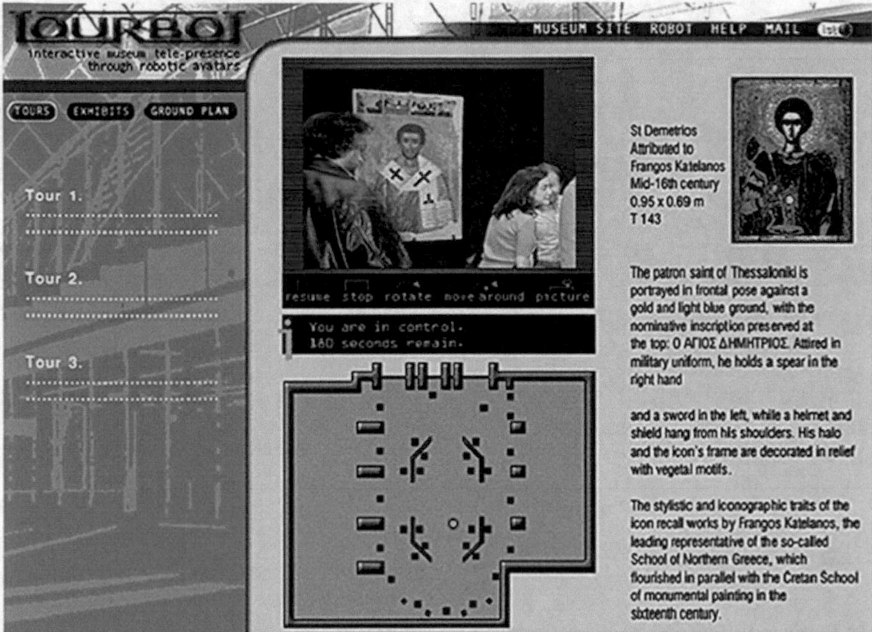

Fig. 18.15 Web interface of the TOURBOT system (reproduced from [35], © 2003 Springer, reprinted with permission)

client-pull and server-push technologies to provide visual feedback of the robot's movements; this includes images taken by the robot as well as a Java-animated map indicating the robot's current position. However, their interfaces do not provide any means to reflect changes in the environment. Three-dimensional graphics visualizations for remote robot control may also allow remote users to carry out manipulation tasks with a mobile robot by controlling a 3-D graphics simulation of the robot. The Web interface developed within TOURBOT and WebFAIR [13] has been designed to provide enhanced functionality and ease of use (Fig. 18.15). Besides providing live streaming video from the exhibition site, the interface also allowed personalized control of the robot. The user is given the possibility to select from a list of predefined guided tours or direct the robot to visit particular exhibits or locations in the exhibition. Furthermore, the user can control the pan–tilt unit of the robot to request the robot to move around an exhibit in order to view it from various directions and to grab high-resolution images.

Onboard Interfaces

In addition to interacting with remote users, robots should interact with on-site visitors as well. For this purpose, in the case of TOURBOT, a properly enhanced version of the Web interface is displayed in a touchscreen mounted at the rear side of the robot. INDIGO (Fig. 18.16) employed also a touchscreen on the robot to be used during interactions, e.g., display information on the exhibits and in cases the

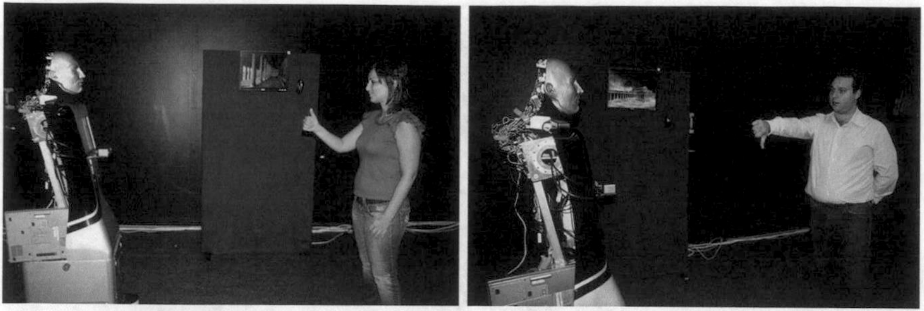

Fig. 18.16 Interaction sessions with the INDIGO robot

input (gesture or speech) from users was not clear the robot prompted them to repeat their answer or use the touchscreen.

18.6 Discussion

As technology becomes progressively available in broader everyday contexts, the number of paradigms of robots in museums is gradually increasing. A robotic avatar can introduce a novel model of augmented environments, allowing human interaction with cultural heritage exhibits and exploration of a remote or virtual site. This chapter provided insight to the development of robotic museum guides featuring human-like interactivity. Accordingly, it exposed the reader to the technical challenges and the specific requirements related to the robot design, navigation capabilities, multimodal interaction, and interfaces to support meaningful social interaction with museum visitors enjoying physical or "virtual" (i.e., remote) presence. Evidently, the field remains too broad to be exhaustively covered in a book chapter. The interested reader is therefore encouraged to treat it as a first acquaintance with the field; references included should serve the purpose for a more in-depth engagement with this challenging and exciting topic.

Acknowledgments This work has been partially supported by the EU Information and Communication Technologies Research Project JAMES (FP7-270435), INDIGO (FP6-045388), and EU FET Proactive Research Project TIMESTORM (H2020-641100).

References

1. C. Breazeal, A. Takanishi, T. Kobayashi, *Social Robots that Interact with People*, Chapter 58 (Springer, 2008), pp. 1349–1370
2. C. Breazeal, Toward sociable robots. Robot. Auton. Syst. **42**(3–4), 167–175 (2003) (Socially Interactive Robots)

3. Reem: Full-Size Humanoid Service Robot. http://pal-robotics.com/en/products/reem/. Last accessed Aug 2016
4. F. Lier, S. Schulz, I. Lütkebohle, *Continuous Integration for Iterative Validation of Simulated Robot Models* (Springer, Berlin, Heidelberg, 2012), pp. 101–112
5. Socibot. https://www.engineeredarts.co.uk/socibot/. Last accessed Apr 2016
6. E. Montalbano, *Slideshow: Tokyo Museum Features Eerily Human Robot Guides. Materials & Assembly Gadget Freak, Electronics & Test* (2014). https://www.designnews.com/materialsassembly/slideshow-tokyo-museum-features-eerily-human-robot-guides/167786772847669. Last accessed Feb 2017
7. S. Konstantopoulos, I. Androutsopoulos, H. Baltzakis, V. Karkaletsis, C. Matheson, A. Tegos, P. Trahanias, in *Indigo: Interaction with Personality and Dialogue Enabled Robots*. Proceedings of the System Demonstrations of the 18th European Conference on Artificial Intelligence, Patras, Greece, July 2008. http://www.ics.forth.gr/indigo/
8. M. Mori, Bukimi no tani [The uncanny valley]. Energy **7**(4), 33–35 (1970)
9. K.F. MacDorman, R.D. Green, C.-C. Ho, C.T. Koch, Too real for comfort? Uncanny responses to computer generated faces. Comput. Human Behav. **25**(3), 695–710 (2009) (Including the Special Issue: Enabling elderly users to create and share self authored multimedia content)
10. A. Tinwell, M. Grimshaw, in *Bridging the Uncanny: An Impossible Traverse?* Proceedings of the 13th International MindTrek Conference: Everyday Life in the Ubiquitous Era, MindTrek'09 (ACM, New York, NY, 2009), pp. 66–73
11. Y. Hurmuzlu, F. Genot, B. Brogliato, Modeling, stability and control of biped robots—a general framework. Automatica **40**(10), 1647–1664 (2004)
12. T. Uchiyama, T. Morita, N. Sawasaki, *Development of Personal Robot* (Springer, Berlin, Heidelberg, 2011), pp. 319–336
13. P. Trahanias, W. Burgard, A. Argyros, D. Hahnel, H. Baltzakis, P. Pfaff, C. Stachniss, TOURBOT and WebFAIR: web-operated mobile robots for tele-presence in populated exhibitions. IEEE Robot. Autom. Mag. **12**(2), 77–89 (2005)
14. S. Thrun, M. Bennewitz, W. Burgard, A.B. Cremers, F. Dellaert, D. Fox, D. Hahnel, C. Rosenberg, N. Roy, J. Schulte, D. Schulz, Minerva: a second-generation museum tour-guide robot. Proc. IEEE ICRA **3**, 1999–2005 (1999)
15. W. Burgard, A.B. Cremers, D. Fox, D. Haehnel, G. Lakemeyer, D. Schulz, W. Steiner, S. Thrun, Experiences with an interactive museum tour-guide robot. Artif. Intell. **114**(1–2), 3–55 (1999)
16. G. Kim, W. Chung, K.R. Kim, M. Kim, S. Han, R.H. Shinn, The autonomous tour-guide robot Jinny. Proc. IEEE/RSJ IROS **4**, 3450–3455 (2004)
17. J.A. Castellanos, J.M.M. Montiel, J. Neira, J.D. Tardos, The SPmap: a probabilistic framework for simultaneous localization and map building. IEEE Trans. Robot. Autom. **15**(5), 948–952 (1999)
18. G. Dissanayake, H. Durrant-Whyte, T. Bailey, A computationally efficient solution to the simultaneous localisation and map building (slam) problem. Proc. IEEE ICRA **2**, 1009–1014 (2000)
19. J.S. Gutmann, K. Konolige, Incremental mapping of large cyclic environments. Proc. IEEE Int. Symp. on Computational Intelligence in Robotics and Automation (CIRA), Monterey, CA, pp. 318–325 (1999). doi: 10.1109/CIRA.1999.810068
20. J.J. Leonard, H Hans Jacob, S. Feder, in *A Computationally Efficient Method for Large-Scale Concurrent Mapping and Localization*. Proceedings of the 9th International Symposium on Robotics Research, pp. 169–176, 1999
21. F. Lu, E. Milios, Globally consistent range scan alignment for environment mapping. Auton. Robots **4**, 333–349 (1997)
22. H. Shatkay, *Learning Models for Robot Navigation*, PhD thesis, Brown University, Providence, RI, USA, 1998
23. S. Thrun, A probabilistic online mapping algorithm for teams of mobile robots. Int. J. Robot. Res. **20**, 2001 (2001)

24. H.P. Moravec, A.E. Elfes, High resolution maps from wide angle sonar. Proc. IEEE ICRA, St. Louis, MO, 116–121 (1985)
25. D. Fox, W. Burgard, S. Thrun, Markov localization for mobile robots in dynamic environments. J. Artif. Intell. Res. (JAIR) **11**, 391–427 (1999)
26. S. Thrun, W. Burgard, D. Fox, A real-time algorithm for mobile robot mapping with applications to multi-robot and 3D mapping. Proc. IEEE ICRA **1**, 321–328 (2000)
27. D. Hähnel, D. Schulz, W. Burgard, Mobile robot mapping in populated environments. Adv. Robot. **17**(7), 579–598 (2003)
28. S. Thrun, M. Beetz, M. Bennewitz, W. Burgard, A.B. Cremers, F. Dellaert, D. Fox, D. Haehnel, C. Rosenberg, N. Roy et al., Probabilistic algorithms and the interactive museum tour-guide robot Minerva. Int. J. Robot. Res. **19**(11), 972–999 (2000)
29. H. Baltzakis, P. Trahanias, Closing multiple loops while mapping features in cyclic environments. Proc. IEEE/RSJ IROS **1**, 717–722 (2003)
30. K.O. Arras, N. Tomatis, R. Siegwart, Multisensor on-the-fly localization using laser and vision. Proc. IEEE/RSJ IROS **1**, 462–467 (2000)
31. J.A. Castellanos, J.M. Martinez, J. Neira, J.D. Tardos, in *Experiments in Multisensor Mobile Robot Localization and Map Building*. Proceedings of 3rd IFAC Symposium on Intelligent Autonomous Vehicles, MACH'ID, pp. 173–178, 1998
32. H. Baltzakis, *A Hybrid Framework for Mobile Robot Navigation Modelling with Switching State Space Networks*, PhD thesis, Department of Computer Science, University of Crete, 2004
33. H. Baltzakis, P. Trahanias, A hybrid framework for mobile robot localization: formulation using switching state-space models. Auton. Robots **15**(2), 169–191 (2003)
34. A.P. Dempster, N.M. Laird, D.B. Rubin, Maximum likelihood from incomplete data via the em algorithm. J. R. Stat. Soc. Ser. B **39**(1), 1–38 (1977)
35. W. Burgard, P. Trahanias, D. Haehnel, M. Moors, D. Schulz, H. Baltzakis, A. Argyros, Telepresence in populated exhibitions through web-operated mobile robots. Auton. Robots **15**(3), 299–316 (2003)
36. W. Burgard, C. Stachniss, D. Haehnel, Mobile robot map learning from range data in dynamic environments, in *Autonomous Navigation in Dynamic Environments*, ed. by C. Laugier, R. Chatila. Springer Tracts in Advanced Robotics, vol 35 (Springer, Berlin, Heidelberg, 2007), pp. 3–28
37. C.C. Wang, C. Thorpe, Simultaneous localization and mapping with detection and tracking of moving objects. Proc. IEEE ICRA, Washington, DC, 2002, pp. 2918–2924. doi: 10.1109/ROBOT.2002.1013675
38. M. Montemerlo, S. Thrun, W. Whittaker, Conditional particle filters for simultaneous mobile robot localization and people-tracking. Proc. IEEE ICRA, 695–701 (2002). doi:10.1109/ROBOT.2002.1013439
39. H. Baltzakis, A. Argyros, P. Trahanias, Fusion of laser and visual data for robot motion planning and collision avoidance. Mach. Vis. Appl. **15**(2), 92–100 (2003)
40. J.C. Latombe, *Robot Motion Planning* (Kluwer Academic Publishers, Boston, MA, 1991)
41. B. Lau, *Techniques for Robot Navigation in Dynamic Real-World Environments*, PhD thesis, University of Freiburg, 2013
42. S. Thrun, A. Buecken, W. Burgard, D. Fox, T. Froehlinghaus, D. Hennig, T. Hofmann, M. Krell, T. Schmidt, *Map Learning and High-Speed Navigation in Rhino*. Technical Report Technical Report IAI-TR-96-3, University of Bonn, Department of Computer Science, July 1996
43. J. Borenstein, Y. Koren, The vector field histogram—fast obstacle avoidance for mobile robots. IEEE Trans. Robot. Autom. **7**(3), 278–288 (1991)
44. O. Khatib, Real-time obstacle avoidance for robot manipulator and mobile robots. Int. J. Robot. Res. **5**(1), 90–98 (1986)
45. D. Fox, W. Burgard, S. Thrun, The dynamic window approach to collision avoidance. IEEE Robot. Autom. Mag **4**(1), 23–33 (1997)

46. A. Foka, P. Trahanias, Predictive control of robot velocity to avoid obstacles in dynamic environments. Proc. IEEE/RSJ IROS **1**, 370–375 (2003)
47. A. Foka, P. Trahanias, Probabilistic autonomous robot navigation in dynamic environments with human motion prediction. Int. J. Soc. Robot. **2**(1), 79–94 (2010)
48. I.R. Nourbakhsh, C. Kunz, T. Willeke, The mobot museum robot installations: a five year experiment. Proc. IEEE/RSJ IROS 3, 3636–3641 (2003). doi: 10.1109/IROS.2003.1249720
49. R. Siegwart, K.O. Arras, S. Bouabdallah, D. Burnier, G. Froidevaux, X. Greppin, B. Jensen, A. Lorotte, L. Mayor, M. Meisser, R. Philippsen, R. Piguet, G. Ramel, G. Terrien, N. Tomatis, Robox at expo.02: a large-scale installation of personal robots. Robot. Auton. Syst. **42**(3–4), 203–222 (2003)
50. J. Cassell, T. Bickmore, M. Billinghurst, L. Campbell, K. Chang, H. Vilhjálmsson, H. Yan, in *Embodiment in Conversational Interfaces: Rea*. Proceedings of the SIGCHI Conference on Human Factors in Computing Systems, CHI'99 (ACM, New York, NY, 1999), pp. 520–527
51. J. Rickel, W.L. Johnson, Animated agents for procedural training in virtual reality: perception, cognition and motor control. Appl. Artif. Intell. **13**(4–5), 343–382 (1999)
52. J. Li, L. Deng, Y. Gong, R. Haeb-Umbach, An overview of noise-robust automatic speech recognition. IEEE/ACM Trans. Audio Speech Lang. Process. **22**(4), 745–777 (2014)
53. R. Lippmann, E. Martin, D. Paul, Multi-style training for robust isolated-word speech recognition. Acoust. Speech Signal Process. **12**, 705–708 (1987) (IEEE International Conference on ICASSP'87)
54. I. Cohen, B. Berdugo, Microphone array post-filtering for non-stationary noise suppression. Proc. IEEE Int. Conf. Acoust. Speech Signal Process. (ICASSP) **1**, I-901–I-904 (2002)
55. S. Konstantopoulos, A. Tegos, D. Bilidas, I. Androutsopoulos, G. Lampouras, P. Malakasiotis, C. Matheson, O. Deroo, in *Adaptive Natural Language Interaction*. Proceedings of the 12th Conference of the European Chapter of the Association for Computational Linguistics: Demonstrations Session, EACL'09 (Association for Computational Linguistics, Stroudsburg, PA, 2009), pp. 37–40
56. N. Dalal, B. Triggs, *Histograms of Oriented Gradients for Human Detection*. CVPR, 2005
57. H. Baltzakis, A. Argyros, M. Lourakis, P. Trahanias, Tracking of human hands and faces through probabilistic fusion of multiple visual cues, in *Computer Vision Systems*, ed. by A. Gasteratos, M. Vincze, J. Tsotsos. Lecture Notes in Computer Science, vol 5008 (Springer, Berlin, Heidelberg, 2008), pp. 33–42
58. M.J. Jones, J.M. Rehg, Statistical color models with application to skin detection. Int. J. Comput. Vis. **46**(1), 81–96 (2002)
59. J. Shotton, A. Fitzgibbon, M. Cook, T. Sharp, M. Finocchio, R. Moore, A. Kipman, A. Blake, Real-time human pose recognition in parts from single depth images. Proc. IEEE CVPR, Providence, RI, 2011, pp. 1297–1304. doi: 10.1109/CVPR.2011.5995316
60. B. Wu, R. Nevatia, Detection and tracking of multiple, partially occluded humans by Bayesian combination of Edgelet part detectors. IJCV **75**(2), 247–266 (2007)
61. H. Baltzakis, A. Argyros. Propagation of Pixel Hypotheses for Multiple Objects Tracking. In *Advances in Visual Computing*. Ed by Bebis G. et al. Lecture Notes in Computer Science, vol 5876. (Springer, Berlin, Heidelberg, 2009) pp. 140–149
62. H. Baltzakis, M. Pateraki, P. Trahanias, Visual tracking of hands, faces and facial features of multiple persons. Mach. Vis. Appl., 1–17 (2012). doi:10.1007/s00138-012-0409-5
63. M.E. Foster, A. Gaschler, M. Giuliani, A. Isard, M. Pateraki, R. Petrick, in *"Two People Walk into a Bar": Dynamic Multi-Party Social Interaction with a Robot Agent*. Proceedings of the 14th ACM International Conference on Multimodal Interaction, Santa Monica, CA, USA, 22–26 October 2012
64. Microsoft Kinect. http://www.xbox.com/en-US/xbox-one/accessories/kinect. Last accessed Feb 2017
65. G. Fanelli, J. Gall, L. Van Gool, Real time head pose estimation with random regression forests. Proc. IEEE CVPR, Providence, RI, pp. 617–624 (2011). doi: 10.1109/CVPR.2011.5995458

66. M. Sigalas, M. Pateraki, P. Trahanias, Full-body pose tracking—the top view reprojection approach. IEEE Trans. Pattern Anal. Mach. Intell. **99**, 1–14 (2015)
67. M. Sigalas, M. Pateraki, P. Trahanias, Visual estimation of attentive cues in HRI: the case of torso and head pose, in *Computer Vision Systems*, ed. by L. Nalpantidis, V. Krueger, J. Eklundh, A. Gasteratos (Springer, New York, NY, 2015), pp. 375–388
68. X. Zabulis, H. Baltzakis, A.A. Argyros, Vision-based hand gesture recognition for human computer interaction, in *The Universal Access Handbook*. Human Factors and Ergonomics (Lawrence Erlbaum Associates Inc., Mahwah, NJ, 2009), pp. 34.1–34.30
69. M. Pateraki, H. Baltzakis, P. Trahanias, Visual estimation of pointed targets for robot guidance via fusion of face pose and hand orientation. Comput. Vis. Image Underst. **120**, 1–13 (2014)
70. M. Sigalas, H. Baltzakis, P. Trahanias, in *Gesture Recognition Based on Arm Tracking for Human–Robot Interaction*. Proceedings of IEEE IROS, Taipei, pp. 5424–5429, 2010
71. K. Goldberg, S. Gentner, C. Sutter, J. Wiegley, The mercury project: a feasibility study for internet robots. IEEE Robot. Autom. Mag. **7**(1), 35–40 (2000)
72. A.L. Taylor, J.T. Wright, in *A Telerobot on the World Wide Web*. National Conference of the Australian Robot Association, 1995

Chapter 19
Digital Cultural Heritage Experience in Ambient Intelligence

Nikolaos Partarakis, Dimitris Grammenos, George Margetis, Emmanouil Zidianakis, Giannis Drossis, Asterios Leonidis, George Metaxakis, Margherita Antona, and Constantine Stephanidis

Abstract This chapter presents recent advances in ambient intelligence technologies (AmI) for digital heritage experience in the context of virtual museums (VM). This is delivered under the light of an integrated and scalable approach towards the creation of AmI heritage environments. More specifically, this chapter presents a framework for representing knowledge and the appropriate mechanisms for personalizing content and user interfaces (UIs) to each individual user of a VM application. Based on the presented framework, a number of enabling technologies are reviewed as employed in alternative application contexts to explore (a) the provision of personalized interaction with artworks, (b) the provision of mixed reality technologies for blending the physical with the virtual world, (c) gamification techniques for educational purposes within the museum context, (d) the usage of gamification as a means to produce interactive art installations and (e) the usage of portable mobile and custom hardware devices as a museum guide and as a means for exploring a museum in the context of a treasure hunt game.

Keywords Ambient intelligence • Gamification • Interaction • Cultural heritage • Virtual museum • Interactive exhibits • Digital exhibits • Augmented games • Tabletop games • Museum guide • Immersive experiences • Mixed reality • Interactive art

---

N. Partarakis (✉) • D. Grammenos • G. Margetis • E. Zidianakis • G. Drossis • A. Leonidis • G. Metaxakis • M. Antona
Foundation for Research and Technology—Hellas (FORTH), Institute of Computer Science, Heraklion, Crete 70013, Greece
e-mail: partarak@ics.forth.gr; gramenos@ics.forth.gr; gmarget@ics.forth.gr; zidian@ics.forth.gr; drossis@ics.forth.gr; leonidis@ics.forth.gr; gmetax@ics.forth.gr; antona@ics.forth.gr

C. Stephanidis
Foundation for Research and Technology—Hellas (FORTH), Institute of Computer Science, Heraklion, Crete 70013, Greece

Department of Computer Science, University of Crete, Voutes University Campus, Heraklion, Greece
e-mail: cs@ics.forth.gr; cs@csd.uoc.gr

M. Ioannides et al. (eds.), *Mixed Reality and Gamification for Cultural Heritage*,
DOI 10.1007/978-3-319-49607-8_19

19.1 Introduction

Today, the term virtual museum (VM) is mainly used to describe initiatives such as 2D and 3D digital collections available on the web, virtual tours to existing physical museums or (in its advanced form) a systematic use of web technology and tools, as well as multimedia content, to communicate aspects of the digital culture and cultural heritage (CH).[1] Recent and current research activities on VMs have identified and systematically advanced new technologies, methods and tools to develop the VM of tomorrow. A wide range of technological challenges related to digital CH have been addressed, including 3D and mass digitization of tangible artefacts/artworks (e.g. Scan4Reco,[2] 3D-COFORM,[3] GRAVITATE[4]), digital repositories, metadata and preservation policies (e.g. Europeana,[5] Athena Plus,[6] DCH-RP[7]), 3D data capture and scanning (e.g. DigiArt,[8] GRAVITATE[9]), digitization of intangible cultural content (i-Treasures[10]), authoring and digital storytelling (e.g. CHESS[11]), and virtual reality (VR) and augmented reality (AR) technologies (e.g. DigiArt,[12] CHESS,[13] iTACITUS[14]), as well as holistic solutions for virtual exhibitions (e.g. Athena Plus[15]). Access to digital content through mobile and web platforms, adaptability, personalisation and multimodal user interaction have equally been addressed. Furthermore, initiatives such as V-Must[16] and eCult[17] have carried out extensive technology watch on VM-related state-of-the-art technologies and applications and have conceived well-documented visions on the VM of tomorrow.[18]

---

[1]Examples of existing virtual museums can be found at http://www.v-must.net/virtual-museums (V-musT.net is a NoE funded by FP7; end date 31/12/15).

[2]http://scan4reco.eu/scan4reco/

[3]http://www.3d-coform.eu/

[4]http://gravitate-project.eu/

[5]http://www.europeana.eu/portal/

[6]http://www.athenaplus.eu/

[7]http://www.dch-rp.eu/

[8]http://digiart-project.eu/

[9]http://gravitate-project.eu/

[10]http://i-treasures.eu/

[11]http://www.chessexperience.eu/

[12]http://digiart-project.eu/

[13]http://www.chessexperience.eu/

[14]http://www.instantreality.org/itacitus/

[15]http://www.athenaplus.eu/

[16]http://www.v-must.net/

[17]http://www.ecultobservatory.eu/tech-catalogue/tech-solutions/all and http://www.v-must.net/technology

[18]http://www.v-must.net/library/documents/d31-theory-design-updated-2014, http://www.ecultobservatory.eu/documents

Despite this progress, several limitations still exist, such as (a) the lack of technology to enhance and deliver digital content in high quality and in universal formats to reduce compatibility issues, (b) the lack of tools for the development of VMs to reduce the complexity and authoring time, (c) the need to integrate the aforementioned technologies under a unified framework for visualizing VMs content, (d) the lack of sufficient mechanisms to provide personalized content and (e) the lack of adaptation mechanisms to present a suitable user interface to individual users of the VM.

This chapter presents a framework for implementing digital cultural heritage application on top of AmI technologies supporting rich interaction and gamification. Based on the presented framework, a number of enabling technologies are reviewed as employed in alternative application contexts.

19.2 Background and Related Work

19.2.1 Virtual Museums

VMs have evolved from digital duplicates of "real" museums or online museums into complex communication systems, strongly connected with narratives, interaction and immersion in 3D-reconstructed scenarios [1]. Currently existing VMs can be classified as:

- **Mobile VMs or micro museums:** Mobile applications to explain history, architecture and/or other artworks visually (indoor virtual archaeology, embedded virtual reconstructions, etc.)
- **On-site interactive installations:** Multi-user environments, aimed at conserving the collective experience typical of the visit to a museum. A common characteristic is the use of 3D models reconstructing monuments, sites, landscapes, etc., which can be explored in most cases in real time, either directly or through a guide [2]
- **Web-delivered VMs:** Virtual museums providing content through the Web. A wide variety of 3D viewers and players have been developed to provide 3D interactive applications "embedded" in browsers, activated by a website exposing specific 3D content. Examples include Google Art, Inventing Europe, MUSEON, etc.
- **Multimedia VMs:** They involve interactive experiences blending video, audio and interactive technologies, usually delivered via CD-ROM or DVD (e.g. "Medieval Dublin: From Vikings to Tudors").
- **Digital Archives:** Increasingly popular, as the amount of digital information increases, together with the wish of the public to gain access to information. Examples include thesaurus of terms, digital repositories considering all possible different metadata schemes, intelligent searching/browsing systems, etc.

- **VMs can be classified by:** (a) **Content,** referring to the actual theme and exhibits of a VM (history, archaeology, natural history, art, etc.); (b) **interaction technology,** related to the user capability of modifying the environment and receiving a feedback to his/her actions (both immersion and interaction concur to realize the belief of actually being in a virtual space [3]; (c) **duration,** referring to the timing of a VM and the consequences in terms of technology, content, installation, and sustainability of the projects (periodic, permanent, temporary); (d) **communication,** referring to the type of communication style used to create a VM. Can be classified in descriptive, narrative or dramatization-based VMs; (e) **level of user immersion**, immersive and non-immersive [3]; (f) **sustainability level**, i.e. the extent to which the museum software, digital content and setup and/or metadata are **r**eusable, portable, maintainable and exchangeable; (g) **type of distribution** refers to the extent to which the VM can be moved from one location to another. It may include *mobile VMs* and *non-distributed VMs* (e.g. on-site installations); and (g) **scope of the VM**, including educational, entertainment, promotional and research.

19.2.2 Knowledge Models for CH

In the cultural heritage domain, the use of ontologies for describing and classifying objects is now a well-established practice. The Getty vocabulary databases, maintained by the Getty Vocabulary Program, provide a solid basis that is a de facto standard in the area.[19] These databases are thesauri compliant with the ISO standard for thesaurus construction. They comprise the Art & Architecture Thesaurus (AAT), the Union List of Artist Names (ULAN) and the Getty Thesaurus for Geographic Names (TGN). The AAT, in particular, contains more than 30,000 concepts, including terms, descriptions, bibliographic citations and other information relating to art. The AAT is organized as a hierarchy with seven levels, called facets, in which a term may have more than one broader term. The Getty Research Institute has also developed a metadata schema, called the Categories for the Description of Works of Art (CDWA), for describing art works. CDWA includes 381 categories and subcategories, a small subset of which are considered the core, in the sense that they represent the minimum information necessary to identify and describe a work. Complementary to the CDWA, the Conceptual Reference Model (CRM) of the International Committee for Documentation of the International Council of Museums (ICOM-CIDOC) has emerged as a conceptual basis for reconciling different metadata schemas.[20] The CRM provides definitions and a formal structure for describing the implicit and explicit concepts and relationships used in cultural heritage documentation. CRM is an ISO standard (21127:2006) that

[19]http://www.getty.edu/research/tools/vocabularies/index.html

[20]http://www.cidoc-crm.org/

has been integrated with the Functional Requirements for Bibliographic Records (FRBR) and the Europeana Data Model,[21] which play the role of upper ontology for integrating metadata schemes of libraries, archives and museums.

19.2.3 Interactive Technologies for Virtual Museums

Virtual Reality (VR) VR provides total sensory immersion through immersion displays and tracking and sensing technologies. Common visualization displays include head-mounted displays and 3D polarizing stereoscopic glasses while inertia and magnetic trackers are the most popular positional and orientation devices. As far as sensing is concerned, a 3D mouse and gloves can be used to create a feeling of control of an actual space. An example of a high-immersion VR environment is Kivotos, a VR environment that uses the CAVE® system, in a room of 3 m by 3 m, where the walls and the floor act as projection screens and in which visitors take off on a journey thanks to stereoscopic 3D glasses.[22,23] As mentioned earlier, virtual exhibitions can be visualized in the web browser in the form of 3D galleries, but they can also be used as a stand-alone interface. In addition, a number of commercial VR software tools and libraries exist, such as Cortona3D, which can be used to generate fast and effectively virtual museum environments. However, the cost of creating and storing the content (i.e. 3D galleries) is considerably high for the medium- and small-sized museums that represent the majority of Cultural Heritage Institutions (CHIs).

Augmented Reality (AR) In addition to VR exhibitions, museum visitors can enjoy an enhanced experience by visualizing, interacting and navigating into museum collections (i.e. artworks) or even by creating museum galleries in an AR environment. The virtual visitors can position virtual artworks anywhere in the real environment by using either sophisticated software methods (i.e. computer vision techniques) or specialized tracking devices (i.e. InertiaCube). Although the AR exhibition is harder to achieve, it offers advantages to museum visitors as compared to Web3D and VR exhibitions. Specifically, in an AR museum exhibition, virtual information (usually 3D objects but also any type of multimedia information, such as textual or pictorial information) is played over video frames captured by a camera, giving users the impression that the virtual cultural artworks actually exist in the real environment. AR has been experimentally applied to make it possible to visualize incomplete or broken real objects as they were in their original state by superimposition of the missing parts [4]. The ARCO system[24] [5]

[21]http://pro.europeana.eu/web/guest/edm-documentation

[22]Foundation of the Hellenic World, available at: http://www.ime.gr

[23]Cortona, VRML Client—Web3D Products, available at: http://www.parallelgraphics.com/products/cortona/

[24]Augmented Representation of Cultural Objects (ARCO) Consortium. Available at: http://www.arco-web.org

provides customized tools for virtual museum environments, ranging from the digitization of museum collections to the tangible visualization of both museum galleries and artworks. ARCO developed tangible interfaces that allow museum visitors to visualize virtual museums in Web3D, VR and AR environments sequentially. A major benefit of an AR-based interface resides in the fact that carefully designed applications can provide novel and intuitive interaction without the need for expensive input devices.

Mixed Reality (MR) MR relies on a combination of VR, AR and the real environment. According to Milgram and Kishino's virtuality continuum, real world and virtual world objects are presented together on a single display [6] with visual representation of real and virtual space [7]. An example of the use of MR techniques in a museum environment is the Situating Hybrid Assemblies in Public Environments (SHAPE) project that uses Hybrid Reality technology to enhance users' social experience and learning in museum and other exhibition environments with regard to cultural artworks and to their related contexts [8]. It proposes the use of a sophisticated device called the Periscope (now called the Augurscope), which is a portable MR interface, inside museum environments to support visitors' interaction and visualization of artworks.

19.2.4 Gamification Techniques for Digital Cultural Heritage

Gamification is the use of game thinking and game mechanics as well as game dynamics and frameworks in a non-game context in order to engage users, solve problems, improve user experience and promote desired behaviours [9]. This can be achieved by using techniques from the fields of psychology and game design. It is used to improve timelines and learning.

Museums are considered ideal environments for experimenting with informal learning technologies [10]. In terms of game-based learning, treasure hunts, mysteries and puzzles are common in museums, as is the use of mobile devices to guide and facilitate the collection of exhibition information to collaboratively solve tasks. A familiar approach is seen in the design of Mystery at the Museum at the Boston Museum of Science [11]. In designing learning games that both engage and support inquiry across school and museum contexts, mobile social media, "smartphone" technologies and ubiquitous Internet access have been pivotal developments [12, 13]. However, finding a balance between guided and open activities and structuring opportunities for social interaction and collaboration are important when designing mobile applications for informal learning settings [14].

19.3 A State-of-the-Art AmI Framework for Digital Cultural Heritage

In this chapter, a state-of-the-art AmI framework for digital cultural heritage is presented. This framework is based on AmI technologies and comprises a set of reusable tools and components used across a number of programming languages and tools for the development of interactive systems for cultural heritage. Three major facilities are offered by this framework: (a) a transparent way to provide seamless interaction between software components and services, (b) a knowledge representation framework to support uniform data storage and exploitation from alternative services and programming languages and (c) a pool of reusable interaction modalities based on a suite of image recognition and vision technologies. A high-level architecture of the framework is presented in Fig. 19.1.

19.3.1 A Service-Oriented Middleware

At a technical level, ambient intelligence (AmI) environments are comprised of a large number of diverse heterogeneous computing systems that constantly interoperate in order to provide a unified and seamless user experience. The comprising computing systems are inevitably heterogeneous, since they cut through many different research domains with many different requirements, goals and capabilities. Requiring all the constituent components to be exclusively developed using a universal set of software and hardware technologies is impractical due to performance, suitability, sustainability and, of course, reusability reasons. Towards this direction, we addressed the issue by developing a software platform that lies between all the diverse computing systems and the applications that utilize them and provide a common consistent view and access methods of the former to the latter, regardless of their implementation technologies [15]. This software platform is referred to as the service middleware for AmI environments.

The service middleware ecosystem comprises of the following four software components: (a) software libraries for facilitating communications and service distribution; (b) a set of core services for providing discovery and deployment functionality for the services infrastructure; (c) development tools that facilitate the creation, usage and deployment of services; and (d) client programs for managing and monitoring the computers that are used for running services [16].

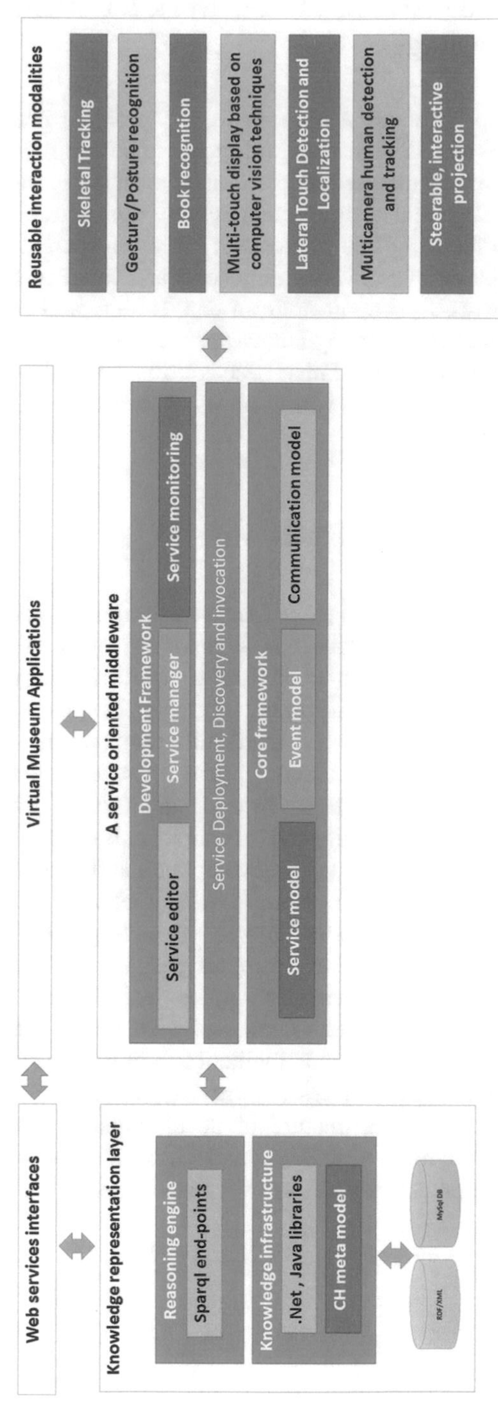

Fig. 19.1 High level architecture (*© 2016 FORTH-ICS*, reprinted with permission)

19.3.2 A Knowledge Representation Layer

In the proposed framework, knowledge is handled through an ontology model. Although the structure of the ontology is modelled using OWL,[25] the actual data are stored either in an XML/OWL format or in a MySQL relational database. The model gets exported to the higher levels of the architecture through a set of programming language classes developed either manually using C# or automatically through the protégé[26] data export facilities. Reasoning engine rules have been defined on the knowledge model using Jess.[27] Two SPARQL query engines have been defined: one that uses the SemWeb.Net Library[28] and one using Jena[29] and Pellet.[30] These query engines submit SPARQL queries to the ontology, and the results of these queries are retrieved in XML and deserialized into meaningful instances of the model. The knowledge infrastructure is exposed to different programming languages and tools in alternative ways: (a) as a middleware service for allowing access from all deployed services, (b) as an IIS and an Apache Tomcat web service to be used by applications not running on the middleware but with support for web services and (c) as a class library both in .Net and Java for direct integration and usage by applications.

19.3.3 A Pool of Reusable Interaction Modalities

The framework facilitates alternative forms of interaction that employ the full set of human perceptual capabilities in order to improve interactive user experience. A pool of reusable computer vision components is employed, each one offering an alternative form of interaction:

- **Skeletal tracking:** The skeletal tracking component reports the position information of each skeleton joint. This component performs geometric transformations on each skeleton joint position constituting every real-time skeleton frame. This happens in order to get the same valid results regardless of the position of the user who may be located everywhere inside the sensor's field of view [17].
- **Gesture/posture recognition:** The gesture/posture recognition module implements the dynamic time warping (DTW) algorithm [18] for measuring the similarity between two skeleton sequences which may vary in time or speed.

[25]OWL Web Ontology Language Reference. W3C Recommendation, 10 February 2004. http://www.w3.org/TR/owl-ref/

[26]Protégé: http://protege.stanford.edu/

[27]Jess: http://herzberg.ca.sandia.gov/

[28]Semantic Web/RDF Library for C#/.NET: http://razor.occams.info/code/semweb/

[29]Apache Jena: https://jena.apache.org/documentation/inference/

[30]Pellet OWL 2 Reasoner for Java: http://clarkparsia.com/pellet/

Additionally, it provides a training platform that allows developers to fine tune their gestures having access to a number of alternative biometric parameters [17].

- **Book recognition:** This component is capable of performing the recognition of book pages and of specific elements of interest within a page, as well as perceiving interaction with actual books and pens/pencils, without requiring any special interaction device [19].
- **Multitouch display based on computer vision techniques:** A multitouch display based on computer vision techniques. The developed system is built upon low-cost, off-the-shelf hardware components and a careful selection of computer vision techniques. The resulting system is capable of detecting and tracking several objects that may move freely on the surface of a wide projection screen. It also provides additional information regarding the detected and tracked objects, such as their orientation, their full contour, etc. [20].
- **Lateral touch detection and localization:** Fingertip contact detection and localization upon planar surfaces to provide interactivity in augmented displays implemented upon these surfaces by projector-camera systems. In contrast to the widely employed approach where user hands are observed from above, lateral camera placement avails increased sensitivity to touch detection [21].
- **Multi-camera human detection and tracking:** A computer vision system that supports non-instrumented, location-based interaction of multiple users with digital representations of large-scale artefacts. The proposed system is based on a camera network that observes multiple humans in front of a very large display. The acquired views are used to volumetrically reconstruct and track the humans robustly and in real time, even in crowded scenes and challenging human configurations [22].
- **Steerable, interactive projection:** Technology to produce a steerable, interactive projection display that has the shape of a disk. Interactivity is provided through sensitivity to the contact of multiple fingertips and is achieved through the use of RGBD cameras [23]. The surface is mounted on two gimbals which, in turn, provide two rotational degrees of freedom. Modulation of surface posture supports the ergonomy of the device but can be, **alternatively**, used as a means of user-interface input. The geometry for mapping visual content and localizing fingertip contacts upon this steerable display is provided, along with pertinent calibration methods for the proposed system [24].

19.4 Applications and Their Deployment in CHIs

This section presents a collection of interactive applications in the context of cultural heritage institutions that explore the proposed AmI framework. These applications are grouped based on the provision of similar functionality to end users in the following categories: (a) personalized interaction with artworks, (b) mixed-reality technologies, (c) gamification techniques for educational purposes, (d) interactive art installations and (e) portable mobile and custom hardware devices.

19.4.1 Personalized Interaction with Artworks

This section presents interactive systems that augment digital reproductions of artefacts to offer personalized interaction. These systems are used to present digital artefacts that are not physically exhibited in museums due to their nature (e.g. murals inside protected monuments).

19.4.1.1 Interacting with Large Digital Reproductions of Murals

Macrographia (see Fig. 19.2) is a system that presents very large images, which visitors can explore by walking around in a room. The images are projected on a screen which takes up one wall of the room and are analysed part by part depending

Fig. 19.2 Macrographia installation "Archaeological Museum of Thessaloniki" (© *2010 FORTH-ICS*, reprinted with permission)

Interaction type	Body tracking	**Number of users**	No limitation
Size	6×2 m	**Usage**	Projection of large murals
Complexity	2 Projectors 1 PC 4 Depth cameras	**Approach**	Multi-camera human detection

on the location of each visitor in the room. Visitors enter the room, and the system follows the movement of each one separately. When someone stands in front of a section of the image, depending on the distance from the screen, the section of the image she/he views and the caption underneath change. There are several layers of information, depending on the size of the room. Visitors can select the language of the accompanying text by entering the room from the left or right side [25].

The system is installed in a room in which a computer vision system tracks the position of visitors [26]. Macrographia can present large scale images of artefacts, with which one or more visitors can concurrently interact by walking around. Visitors enter the room from an entrance opposite the display. The vision system assigns a unique ID number to each person entering the room. As help signs illustrate, visitors entering the room from the right-hand side are considered to be speakers of one language, for example, English, while those from the left-hand side of another, for example, Greek. When at least one person is in the room, a piece of music starts to play. The room is conceptually split in several zones of interest, delimited by different themes presented on the projected image. These zones divide the room in vertical slices. The room is also split in several horizontal zones that run parallel to the projected image, which are delimited by their distance from it. Thus, a grid is created, comprising many interaction slots. When a visitor is located over a slot, the respective projected image part changes and, depending on the slot's distance from the wall, visitors can see enriched images, accompanied by related information.

All information is presented in the user's preferred language. Since users are associated with a unique ID, the system keeps track of the information they have accessed, as well as of the time they have spent on each slot.

Apart from location-sensing, macrographia also supports two additional types of interaction: (a) a kiosk and (b) mobile phones. The kiosk offers an overview of the projected image, an introductory text and two buttons for changing the user's language. All information is automatically presented in the visitor's preferred language. Furthermore, the wall piece in front of which the visitor has spent most of the time is highlighted. Mobile phones are used as multimedia guides, automatically presenting images and text (that can also be read aloud) related to the visitor's current position.

19.4.1.2 Interacting with Digital Reproductions of Paintings

The "personalized multi-user painting" is a suite of tools to allow the augmentation of interaction with paintings using a collection of alternative interaction devices (projection, portable devices, and mounted displays). Its purpose is to provide interaction where no interaction exists (making physical artefacts interactive) and provide interactive digital artefacts where no artefacts exist by importing both an artefact and the means to interact with it within the cultural heritage institutions experience [27]. It comprises a number of devices for content provision and a number of modalities for user interaction. As shown in Fig. 19.3, the main section

Fig. 19.3 The interactive digital exhibit (© *2014 FORTH-ICS*, reprinted with permission)

Interaction type	Body Tracking and touch	**Number of users**	2 With body tracking 2 Using tablets 2 Using tablets 2 Using captions Unlimited using (mobile phones)
Size	Variable	**Usage**	Projection of painting
Complexity	1 Projectors 4 Tablets 1 Depth cameras Unlimited mobile phones	**Approach**	Single-camera body tracking

of the exhibition wall is occupied by a digital representation of an exhibit in two variations. The first variation is a fully digital exhibit where the exhibit itself is projected through the usage of a short-throw projector, while the second one is an actual physical painting. In both cases, skeleton tracking is used to track the location and distance of visitors. The installed tracking technology supports the presentation of information about points of interest using body tracking (two visitors are supported on the body tracking mode while three are supported for the hand tracking). At the sides of the exhibit, two tablets are mounted on the wall or on two portable stands to act as captions of the painting. The captions, based on the visitor profiles, present various information such as description, videos, points of interests, deep zoom representation of the painting, full artefact info and information from external sources. These tablets are also equipped with embedded web cameras for QR code recognition. Visitors' mobile phones are used for accessing information about the exhibit by scanning the QR codes (from the captions). Portable tablets, rented or carried by visitors, can also be employed as information displays.

19.4.2 *Mixed-Reality Technologies*

The term mixed reality technology in this chapter is used to denote the mixing of physical artefacts and machinery with digital information and interactive systems to produce a unique sensory experience.

19.4.2.1 Augmenting Traditional Games with Non-ICT

The mixed reality game presented in Fig. 19.4 is a collaborative game where children can solve puzzles either in a cooperative or in a competitive manner [28]. Between the two large touch displays, there is a wooden ball game activated through a rotating physical controller. When the ball is activated by the controller, it is transmitted via the displays (in its digital form). There the virtual avatar of Eleftherios Venizelos, a Greek politician of the early twentieth century, appears with a golf club to push the ball back to its physical form. Then through the game, the ball enters the second display and falls within a golf hole to appear again in its physical form in the wooden game setup.

19.4.2.2 Making Traditional Artefacts Interactive

The oil mill is an innovative interactive system presenting traditional Cretan products and recipes. The oil mill incorporates a miniature stone mill, through which it is possible to browse through an introduction to Cretan diet and cooking. Users can browse through a digital album about Cretan diet, by rotating the metal handle of the mill, while real oil flows from one end of the system. Users can also send information provided by the system (e.g. recipes, information about traditional products) by e-mail. The system also comprises lighted glass showcases containing museum replicas of pottery.

The oil mill aims at providing information related to Greek culture and tradition, combining real traditional artefacts with digital content. The technology that lies underneath the system is able to augment any physical object towards natural user interaction for browsing digital content related to a specific thematic area (e.g. Cretan diet as shown in Fig. 19.5).

Fig. 19.4 An interactive puzzle game for children "House of El. Venizelos city of Chania" (© *2015 FORTH-ICS*, reprinted with permission)

Interaction type	Multitouch	**Number of users**	Maximum 10
Size	Wall 5 × 2.5 m	**Usage**	Cooperative gaming
Complexity	2 Screens 55″ One physical ball game Various sensors	**Approach**	Distributed service-oriented communication of devices

19.4.2.3 Alternative Forms of Interaction with Terrain-Based Information

PaperView is a **tabletop augmented reality** system that supports the exploration of **terrain-based information** (e.g. areas of interest on a 2D map or a 3D scale model) using rectangular pieces of **plain cardboard**. The system allows users to study information and interactive multimedia, using the cardboards as individual interactive screens; these cardboard screens can be lifted and held at various angles. Multiple users can concurrently use the table [29]. When a user places a cardboard piece over the table surface, an image is projected on it, adding detail to the surface image. Furthermore, a pointer (i.e. a magnifying glass) is projected on the paper's centre, which assists the user in exploring the surface, guiding her/him to the

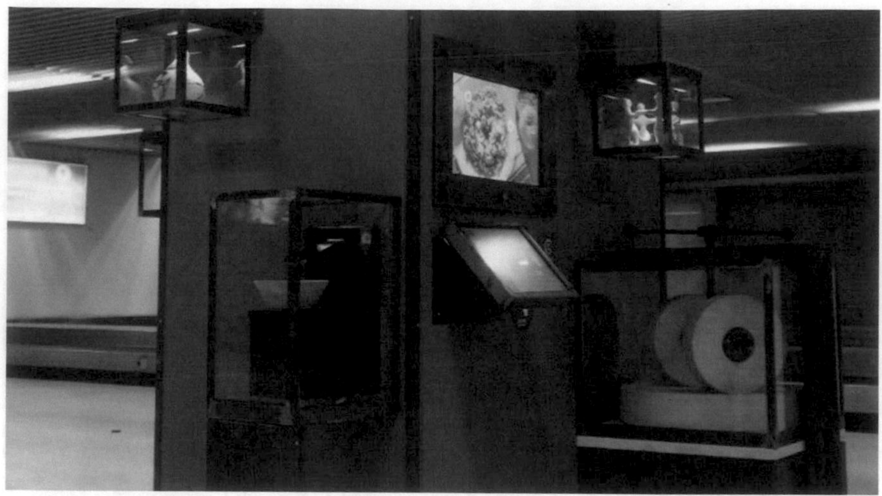

Fig. 19.5 An exemplary setup of the oil mill "Kazantzakis Airport of Heraklion" (© *2013 FORTH-ICS,* reprinted with permission)

Interaction type	Multitouch	**Number of users**	Single user
Size	Depends on the physical exhibits	**Usage**	Augmentation of physical artefacts
Complexity	1 Touch screen 32″ 1 Touch screen 22″ Sensors	**Approach**	Interaction with digital media through physical objects

information hotspots available. When a hotspot is selected, a multimedia slideshow starts. The slideshow comprises a series of pages, each of which may contain any combination of text, images and videos. At the bottom area of the slideshow, a toolbar is projected containing an indication of the current page and the total number of pages available, as well as buttons for moving to the next/previous page (Fig. 19.6).

19.4.2.4 Interacting with Moving Surfaces

360^2 is an interactive installation that supports exploring artefacts through physical and multitouch interaction with a **double rotating gimbal** (i.e. a non-instrumented disk that can dynamically rotate around two axes) [23]. While the user manipulates the disk, the system uses a projector to visualize a display upon it. A depth camera is used to estimate the pose of the surface and multiple simultaneous fingertip contacts

Fig. 19.6 PaperView "Heraklion Info Point"(© *2015 FORTH-ICS*, reprinted with permission)

Interaction type	Cardboard for information display and touch	**Number of users**	Maximum 8 (limited by the size of the table)
Size	Table 1 × 2 m	**Usage**	Augmentation of terrain-based information
Complexity	Projector, high-resolution camera	**Approach**	Augmentation of analogue media with information And touch based interaction on non-technological surfaces

upon it. The estimates are transformed into meaningful user input, availing both fingertip contact and disk pose information. Besides the provision of **augmented multitouch interaction**, such an achievement can serve two distinct functions. On one hand, the rotation mechanism can be used as a means for easily and intuitively browsing and interacting with alternative, dynamically changing, projection views. On the other hand, the high flexibility and extensive range of projection poses supported by the system can be used in order to dynamically personalize the physical properties of an interactive projection surface to the ergonomic preferences and needs of users [24] (Fig. 19.7).

19.4.3 Gamification Techniques for Learning Purposes

This section presents the use of gamification techniques for educational purposes in cultural heritage settings. More specifically, the systems presented in this section

Fig. 19.7 The rotating disk system presenting the numismatic collection of Alpha Bank "Archaeological Museum of Thessaloniki" (© *2014 FORTH-ICS*, reprinted with permission)

Interaction type	Single touch	**Number of users**	Single user
Size	Depents on the size of the disk	**Usage**	Presentation of dual-sided rounded objects and or 3D models
Complexity	1 Projector 1 Depth sensor 1 High-resolution camera	**Approach**	Touch based interaction on non-technological surfaces

are: (a) interactive wall based games, (b) digital word games that can deliver educational info, (c) interactive animations, (d) interactive game surfaces for children and (e) immersive representations of information.

19.4.3.1 Interactive "Wall-Based" Games

Interactive "wall-based" games are defined as games that can be played standing in front a projection which is the game screen and can use their body as the input controller. The interactive wall supports **games** that can be played by one, two or more players simultaneously, using their entire body, in a space of about 3 × 3 m comprising a large projection area. Players control the game using their **"virtual" shadows** which are projected on the screen and follow their **body movements** [9, 30]. The rationale for using the players' shadow is twofold. On the one hand, it is easier for people, especially "non-game players", to identify their shadow rather than an avatar, thus achieving a higher level of control and immersion. On the other hand, this approach allows for maximum flexibility regarding the number, posture and size of players, as well instantly joining and leaving the game, thus maximizing the opportunities for social interaction. Players have to use their shadows to direct specific items in (e.g. products) or away from (e.g. garbage) their baskets. Also, in some game variations, players may also have to put different items in each different basket (see Fig. 19.8).

19.4.3.2 Playing with Words

Cryptolexon, the hidden crossword puzzle, combines entertainment with knowledge. Within the matrix of letters, significant words are hidden. Once a word is discovered, multimedia information about it is displayed. The system uses a touch screen. Users can find the hidden words on the touch screen by dragging their finger from the start to the end of each word or, alternatively, by touching each word's first and last letter (Fig. 19.9).

Fig. 19.8 Interactive wall "House of El. Venizelos at the city of Chania" (© *2015 FORTH-ICS*, reprinted with permission)

Interaction type	Full-body interaction	**Number of users**	Maximum that can fit in front of the projection
Size	3 × 2 m	**Usage**	Shadow-based games
Complexity	1 Project and 1 depth camera	**Approach**	Interaction with virtual shadow

19.4.3.3 Learning Through Interactive Animations

Interactive animations can be used to produce game-like edutainment experiences in the context of cultural heritage institutions. An example is the technology kiosk installed at the Archaeological Museum of Heraklion where children can learn how ancient metallic and clay items were created. To do so, children should successfully complete a series of mini games that interleave animations with riddle-solving parts. An example of the "ancient technology kiosk" is presented in Fig. 19.10.

Fig. 19.9 Cryptolexon "House of El. Venizelos at the city of Chania" (© *2015 FORTH-ICS*, reprinted with permission)

Interaction type	Touch	**Number of users**	Single user
Size	Depends on the installation the minimum is the size of a 32″ touch display	**Usage**	Word-based gaming
Complexity	1 Touch display	**Approach**	Puzzle gaming

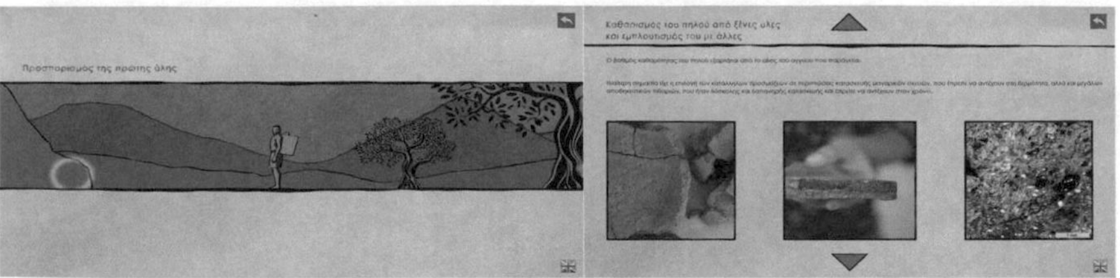

Fig. 19.10 *Left*: interacting with animated character. *Right*: presentation of educational material (© *2013 FORTH-ICS,* reprinted with permission)

Interaction type	Touch	**Number of users**	Single user
Size	Depends on the installation. Minimum is the size of a 32″ display	**Usage**	Interaction with animations
Complexity	1 Display 32″	**Approach**	Gaming

19.4.3.4 Experimenting with Interactive Surfaces for Children

Interactive surfaces can be employed by cultural heritage institutions to augment the experience provided to visitors through an easy-to-deploy and easy-to-maintain single digital exhibit. An interactive surface comes with embedded applications that can be personalized to meet the demands of third parties or integrate new applications on demand. Furthermore, it can integrate a number of ready-to-use, handcrafted physical objects that are used for interacting [31].

A setup of such an interactive surface can embed a number of applications (see Fig. 19.11), such as:

- The **Art River**: A river of information that users can interact with. Interaction happens through augmented rocks interlinked with information elements.
- The **Museum Coffee Table**: A place where parents get access to more information about exhibits while children get entertained through games.
- The **Puzzle**: An interactive puzzle, inspired by the lives and works of famous artists.
- **Pick and Match**: A card-based memory game employing cards with art content.
- The **Art Collector**: An augmented board game in which players are asked questions regarding artistic creation facts and locations for each continent.
- **Paint it**: A painting application allowing children to make their first steps in painting by exploring and learning the principles of colour theory.

Fig. 19.11 A suite of games for the interactive surface (© *2014 FORTH-ICS,* reprinted with permission)

Interaction type	Multitouch and physical objects	**Number of users**	<30
Size	A 42″ sized table	**Usage**	Table based edu-games
Complexity	A multitouch table with object recognition capabilities	**Approach**	Interaction through the usage of physical objects

19.4.3.5 Interacting with Immersive Representations of Information

Immersive environments integrating information that can be explored by users have been explored as a means of producing alternative experiences for CHIs. TimeViewer is an interactive system that presents information with temporal characteristics in a large-scale display, while user interaction is achieved through remote gestures [32]. Besides representing information as a traditional two-dimensional timeline, the system also supports three-dimensional information representation in a "time tunnel", i.e. a corridor along which the events are placed in chronological order. User interaction in the time tunnel is accomplished through full-body kinesthetic interaction. TimeViewer offers a rich and immersive visualization of any kind of temporal information. The content of the system can be provided through existing formal data models, while the visualization is automatically created (see Fig. 19.12).

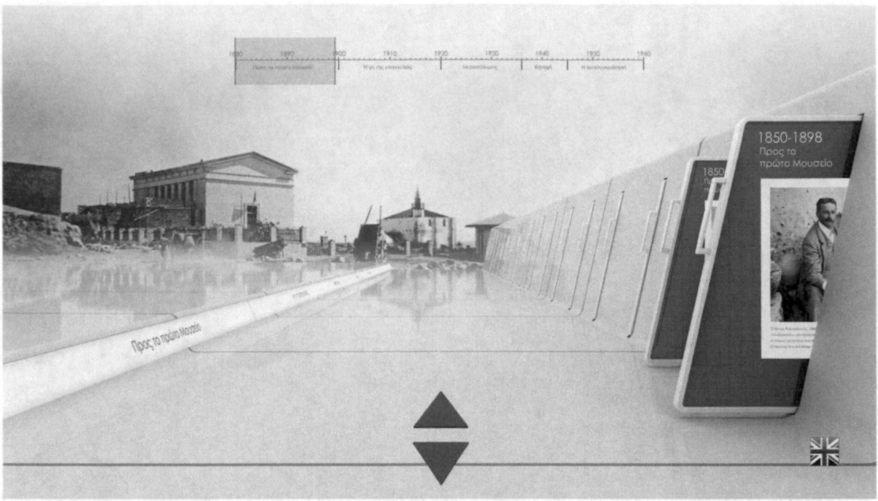

Fig. 19.12 TimeViewer "Archaeological Museum of Heraklion" (© *2016 FORTH-ICS*, reprinted with permission)

Interaction type	Hand tracking, gestures	**Number of users**	Single user
Size	3 × 2 m	**Usage**	Visualization of timelines
Complexity	1 Projector and 1 depth camera	**Approach**	Interaction with information in immersive environments

19.4.4 Interactive Art Installations

In this section, interactive art installations are presented. These installations combine art and ICT while several hardware controllers and mechanical devices are used as a means of empowering interaction with art. This is achieved through the provision of alternative forms of interaction with digital content and mechanical devices that are integrated within the artwork. The output of this interaction is both digital (altering the content presented by the artwork), electrical (e.g. altering the lighting scheme for revealing "secret" areas) and mechanical (e.g. setting mechanical elements to movement).

19.4.4.1 An Interactive Artwork Inspired by the History of the City of Heraklion

At the main info point for visitors of the city centre of Heraklion, a composition that combines technology and art was created as a means to produce a focal point not only for the historical building of the Vikelaia Public Library but also for the city

Fig. 19.13 Interactive sculpture inspired by the history of the city of Heraklion "Heraklion Info Point" (© *2015 FORTH-ICS,* reprinted with permission)

Interaction type	Manipulation of physical objects embedded in the artwork	**Number of users**	Maximum 4
Size	4×3 m	**Usage**	Interactive art
Complexity	4 Displays LED lighting Hardware parts Electronics Analogue moving parts	**Approach**	Interaction with physical controls to produce digital output

centre. This was materialized through a double-sided sculpture where visitors can interact from within the info point. This interaction is mirrored on the outer side and viewed by the people walking by in the historical centre of the city. Inspiration for this work of art was the mythical labyrinth, texts from N. Kazantzakis and the cultural tradition of the city. Visitors are invited to touch the mechanical devices embedded in the sculpture so as to reveal the scripture and set the ancient device back to life (Fig. 19.13).

19.4.4.2 An Interactive Sculpture Inspired by the Phaistos Disc

At the Kazantzakis airport of Heraklion, an interactive sculpture was built inspired by the ancient disk of Phaistos. The main idea of the exhibit was the presentation of the disk through the mixture of the depicted symbols within a large space of 6×6 m. The sculpture is built using a collection of hand-crafted cubes, each one containing computer-controlled internal lighting and in each side the symbols from the disk. The main area of the sculpture is occupied by a large interactive display where users can browse multimedia content using hand tracking. While interacting, the sculpture is activated, and various light patterns are employed to give movement to the composition (Fig. 19.14).

Fig. 19.14 Interactive sculpture inspired by the ancient Phaistos Disc "Heraklion Kazantzakis Airport" (© *2013 FORTH-ICS*, reprinted with permission)

Interaction type	Hand tracking	**Number of users**	One in each side
Size	$6 \times 2 \times 6$ m	**Usage**	Interaction with art while browsing information
Complexity	2 Displays 2 Depth camera LED lighting Various sensors and electronic devices	**Approach**	Combining information with art

19.4.4.3 An Interactive Sculpture Inspired by the Antikythera Mechanism

An impressive metal structure has been created and installed upon one of the conveyor belts of the airport of Chania. The sculpture also integrates two large displays where the users can interact from a distance using hand gestures. Interaction gives movement to the composition, and a combination of mechanical elements, lights and micro devices contribute to a unique experience not only for the users but also for all people standing by the conveyor belt as shown in Fig. 19.15.

19.4.5 Portable Mobile and Custom Hardware Devices

This section presents technologies that can be considered as mobile devices for CHIs, including both applications that are installed and run in the visitor's mobile phone or custom hardware devices that are provided to visitors by the CHI.

Fig. 19.15 Interactive sculpture inspired by the Antikythera mechanism "Chania Daskalogiannis Airport" (© *2013 FORTH-ICS*, reprinted with permission)

Interaction type	Hand tracking	**Number of users**	One in each side
Size	6 × 1 × 3 m	**Usage**	Interaction with art while browsing information
Complexity	2 Displays 2 Depth camera LED lighting Various sensors and electronic devices	**Approach**	Combining information with art

19.4.5.1 Museum Guide

The "Museum Guide" is a mobile application that can be installed on user-owned mobile devices. The main purpose of this system is to take advantage of the near ubiquity of mobile devices to create a rich museum touring guide that escorts the user during their visit to a museum [33].

More specifically, the visitors' experience is enhanced through (see Fig. 19.16):

- Area information and guidance: Visitors are able to identify, with relative precision, where they are located within the museum and can easily find their way around it, whether they wish to visit a specific exhibition room or a utility area of the building.

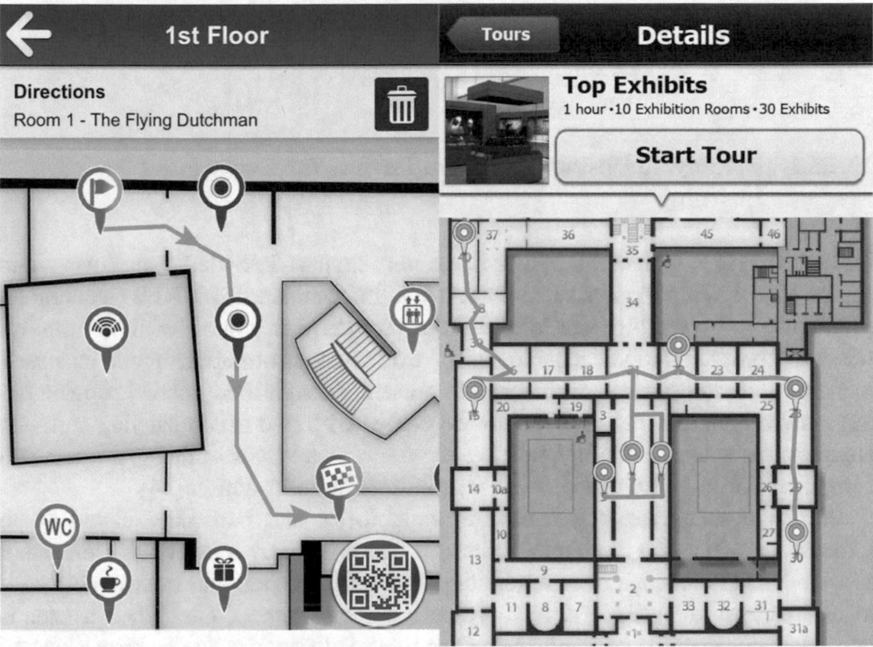

Fig. 19.16 *Left*: a route defined by the visitor. *Right*: overview of a tour (© *2013 FORTH-ICS*, reprinted with permission)

Interaction type	Touch	**Number of users**	Single user
Size	Size of a handheld device	**Usage**	Terrain-based information
Complexity	Handheld device	**Approach**	Terrain and POIs visualization

- Thematic information: Visitors can receive detailed information (i.e. textual descriptions, photographs, audio and video content) regarding the museum's permanent and any temporary exhibitions, its collections, and individual exhibits.
- Tour creation: A set of predefined tours, focusing on specific collections or exhibits, is available to the visitor.

In order to identify the visitor's location in the museum, the use of QR codes was adopted. Each public building area (e.g. cafeteria, gift shop, WC, etc.) has been assigned its own code, as has each individual exhibit within the museum. Through the use of their device's built-in camera, a visitor can inform the application of their current location or identify an exhibit they may be interested in finding more about.

With always available information and multimedia regarding all exhibits and other points of interest and the ability to tailor their experience to their needs, visitors are essentially accompanied by a comprehensive, intelligent guide that makes their museum experience not only richer but also more efficient.

19.4.5.2 Employing Custom Hardware Devices for Exploratory Learning

InfoScope is a novel mobile device that can support knowledge discovery and exploratory playing in physical environments. InfoScope utilizes RFID technology to provide audio guiding and localized question/answer games, while it employs wireless communication technologies to exchange information about its user's interests with computer platforms and to present through them related supplementary multimedia information. The device comes with two accompanying software components: one for editing/updating its contents and one running on personal computers for providing supplementary multimedia information [34].

InfoScope integrates RFID reading capabilities and can play related audio information which can be adapted to its user's profile (e.g. language, age, interests). The device is embedded in an ergonomically designed shell and is extremely easy to use, as it mimics the use of a typical doctor's stethoscope. When a user is interested in a specific item, all she/he has to do is to put the device over a related RFID tag in order to listen to a corresponding audio description. Additionally, by "listening to" appropriate tags, the user can adapt the audio descriptions to her personal profile traits. Beyond localized information presentation, InfoScope supports exploratory gaming in physical environments through question/answer games, where a tag is used to trigger a question that has to be answered by "listening to" the tag of the corresponding place/item and has been installed at the House of El. Venizelos at the city of Chania in the context of the museum's educational activities for children as shown in Fig. 19.17.

Fig. 19.17 InfoScope device and PC docking station "House of El. Venizelos at the city of Chania" (© *2015 FORTH-ICS,* reprinted with permission)

Interaction type	Touch using the device on RFID tags	**Number of users**	Single user
Size	5 × 5 × 15 cm	**Usage**	Presentation of tagged audio information
Complexity	Portable InfoScope Docking station with charging station and touch display	**Approach**	Interaction using portable audio guides

19.5 Lessons Learned

This chapter presents an AmI framework employed in the context of various interactive applications hosted over the years in numerous installations. This framework should be considered a living organism that was not developed in its current state from the beginning but rather evolved in its current state through an evolutionary process that involved a lot of experimentation and trial and error. The main building block of the success of this framework was that it was designed by the beginning to be simple, powerful and expandable. Prior to producing anything, the need for a service-oriented infrastructure that could unite heterogeneous computing components, applications, services and sensors was visualized. This was substantial and was materialized in the form of a distributed service-oriented middleware that could support any computing platform, software development toolkit and programming language. The middleware was developed as a separate product from the beginning and tested so as to ensure that the glue for developing truly distributed AmI environments and applications existed. Then the second step was to envision how interaction would be bound to applications in such environments so as to ensure that applications will still operate under any circumstances and regardless of the way that the user desires to interact (hand tracking, touch, gestures, etc.). To achieve a total separation of the interaction modalities with the systems receiving input, a decision was made to develop autonomous pluggable service-oriented modalities that would become available to applications through the middleware. Thus all the alternative modalities were developed and tested individually over the years and became available to applications through the middleware. The same was followed for knowledge representation. A knowledge base was developed in a semantic format, and a querying mechanism was developed and exposed through the middleware. The coming together of the above measures made possible the development of applications in a multitude of programming languages (c#, ActionScript, Java, Python, Delphi, etc.), tools (Visual Studio, Flex Builder, Eclipse, MonoDevelop, etc.) and frameworks (.Net, Windows Forms, WPF, Adobe Flash, etc.) that use and reuse the presented infrastructure. This for certain boosted development and productivity and allowed the facilitation of experts from various application domains and backgrounds. Using the infrastructure, it was made possible even for designers to produce interactive applications with limited programming expertise and tool knowledge.

19.6 Conclusions and Future Work

This chapter has presented a state-of-the-art AmI framework for digital cultural heritage. This framework has provided the building blocks to support the development of a number of applications for digital cultural heritage, offering a novel form of information presentation, interaction and learning in CHIs. Several installations of applications were explored addressing a number of alternative topics: (a) personalized interaction with artworks, (b) mixed-reality technologies, (c) gamification techniques for education purposes, (d) gamification as a means to produce interactive art installations and (e) portable mobile and custom hardware devices. Although these applications were built on top of heterogeneous technologies, programming languages and platforms, all of them facilitate the versatile framework as a provider of key enabling technologies (intercommunication, knowledge management and interaction).

Although the presented framework has already been practically exploited in the context of numerous developments and evaluated through interactive installations in public spaces, there are a number of directions where significant progress can be achieved in the future. A major research line towards this direction is the support for integrating a number of linked data end points to the knowledge layer of the framework. This will make the integration of existing data sources feasible, thus contributing to a more pluralistic representation of knowledge and the reuse of existing knowledge. Furthermore, although the interaction metaphors have been abstracted and modelled separately, the user interface currently is built ad hoc for each interactive system instantiation. In the future, it is expected that the development of a common reusable UI toolkit for interactive applications for cultural heritage will greatly boost development and significantly reduce development time. Moreover, some of the presented systems integrate some form of personalization mechanisms so as to present more focused information to each visitor. This is currently achieved at the knowledge and UI level for each application individually. In the future, it is planned to develop an information personalization layer integrated into the knowledge representation, so as to centrally store user profiles and produce dynamically the required content personalization prior to the extraction of content by each interactive application. Finally, a very important path of improvement is planned through the exploitation of the log data collected in each in vivo installation. The analysis of this very rich material can provide feedback on how museum visitors interact with the system, detect problems and help redesign and improve each application as well as the framework as a whole.

Acknowledgements This work is supported by the FORTH-ICS internal RTD Programme "Ambient Intelligence and Smart Environments".[31]

References

1. D. Ferdani, A. Pagano, M. Farouk, Terminology, definitions and types for virtual museums. (2014), Retrieved from http://www.v-must.net/
2. M. Forte, A. Siliotti, *Virtual Archaeology: Great Discoveries Brought to Life Through Virtual Reality* (Thames & Hudson, London, 1997)
3. M. Carrozzino, M. Bergamasco, Beyond virtual museums: Experiencing immersive virtual reality in real museums. J. Cultural Herit. **11**, 452–458 (2010)
4. F. Liarokapis, M. White, Augmented reality techniques for museum environments. Mediterranean J. Comput. Netw. **1**(2), 90–96 (2005)
5. M. White, N. Mourkoussis, J. Darcy, P. Petridis, F. Liarokapis, P. Lister, & M. Stawniak, *ARCO-an architecture for digitization, management and presentation of virtual exhibitions*. In Computer Graphics International, 2004. Proceedings (2004, June), pp. 622–625. IEEE.
6. P. Milgram, F. Kishino, A taxonomy of mixed reality visual displays. IEICE TRANSACTIONS on Information and Systems **77**(12), 1321–1329 (1994)
7. C.E. Hughes, C.B. Stapleton, D.E. Hughes, E.M. Smith, Mixed reality in education, entertainment, and training. IEEE Comput. Graph. Appl. **25**(6), 24–30 (2005)
8. T. Hall, L. Ciolfi, L. Bannon, M. Fraser, S. Benford, J. Bowers, M. Flintham, The visitor as virtual archaeologist: explorations in mixed reality technology to enhance educational and social interaction in the museum, in *Proceedings of the 2001 Conference on Virtual Reality, Archeology, and Cultural Heritage* (ACM, New York, 2001), pp. 91–96
9. D. Grammenos, G. Margetis, P. Koutlemanis, X. Zabulis, 53.090 virtual rusks = 510 real smiles—Using a fun exergame installation for advertising traditional food products, in *Advances in Computer Entertainment*, ed. by A. Nijholt, T. Romão, D. Reidsma (Springer, Berlin, Heidelberg, 2012), pp. 214–229. doi:10.1007/2F978-3-642-34292-9_15

[31]FORTH-ICS AmI Programme: http://www.ics.forth.gr/index_main.php?l=e&c=4

10. P. Pierroux, L. Bannon, V. Kaptelinin, K. Walker, T. Hall, D. Stuedahl, *MUSTEL: Framing the Design of Technology-Enhanced Learning Activities for Museum Visitors* (International Cultural Heritage Informatics Meeting Proceedings (ICHIM), Toronto, 2007)
11. E. Klopfer, J. Perry, K. Squire, M.F. Jan, & C. Steinkuehler, Mystery at the museum: A collaborative game for museum education. In *Proceedings of th 2005 conference on Computer support for collaborative learning: learning 2005: the next 10 years!* (International Society of the Learning Sciences, 2005, May), pp. 316–320.
12. J. Bowen, J. Bradburne, A. Burch, L. Dierking, J. Falk, S.F. Fantoni, P. Lonsdale, *Digital Technologies and the Museum Experience: Handheld Guides and Other Media* (Rowman Altamira, Lanham, 2008)
13. J. Wishart, P. Triggs, MuseumScouts: Exploring how schools, museums and interactive technologies can work together to support learning. Comput. Educ. **54**(3), 669–678 (2010)
14. P. Pierroux, I. Krange, I. Sem, Bridging Contexts and Interpretations: Mobile Blogging on Art Museum Field Trips. Mediekultur. J. Media Commun. Res. **50**, 25–44 (2011)
15. I. Georgalis, Y. Tanaka, N. Spyratos, C. Stephanidis, Programming smart object federations for simulating and implementing ambient intelligence scenarios, in *Proceedings of the 3rd International Conference on Pervasive and Embedded Computing and Communication Systems (PECCS 2013), Barcelona, Spain, 19–21 February*, ed. by C. Benavente-Peces, J. Filipethe (SciTePress, Portugal, 2013), pp. 5–15. ISBN 978-989-8565-43-3
16. I. Georgalis, D. Grammenos, C. Stephanidis, *Middleware for Ambient Intelligence Environments: Reviewing Requirements and Communication Technologies*. In Universal Access in Human-Computer Interaction. Intelligent and Ubiquitous Interaction Environments (Springer, Berlin Heidelberg, 2009), pp. 168–177
17. E. Zidianakis, N. Partarakis, M. Antona, C. Stephanidis, Building a sensory infrastructure to support interaction and monitoring in ambient intelligence environments, in *Distributed, Ambient, and Pervasive Interactions* (Springer, Berlin, 2014), pp. 519–529
18. H. Sakoe, S. Chiba, Dynamic programming algorithm optimization for spoken word recognition. IEEE Trans. on Acoust., Speech, and Signal Process, ASSP **26**, 43–49 (1978)
19. G. Margetis, X. Zabulis, P. Koutlemanis, M. Antona, C. Stephanidis, Augmented interaction with physical books in an Ambient Intelligence learning environment. Multimed. Tools Appl. **67**(2), 473–495 (2013)
20. D. Michel, A.A. Argyros, D. Grammenos, X. Zabulis, & T. Sarmis. Building a multi-touch display based on computer vision techniques. In MVA (2009), pp. 74–77.
21. A. Ntelidakis, X. Zabulis, D. Grammenos, P. Koutlemanis, *Lateral touch detection and localization for interactive, augmented planar surfaces*. International Symposium on Visual Computing, Las Vegas, Nevada, USA (Springer, Switzerland, 2015)
22. X. Zabulis, D. Grammenos, T. Sarmis, K. Tzevanidis, P. Padeleris, P. Koutlemanis, A.A. Argyros, Multicamera human detection and tracking supporting natural interaction with large scale displays. Machine Vision Appl. J **24**, 319–336 (2013). doi:10.1007/s00138-012-0408-6
23. X. Zabulis, P. Koutlemanis, D. Grammenos, Augmented multitouch interaction upon a 2-DOF rotating disk, in *Proceedings of the 8th International Symposium on Advances in Visual Computing (ISVC 2012), Rethymnon, Crete, Greece, 16–18 July 2012*, ed. by G. Bebis et al. (Springer, Berlin, 2012), pp. 642–653 (LNCS 7431)
24. P. Koutlemanis, A. Ntelidakis, X. Zabulis, D. Grammenos, I. Adami, A steerable multitouch display for surface computing and its evaluation. Int. J. Artif. Intell. Tools **22**(06), 1360016 (2013)
25. D. Grammenos, X. Zabulis, D. Michel, P. Padeleris, T. Sarmis, G. Georgalis, P. Koutlemanis, K. Tzevanidis, A. Argyros, M. Sifakis, P. Adam-Veleni, C. Stephanidis, Macedonia from Fragments to Pixels: A Permanent Exhibition of Interactive Systems at the Archaeological Museum of Thessaloniki, in *Progress in Cultural Heritage Preservation, Proceedings of the 4th International Conference EuroMed 2012, Limassol, Cyprus, 29 October–3 November,*

ed. by M. Ioannides, D. Fritsch, J. Leissner, R. Davies, F. Remondino, R. Caffo (Springer, Berlin, 2012), pp. 602–609 [LNCS: 7616]
26. G. Galanakis, X. Zabulis, P. Koutlemanis, S. Paparoulis, & V. Kouroumalis, Tracking persons using a network of RGBD cameras, In *The Proceedings of the 7th ACM International Conference on PErvasive Technologies Related to Assistive Environments* (PETRA 2014), Rhodes, Greece, 27–30 May.
27. N. Partarakis, M. Antona, & C. Stephanidis, Adaptable, personalizable and multi user museum exhibits. In the Proceedings of the CHI2014 Workshop Curating the Digital: Spaces for Art and Interaction, Toronto, Canada. 26–27 April (2014).
28. D. Grammenos, A. Chatziantoniou, Jigsaw together: A distributed collaborative game for players with diverse skills and preferences, in *Proceedings of the 13th International Conference on Interaction Design & Children, June 17–20, 2014, Aarhus, Denmark* (ACM, New York, 2014), pp. 205–208
29. D. Grammenos, D. Michel, X. Zabulis, A. Argyros, PaperView: augmenting physical surfaces with location-aware digital information, in *The Proceedings of the 5th International Conference on Tangible, Embedded, and Embodied Interaction (TEI 2011), Funchal, Portugal, 23–26 January* (ACM Press, New York, 2011), pp. 57–60
30. D. Grammenos, G. Margetis, P. Koutlemanis, X. Zabulis, Paximadaki, the game: Creating an advergame for promoting traditional food products, in *Proceeding of the 16th International Academic MindTrek Conference (MindTrek '12)* (ACM, New York, 2012), pp. 287–290. doi:10.1145/2393132.2393195 (free download from the ACM Digital Library)
31. N. Partarakis, E. Zidianakis, M. Antona, C. Stephanidis, Art and Coffee in the Museum, in *Distributed, Ambient, and Pervasive Interactions—Volume 21 of the combined Proceedings of the 17th International Conference on Human-Computer Interaction (HCI International 2015), Los Angeles, CA, USA, 2–7 August*, ed. by N. Streitz, P. Markopoulos (Berlin, Lecture Notes in Computer Science Series of Springer, 2015), pp. 370–381. ISBN 978-3-319-20803-9
32. G. Drossis, D. Grammenos, I. Adami, C. Stephanidis, 3D visualization and multimodal interaction with temporal information using timelines. Proceedings of INTERACT 2013 Lecture Notes in Computer Science **8119**, 214–231 (2013). Springer
33. G. Kapnas, A. Leonidis, M. Korozi, S. Ntoa, G. Margetis, C. Stephanidis, A Museum Guide Application for Deployment on User-Owned Mobile Devices, in *HCI International 2013—Posters' Extended Abstracts, Part II—Volume 29 of the combined Proceedings of HCI International 2013 (15th International Conference on Human-Computer Interaction), Las Vegas, Nevada, USA, 21–26 July*, ed. by C. Stephanidis (Communications in Computer and Information Science, Berlin, 2013), pp. 253–257. ISBN 978-3-642-39475-1
34. D. Grammenos, *Infoscope: A mobile device supporting exploratory and playful knowledge discovery in physical environments.* HCI International 2013—Posters' Extended Abstracts (Springer, Berlin, 2013), pp. 647–651

Chapter 20
Storytelling and Digital Epigraphy-Based Narratives in Linked Open Data

Pietro Liuzzo, Francesco Mambrini, and Philipp Franck

Abstract Carefully curated digital collections, structured with rich metadata sets and accessible via search engines and APIs, are not enough for users anymore. Multimedia narratives on the web and other digital "wayfindings" help a wider audience access the content of digital collections and also familiarize them with the research products that are published online. Digital humanists, then, face a twofold challenge: how to create scientific-oriented resources that serve the need of both scholars and general users and how to introduce nonspecialists to the digital collections produced by academics. The case of epigraphy is interesting, as there are already several examples of how niche content can be introduced to a wider public using multiple tools. This chapter illustrates the effort made by the Europeana network of Ancient Greek and Latin Epigraphy (EAGLE) in both integrating the largest collections of digitized inscriptions in Europe in a single database and providing users with tools for research, interaction, and fact finding. In particular, we will focus on the web-based storytelling tools that help users build engaging multimedia narrative based on inscriptions and ancient monuments and on a virtual exhibition that showcases some of the most spectacular items in the EAGLE collection.

Keywords Digital epigraphy • Digital storytelling • Virtual exhibitions • Linked open data

P. Liuzzo (✉)
Hamburg University, Alsterterrasse 1, 20354 Hamburg, Germany
e-mail: pietro.liuzzo@uni-hamburg.de

F. Mambrini • P. Franck
Deutsches Archäologisches Institut, Podbielskiallee 69-71, 14195 Berlin, Germany
e-mail: francesco.mambrini@dainst.de; philipp.franck@dainst.de

M. Ioannides et al. (eds.), *Mixed Reality and Gamification for Cultural Heritage*,
DOI 10.1007/978-3-319-49607-8_20

20.1 Introduction: "Every Inscription Has a Story to Tell"

The shift to digital formats has opened a wide range of opportunities in the field of Latin and Greek epigraphy, the science that is concerned with the task of editing and understanding the complex cultural artifacts that we call "inscriptions."[1] The current trend toward the use of a standard format (named EpiDoc)[2] to encode textual information and toward the adoption of Linked Open Data has redefined the concept of "editing" inscriptions in Greek and Latin. Nowadays, it is hardly possible to imagine a publication of those crucial sources for the study of the ancient civilizations that do not include several digital images of the text carrier, maps, and links to gazetteers or prosopographical indexes;[3] while several projects have already explored that road,[4] others, like the *Digital Marmor Parium*,[5] are planning to attempt the encoding of even more complex linguistic information, such as syntax or event structure.

In their conceptual model, however, these digital publications have remained focused on the production of critical editions of the texts, enriched with layers of more or less erudite apparatuses that can be now accessed interactively and (for the most part) freely online. Similar editions make for indispensable and very powerful research tools. However, given the scale that such an intense work of editing and linking to the available resources require, the question of how "accessible" our digitized inscriptions in truth are becomes unavoidable. Is a digital critical edition with maps, indexes, and images able to have the impact on society that, for example, public granting institutions would require?

In fact, ancient inscriptions make for a very interesting case in the debate between cultural heritage and society.[6] On the one hand, inscriptions require a very hard and specialized training to be read and interpreted. Epigraphy is a very active field of research that counts a number of devoted enthusiasts, inside and outside academia. On the other hand, however, names, places, and events, not to mention the (often tormented) histories of the monuments or objects where the texts were inscribed or their aesthetic quality, are a direct gateway to the ancient world.

[1] On the evolving paradigms of epigraphy from the past to the digital age see especially [4]. On the problematic definition of what we ordinarily call "inscriptions" see [2].

[2] A specification of the Text Encoding Initiative (TEI) [5].

[3] See the latest published digital project such as the Roman Inscriptions of Britain (http://romaninscriptionsofbritain.org/) or The Inscriptiones Orae Septentrionalis Ponti Eusini (http://iospe.cch.kcl.ac.uk/index.html).

[4] The inscriptions of Aphrodisia [6] set a fundamental precedent. For an overview of the rich panorama of projects in digital epigraphy, readers may refer to the contributions published in [7]. The EpiDoc community is also promoting regular training workshops: on the experience see now [8].

[5] Information can be found on the project website: http://www.dh.uni-leipzig.de/wo/projects/open-greek-and-latin-project/digital-marmor-parium/; for further discussion see [3].

[6] On the presence of inscriptions in our cultural landscape, even beyond the restricted circle of specialists, see the recent contribution by Orlandi [9], who also dwells on the advantages of digital technologies in fostering the relations between inscribed monuments and society.

Even if the historical significance of those monuments and texts is difficult to reconstruct, the results are often immediately informative and appealing also to nonspecialists. Examples of such individual and collective "stories", that it is possible to tell starting from inscriptions, can be multiplied.[7]

The EAGLE project,[8] a best-practice network co-funded by the EU Commission, aims to address both sides of the equation: namely, it aims to provide both a large collection of digitized critical editions and an access point for the wider public into the world of ancient inscriptions.

The first goal of the project is in fact to collect the vast majority of the surviving inscriptions of the Greco-Roman world, scattered among 25 different European countries; this goal entails an effort to harmonize the available metadata about them in a standardized information schema and to make the materials accessible in a single readily searchable database.[9] On the other hand, the project attempts also to highlight the historical meaning of the collected objects, by emphasizing the connection between the materials and other data (such as images, scholarly and popular narratives about antiquity, maps, and videos) available online; also, we intended to provide an environment where users could create and share their own narratives about inscriptions, using the items collected within EAGLE as well as content from the main repositories on the web.

The results of the efforts in content aggregation and curation are documented elsewhere.[10] In this chapter, we focus on the second task. In the first section, we present the EAGLE Storytelling App and the environment dedicated to the published "Stories" on the official EAGLE website. In the second section, we illustrate "Sign of Life," the virtual exhibition that was set up to guide the viewers through a series of thematic explorations of some inscribed monuments published by EAGLE.

20.2 The EAGLE Storytelling App

20.2.1 Design, Rationale, and Intended Users

The Storytelling App is a web software that is integrated within the portal of the project;[11] it assists users with a registered account to create narratives based on

[7]For a very entertaining and at the same time scientifically rigorous overview of individual stories that can be told from the inscription of ancient Emona (actual Ljubljana in Slovenia), see the book by Šašel Kos [10].

[8]http://www.eagle-network.eu/ on which see [9].

[9]The search interface can now be reached at: http://www.eagle-network.eu/resources/search-inscriptions/

[10]An updated list of the technical reports and of the published paper produced in the context of EAGLE is maintained at: http://www.eagle-network.eu/about/documents-deliverables/

[11]The access page of the applications and of the published content is http://www.eagle-network.eu/stories. For a user manual and an introduction to the application design, see [11].

ancient inscriptions and to publish them online. The design of the application evolved around five basic requirements. Primarily, the design intended to ensure the user-friendliness of the interfaces, the support for multimedia content, the integration with the other services provided by EAGLE as well as the interoperability with the other online databases and resources for ancient history.

Multimediality is especially important when dealing with ancient inscriptions. Although this aspect is often overlooked in favor of an exclusively textual approach, it must be kept in mind that the ancient inscriptions are in themselves complex multimedia objects, where the physical features of the text carrier and (in the case of greater public monuments) its spatial collocation contribute to the overall meaning together with the written words. One of the key features of the app is therefore to help authors to search and include within their narratives the most relevant visual (such as images and videos) or interactive content (like maps that localize modern and ancient sites) that help the readers contextualize the inscribed objects, to imagine their visual impact or their reconstruction.

The application was designed as a plug-in for WordPress, the same content management system that is used for the project web portal. The plug-in increases the functionality of the WordPress page editor by supporting the inclusion of multimedia content from a number of repositories related to the ancient world. Thus, the application adds a new toolkit for professional working with online-edited content for ancient history while at the same time allowing for a seamless integration in the general "look and feel" of the project web portal.[12]

Currently, the publication of new content in the dedicated "Stories" section is open to everyone: all the users that register an account with EAGLE can write and publish their content without further requirement. The application was designed to serve an immediate need of visibility within the consortium of the project partners. The EAGLE Network is not only unique in terms of the vast collections that it brings together. Another asset that the project is joining is the expertise of the specialists that work to maintain and edit the inscriptions that are part of EAGLE.[13] All the content providers, some of which are assembling collections dedicated to the ancient history of specific regions of the Greco-Roman world, with strong connections to the history of the community where they are based (such as Cyprus, Slovenia, or modern Romania),[14] in joining a large network were also extremely motivated to "showcase" some of the most valuable objects in their keeping.

This need for visibility contributed to identify our first use case and potential group of intended users. Not differently from the EAGLE partners, curators of both digital and museum collections may benefit from an environment that allows them to give visibility to some selected objects in their keeping, by pointing the

---

[12]These two aspects are, however, kept apart in the application design: see the section below on modularity and extensibility.

[13]A full list of the project partners is maintained at: http://www.eagle-network.eu/about/partners/

[14]On the inscriptions from ancient Ljubljana (Emona), see [12, 10]; on ancient Dacia, see [13].

audience's attention to their historical significance, their relations with their broader context, in an interactive and appealing way.

Teachers and students of ancient history were other figures that we intended to target. While the translation of inscriptions is an exercise of primary importance, the work of historical interpretation of an inscription does not end with a rendering of the text in a modern language. Contextualizing the text, in any possible sense of the concept of "context" (involving, for instance, its relation with the text carrier, or with its spatial context and its current place of preservation, and many more aspects), is also a fundamental task of epigraphic research that students are trained to attempt.

With our Storytelling App, we aimed to provide a web environment to record and share the results of this interpretative work.[15]

20.2.2 The EAGLE Stories

The point of access to the world of the EAGLE stories and to the Storytelling App is the dedicated "Stories" page on the project web portal.[16] On this page, visitors can first of all browse, search, and read the content that other users have already published. The readers find previews of all the published content and have multiple options to browse the collection. Among them, greater prominence is given to an interactive map that displays the locations referenced in the published stories: by clicking on any of the places, the readers can access the relevant stories directly (Fig. 20.1). Other filters allow readers to search the content by author or by keyword or to search the full text of the stories for any given term.

Although authors are not constrained to follow a model and a full latitude is given to them to structure their content as they like, a typical story includes a series of text paragraphs intermingled with images and other interactive content. In particular, content embedded from databases on historical sources and ancient civilizations are displayed as boxes with a thumbnail and a preview containing a limited set of information (Fig. 20.2). By clicking on the box, users can visualize the rest of the description, like the full text of an inscription, the full set of metadata for images, or a larger series of paragraphs for voices in online encyclopedias.

Two buttons allow users to visualize any given record in their original website or to trigger a search in the EAGLE portal to identify all the stories that include the same digital object within their text. Thanks to this functionality, users can continue studying a single object or a single place by reading other stories that make

[15]Another aspect that our application is designed to encourage is creative writing; in the final stage of the development, a contest was also organized to award the best story written using the storytelling app [22, 23]. The selected stories are collected in an e-book available at: http://www.eagle-network.eu/results-of-the-eagle-1st-short-story-contest/

[16]http://www.eagle-network.eu/stories/

Fig. 20.1 The "Stories" page from the EAGLE website (©2016, EU CIP EAGLE, contract nr. 325122, reprinted with permission)

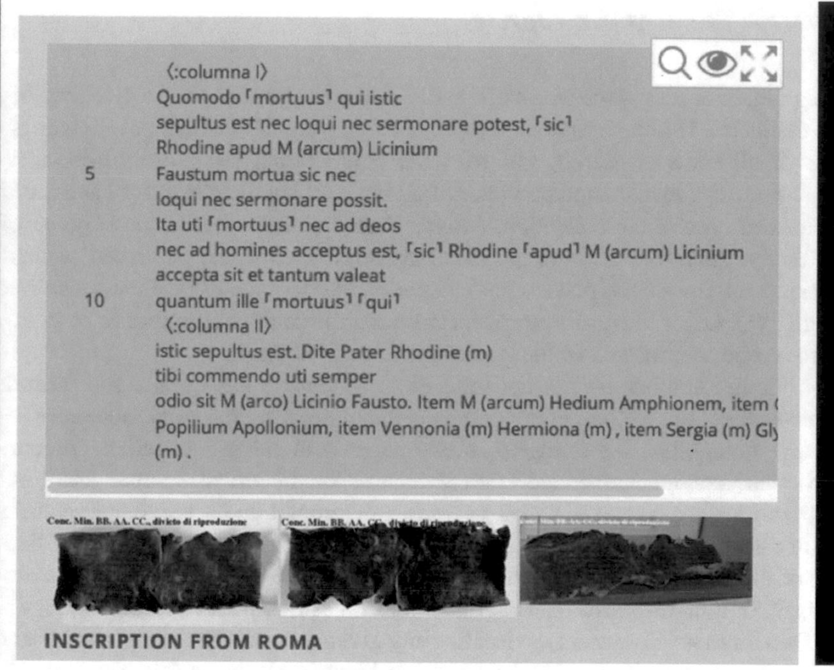

Fig. 20.2 A multimedia box with an inscription from the Storytelling App (©2016, EU CIP EAGLE, contract nr. 325122, reprinted with permission)

reference to it. At the same time, this index of referenced objects can be leveraged also in the opposite direction: a database of inscriptions or of other archaeological objects may include the links to all the stories that embed items from their collections. The EAGLE portal, for instance, provides links to the related stories in the results returned by the search engine.

20.2.3 The Storytelling App for Authors

The Storytelling App assists the authors in handling content from online repositories about ancient monuments and inscriptions. In addition to the WordPress default interface to insert images and other content from the multimedia gallery, our plug-in offers some specific functions to interrogate a series of supported external databases and insert the selected content within the text. The items retrieved from this interface are then visualized as the interactive boxes described above.

While the WordPress editor natively supports embedding from popular websites such as Flickr or YouTube, the Storytelling App is unique in the panorama of actual Digital Humanities for its ability to extend the same behavior with content from repositories related to antiquity. First of all, the plug-in allows to retrieve items from the EAGLE collection itself; in addition to a simplified search interface that is available from within the story editor, the authors, who must have a registered EAGLE account to access the authoring capabilities of our app, can use their account to perform more elaborate queries with the inscription search engine on the EAGLE web portal and then save the desired items in their personal space; those saved items from the regular search engine are immediately available in the Storytelling App. Maps can be loaded by searching for any ancient or modern location in the iDAI.gazetteer[17] or in Pelagios, using the Pleiades gazetteer (Fig. 20.3).[18] Other Linked Open Data from the Pelagios network[19] are also supported for retrieval and inclusion. Sources for further readings or introductory explanations of concepts or events can be added by embedding links to entries in online encyclopedias. Currently, the Ancient History Encyclopedia[20] and Wikipedia (with the option to include articles in any of the available languages of the free encyclopedia) are supported as content source. Texts, images, and videos from Europeana[21] can also be searched and included into the stories.

The app was designed so that multiple methods to retrieve and embed content are supported. The search interface reproduced in Fig. 20.3 is the most direct. However, authors that are more familiar with the original datasources, or want to perform more sophisticated queries that are not supported in the simple search functions of the story editor, can paste the URL of any item from the supported repositories directly in the text. Finally, content can be embedded using the syntax of "shortcodes" in WordPress, by specifying the source to retrieve the content (e.g., "idai" for the iDAI.gazetteer) and the ID of the desired object.

[17]https://gazetteer.dainst.org/

[18]http://pleiades.stoa.org/

[19]http://commons.pelagios.org/

[20]http://www.ancient.eu/

[21]http://www.europeana.eu/

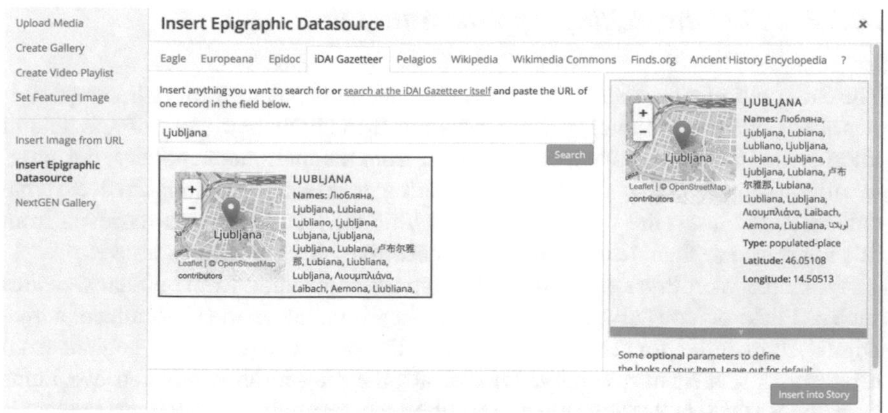

Fig. 20.3 Maps in the Storytelling App visual editor (©2016, EU CIP EAGLE, contract nr. 325122, reprinted with permission)

20.2.4 The EpiDoc Generic Renderer

While EAGLE aims to create the largest online collection of Greco-Roman inscriptions, the number of digital projects in digital epigraphy is growing daily. Several new projects are producing digital editions of inscriptions, and it is foreseeable that many more will come in the future; one notable example is, for instance, the *Digital Marmor Parium* that we have mentioned above. As we said in the Introduction, one important aspect of the current practice of digital epigraphy is the adoption of EpiDoc to encode the textual information. One crucial feature of the Storytelling App, which is aimed to ensure the synergy of the application with the community of digital epigraphists at large, is the ability to handle any inscription published online that conforms to the guidelines of EpiDoc. By pasting the URL of any EpiDoc-compliant text into the "Epidoc" tab of the plug-in (or directly into the story), authors can embed a box displaying the text and information about the inscription within their story. The inserted inscription will be visualized exactly as all the other items from the EAGLE collection (as reproduced in Fig. 20.2 above).

Whereas there are several projects using the standard, most of which offer also a human-readable rendering of the editions (mostly into HTML), a generic parser and renderer of EpiDoc XML was not previously available. Its implementation proved more challenging than it was originally foreseen, but it can be considered one of the main acquisitions of the EAGLE services.

Although EpiDoc is a widely accepted international standard, in the real world there are almost as many different implementations of it as there are projects that make use of it. This situation is not only the result of the different versions of EpiDoc that were developed over time, but it also originates from the varying need of the different epigraphy projects. Last but not least, some details in the XML syntax depend on the habits of the editors and, even more, on the settings of the used

XML-editing software. These small differences are of no concern, if editors keep their EpiDoc files in the environments (website, desktop editor) they were originally intended for; most of them do not even become noticeable when developers work with single files at time. However, the project of a "generic reader" for the Storytelling App aimed to deal with EpiDoc editions at a bigger scale and at a "project-agnostic" level: the reader must be prepared to handle XML code coming from different projects, encoded by different authors with the help of different XML editors. At this scale, apparently "trivial" differences (such as the definition of the document scheme or of namespaces) become very problematic.

In order to cope with these issues, we developed an EpiDoc renderer as a PHP class which investigates the EpiDoc file provided in input, modifies it if necessary, and sets up the XSLT Parser with the appropriate settings.

The EpiDoc Converter that powers the renderer of the Storytelling App is an acquisition that can be useful to the community of digital epigraphists even beyond the application; for this reason, we decided to run it as a public service hosted by the Deutsches Archäologisches Institut.[22] The service is available through a simple API where users can provide an EpiDoc file, customize the appropriate settings, and receive their edition rendered as HTML. The options allow users to specify, for instance, whether they want to render the whole file or just the <edition>-part or if they want to receive a full HTML page or just a snippet.

Potentially, the service can ease significantly the work of all projects or editors that want to adopt EpiDoc to produce online editions of inscriptions but are not capable of (or are not willing to) handling the visualization aspects. By calling the DAI-run service, editors can outsource the rendering work to an external service, without the need to program one for themselves.

20.2.5 Beyond EAGLE: Modularity and Extensibility

The Storytelling App was designed from the start to interact with the online community of digital classicists, for the app is programmed to integrate content from data repositories maintained by other projects around the world side by side with objects from the EAGLE collection. The generic EpiDoc Converter, which extends the range of content that is available to authors to virtually all present and future EpiDoc-compliant editions of the texts, marks another step toward the interoperability in the domain of epigraphy, archaeology, and ancient history. Furthermore, the source code of the app introduces an abstract class that can be used by developers to add new data sources and support for new repositories with little effort; this feature is also intended to support the extension of the application.

Structurally, the modularity and extensibility of the application is also insured at the level of design by separating the code in two different plug-ins, namely, a generic

[22]The public API and a web demonstrators can be accessed at: http://epidoc.dainst.org/

and an EAGLE-specific part. The latter implements the structural compatibility of the application with the rest of the web portal and implements a limited number of changes to the WordPress theme of the website. The generic plug-in, on the other hand, contains the core functionality and, thanks to its separation from the EAGLE-specific components, is reusable on any other WordPress blogs and websites.

The app is now published on the official plug-in repository of WordPress, where users can also view and download the source code.[23]

20.3 Signs of Life: The EAGLE Virtual Exhibition

Signs of Life is a virtual exhibition on epigraphy.[24] With an organized narrative, it provides a path through contents in the EAGLE Network and is a sort of long story about epigraphy.

This virtual exhibition aims at providing users with both a general introduction to some aspects of Greek and Roman epigraphy and at showcasing a large amount of projects and resources available for further enquiry. It is designed thus to meet the needs of those who have no clear notion of what epigraphy is but also to connect contents and resources for people who do know about epigraphy but might not be aware of the existence of some research tool or product already available online.[25]

Signs of Life, curated by the EAGLE Best Practice Network, has been designed during the Fifth EAGLE International Event in Nicosia (11–12 March 2015) with a simple but effective structure: six rooms which introduce the reader and visitor to some key aspects of epigraphy, presenting them with sample inscriptions and a brief narrative.

There are two ways in which the users can access the exhibition. One is simply reading the web version, a hypertext with a coherent narrative and functionalities to explore further related resources.[26] The other is entering the Virtual Museum for a

---

[23]https://wordpress.org/plugins/eagle-storytelling-application/

[24]The exhibition can be accessed at: http://www.eagle-network.eu/virtual-exhibition/. This is not the first virtual exhibition about epigraphy, but previous examples were dedicated to very specific contents. See, e.g., the Vindolanda Tablets Virtual Exhibition at http://vindolanda.csad.ox.ac.uk/exhibition/index.shtml and the virtual exhibition about Mount Testaccio at http://ceipac.ub.edu/MOSTRA/u_expo.htm. On virtual exhibitions, see [14] and [15]. On terms and definitions about Virtual Museums, see [16]. Many more examples of digital exhibition are archaeology based and aimed at tourists. See [17] for more about virtual exhibitions and cultural heritage.

[25]On the types of users of epigraphy and epigraphic contents, readers are referred to several studies published in [7], especially [18] on the users of digital epigraphy in general, [12] on examples of epigraphic work in primary schools in Slovenia, [19] for interaction between the Ashmolean Museum and high schools, and [13] on the knowledge of epigraphy by university students in Romania.

[26]For example, the stories in [10]. Wherever possible also connection to other EAGLE resources is given, especially to the EAGLE Storytelling App, the EAGLE MediaWiki (retrievable at: http://www.eagle-network.eu/wiki), and the controlled vocabularies of EAGLE (http://www.eagle-network.eu/resources/vocabularies).

fully interactive and immersive tour, free of the narrative structure and only organized according to the macro structure.[27] In this way the user who prefers to delve into the contents and read them can start from the web version and follow the narrative through, while the more interaction-oriented user can experience the contents with a more physical approach, walking in the 3D environment; as no path is indicated within the alveolar structure of the virtual environment, spectators are also free to select what to look at more closely without any precise order.

The contents of both views are the same, but the two environments are tailored for different kinds of users. From each page of the hypertext version, the user can jump back into the 3D environment and vice versa, so that also a mixed experience is fully possible: the two ways of exploring the contents are studied to support one another.

One major challenge was of course to find 3D models of the selected items. There are indeed collections of 3D models including inscriptions, and some models of a specimen of items is also available; these, however, remain a very small minority and cannot encompass monumental inscriptions. Moreover, as in a real museum, how to display an inscription is not a trivial problem to solve in a Virtual Museum as well. Some inscribed monument can require space as viewers must be able to inspect texts both in front and in the back; some others might be very small and require closeup inspection. In essence, the 3D environment ends up presenting a lot of 2D photos on the walls of the environment but remains conceptually valuable and open to host further models, as more and more companies are open also to produce such on demand.[28]

20.3.1 Aims and Objectives

The main aim of *Signs of Life* is to take Epigraphy "*Outside the Echo Chamber*," to quote the title of a recent publication [1], and present it to a much wider range of possibly interested readers. A new reader or visitor of the exhibition will see a part or all the exhibition and hopefully end his tour with an idea of what epigraphy is about. At the same time, an experienced reader going through the exhibition might find interesting tools, visualizations, and contents for teaching at secondary school level but also for introductory university classes or for amateurs, if not for his own research. The exhibition contains organized references to many resources available online, providing also pathways to them for people who might not be aware of interesting products or visualizations.

---

[27]The virtual tour was developed using Unity by Panayiotis Kyriakou at the Cyprus Institute. See [17], pp. 17–18 for the state of the art on current technologies and tools for virtual exhibitions.

[28]Museo Techniki (http://www.museotechniki.com), for instance, is a company that produces 3D models also for educational purposes; they have provided *Signs of Life* with some of the showcased models made from photos shared in Wikimedia Commons.

20.3.2 Structure

After the Introduction, which also links to a discussion and definition of what epigraphy is [2], *Signs of Life* is organized in the following rooms:

- Inscriptions which changed history
- Scripts and alphabets
- Objects and the relation between image, text, and context
- Emotions in inscriptions
- The stone cutter: methods and mistakes
- Digital technologies for epigraphy

In the Introduction, the reader learns about epigraphy as a discipline in general with some definitions and a gentle introduction to the subject. Some answers are given to what an inscription is and what it tells us. Throughout the narrative, the focus is kept on this line, to provide the reader not just with bare data, which would not be that useful, but with a parsed interpretation in the context of the exhibition of a monument or text, making sense in the context. For this reason not all text are reported and translated.

In Room 1—*Inscriptions which changed History*—a selection of inscriptions which are very important for history is provided together with examples of what makes inscriptions relevant for historical reconstruction and the study of history, although this aspect might not be immediately visible to the reader of the text itself. The examples should make evident to the reader that it is not simply the object or the text that is relevant, but it is the connection between several aspects and with other documents that brings a text to life and makes it important.

Room 2—*Scripts and Alphabets*—details another area of great interest in cross-disciplinary fields, thus extending the range of the contents to a much wider and deeper audience than just the circle of specialists in Greco-Roman epigraphy. Scripts and alphabets are indeed a topic of great interest and significance for different researchers and from different perspectives, cutting across time and space.

A key theoretical point is demonstrated by the items in Room 3—*Objects and the relation between image, text, and context*, which faces directly the issue of the relation between a monument, the text, and images it carries and the context in which it is placed.[29]

This first part of the exhibition with its examples takes the readers to a good understanding of the subject matter and allows them to go into more details and start looking at the content of the inscribed text.

Instead of describing typologies of documents that can be attested in inscriptions, as a manual of epigraphy usually does, Room 4—*Emotions in Inscriptions*—looks at the contents of inscriptions from a specific angle, which is especially appealing to the potential audience, by taking into account some specific emotions involved in the texts and pointing out concrete examples. If the political

[29] See the "Introduction" in [7], as well as [20].

significance of a text read in its historical context is very interesting for the history amateur, this kind of insight which is brought with empathy closer to the life of ancient people interests also more general users.

A further aspect, which is important for researchers and at least interesting to the reader, is presented in Room 5—*The stone cutter: methods and mistakes*. The world of stonecutters and what we learn from their products about them might sound more technical, but nevertheless, by showing how inscriptions could be produced and what common mistakes and phenomena could occur takes the reader closer to the life and experience of this specific class of the ancient society. On the other side, together with Room 2, this section of the exhibition presents some of the less obvious difficulties with which researchers in epigraphy are confronted.

The final room exhibits 3D models of inscriptions to give the three-dimensional effect of the monuments in scale; this part is accessible in full only in the immersive environment.

Each room has several inscriptions for which a link to metadata is given, in addition to one or more photos and a contextualization in the path of the exhibition. Throughout the text, there are links to other related contents, especially definitions of keywords, videos, 3D models, and geographical information but also further interesting contents from other online resources (texts, papyri, etc.); in this way, the reader is invited to look as much as possible at these objects from different perspectives (historical, archaeological, artistic, etc.). The unexperienced user should always find definitions for terms that are specifically defined in the context of epigraphy, and the researcher might look up and quickly check the content, seeing quoted text or place information directly.[30]

Just like in the rationale of the Storytelling App (see the previous section), *Signs of Life* intends to provide the viewers, and especially the "newbies" who start on the EAGLE website without prior knowledge of epigraphy, with an effective *viaticum* not just to the other functionalities of the EAGLE portal but also to other networked resources for ancient history. This is done using mixed media types and offering an immersive experience although with the limitation of the availability of data, so that the cultural heritage sector gains guided access to inscriptions as a specific type of subject for which often a specialist is not available. Small and medium collections could reuse the exhibition as an introduction to their *lapidaria* in the same way a teacher could use it to introduce their students to epigraphy.

20.3.3 Functionalities

The Introduction page provides an overview on the theme of the entire exhibition. Each page has always a side and a bottom navigation tool, images, text, and links,

[30]On the importance of this aspect, see [21].

with a double level of bold for text, to give two degrees of emphasis to long text which the user might skim through only, building on real exhibition experiences.

As in the Storytelling App, also in the virtual exhibition, some functionalities are used to support the reader in contextualizing the contents. For example, each room has its own introduction and allows a navigation at room level only. Once the user enters a room and starts to see the items, navigation is also provided among the items keeping track of the position of the user in the contents. Ancient Place Names are linked to the Pleiades gazetteer[31] and, with the use of a javascript library available online,[32] related contents are visualized together with a small map of the mentioned place in a small pop-up window. This is a way in which the exhibition exploits Linked Open Data resources seamlessly to enrich and edit its contents. Although its aim is not to make Linked Data available, the exhibition uses the potential offered by projects publishing data and building tools to display this data as an end product, thus providing direct evidence of the importance of such work to its users.

At the end of each page, relevant related stories or links to external resources are provided, especially to those interactive tools about epigraphy which are openly available and accessible online, like interactive maps. Where possible, interactive contents are directly embedded, like the timeline of the Parian Marble [3], the map of places mentioned on the Vicarello Beckers[33], or the graph of attested languages and their relation provided by Trismegistos.[34]

Images from participating archives[35] and from Wikimedia Commons are visualized as slideshows, as static images, or, when they are exposed with a IIIF protocol,[36] with Openseadragon[37] as zoomable images in a simple viewer.

The user experience is also extended with some games and extras embedded in the exhibition. In the quizzes the user can try his or her knowledge and see the solutions, to learn while playing in a simple and intuitive way.

20.4 Conclusions

Signs of Life and the Storytelling App are products of an international collaborative effort by the EAGLE Best Practice Network to create resources that introduce the wide public to epigraphy (mainly Greek and Latin); in this, they share a common approach to the task, which does not give up on the complexity of the discipline but

[31] http://pleiades.stoa.org/

[32] http://isawnyu.github.io/awld-js/

[33] http://pelagios-project.blogspot.co.uk/2013/10/iwp2-pelagios-and-beakers-of-vicarello_17.html

[34] http://www.trismegistos.org/network/10_2015_11_18/

[35] http://www.eagle-network.eu/about/partners/

[36] http://iiif.io/

[37] https://openseadragon.github.io/

diversify contents and functionalities to meet different needs. In both cases, the use of available Linked Open Data maintained by the international community is leveraged to evoke the notion of the "historical context" of which every inscription is part.

This approach reflects in part the guidelines of the Europeana Strategy 2020 and aims to contribute to the main task of reaching out to people with content of high complexity. The virtual exhibition as well as the stories help the user find contents and make his or her away within a vast amount of data which is otherwise impossible to master without previous knowledge. These products reuse data from Europeana and other sources to design pathways and introduce the user in a gentle way, thus improving the access and usability of contents. Especially the Storytelling App offers to its users the possibility to easily integrate such content in their own products using a very popular platform, thus allowing for an easy and straightforward facilitation in content retrievability and representation, some of the major problems hindering digital resources reuse. The contents produced are simple and thus easy to integrate with other resources, like the Ancient History Encyclopedia which uses the Storytelling App and its contents.

Choices and selection of content, organization, and display face the challenge to meet the needs of users without simplification; instead, they require digital editors and curators to focus on the relevant information in each context. This is what makes the interaction with such a kind of "niche content" interesting rather than pedantic: by giving meaning to information, we encourage deeper research and reading rather than keep people insulated from complications. The relation and connection between content and external resources should leverage the richness of available online resources, which is often unknown to beginners as well as to experienced users.

Linked Data as such is a mine from which end products such as stories or an exhibition can be dug out to enrich the selected and curated contents they present to the public. Authors and readers in their turn benefit too from a facilitated authoring and editing environment and from the use of enhanced contents, for they can access a vast repertoire of already edited materials; on the other hand, editors and curators should not overwhelm them by the number of connections proposed and need to provide clear guidance to their audience through each connection.

Stories, narratives, and other end products are vital to the meaning of the underlying data as they make it readable and thus accessible to the end users. Academically curated data and digital products present a challenge to their editors and authors, which is to make themselves relevant and usable not just for machines; tools to facilitate the perusal and presentation of such resources are more relevant and needed each day, as more data become available.

The efforts put forth by the EAGLE consortium in the field of epigraphy in this direction are an example of how also very closed niches of interests can be opened to the wide public thanks to the use of carefully curated data and authoring tools to present them "in context." Our hope is that they will offer occasions for further interaction.

Acknowledgments This work has been funded by the EU EAGLE Best Practice Network project: Grant Agreement CIP 325122, call CIP-ICT-PSP-2012-6.

References

1. G. Bodard, M. Romanello (eds.), *Digital classics outside the echo-chamber: teaching, knowledge exchange and public engagement* (Ubiquity Press, London, 2016)
2. S. Panciera, What is an Inscription? Problems of definition and identity of an historical source. Z. Papyrol. Epigr. **182**, 1–10 (2012)
3. M. Berti, S. Stoyanova, Digital Marmor Parium for a digital edition of a Greek chronicle, in *Information Technologies for Epigraphy and Cultural Heritage. Proceedings of the First EAGLE International Conference* (La Sapienza University Press, Rome, 2014), pp. 319–324
4. H. Cayless, Ch. Roueché, G. Bodard, T. Elliott, Epigraphy in 2017. Digit. Humanit. Q. **3**(1), (2009), http://digitalhumanities.org/dhq/vol/3/1/000030/000030.html
5. T. Elliot et al., *EpiDoc: Epigraphic Documents in TEI XML* (2006–2016), http://epidoc.sf.net
6. G. Bodard, The inscriptions of Aphrodisias as electronic publication: a user's perspective and a proposed paradigm. Digit. Mediev. **4**, http://digitalmedievalist.org/journal/4/bodard/
7. S. Orlandi, R. Santucci, V. Casarosa, P.M. Liuzzo (eds.), in *Information Technologies for Epigraphy and Cultural Heritage*. Proceedings of the First EAGLE International Conference (La Sapienza University Press, Rome, 2014)
8. G. Bodard, S. Stoyanova, Epigraphers and encoders: strategies for teaching and learning digital epigraphy, in *Digital Classics Outside the Echo-Chamber: Teaching, Knowledge Exchange and Public Engagement* (Ubiquity Press, London, 2016), pp. 51–68. doi:10.5334/bat.d
9. S. Orlandi, Ancient inscriptions between citizens and scholars: the double soul of the EAGLE project, in *Digital Classics Outside the Echo-Chamber: Teaching, Knowledge Exchange and Public Engagement* (Ubiquity Press, London, 2016), pp. 205–221. doi:10.5334/bat.l
10. M. Šašel Kos, *The Disappearing Tombstone and Other Stories from Emona* (Založba ZRC, Ljubljana, 2015)
11. W. Schmidle, F. Mambrini, P. Franck, *The EAGLE Flagship Storytelling Application*. EAGLE Deliverable D5.4.2 (2015), http://www.eagle-network.eu/wp-content/uploads/2013/06/EAGLE_D5.4.2_Second-release-of-the-EAGLE-Flagship-Storytelling-Application_v1_0.pdf
12. A. Ragolič, Epigraphy as a tool for learning Latin: the case of the Prežihov Voranc Primary School in Ljubljana, Slovenia, in *Information Technologies for Epigraphy and Cultural Heritage. Proceedings of the First EAGLE International Conference* (La Sapienza University Press, Rome, 2014), pp. 205–220
13. R. Varga, (Digital) epigraphy as viewed by Romanian archaeology/classics students, in *Information Technologies for Epigraphy and Cultural Heritage. Proceedings of the First EAGLE International Conference* (La Sapienza University Press, Rome, 2014), pp. 233–238
14. S. Hermon, S. Hazan, in *Rethinking the Virtual Museum*. Digital Heritage International Congress (DigitalHeritage) Marseille, pp. 625–632, 2013. doi:10.1109/DigitalHeritage.2013.6744829
15. S. Hazan, The digital exhibition—considered in the long-term. Uncommon Cult. **6**(1), (2015), http://uncommonculture.org/ojs/index.php/UC/article/view/6069/4620
16. D. Ferdani, A. Pagano, M. Farouk, *Terminology, Definitions and Types for Virtual Museums*. V-Must.net, Deliverable 2.1c (2014), http://www.v-must.net/sites/default/files/D2.1c%20V_Must_TERMINOLOGY_V2014_FINAL.pdf
17. V. Vassallo, P.M. Liuzzo, *Epigraphy Virtual Exhibition*. EAGLE Deliverable 2.7 (2016), http://www.eagle-network.eu/repository/eagle/WP1%20-%20Project%20management/Deliverables/EAGLE_D2.7_Epigraphy%20Virtual%20Exhibition_v1.0.pdf

18. L. Löser, in *Meeting the Needs of Today's Audiences of Epigraphy with Digital Editions*. Proceedings of the Second EAGLE International Conference, Rome, 27–29 January 2016 (forthcoming)
19. J. Masséglia, in *The Ashmolean Latin Inscriptions Project (AshLI)*. Proceedings of the Second EAGLE International Conference, Rome, 27–29 January 2016 (forthcoming)
20. E. Santin, E. Morlock, The inscription between text and object, in *Information Technologies for Epigraphy and Cultural Heritage. Proceedings of the First EAGLE International Conference* (La Sapienza University Press, Rome, 2014), pp. 325–349
21. E. Bozia, A. Barmpoutis, R. Wagman, Open-access epigraphy: electronic dissemination of 3D-digitized archaeological material, in *Information Technologies for Epigraphy and Cultural Heritage. Proceedings of the First EAGLE International Conference* (La Sapienza University Press, Rome, 2014), pp. 421–435
22. J. Lehmann, M. Lalmas, E. Yom-Tov, G. Dupret, Models of user engagement, in *User Modeling, Adaptation, and Personalization, Lecture Notes in Computer Science* (Springer, Berlin, 2012), pp. 164–175
23. G. Palma, M. Baldassari, M. Favilla, R. Scopigno, Storytelling of a coin collection by means of RTI images: the case of the Simoneschi Collection in Palazzo Blu, in *Museums and the Web 2013*. (2014), http://mwf2014.museumsandtheweb.com/paper/storytelling-of-a-coin-collection-by-means-of-rti-images-the-case-of-the-simoneschi-collection-in-palazzo-blu/

Part VIII
Museum Applications

Chapter 21
AM-Based Evaluation, Reconstruction, and Improvement of Cultural Heritage Artifacts

Andreas Gebhardt

Abstract Modern imaging and scanning processes and digital manufacturing methods like additive manufacturing (AM, also known as rapid prototyping) are very important tools for documentation and the support of research in the field of cultural heritage artifacts. This chapter presents the data handling and the capabilities of the most important AM processes and materials used. Many samples linked to medical applications that are closely related to cultural heritage artifacts show successful applications for both documentation and scientific research. Having once obtained the 3D data set, AM opens up business cases for marketing and customized production of cultural heritage artifacts. Examples are giveaways made from plastics as well as precious one-offs made from metal.

Keywords Additive manufacturing (AM) • Rapid prototyping (RP) • Computerized tomography (CT) • Digital manufacturing • Stereolithography • Selective laser melting (SLM) • 3D printing • Extrusion • Tiye • Nefertiti • Fibula • Celts

21.1 Introduction

There are various reasons why people want to have three-dimensional pictures or statues from cultural heritage artifacts. Mostly, a physical copy is wanted in order to touch a "non touchable" unique original. Often there is an educational background that additionally requires a segmentation to underline special topics, such as hidden structures or lost details. More and more scientific documentation is the reason for 3D modeling and manufacturing. One aim is to support the classical 2D paperwork, but new aspects are added by in situ 3D documentation during excavation.

A. Gebhardt (✉)
Aachen University of Applied Sciences, Bayernallee 11, 52066 Aachen, Germany
e-mail: gebhardt@fh-aachen.de

M. Ioannides et al. (eds.), *Mixed Reality and Gamification for Cultural Heritage*,
DOI 10.1007/978-3-319-49607-8_21

Additive manufacturing (AM) or 3D printing is an already proven but still new method that improves tremendously due to a strong technical development supported by scientists and machine developers in many countries worldwide.

AM can be split into three subtasks; data acquisition, 3D printing process including postprocessing, and finishing. While the 3D printing process gets increasingly at least partly automated, the finishing still is characterized by manual subtasks.

21.2 Entry Point and Precondition: Solid 3D CAD Model and Dataflow

While most of the technical 3D printed models are part of a product development process and therefore are based on 3D CAD data, this is not so for cultural heritage artifacts. Cultural heritage artifacts mainly have a character of documentation, frequently linked to restoration work. As they usually represent humanoid structures, they cannot be designed using technical rules and in most the cases cannot even be represented by technical (CAD) software. Therefore, the standard method of data acquisition is scanning as far as the outer appearance is concerned, and all kinds of medical imaging including computed tomography of internal structures are touched.

In the 1990s, medical computed tomography (CT) scanners needed to be used. The applicable X-ray dose was low in order to save the (human) patient, and the process was very expensive. Today CT scanners are available also for technical documentation and quality control, making them cheaper, easy to handle, and free from medical restrictions such as high X-ray doses.

Medical imaging processes such as CT or ultrasonic (US) are the front end of the dataflow. A common format for medical images is DICOM. Special software allows a suitable threshold selection and a 3D reconstruction that provide the basis for a set of STL data that can be processed in any 3D printer or AM machine.

Figure 21.1 shows the dataflow using the example of the imaging, segmentation, and reconstruction of a human skull which is pretty much the same with cultural heritage data acquisition.

The process chain starts with the indication calling for a model (Fig. 21.1). The processes are determined by the material to be investigated. Computed tomography (CT) is used for reproducing solid material like bone structures, wood, low-density stone, etc. Magnetic resonance imaging (MRI) and ultrasonic processes (US) are used for soft tissue garments and fabrics. Positron emission tomography (PET) and single-photon emission computed tomography (SPECT) are for the reproduction of circulatory and metabolic disorders. Although CT images, for example, also contain layer information, they cannot be used directly in the 3D printing machine as the layer thickness is 1–2 mm (minimum 0.5 mm) and therefore is significantly thicker than those used in additive manufacturing (approx. 0.1 mm).

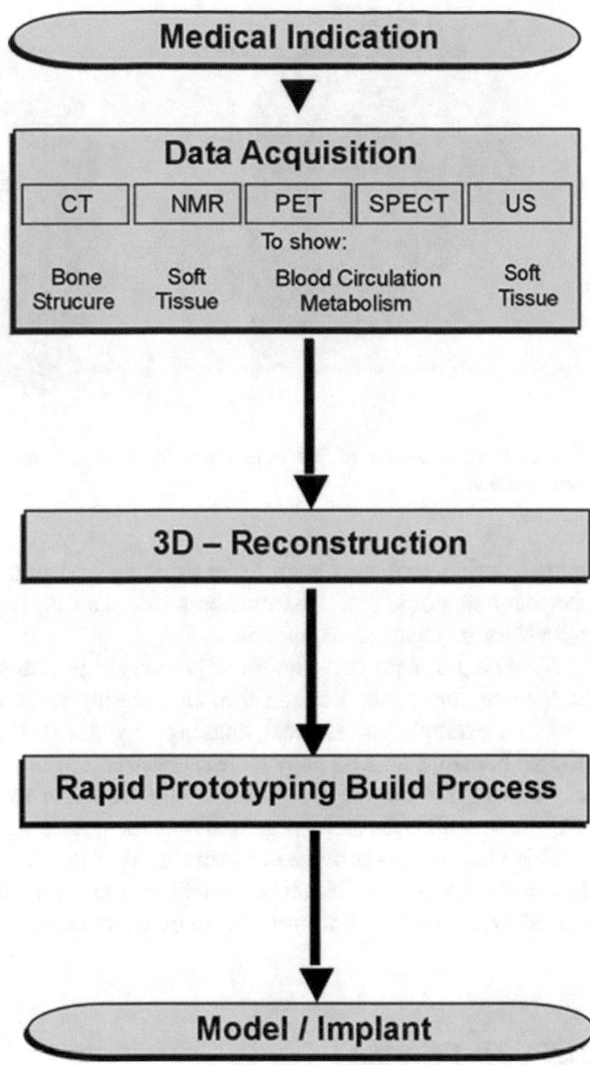

Fig. 21.1 Process chain for the production of an anatomic facsimile model

Using special image analysis processes, 3D images are reconstructed from the scanned layers. Each layer is segmented depending on its required structure. If solid and flexible materials like bone and soft tissue are to be reproduced simultaneously, as is the case, for example, with the larynx, single partial images may be superimposed. From the segmented layer information, a virtual picture is created on the computer screen (Fig. 21.1) with the aid of 3D reconstruction processes. Modern CT scanners and image analysis devices are able not only to provide output media and data structures for the daily routine but also to produce STL data and to address 3D printers directly. If this is not directly possible, special programs, for example, MIMICS (materialize), are used. They also handle specific additive

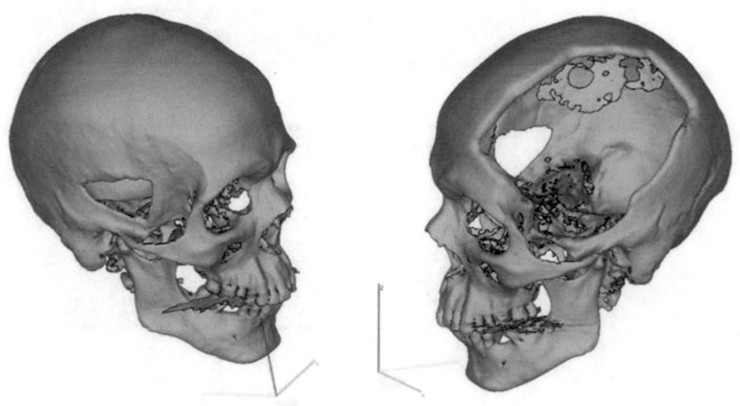

Fig. 21.2 Visualization of 3D data obtained from CT scans after segmentation and 3D reconstruction

manufacturing problems such as positioning and orientation in the build space, necessary supports, etc. This creates a raw data basis that is equivalent to CAD models for mechanical engineering.

Following this process chain until the rapid prototyping [1] or AM entry point leads to the input data needed for manufacturing an additively made part.

As an example for medical imaging in order to receive a scaled model of a (living) human, Fig. 21.2 shows the reconstructed data of a human skull. Although it is a living person, the procedure is applicable for the reconstruction of cultural artifacts as well and can be regarded as a standard process chain.

This kind of data provides the starting point for further digital treatment. The data can be scaled, details can be cut and enlarged, and different parts can be treated separately, i.e., colored or prepared to be made from different materials.

21.3 3D Printing

3D printing (3DP) is a rather new but already quite common method for making scaled physical objects from a 3D data set. As the process works layer by layer, it allows to make almost any shape or geometry and preferably can be used to fabricate nonrectangular structures as they occur in historic artifacts. Figure 21.3 shows a skull made by 3D printing (inkjet powder-binder process).

The disadvantage of 3D printing is that the models show a stair-stepping structure on its surface due to the equidistant layers. Stair stepping can be reduced by process optimization and eliminated by manual postprocessing and finishing.

Having the data, the decision has to be made on which AM process should be used. This mainly depends on the further application.

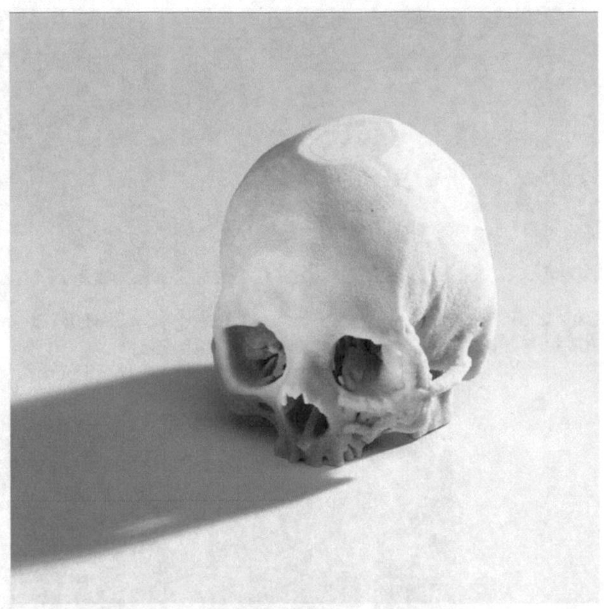

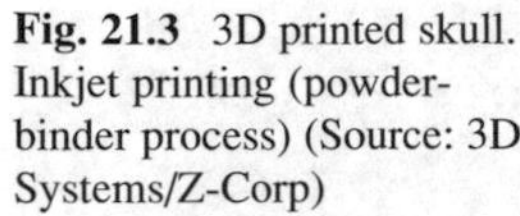

Fig. 21.3 3D printed skull. Inkjet printing (powder-binder process) (Source: 3D Systems/Z-Corp)

The different 3D printing processes, its pros and cons, the materials used, and suitable finishing procedures are described in detail in [2] and will not be repeated here. We will just discuss a few important characteristics that support the application of printed parts for making cultural heritage artifacts. Properties like transparency, rigidity, durability, surface quality, color, and others are to be taken into account.

Figure 21.4 shows the facial bone structures of a skull, both made from the identical 3D CAD data. An additive manufactured model obtained from laser stereolithography (left) and from 3D printing (inkjet powder-binder process, right) is displayed.

Because of the good surface quality and the detailed reproduction, laser stereolithography (Fig. 21.4, left) and polymer jetting are used preferably to make fine structured models such as skulls and other human bone structures. Interior hollow structures like the frontal sinus or the filigree subcranial bone structure can be reproduced best by these processes.

Laser sintering, 3D printing, fused layer manufacturing (extrusion, FDM), and layer laminate modeling (LOM) deliver suitable models as well and are used for this. For sintering and FDM, there are special approved materials available that are colored, transparent, or flexible. Some can be sterilized which mostly is not important for cultural heritage artifacts.

On Fig. 21.4, right, a skull made by 3D printing (powder-binder process) can be seen, which is made from the identical data set as the stereolithography skull on Fig. 21.4, left. The differences can be seen clearly. 3D printing delivers slightly less details and a rough surface. The model is not transparent. Whether this is a disadvantage or not depends on the intended use. But definitely the process is quick and cheap.

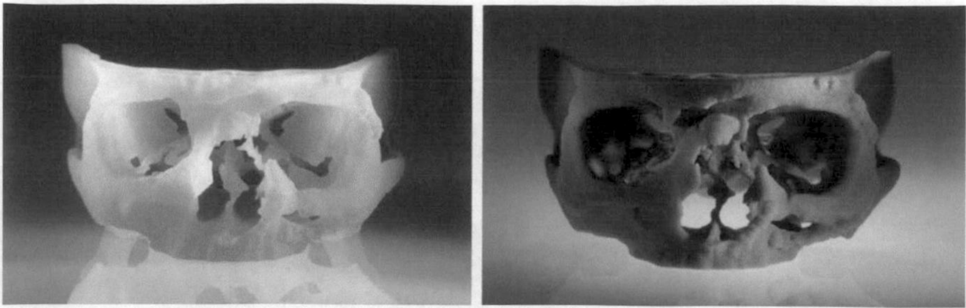

Fig. 21.4 Facsimile of a human skull based on CT data, stereolithography, *left*; 3D printing (powder-binder process), *right* (Source: CP-GmbH)

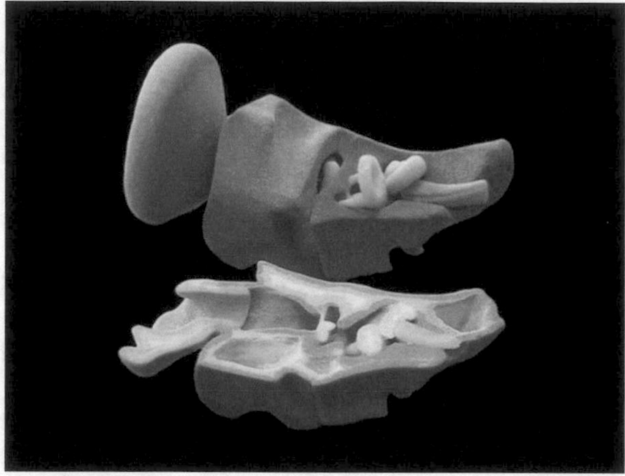

Fig. 21.5 Cutaway model of an ear. Colored inkjet printing (powder-binder process) (Source: CP-GmbH)

As today we have a great variety of additive manufacturing processes, materials, color (Fig. 21.5), flexibility and transparency, and machines, the user should do some basic market research in order to identify the best process for this task.

21.4 Applications

21.4.1 3D Printed Models

The additively manufactured model mostly is used directly as a one-off, or just a few copies are printed. If more copies are required, the print is treated as a master model for further copying processes. In any case, a treatment called finishing is needed. It includes manual work like infiltration, grinding, varnishing, and related handy tasks.

Figure 21.6 shows a complete human skeleton, made by 3D printing (inkjet powder-binder process). The data are based on MRT scans obtained from a living person. It obviously is very well suited to display a historic situation, i.e., close to or even on an excavation site.

As an example of stone structures, Fig. 21.7 displays a model of the Roman Colosseum. The data were taken as a printable data set from the Thingiverse Internet platform and printed using a personal grade (DIY) 3D printer (or fabber) using PLA filament.

Different colors, materials such as metals, and a higher amount or copies often can be reproduced more readily with the aid of molding processes. One of the most prominent processes is vacuum casting (room temperature vulcanization, RTV). Depending on the requirements of the special task, it may be necessary to produce several models by molding processes.

Even the creative work of artists can be supported successfully by AM. To work out a sculpture, a first handmade model can be scanned and transformed into an AM part made of polyamide (by sintering) or a material close to plaster (by 3D printing). This master can be worked out manually to express the intention of the artist and transfer it via a wax pattern into a small series made from brass.

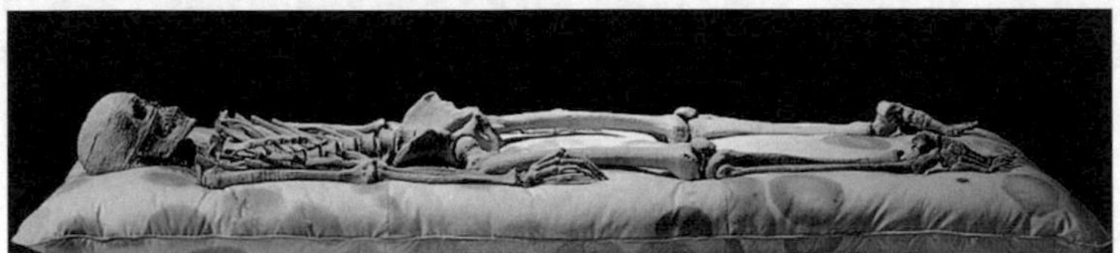

Fig. 21.6 Complete human skeleton. 3D printing (inkjet powder-binder process) (Source: CP-GmbH)

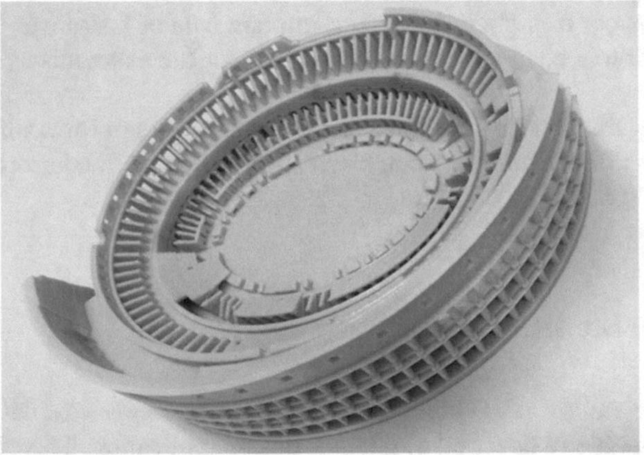

Fig. 21.7 Reproduction of the Roman Colosseum. Plastic filament printer (Source: Data Thingiverse; Print, GoetheLab, FH Aachen)

Fig. 21.8 Artistic sculpture by Alisa Minyukova, NY (*white*, *right*) and RTV copy made from wax (*red*, *left*) used as a lost wax casting model. Castings made from brass (*center*) (Source: CP-GmbH)

As an example, the sculpture of Alexander Pushkin, made by the NY-based artist Alisa Minyukova, is shown on Fig. 21.8 and demonstrates the process. An RTV copy (red, left) of the sculpture (white, right) is made to be used as a lost wax casting model in order to do a small series of castings made from brass (center).

21.4.2 Integrating and Improving Cultural Heritage Artifacts

The 3D data also can be used in a reverse engineering process. Good examples are implants designed to fit in bone structures. Figure 21.9 shows the bone side situation on the CT image. It is obvious that the implant cannot just cover the defect but needs to undergo a complex 3D design, mainly for the exact reconstruction of the orbita bow.

3D printing then can be used either to make a wax pattern for casting the implant or to directly print it from implantable material such as titanium using selective laser melting (SLM) [3].

21.5 Case Studies

Regarding the variety of 3D printing processes and machines available today, it is barely not possible to cover all possible types of application. Therefore, based on this general information, some case studies are presented to underline special applications closely linked to cultural heritage artifacts and research.

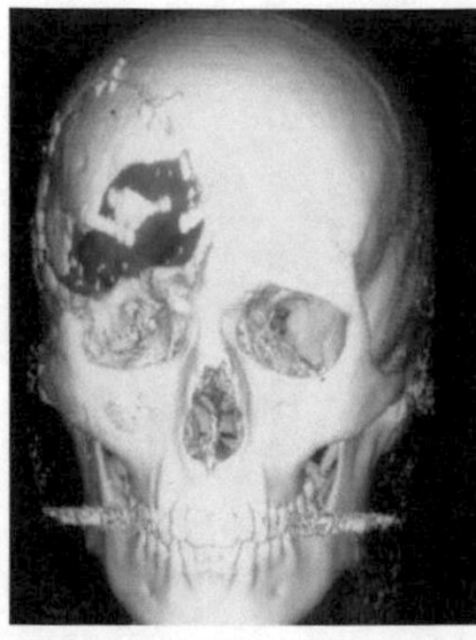
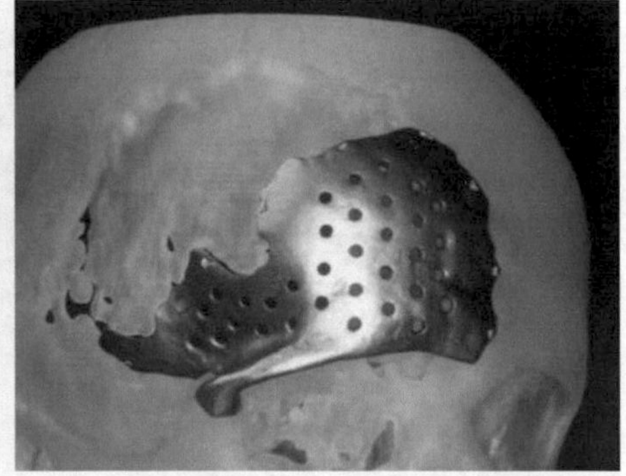

Fig. 21.9 Skull with defect. CT image after 3D reconstruction (*left*), Craniofacial implant including orbita bow (*right*) [Source: CP-GmbH, Charité Hospital Berlin (Prof. Bier)]

21.5.1 Reconstruction of Missing Parts

3D printing opens up interesting opportunities for people who are reconstructing missing parts. Dealing with human bodies is the most challenging application, but the reconstruction of missing parts of historic busts, buildings, and housewares follows the same system.

The picture shows a female that lost not just an eye but a representative portion of her face. The patient has been taken into a CT scanner to obtain the geometry of the defect as is and the good side just from outside. Then the episthesis has been designed virtually starting with mirroring the good side followed by optimization and fit in on the defect side (Fig. 21.10).

The data have been 3D printed and worked out by anaplastologists, Fig. 21.8.

21.5.2 Big Objects

21.5.2.1 Group of Persons

The 3D data needed for the reproduction of human sculptures can be obtained very easily by 3D body scanning. This was done at an exhibition designed by the artist Karin Sander at the "Staatsgalerie Stuttgart." The exhibits were generated by body scanning and 3D printing of the visitors. At the opening there were only empty shelves. At the finissage, all shelves were covered by a great number of 1:7 scale sculptures of the visitors. For this, monochromatic 3D printing is a suitable process, because it is quick, cheap, and the details are sufficient. Figure 21.11 shows a group of persons.

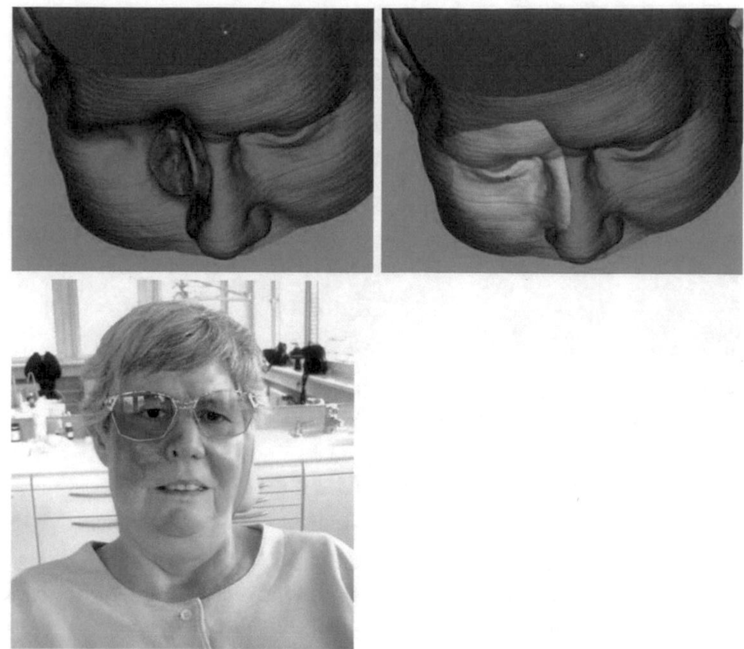

Fig. 21.10 Reconstruction of missing body parts based on scans, above. Final situation after fit in of the episthesis (Source: CP-GmbH, Horlitz)

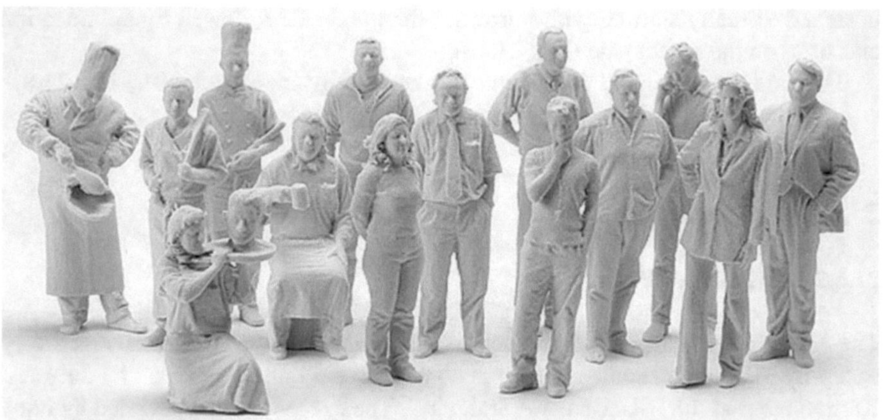

Fig. 21.11 Body scanning and 3D printing (3D Systems/Z-Corp). Plaster-ceramics (Source: Karin Sander/GoetheLab FH-Aachen)

21.5.2.2 The CHIO Horse

The International Horse Championship (CHIO) at Aachen is one of the most prestigious events worldwide. Among the regular trophies, there are trophies of

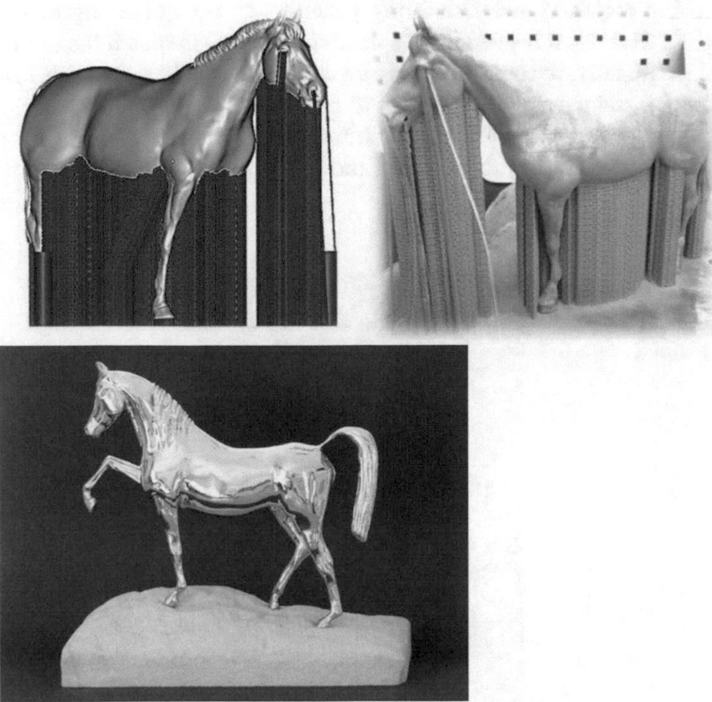

Fig. 21.12 CHIO trophy "Altis MidMesh". Stainless steel. Print data with supports (*red*) prepared for printing (*above*, *left*), SLM model with supports after the build (*above*, *right*), final sculpture (Source: Otto Junker GmbH, GoetheLab FH Aachen)

honor like the "Altis MidMesh" prize. It was made by scanning a living horse using multicamera scanners, data preparation, selective metal sintering (SLM) manual postprocessing, and multistage hand polishing to mirror quality. Figure 21.12 shows the scan date including the support structures (red) prepared for printing (above, left), the model including supports after the build (above, right), and the final sculpture.

It is a very good example for the treatment of big and complex and even moving structures.

21.5.2.3 The Sword of Messieur Dominique Perrault

The French architect Dominique Perrault was elected as one of the 56 members of the French Academy of Fine Arts, division of the "Institut de France" in June 2016. Following a century-old tradition, every new member brings his own sword, representing his style and capabilities. Perrault did not follow the tradition and designed a sword that resembles a rebar, resulting in a new formal language and showing a different haptic quality (Fig. 21.13d). It was printed in an upright position using the SLM metal sintering process and doing the engravings in the process (Fig. 21.13c). It needed to be split in five pieces to match the build volume (Fig. 21.13a). Finally, it was assembled by laser welding. The sword was selectively surface treated and the tip was polished to mirror quality (Fig. 21.13b).

The example demonstrates that all kinds of tools can be made by additive manufacturing, even if they do not fit in the build space of the printer.

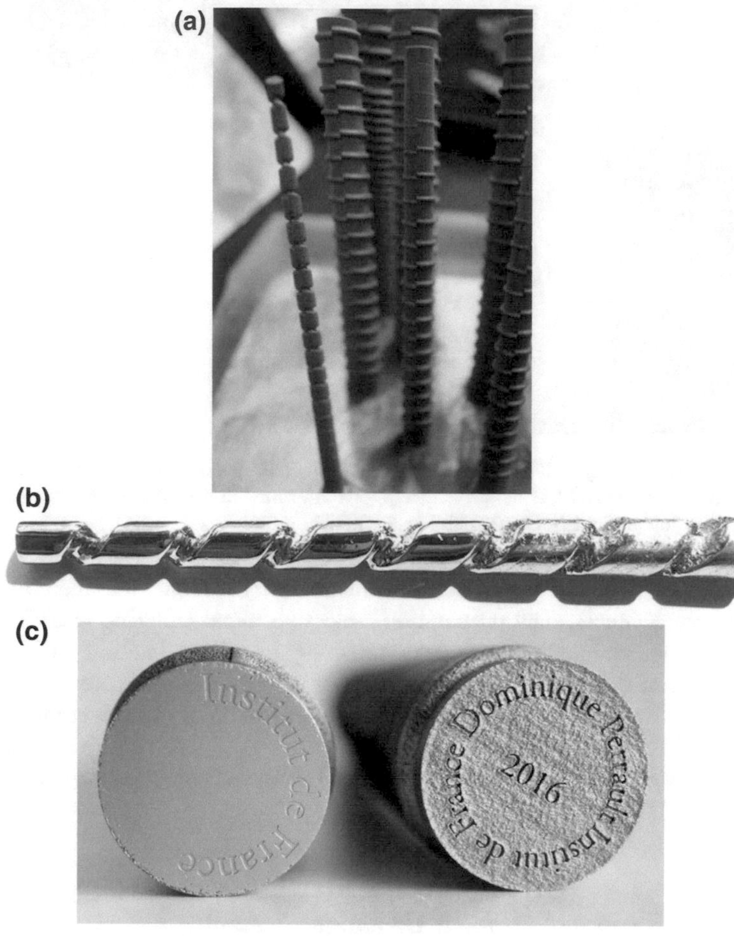

Fig. 21.13 (**a**) Situation in the SLM build space. (**b**) Polished tip. (**c**) Engravings on the handle. (**d**) Messieur Dominique Perrault with his sword after the ceremony (© 2016 Andreas Gebhardt, reprinted with permission)

Fig. 21.13 (continued)

21.6 Scientific Investigations

21.6.1 The Bust of the Egyptian Queen Tiye

The small bust of Tiye, the principal wife of King Amenophis III and consequently the queen of Egypt (18th dynasty; 1413–1377 BC), wrongly stands in the shadow of the world-famous one of her daughter-in-law Nefertiti. From the researchers' point of view, she is even more interesting.

The small (its overall height is just about 10 cm) but beautiful bust consists of a wooden skull with carved face framed by a helmetlike bonnet (Fig. 21.14). The bonnet is made from some kind of paper machée that covers almost the total skull. In the middle of the forehead, two tubelike structures penetrate the bonnet that assumedly have been linked to the traditional snakes that are missing. The tubes belong to a golden jewelry that is supposed to cover almost the entire head but mostly is invisibly hidden under the bonnet. A headband covers the upper section of

Fig. 21.14 The bust of queen Tiye as it appears today (Source: Egyptian Museum Berlin) (© 2005 Egyptian Museum Berlin, reprinted with permission)

the forehead. Another visible part of the jewelry is a decorated golden stud that is supposed to be linked to the jewelry. Almost three quarters of it can be seen clearly at her left ear. A similar one is assumed on the right side (Fig. 21.14).

At any time, researchers wanted to know the construction of the entire bust and all of its elements. As in the 1920s X-ray became available, the bust was taken for investigation. Impressive pictures showed all parts including the wooden base, the bonnet, and the jewelry (Fig. 21.15). Surprisingly, the wooden face was covered with another, so far invisible, silver bonnet that seemed to show the original appearance before the paper machée bonnet was applied. This was done to indicate the change of the social status of a queen to the one of a goddess after the death of her husband [2].

Although the X-rays delivered a clear impression of the whole arrangement, it remained two-dimensional, thus leaving many questions open. Especially the manual replication of its elements, mainly the jewelry, was almost not possible because of the lack of 3D information.

At that time, the researchers discussed a possible disassembly of the bust. Therefore, a precise and scaled physical 3D copy would be of great interest in order to plan the procedure and to train the people who would do it. But it was not available in that time.

In the late 1990s, a commercial high-power CT scanner, designed for material testing but for medical application, was available at the German Federal Institute for Materials Research and Testing (BAM) in Berlin. After a long-lasting procedure, a set of layer data was obtained. A virtual 3D reconstruction was used to obtain a 3D data set of all features. For the first time, the whole arrangement could be regarded continuously from any side, and all details were clearly visible including its interdependencies (Fig. 21.16). The result proved all assumptions concerning the jewelry and the silver bonnet.

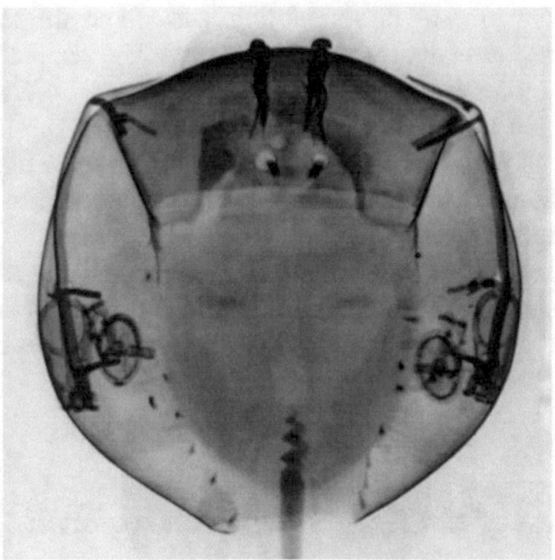

Fig. 21.15 X-ray of the bust of queen Tiye taken in the early 1920s (Source: Wildung) (© 1995, Wildung, reprinted with permission)

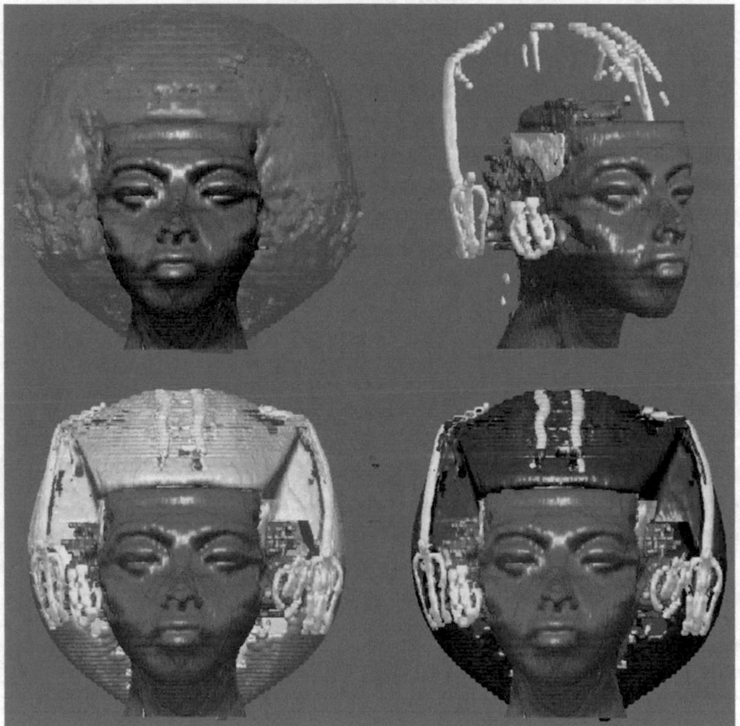

Fig. 21.16 3D reconstruction from CT scans of the bust of queen Tiye. All elements are clearly visible (Source: Illerhaus, BAM) (© 2004 Illerhaus, reprinted with permission)

Consequently, the idea of disassembling was given up. But soon didactical reasons caused a new demand for making a copy. The people responsible for the Egyptian Museum in Berlin, first of all the director Prof. D. Wildung [4] (until the end of 2009), wanted to demonstrate the complexity of the bust to the visitors. Therefore, a set of all parts was needed. It was planned to be displayed close to the original. A 2:1 scale was chosen to make details visible and to make sure that the model was not a replica but a supporting tool.

From this data, stereolithography models were made using additive manufacturing because of its ability to process fine details and make a smooth surface. All parts, including the jewelry but the face and the silver bonnet as well, were made using AM and decorated close to the original (Fig. 21.17).

21.6.2 The Bust of the Egyptian Queen Nefertiti

Some cultural heritage artifacts keep interior secrets even if they appear as a monolithic statue. A very impressive example is the world-famous statue of Nefertiti (ca. 1370 BC–ca. 1330 BC) made around 1340 BC. Nefertiti was the Great Royal Wife of the Egyptian Pharaoh Akhenaton.

The bust appears today like it was found in 1912 at the workshop of the sculptor Thutmosis at Amarna who supposedly made it. It is a colored bust made from a monolithic limestone with a height of approximately 50 cm (Fig. 21.18).

To obtain a smooth surface and to be able to apply the bright colors we can see even now, the limestone was covered with a layer of plaster. It was a guess since many years, but could not be proved, that the application of the plaster was used for some kind of cosmetic improvement too. But as the layer thickness of the plaster could not be investigated without at least partly destroying the original, it was a taboo to touch it.

Fig. 21.17 Bust of queen Tiye. Main elements made by AM: Jewelry (on top of the supports), face, bonnet. Stereolithography. Scale: 2:1 (Source: CP-GmbH © 2009, CP GmbH, Germany, reprinted with permission)

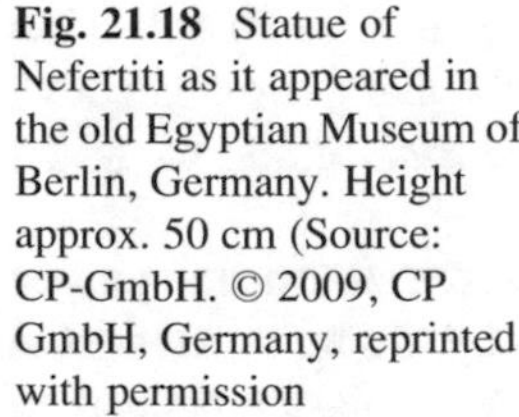

Fig. 21.18 Statue of Nefertiti as it appeared in the old Egyptian Museum of Berlin, Germany. Height approx. 50 cm (Source: CP-GmbH. © 2009, CP GmbH, Germany, reprinted with permission

The use of X-rays did not show reasonable results as the skin-like plaster layer needs to be investigated in all three dimensions in order to obtain a clear picture of the distribution of the layer thickness. Even the first CT scanners did not deliver a sufficient result, because of its comparably big scan layers (2.5 mm) and its low power designed to monitor human structures but stones.

The investigation of the bust confirmed that, while making the bust in the antique, Nefertiti herself served as a model. So, the ancient sculptor made a real copy of her, including all human imperfections like a clearly visible asymmetry of her shoulders. After sculpturing he used plaster to improve the bust. This result could be clearly verified by the CT scans and the limestone-plaster distribution obtained from virtual 3D reconstruction on the computer. But because of the low resolution due to the big CT layer thickness, and the stair-stepping pattern on the surface caused by this, it remained only a qualitative result.

Knowing about the imperfections of the data as well as of the AM of these days, a first model of the visible bust was made using the AM process of stereolithography. Because the build space of the machine was limited, a two-piece bust with a reduced scale of 1:0.7 was made. In 1994, this was the first model worldwide obtained from the data of the original bust (Fig. 21.20, left).

In 2006, a new generation of CT scanners was available at the Siemens Imaging Science Institute (ISI) at the Charité hospital in Berlin, Germany. The high resolution obtained from this device and the advanced computer technology that allowed separating even comparably small differences of density that is needed to distinguish plaster from limestone led to impressively improved results. It led to more detailed information about the plaster-limestone distribution including areas where the plaster was just absorbed by the surface but did cause no measurable solid layer.

The plaster can be seen as yellow areas with the color density as an indicator of the layer thickness (Fig. 21.17). Many areas show just a powder like yellow shadow. This indicates that the plaster was just used to improve the surface and to get an even ground for painting.

The first idea was to make a 1:1 scale 3D bust showing just the skin-like plaster layer, but it was given up because of the instability caused by the many areas that are covered with no or almost only a neglectable amount of plaster needed to smoothen the surface for painting reasons. According to Fig. 21.19, the plaster distribution can be studied very well just with the scans.

The improved 3D data were very useful to make a high-quality 3D copy. As the AM technology improved as well, a much more accurate 1:1 scale model with better surface quality was obtained (Figs. 21.20, right and 21.21). It was made for display. To underline that it was a replica, it was painted white.

The model bust was used for various purposes. The most prominent display was on 5 October 2009, two weeks before the official opening of the restored Egyptian Museum in Berlin (19 October 2009). The British Royal Highness, Prince Charles and his spouse Camilla, visited the future official presentation site of Nefertiti. At the spot where the original was going to be placed shortly after, the model was displayed to give the Royal visitors an idea of the future situation (Fig. 21.21).

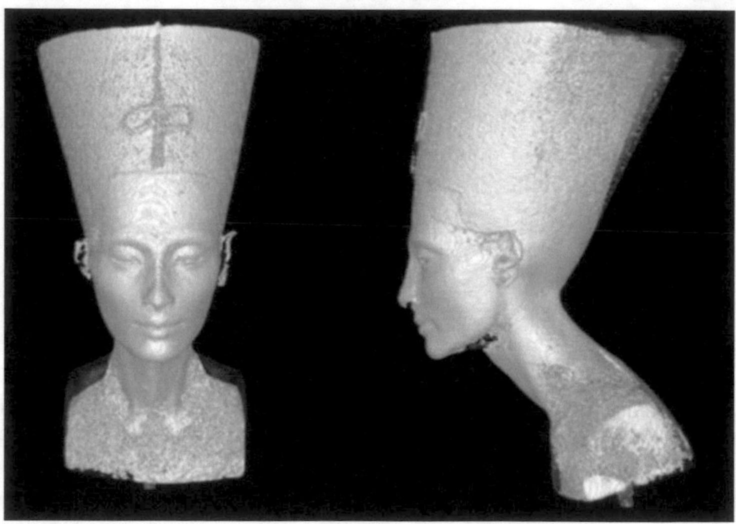

Fig. 21.19 Digital reconstruction of the bust of Nefertiti. Limestone-plaster distribution according to the improved CT scan in 2006 (Source: Siemens. © 2008 Siemens, reprinted with permission)

Fig. 21.20 Bust of Nefertiti made by AM (stereolithography), detail. Model based on the first CT scan (1994, *left*, unpainted) and on the improved one (2006, *right*, *painted white*) (Source: CP-GmbH. © 2008 CP-GmbH, reprinted with permission)

Fig. 21.21 His Royal Highness Prince Charles during the visit of the new Egyptian Museum in Berlin prior to the official opening. The model bust was used to indicate the later position of the original (Source: ZDF. © 2009 ZDF, reprinted with permission)

21.7 Commercial Aspects

More and more even museums are forced to generate income. As most of them bear unique artifacts, the easiest way to do so is manufacturing and selling a limited amount of exclusive copies.

Having once obtained the data, 3D printing opens up a great variety of commercially usable artifacts. Besides the 1:1 scale bust made from polyamide on Figs. 21.20 and 21.21, especially smaller objects are attractive. With the help of an SLM machine designed for dental and jewelry applications, the bust was built with silver (DDMC), Figs. 21.20 and 21.21. As can be seen in Fig. 21.22, the process requires supports that need to be removed after the build, and it needs professional polishing that must be made by hand. The bust is about 3 cm high, and due to a wall thickness of less than 1 mm, it requires only a small amount of silver.

Another commercial application to reach even small-budget customers is made from ABS by Extrusion (FDM). The 5 cm high bust (Fig. 21.23) clearly shows the extrusion marks but overall represents the original very well.

Fig. 21.22 Bust of Nefertiti. SLM, Silver (Source: GoetheLab, FH Aachen © 2012 GoetheLab, FH Aachen, reprinted with permission)

Fig. 21.23 Scaled bust of queen Nefertiti, FDM (ABS), height ca. 5 cm (Source: GoetheLab, FH Aachen © 2012 GoetheLab, FH Aachen, reprinted with permission)

Using FDM (extrusion) even small series can be made economically as shown on Fig. 21.24. The sculptures on Fig. 21.21 are put on a socket each and still are with supports that can be washed out using a cleaning station.

Mainly in the region of Hallein, Austriche, there are excavating fields with huge amounts of Celtic garment pins (fibulas) made from metal. It is suggested to let the customers select their "personal" one and directly scan and print it on site. The business case behind it is to sell individual "one-offs" with certificates. For demonstration, the process was realized with the pin displayed on Fig. 21.25.

The same can be done with all kinds of cultural heritage artifacts such as coins, vases, jewelry, and many more.

Fig. 21.24 Bust of Nefertiti. Small series of FDM parts made from ABS, still on the build platform and with supports [Source: GoetheLab, FH Aachen (© 2012 GoetheLab, FH Aachen, reprinted with permission)]

Fig. 21.25 Celtic garment pin (fibula). Scanned and made from metal by SLM (Source: GoetheLab FH Aachen © 2013 GoetheLab FH Aachen, reprinted with permission)

Fig. 21.26 Small series of sculptures made from brass by additive manufacturing and lost wax casting (Source: GoetheLab FH Aachen © 2012 GoetheLab FH Aachen, reprinted with permission)

Even high-priced exclusive series can be made by using the lost wax process chain, discussed above (Fig. 21.26).

21.8 Conclusion

3D printing or additive manufacturing is a valuable method to support the visualization, investigation, and production of physical models of cultural heritage artifacts. In conjunction with today's scanners, not only scientific research is supported but a decentralized low-budget production can be installed in any museum.

References

1. A. Gebhardt, Rapid prototyping of metallic parts: state of the art and trends, in *Expolaser 2005 Conference: Laser Tool: State of the Art and Trends* (Piacenza, 2005)
2. A. Gebhardt, *Additive Manufacturing* (Hanser Publications Cincinnati, Ohio, 2016)
3. A. Gebhardt, F.-M. Schmidt, J. Hötter, J. Sokalla, P. Sokalla, Additive manufacturing by selective laser melting, in *6th International Conference on Laser Assisted Net Shape*, LANE 2010, Erlangen (2010)
4. D. Wildung, Metamorphosen eiener Königin (Metamorphoses of a Queen): Neue Ergebnisse zur Ikonographie des Berliner Kopfes de Teje mit Hilfe der Computertomographie. Antike Welt. **26**, 245–249 (1995)

Chapter 22
The Willing Suspension of Disbelief: The Tangible and the Intangible of Heritage Education in E-Learning and Virtual Museums

Susan Hazan and Anna Lobovikov Katz

Abstract Narratives spun around a series of physical objects in a virtual environment may produce a truly compelling story, but does their potency draw on the fact that in spite of their intangible delivery their provenance is clearly deeply rooted in their museum provenance? We trust, either by what we witness with our own eyes or perhaps by what we instinctively know to be true. An institution, such as a museum, is devoted to the custodian care to their collections, and the publics' certainty of this responsibility cues us to willingly suspend our own disbelief, even when encountered online where we cannot see the physical objects.

Based on a methodology, developed by an EU project for heritage education, we evaluate a specific cultural heritage platform both quantitatively and qualitatively in order to explore how online visitors experience virtual heritage. We will also explore the ways in which educational methodologies can now be enhanced by these narratives and how material objects and physical environments can forge meaningful connections for students as well as museum visitors to explore.

This chapter considers e-learning through the virtual texts, digital images of museum objects and historic sites to sustain the relationship between the tangible and intangible (Galla, Frequently Asked Questions about Intangible Heritage. *ICOM News*, No. 4, 2003) and investigates the ways in which narratives fold into cultural heritage—or unwraps from them into the virtual reality. We argue that linking to the ancient world or historical texts may well open up new pathways for self-directed learning and creative ways of thinking about ourselves—past and present.

S. Hazan (✉)
The Israel Museum, Jerusalem, Israel
e-mail: shazan@imj.org.il

A.L. Katz
Technion – Israel Institute of Technology, Haifa, Israel
e-mail: anna@technion.ac.il

M. Ioannides et al. (eds.), *Mixed Reality and Gamification for Cultural Heritage*,
DOI 10.1007/978-3-319-49607-8_22

Keywords E-learning • Virtual museum • Shuttle learning • Bible • Old Testament • Manuscript

22.1 Introduction: The Willing Suspension of Disbelief

When we visit a library or archive, we typically expect to find printed materials, books, publications and documents. However, when we go to a museum—either in person or online—we expect a very different kind of experience. The very notion of 'the museum' sets up a certain expectation, and we presume that we will discover exceptional and often extraordinary kinds of objects. Accordingly, when these very same objects are delivered online, they are managed very differently from the way books are managed by libraries or the way that archives are managed as hierarchal documents. As the footprint of the physical museum, an online museum is therefore orchestrated to convey the singular and often unique nature of the objects, as well as the very quintessence of the physical museum [1]. This means that as objects and works of art make their screen debut, these kinds of platforms need to communicate not only the physicality of the objects but also be able to signify the entirety of the museum experience.

While recent studies often extol the benefits of using mixed reality (VR and AR) in CH applications, particularly those employing gamification principles, our research ponders the qualitative experience of end users who are not only once removed from the physical objects (located somewhere else in a museum) but also have to suspend their disbelief when engaging with a mere digital image of the absent object. We question, therefore, whether the digital CH object is potent enough to fulfil this role and whether narratives built upon digital objects serve to deliver narratives both convincingly and meaningfully.

The chapter explores the role of tangible cultural heritage objects (CHO) in virtual learning. Our case study, *Visualizing Isaiah* (see Fig. 22.1), examines the contribution of images of real museum objects in a text-driven, virtual museum project. It questions and explores the potential restraints of these kinds of contributions as well as their significance for virtual visitors.

The term 'willing suspension of disbelief' was penned by the poet Samuel Taylor Coleridge in [2], who suggested that if a writer could inspire 'human interest and a semblance of truth' into a work of fiction, the reader would be able to suspend judgement concerning the implausibility of the narrative. In the context of the museum, we are pre-cued to suspend our disbelief by the very idea of a museum as a 'place of truth', and we readily deposit our scepticism at the door as we enter into the narrative and encounter the material objects, incontestably set up in front of us. Of course we are not suggesting that museums create works of fiction, but they do set up a specific scenario for us to experience, and they presumably expect that their visitors will concur with the storyline [3].

But does this carry over to the online narrative? Does peering through a screen to the digital agents of the objects disrupt this compliance in any way? Does the

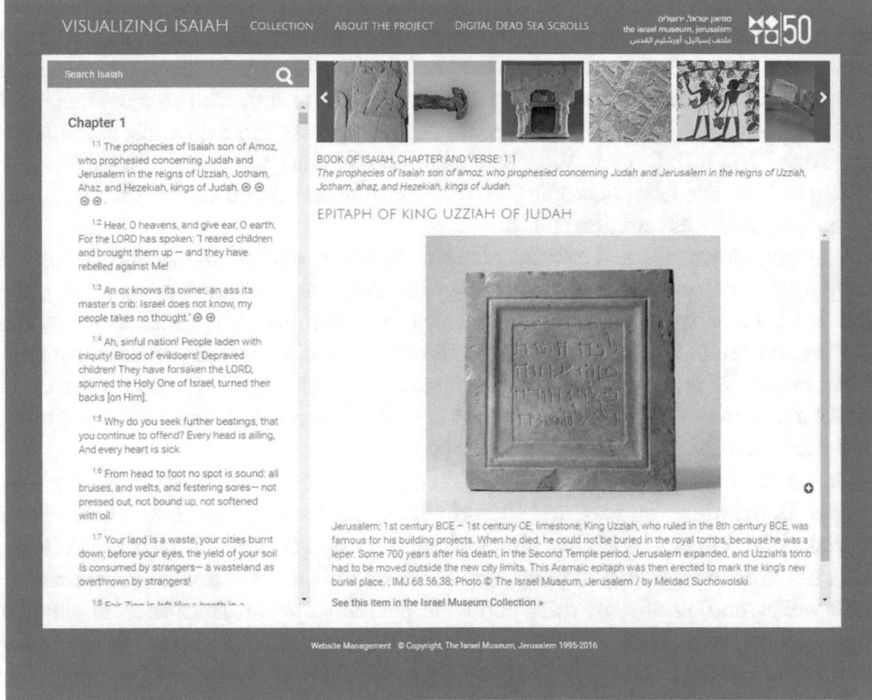

Fig. 22.1 Visualizing Isaiah website screenshot © 2016 S. Hazan, reprinted with permission

storyline still hold water? Baudrillard cautions us that all mediated experiences, in fact, have been subsumed in the totalization of the electronic surrogate—the Baudrillard simulation [4, p. 6]. However, the experience of dislocated presence is disturbingly familiar, not only from a virtual museum but from television. Marc Augé [5, p. 32] reminds us of 'the false familiarity the small screen establishes between the viewers and the actors of big-scale history, whose profiles become as well known to us as those of soap-opera heroes and international artistic or sporting stars'. Sometimes the balance is tipped even further when it seems that we are more at home with our favourite soap opera characters than we are with our own lives. After more than five decades of television viewing and almost a century of telephonic communications, we have become comfortable with life in a media-saturated society and have learned to chart these waters with confidence.

But while, in fact, we are able to take these experiences with us when we visit a museum, are we just as prepared to slip effortlessly into screen mode to view the virtual museum [6]? What is it that makes the virtual museum an equally extraordinary place? The location (in a museum) sets it apart from all the other kinds of mediated experiences we confront every day of our lives in our own home, place of work or in other public places. In an engaging discussion on the performance of self-online, Sherry Turkle points out how notions of the decentering or the 'realignment of self' present new permutations and possibilities [7]. These kinds of online projects represent a kind of decentering of the museum: a shift in location in our encounter with primary museum objects. Lawrence Weschler—who described the museum in his popular book, *Mr. Wilson's Cabinet of Wonder*—discusses this point with John Walsh, then director of the J. Paul Getty Museum, who concurs that most of the institutional-historical allusions at Wilson's purely fantastic museum turn out to be true [8, p. 60]. Even in Weschler's fantastic cabinet of curiosities, we are able to suspend our disbelief and dive into the narrative and dwell on our own interpretations, experiences and delectation.

The project we selected to think about these ideas, *Visualizing Isaiah*, is nestled securely in a museum website and clearly identified as such. In this case we argue that this is no 'displacement' of the physical museum but an argumentation of the physical museum. Clearly, as we encounter these specific objects, we are confident that these are, in reality, physical objects that are part of a collection that is managed by the museum—however reproduced yet greatly reduced to a tiny screen and often delivered directly into the palm of your hand.

In his seminal essay, *The Work of Art in the Age of Mechanical Reproduction*, Walter Benjamin discusses art. 'In principle, the work of art has always been reproducible. Objects made by humans could always be copied by humans. Replicas were made by pupils in practicing for their craft, by masters in disseminating their works, and, finally, by third parties in pursuit of profit. But the technological reproduction of artworks is something new' [9]. Benjamin describes in his essay how the loss of the aura, crucial to the object-orientated museum and implicit in the presentation of the artwork, is the idea that the museum acts as a stage to present the *original* object. But why is this originality or presumed lack of originality so critical to the museum experience? Andrea Witcomb draws on Benjamin and the logic operating in nineteeth-century museum practice. 'This is the opposition', Witcomb argues, 'between a copy and its original, an opposition which privileges the original as more important, more precious, than a copy' [10, p. 106]. Witcomb describes how special attention was given to demonstrate the originality of an object and argues how 'originality could no longer be taken for granted. It had to be constructed and guaranteed'. She describes how great care was taken not only to locate originality but also to present the original through erecting a symbolic barrier that was set up 'between viewer and artefact, between subject and object' (ibid). This physical and symbolic barrier, Witcomb argues, 'served to signify the monetary value of the artefact, thus mixing auratic with monetary values, aesthetics with commercial values' (ibid). In this way the visitor was assured that the objects encountered in the museum were valuable, in some way special, and possibly even exemplary but, at the least, worthy of taking the time to make a special trip to a dedicated space that guarantees the engagement with the original.

Underlying our desire to encounter the unique and original, Jesse Prinz and his team undertook a fascinating experiment: 'We told test subjects to imagine that the Mona Lisa was destroyed in a fire, but that there happened to be a perfect copy that even experts couldn't tell from the original. If they could see just one or the other, would they rather see the ashes of the original Mona Lisa or a perfect duplicate?

Eighty per cent of our respondents chose the ashes: apparently we disvalue copies and attribute almost magical significance to originals' [11].

Different objects, however, transverse the museum's potential space in different ways. We often consider a museum to be populated with wondrous objects; however, the sometimes banal object found in a local museum resonates with visitors precisely through their familiarity with the objects, even though they may belong more to the past than they do to the present. The connections between home and museum serve to forge closer bonds and a closer identification with the exhibition, and 'the' story effortlessly becomes 'their' story as the mimetic object slips easily into collective memory. Some objects, however, are temporally or spatially detached from the visitor's own life and, when encountered on display, demand that the distance between the visitor's own entrance narrative and the object's provenance be resolved in order for the encounter to be meaningful.

The entrance narrative, according to Doering [12], is the visitor's own internal storyline. The entrance narrative, she argues, is marked with three distinct components: a fundamental way that individuals construe and contemplate the world, their own information about the exhibition and their own personal experiences, emotions and memories. When objects, for example, from a distant historical period and a culture that is very different from their own are displayed, there may be little bearing on a visitor's own storyline. The potential discrepancies between time and space need to be bridged through new indexes to enable the visitor to be able to make his first step into the narrative and to bridge the gap between the exhibition's narrative and his own. We are interested to see if there is a connection in our visitors' own entrance narrative—in our case the Book of Isaiah—http://www.imj.org.il/isaiah. Does familiarity with the Bible book, from school, home or place of worship, for example, effect how the online storyline is appropriated by the user?

22.2 Visualizing Isaiah, the Project

The objects from Visualizing Isaiah, according to the Israel Museum exhibition curator, Dr. Eran Arie, Frieder Burda Curator of Iron Age and Persian Period Archaeology, fall into different categories:

1. Rare inscriptions that allude to important figures from the Book of Isaiah, among them Hezekiah, King of Judah; Sennacherib, King of Assyria; and others.
2. Inscriptions that reference persons and official functionaries that share the same names as those appearing in the Book of Isaiah but clearly do not indicate the same people. These authentic artefacts from Biblical times attest to the widespread use of names that are mentioned by the prophet.
3. Objects and utensils that were in use during this period of the kind which might have been used by the prophet himself—for example, cult objects, jewellery, everyday artefacts and more. These objects would have been in the prophet's vicinity and would have provided the material context for his prophecies.

4. Various symbols—mainly from the animal and plant kingdoms—which the prophet drew upon metaphorically. These symbols were also prevalent in Ancient Near Eastern art, as can be seen in archaeological discoveries of the period.

Visualizing Isaiah therefore brings together objects and text, the reverential and every day. Clearly, archaeological objects cannot prove the existence of the prophet or the veracity of his prophecies. They can only provide a backdrop of imagery and mimetics that illustrate the context in which the prophet—or those who penned his words—lived and worked. Thus the aim of *Visualizing Isaiah* is not to prove the veracity of the Biblical text but to draw the public closer to the world of concepts and material culture and to the natural environment of those times.

Whether located in the physical museum or projected online, the story told here in this project is intrinsically the same. Pierre Lévy takes exception to the ideas of real and virtual as dialectical counterparts and argues that 'virtualization, or the transition to a problematic, in no way implies a disappearance in illusion or dematerialization. Rather it should be understood as a form of 'desubstantation' [...] the body as flame, the text as flux' [13, p. 169]. To avoid locating real and virtual in such a dichotomy, he likens this desubstantation to the Moebius effect, 'which organizes the endless loop of the interior and exterior—the sharing of private elements and the subjective integration of public items' (ibid. p. 169). We argue that the integration of the material and dematerialized, the tangible and intangible, creates new forms of museum hybridity that is continuously modifying the museum experience. Bringing together practices that have traditionally revolved around the tangible object with the emerging methods of collecting and displaying art that refuses to remain fixed within its four walls, the museum now functions in an endless loop of interior and exterior presence (Fig. 22.2).

There are many ways in which museums flow through bespoke networks, harnessing a whole range of digital solutions to advance their institutional mission. Museums have adapted evolving technologies to their own agendas, other sectors and sister institutions, such as libraries and archives, and have also evolved their own kind of hybridization of the old with the new. As libraries and archives integrate similar technologies and strategies available to them, their institutional identity will resemble the system that they have evolved from, rather than an entirely new technologically driven entity. In the same way that these kinds of projects move into electronic networks while preserving their institutional integrity, they move into spaces that resemble their own provenance steadfastly nestled in the arms of the notion of the museum [14].

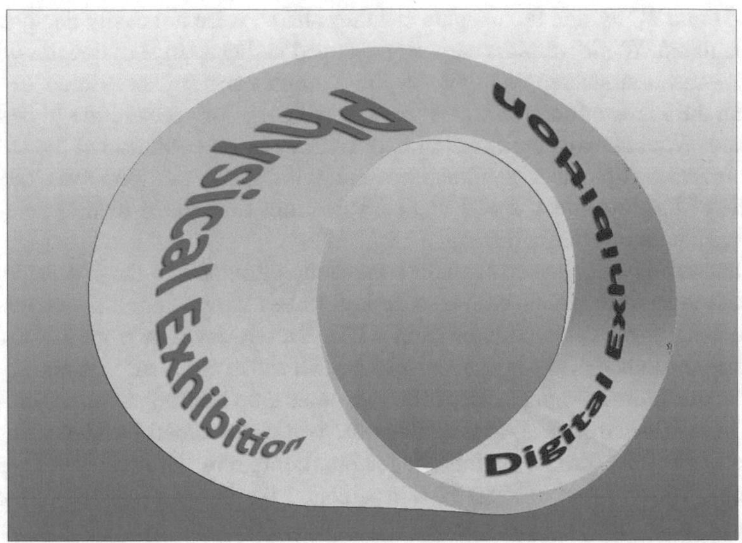

Fig. 22.2 Moebius effect: the physical and virtual © 2016 S. Hazan, reprinted with permission

22.3 Text-Object-Text Loop and the Online Museum

Since their discovery in 1947, the Dead Sea Scrolls [15] have held a unique attraction for both scholar and layman alike. Those who may be curious about a time when it is said that Jesus of Nazareth lived and preached and those who are interested in the Second Temple period in the Land of Israel sense that these primary texts could throw new light on society at the nascent period of Christianity and pre-Rabbinic Judaism. Access to the scrolls, written in Hebrew, Greek and Aramaic, was initially granted only to a handful of scholars, however, and they were unwilling to share their own research with the larger community those first years after the discovery.

Access to the ancient texts gradually opened up through the distribution of images of the scrolls, the research surrounding them as well as the translations and transliterations of the ancient scripts. Later on, books and print publications were to appear, and gradually the circle widened as microfiche, as well as CD-ROMs, started appearing, until eventually parts of the scrolls began to make their appearance online.

Still, intellectual access to the scrolls was limited to a small group: those with the ability to be able to read, decipher and translate their message. The international scholarly community who made the Dead Sea Scrolls their life work shared a vocabulary that enabled only academic discourse. Discussions that revolved around the scrolls, their graphic quality, the scribal features and their historical message were elucidated in a lingua franca that was not actually expressed in a language easily shared by outsiders. Scholars referred to specific texts by cryptically calling the fragments by their identification numbers, such as 11QPsa, 4Q179, CD,

1Q59–61 and 2Q18, and the insights that they shared were not easily deciphered by the uninitiated. While scholars earnestly engaged in these kinds of debates with one another—discussions dappled with cryptic footnotes and savant references—these were not the kinds of conversations that made it easy for you and me to be able to jump into. What actually stood out in stark contrast to the evolution of the Dead Sea Scrolls scholarship—at a snail's pace and with great caution—was the exact opposite of the breakneck speed that conversations take place today at electronic pathways and social networks.

At the same time, the scrolls held a magnetic attraction to those outside of the cabal and those individuals who also desired to be able to share the conversations after hearing about them perhaps from a Dan Brown novel or from TV and were more than curious to see for themselves what all the excitement was about.

Important archaeological discoveries made in the Qumran caves in the Judean desert from 1947 onwards—among them the world-renowned Dead Sea Scrolls—include some 230 scrolls, mainly fragments, containing Biblical passages. It is interesting to note that among these fragments, the Book of Isaiah is the most popular; to date, there is evidence of 21(!) copies of the book. The most remarkable among them, the Great Isaiah Scroll, which comprises the entire Book of Isaiah with all of its 66 chapters, is the only Biblical book to have been discovered in its entirety at Qumran. The online project *Visualizing Isaiah* invites remote visitors on a journey through a rich selection of objects from the museum's collections that portray the era of the prophet Isaiah.

Isaiah, son of Amoz, one of the major prophets, lived in Jerusalem, the capital of the kingdom of Judah, between the late eighth century and early seventh century BCE, under the rule of kings Uzziah, Jotham, Ahaz and Hezekiah. These were the days of the First Temple, also known in modern research as the Iron Age. They were turbulent times during which the Assyrian Empire dominated the Ancient Near East unchallenged. In 721 BC, during the time of the prophet, the Northern Kingdom of Israel was destroyed by Sargon, king of Assyria, while 20 years later, the Southern Kingdom of Judah was ravaged by Sargon's son, Sennacherib.

The majority of the objects included in *Visualizing Isaiah* are drawn from the Israel Museum's permanent collection with the addition of objects from sister institutions and historical sites, e.g. obelisks, capitals of a column, altars and tombstones located in the public domain. The museum also hosts the online platform, framing it as typical virtual exhibition.

Visualizing Isaiah provides a unique opportunity for non-Hebrew virtual visitor, to read an English translation of the ancient Hebrew manuscript while viewing images as verse and chapter unfold. The questionnaire sought to understand how virtual visitors become aware of the connection between word and image. Do they find this evocative and/or meaningful?

Linking objects to the Biblical text brings up many questions both for the authors of the project and the community of users as they interact with the manuscript. For example, for those who may be familiar with the Book of Isaiah before their virtual visit, we questioned whether the encounter with tangible objects would impact their understanding of the chapter in any way. In what way do the images of these real objects impact the (re-)reading of the ancient text? Does this compilation of text and image contribute to a deeper or richer interpretation of the text, or could it be seen as a distraction or even create antipathy in the reading of the traditional Biblical narrative?

22.4 The Virtual and the Physical in Heritage-Related Education: Lesson from an EU Project

Educational Linkage Approach In Cultural Heritage (ELAICH) was a European project that was carried out in the framework of Euromed Heritage Programme 4 (2009–2012)—ELAICH ENPI-2008/150–583 [16]. The educational e-learning toolkit was developed by this project to enable educators and heritage authorities to introduce the values of cultural heritage and principles and the challenges of its preservation to youth [17]. The principal ELAICH product—ELAICH e-learning toolkit—is open and accessible to school teachers throughout the ELAICH e-learning platform without charge or registration [18]. According to EU requirements, ELAICH has been developed for youth but is also appropriate and available for everyone. ELAICH makes science accessible to citizens, presenting results of scientific research and supporting a range of different kinds of scientific inquiry.

ELAICH connects between the virtual and the material in a way both similar and different from *Visualizing Isaiah*, which is, in itself, an entire e-learning course, with its own internal logic and recommended path. In addition to interacting with the linear text, the project enhances visual analysis, applicable to heritage preservation. The ELAICH educational toolkit acts as an accessible e-learning platform, enabling remote students to develop understanding and acquire basic knowledge of the contemporary conservation of historic buildings and sites (built heritage). These kinds of online experiences offer opportunities for learning, studying and collecting data in the context of analyzing historic buildings/gardens while focusing on research qualities, such as accuracy, responsibility, analysis and synthesis [19] (Fig. 22.3).

The 'shuttle online–offline (on-site)' learning was first described in 2015 by Lobovikov-Katz [20] as a combined online–offline educational approach and was first developed and applied by her as part of the ELAICH pilot course, organized in Israel, Haifa, in the first year of the project, as well as the core idea 'from website to historic site': 'from learning by means of an "intangible" website to an on-site study of "tangible" historic site'. We find this shuttle learning relevant to a process experienced by the virtual learners in *Visualizing Isaiah*.

What we learned from our ELAICH online learning sessions were the ways in which students were able to analyze virtual images of, e.g. stone details or patterns of stone deterioration, a potential learning moment that would possibly help them make the connection to a building they would study at a historic site. In this way, combining online and on-site learning helps to 'add a new dimension' to virtual

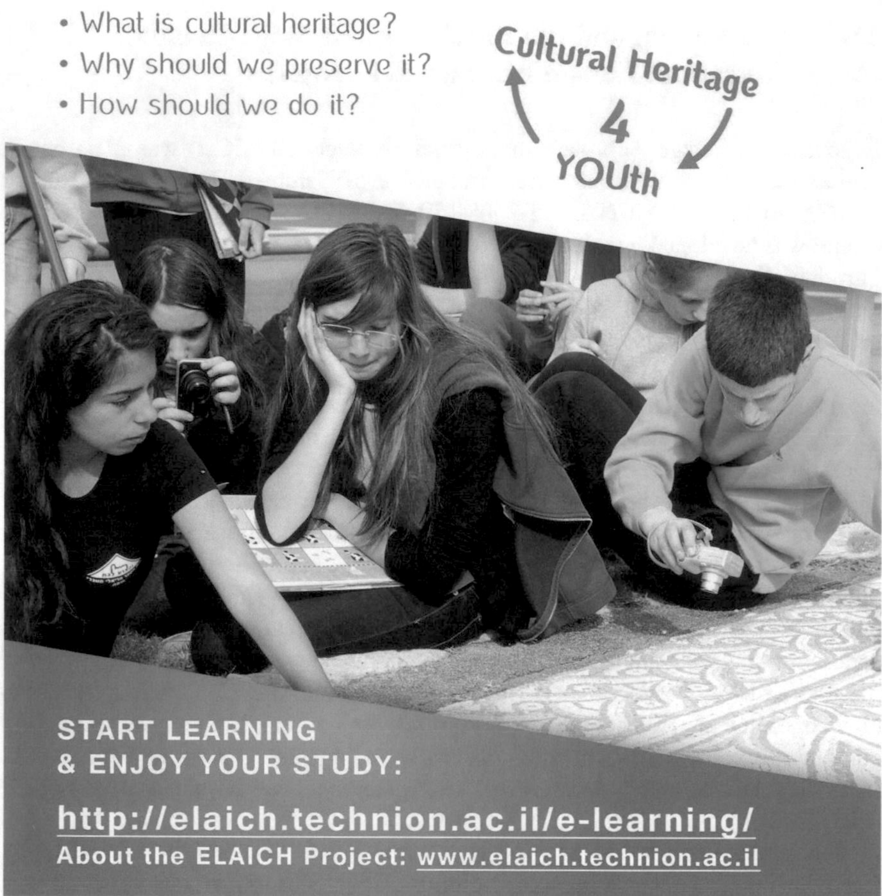

ELAICH - FROM learning by means of an "INTANGIBLE" WEB SITE TO an on-site study of "TANGIBLE" HISTORIC SITE
• What is cultural heritage?
• Why should we preserve it?
• How should we do it?
Cultural Heritage
4
YOUth
START LEARNING
& ENJOY YOUR STUDY:
http://elaich.technion.ac.il/e-learning/
About the ELAICH Project: www.elaich.technion.ac.il

Fig. 22.3 From intangible to tangible, 'From Website to Historic Site'. From the ELAICH leaflet © 2016 Lobovikov Katz, reprinted with permission

images, to essentially make them more familiar and more 'real'. At the same time, when visiting a historic building after developing a basic understanding of its materials, similar architecture or relevant conservation problems, we hoped that this would facilitate a deeper understanding of a specific building and also help to reinforce the knowledge acquired through online learning [21].

In the context of *Visualizing Isaiah* and based on our previous experience from ELAICH, we were interested to find out whether our users could use the juxtaposition of text and image to enable new kinds of learning and meaningful experience.

22.5 Visualizing Isaiah Questionnaires: Quantitative and Qualitative Evaluation

These questions and others were examined in our survey which was distributed as an anonymous questionnaire and over a period of 4 weeks when we received 34 full responses. The questionnaire was predicated on users visiting the site prior to answering the questions, and, from the results received, it was clear that all had diligently done so, basing their responses on what appears as a close reading of the project. The questionnaire was composed of 20 questions:

1. Vocational preferences
2. Professional area of expertise
3. Academic qualifications
4. Age
5. Whether users had actually visited the Israel Museum
6. Whether they live within visiting distance of the Israel Museum, located in Jerusalem, Israel
7. Whether they had visited a virtual museum before
8. Whether they had come across the Book of Isaiah before they were directed to this website
9. Whether they had heard of any of the people mentioned in the Book of Isaiah before—suggesting
   - King Uzziah of Judah
   - Chemosham (son of) Chemoshel the scribe
   - King Hezekiah
   - King Sennacherib of Assyria
10. Whether they had heard of any of the subjects mentioned in the Book of Isaiah before
11. Whether they had ever visited a historic site connected with the Book of Isaiah
12. Whether they knew about this connection at the time of the visit
13. Isaiah, Chap. 7, Verse 2

    > Now, when it was reported to the House of David that Aram had allied itself with Ephraim, their hearts and the hearts of their people trembled as trees of the forest sway before a wind.

    The stone inscription commemorating the military victories of Hazael, king of Aram, contains the earliest reference to the Davidic dynasty outside the Bible.

We questioned whether this enhanced the Book of Isaiah in their eyes—suggesting three options:

- The connection between the stone inscriptions is mere coincidence.
- The stone inscription could refer to the same David that is referred to in the Isaiah text.
- This is the physical proof of the House of David that is mentioned in the Book of Isaiah.

14. Whether they preferred to start from the images and from them go to the text
15. Whether they felt different about the objects that once stood in the open air and were often part of a building (e.g. column capital, altar, tombstone, etc.) in comparison with small objects usually used in the houses (e.g. jewellery, coins, pottery)
16. What objects in their eyes better contribute to a fuller understanding of the text
17. Whether they had come across any of the objects in a physical exhibition
18. Whether they had ever visited historic sites associated with any of the objects which appear in the images of *Visualizing Isaiah*
19. Whether they would say that the related objects appear more 'real' to you, following the visit
20. Ending with a request to summarize their experience of *Visualizing Isaiah*

The first series of questions is related to the background of our users. Our respondents were representative of the cultural heritage community, as reflected both in their vocational preferences and professional affiliation. This was probably due to the authors' mode of distribution: MUSEUM-L email distribution list, Facebook and direct email. This weighted the responses as we were approaching users who were intrinsically preselected to feel at home with this kind of experience. Having said this, within the restrictions of acting within this sector, we were still able to learn a lot about this project (Figs. 22.4 and 22.5).

Our respondents were self-identified as academic, with a majority in the MA/MSC range or higher with an equal distribution between age groups. More interesting for our investigations was the overwhelming percentage (76.4 %) of users who had never visited the Israel Museum and were not located within visiting distance of the museum (over 90 %). This made this group an excellent case study for us to investigate those who were experiencing the project exclusively over their screen.

In order to understand whether our users were familiar with the Book of Isaiah, we asked where they had encountered the narrative (Fig. 22.6).

Clearly our respondents (73 %) were familiar with the Bible chapter, with over one third identifying that they are related to the text in the contest of a place of worship with only slightly more than one quarter who had never come across the Book of Isaiah before.

Where things began to get interesting was with the question of whether our respondents were familiar with the characters mentioned in the narrative. The high percentage of positive answers indicated how our users were invested in the Book

Answer Choices	Responses	
History	60.61%	20
Arts	39.39%	13
Humanities	51.52%	17
STEM (Science, technology, engineering, mathematics)	24.24%	8
Sport	9.09%	3
Music	12.12%	4
Other	3.03%	1
Other (please specify)	15.15%	5

Fig. 22.4 Q1: How would you describe your vocational preferences? © 2016 Hazan/Lobovikov Katz, reprinted with permission

Answer Choices	Responses	
History	42.42%	14
Arts	18.18%	6
Humanities	27.27%	9
STEM (Science, technology, engineering, mathematics)	18.18%	6
Music	3.03%	1
Other	3.03%	1
Other (please specify)	39.39%	13

Fig. 22.5 Q2: What is your professional area of expertise? © 2016 Hazan/Lobovikov Katz, reprinted with permission

Answer Choices	Responses	
In a place of worship	33.33%	11
In school	18.18%	6
At home	21.21%	7
I have never come across the Book of Isaiah before	27.27%	9

Fig. 22.6 Q8: Where had you come across the Book of Isaiah before you came to this website? © 2016 Hazan/Lobovikov Katz, reprinted with permission

of Isaiah and were well versed with the characters described in the narrative (Fig. 22.7).

In addition to the characters mentioned, we also asked whether they had heard of any of the ideas in the narrative (Fig. 22.8).

The largest group had heard of at least one or two of the ideas, while at the same time only 3 % indicated that they had a specific interest prior to the experience with the platform, and 85 % had never visited a historical site before. When we quoted from Isaiah (Chap. 7, Verse 2) and asked how this enhanced the Book of Isaiah in their eyes, the majority stated that the stone inscription 'could' relate to the earliest reference to the David dynasty outside of the Bible, while a full quarter stated that they see this as the physical proof of the House of David that is mentioned in the Bible (Fig. 22.9).

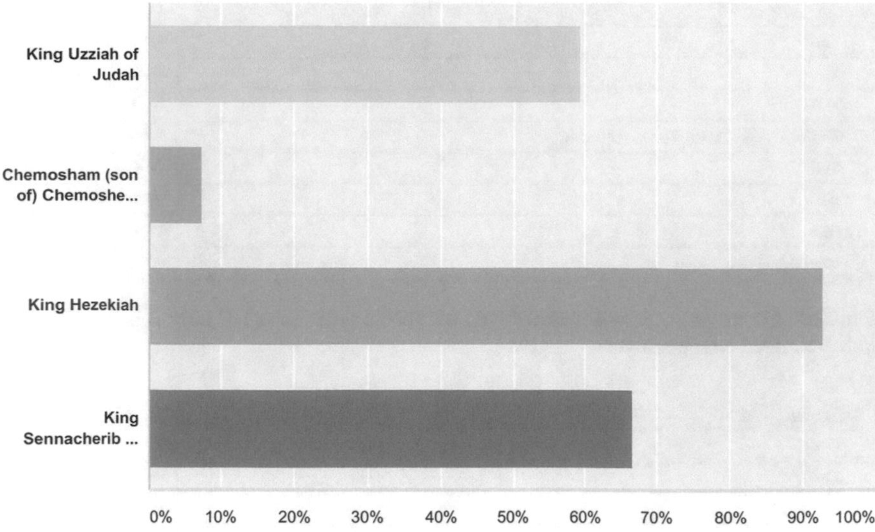

Fig. 22.7 Q9: Have you heard of any of the people mentioned in the Book of Isaiah before? © 2016 Hazan/Lobovikov Katz, reprinted with permission

Answer Choices	Responses	
No	15.15%	5
One or two of the ideas	51.52%	17
Quite a lot	30.30%	10
I already had a specific interest in the Book of Isaiah before	3.03%	1

Fig. 22.8 Q10: Have you heard of any of the subjects mentioned in the Book of Isaiah before? © 2016 Hazan/Lobovikov Katz, reprinted with permission

Answer Choices	Responses	
The connection between the stone inscription is mere coincidence	0.00%	0
The stone inscription could refer to the same David that is referred to in the Isaiah text	74.19%	23
This is the physical proof of the House of David that is mentioned in the Book of Isaiah	25.81%	8

Fig. 22.9 Q13: Isaiah, Chap. 7, Verse 2 'Now, when it was reported to the House of David that Aram had allied itself with Ephraim, their hearts and the hearts of their people trembled as trees of the forest sway before a wind'. The stone inscription commemorating the military victories of Hazael, king of Aram, contains the earliest reference to the Davidic dynasty outside the Bible. How does this enhance the Book of Isaiah in your eyes? © 2016 Hazan/Lobovikov Katz, reprinted with permission

So with a healthy scepticism, our respondents do then see either a possible or even concrete (25 %) connection, perhaps even affirmation of the Biblical story as indicated by the museum object. Although we hadn't asked about their private religious belief system, we could begin to see how the empirical evidence of a

Answer Choices	Responses	
No - I prefer to explore with the text itself	15.15%	5
I prefer to search on the images	21.21%	7
I find both the images and the text useful to search the narrative	63.64%	21

Fig. 22.10 Q14: Concerning the website—do you prefer to start from the images and from them go to the text? © 2016 Hazan/Lobovikov Katz, reprinted with permission

museum object could serve to create a certain concomitance between Biblical narrative and museum object—even with a digital surrogate. While the response group was very limited (34 responses) and the 20 questions too brief to be comprehensive, we do see some sort of indication here and would be encouraged to investigate this simultaneity further in the future.

We were also interested in the ways users moved through the narrative. In questioning whether users preferred the text or images as a means of navigating the experience, they responded as follows (Fig. 22.10):

This response perhaps was unsurprising and a pleasant result for the authors of the project who had tried to offer both options as intuitive navigation tools and were gratified to see that both were (almost) equally appreciated.

Perhaps the most interesting of the responses was the final question that asked users to sum up their experiences with the project. Here is a selection of these comments:

Several appreciated the project and wished to share this with us.

> This is the first time I have heard about this exhibit. I will be searching for a glimpse of the project.
>
> Wonderful to have access to this material online.
>
> Enjoyed and learned.
>
> The descriptive text was a good length; I did not feel overwhelmed by it, and yet it was a decent amount of information. The object photographs were very interesting, and I liked the automated link between the images and the scriptural text. This virtual exhibit is a very interesting concept—I don't know of any other virtual exhibits based upon scriptural texts.
>
> Fascinating, easily navigated, and clear links between the text and images, and objects which relate to each other. Really enjoyable visit.

At the same time, there were others who read the narrative and images in opposition.

> The site was slow. I did not see a strong connection between some of the objects and the text. Perhaps more interpretation connecting the two could help. The clothing Egyptians pressing grapes for example was not stained, which was point of the analogy in the text.

We were looking for an affirmation of the suspension of disbelief—the ability to trust in the veracity of the museum experience—and specifically in the *Visualizing Isaiah* project, even when visitors were encountering the digital surrogate:

> I find the archaeological artifacts to be helpful to visualize the world in which the historical events of the Book of Isaiah took place. I especially like how I can look just at the artifacts and that I can see how the artifacts connect to and illuminate the text of Isaiah.

I really enjoyed this online exhibit. I found the approach, i.e. connecting passages from Isaiah to the artifacts was both interesting and refreshing. In North America religious references and contexts tend not to be explored in museums or at historic sites, and artifacts with a religious association are treated merely as objects or pieces of art, so it was great to see the artifacts tied back not only to their history, but their religious history as well.

While the historical connections between text and artifact are intriguing, I find the objects themselves both fascinating and awe-inspiring. I guess I might have been accused of idolatry in Isaiah's time! I have always loved hand-crafted items, and this collection is beyond wonderful. I plan to go back and show the exhibit to my husband, a retired church educator. It will be interesting to hear his responses.

A great experience for accessing objects and the text of Isaiah with no need to be there physically.

It provides a really good contextual experience for the text which is always difficult to study and analyze. The visualization project provides a perfect framework to explore it!

Brings a reality and a connection for me to the story of Isaiah.

Yet only one of our 34 respondents stated that they preferred the physicality of the museum experience:

I enjoyed the introduction. I like the cross-section of objects all contributing to the story. I didn't stay on the site long—being of a slightly older generation I still prefer to see the actual things in the field or museum, and don't enjoy the 'click through and back' travel of website enough to keep at it for long.

22.6 Conclusions

The qualitative and quantitative analysis of the questionnaires indicates that, for a significant number of survey participants, *Visualizing Isaiah* conveys a satisfying contextualization and even conviction of the Isaiah narrative. Through moving through the experience via digital images, the majority of the virtual visitors were able to concur with the historical context and material associations with the ancient text. In addition, around 20 % of the respondents stated that they actually prefer to start from images and from there continue to move through the text.

For those who are unable to read the original Hebrew, the English translation together with the digital objects makes the ancient scroll, perhaps for the first time for some, directly accessible. This immediate access to the ancient text might have also contributed to reinforcing the feeling of 'original' and re-enforce the connection between the perception of authenticity in the text and of validity of the images of the museum objects.

The functionality of the online tools in the two examples *Visualizing Isaiah* and 'ELAICH' is yet different. *Visualizing Isaiah* provides tools to enrich the user's experience and to create a flexible e-environment where users are free to explore and move through the narrative along their chosen path, in spite of the obvious linearity of the Bible narrative. Alternatively, 'ELAICH' offers users direct access into any point of the e-learning platform at any stage, opening an entire e-learning course, with its own internal structure and recommended path. Both systems, however, facilitate knowledge acquisition and develop a more meaningful engagement with the material, while at the same time hone a specific skill in visual analysis, truly advantageous for cultural heritage preservation.

The framing of *Virtual Isaiah* in the museum context, taken together with the statement that (most of) the objects come from the museum collection, clearly contributes to the confidence in the resources as 'real objects'. Users know that should they walk into the museum tomorrow, they are confident that they will be able to encounter the very same objects in their material form. Perhaps that is the way that the trust in the museum is transposed to the virtual, and the remote visitor is able to suspend his or her disbelief and dive into the story.

This chapter considers e-learning through the virtual texts, and digital images of museum objects, and historic sites to sustain the relationship between the tangible and intangible [22] and investigates the ways in which narratives fold into cultural heritage—or unwraps from them into the virtual reality. We argue that linking to the ancient world or historical texts opens up new pathways for self-directed learning and new and creative ways of thinking about our selfves—past and present.

Acknowledgements These artefacts shed light on the material culture of Isaiah's times, serving as a backdrop to many of his prophecies. Only a small number of the objects included here are from institutions or archaeological sites outside of the Israel Museum.

Curated by Dr. Eran Arie, Frieder Burda Curator of Iron Age and Persian Period Archaeology and Dr. Susan Hazan, Curator of New Media, The Israel Museum, Jerusalem

Visualizing Isaiah was first envisioned and funded by George Blumenthal and the Centre for Online Judaic Studies in order to provide greater access to Biblical texts and the Archaeology of Ancient Israel. http://cojs.org/ (accessed 29.5.16).

Photographs by Ardon Bar-Hama were generously supported by George Blumenthal.

The ELAICH project has received funding from the European Union in the framework of EuroMed Heritage 4 Programme under ELAICH grant agreement n° ENPI-2008/150–583 and was developed by the ELAICH Consortium, led by Technion—Israel Institute of Technology. The authors' appreciation is addressed to all research teams of the ELAICH Consortium for their contribution to the project.

References

1. S. Hazan, Facet Publishing "User Studies for Digital Library Development", *Holding the Museum in the Palm of your Hand* (2012)
2. S.T. Coleridge, *Biographia Literaria or Biographical Sketches of My Literary Life and Opinions* (R. Fenner, London, 1817)
3. S. Hazan, S. Hermon, *The Responsive Museum*, Proceedings, NODEM, Network of Design and Digital Heritage. (Interactive Institute Swedish ICT, Stockholm, 2013)
4. J. Baudrillard, *Simulacra and Simulation* (University of Michigan Press, Ann Arbor, 2000)
5. M. Augé, *Non-places: An Introduction to an Anthropology of Supermodernity* (trans: J. Howe) (Verso, London, 1995)
6. A. Malraux, Le musée imaginaire, in *Les voix du silence* (Nouvelle Revue, Paris, 1967)

7. S. Turkle, *Life on the Screen: Identity in the Age of the Internet* (Weidenfeld and Nicolson, London, 1995)
8. L. Weschler, *Mr. Wilson's Cabinet of Wonder: Pronged Ants, Horned Humans, Mice on Toast and Other Marvels of Jurassic Technology* (Vintage, New York, 1995)
9. W. Benjamin, *The Work of Art in the Age of Mechanical Reproduction*. in *Illustrations*: *Walter Benjamin – Essays and Reflections*, ed. by Arendt Hannah (Schocken Books, New York, 1936), 1985, pp. 217–251
10. A. Witcomb, *Re-imagining the Museum: Beyond the Mausoleum* (Routledge, London, 2003)
11. J. Prinz, *How Wonder Works* (2013), https://aeon.co/essays/why-wonder-is-the-most-human-of-all-emotions. Accessed 28 May 2016
12. Z.D. Doering, *Strangers, Guests or Clients? Visitor Experiences in Museums* (Smithsonian Institution, Washington, DC, 1999)
13. P. Lévy, *Becoming Virtual, Reality in the Digital Age* (Plenum Trade, New York, 1998)
14. S. Hazan, *Performing the Museum in an Age of Digital Reproduction*. ISSN: 2057-519X (Online) (2015)
15. S. Hazan, *The Digital Dead Sea Scrolls – Working on a Google Cloud*, in Proceedings, Museums and the Web 2011 (San Diego, 2011), http://www.museumsandtheweb.com/mw2012/papers/the_digital_dead_sea_scrolls_working_on_a_goog. Accessed 22 Apr 2016
16. ELAICH Manual, in *ELAICH Educational Toolkit for educators and heritage authorities* ed. by A. Lobovikov-Katz (available in English, Italian, Greek, Hebrew, Arabic, Maltese) Printed version: Technion (2012). On-line version: http://elaich.technion.ac.il/e-learning. Accessed 29 May 2016
17. A. Lobovikov-Katz, A. Konstanti, K. Labropoulos, A. Moropoulou, J.A. Cassar, R. De Angelis, *The EUROMED 4 Project "ELAICH": e-tools for a teaching environment on EU Mediterranean cultural heritage*, Progress in Cultural Heritage Preservation, Lecture Notes in Computer Science, LNCS 7616 (Springer, 2012)
18. A. Lobovikov-Katz, A. Moropoulou, A. Konstanti, P. Ortiz Calderón, R. Van Grieken, S.G. F. Worth Izzo, Tangible versus intangible in e-learning on cultural heritage: from online learning to on-site study of historic sites, in *Digital Heritage. Progress in Cultural Heritage: Documentation, Preservation and Protection*, ed. by M. Ioannides, N. Magnenat-Thalmann, E. Fink, R. Žarnić, A.-Y. Yen, E. Quak. LNCS, Vol. 8740 (Springer, New York, 2014), pp. 819–828
19. A. Lobovikov-Katz, Heritage education for heritage conservation (Contribution of educational codes to study of deterioration of natural building stone in historic monuments). Strain **45**(5), 480–484 (2009). Article first published online: 18 November 2008
20. A. Lobovikov-Katz, *The virtual and the real: e-learning in interdisciplinary education – the case of cultural heritage*, The 13th Annual MEITAL National Conference "New Technologies and Their Evaluation in Online Teaching and Learning" Haifa, 2015, pp. 58–63
21. M. Mortara, C.E. Catalano, F. Bellotti, G. Fiucci, M. Houry-Panchetti, P. Petridis, Learning cultural heritage by serious games. J. Cult. Herit. **15**(3), 318–325 (2014). doi:10.1016/j.culher.2013.04.004. Accessed 29 May 2016
22. A. Galla, *Frequently Asked Questions about Intangible Heritage*, ICOM News, No. 4 (2003)

Chapter 23
Modelling of Static and Moving Objects: Digitizing Tangible and Intangible Cultural Heritage

Nikolaos Doulamis, Anastasios Doulamis, Charalabos Ioannidis, Michael Klein, and Marinos Ioannides

Abstract From the ancient library of Alexandria 2300 years ago, cultural collections have a common fundamental base; to gather, preserve and promote knowledge helping the intellectual and cognitive evolution of humanity. Nowadays the information revolution has given scientists, educators, researchers and individuals the ability not only to use a variety of digital libraries as a source of information but also to contribute to these libraries by uploading data that they create, leading to a massive production of digital data that we need to verify, manage, archive, preserve and reuse. Cultural heritage (CH) data is a category in digital libraries that needs our attention the most, because of their crucial role in helping us to interact with the past and learn, promote and preserve our cultural assets. Digital documentation of tangible and intangible heritage, data formats and standards, metadata and semantics, linked data, crowdsourcing and cloud, the use and reuse of data and copyright issues are the rising challenges that we try to address in this chapter, through literature research and best practice examples. At the end of this analysis, this chapter tries to predict the future of Digital Heritage Libraries, where 3D digital assets will be part of augmented, virtual and mixed reality experiences.

Keywords 4D modelling • Tangible and intangible cultural heritage • 3D reconstruction • Semantics • Laban motion analysis

---

N. Doulamis (✉) • A. Doulamis • C. Ioannidis
National Technical University of Athens, 9th, Heroon Polytechniou, Zografou, Athens
e-mail: ndoulam@cs.ntua.gr; adoulam@cs.ntua.gr; cion@survey.ntua.gr

M. Klein
7Reasons Ltd, Vienna, Austria
e-mail: mk@7reasons.net

M. Ioannides
Digital Heritage Research Lab, Cyprus University of Technology, 30 Archbishop Kyperlanou, Limassol 3036, Cyprus
e-mail: marinos.ioannides@cut.ac.cy

M. Ioannides et al. (eds.), *Mixed Reality and Gamification for Cultural Heritage*,
DOI 10.1007/978-3-319-49607-8_23

23.1 Introduction

An innovative four-dimensional (4D; 3D geometry + time) framework is introduced in this chapter to improve the automation and cost-effectiveness of 3D capturing of cultural heritage (CH) assets and to provide new personalized tools and services to different CH actors (researchers, curators and creative industries) in analysing, documenting, understanding and experiencing unique cultural diversity [1]. Both tangible and intangible CH assets are examined. The first case covers outdoor CH objects, which are most sensitive to environmental, natural phenomena and man-made factors, implying an imminent need for a spatio-temporal assessment to identify regions of material degradation and structuring problems. The latter covers a significant part of our cultural legacy including 'the practices, representations, expressions, knowledge, skills—as well as the instruments, objects, artefacts and cultural spaces' [2].

Currently, 3D digital models are generated under a spatial–temporal independent framework. This means that digitalization information of common parts (surfaces) of an object is not exploited to digitalize similar surfaces of the same or other objects. Furthermore, the digitization process at a current time instance does not exploit results from reconstructions obtained at previous time instances. As an additional drawback, one can also refer to the lack of a semantic enrichment of the digital information to assist CH community users in their research and work.

4D modelling is also a very important aspect of human creativity. Human creativity is characterized by the tangible and intangible dimension. Although many research works have been proposed in the literature on modelling, representation and archiving of the tangible dimension of human creativity (e.g. digitization and archiving of a book or 3D representation of a monument), the intangible dimension is somehow underestimated [3]. Intangible human creativity aspects include human expressions, especially in the case of performing arts, the style as well as the movement and the respective interaction with other objects (including humans) and the environment. Transforming the intangible elements of human creativity into tangible digits is very important for research excellence and competitiveness since the respective research boosts the creative industry sector in diverse areas such as advertising, architecture, media production, fashion and films [4]. This makes 4D modelling too complex to be validated under real-life, large-scale application domains [5, 6].

Digitalizing CH assets (tangible or intangible) is one of the most salient research actions in the cultural community [7]. This assists conservators to check how restoration methods affect an object or how materials decay through time, archaeologists to better document an item, curators to properly display them and the creative industries to digitalize intangible content (e.g. dances) in a efficiently way worldwide. The construction of high-fidelity 3D models is a time-consuming task, with limited functionalities since it cannot capture temporal properties of an item (how it behaves in time). In addition, the time required to obtain a precise model is often too high due to the manual effort needed to be interwoven in the reconstruction process [1]. For this reason, 3D digitalization is mainly applied to individualized items of museums' collections, to indoor cultural assets where temporal variations are minimal and to famous sites/museums where adequate financial resources can be given to perform such a digitalization.

The proposed 4D modelling scheme refers to a proper combination of tangible and intangible CH assets. This is very important for virtual reality (VR) applications. The combination of intangible and tangible content adds value to the 'lifeless' cultural heritage information since it provides the 'reasons' for building and creating a CH monument. Imagine a dance hall. This is an empty building, but when we add the dancers and the style of the dancing and we embed 3D moving objects, we transform the 'lifeless' walls into a vivid CH monument. VR scenarios and applications can animate these models. For this reason, a 4D viewer has been developed in this chapter to demonstrate the significance of the models.

Such a concept has great impact on CH experiences for the elderly and people of special needs. A large number of our society, especially in the ageing Europe, are not capable of travelling to several archaeological sites to share unique cultural experiences either due to limitations in physical access or due to the fatigue of the trip. This part of our society mainly refers to the elderly and people with special needs. The personalized augmented/virtual reality services provide this category of people unique experiences of cultural site navigation and storytelling, making them communicants of Europe's unique culture. It also provides new experiences on sharing cultural heritage objects for place where a visitor have not visited. Furthermore, the chapter strengthens the creation of e-museums, cultural diversity and employability.

In this chapter, a conceptual framework for 4D modelling (3D geometry plus time) of both tangible and intangible (concentrated on digitalizing dances) CH assets is introduced. The new model is suitable for monitoring spatial–temporal evolutions of CH items.

23.2 State of the Art in 4D CH Modelling

23.2.1 4D Modelling of Tangible CH Assets

Nowadays, several methods exist in 3D modelling. Examples include (i) image-based methods that exploit photogrammetric aspects in creating high-fidelity 3D textured models [8]; (ii) photometric stereo that exploits light reflection properties for 3D modelling [9]; (iii) real-time depth sensors, such as Kinect, to create cost-effective but low-fidelity RGBD images [10]; (iv) structured light technologies with the capability of simultaneously capturing the 3D geometry and texture [11]; and (v) laser scanning for large-scale automated 3D reconstruction [12]. However, each of the aforementioned methods presents advantages/disadvantages, making high-fidelity 3D modelling of CH assets a complex decision-making process.

Photogrammetric stereo presents the advantage of creating high-fidelity 3D point clouds, but the respective accuracy significantly falls in cases of uniform texture images, which is usually the case in cultural assets. Additionally, significant effort may be required in cases where the use of different platforms (terrestrial, e.g. scaffolds, or aerial, e.g. UAVs) is needed to obtain the different views of images, especially in objects or regions where no physical access is permitted. On the other hand, photometric stereo can be applied either for improving the results of image-based matching or for reconstructing transparent/specular surfaces, where conventional methods fail. Real-time depth sensors, such as Kinect, present the advantage of providing cost-effective 3D modelling. However, the respective 3D meshes are of low resolution and therefore not suitable for many CH applications (e.g. conservation, monitoring). Structured light 3D reconstruction methods are suitable for small-scale objects and present difficulties in outdoor scanning. Finally, 3D laser scanning presents the advantage of automation, but the creating point clouds present a large amount of noise due to the failure of reflection of the laser beams. Additionally, the respective cost of 3D modelling is high, as using and maintaining 3D laser scanner devices is expensive.

However, despite the existence of several 3D capturing methods, 3D modelling is currently performed under an isolated and fragmented solution without taking into consideration the advantages/disadvantages of each technology as well as the requirements of the respective application domain (e.g. uniform regions, transparent surfaces, low- versus high-resolution 3D modelling, large versus small dimension modelling) [1]. In particular, each research institution and/or enterprise adopts a specific 3D modelling policy at which they have specialized, without integrating/fusing several methods together for improving cost-effectiveness while simultaneously retaining high-fidelity reconstruction accuracy. In this context, integration means that the advantages of one method are used to adjust the operation (or parameters) of other 3D modelling approaches, improving both the resolution accuracy and the respective cost. For example, suppose that an initial 3D modelling obtained from low-fidelity depth sensors was done. By applying 3D processing algorithms, the regions that need more accuracy in 3D reconstruction (e.g. regions of complex geometric features) can be determined compared with the surfaces that need low-resolution accuracy (e.g. regions of simple geometry).

Another important limitation of the existing 3D modelling methods is the lack of automation in 3D modelling decision-making. Automation means the determination of the parameters that define (i) the regions (part of an object or a surface) of 3D modelling, (ii) the scale (e.g. the respective resolution), (iii) the respective 3D technologies (or a combination of them) and (iv) the time instance at which 3D modelling is performed. This quartet (region, scale, time, technology) determines the main parameter that automates decision-making in 3D modelling. Then, through the aid of robotic methods, such as UAVs, the 3D modelling processing can be automated, reducing the cost of the 3D reconstruction.

Weather, humidity and environmental conditions significantly affect the state of an outdoor cultural resource [13]. Additionally, geological landslides and earthquakes can damage the structural state of a CH asset. For this reason, spatial–

temporal 3D modelling is required to capture the dynamic behaviour of an open cultural resource. In addition, an archaeological site is a live place where several reconstruction and conservation works take place. Before a spatial modification, high-fidelity 3D modelling techniques need to be implemented to capture the current state of the monument. Archaeologist, conservators and engineers have a benchmark before any action takes place [14, 15]. The same is evident during an excavation phase where several temporal changes are encountered. Therefore, 3D scanning should take place after any spatial–temporal change to record and monitor the excavation process.

23.2.2 4D Modelling of Intangible CH Assets

23.2.2.1 Digitalizing Intangible Cultural Heritage Content

Intangible cultural heritage (ICH) is a very important mainspring of cultural diversity and a guarantee of sustainable development, as underscored in the UNESCO Recommendation on the safeguarding of Traditional Culture and folklore of 1989 [1]. Improving the digitization technology regarding capturing, modelling and mathematical representation of performance arts and especially folklore dances is critical in (i) promoting cultural diversity to the children and the youth through the safeguard of traditional performance arts, (ii) making local communities and especially indigenous people aware of the richness of their intangible heritage and (iii) strengthening cooperation and intercultural dialogue between people, different cultures and countries.

However, despite the recent progress in digitization technology, especially in the area of 3D virtual reconstruction (see the research achievements of the projects 3D-COFORM, EPOCH, IMPACT, PRESTOSPACE, V-CITY [16–20]), digitization of intangible cultural assets and especially of folklore performing arts presents many technological challenges that make the overall process a very demanding task. This is mainly due to the fact that folklore performances present a series of challenges ranging from digitization and computer vision to spatio-temporal (4D) dynamic modelling and virtual scene generation. The research challenges stem from the complex geometry of the dance in the spatio-temporal space, the highly complex background scenes of quite dynamic and changing conditions as well as the interaction of the moving objects with each other and with the environment.

Currently, digitization of intangible cultural assets is based on simple audiovisual recordings, a static and monolithic digitization approach. Audiovisual capturing, even with the use of the current advanced stereoscopic 3D camcorders, lacks of cost-effective and innovative preservation of the structure, the geometry and all other related information of the dance [21]. Therefore, such type of digitization is not suitable for preserving and promoting the intangible cultural heritage. Traditional performing arts present highly complex geometrical characteristics that fail to be captured through a simple AV capturing, even in a 3D digitization mode. Dancers use internal and external cues to express their feelings and concepts, from the most abstract ideas to very concrete human situations in a highly creative manner, wherein a body or bodies in time and space are the central tools of the choreographic process. This complex process requires advanced computational models able to describe the series of the composed dance phases a performance consists of.

Simple AV digitization presents difficulties in creating virtual surrogates through the enrichment of the created 3D objects with knowledge beyond the physical objects. This is mainly due to the fact that the structure of the choreographic performance is lost in trillions of pixels of no semantic information. However, creation of virtual surrogates and virtual enrichment policies is critical, since they add value to the captured cultural assets and promote awareness, easy archiving and the reuse of the digitized content.

To address the aforementioned difficulties, the National Science Foundation of the USA supports a programme for developing a Tele-Immersive Dance: A Human/Computer Creative Environment [22, 23]. The purpose of this project is to design a symbiotic creativity framework for dance choreography based on Laban Movement Analysis (LMA) [24]. The system exploits a tele-immersion architecture of 3D capturing the movements of a dancer and then exploits computational models for modelling human creativity [25]. However, the focus of this US-supported research is on the creation of a collaborative synchronized framework instead of archiving, preserving and adding value to the intangible cultural assets of folklore performing arts.

Another research is supported by the Japanese Research Framework [26]. The model is focused on Japanese traditional performing arts. The system generates sequences of 3D actor models of the performances from a multi-view video. However, such approaches do not deal with the problem of symbolic representation, which is very critical for preserving and adding value to the intangible cultural heritage of Europe. In addition, 3D modelling is performed using a graph cut approach, and no motion information is considered, increasing the cost for modelling. Finally, Japanese performances consist of one person of slow motion and are quite different from the European ones.

The third research approach is based on the Motion Bank project of the Fraunhofer Institute [27]. Motion Bank was a 4-year research project providing a broad context for research into choreographic practice. The main focus is on the creation of online digital scores in collaboration with guest choreographers to be made publicly available via the Motion Bank website. Both these unique score productions and development of related teaching applications will be undertaken with and rely on the expertise and experience of the collaborative partners.

23.2.2.2 3D Modelling of Moving Objects

Modelling in computer graphics is a process to create a computer mathematical structure which represents accurately the real object (model), which by definition is an abstract representation that reflects the characteristics of a given entity either physical or conceptual. 3D motion modelling is a process in which the entity to be modelled is the movement of an object in 3D space. This process uses low-level features that correlate to a kinematic description of a motion, and it relies on computational geometry techniques, i.e., skeleton extraction, division of space into subspaces and mesh reconstruction.

Menier et al. [28] present an approach to recover body motions from multiple views using a 3D skeletal model, which is an a priori articulated model consisting of a kinematic chain of segments representing a body pose. Motion recovery of the user is addressed like a propagation problem which consists in predicting a likely pose by knowing the previous poses. In [29], an approach for simultaneously reconstructing 3D human motion and full-body skeletal size from a small set of 2D image features is presented. To resolve the problem of ambiguity for skeleton reconstruction, a large set of pre-processed human motion examples and pre recorded human skeleton data is required. In [30], an approach that recovers the movement of the skeleton, as well as the possibly non-rigid temporal deformation of the 3D surface, by using an articulated template model and silhouettes from a multi-view image sequence is presented. This way, large-scale deformations and fast movements are captured by the skeleton pose, while small-scale deformations are captured by the surface to the silhouette.

This method exceeds the performance of related methods, on HumanEva benchmark, since both accurate skeleton and surface motion are found fully automatically. In [31], to capture 3D motion, a polyhedral mesh with fixed topology that represents the instantaneous geometry of the observed scene is used. The initial mesh is constructed in the first frame using the PVMS software, which is based on the algorithm of [32] that outperforms all other algorithms submitted by that time according to a quantitative evaluation on the Middlebury benchmark [33]. To overcome the problem of accumulated drift, a strategy called 'track to first' is applied [34]. In [35], a volumetric approach to 3D motion modelling is proposed. At each time instant, the shape of the scene is estimated as a 3D voxel model, and then, based on a hierarchical version of the Lucas–Kanade algorithm for optical flow estimation, a 3D motion vector is computed for every voxel in the scene. Another volumetric approach uses silhouette volume intersection to generate the 3D voxel representation of the object shape [36]. The main drawback of this approach is that the 3D voxel computation and high-fidelity texture mapping algorithm are repeated independently for each captured frame in order to create a 3D motion picture. In [37], a work that extends the probabilistic latent semantic analysis for 3D human motion tracking is proposed. This work is based on a semi-supervised learning and is capable of describing the mapping of image features to 3D human pose estimates. For human motion modelling, a 3D posture of the human figure as well as an intrinsic representation of the motion are recovered.

23.2.2.3 Symbolic Representation and Semantic Signature Extraction

The topic of transforming choreographies into symbolic representations is addressed within the project 'Synchronous Objects' realized by William Forsythe and the Ohio State University (www.synchronousobjects.org) [38]. The idea of this project was to extract choreographic building blocks, to quantify them and to repurpose this information visually and qualitatively. Thereby the dances have been captured in top and front view. The dances have been interactively marked by animators frame by frame with the aim to track their movements. On the captured video data, different patterns have been identified and have been linked to attribute data as cues (here it was noted when a dancer is giving a cue for another dancer to move and who is receiving it) or alignments (identified motion patterns).

23.3 The Proposed 4D Modelling Procedure

Figure 23.1 presents an overview of the proposed scheme for 4D modelling both of tangible and intangible CH assets.

The system consists of two subsystems; the first refers to tangible CH modelling. It includes 3D digitalization issues of CH objects and a change history map. Regarding the intangible CH analysis subsystem, we should include methods for

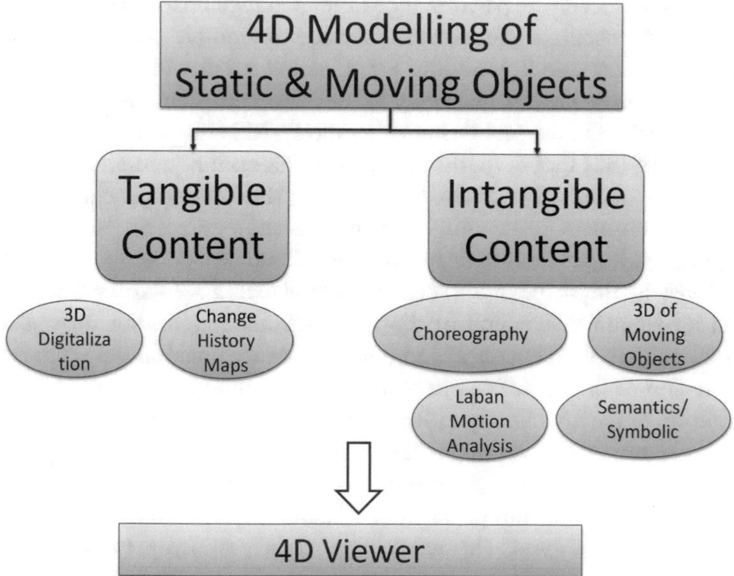

Fig. 23.1 An overview of proposed holistic approach for 4D modelling of tangible and intangible cultural heritage objects

choreographic analysis, 3D modelling of moving objects, Laban Motion Analysis (LMA) and semantic/symbolic representation.

23.3.1 4D Modelling of Tangible CH Assets

Figure 23.2 presents the main research workflow of the proposed scheme for 4D modelling of tangible cultural content [5].

Initially, scenarios and use cases need to be defined. This includes selection of the regions for which the model will be applied in terms of their importance in spatial–temporal monitoring, material degradation, structural distortions and need for restorations. Additionally, surfaces of different properties will be selected (smooth versus rough, transparent versus opaque, uniform versus non-uniform, small versus large scale) to verify the effect of different 3D capturing methodologies in 3D reconstruction precision. Also, models that simulate how a specific material behaves on external factors (humidity, temperature, pollution, etc.) need to be introduced. Finally, a set of annotation data (ground-truth set) that contains representative examples of different material conditions along with visual features should be created, and metadata and respective structures which are included as semantic-aware information of the 4D model should be defined.

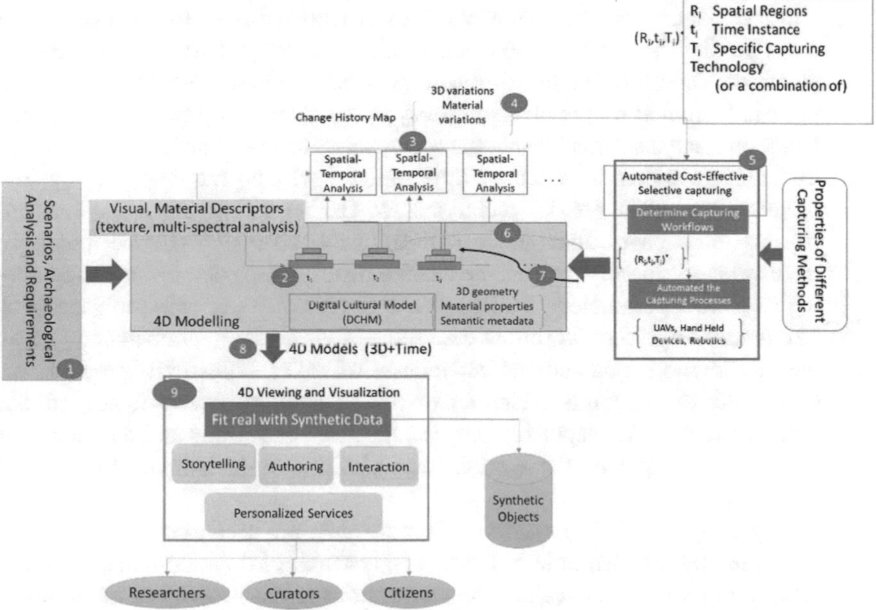

Fig. 23.2 The concept and main steps of the 4D modelling for static objects

The following step is to proceed with the creation of an initial high-fidelity 3D model exploiting photogrammetric methods. Different 3D capturing methods will be applied for surfaces of different features. For example, photometry stereo will be used for transparent surfaces, whereas stereo-photogrammetry will be considered for opaque regions. This initial 3D representation will be used: (a) to provide a cost-effective 4D digitalization framework at the forthcoming time periods (predictive capturing) and (b) as benchmark to validate how the fusion of 3D capturing methods improves cost-effectiveness while keeping the same accuracy.

The most crucial part is the detection of spatial–temporal differences between two consecutive generated 3D digital models. To do this, the main actions to do this are:

(i) *Registration and affine-invariant transformation of 3D digital models*. Estimation of 3D differences is not a straightforward research task, since usually the obtained 3D models have different orientations and registration properties. For this, the first step is to create 3D models of common orientation, position and scale. To simplify processing requirements, firstly an estimation of the medial axis of the 3D captured objects and then the application of 3D template matching methods to minimize the difference between the two medial axes' skeletons should be done.

(ii) *Creation of change history maps*. Change history maps are created by processing consecutive 3D surfaces. The maps indicate differences in 3D shape-related domain and material model features. They provide useful information that automates the 3D capturing process and introduces a cost-effective 3D acquisition framework. This is achieved since the change history maps predict the spatial regions where high- or low- fidelity 3D capturing is required. Therefore, at the forthcoming time intervals, the 3D acquisition process is guided by the change history maps generated through the spatial–temporal analysis. This means that regions that have not undergone a significant change either in space or time domain will be monitored using low accuracy and data density techniques at the next time intervals. Instead, regions that have undergone a 'significant change' will be precisely reconstructed. In other words, the change history maps determine the capturing workflow parameters, leading to a cost-effective periodic monitoring of CH assets. Capturing workflow determines four critical parameters as far as the automation and cost-effectiveness of 3D acquisition process are concerned: the region at which a new 3D acquisition process is needed, the time of the next 3D capturing process, the scale (accuracy and data density) and the technique or the combination (fusion) of techniques for the 3D acquisition.

(iii) *4D model updating*. The results of the procedure are used to update/create 4D digital models at each time instance. The research of this step will be focused on creating multilevel scalable representations (from low-resolution to high-fidelity scales) exploiting only partial time-varying 3D reconstructions. This is achieved by combining knowledge from partial 3D modelling results of previous time periods.

The final step is to include augmented reality algorithms, computer graphics techniques and interactive presentation methods for publishing the acquired 4D models at different contextual conditions, creating new dimensions in the way that tangible cultural heritage assets are studied, visualized, curated, reused and monitored. In particular, the mobile augmented reality environment with highly interactive capabilities and media publishing methods that enrich the captured 3D objects with virtual digital surrogates to provide personalized services to different CH actors are supported.

23.3.2 *4D Modelling of Intangible CH Assets*

To achieve a reliable 4D modelling of intangible cultural heritage (ICH) assets, such as dances, a new pioneer framework should be adopted. The research tools needed to be applied are depicted in Fig. 23.3. The goals are to (a) explore a scalable capturing framework as regards 3D reconstruction of ICH in terms of accuracy and cost-effectiveness, (b) develop the captured visual 3D signals into symbolic data that represent the overall human creativity, (c) define an interoperable Intangible

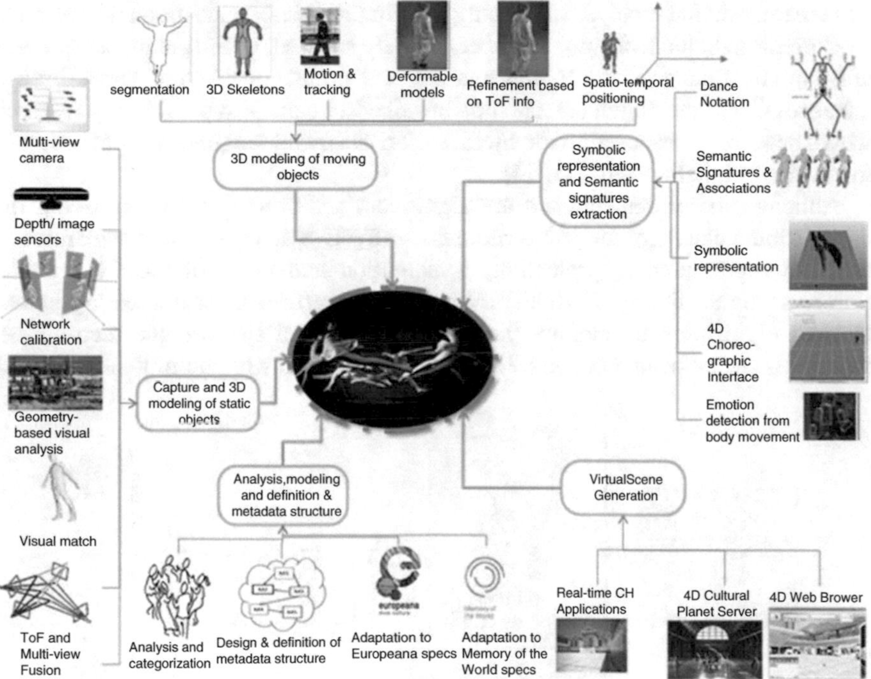

Fig. 23.3 The main research components towards an intangible cultural heritage content (ICH) digitalization

Cultural Metadata Interface (ICMI) for folklore performing arts and (d) nominate the appropriate codification of the extracted symbolic data structures in an interoperable form that permits interconnection with existing specifications of national digital cultural repositories or international digital cultural repositories like the EU digital library EUROPEANA [39] and UNESCO's Memory of the World [40] (Fig. 23.4).

Exploring the digitization technology regarding folklore performances constitutes a significant impact. On the one hand, the multicultural intangible dimension is documented, preserved and made available to everybody on the Internet. On the other hand, the multifaceted value to the intangible cultural content for usage in education, tourism, art, media, science and leisure settings is added. Finally, this contributes for new jobs and skills and to the EU's strategy to deliver smart sustainable and inclusive growth and implements the knowledge triangle by connecting the education, research and industry by supporting and boosting innovative enterprise to develop their technological breakthroughs into viable products in the area of ICH digitalization and preservation, with real commercial potential.

During the twentieth century, there were several attempts to model human creativity in performing arts. In the 1920s, Rudolf Laban developed a system of movement notation that eventually evolved into modern-day LMA [24], which provides a language for describing, visualizing, interpreting and documenting all varieties of human movement, in an attempt to preserve classic choreographies. In the early 2000s, LMA was extensively used for analysing dance performances [41] and creating digital archives of dancing [42] in the area of education and research.

Currently, digital technology has been widely adopted, which greatly accelerates efforts and efficiency of CH preservation and protection. At the same time, it enhances CH in the digital era, creating enriched virtual surrogates. Many research works have been proposed in the literature on archiving tangible cultural assets in the form of digital content [43, 44].

Although the aforementioned are significant achievements for improving the digitization technology towards a more cost-effective automated and semantically enriched representation, protection, presentation and reuse of the CH via the European digital library EUROPEANA, very few efforts exist in creating breakthrough digitization technology (i.e. audio, visual and stereoscopic recordings), improving the e-documentation (3D modelling enriched with multimedia metadata

Fig. 23.4 Framework of the proposed intangible cultural content digitalization

and ontologies), e-preservation (standards) and the reuse of ICH traditional music and fashion, folklore, handicraft, etc. Some efforts towards this goal have been introduced by the Transforming Intangible Folkloric Performing Arts into Tangible Choreographic Digital Objects (TERPSICHORE) H2020 project [45]. The main goal of the TERPSICHORE project is the transformation of intangible cultural heritage content to 3D virtual content, through the development and exploitation of affordable digitization technology. Towards this direction, fusion of different scientific and technological fields, such as capturing technology, computer vision and learning, 3D modelling and reconstruction, virtual reality, computer graphics and data aggregation for metadata extraction, is necessary.

23.3.2.1 Choreographic Analysis, Design and Modelling

The main research objective in this section is to analyse the spatial specifications, the attributes and the properties of folklore traditional performing arts. The analysis describes all the aspects that are needed for recording human creativity based on tradition; thus, apart from the human movement, the way of expression, the associated emotional characteristics, the style as well as additional contextual data, such as climate conditions, social-cultural factors, stylistic variations and the accompanied untold scenarios and stories, should be recorded. All the aforementioned specifications will be surveyed in such a way as to derive an interoperable description framework based on which we are able to design and define the Intangible Cultural Metadata Interface (ICMI). ICMI aims at specifying a set of metadata that are necessary for representing the rich intangible cultural heritage information, especially in the case of folklore traditional performing arts. In addition, ICMI introduces an interoperable description scheme framework able to specify the metadata structure and the relations between the extracted metadata. Thus, ICMI specifies not only the appropriate metadata for representing human creativity but also the structure and semantics of relations between its components. Figure 23.5 presents an indicative description framework of the basic metadata elements used for the description of folklore performing arts. As is observed, the metadata of the ICMI are divided into four main categories: the low-level feature metadata, the contextual and environmental metadata, the sociocultural factors and the emotional attributes.

The pool of the basic metadata used for describing the intangible cultural assets of traditional folklore performing arts is framed with a metadata structure format able to interoperably represent the semantics relations between the metadata components of Fig. 23.5. Special emphasis should be given in order to align the ICMI format with existing specifications of digital cultural libraries, such as EUROPEANA and UNESCO's Memory of the World, since this will allow the easy archiving, usage and reusage of the digitized intangible cultural content with the content of large digital cultural repositories.

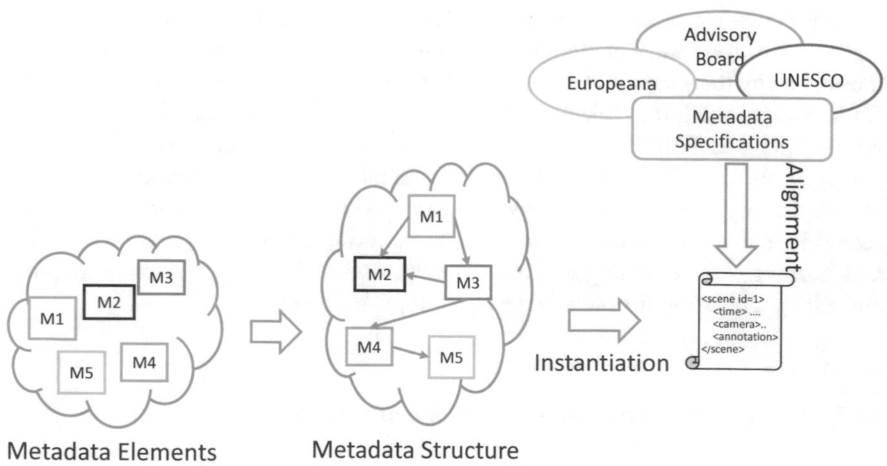

Fig. 23.5 Description of the basic metadata elements used for representing the folklore performing arts

23.3.2.2 Capture and 3D Modelling of Static Objects

Another important research issue deals with technologies able to capture and virtually 3D reconstruct traditional performing arts under an affordable, cost-effective and accurate digitization framework. To do this, an innovative technological framework able to combine advanced technologies in the area of photogrammetry and computer vision should be introduced. *A scalable capturing framework* that combines 3D modelling technology through a set of multi-view stereo camera architecture and low-cost depth sensors (Kinect^{TM}) is necessary to be adopted. The balance of using multi-view stereo imaging (high-resolution cameras plus dense image matching techniques) and low-cost depth sensors able to generate depth information in real time is obtained in terms of accuracy and cost-effectiveness. In other words, the fusion of the information from different sensors in order to increase the accuracy or reduce the number of cameras necessary for data capturing remains a challenge.

As regards the multi-view imaging architecture, the 3D information is extracted by applying dense image matching techniques. For each stereo model observing common content, a correspondence is determined for each pixel individually. By using these correspondences between all stereo models, all 3D points can be triangulated based on their viewing rays at once. This leads to a very dense and accurate point cloud. In order to acquire the movements in time, this step is performed for each frame in time for all synchronized cameras—leading to 3D point clouds for each time stamp. However, this is a computational-intensive process that increases the total cost of digitization. 3D modelling tools appropriately designed for time-varying shapes should be used. Such methodologies exploit motion information as well as tracking methods. Subsequently, a volumetric

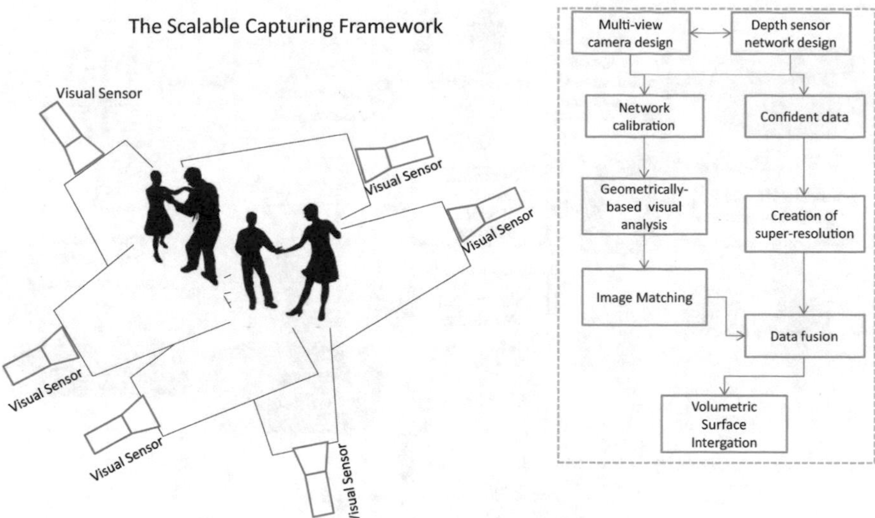

Fig. 23.6 A representation of the methodology resulting in a scalable capturing framework in terms of accuracy and performance

integration of this depth information not only enables the extraction of a volumetric representation but also enables to fill small gaps and reduces noise.

The fusion process should be performed under a calibrated network of cameras or depth sensors. Network calibration is very important since it allows the implementation of super-resolution methods and detection of confidence data as obtained either by the depth sensors or the multi-view imaging. The use of self-calibration methodologies able to automatically calibrate the network of cameras and depth sensors using computer vision tools is a major research issue. Figure 23.6 presents the aforementioned methodology.

23.3.2.3 3D Modelling of Moving Objects

Another research field includes imaging methodologies based on the combination of photogrammetric, computer vision and computer graphics techniques able to automate the 3D modelling procedure of moving objects. Towards this direction, initially, segmentation algorithms able to isolate the foreground objects from the background are applied. This step is critical since it allows the human objects to be separated from the background content. The foreground objects are dynamically updated through the motion estimation captured by the capturing layer. On the contrary, background content is updated by the information provided by the depth sensor network. A set of deformable models is used to describe the human movement. These set of deformable models are provided dealing with the analysis, design and modelling of folklore traditional performing arts.

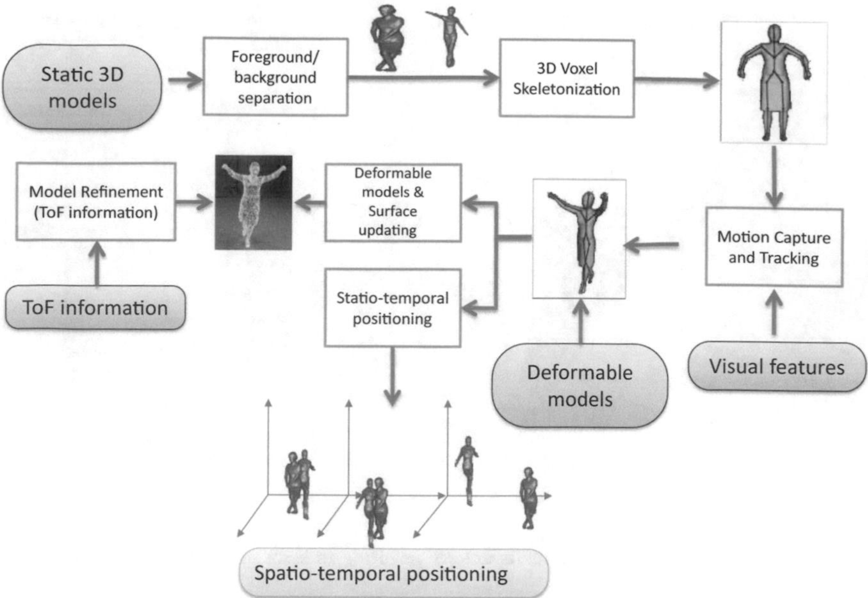

Fig. 23.7 The 3D modelling methodology for moving objects

In order to allow a cost-effective 3D digitization process, a voxel 3D skeletonization is performed. In this way, we are able to reduce the amount of information needed to describe the human object; therefore, a reduction of the cost of processing resulting in more accurate and cost-effective 3D modelling of moving objects is possible. 3D skeletons are medial axes that transform and encode mostly motion information. 3D skeletons separate motion estimation from shape, and thus, they allow a more accurate 3D model updating through time.

The derived 3D skeletons are tracked in time using motion capture and tracking computer vision methodologies. Tracking process is assisted through the selection of appropriate geometrically enriched data. By taking into consideration motion tracking, which is performed on the 3D skeletons to increase accuracy and computational efficiency, as well as the set of deformable models appropriate for a specific folklore performance, we are able to automatically update the detected 3D models to fit the properties of the current human movement and shape constraints as obtained by the static 3D models.

Despite the efficiency of the aforementioned methodology, possible errors (in the 3D skeletonization and tracking process) generate erroneous virtual 3D reconstructions. To address this difficulty, we enhance the results of the 3D modelling of moving objects using information derived from the depth sensor network. In this case, we are able to exploit the depth information to improve 3D modelling accuracy. Figure 23.7 describes this architecture.

23.3.2.4 Symbolic Representation and Extraction of Semantic Signatures

3D modelling is critical for encoding the complex 3D reconstructions of performing arts into a set of compact semantic signatures in a similar way that a music song is encoded using a music score. For this reason, computational geometry algorithms are used to decode the spatial–temporal trajectory of the performances. This includes methodologies for positioning both in 3D and temporal space. Then, semantic signatures and respective spatial–temporal associations are extracted to represent the performances with high-level concepts. It is clear that semantic analysis aids the digitization and computer vision process and vice versa.

The visualization of scores fosters the understanding of the dance, and it helps visitors, dancers and choreographs to comprehend the structure and the intension of the dance. A more formalized documentation of the dance will be supported with an automated mapping of capturing data to formal and abstract choreographic notations ('symbolic representations'). Hereby, the captured dance could be coded using traditional approaches like the LMA or modern ballet notation forms like the 'peacemaker' from William Forsythe and David Kern.

Beside the abstract visualization, the complete reconstructed 4D scenario can be visualized within an interactive WebViewer. This interactive WebViewer links the extracted symbolic representations to the 4D reconstruction of the choreography. Within this WebViewer, beside different viewpoints, also the perspective of a specific dance can be chosen.

23.4 4D Viewer

The virtual reality (VR) viewer is an attempt to create an end-user software which manages the presentation of the various data sets (imagery, 3D scans, 3D models, etc.).

The main role of a 4D viewer is to depict not only the 3D geometry of a CH asset but also its evolution in time. Time parameter captures the same content passing through time changes. For example, a street view or a monument during different time periods creates a historical timeline of cultural value. Also, the different possible angle views of the street/object of interest (different users uploading the same street but with different shooting angles and time parameters) could provide related input for systems or algorithms that construct 3D objects from 2D images. Such extensibility has a huge impact in the field of cultural heritage especially for city views and city momentums where big data manipulation over the web can be easily controlled by any end user using parameters to scroll through (i) time and (ii) 3D object manipulation [46].

Fig. 23.8 3D reconstruction using the images obtained from ranking algorithm. The object of interest is the Archangelos Michael church, *left* to *right*: point cloud, 3D mesh and textured 3D mesh

This is also very important in searching CH content taking into account time constraints, for instance, image of a monument under different weather conditions or its impact on different climate phenomena and material decay factors.

As an example, Fig. 23.8 presents the 3D model of Archangelos Michael church with different information levels [47]. The viewer allows the user to access different information through various functions. It is designed with a user-friendly interface for an intuitive working experience. They can be viewed from all sides, as well as from outside and inside. With the slice tool, the model can be cut and inspected deeper.

On the bottom of the screen, a slider is provided that allows the user to move through different time periods accompanied with the images of the monument in the current period. Sliding over the images, the user can navigate in time and across different parts of the model (Fig. 23.9).

The system also includes an information box in which metadata and in the case of additional reconstructions also para-data of the site together with its context (period, special morphology, references, additional images) are presented as well as links to architectural, historical, artistic, social, religious or political interest information (Fig. 23.10).

Fig. 23.9 The timeline feature in the VR viewer

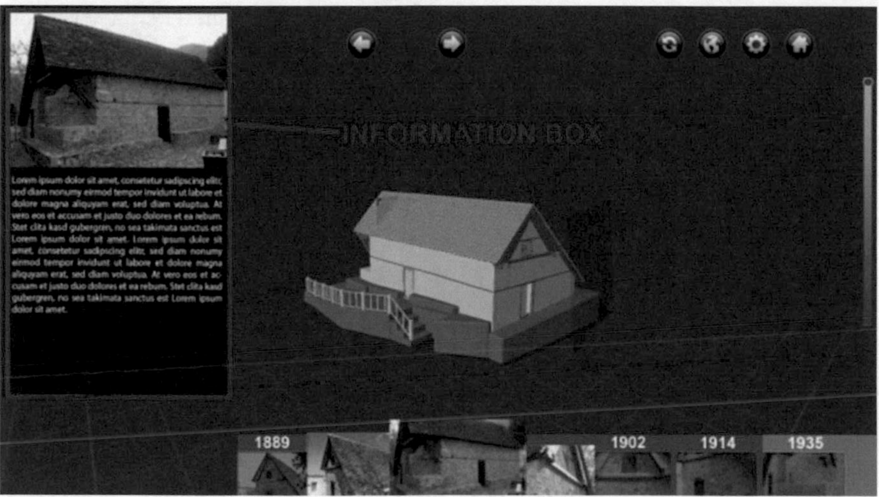

Fig. 23.10 The information box feature in the VR viewer

The slice tool enables the user to view an intersection of the reconstructed model with the help of a slicing plane (Fig. 23.11). This provides an insight to the interior construction of the model. With this tool the inner image overlays are also accessed.

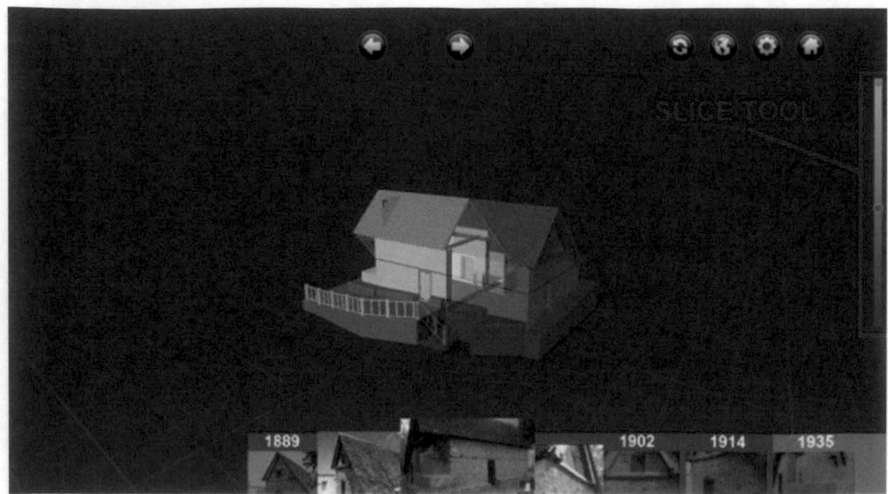

Fig. 23.11 The slice tool in the VR viewer

23.5 Conclusions

Geometry is not enough when we are focusing on moving cultural heritage objects, such as the ones called intangible heritage or for tangible outdoor assets that undergo material degradation. For the latter case, weather conditions, natural phenomena (e.g. flooding, rains, wind, earthquakes) or man-made destructions (wars, urbanization, pollution) may decay parts of the CH assets, demonstrating an imminent need for time-evolved reconstruction. To handle this challenge, the concept of 4D modelling (3D geometry plus time) is developed, both for tangible and intangible cultural heritage objects. For intangible assets, the concept of change history maps is introduced. Change history maps can receive information from semantic sources regarding the most salient parts of an item, its geometric details or other attributes that need to be protected.

A pipeline for 4D modelling of moving objects is also presented, focusing on human dance as one of the most salient parts of intangible cultural heritage. The pipeline includes the exploitation of novel computer vision mechanisms, LMA and symbolic representation of the content.

A 4D viewer is needed to depict content evolution through time. The viewer allows users to manipulate the 3D content, observe its evolution in time, compare 3D models in time, etc. Thus, the 4D viewer can be seen as a reliable means for managing the derived 4D models.

Acknowledgement This work is supported by the FP7 project Four Dimensional Cultural Heritage World (4D CH World) funded by the European Union under the grant agreement 324523 and the H0202 project Transforming Intangible Folkloric Performing Arts into Tangible Choreographic Digital Objects (TERPSICHORE) funded by RISE European Union programme under the grant agreement 691218.

References

1. G. Kyriakaki, A. Doulamis, N. Doulamis, M. Ioannides, K. Makantasis, E. Protopapadakis, A. Hadjiprocopis, K. Wenzel, D. Fritsch, M. Klein, G. Weinlinger, 4D reconstruction of tangible cultural heritage objects from web-retrieved images. Int. J. Herit. Digit. Era **3**(2), 431–452 (2014)
2. UNESCO Culture Sector—Intangible Heritage—2003 Convention [Online]. Available http://www.unesco.org/culture/ich/index.php?lg=en&pg=00022. Accessed 30 Dec 2012
3. K. Dimitropoulos, P. Barmpoutis, A. Kitsikidis, N. Grammalidis, in *Extracting Dynamics from Multi-Dimensional Time-Evolving Data Using a Bag of Higher-Order Linear Dynamical Systems*. 11th International Conference on Computer Vision Theory and Applications (VISAPP 2016), Rome, Italy, 27–29 February 2016
4. A. Nakazawa, A.N. Shinchiro, S. Kudoh, K. Ikeuchi, in *Digital Archive of Human Dance Motions*, ed. by Reidsma et al. International Conference on Virtual Systems and Multimedia (VSMM2002), pp. 180–188, 2002
5. M. Ioannides, A. Hadjiprocopis, N. Doulamis, A. Doulamis, E. Protopapadakis, K. Makantasis, P. Santos, D. Fellner, A. Stork, O. Balet, M.J. Julien, G. Weinlinger, P.S. Johnson, M. Klein, D. Fritsch, Online 4D reconstruction using multi-images available under open access. ISPRS Ann. Photogramm. Remote Sens. Spat. Inf. Sci. Strasbourg **II-5/W1**, 169–174, 2–6 September 2013
6. A. Doulamis, M. Ioannides, N. Doulamis, A. Hadjiprocopis, D. Fritsch, O. Balet, M. Julien, E. Protopapadakis, K. Makantasis, G. Weinlinger, P. S. Johnsons, M. Klein, D. Fellner, A. Stork, P. Santos, 4D reconstruction of the past. SPIE Int. Soc. Opt. Eng. **8795-87950J** (2013)
7. G. Pavlidis, A. Koutsoudis, F. Arnaoutoglou, V. Tsioukas, C. Chamzas, Methods for 3D digitization of cultural heritage. J. Cult. Herit. **8**(1), 93–98 (2007)
8. M.T. Ioannou, A. Georgopoulos, *Evaluating Large Scale Orthophotos Derived from High Resolution Satellite Imagery*. SPIE 1st International Conference on Remote Sensing and Geoinformation of the Environment, 879515, Cyprus, 5 August 2013
9. V. Argyriou, S. Zafeiriou, M. Petrou, Optimal illumination directions for faces and rough surfaces for single and multiple light imaging using class-specific prior knowledge. Comput. Vis. Image Underst. **125**, 16–36 (2014)
10. S. Izadi, D. Kim, O. Hilliges, D. Molyneaux, R. Newcombe, P. Kohli, J. Shotton, S. Hodges, D. Freeman, A. Davison, A. Fitzgibbon, in *KinectFusion: Real-Time 3D Reconstruction and Interaction Using a Moving Depth Camera*. ACM UIST'11, Santa Barbara, CA, USA, pp. 559–568, 16–19 October 2011
11. R. Orghidan, J. Salvi, M. Gordan, C. Florea, J. Batlle, Structured light self-calibration with vanishing points. Mach. Vis. Appl. **25**(2), 489–500 (2014)
12. H. Huang, C. Brenner, M. Sester, A generative statistical approach to automatic 3D building roof reconstruction from laser scanning data. ISPRS J. Photogramm. Remote Sens. **79**, 29–43 (2013)
13. A. Doulamis, A. Kioussi, M. Karoglou, N. Matsatsinis, A. Moropoulou, in *Collective Intelligence in Cultural Heritage Protection*. International Conference on Cultural Heritage, Limassol, Cyprus, published in Lectures Notes in Computer Science (Springer Press, 2012), pp. 310–339
14. A. Kioussi, M. Karoglou, A. Doulamis, K. Lakiotaki, N. Matsatsinis, A. Moropoulou, in *Decision Making on Cultural Heritage Consolidation Materials Using Computational Intelligence Tools*. International Conference on Cultural Heritage Preservation, Slit Croatia, May 2012
15. A. Doulamis, A. Kioussi, A. Moropoulou, in *New Visual-Based Diagnostic Protocol for Cultural Heritage exploiting the MPEG-7 Standard*. 6th International Conference on Emerging Technologies in Non-Destructive Testing, May 2015

16. 3D-COFORM—Tools and Expertise for 3D Collection Formation, [Online]. Available at http://www.3d-coform.eu/. Accessed 01 Jan 2012
17. PRESTOSPACE—Preservation Towards Storage and Access. Standardised Practices for Audio-visual Contents in Europe [Online]. Available at http://prestospace.org/. Accessed 01 Jan 2013
18. IMPACT—IMProving ACcess to Text [Online]. Available at http://www.impact-project.eu/. Accessed 01 Jan 2013
19. V-City—The Virtual City [Online]. Available at http://vcity.diginext.fr/EN/index.html. Accessed 01 Jan 2012
20. EPOCH—Excellence in Processing Open Cultural Heritage [Online]. Available at http://www.epoch-net.org/. Accessed 01 Jan 2012
21. F. Bressan, S. Canazza, A. Roda, N. Orio, in *Preserving Today for Tomorrow: A Case Study of an Archive of Interactive Music Installations*. Proceedings of WEMIS-Workshop on Exploring Musical Information Spaces, 2009
22. R. Sheppard, M. Kamali, R. Rivas, M. Tamai, Z. Yang, W. Wu, K. Nahrstedt, in *Advancing Interactive Collaborative Mediums Through Tele-immersive Dance (TED): A Symbiotic Creativity and Design Environment for Art and Computer Science*. Proceedings of ACM International Conference on Multimedia, pp. 579–588, 2008
23. K. Nahrstedt, R. Bajcsy, L. Wymore, R. Sheppard, K. Mezur, Computation model of human creativity in dance choreography. Proc. Assoc. Adv. Artif. Intell. (AAAI) Spring Symp. **61**, 61801–61805 (2008)
24. J. Pforsich, *Handbook for Laban Movement Analysis* (Janis Pforsich, New York, NY, 1977)
25. R. Sheppard, *Video Lectures* (University of Illinois at Urbana-Champaign, 2012) [Online]. Available at http://videolectures.net/aaai08_sheppard_tid. Accessed 01 Jan 2012
26. K. Hisatomi, M. Katayama, K. Tomiyama, Y. Iwadate, 3D archive system for traditional performing arts. Int. J. Comput. Vis. **94**(1), 78–98 (2011)
27. Motion Bank Project, Fraunhofer [Online]. Available at http://www.igd.fraunhofer.de/en/Institut/Abteilungen/Virtuelle-und-Erweiterte-Realit%C3%A4t/Projekte/Motion-Bank. Accessed 01 Jan 2012
28. C. Menier, E. Boyer, B. Raffin, in *3D Skeleton-Based Body Pose Recovery*. 3rd International Symposium on 3D Data Processing, Visualization and Transmission, Chapel Hill, NC, pp. 389–396, 14–16 June 2006
29. Y.L. Chen, J. Chai, 3D reconstruction of human motion and skeleton from uncalibrated monocular video. Comput. Vis. ACCV 2009 **5994**, 71–82 (2010)
30. J. Gall, C. Stoll, E. de Aguiar, C. Theobalt, B. Rosenhahn, H.P. Seidel, in *Motion Capture Using Joint Skeleton Tracking and Surface Estimation*. Proceedings of IEEE Conference on Computer Vision and Pattern Recognition CVPR 2009, pp. 1746–1753, 20–25 June 2009
31. Y. Furukawa, J. Ponce, R. Ronfard, G. Taubin, Dense 3D motion capture from synchronized video streams. Image Geometry Process. 3-D Cinematograph. **5**, 193–211 (2010)
32. Y. Furukawa, J. Ponce, Accurate, dense, and robust multi-view stereopsis. IEEE Trans. Pattern Anal. Mach. Intell. **32**(8), 1362–1376 (2010)
33. S.M. Seitz, B. Curless, J. Diebel, D. Scharstein, R. Szeliski, *Multi-View Stereo Evaluation* (2010), http://vision.middlebury.edu/mview/
34. A. Buchanan, A. Fitzgibbon, Interactive feature tracking using k-d trees and dynamic programming. Proc. Comput. Vis. Pattern Recognit. **1**, 626–633 (2006)
35. S. Vedula, S. Baker, T. Kanade, Image-based spatio-temporal modeling and view interpolation of dynamic events. ACM Trans. Graph. **24**(2), 240–261 (2005)
36. T. Matsuyama, W. Xiaojun, T. Takai, T. Wada, Real-time dynamic 3-D object shape reconstruction and high-fidelity texture mapping for 3-D video. IEEE Trans. Circuits Syst. Video Technol. **14**(3), 357–369 (2004)
37. K. Moon, V. Pavlovic, *3D Human Motion Tracking Using Dynamic Probabilistic Latent Semantic Analysis*. Proceedings of Canadian Conference on Computer and Robot Vision (CRV '08), pp. 155–162, 28–30 May 2008

38. www.synchronousobjects.org
39. Europeana—Homepage, Europeana [Online]. Available http://www.europeana.eu/portal/. Accessed 30 Dec 2012
40. Memory of the World|United Nations Educational, Scientific and Cultural Organization [Online]. Available http://www.unesco.org/new/en/communication-and-information/flagship-project-activities/memory-of-the-world/homepage/. Accessed 30 Dec 2012
41. E. Davis, *BEYOND DANCE Laban's Legacy of Movement Analysis* (Brechin Books, London, 2001)
42. J. Newlove, J. Dalby, *LABAN for All* (Nick Hern Books, London, 2004)
43. R. Li, T. Luo, H. Zha, 3D digitization and its applications in cultural heritage, EuroMED 2010, in *Lecture Notes in Computer Science*, ed. by M. Ioannides, D. Fellner, A. Georgopoulos, D.G. Hadjimitsis, vol 6436 (Springer, Berlin, Heidelberg, 2010), pp. 381–388
44. J.A. Magán Wals, M. Palafox Parejo, E. Tardón González, A. Sanz Cabrerizo, Mass digitization at the complutense university library: access to and preservation of its cultural heritage. LIBER Q. J. Eur. Res. Libr. [Online] (2011). Available http://liber.library.uu.nl/. Accessed 30 Dec 2012
45. http://cordis.europa.eu/project/rcn/199950_en.html. Accessed 1 Jun 2016
46. E. Sardis, V. Anagnostopoulos, N. Doulamis, T. Varvarigou, G. Kyriakaki, in *From 2D to 3D and 4D Using Timelines in Mobile Cultural Experiences*. (Euromed 2014, Limassol, Cyprus, 2012)
47. A. Doulamis, N. Doulamis, K. Makantasis, M. Klein, in *A 4D Virtual/Augmented Reality Viewer Exploiting Unstructured Web-Based Image Data*. Proceedings of 10th International Conference on Computer Vision Theory and Applications (VISAPP), vol 2, Berlin, Germany, pp. 631–639, 2015

Index

M. Ioannides et al. (eds.), *Mixed Reality and Gamification for Cultural Heritage*,
DOI 10.1007/978-3-319-49607-8

M

N

O

P

R

S

T

Printed in the United States
By Bookmasters